Missouri River

Yellowstone River

Winter Camp 1804-1805

RETURN ROUTE

OUTWARD ROUTE

Platte River

Missouri River

St. Louis

D1068518

Letters of the
Lewis and Clark Expedition

Letters of the
Lewis and Clark Expedition

WITH RELATED DOCUMENTS

1783-1854

Edited by Donald Jackson

University of Illinois Press

Urbana, 1962

Second printing (with minor changes), 1963.

Foreword

When they turned their boats against the current of the Missouri and set out "under a jentle brease," Meriwether Lewis and William Clark were to become the writingest explorers of their time. They wrote constantly and abundantly, afloat and ashore, legibly and illegibly, and always with an urgent sense of purpose. This book contains a fraction of what they wrote.

Much that they did not write is here, also, for it is no longer useful to think of the Lewis and Clark Expedition as the personal story of two men. Their journey to the Pacific and return in 1804–06 was an enterprise of many aims and a product of many minds. It was made possible by soldiers like Russell Bissell, Moses Hooke, and Amos Stoddard; frontier civilians like Elijah Galusha, Charles Gratiot, and John Hay; scientists like Robert Patterson, Benjamin Rush, and Caspar Wistar; government officials like Henry Dearborn, Albert Gallatin, and—more than any of these—Thomas Jefferson. The concern these men felt for the success of the expedition and the care they gave to its execution are evident in the pages that follow.

Out of context, some of the documents do not appear to be relevant. Jefferson delivers an address of welcome to a party of Osage Indians. The Inspector General orders a lance corporal and seven privates to march from Carlisle to Pittsburgh. Pierre Chouteau reports on his successful trip to return a Mandan chief and his family to their village. Robert Barnhill bills the War Department for two pistols with secret triggers. Charles Willson Peale reports on the health of a prairie dog. Nicholas Biddle asks a friend in Paris to send him a rare book. Only when the expedition is viewed in its many aspects do such items fall into place. The documents cover these major phases of the expedition story:

(a) Early proposals and attempts to explore the West, before the Lewis and Clark Expedition.

[v]

(b) The months of preparation, procurement of equipment, training of personnel.

(c) The journey itself, beginning with Lewis's voyage down the Ohio in the summer of 1803 and ending with the return of the expedition from the Pacific in September 1806.

(d) Financial records of the expedition.

(e) Foreign reaction: the inclination of Spanish officials to intercept the party.

(f) The expedition as a diplomatic mission to the Indians: Lewis's recruitment of chiefs and warriors to visit Washington and other eastern cities; the procedures by which these men were transported, cared for, and counseled.

(g) The expedition as a scientific reconnaissance: the evaluation by contemporary zoologists, botanists, and geologists of the specimens and descriptions obtained by the explorers.

(h) Publication of findings: early failure to achieve publication, and the long struggle of Jefferson, Clark, and Nicholas Biddle to produce a narrative; final deposit of the manuscript journals with the American Philosophical Society.

(i) Brief coverage of Lewis's violent death in 1809, because of its relation to publication of his journals.

(j) Some miscellaneous documents, extending into later years and mainly providing biographical data about other members of the expedition.

In matters related directly to the planning and completion of the expedition, I have attempted to present all the extant non-journal material. My coverage of other aspects, such as the handling of Indian delegations, and the Spanish reaction to the expedition, is less exhaustive. Of the 428 items in the volume, more than half have not appeared in print. The rest have been published in scattered sources, some difficult to obtain, and they have not always been correctly transcribed or adequately annotated.

No one should attempt to understand the expedition from a study of this compilation alone; it is complementary to the journals. An eight-volume edition of the journals appeared in 1904–05, after a century of postponement. It is listed in the bibliography under JOURNALS, while related journals or personal narratives are listed under BIDDLE, BIDDLE-COUES, GASS, and LEWIS & ORDWAY. A concise, abridged edition of the journals in one volume is Bernard DeVoto's *The Journals of Lewis and Clark* (Boston, 1953).

New journal material is still coming to light. A collection of Clark's field notes, now in the Western Americana Collection of Yale University Library, is being edited for publication by Ernest S. Osgood. Private Robert Frazer's journal and Sergeant Nathaniel Pryor's (if he kept one) are still unaccounted for. No journal of Lewis's has been located for the first leg of the expedition, from St. Louis to the winter camp in the Mandan country.

EDITORIAL PROCEDURES

The Documents

The original text is followed as closely as the demands of typography will permit, with several departures based on common sense and the current practice of scholars. Missing periods at the ends of sentences are supplied, dashes terminating sentences are supplanted by periods, and superfluous dashes after periods are omitted. In abbreviations, raised letters are brought down and a period supplied if modern usage calls for one. Words underscored in manuscript are italicized. A few recurring abbreviations are standardized (and so, for example, Jefferson's US. and Lewis's U'S. both become U.S.). The complimentary closing is run in with the preceding paragraph, and a comma is used if no other end punctuation is present. Procedures for dealing with missing or illegible words, conjectural readings, etc., are shown in the list of symbols, pp. ix–x. When in doubt as to how to proceed in a trivial matter I silently follow modern practice; if the question is more important I explain the situation in a note.

Of all the details that vex the transcriber of historical documents, one of the most puzzling—but certainly not the most important—is capitalization. I follow the original, resorting to modern practice where the writer's intention is not clear. Some writers now and then fail to begin sentences with a capital letter, and Jefferson almost never does so, but I follow Boyd in the *Papers of Thomas Jefferson* and use a capital at the beginning of every sentence.

But in the matter of capitalization, one man has utterly bested me. William Clark, a creative speller, is also a versatile capitalizer—especially in handling words beginning with *s*. After many attempts to work out a sane norm I have retired in confusion. Clark uses four kinds of initial *s* and each can be interpreted as a capital. "I send my Sister Croghan Some Seeds of Several Kinds of Grapes," he writes, and no one will insist that he really means to capitalize all those words. I settle the matter for him by putting every initial *s* in lower case, regardless of form, except where it is crystal clear that Clark means to capitalize. I cope with his other capitals as best I can, promising little in the way of consistency.

[*vii*]

In the days when mail from the frontiers was slow and difficult, letter writers seldom confined themselves to a single topic. It is not unusual to find a substantial passage on Lewis and Clark midway in a ten-page letter about civil or Indian affairs. When extraneous portions of a letter are long, I delete them and indicate the deletion by a symbol. If they do not bulk large I often let them stand, preferring when possible to present the full text of a letter. If a manuscript contains only a brief reference to the expedition, I am most likely to quote the passage in a footnote to some related letter.

Jefferson's file copies before 1804 are letterpress copies, made by transferring the image under pressure to a sheet of dampened tissue. They often are badly blurred. In 1804 he began to use his famous polygraph, a device for reproducing one or more copies of a letter as he wrote the original. The reader may assume that virtually all of the "sender's copies" of Jefferson's letters are either letterpress or polygraph versions.

The Notes

The first manuscript indicated is the one from which the transcription has been made; other copies, if any, are listed next. If endorsements or addresses are routine, their presence is merely noted, but if they contribute useful information they are quoted in full. Jefferson faithfully endorsed his incoming letters with name of sender, date of letter, date of receipt, and sometimes subject. The date of receipt which I give for Jefferson's letters is always taken from the endorsement, unless it is identified as coming from his own compilation of letters sent and received, which I refer to as his "index of letters."

Material taken from printed texts is so indicated (Printed, NASATIR, 1:330–31), but no attempt is made to record other printed versions.

Senders, receivers, and persons referred to in the manuscripts are briefly identified at first mention. For senders and receivers, this identification is made in the first paragraph of the notes and no reference number is used. The reader can easily find the identification of an individual by locating in the index the page on which he is first mentioned.

No source is cited for the kind of biographical information to be found in standard directories, genealogies, and similar aids.

Names of authors in SMALL CAPITALS are citations to sources listed in the bibliography on pp. 680–93. This device enables me to keep many long titles and other impedimenta out of the notes. In the case of two or more works by authors with the same surname, I assign a number, as in SMITH (1). When a published work is being discussed, not merely cited, I often list it fully by author and title in the notes.

SYMBOLS

Libraries and archives, as designated by the National Union Catalog of the Library of Congress:

CaBVa	Vancouver Public Library, B.C.
CSmH	Henry E. Huntington Library, San Marino, Calif.
CtY	Yale University Library, New Haven, Conn.
CU-B	Bancroft Library, University of California, Berkeley
DLC	Library of Congress. Used alone, this symbol designates the Jefferson Papers; other collections are specified, as DLC—Biddle, etc.
DNA	National Archives. Always followed by an RG or record group number, plus any other file numbers required for identification.
Ia-HA	Iowa State Department of History and Archives, Des Moines
ICHi	Chicago Historical Society Library
ICN	Newberry Library, Chicago
IHi	Illinois State Historical Library, Springfield
InU	Indiana University Library, Bloomington
IU-Hi	Illinois Historical Survey, University of Illinois, Urbana
KHi	Kansas State Historical Society Library, Topeka
KyLoF	Filson Club Library, Louisville, Ky.
MB	Boston Public Library
MH	Harvard University Library, Cambridge, Mass.
MHi	Massachusetts Historical Society Library, Boston
MiU-C	William L. Clements Library, University of Michigan, Ann Arbor
MoSHi	Missouri Historical Society Library, St. Louis
MsAr	Mississippi State Department of Archives and History, Jackson
MtHi	Montana Historical Society Library, Helena
NBLiHi	Long Island Historical Society Library, Brooklyn
NhD	Dartmouth College Library, Hanover, N.H.
NHi	New-York Historical Society Library, New York
NjP	Princeton University Library, Princeton, N.J.
NN	New York Public Library
OrHi	Oregon Historical Society Library, Portland
PHC	Haverford College Library, Haverford, Pa.
PHi	Historical Society of Pennsylvania Library, Philadelphia
PPAmP	American Philosophical Society Library, Philadelphia
PPi	University of Pittsburgh Library
ViHi	Virginia Historical Society Library, Richmond

[*ix*]

ViU	Alderman Library, University of Virginia, Charlottesville
ViWC	Colonial Williamsburg Library, Va.
WHi	State Historical Society of Wisconsin Library, Madison

Other symbols and editorial aids:

AD	Autograph document
ADS	Autograph document, signed
AL	Autograph letter
ALS	Autograph letter, signed
D	Document
DS	Document, signed
Lbk	Letterbook copy
RC	Receiver's copy
RG	Record Group in the National Archives
SC	Sender's copy
[ ]	Word or phrase supplied or corrected. Editorial remarks within text are italicized and enclosed in square brackets.
[?]	Conjectural reading, or conjectural identification of an addressee.
[. . .]	A word or two missing or illegible. Longer omissions are specified in footnotes.
< >	Word or phrase deleted from manuscript, usually by sender. The words are set in italics.
. . . .	Unrelated matter deleted by the editor. The symbol stands alone, centered on a separate line.

Contents

[*xiii*]

[*xvi*]

A section of illustrations appears after page 106

Letters of the
Lewis and Clark Expedition
WITH RELATED DOCUMENTS
1783-1854

---

1. Jefferson to James Wilkinson

Dear General   Washington Feb. 23. 1801.
   I take the liberty of asking the protection of your cover for a letter[1] to Lieut. Meriwether Lewis, not knowing where he may be. In selecting a private secretary, I have thought it would be advantageous to take one who possessing a knolege of the Western country, of the army & it's situation, might sometimes aid us with informations of interest, which we may not otherwise possess.[2] A personal acquaintance with him, owing from his being of my neighborhood, has induced me to select him, if his presence can be dispensed with, without injury to the service. Altho' the public ought justly to be relieved from the charge of pay and rations while absent from his post, yet I should propose that he might retain his rank & right to rise. I have desired[?] him to wait on you and to recieve your pleasure on this subject, and I would sollicit such arrangements from you as might enable him to wind up whatever affairs he is engaged in as speedily as the public, & his own, interest would permit, without injury [to] either. Should he not be with you, I will ask the favor of you to avail [yourself] of the best conveyance of this which may occur. I pray you to accept assurances of high consideration & regard, Dear Genl. Your most obedt. & most humble servt.

                                                TH: JEFFERSON

   ALS, SC (DLC). James Wilkinson (1757–1825), commanding general of the U.S. Army, was governor of the Territory of Louisiana from July 1805 until Lewis's appointment in March 1807.
   1. Jefferson sent both letters to Tarleton Bates (1775–1806), a young Pittsburgh businessman who was Lewis's friend. Bates acknowledged receipt

[1]

of the letters 6 March (DLC), saying he had delivered Lewis's personally but had forwarded Wilkinson's, since the General was on his way to Washington.

2. It is perhaps too easy to find in this statement the suggestion that Jefferson already had decided to send Lewis on a western expedition. The President had no need to hint of such plans to Wilkinson, and probably would not have done so, for any steps he might have been taking to organize an expedition at this time would have been highly secret. But the President did need to give Wilkinson some reason for taking away one of his paymasters, and so he speaks (here and in the letter to Lewis below) of Lewis's knowledge of the West and of the "informations of interest" he can gather. This may mean simply that Lewis knew the posts along the Ohio, had ranged far into the interior of the country, and showed an interest in some of the pursuits which fascinated Jefferson—botany, zoology, geography, and ethnology.

2. Jefferson to Lewis

Dear Sir   Washington Feb. 23. 1801.

The appointment to the Presidency of the U.S. has rendered it necessary for me to have a private secretary, and in selecting one I have thought it important to respect not only his capacity to aid in the private concerns of the household, but also to contribute to the mass of information which it is interesting for the administration to acquire. Your knolege of the Western country, of the army and of all it's interests & relations has rendered it desireable for public as well as private purposes that you should be engaged in that office. In point of profit it has little to offer; the salary being only 500. D. which would scarcely be more than an equivalent for your pay & rations, which you would be obliged to relinquish while withdrawn from active service, but retaining your rank & right to rise. But it would be an easier office,[1] would make you know & be known to characters of influence in the affairs of our country, and give you the advantage of their wisdom. You would of course save also the expence of subsistence & lodging as you would be one of my family. If these or any other views which your own reflections may suggest should present the office of my private secretary as worthy of acceptance you will make me happy in accepting it. It has been sollicited by several, who will have no answer till I hear from you. Should you accept, it would be necessary that you should wind up whatever affairs you are engaged in as expeditiously as your own & the public interest will admit, & adjourn to this place: and that immediately on receipt of this you inform me by letter of your determination. It would also be

[2]

necessary that you wait on Genl. Wilkinson & obtain his approbation, & his aid in making such arrangements as may render your absence as little injurious to the service as may be. I write to him on this subject. Accept assurances of the esteem of Dear Sir your friend & servt.

TH: JEFFERSON

ALS, SC (DLC). Reply is No. 3.

1. Jefferson later described the duties of secretary in a letter of 26 March 1804 to William A. Burwell. "The office itself is more in the nature of that of an Aid de camp, than a mere Secretary. The writing is not considerable, because I write my own letters & copy them in a press. The care of our company, execution of some commissions in the town occasionally, messages to Congress, occasional conferences & explanations with particular members, with the offices, & inhabitants of the place where it cannot so well be done in writing, constitute the chief business. . . . A servant of the house to render you the offices you may need, & a horse in the stable always at your service . . ." (DLC).

3. Lewis to Jefferson

Dear Sir,   Pittsburgh, March 10th 1801.

Not untill two late on friday last to answer by that days mail, did I receive your much esteemed favour of the 23rd Ult. In it you have thought proper so far to honour me with your confidence, as to express a wish that I should accept the place of your private Secretary; I most cordially acquiesce, and with pleasure accept the office, nor were further motives necessary to induce my complyance, than that you Sir should conceive that in the discharge of the duties of that office, I could be servicable to my country, or ucefull to youreself: permit me here Sir to do further justice to my feelings, by expressing the lively sensibility with which I received this mark of your confidence and esteem.

I did not reach this place on my return from D,Etroit, untill late on the night of the 5th inst., five days after the departure of Genl. Wilkinson, my report therefore on the subject of your letter was immediately made to Colo. Hamtramck, the commanding officer at this place;[1] since which, not a moment has been lost in making the necessary arrangements in order to get forward to the City of Washington with all possible despatch: rest assured I shall not relax in my exertions. Receive I pray you Sir, the most undisembled assureance, of the attatchment and friendship of Your most obedient, & Very Humble Servt.,

MERIWETHER LEWIS

[3]

ALS, RC (DLC). Endorsed; received 20 March 1801.

1. Wilkinson's consent was only a formality, and Lewis would soon be seeing the General in Washington. Col. John Francis Hamtramck (d. 1803), commanding the First Infantry, of course had ample authority to order the young lieutenant east. A document (DNA, RG 92, Box 560A) dated 9 March 1801 and headed "Return of Transportn. wanting for the purpose of conveying the baggage and papers of Lieut. M. Lewis 1st. U.S. Infty. Regt. to the City of Washington" contains the following notation in Lewis's hand: "The Quarter Master Genl. will be so good as to furnish three Pack Horses, two pack-saddles compleat with girths and croopers, four temporary boxes (2 feet long, 1 foot 2 Inches wide, and 1 foot eight inches deep) and [*blank*] lbs. lash rope." One of the horses went lame, the roads were difficult after spring rains, and Lewis did not reach Washington until 1 April. Jefferson had departed for Virginia the day before, leaving word that Lewis might follow him for a few days of relaxation; but Lewis decided to stay and turn over his records to Lt. Ninian Pinkney, of Maryland, who was succeeding him as paymaster of the First Infantry (Lewis to Jefferson, 5 April 1803, DLC).

4. Carlos Martínez de Yrujo to Pedro Cevallos

No. 313—   [2 December 1802]

"Notice of a project communicated by the President to send travelers to explore the course of the Missouri River, and for them to penetrate as far as the Southern Ocean."

Most Excellent *Señor*

My Dear Sir: The President asked me the other day in a frank and confident tone, if our Court would take it badly, that the Congress decree the formation of a group of travelers, who would form a small caravan and go and explore the course of the Missouri River in which they would nominally have the objective of investigating everything which might contribute to the progress of commerce; but that in reality it would have no other view than the advancement of the geography. He said they would give it the denomination of mercantile, inasmuch as only in this way would the Congress have the power of voting the necessary funds; it not being possible to appropriate funds for a society, or a purely literary expedition, since there does not exist in the constitution any clause which would give it the authority for this effect. I replied to him that making use of the same frankness with which he honored me, I would take the liberty of telling him, that I persuaded myself that an expedition of this nature could not fail to give umbrage to our Government. Then he replied to me that he did not see the motive why they [our government] should have the least fear, inasmuch as its object would not be other than to observe the

[4]

territories which are found between 40° and 60° [north latitude] from the mouth of the Missouri to the Pacific Ocean, and unite the discoveries that these men would make with those which the celebrated Makensi made in 1793, and be sure if it were possible in that district to establish a continual communication, or little interrupted, by water as far as the South Sea. I told him then that this was already a determined point, as much by the fruitless attempts made with this objective by the Jesuits in Northern California, as by the particular surveys later made by the Captains Cook, Maurelle, Martinez, Vancouver, Cuadra, and lately by the *Señores* Malespina, and Bustamente,[1] who had reconnoitered in the most careful and scrupulous manner all that coast, from the south of the famous strait of Juan de Fucca, situated at 45° latitude, up to the Bucareli River, which the English call Cook River situated at 60° north latitude, and that all these examinations and attempts evidently prove there does not exist this passage of the Northwest, sought with so much anxiety by the most famous navigators of all the nations in the last two centuries, and that it has not existed except in the most exalted imaginations of our Ferrer Maldonado, and Mr. Basq,[2] French geographer. I added that although Miers[3] in these later times had inclined to believe in the existence of this passage, his error had been later demonstrated by the surveys which had been made of the points where it was supposed to exist. Finally that Mackinsee's[4] second trip, in which he penetrated in 1793 up to the Pacific Ocean, shows that there does not exist such a communication by water, since although he arrived in his canoe up to the river of la Paz [Peace river] and not very far from a considerable cordillera of mountains which runs north and south parallel to the ocean coast between 50° and 60° he found himself later in the necessity of traveling by land a very great distance, and the practical [experienced] Indians of the country could not give him news of any considerable river whatsoever which from those mountains, which must be without doubt the source of the waters of the west in that vicinity, empties into the Pacific Ocean. This account of useless and fruitless attempts it seems to me calmed his spirit with which he began to talk to me of the subject.

The President has been all his life a man of letters, very speculative and a lover of glory, and it would be possible he might attempt to perpetuate the fame of his administration not ony by the measures of frugality and economy which characterize him, but also by discovering or attempting at least to discover the way by which the Americans may some day extend their population and their influence up to the coasts of the South Sea.

[5]

I do not know what might be his final decision concerning this point, but I shall be on the lookout to see if it is attempted to realize or not this idea by the Congress, and in case of trying to carry it into effect I shall notify Your Excellency in order that it may please you to communicate to me His Majesty's orders concerning this issue.

May God keep Your Excellency many years.

Washington December 2, 1802

   Most Excellent *Señor*

Your most attentive and constant servant, kisses the hand of Your Excellency

CARLOS MARTÍNEZ DE YRUJO [rubric]

Most Excellent *Señor* Don Pedro Cevallos

[Decree] "That His Majesty has seen with satisfaction that by their erudite reflections the President's project has been abandoned.

February 19, 1803.

Printed, NASATIR (2), 2:712–14. The Spanish original is in the Archivo Histórico Nacional (Madrid), Papeles de Estado, legajo 5630, apartado 2. Carlos Martínez, Marqués de Casa Yrujo (1763–1824), was Spanish minister to the U.S. from 1796 to 1806. Pedro Cevallos or Ceballos (1764–1840) was minister of foreign affairs in the Spanish government. I am grateful to A. P. Nasatir and to John Francis McDermott of the St. Louis Historical Documents Foundation for permission to publish several translated documents from Nasatir's *Before Lewis and Clark*. I have resisted the temptation to include all the material bearing on Spanish reaction to Lewis and Clark; it is too voluminous, and I am content to know that more of it will appear when Nasatir and Noel M. Loomis begin to publish on the genesis of the Santa Fe Trail.

1. Here Yrujo begins to summarize his knowledge of explorations along the Pacific coast of North America. Capt. James Cook (1728–79) was killed by Hawaiians after his ship *Resolution* failed to find the Northwest Passage. Antonio Francisco Mourelle was a Spanish naval officer who voyaged along the Northwest coast in 1779. Esteban José Martinez, another Spanish officer, explored the region in 1788. The English explorer George Vancouver (1758–98) studied the area in 1792–94 and his *Voyage* was published posthumously in 1798. Juan Francisco de la Bodega y Cuadra, a Spanish naval officer, almost discovered the Strait of Juan de Fuca in 1775. Alejandro Malespina, a commander in the Spanish navy, and José Bustamente y Guerra reconnoitered Yakutat Bay in 1791. WAGNER discusses these and other voyages, and their cartographic results.

2. Lorenzo Ferrer Maldonaldo, Spanish author of a fictitious narrative of a voyage (1588) during which he claimed to have found a Northwest Passage. I have not identified "Mr. Basq."

3. John Meares, an English voyager, visited Nootka in 1786.

4. Sir Alexander Mackenzie (1755?–1820) was first to cross the North American continent north of Mexico. Later correspondence will show the degree to which Jefferson, Lewis, and Clark were aware of his work and influenced by it.

5. George Rogers Clark to Jefferson

Sir   Falls of Ohio 12th December 1802

I latterly had the pleasure of the perrusial of a letter[1] from the Secretary of War to my brother on the subject of the post of Fort Jifferson on the Mississippi—his answer to that letter completely discribed the place. A Military Post & Trading Town there, must be obvious to every man of observation that is acquainted with the Geography of the Countrey. I was the more pleased as I had Contemplated the importance of that spot from my earliest acquaintance with the Western Countrey.

When I was ordered [to] fix the garrison at or near the Mouth of the Ohio in the year 1780 I lay three weeks in the point and explored the banks of the river and Countrey before I fixed on the spot to build a Fort—and if my Instructions had not have been to place the Garrison South of the Ohio I certainly should have advised a Fortress in the point. I marked the ground the annual inundations flooded, it is about *five* feet, and from that to *seven* feet is the depth of the water that covers this butifull Tract of bottom, which may be raised for a City of any size, by the earth thrown out of the canals, cut through the City, and those canals may be kept pure by turning the Cash [Cache] River through them. I thus drew the plan and have been improving on it frequently to the present time. What caused me to view this ground with more attention was that the Spanish shore oppos'd. so high that a small expense would free two or three hundred acres of land.

This circumstance induced me to think that it would be necessary for us, at least to have a fortress in this point as a Key to the enterance of the Ohio. Those were my Ideas while on the ground. I segest to you, Sir, if worthey your attention, any further information, and the best perhaps that can be obtained of that country, may be got from my brother William, who is now settled at Clarksville in the Indiana Territory. I have long since laid aside all Idea of Public affairs, by bad fortune, and ill health. I have become incapable of persuing those enterpriseing & active persuits which I have been fond of from my youth—but I will with the greatest pleasure give my bro. William every information in my power on this, or any other

[7]

point which may be of Service to your Administration. He is well quallified almost for any business.[2] If it should be in your power to confur on him any post of Honor and profit, in this Countrey in which we live, it will exceedingly gratify me. I seem to [. . .] a right to expect such a gratification when asked for—but what will greatly highten it is, that I am sure it gives you pleasure to have it in your power to do me a Service. With the greatest assurrance of your prosperity I have the honor to be your ever sincere

G. R. CLARK

N.B. Mr. Hurst[3] the gentleman whome will hand you this letter, is a young Lawyer from Vincennes a Man of integrity and a good republican whom I beg leave to recommend to you.

G. R. C.

ALS, RC (DLC); SC (WHi). Endorsed; received 7 Jan. 1803. George Rogers Clark (1752–1818) was William's brother, famed for his conquest of the Northwest during the Revolution. "Falls of Ohio" may mean Louisville, Ky., on the south bank of the river, or the little village of Clarksville in Indiana Territory on the north bank.

1. Jefferson had asked the Secretary of War to specify the best site for a military post at the mouth of the Ohio, and the Secretary had forwarded the inquiry to William Clark for reply (JAMES (3), 460). William had inspected the site of Fort Jefferson a few years earlier and had made a brief record of his visit, describing the terrain and location on a slip of paper headed "Notes about old Fort Jefferson below the Mouth of the Ohio in 1795" (MoSHi).

2. The business that Jefferson would soon consider William qualified for was an employment once offered to George. George was now a man of lessening influence, inclined to drink, bitter over financial losses incurred in military service, and soon to be described by a visitor as "frail and helpless." But in 1783 he had been Jefferson's choice to lead an expedition to the Pacific. For an exchange of letters between the two men on that subject, see Nos. 412 and 413 in Appendix I.

3. Henry Hurst (1769–1855), a Vincennes attorney who was later an officer on William Henry Harrison's staff and still later a member of the Indiana legislature.

6. Lewis's Estimate of Expenses

[1803]

Recapitulation of an estimate of the sum necessary to carry into effort the Missie. expedicion—

Mathematical Instruments	$217
Arms & Accoutrements extraordinary	" 81
Camp Ecquipage	"255
Medecine & packing	" 55
Means of transportation	"430

Indian presents . . . . "696
Provisions extraordinary . . . . "224
Materials for making up the various articles into portable
  packs . . . . " 55
For the pay of hunters guides & Interpreters . . . . . . "300
In silver coin to defray the expences of the party from Nashville
  to the last white settlement on the Missisourie . . . . . "100
Contingencies . . . . " 87
                                                   $2,500

AD, RC (DLC). Endorsed by Jefferson, "Lewis Meriwether. Missouri Estimate." This undated document in Lewis's hand must have been written before Jefferson's confidential message to Congress (No. 8), and may have been written in late December 1802 when Jefferson was sounding out the Spanish minister. Because of this document, the sum of $2,500 has become firmly implanted in the literature as the total cost of the expedition. At this early stage, Lewis could not know how many times he would need to multiply the amount of his first guess. Bits of data about the financial aspects of the project are scattered throughout this volume, but see especially the procurement documents under Nos. 53–57 and the financial summaries under No. 277. I suspect that Jefferson and Lewis set the original estimate as low as possible to avoid congressional criticism. It must also be remembered that at first Lewis planned to take only a dozen men with him.

7. Cipher for Correspondence with Jefferson

[1803]

Suppose the key word to be 'antipodes'

Write it thus   a n t i p o d e s a n t i p o d e s a n t i p o d e s
to be cyphered t h e m a n w h o s e m i n d o n v i r t u e b e n t
                    u v y u g b & m g t s f r c s s s n j e m c u g i t m
then copy out the cyphered line thus. uvyvgb&mgtsfrcsssnjemcugitm
numbers are thus. 18. is *bu*. 1798 is thus *bubg*
The method is this.
Look for
t in the 1st vertical column, & a in the 1st horizontal one, gives u
h . . . . n v
e . . . . t . . . . y
m . . . . i . . . . u
a . . . . p . . . . g
n . . . . o . . . . b

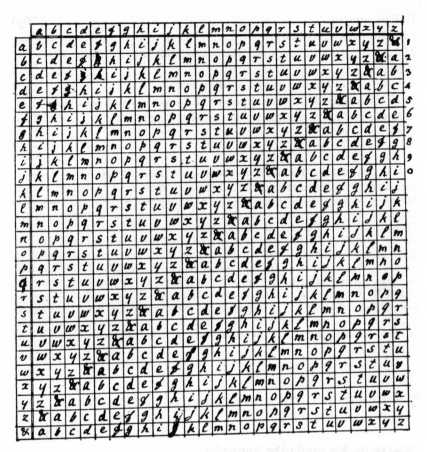

AD, SC (DLC). Endorsed, "Cypher establd. with Captain Lewis. Key. Artichokes." For notes on the operation of the cipher, see "Method of using Mr. [Robert] Patterson's cypher," fol. 22130 (DLC), and the documents that follow. For another copy of the cipher given to Lewis, apparently an earlier one, see fol. 22136. On that one a sample message encoded by Jefferson reads, "I am at the head of the Missouri. All well, and the Indians so far friendly." The key word is the same: artichokes. Apparently no occasion for Lewis to use this form of communication arose during the expedition. The cipher and Jefferson's explanation have been transposed here to avoid a difficulty in paging.

8. Jefferson's Message to Congress

Confidential. [18 January 1803]

Gentlemen of the Senate and of the House of Representatives.

As the continuance of the Act for establishing trading houses with the Indian tribes will be under the consideration of the legislature at it's present session, I think it my duty to communicate the views which have guided me in the execution of that act; in order that you may decide on the policy of continuing it, in the present or any other form, or to discontinue it altogether if that shall, on the whole, seem most for the public good.

The Indian tribes residing within the limits of the U.S. have for a considerable time been growing more & more uneasy at the constant diminution of the territory they occupy, altho' effected by their own voluntary sales: and the policy has long been gaining strength with them of refusing absolutely all further sale on any conditions, insomuch that, at this time, it hazards their friendship, and excites dangerous jealousies & perturbations in their minds to make any overture for the purchase of the smallest portions of their land. A very few tribes only are not yet obstinately in these dispositions. In order peaceably to counteract this policy of theirs, and to provide an extension of territory which the rapid increase of our numbers will call for, two measures are deemed expedient. First, to encourage them to abandon hunting, to apply to the raising [of] stock, to agriculture and domestic manufacture, and thereby prove to themselves that less land & labour will maintain them in this, better than in their former mode of living. The extensive forests necessary in the hunting life, will then become useless, & they will see advantage in exchanging them for the means of improving their farms, & of increasing their domestic comforts. Secondly to multiply trading houses among them, & place within their reach those things which will contribute more to their domestic comfort than the possession of extensive, but uncultivated wilds. Experience & reflection will develope to them the wisdom of exchanging what they can spare & we want, for what we can spare and they want. In leading them thus to agriculture, to manufactures & civilization, in bringing together their & our settlements, & in preparing them ultimately to participate in the benefits of our government, I trust and believe we are acting for their greatest good. At these trading houses we have pursued the principles of the act of Congress, which directs that the commerce shall be carried on liberally, & requires only that the capital stock shall not be diminished. We consequently undersell private traders, foreign & domestic, drive them from the competition, & thus, with the good will of the Indians, rid ourselves of a description of men who are constantly endeavoring to excite in the Indian mind suspicions, fears & irritations towards us. A letter now inclosed shows the effect of our competition on the operations of the traders, while the Indians, percieving the advantage of purchasing from us, are

[11]

solliciting generally our establishment of trading houses among them. In one quarter this is particularly interesting. The legislature, reflecting on the late occurrences on the Missisipi, must be sensible how desireable it is to possess a respectable breadth of country on that river, from our Southern limit to the Illinois at least; so that we may present as firm a front on that as on our Eastern border. We possess what is below the Yazoo, & can probably acquire a certain breadth from the Illinois & Wabash to the Ohio. But between the Ohio and Yazoo, the country all belongs to the Chickasaws, the most friendly tribe within our limits, but the most decided against the alienation of lands. The portion of their country most important for us is exactly that which they do not inhabit. Their settlements are not on the Missisipi, but in the interior country. They have lately shown a desire to become agricultural, and this leads to the desire of buying implements & comforts. In the strengthening and gratifying of these wants, I see the only prospect of planting on the Missisipi itself the means of it's own safety. Duty has required me to submit these views to the judgment of the legislature. But as their disclosure might embarrass & defeat their effect, they are committed to the special confidence of the two houses.

While the extension of the public commerce among the Indian tribes may deprive of that source of profit such of our citizens as are engaged in it, it might be worthy the attention of Congress, in their care of individual as well as of the general interest to point in another direction the enterprize of these citizens, as profitably for themselves, and more usefully for the public. The river Missouri, & the Indians inhabiting it, are not as well known as is rendered desireable by their connection with the Missisipi, & consequently with us. It is however understood that the country on that river is inhabited by numerous tribes, who furnish great supplies of furs & peltry to the trade of another nation carried on in a high latitude, through an infinite number of portages and lakes, shut up by ice through a long season. The commerce on that line could bear no competition with that of the Missouri, traversing a moderate climate, offering according to the best accounts a continued navigation from it's source, and, possibly with a single portage, from the Western ocean, and finding to the Atlantic a choice of channels through the Illinois or Wabash, the Lakes and Hudson, through the Ohio and Susquehanna or Potomac or James rivers, and through the Tennessee and Savannah rivers. An intelligent officer with ten or twelve chosen men, fit for the enterprize and willing to undertake it, taken from our posts, where they may be spared without inconvenience, might explore the whole line, even to the Western ocean, have conferences with the natives on the subject of commercial intercourse, get admission among them for our traders as others are admitted, agree on convenient deposits for an interchange of articles, and return with the information acquired in the course of two summers. Their arms & accoutrements, some instruments of observation, & light & cheap presents for the Indians would be all the apparatus they could carry, and with an expectation of a soldier's portion of land on their return would constitute the whole expense. Their pay would be going on, whether here or there. While other civilized nations have encountered great expense to enlarge the boundaries of knowledge, by undertaking voyages of discovery, & for other literary purposes, in various parts and directions, our nation seems to owe to the same object, as well as to its own interest, to explore this, the only line of easy communication across the continent, and so directly traversing our own part of it. The interests of commerce place the principal object within the constitutional powers and care of Congress, and that it should incidentally advance the geographical knowledge of our own continent can not but be an additional gratification. The nation claiming the territory, regarding this as a literary pursuit which it is in the habit of permitting within it's dominions, would not be disposed to view it with jealousy, even if the expiring state of it's interest there did not render it a matter of indifference. The appropriation of two thousand five hundred dollars 'for the purpose of extending the external commerce of the U.S.,' while understood and considered by the Executive as giving the legislative sanction, would cover the undertaking from notice, and prevent the obstructions which interested individuals might otherwise previously prepare in it's way.

TH: JEFFERSON
Jan. 18. 1803.

ADS, SC (DLC).

Jefferson seems to have included his request for a special appropriation in an early draft of his regular message to Congress, which he circulated among his cabinet members according to his custom. In response he got a comment from Albert Gallatin, his Secretary of the Treasury, that the proposal for western exploration ought to be the subject of a confidential message, "as it contemplates an expedition out of our own territory. . . ." Gallatin continued, "I feel warmly interested in this plan, & will suggest the propriety that Gen. Dearborn should write immediately to procure 'Vancouver's Survey' one copy of which, the only one I believe in America, is advertised by F. Nichols No. 70 Chesnut St. Philada. Price with all the charts 55 dollars" (DLC, received by Jefferson 21 Nov. 1802).

Perhaps as a result of Gallatin's reaction, Jefferson did not retain the subject in his annual message to Congress, 15 Dec. 1802 (DLC). The confidential message above was passed as requested, and became a law 28 Feb. 1803 (*Annals of the Congress of the United States*, 12:103).

Jefferson tried hard to keep the projected expedition secret. But from whom? Surely not from the British, French, and Spanish, to whom he was giving disarming reassurances that the exploration was mainly literary. He feared, instead, the intervention of his political enemies. We see an indication of this when Attorney General Levi Lincoln writes (No. 26) of "the perverse, hostile, and malignant state of the opposition" which has the capacity to arouse public sentiment against the executive. And so the word goes out that the expedition is bound up the Mississippi. Except when he is writing to men who need to know the real destination, or to Europeans who are too far away to be security risks, Jefferson speaks in these terms. As late as 13 July 1803 he tells Caesar A. Rodney, "Capt. Lewis left this on the 5th on his journey up the Missisipi" (DLC). But the cloak of secrecy may have leaked a good deal of light. When Lewis asked Clark to accompany him, and cautioned him not to reveal the destination, Clark replied that word of the expedition had been abroad in Louisville for several weeks (No. 74). Whether or not the true destination was known, Clark did not make clear.

9. Carlos Martínez de Yrujo to Pedro Cevallos

No. 320   [31 January 1803]
The Marqués de Casa Yrujo to Most Excellent *Señor* Don Pedro Cevallos.

"Gives notice of the President having passed to the Senate the project of sending travelers to explore the course of the Missouri, of which he gave account in the letter no. 313."

Most Excellent *Señor*

Dear Sir:

In my letter No. 313 I notified Your Excellency that the President of the United States had a project directed to send travelers in order to explore the course of the Missouri River, who continuing their expedition up to the North West Coast, they were to examine the possibility or impossibility of communications by water, between the Atlantic Ocean and the Southern Ocean, and contribute to advance the geography of the North of America. I also told Your Excellency the conversation which pertaining to this project, the President had with me concerning this plan, he desiring to know whether our Court would refuse to grant the necessary passports to the travelers, and all of which I judged opportune to reply to you concerning the particular. I thought that in consequence he would desist in his attempt, and in this way I hinted this to Your

Excellency, but later I have learned that he has communicated his design to the Senate, which has already taken a step towards the execution. Nevertheless I have understood that the good judgment of the Senate does not see the advantages that the President proposes in this expedition, and that on the contrary, they feared it might offend one of the European nations, and consequently it is very probable that the project will not proceed. But since I promised to give to Your Excellency news of any latest occurrence, I thought I should communicate this to you for your intelligence.

May God keep Your Excellency many years.

Washington, January 31, 1803.

Most Excellent *Señor.*

Your most attentive and constant servant kisses Your Excellency's Hand.

THE MARQUÉS DE CASA YRUJO

[rubric]

Most Excellent *Señor* Don Pedro Cevallos.

Printed, NASATIR (2), 2:715–16. The Spanish original is in the Archivo Histórico Nacional (Madrid), Papeles de Estado, legajo 5630, apartado 3.

10. Jefferson to Bernard Lacépède

Dear Sir   Washington Feb. 24. 1803.

I have just recieved from Mr. Paine[1] the copy of your Discours l'ouverture de l'an IX.[2] which you were so good as to send me. A rapid view of parts of it only assures me of the pleasure I shall recieve from a deliberate perusal of the whole the first moment I have to spare. I was struck with the prophetic spirit of the passage pa. 10. 11. "bientot de courageux voyageurs visiteront les sources du Missisipi et du Missouri, que l'oeil d'un European n'a pas encore entrevues." It happens that we are now actually sending off a small party to explore the Missouri to it's source, and whatever other river, heading nearest with that, runs into the Western ocean; to enlarge our knolege of the geography of our continent, by adding information of that interesting line of communication across it, and to give us a general view of it's population, natural history, productions, soil & climate. It is not improbable that this voyage of discovery will procure us further information of the Mammoth, & of the Megatherium also, mentioned by you page 6. For you have possibly seen in our

[15]

Philosophical transactions, that, before we had seen the account of that animal by Mr. Cuvier,[3] we had found here some remains of an enormous animal incognitum, whom, from the disproportionate length of h[is] claw, we had denominated Megalonyx,[4] and which is probably the same animal; and that there are symptoms of it's late and present existence. The route we are exploring will perhaps bring us further evidence of it, and may be accomplished in two summers.

·   ·   ·   ·

I pray you to accept assurances of my great consideration and respect.

TH: JEFFERSON

ALS, SC (DLC). Reply is No. 35. Bernard Germain Etienne de la Ville sur Illion, Comte de Lacépède (1756–1825), was a French naturalist who corresponded frequently with Jefferson.

1. Thomas Paine (1737–1809), the American political philosopher.
2. *Discours d'ouverture et de clôture du cours de zoologie donné dans le Muséum national d'histoire naturelle, l'an ix de la république* (Paris [1801]).
3. Georges Leopold Chrétien, Baron Cuvier (1769–1832), French naturalist and comparative anatomist.
4. Jefferson's interest in the fossil remains of the giant ground sloth reflects his fascination with mammalian paleontology, a science so new that its founder, Cuvier, was still living. The speculation that the creature might still exist demonstrates the primitive state of knowledge in that field; but not so much, perhaps, as the speculation of Henri Marie Blainville (1777–1850) that Jefferson's megalonyx was no other than the grizzly bear. See Blainville's unsigned article, "Note sur l'our gris d'Amerique," *Journal de physique, de chimie, d'histoire naturelle et des artes*, 81 (Dec. 1815), 416–19. His contemporaries were skeptical. "What he says is very cleaver," said José Corrèa da Serra, "but not sufficient to bring conviction, and he himself avows it" (to Jefferson, 16 June 1816, DLC).

11. Jefferson to Benjamin Smith Barton

Dear Sir   Washington Feb. 27. 1803.

I inclose you a copy of two discourses sent you by Mr. La Cepede through the hands of Mr. Paine, who delivered them with some sent me. What follows in this letter is strictly confidential. You know we have been many years wishing to have the Missouri explored & whatever river, heading with that, runs into the Western ocean. Congress, in some secret proceedings, have yielded to a proposition I made them for permitting me to have it done: it is to be undertaken immediately, with a party of about ten, & I have appointed Capt. Lewis, my secretary, to conduct it. It was impossible to find a character who to a compleat science in botany, natural history, mineralogy & astronomy, joined the firmness of constitution & character, prudence, habits adapted to the woods, & a familiarity with the Indian manners & character, requisite for this undertaking. All the latter qualifications Capt. Lewis has. Altho' no regular botanist &c. he possesses a remarkable store of accurate observation on all the subjects of the three kingdoms, & will therefore readily single out whatever presents itself new to him in either: and he has qualified himself for taking those observations of longitude & latitude necessary to fix the geography of the line he passes through. In order to draw his attention at once to the objects most desirable, I must ask the favor of you to prepare for him a note of those in the lines of botany, zoology, or of Indian history which you think most worthy of inquiry & observation. He will be with you in Philadelphia in two or three weeks, & will wait on you, and receive thankfully on paper, and any verbal communications which you may be so good as to make to him. I make no apology for this trouble, because I know that the same wish to promote science which has induced me to bring forward this proposition, will induce you to aid in promoting it. Accept assurances of my friendly esteem & high respect.

TH: JEFFERSON

ALS, SC (DLC); RC (PHi); transcript (ViWC). Benjamin Smith Barton (1766–1815), physician, naturalist, and lecturer at the University of Pennsylvania, will figure in Jefferson's later attempts to achieve publication of the Lewis and Clark journals.

12. Jefferson to Caspar Wistar

Dear Sir   Washington Feb. 28. 1803

The inclosed sheets may contain some details which perhaps may be thought interesting enough for the transactions of our society. They were forwarded to me by Mr. Dunbar[1] with a couple of vocabularies which I retain to be added to my collection.

What follows is to be perfectly confidential. I have at length succeeded in procuring an essay to be made of exploring the Missouri & whatever river, heading with that, runs into the Western ocean. Congress by a secret authority enables me to do it. A party of about 10. chosen men headed by an officer will immediately set out. We cannot in the U.S. find a person who to courage, prudence, habits

[17]

& health adapted to the woods, & some familiarity with the Indian character, joins a perfect knolege of botany, natural history, mineralogy & astronomy, all of which would be desireable. To the first qualifications Capt. Lewis my secretary adds a great mass of accurate observation made on the different subjects of the three kingdoms as existing in these states, not under their scientific forms, but so as that he will readily seize whatever is new in the country he passes thro, and give us accounts of new things only: and he has qualified himself for fixing the longitude & latitude of the different points in the line he will go over. I have thought it would be useful to confine his attention to those objects only on which information is most deficient & most desireable: & therefore would thank you to make a note on paper of those which occur to you as most desireable for him to attend to. He will be in Philadelphia within two or three weeks & will call on you. Any advice or hints you can give him will be thankfully received & usefully applied. I presume he will complete his tour there & back in two seasons. Accept assurances of my sincere esteem & high respect.

TH: JEFFERSON

ALS, SC (DLC). Caspar Wistar (1761–1818) was professor of anatomy at the University of Pennsylvania, and successor to Jefferson in 1815 as president of the American Philosophical Society.

1. William Dunbar (1749–1810), Scottish scientist and planter who settled on the Mississippi near Natchez in 1792, and who carried on a correspondence with Jefferson for many years. See later references to his exploration of his region, and a discussion (Nos. 151, 157) of how to find the longitude without a timepiece.

13. Jefferson to Benjamin Rush

Dear Sir   Washington Feb. 28. 1803

I wish to mention to you in confidence that I have obtained authority from Congress to undertake the long desired object of exploring the Missouri & whatever river, heading with that, leads into the Western ocean. About 10. chosen woodsmen headed by Capt. Lewis my secretary, will set out on it immediately & probably accomplish it in two seasons. Capt. Lewis is brave, prudent, habituated to the woods, & familiar with Indian manners & character. He is not regularly educated, but he possesses a great mass of accurate observation on all the subjects of nature which present themselves here, & will therefore readily select those only in his new route which shall

be new. He has qualified himself for those observations of longitude
& latitude necessary to fix the points of the line he will go over. It
would be very useful to state for him those objects on which it is
most desirable he should bring us information. For this purpose I
ask the favor of you to prepare some notes of such particulars as may
occur in his journey & which you think should draw his attention
& enquiry. He will be in Philadelphia about 2. or 3. weeks hence &
will wait on you.

.   .   .   .

I pray you to accept assurances of my affectionate friendship &
sincere respect.

TH: JEFFERSON

ALS, SC (DLC); RC (CU-B). Benjamin Rush (1745?-1813) was a leading
physician and a professor of medicine at the University of Pennsylvania. To
this letter Rush replied 12 March 1803: "I shall expect to see Mr. Lewis
in Philadelphia, and shall not fail of furnishing him with a number of
questions calculated to increase our knowledge of subjects connected with
medicine" (RUSH LETTERS, 2:858). See No. 43 for the rules of health he gave
to Lewis, and No. 101 for a list of questions in medicine and ethnology.

14. Lewis's British Passport

[28 February 1803]

The undersigned, chargé d'affaires of his Britannic Majesty in the
United States of America, &c., certifies to all to whom these presents
shall come, that the bearer, Captain Merriwether Lewis, citizen of
the United States of America, is sent (under the authority of the said
United States) to explore the headwaters and shores of the Missoury
and the western parts of the North American continent, and that he
carries with him no merchandise other than that which is necessary
to assure a favorable reception among the native tribes, and to advance
the scientific and literary objects of his voyage. I therefore pray all
to whom these presents shall come, either his Majesty's superin-
tendents of Indian affairs or subjects of his Majesty who are engaged
in trade with the said tribes, not only to permit the said Captain
Lewis to pass without hindrance or impediment whatsoever, but also
to render him all the aid and all the protection which shall depend
upon them, and finally to advance by all possible means the object
of his voyage, which he has undertaken with a scientific motive only,
and the protection and fulfillment of which is of interest to all civilized
nations.

Given at the city of Washington the 28th of February 1803.

EDWD. THORNTON

Copia

Delassus

Transcript, Archivo General de Indias (Seville), Papeles de Cuba, legajo 2368. The transcript, in French, was made by Carlos Dehault Delassus (1764–1842), lieutenant governor of Upper Louisiana. Edward Thornton (1766–1852) was British chargé d'affaires in the U.S. from Nov. 1800 to Nov. 1803.

It was logical for Lewis to carry a British passport in the French language, since the British subjects he was most likely to meet would have been French-speaking traders from Canada. It is possible, however, that he asked John Hay in Cahokia to translate the document into French, upon learning that Delassus did not read English (see No. 99). One might have expected Thornton to send a copy along with his letter to Lord Hawkesbury (No. 28), but there is no copy in the Public Record Office, London.

15. Lewis's French Passport

[1 March 1803]

The Commissioner General of Trade Relations chargé d'affaires of the French Republic, undersigned, requests all those to whom this present shall be delivered, officials of the government of the French Republic, captains and commanders of vessels or land forces of the Republic, and moreover all French Citizens, to give protection and aid to the bearer, Captain Merriwether Lewis, Citizen of the United States, who, by authority of the President of the said United States, is setting out on a voyage of discovery with the purpose of exploring the Missouri river and the western regions of the Northern Continent. The undersigned certifies that Captain Merriwether Lewis has no purpose other than the above, that he carries with him only the goods and merchandise fitting to make him well received by the Indians, and his voyage being of a purely scientific nature, and in its end of equal interest to all the civilized world, the undersigned repeats the invitation to all those who may be requested to give him aid and assistance, likewise his travelling companions who are in number [*blank*].

Given at Georgetown near the town of Washington, 10 Ventose year 11 (1st March 1803) and sealed with the seal of the legation.

L. A. PICHON

Transcript (DLC) from Correspondance Politique, Affaires Étrangères, E.-U., 55:320. This is a translation. The signer, Louis André, Baron Pichon (1771–1850), was secretary of the legation of France to the U.S.

16. Jefferson to Robert Patterson

Dear Sir   Washington Mar. 2. 1803.

I am now able to inform you, tho' I must do it confidentially, that we are at length likely to get the Missouri explored, & whatever river heading with that, leads into the Western ocean. Congress by a secret act has authorised me to do it. I propose to send immediately a party of about ten men with Capt. Lewis, my secretary, at their head. If we could have got a person perfectly skilled in botany, natural history, mineralogy, astronomy, with at the same time the necessary firmness of body & mind, habits of living in the woods & familiarity with the Indian character, it would have been better. But I know of no such character who would undertake an enterprise so perilous. To all the latter qualities Capt. Lewis joins a great stock of <scientific> accurate observation on the subjects of the three kingdoms which are found in our own country but not according to their scientific nomenclatures. But he will be able to seize for examination & description such things only as he shall meet with new. He has been for some time qualifying himself for taking observations of longitude & latitude to fix the geographical points of the line he will pass over, but little means are possessed here of doing that; and it is the particular part in which you could give him valuable instruction, & he will receive it thankfully & employ it usefully. The instruments thought best to be carried for this purpose are a good theodolite & a Hadley. He will be in Philadelphia 2. or 3. weeks hence to procure instruments & will take the liberty to call on you; and I shall be particularly obliged to you for any advice or instruction you can give him. I think it adviseable that nothing should be said of this till he shall have got beyond the reach of any obstacles which might be prepared for him by those who would not like the enterprise. Accept assurances of my sincere esteem & great respect.

TH: JEFFERSON

ALS, SC (DLC); RC (NBLiHi). Reply is No. 22. Robert Patterson (1743–1824) was professor of mathematics at the University of Pennsylvania and later director of the U.S. mint at Philadelphia.

17. Louis André Pichon to Jefferson

[4 March 1803]

Mr. Pichon with his respects incloses herewith the passport which the President of the United States did him the honor to ask and returns the passport of Mr. Thornton which had been communicated as a model.

G. Town 4th March.

AL, RC (DLC).

18. Louis André Pichon to the Minister of Foreign Affairs

Citizen Minister,   Georgetown 13 Ventose Year 11 [4 March 1803]
   Yesterday at midnight the power of this Congress, the Seventh held under the existing Constitution, came to an end. This assembly was busy up to the last moment of its existence, and, as is the custom, to speed business, the President spent the night at the Capitol to sign the acts. As I have had the honor of telling you, Citizen Minister, the next Congress will reconvene, according to the adjournment pronounced by the former, on the first Monday of the month of next November. Mr. Jefferson leaves tomorrow or later for Monticello, where he must remain until the end of March.

   Citizen Minister, the President, at whose residence I was yesterday, expressed the wish that, before his departure, I would grant him a passport, of which I have the honor to send you the attached copy, and the purpose of which I must explain to you. For a long time Mr. Jefferson has been concerned with the means of exploring the sources of the Missouri beyond which he supposes must be found those of the river Origan which flows into the Pacific Ocean, and of which only the mouth is known; I believe that is the river named, if I am not mistaken, the river Colombia by the explorer McKenzie. As a result he has planned an expedition destined to this discovery and for which he has obtained from Congress a small sum of money; this appropriation, however, could not be made directly for this purpose on account of the scruples they have over the right of the general Government to do anything which might tend toward the encouragement of the Sciences. The thing was voted through with the indefinite end of encouraging foreign trade, and they even assure me that the President's personal influence was necessary to obtain this small appropriation which I believe [does not amount to] 5000 Dollars.

   The President, then, who has this expedition very much at heart, asked me for a passport yesterday. He explained his purpose to me, on the big map by Arrow Smith.[1] Citizen Minister, the only observation I allowed myself to make was to ask Mr. Jefferson whether the

Minister from Spain was granting a passport. He replied that he ought to grant one [qu'il devait le donner]. I asked him to give me a memorandum on how to carry it out. He entrusted me with that of the English chargé d'affaires, Mr. Thornton. I copied mine almost exactly from that and I even copied the date, that of 1 March,[2] which is what makes my passport appear antedated when compared to this letter. Citizen Minister, I did not think I should allow myself any other reflection on the wish which the President expressed to me and, truly, the request did not appear to demand it.

As you see, Citizen Minister, the expedition is entrusted to a Capt. Merrywether; I have not been able to determine the number of men who are accompanying him. The President told me that it would be eight or ten, if my memory is correct. The travelers must return by sea. They will find an opportunity on the Northwest coast, even by American ships. That is perhaps the only detail of the expedition in which a French passport might be of some use. Citizen Minister, accept my respects,

L. A. PICHON

Transcript (DLC) from Correspondance Politique, Affaires Étrangères, E.-U., 55:318. This is a translation. The minister of foreign affairs was Charles Maurice de Talleyrand (1754–1838).

1. Aaron Arrowsmith (1750–1832), English geographer and cartographer.

2. In the French version of the British passport, the only one that I have located, the date is 28 Feb.

19. Andrew Ellicott to Jefferson

Dear Sir   Lancaster March 6th 1803.

Your agreeable favour of the 26th Ult. has been duly received, and the contents noted. I shall be very happy to see Captn. Lewis, and will with pleasure give him all the information, and instruction, in my power. The necessary apparatus for his intended, and very interesting expedition, you will find mentioned in the last paragraph of the 42d page of my printed observations made in our southern country,[1] a copy of which I left with you. But exclusive of the watch, I would recommend one of Arnolds chronometers, (if it could be had,) for reasons which I will fully explain to Mr. Lewis.

Mr. Lewis's first object must be, to acquire a facility, and dexterity, in making the observations; which can only be attained by practice; in this he shall have all the assistance I can give him with aid of my apparatus. It is not to be expected that the calculations can be made till after his return, because the transportation of the books, and tables, necessary for that purpose, would be found inconvenient on such a journey. The observations on which Arrow.smith has constructed his map[2] of the northern part of this country, were all calculated in England.

The week before last I adapted a grid-iron pendulum to my regulator, it is the first ever made in this country, and was the work of six sundays, the duties of my office not allowing any other time:—the rods, and bob of this pendulum together, weigh 18 pounds.

I had a midling good observation on the beginning of the eclipse of the sun on the evening of the 21st of last month.

I am in hopes Mr. Madison forwarded my observations to the national institute by Mr. Munroe. Those on the 4th satellite of Jupiter, have been lately written for by both la Lande, and Delambre.[3] I have the honor to be with great respect and esteem your friend and hbl. servt.

Andw. Ellicott.

By a practice of more than twenty years, I have constantly found water preferable to any other fluid for an artificial, or portable horizon.[4] The reflection of the Sun from the water it is true, will be fainter than that from the specula, unless the Telescope of the Sextant be directed nearly off the foliated part of the horizon speculum. This direction can be easily given to it, by a screw for that purpose, and which carries the Telescope parallel to the plane of the Sextant.

Altho the meridian altitude of the sun, when it exceeds 60°, cannot be taken with a Sextant from the artificial horizon; yet the latitude may be accurately determined by using the altitude of the sun, and the horary angles formed in taking equal altitudes to ascertain the error, and rate of going of either a clock, or watch. This method I have constantly used when the meridional altitude of the sun exceeded 60°, and am convinced from a long experience, that the latitude may be deduced from such observations nearly, if not quite as accurately, as from the sun's meridional altitude. By many trials made at this place, the latitude in no case, differs so much as half a minute from that settled by the Zenith Sector.

The equal altitudes ought always to be taken at least two hours before, and after noon.

If the distance of the moon, from the sun, be taken immediately before the morning equal altitudes, or after those of the afternoon, or both if the position of the moon will permit, every requisite for determining with accuracy both the latitude, and longitude, will be had. I do not find that this method has been practised by any

[24]

person but myself, the theory has however been long understood.

After the forenoon equal altitudes have been taken, the sextant should be carefully laid away, and the index not moved, till the afternoon ones are taken, and if the latitude is to be deduced from the observations, the altitude must be carefully counted off, but if the time only is wanted, the degrees, minutes, and seconds of altitude are of no importance.

It is rather better to have the vessel which contains the water for the artificial horizon unconnected with the talk [talc], or isinglass cover, because the wind is sometimes so violent, as to shake the cover, and consequently if the two parts are connected, an undulatory motion will be communicated to the water.

It will be a necessary precaution, to have the Chronometer, with its case, tied up in a bladder when not in use,—it will privent its being injured if by accident it should be thrown in the water by the overturning of a canoe, or other accident.[5]

A. E.

ALS, RC (DLC). Endorsed; received 18 March 1803. Andrew Ellicott (1754–1820) of Lancaster, Pa., was an astronomer and surveyor.

1. *The journal of Andrew Ellicott . . . for determining the boundary between the United States and the possessions of his Catholic Majesty in America* (Philadelphia, 1803).

2. Jefferson ordered a copy of this map 17 June 1803 (SOWERBY, 4:102), and Lewis probably carried one with him to the Pacific.

3. Here Ellicott mentions James Madison (1751–1836), then Secretary of State; James Monroe (1758–1831), then special envoy to France; Joseph Jérôme le Français de Lalande (1732–1807), French astronomer; and Jean Baptiste Delambre (1749–1822), French astronomer and secretary of the National Institute of France. Ellicott had proposed Delambre for membership in the American Philosophical Society in a letter of 17 Jan. 1803 to Robert Patterson (PPAmP).

4. Robert Patterson described the artificial horizon as a device which, "by means of a reflecting sextant, answers the purpose of measuring all altitudes of the sun, or any other visible object, from 0 to 90° as well as alt. depressions not exceeding 50° with great ease and accuracy" (to Jefferson, 24 Oct. 1815, DLC). In a letter of 28 Nov. 1815 he gave Jefferson complete instructions for use of an artificial horizon which he had just sent.

5. A contemporary copy of these notes in PPAmP contains some added comments by Thomas Whitney, in the hand of John Vaughan.

20. Edward Thornton to Lord Hawkesbury

My Lord,   Philadelphia 9th March 1803.

One of the two Acts of Congress, passed in secret sessions of the two Houses, and discussed with closed doors, relates to the encouragement and extension of the external commerce of the United States, and appropriates the sum of two thousand five hundred dollars for that purpose; and it requires some explanation to make Your Lordship aware of the necessity of secrecy on a subject, which has been very often examined before, and which on the face of it does not present any circumstance requiring concealment.

The President has for some years past had it in view to set on foot an expedition entirely of a scientific nature for exploring the Western Continent of America by the route of the Great River Missouri, and for tracing the proximity of the sources of this river to the streams, which fall on the other side into the Pacific Ocean. He supposes this to be the most natural and direct water-communication between the two Oceans, and he is ambitious in his character of a man of letters and of science, of distinguishing his Presidency by a discovery, now the only one left to his enterprize—the Northern Communication having been so ably explored and ascertained by Sir Alexander Mackenzie's journeys.

But the constitution of the United States according to the comments of the most able jurists of the country does not permit the general government to offer bounties for the promotion of discoveries or for the advancement of science; and motives of prudence and humanity would equally prevent him from sending persons on an expedition of much peril and not strictly within the limits of legislative authority without apprizing the Congress of the real state of the case. A certain degree of secrecy was absolutely necessary before the commencement at least of the expedition: and it is with this view that the Congress have received the President's communication with closed doors, and have in the same manner authorized an appropriation with the ostensible object of extending the external commerce of the country, but with a complete understanding of the real nature of the plan in contemplation.

This is the state of the case, as the President himself represented it to me a day or two before I left Washington, requesting at the same time, if I felt it consistent with my duty, to furnish the Gentleman, whom he has selected for this enterprize, with a passport, that might secure him as far as related to His Majesty's subjects from groundless suspicions, and that would explain its real object, which is exclusively scientific. He assured me that it was in no shape his wish to encourage commerce with distant or indeed with any Indian tribes, which could only be done by attracting them towards the territory of the Union, or by withdrawing the white inhabitants from their proper business of agriculture, and that the Gentleman

[26]

entrusted with the conduct of the business would carry no articles of commerce whatever except such as would be indispensably necessary to secure him a favourable reception and passage through the Indian tribes dispersed on the banks of the Missouri.

The Gentleman he has selected for the journey is his Secretary, Captain Merriwether Lewis, a person in the vigour of his age, of a hardy constitution, and already acquainted with the manners of the Indians by his residence in the Western Settlements. He is to be accompanied by a small party of eight or ten boatmen of his own selection, and such Indian hunters as he can prevail upon to accompany him. It did not appear to me that any injurious consequences could arise from granting a passport on the terms and with the views expressed by Mr. Jefferson, and I hope Your Lordship will not think that in paying this mark of personal attention to the President's wishes, I have materially exceeded the limits of my duty.

The apprehended occupation of Louisiana by the French seems to have accelerated the determination of the President, as he thinks it certain that on their arrival they will instantly set on foot enterprizes of a similar nature. I have the honour to be etc.

EDWD. THORNTON

Transcript (DLC—Foreign Office Records) from the Public Record Office, London, F.O. 5, vol. 38, pp. 56–59. In the original records this letter now forms pp. 105–07. Robert Banks Jenkinson, Lord Hawkesbury (1770–1828), was British secretary of state for foreign affairs, 1801–04. His office was kept informed of the progress of the expedition, receiving clippings of newspaper versions of Lewis's letter to Jefferson, 7 April 1805, and Clark's to Harrison, 2 April 1805 (F.O. 5, vol. 45, p. 252); Jefferson's message to Congress of 19 Feb. 1806 (F.O. 97, vol. 6, p. 252); and a report of 2 Nov. 1806 announcing the arrival of Lewis and Clark in St. Louis (F.O. 5, vol. 49, p. 215).

21. Albert Gallatin to Jefferson

Dear Sir   Washington 14th March 1803

. . . .

I have issued a Warrant for the 2,500 dollars appropriated for the extension of the external commerce of the United States in favor of T. Tucker[1] as Treasurer of the Military Department, which will, of course, place the whole sum subject to the drafts of Gen. Dearborn[2] as Secy. of War; but it is necessary that I should have for that purpose your authorization: a form is herein enclosed. Capn. Lewis leaves this place to morrow morning. I have requested Mr. King[3] to project a blank map to extend from 88 to 126° West longitude from Greenwich & from 30° to 55° north latitude; which will give us the whole course of the Mississipi and the whole coast of the Pacific ocean within the same latitudes together with a sufficient space to the North to include all the head waters of the Port Nelson River. In this I intend to insert the course of the Mississipi as high up as the Ohio from Ellicot's, the coast of the Pacific from Cook & Vancouver, the north bend of the Missouri & such other of its waters as are there delineated from the three maps of Arrowsmith & from that of Mackenzie, and the Rio Norte and other parts of the Missoury from Danville & Delisle.[4] The most difficult point to ascertain is the latitude of the sources of the Rio Norte; and it is important, in order to know whether there would be any danger in following a more southerly branch of the Missouri than that delineated in Mackenzie's & in the manuscript transcribed from Mr. Thornton's[5] map by Cap. Lewis. I mention this because you may perhaps have some book at Monticello, which might throw some light on that subject or at least on the latitude & longitude of Santa Fe.

I do not perceive that there will be any thing of importance to be done in this department till you return. With rispect & attachment Your obedt. Servt.

ALBERT GALLATIN

ALS, RC (DLC). Endorsed; received 18 March 1803.

1. Thomas Tudor Tucker (1745–1828), Treasurer of the U.S.

2. Henry A. Dearborn (1751–1829), Jefferson's Secretary of War.

3. Nicholas King, a cartographer and draftsman who had come from England in 1796, was surveyor of the city of Washington, 1803–12, and the producer of several important American maps. He made one, perhaps two, copies of the map that Clark prepared during the winter of 1804–05 (FRIIS, 348–49). Lewis left among his papers a recipe for making wine which he had obtained from "Mr. King of Washington" (Lewis's account book, MoSHi).

4. Jean Baptiste d'Anville (1697–1782), French geographer and cartographer whose *Atlas général* was published between 1737 and 1780; Guillaume Delisle (1675–1726), French cartographer whose map of 1718 was a pioneer rendering of the American West.

5. This might be Edward Thornton, the English chargé d'affaires, but more likely is English cartographer John Thornton, whose *Atlas maritimus* was published in London, 1703.

22. Robert Patterson to Jefferson

Sir   Philadelphia March 15th 1803.

I have been honoured with your favour of the 2d and thank you for your confidence, which I will never abuse. I am preparing a set of astronomical formula for Mr. L. and will, with the greatest pleasure, render him every assistance in my power. I take the liberty of subjoining the formula which I commonly use for computing the longitude from the common lunar observation, illustrated by an example. The other formula for computing the time, alts. &c are all expressed in the same manner, viz. by the common algebraic signs; which renders the process extremely easy even to boys or common sailors of but moderate capacities.

Example

Suppose the apparent angular distance of the sun & moon's nearest limbs (by taking the mean of a set of observations) to be 110° 2' 30" the app. alt of ⊙'s lower limb measuring 20° 40' and that of)'s lower limb 35° 24' height of the eye 18 feet, estimated Greenwich time Sept. 18th 1798 about 6 hours p.m. time at place of observation, allowing for error of watch, or computed from the sun's alt. & lat. of place 4ʰ 20ᵐ 30ˢ p.m. apparent time. Reqd. the longitude of the place of observation, from the merid. of Greenwich.

Solution.

From the app. alts. of the lower limbs of ⊙ &) find the app. alts. of their centers by subtracting the dip corresponding to the height of the eye, and adding the app. semidiameters: Also from the app. dist. of limbs find the app. dist. of centers by adding the semidiameters. The longitude may then be computed by the following formula, in which the capital letters represent the corresponding arches in the adjoining column; & the small letters, the logarithmic functions of those arches. When the small letter is omitted, the arch is found from the log. funct. The logs. need not be taken out to more than 4 decimal places, and to the nearest minute only of their corresponding arches except in the case of proportional logs. Where an ambiguous sign [. . .] as ± or ∓ (expressing the sum or difference) the one or the other is to be used as directed in the explanatory note to which the number in the margin refers

110°	2'	30"		20°	40'	00"	35° 26' 00"	
	15	59			3	18	3 18	dip
	15	20		20	36	42	35 20 42	
110	33	49	app. dist.		15	59	15 20	sem. diam.
			cents.	20	52	41	35 36 2	app. alt of cents.

[29]

Explanatory notes

1. Add when C is greater than B otherwise subtract

2. Subtract when C is greater than B otherwise add

3. Subtract when either H or I exceeds 90°, or when H is greater than I, otherwise add.

4. Add when either H or I exceeds 90°, or when H is less than I, otherwise subt.

5. In tab. 13 (req. tab.) under the nearest degree to Q at top find two numbers, one opp. the nearest min. to ☽'s corr. of alt. found in tab. 8, and the other opp. the nearest min. to 1st. corr. (N) and the diff. of those two numbers will be the 3d corr. This corr. may generally be omitted.

6. Add when Q is less than 90°. Otherwise sub.

7. These are to be found in N.A. from p. 8th to p. 11th of the month, and the sun or star from which the moons dist. was obsd. taking out the two differences which are next greater, & next less than the true dist. (S) calling that the *preceding* dist. which comes first in the order of time, and the other the *folling* dist.

8. The Gr. time and time at place of ob. must both be reckoned from the same no.[?].

9. When Y is greater than Z the long. is W. Otherwise it is E. and when the long comes out more than 12 hours or 180 subt. it from 24^h or 360° & change its name.

Formula

App. dist. of cents.	A	110 33 49			
☽'s app. alt.	B	35 36	[...]	b	10.2350
☉ or ✱'s app. alt.	C	20 53			
½B + C	D	28 14	tan	d	9.7299
C ~ D	E	7 21	cot	e	10.8894
½A	F	55 17	tan	f	10.1593
d + e + f − 20	G	80 33	tan	−	10.7786
1 F $\overset{+}{\underset{-}{}}$ G	H	25 16			
2 F $\overset{+}{\underset{-}{}}$ G	I	135 50	tan	i	9.9874
☽'s hor. par. N.A. page 7.	K	55 42	pr log k		·5994
b + i + k − 20	L	27 8	pr log −		.8218

[30]

Refr. of I (consid. as an alt.)			
Tab. I (req. tables)	M		59
L − M = 1st corr.	N	26	9
3 A ± N	O 110	7	40
Ref. of H for *, refr-par for			
⊙ = 2d corr	P	1	54
4 O ± P	Q 110	9	34
5 Corr. from Tab. 13 = 3d corr.	R		4
6 Q ± R = true dist. of cents.	S 110	9	30
7 Preceeding dist. in N.A.	T 110	2	21
7 Following dist. in N.A.	U 111	27	47
T ~ S	V	7	9	pr log v	1.4010
T ~ U	W	1 25	26	pr log w	3236
v − w	X	15	4	pr log −	1.0774
8 Hour above T, in N.A., + X =			
true Green time	Y	6 15	4
8 Time at pl. of obs.	Z	4 20	30
9 Y ~ Z = long. in time	A	1 54	34
9 A ÷ 4 = long. in degrees &c.	B	28° 38½′ West	

Note, the logarithmetical part of the operation may, with sufficient accuracy be wrought in Gunters scale thus

1 Extend the compassers from Tang. E to Tang. D, and that ext. will reach from Tang. F to Tang. G.

2 Extend from Tang. I to sine B and that extent will reach (on the line of numbers) from K to L

3 Extend (on the line of numbers) from W to 180^m and that extent will reach from V to X

I am, Sir, with the most perfect respect & esteem, your obedient Servant,

R. PATTERSON

ALS, RC (DLC). Endorsed; received 4 April 1803.

23. Jefferson to Albert Gallatin

Dear Sir   Monticello Mar. 20. 1803.
    Your's of the 14th is recieved and I have written to Mr. Madison to issue a commission to Edward Turner of Kentucky to be Register

of the land office at Natchez. A commission has issued to Trist vice Carmichael. Thompson and Watson may await my return. I now inclose the power for transferring the 2500. D. to the disposal of the Secretary at War.

I do not find in my library any thing which can throw light on the geography of the Rio Norte. I do not believe that in modern times any thing has been added to the information given as to that river in early times. Of this information Mitchell [1] had the benefit. His map was made under public patronage & with all the information that could procure him. That it was made with great care we know from what is laid down in those Western parts with which we have lately become acquainted. Certainly we find his map much nearer the truth than could have been expected considering when it was made. Hence I conclude that his delineation of the Rio Norte is more to be credited than any other, not excepting Danville & Delisle. Accept my best [. . .].

TH: JEFFERSON

ALS, SC (DLC); RC (NHi).
1. John Mitchell (d. 1768), English cartographer, produced in 1755 a map entitled *Map of the British and French dominions in North America . . .* which was later used in various boundary negotiations.

24. Albert Gallatin to Jefferson

Dear Sir [13 April 1803]

I perceive nothing in the enclosed [1] which should in my opinion require alteration. Perhaps something might be added.

The present aspect of affairs may, ere long, render it necessary that we should, by taking immediate possession, prevent G. B. from doing the same. Hence a perfect knowledge of the posts, establishments & force kept by Spain in upper Louisiana, and also of the most proper station to occupy, for the purpose of preventing effectually the occupying of any part of the Missouri country by G. B., seems important. With that view the present communications of the British with the Missouri, either from the Mississipi, or, which is still more in point, from the waters emptying in Lake Winnipec & generally in Hudson bay, should be well ascertained, as well as the mode in which a small but sufficient force could best be conveyed to the most proper point from whence to prevent any attempt from Lake Winnipec.

But whatever may be the issue of the present difficulties, the future destinies of the Missouri country are of vast importance to the United States, it being perhaps the only large tract of country, and certainly the *first* which lying out of the boundaries of the Union will be settled by the people of the U. States. The precise extent, therefore, of the country drained by all the waters emptying into that river, and consequently the length & directions of all the principal branches ought to be, as far as practicable, ascertained as well as that particular branch which may be followed for the purpose of examining the communications with the Pacific Ocean. That tract of country is bounded on the north by the Waters of Hudson's bay, the extent of which southwardly is tolerably ascertained by Mackenzie & others; Westwardly by the Waters of the Columbia & other rivers emptying into the Pacific, which it is the principal object of this voyage to explore; and Southwardly, it is presumed, by the waters of Rio Norte. How far these extend Northwardly & confine the waters of the Missouri it is important to know, as their position would generally determine the extent of territory watered by the Missouri. It is presumable, from analogy that the Waters of Hudson's bay which interlock with the many northerly streams of the Missouri are divided from them by elevated lands interspersed with lakes, but not by any regular chain of mountains. By the same analogy, (for within the United States & known parts of North America the spring of every river north of 42° latitude issues from a lake, and south of 41° from a mountain,) it is probable that the northern branches of the Rio Norte are separated from the southern streams of the Kanses & Missouri rivers by a chain of mountains running westwardly till it unites with the chain which divides the waters of Missouri & other rivers from those emptying into the Pacific. Hence it is presumable that the distance of that east & west chain from the Missouri will generally show the extent of country watered by this river. And although C[apt]n L. going westwardly toward his main object may not personally become acquainted with the country lying south of his track, yet so far as he may collect information on that subject & also on the communications with the Rio Norte or other southern rivers if any others, which is not probable, interlocks with the Missouri, it would be a desirable object. The great object to ascertain is whether from its extent & fertility that country is susceptible of a large population, in the same manner as the corresponding tract on the Ohio. Besides the general opinion which may be formed of its fertility, some more specific instructions on the signs of the soil might be given—the two principal of which are the *prevailing* species of timber whether oak—beech—pine—or barren, and the

[33]

evenness or mountainous & rocky situation of the land. Those two circumstances do generally determine in America the quantity of soil fit for cultivation in any one large tract of country; for I presume there are no swamps in that part of the world. But several more signs might be added to which the traveller should pay attention.

I think C. L. ought to take, on the Spanish side of the Illinois settlement, some person who had navigated the Missouri as high as possible & it might not be amiss to try to winter with the traders *from that quarter* who go to the farthest tribe of Indians in the proper direction. A boat or canoe might be hired there (at the Illinois) to carry up to that spot a sufficient quantity of flour to enable him to winter there with comfort so that his band should be fresh & in good spirits in the spring. Respectfully your obt. Servt.

ALBERT GALLATIN

ALS, RC (DLC). Endorsed; received 13 April 1803.
1. Jefferson had sent to his cabinet members a draft of his instructions to Lewis, the final version of which appears herein as No. 47. Gallatin's reply is a useful one, and predictably so, considering his own interest in linguistics, ethnology, and geography.

25. James Madison's Notes

[14 April 1803]

1. Quer. if the laws give any authority at present beyond the limits of the U.S.?
2. "This Mission having reference to the commerce"—may repell, more than the expression used, the criticism of illicit principal objects of the measure.
3. including the fish"
4. if practicable he might note occasionally the variations of the head &c.

AD, RC (DLC). Endorsed. Date of receipt is shown.

26. Levi Lincoln to Jefferson

Sir   Washington April 17 1803
From the perusal, & reperusal of your Instructions for Capt. Lewis nothing of importance has suggested itself to my mind which has not been particularly attended to.

[34]

I consider the enterprise of national consequence, and, to a degree, personally hazardous, to the projectors & individual adventurers. In the perverse, hostile, and malig[n]ant state of the opposition, with their facility, of imposing on the public mind, & producing excitements, every measure originating with the executive will be attacked, with a virulence in proportion, to the patriotism of the motive, the wisdom of the means, & the probable utility of its execution. The greatest success, will but stop that mouth of clamor, which must be met with the merits of the projection, in case of its fa[i]lure, or serious disaster. In this view of the subject may not some new aspects be usefully given to the undertaking, and others made more prominent? Would it not be well to those particulars which have a principal reference to oppening & promoting, a knowledge of the country, friendship & trade with its inhabitants, and their improvements in the arts of husbandry, to add more explicitly those articles which have for their object the improvement of the mind, & the preservation of the body—Such as the ideas the various tribes or nations possess of a supreme being, their worships, their religion, the agency it has in their respective govts. in war, & in peace, its influence on their manners —their actions which are crimes against their society, & the punishments—their ideas of property, & the tenures by which they claim it —& also the probability of impressing their minds with a sense of an *improved religion* & morality & the means by which it could be effected. Besides religion & morality making a very important article in the history of all countries as an object of attention, If the enterprise appears to be, an attempt to advance them, it will by many people, on that account, be justified, however calamitous the issue.

Would it not be well also to mention the diseases incident to various climates, situations, and seasons, the age most liable to them, the method of treating them, the medicinal articles applied, the age which is considered as old, & the manner of life most condusive to it &c? If any plants or roots of uncommon virtues as medicine should be found, would it not be an object to procure the seed?

As Capt. Lewis may have in his company, some who have not had the small pox, would it not be best to carry some of the matter for the kine pox with him? [1]

From my ideas of Capt. Lewis he will be much more likely, in case of difficulty, to push too far, than to rec[e]de too soon. Would it not be well to change the term, '*certain* destruction' into *probable* destruction & to add—that these dangers are never to be encountered, which vigilance precaution & attention can secure against, at a reasonable expense.

[35]

The foregoing ideas, indigested, and unimportant in themselves as most of them are, I communicate them for your inspection, without reserve. I have always understood, that Story's deficiency was not so much from the want of strength of intellect, as the want of discretion, & correctness of morals.[2] I am Sir most respectfully your most obt. Servt.

LEVI LINCOLN

ALS, RC (DLC). Endorsed; received 18 April 1803. Levi Lincoln (1782–1868) was Attorney General of the U.S., 1801–04.

1. Jefferson did not need to be reminded of this; he had administered the vaccine himself in 1801 and corresponded on the subject of smallpox with Dr. Benjamin Waterhouse, of Cambridge, Mass. Waterhouse had sent him a tract on "kine pox" 1 March 1803 (DLC).

2. A change of subject. Lincoln is referring to Joseph Story, who had been appointed naval officer for the cities of Salem and Beverley, Mass. A discussion had developed about his fitness for office.

27. Andrew Ellicott to Jefferson

Dear Sir   Lancaster April 18th 1803

A few days ago I received a letter from Mr. John Vaughan[1] from which the following is an extract, "I am desired by a person in the District of Maine Kennebeck River, to enquire as soon as may be of Mr. Ellicott the cost of a Box, with the sextant, and portable horizon, and a place for an Arnold watch, (such as Mr. Ellicott describes in the 5th Vol. of the Phil: Trans.,) we have the watch, and wish for the rest made under the inspection of Mr. E. if possible if it can be done reasonably in order to settle longitudes, and latitudes, in this country."

I immediately replied to Mr. Vaughan's letter, and undertook to have the apparatus for an artificial, or portable horizon, made in this place under my own inspection.

Notwithstanding the manner in which this business is covered, I feel a strong presumption that the apparatus is for Captn. Lewis, and under this impression I have enclosed a few remarks for his use.

I expect shortly to have a work out of the press on which I have been engaged for some time, and which has been much longer delayed than I intended, owing to the little time I have to spare from manual labour, and the duties of my office. As soon as this work is handed to the Publick, I intend publishing a small treatise on practical astronomy as connected with geography, for the use of such persons as may be exploring our extensive western regions, and capable of making the necessary observations.

[36]

In a few weeks I shall have another communication ready for the National Institute, a body of men, from whom I have received much more attention than from any in my own country. The celebrated la Lande[2] is dead, he has not perhaps left an equal behind:—he sent me his works shortly after I came to this place. Delambre has likewise promised me a large work on which he has been long employed, it will be published this summer.

My new pendulum, which was the work of five sundays,[3] exceeds my warmest expectations. I am sir, with sentiments of great esteem, your sincere friend and Hbl. Servt.

ANDW. ELLICOTT

ALS, RC (DLC). Endorsed; received 20 April 1803.

1. John Vaughan (1756–1841), librarian and treasurer of the American Philosophical Society.

2. The *Encyclopaedia Britannica*, however, gives 4 April 1807 as the date of Lalande's death.

3. It was "the work of six sundays" in No. 19.

28. Lewis to Jefferson

Sir, Lancaster Apl. 20th 1803.

With a view to forward as much as possible the preparations which must necessarily be made in the Western country previous to my final departu[r]e, as also to prevent the delay, which would attatch to their being made after my arrival in that quarter, I have taken the following measures, which I hope will meet your approbation; they appear to me to be as complete as my present view of the subject will admit my making them and I trust the result will prove as favorable as wished for.

I have writen triplicates to Mr. John Conner[1] accepting his services as an Interpreter; he is the young man I recollect mentioning to you as having proffered his services to accompany me: to him I have communicated the real extent and objects of my mission, but with strict injunctions to secrecy. He is directed to bring with him two Indians, provided he can engage such as perfectly answer the description given him. I have informed him of the military posts at which I shall touch on the Ohio and Mississippi rivers, and the probable time of my arrival at each, leaving it discretionary with himself to meet me at either: in these letters are inclosed triplicates addressed to the Commandants of those posts, recommending Mr. Conner to their good offices, and requesting for him every aid in their power to bestow, should he be in want of assistance to enable him to get forwa[r]d in due time. The circumstance of Mr. Conner's residence being at the Delleware Town on White river, and distant of course from any post office, induced me to give these letters different conveyances, which I did by inclosing them by different mails to three gentlemen of my acquaintance in that country, two of whom, Capts. M'Clelland & Hamilton, live within twenty seven miles of the town; they are requested, and I am confident will find the means of conveying the letters to him; the other with a similar request was inclosed to Capt. Findley of Cincinnatti, in whose exertions tho' more distant, I have equal confidence.[2]

I have also written to Majr. MacRea,[3] the Commandant of South West Point, and to several officers of my acquaintance who constitute that garrison, stating to them that my destination was up the Mississippi for the purpose of accomplishing the objects, which we agreed on as most proper to be declared publicly: the qualifications of the men are mentioned, and they are requested to look out in time for such volunteers as will answer that description; the inducements for those persons engaging in this service were also stated. The garrison of South West Point must form my first resourse for the scelection of my party, which I shall afterwards change as circumstances may seem to recommend; and with a view to this change, I have written in a similar manner to the officers commanding the posts of Massac, Kaskaskais and Illinois,[4] the posts at which I shall touch previous to ascending the Missouri, and subsequent to my departure from S.W. Point. The men in every instance are to be engaged conditionally, or subject to my approval or otherwise.

I have also written to Dr. Dickson,[5] at Nashville, and requested him to contract in my behalf with some confidential boat-builder at that place, to prepare a boat for me as soon as possible, and to purchase a large light wooden canoe: for this purpose I inclosed the Dr. 50. Dollars, which sum I did not concieve equal by any means to the purchase of the two vessels, but supposed it sufficient for the purchase of the canoe, and to answer also as a small advance to the boat-builder: a discription of these vessels was given. The objects of my mission are stated to him as beforementioned to the several officers.

I have also written to Genl. Irwine[6] of Philadelphia, requesting that he will have in a state of prepareation some articles which are necessary for me, and which will be most difficult to obtain, or may take the greates[t] length of time in their prepareation.

My detention at Harper's Ferry was unavoidable for one month, a period much greater than could reasonably have been calculated on;

my greatest difficulty was the frame of the canoe, which could not be completed without my personal attention to such portion of it as would enable the workmen to understand the design perfectly; other inducements seemed with equal force to urge my waiting the issue of a full experiment, arising as well from a wish to incur no expence unnecessarily, as from an unwillingness to risk any calculation on the advantages of this canoe in which hereafter I might possibly be deceived; experiment was necessary also to determine it's dementions: I therefore resolved to g[i]ve it a fair trial, and accordingly prepared two sections of it with the same materials, of which they must of necessity be composed when completed for servise on my voyage; they were of two disc[r]iptions, the one curved, or in the shape necessary for the stem and stern, the other simicilindrical, or in the form of those sections which constitute the body of the canoe. The experiment and it's result wer[e] as follow.

Dementions.

Curved Section.	F.	I.	Simicilindrical Section.	F.	I.
Length of Keel from junction of section to commencement of curve	1	2	Length of Keel	4	6
			ditto Beam	4	10
			Debth of Hole	2	2
Length of curve	4	5	Note—The curve of the body		
Width of broad end	4	10	of the canoe was formed by a		
Debth of Do. Do.	2	2	suspended cord.		

Weight of the Materials.

Curved Section.	lbs.	Simicilindrical Section	
Iron	22	Iron	22
Hide	25	Hide	30
Wood	10	Wood	12
Bark	21	Bark	25
Total	78	Total	89

Competent to a

Burthen of 850 lbs.   Burthen of 920 lbs.

Necessary to be transported by land.

Iron and Hide of Curved Section	47	
Iron and Hide of Simicilindrical Do.	52	99 lbs.
Burthen of Curved Section	850	
Do. Do. Simicilindrical	920	1,770 lbs.

Thus the weight of this vessel competent to the burthen of 1,770 lbs. amount to no more than 99 lbs. The bark and wood, when it

[39]

becomes necessary to transport the vessel to any considerable distances, may be discarded; as those articles are reaidily obtained for the purposes of this canoe, at all seasons of the year, and in every quarter of the country, which is tolerably furnished with forest trees. When these sections were united they appeared to acquire an additional strength and firmness, and I am confident that in cases of emergency they would be competent to 150 lbs. more than the burthen already stated. Altho' the weight of the articles employed in the construction of a canoe on this plan, have considerably exceeded the estimat I had previously made, yet they do not weigh more than those which form a bark canoe of equal dementions, and in my opinion is much preferable to it in many respects; it is much stronger, will carry its burthen with equal ease, and greater security; and when the Bark and wood are discarded, will be much lighter, and can be transported with more safety and ease. I was induced from the result of this experiment to direct the iron frame of the canoe to be completed.

My Rifles,[7] Tomahawks & knives are preparing at Harper's Ferry, and are already in a state of forwardness that leaves me little doubt of their being in readiness in due time.

I arrived at this place yesterday, called on Mr. Ellicot, and have this day commenced, under his direction, my observations &c to perfect myself in the use and application of the instruments. Mr. Ellicot is extreemly friendly and attentive, and I am confident is disposed to render me every aid in his power: he thinks it will be necessary I should remain here ten or twelve days.[8]

Being fully impressed with the necessity of seting out as early as possible, you may rest assured that not a moment shall be lost in making the necessary preparations. I still think it practicable to reach the mouth of the Missouri by the 1st of August. I am Sir, with much esteem and regard Your Most Obt. Servt.

MERIWETHER LEWIS.

ALS, RC (DLC). Endorsed; received 25 April 1803.

1. John Conner (1775–1826), interpreter and Indian trader, had lived since childhood among the Shawnees and Delawares, and was now established in Buckongahelas' Town on the White River, about three miles southeast of present Muncie, Ind. His usefulness to Lewis would have been limited by the fact that he knew only the languages of the Shawnees, Delawares, Chippewas, and perhaps the Wyandots. Later he became an early settler of Indianapolis and a member of the Indiana state legislature. For a biography of John and his brother William, see THOMPSON.

2. It is not possible to identify with certainty the men Lewis names here. He says that "M'Clelland" and Hamilton live within twenty-seven miles of Conner, and I suspect he means to indicate that they live in Hamilton, Ohio—particularly in view of his later statement (No. 80) that Conner

[40]

lives twenty-four miles from Fort Hamilton. Fort Hamilton had been evacuated and torn down in the summer of 1796, but the town of Hamilton remained and a man named McClellan did live there. He was Robert McClellan (1770–1816), who had been a scout under Anthony Wayne and who later lived in Hamilton with his brother William. Lewis and Clark will meet him when they are descending the Missouri, 12 Sept. 1806, as he makes his way upstream on a fur-trading venture. Another possibility is Capt. John McClallen, a regular army man, appointed captain of artillerists in 1802. He, too, entered the fur trade after his army service, and Lewis and Clark will meet him 17 Sept. 1806 after they part with Robert McClellan. The man named Hamilton is also difficult. The library of the Indiana Historical Society contains a letter of 22 July 1798 from John Hamilton, of Cincinnati, to Governor Arthur St. Clair, asking help in obtaining payment for horses stolen by Indians. A man by this name also figures in the letters of William Henry Harrison, but not until 1813. In TERR. PAPERS, 3:68, Maj. Israel Ludlow is quoted 2 Sept. 1799 as saying, "Capt. Hamilton who was employed to interpret for me, together with Lieut. Stall who commanded the Escort . . . were met by a party of Indians," etc. And, finally, James Hamilton was a wagoner delivering stores to Fort Pitt in 1793, as listed in the Isaac Craig Papers (PPi). I identify "Capt. Findley" as James Findlay (1770–1835), a Cincinnati attorney and, in 1803, a member of the Ohio state legislature. He later served as mayor of Cincinnati and a U.S. representative from Ohio.

3. William McRae, of Pennsylvania, was appointed to the Corps of Artillerists in 1802, and at the time of this letter was commanding a post on the Clinch River, near Knoxville, Tenn.

4. Fort Massac and the post at Kaskaskia were going concerns, but by "Illinois" Lewis probably means the post which was scheduled to be built at Cahokia, across the river from St. Louis. By letter of 19 July 1803, the Secretary of War abandoned this plan (Dearborn to Stoddard, DNA, RG 107).

5. William Dickson (1770–1816), U.S. representative from Tennessee.

6. William Irvine (1741–1804), physician, Revolutionary War officer, member of the Continental Congress, and now (1801–04) superintendent of military stores with headquarters at Philadelphia.

7. See RUSSELL for a summary view of firearms used on the expedition.

8. Lewis's aids for astronomical observation included the formulas of both Robert Patterson and Andrew Ellicott. On some notes about a lunar calculation of 23 Feb. 1805, at Fort Mandan, Lewis mentions "Mr. Elicot's formula" (Clark field notes, CtY). While staying with Ellicott in Lancaster, Lewis wrote Jefferson a letter introducing Andrew's brother Joseph, who was about to visit Washington, describing him as "a judge and resident of the western part of the State of New York—he is a good republican, and a man of good information and reputation" (27 April 1803, DLC).

29. Jefferson to Lewis Harvie

Dear Sir   Washington Apr. 22 1803.
    Since my return to this place I have been in the daily expectation

that the stage of the day would bring back Capt. Lewis, and that then within a few days he would set out on his Missisipi expedition. It was only the day before yesterday I learned that he had been detained at Harper's ferry a month instead of a week, and that he is probably but about this time arriving at Philadelphia, where his stay is uncertain, tho' probably 1, 2, or 3 weeks, after which he will return here for some days only. This at least is the present view I have of his movements. I have delayed writing to you, because my great regard for Capt. Lewis made me unwilling to show a haste to fill his place before he was gone, & to counteract also a malignant & unfounded report that I was parting with him from dissatisfaction, a thing impossible either from his conduct or my dispositions towards him. I shall probably receive a letter from him on his arrival at Philadelphia, informing me when he expects to be back here, and will have the pleasure of communicating to you the earliest conjecture I can form myself for your government.[1] It cannot now be many days. You will have seen the letter of the Spanish minister, which we have forwarded to N. Orleans with an order from Spain to take off immediately the suspension of our right of deposit. To this I can add that we have formal assurances that the treaty of cession of Louisiana to France contained this clause 'Saving the rights acquired by other powers in virtue of treaties made with them by Spain.' That cession is probably not yet finally settled between those powers, which has occasioned an unwillingness in them to say any thing of it to other powers[?]. Spain has been very sensible of our friendly forbearance, and of our dispositions towards her, on the late occasion, and to manifest her sense of it has broken through the reserve which circumstances had laid her under with respect to the cession of Louisiana. Accept my affectionate salutations & assurances of esteem & respect.

TH. JEFFERSON

ALS, SC (DLC). Lewis Harvie (1782–1807) was now to become Jefferson's secretary and later would serve as representative to the General Assembly of Virginia from Richmond during the sessions of 1805–06 and 1806–07.

1. When this letter was written, Harvie was waiting in Georgetown for orders to take up residence with the President. And when, on 28 May, Lewis still had not returned from Philadelphia, Jefferson wrote Harvie to come on as soon as convenient and assume Lewis's duties. The steps which led to Harvie's appointment are these: Early in 1803, Lewis had written to William Brent, offering him the post of secretary to the President. Brent had replied (to Jefferson) that his business affairs were enlarging and that he could not serve permanently, but that he would gladly serve for a brief time "until he [Jefferson] shall have an opportunity of supplying my place" (25 Feb. 1803). Instead, Jefferson wrote on 28 Feb. to Harvie in Richmond, offering him the position. Jefferson's letter indicates that Harvie had

once applied for the post, after it already had been offered to Lewis. Now Jefferson explained that the position was open again, since Lewis would be involved in "some object in the Western country which will probably employ him a year or two. . . ." Harvie replied 12 March 1803 that he had been planning to study law under John Mason in Georgetown, then set up practice in Baltimore, but that he would delay his studies to serve Jefferson. "The duties of the office, I trust will not be incompatible with my bestowing a portion of the day on other avocations. . . ." Within less than a year after accepting the post, Harvie was assigned a mission to France (Pichon to Gallatin, 20 Jan. 1804), and was succeeded as secretary by William Burwell (1780–1821). All letters cited in this note are in DLC.

30. Jefferson to Lewis

Dear Sir   Washington Apr. 23, 1803.

I have not been able to hear any thing of you since Mar. 7. till two or three days ago. Lieut. Wilson told me you would leave Frederic the 18th inst. & that you had been detained till then at Harper's ferry, where Capt. Murray also told me he had seen you.[1] I have no doubt you have used every possible exertion to get off, and therefore we have only to lament what cannot be helped, as the delay of a month now may lose a year in the end. Will you be so good as to call on Doctr. Bollman[2] with my compliments & pay him for some wine sent me? I suppose it will be about 12 Doll. but it must be whatever he says. I will also thank you to purchase for me a Leopard or tyger's skin, such as the covers of our saddles were cut out of. In North 3d street & North 4th street a few doors only from Market street there used to be a considerable furrier's store in each. At one of these it was that I saw a robe of what they called the Peruvian sheep, and I took to be of the Lama or Vigogna. It was made up of several skins, & was of the price of 12 D. If there be such a thing there now, you can either observe & report it to me, or if you think it good (for I have almost forgot it) I would take it at once. Let me hear from you on your receipt of this, and inform me of your prospect of getting off. I have letters here for you from your friends in Albemarle. Accept my affectionate salutations.

TH: JEFFERSON

ALS, SC (DLC).

1. There are two possible Wilsons: John, appointed to the Second Infantry as second lieutenant in 1800, and James, appointed lieutenant in the Second Artillerists in 1801. Capt. Murray is probably William Augustus Murray, of New York, appointed first lieutenant of artillerists in 1802.

2. Justus Erich Bollman (1769–1821), who later became an ally of Aaron Burr.

31. Jefferson to Lewis

Dear Sir   Washington April 27. 1803

Your's of the 20th from Lancaster was recieved the night before last. Not having heard from you since the time of my leaving Washington, I had written to you on the 23d and lodged it in Philadelphia. You will therefore probably receive that & this together. I inclose you a copy of the rough draught of the instructions I have prepared for you, that you may have time to consider them & to propose any modifications which may occur to yourself as useful. Your destination being known to Mr. Patterson, Doctrs. Wistar, Rush & Barton, these instructions may be submitted to their perusal. A considerable portion of them being within the field of the Philosophical society, which once undertook the same mission, I think it my duty to consult some of it's members, limiting the communication by the necessity of secrecy in a good degree. These gentlemen will suggest any additions they will think useful, as has been before asked of them. We have recieved information that Connor cultivates in the first degree the patronage of the British government; to which he values ours as only secondary. As it is possible however that his passion for this expedition may overrule that for the British, and as I do not see that the British agents will necessarily be disposed to counterwork us, I think Connor's qualifications make it desireable to engage him, and that the communication to him will be as useful, as it was certainly proper under our former impression of him. The idea that you are going to explore the Missisipi has been generally given out: it satisfies public curiosity, and masks sufficiently the real destination. I shall be glad to hear from you, as soon after your arrival at Philadelphia as you can form an idea when you will leave, & when be [here.] Accept assurances of my constant & sincere affection.

TH: JEFFERSON

ALS, SC (DLC). A very poor letterpress copy. Reply is No. 36. For the instructions which Jefferson enclosed, see No. 47. The letter of 23 April mentioned in the second sentence has not been found.

32. Jefferson to Lewis

Th: Jefferson to Capt. Lewis.   [30 April 1803]

I think we spoke together of your carrying some steel or cast iron corn mills to give to the Indians or to trade with them, as well as for your own use. Lest however I should be mistaken, I mention them

[44]

now. I make no doubt you have consulted with Mr. Ellicot as to the best instruments to carry. I would wish that nothing that passed between us here should prevent your following his advice, which is certainly the best. Should a time-piece be requisite, it is probable Mr. Garnet[1] can furnish you one. Neither Ellicot nor Garnet have given me their opinion on the substituting a meridian at land, instead of observations of time, for ascertaining longitude by the lunar motions. I presume therfore it will not answer. Accept my affectionate salutations.

Washington Apr. 30. 1803.

AL, SC (DLC).
1. John Garnett (c.1751–1820) of New Brunswick, N.J., publisher of tables requisite and nautical almanacs for use in astronomical observations. It appears that he had not issued any tables at this time, but he already had published an American version of that old standard, *The nautical almanac.* He wrote Robert Patterson 10 June 1805 that he was sending him a set of the almanacs for 1803–07, and that he now had a set of requisite tables in press (PPAmP).

33. Andrew Ellicott to John Vaughan

Dear Sir   Lancaster May 7th 1803
This will be handed to you by my friend Captn. Lewis Secretary to the President of the U.S. Your attention to him will confer an obligation on me.

I have forwarded by this opportunity the apparatus for forming the artificial horizon, with some remarks relative its use. The *talc* is very delicate, and easily injured,—it should therefore be handled with caution. And for fear of accidents the person using the apparatus should not be without some spare pieces.

I wish Mr. Delambre's Diploma forwarded to me as soon as it is made out. I am with great esteem your friend and Hbl. Servt.

ANDW. ELLICOTT.

ALS, RC (PPAmP). Endorsed. Lewis had arrived in Philadelphia by 10 May, when he was seen by Isaac Briggs (Briggs to Jefferson, 17 May 1803, DLC). Jefferson had appointed Briggs surveyor of the lands south of Tennessee, and he was on the point of leaving for the West. He conferred with Lewis on 10 and 11 May.

34. Andrew Ellicott to Robert Patterson

Dear Sir   Lancaster May 7th 1803.
This will be handed to you by my friend Captn. Lewis, Secretary

to the President of the U.S.—every attention you shew to him, will confer an obligation on me.

As the President has already written to you on the subject of Captn. Lewis's intended journey, it will be unnecessary for me to say any thing upon that subject. Such information as may appear necessary, together with your formula's for the longitude, I am sure you will communicate with pleasure.

I wish Mr. Delambre's diploma to be forwarded to me by the first opportunity, that I may transmit it with a communication which I shall have ready for him in a few days. I am with great esteem your friend and Hbl. Servt.

ANDW. ELLICOTT

ALS, RC (PPAmP).

35. Bernard Lacépède to Jefferson

Monsieur President [13 May 1803]

I hasten to have the honor of thanking you for the letter which you have kindly sent to me by Monsieur Monroe. This letter, Monsieur President, is a mark of your esteem and consequently a very honorable testimonial for me. I shall preserve it, moreover, as a monument for history. It is so seldom that one sees the chief magistrate of a great nation unite the enlightenment and solicitude [les lumieres et les soins] which the well-being of his fellow-citizens demands with the boundless knowledge and the labors of a celebrated philosopher.

It is never a mistake to predict that a great and useful undertaking will be carried out by a nation which is free and governed by a leader worthy of that nation. It was therefore without surprise but with much satisfaction that I learned from your letter that you are going to have the sources of the Missouri explored, and to seek a river which, at its source, is near to the source of the Missouri, and bears its waters to the great northern ocean. This river which you wish to discover could well be the *Colombia* which Monsieur Gray,[1] your fellow-citizen, discovered in 1788, or 1789. Monsieur Broughthon,[2] one of Captain Vancouver's companions, went up that river for one hundred *miles,* in December 1792. He stopped at a point which he named *Vancouver,* and which is situated at 45° N. and 237° E., reckoning from the London meridian. At that point, the river *Colombia* is still a quarter of a mile wide, and the depth varies between 12 and thirty-six English feet. The river is then still far from its source at Van-

[46]

couver Point; and yet, from this point one sees Mount Hood, at a distance of twenty leagues; now this Mount Hood could well be a dependence of the *Stony Mountains*, of which Monsieur Fiedler[3] saw the beginning at about 40° N., and the source of the Missouri probably is in the *Stony Mountains* between the 40th and 45th parallels. If your nation could establish an easy communication route by river, canal and *short* portages, between New Yorck, for example, and the town which would be built at the mouth of the Columbia, what a route that would be for trade from Europe, from Asia, and from America, whose northern products would arrive at this route by the Great Lakes and the upper Mississippi, while the southern products of the New World would arrive there by the lower Mississippi and by the Rio Norte of New Mexico, the source of which is near the 40th parallel! What greater means to civilization than these new communication routes!

Nevertheless, whatever may be the success of the expedition you are going to make, it will be extremely useful for the progress of industry, the sciences, and especially natural history. May your fellow-citizens, by the wisdom of their choice, preserve forever their liberty, their government, and the peace! Hitherto, the movement of enlightenment has been from east to west. The inhabitants of the United States, if they do not reject their destiny, will one day halt and reverse this movement.

Buffon[4] died without being able to make use of the very valuable present you had given him. The American animals on which he had reported were the species of reindeer, that of the roe [chevreuil] and that of the cougar.

The fifth and last volume of my history of fishes is going to appear. I am now writing the history of cetaceans. The advantage which the National Institute has of counting you among its members leads me to hope that you will kindly allow me to present you with a complimentary copy of these various works.

If my health had not been completely upset by the terrible misfortune I had last winter of losing a dear wife, I would plan to come to your continent one day, to see your young nature, your happy nation and her honorable chief magistrate; but good fortune is no longer meant for me. Monsieur President, accept the expression of my humble admiration, my keen recognition and my respect.

Paris, 23 floreal, year 11—13 May 1803.   B. G. E. C. LACEPÈDE.

ALS, RC (DLC). Endorsed; received 14 July 1803. This is a translation.
   1. Robert Gray (1755–1806) took his merchant vessel, *Columbia,* into the river in 1792.

2. William Robert Broughton (1762–1821), a British naval captain, explored with Vancouver and published accounts of his voyages.

3. In 1792, Peter Fidler entered the Rockies southwest of Calgary, Alberta, Canada, on behalf of the Hudson's Bay Company. He was once thought to have journeyed down along the mountains into what is now U.S. territory, but this misconception seems to have arisen from his faulty astronomical calculations. Because Fidler's latitudes appeared on Arrowsmith's 1795 map of North America, they were an important factor in the thinking of contemporary geographers. They will bother Lewis during the expedition when he tries to reconcile them with his own observations.

4. Georges Louis Leclerc, Comte de Buffon (1707–88), French naturalist whose major work was *Histoire naturelle* in 44 vols., published in 1749–1804.

36. Lewis to Jefferson

Dear Sir,   Philadelphia, May 14th 1803.

In your instructions to me you mention that the instruments for ascertaining by celestial observations the geography of the country through which I shall pass, *have been already provided:* I shall not therefore purchase any articles of that discription untill I hear further from you on this subject. Will you be so good as to inform me what instruments have been provided? and where they are?—it may be possible that some instrument has been omitted, which Mr. Patterson, Mr. Ellicott and those gentlemen to whom you have referred me in this place, may deem necessary for me, and if so the deficiency can be supplyed in time.

Mr. Patterson and Mr. Ellicott both disapprove of the Theodolite as applicable to my purposes; they think it a delicate instrument, difficult of transportation, and one that would be very liable to get out of order; they also state that in it's application to any observations for obtaining the Longitude, it would be liable to many objections, and to much more inacuracy than the Sextant. The instruments these gentlemen recommend, and which indeed they think indispensibly necessary, are, two Sextants, (one of which, must be constructed for the *back observation,*) an artificial Horizon or two; a good Arnald's watch or Chronometer, a Surveyor's Compass with a ball and socket and two pole chain, and a set of plotting instruments. By means of the Sextant fixed for the back observation and an artificial Horizon also constructed for the purpose, the meridian altitude of the Sun may always be taken, altho it should even exceed eighty degrees: for this valuable problem I am indebted to Mr. Patterson.

As a perfect knolege of the time will be of the first importance in all my Astronomical observations, it is necessary that the time-

[48]

keeper intended for this expedition should be put in the best possible order, if therefore Sir, one has been procured for me, and you are not perfectly assured of her being in good order, it would be best perhaps to send her to me by some safe hand (should any such conveyance offer in time); Mr. Voit[1] could then clean her, and Mr. Ellicott has promised to regulate her, which, I believe he has the means of doing just now, more perfectly than it can be done any where else in the U. States.

I cannot yet say what day it will be in my power to leave this place. Your different orders have been attended to, and the result you shall have in a day or two. I am Sir, with every sentiment of gratitude and respect—Your most Obt. & very Humble Servt.

MERIWETHER LEWIS.

ALS, RC (DLC). Endorsed; received 16 May 1803. Reply is No. 37.

1. Henry Voigt, a watchmaker and the coiner of the U.S. mint at Philadelphia. In a letter to Jefferson of 20 Dec. 1802 (DLC) he indicates that he has held that position for several years; he speaks gratefully of the asylum he has received in America, but does not mention the country of his origin. Under No. 55 see Thomas Parker's bill for the sale of a gold chronometer to Lewis, and Voigt's bill for cleaning and adjusting the instrument.

37. Jefferson to Lewis

Dear Sir   Washington May 16. 1803.

Yours of the 14th is this moment received, & I hasten to answer it by return of post, that no time may be lost. The copy of instructions sent you are only a rough draught for consideration. They will not be signed or *dated* till your departure. Presuming you would procure all the necessary instruments at Philadelphia, which is a principal object of your journey there, the instructions say that the necessary instruments *'have been* provided,' which will be true when they receive their ultimate form, date & signature, tho' nothing was provided at the time of writing the rough draught. This will serve to correct the impression which has been misunderstood, and to let you know you are relied on to provide every thing for yourself. With respect to the Theodolite, I wish you to be governed entirely by the advice of Mr. Patterson & Mr. Ellicott: as also as to the time piece & whatever else they think best. Mr. Garnett told us he had some good ones still on hand; which I remind you of, lest you should not be able to get one in Philadelphia. Accept my affectionate salutations.

TH: JEFFERSON

ALS, SC (DLC).

[49]

38. Benjamin Rush to Lewis

Questions to Merryweather Lewis before he went up the Missouri.

I. Physical history & medicine?

What are the *acute* diseases of the Indians? Is the bilious fever ever attended with a black vomit.

Is Goiture, apoplexy, palsy, Epilepsy, madness [. . .] ven. Disease known among them?

What is their state of life as to longevity?

At what age do the women *begin* & *cease* to menstruate?

At what age do they marry? How long do they suckle the Children?

What is the provision of their Childrn. after being weaned?

The state of the pulse as to *frequency* in the morning, at noon & at night—before & after eating? What is its state in childhood. Adult life, & old age? The number of strokes counted by the quarter of a minute by glass, and multiplied by four will give its frequency in a minute.

What are their Remidies?

Are artificial discharges of blood ever used among them?

In what manner do they induce sweating?

Do they ever used voluntary fasting?

At what *time* do they rise—their Baths?

What is the diet—manner of cooking—& times of eating among the Indians? How do they preserve their food?

II. Morals

1. What are their vices?

2. Is Suicide common among them?—ever from love?

3. Do they employ any substitute for ardent spirits to promote intoxication?

4. Is murder common among them, & do they punish it with death?

III. Religion

1. What Affinity between their religious Ceremonies & those of the Jews?

2. Do they use animal Sacrifices in their worship?

3. What are the principal Objects of their worship?

4. How do they dispose of their dead, and with what Ceremonies do they inter them?

May 17. 1803.   B. RUSH

ADS, SC (PPAmP—Rush's commonplace book, 266–67).

See also No. 101, in which Clark combines these and other subjects of inquiry. Rush's interest in these matters began as early as 1774, when he published *An oration, delivered before the American Philosophical Society, held at Philadelphia. Containing an enquiry into the natural history of medicine among the Indians in North-America* (Philadelphia [1774]). In 1790 he gave a brief list of questions to "Col. McIlvery," who probably was the Creek chief Alexander McGillivray (RUSH, 188–89). He gave a similar list to Timothy Pickering in 1791, when Pickering was about to depart on a mission to the Senecas (RUSH LETTERS, 1:580–81). The Pickering list is quite different from this one, although some of the questions are duplicated. The questions to Pickering include: Are they ever afflicted with piles or swelled feet from walking? Are their excretions by stool regular? Is the passion for the female sex as strong and as much disposed to excess and irregularity as among civilized people? Do the faculties of the mind decay sooner among Indians than among civilized people?

39. Lewis to Andrew Ellicott

Dear Sir,   Philadelphia May 27th 1803.

I have at length been enabled to procure a Chronometer which you will receive by the hands of Mr. Barton who has been so obliging as to take charge of her, you will also receive with her a screw-driver and kee, the in[n]er cases of the Chronometer are confined by a screw. She is wound up and the works are stoped by inscerting a hog's bristle which you will discover by examineation. She has been cleaned by Mr. Voit, and her rate of going asscertained by observation to be 14″ too slow in 24 h. I shall write you again in a few days more particularly you will therefore pardon the brevity of this communication. My sinceer respects to Mrs. Ellicott and the family and believe me your friend & Obt. Servt.

                                          MERIWETHER LEWIS.

ALS, RC (PHi). Addressed.

40. Lewis to Jefferson

Dear Sir,   Philadelphia May 29th 1803.

I have at length so far succeeded in making the necessary preparations for my intended journey as to be enabled to fix on the sixth or seventh of June as the probable time of my departu[r]e for Washington. All the article[s] have been either procured, or are in such state of forwardness in the hands of the workmen as to induce me to hope that my stay here after that period will be unnecessary; indeed it is probable that I might set out by the middle of this week, was it not for a wish to attend Mr. Patterson a few days longer; this, Mr.

[51]

Patterson recommends: he has been extreemly obliging to me since my arrival here, but his avocations for the last ten days have been such, as rendered it impossible for him to afford me the benefit of his instructions; in the mean time I have employed myself in attending more immediately to the objects of my equipment, and am now more at leasure to pursue with effect the subjects to which, he may think proper to direct my attention.

Agreeably to your instructions the draught of your orders prepared for my government, has been submitted to Mr. Patterson, and to Drs. Rush Barton & Wister; they approve of them very highly: Dr. Rush has favored me with some abstract queries under the several heads of *Physical History, medicine, Morals* and *Religeon* of the Indians, which I have no doubt will be servicable in directing my inquiries among that people: Drs. Barton and Wister have each promised to contribute in like manner any thing, which may suggest itself to them as being of any importance in furthering the objects of this expedition. Dr. Barton has sometimes flattered me with the pleasure of his company as far as the Illinois; this event would be extreemly pleasing to me for many reasons; I fear the Dr. will not carry this design into effect; he tells me that his health has been pretty good latterly, and that he is determined to travel in some direction two or three months during the ensuing summer and autumn.

I paid Mr. Dufief[1] 74$ and Dr. Bolman 18$. I have also purchased a Vigogna Blanket, of which I hope you will approve; it is about the size of a common three point Blanket, the skins appear to be too thin for rough service, tho' it is a very pretty thing; it is the best I could find, the price was 10$. The Tiger's skin you requested I have not been able to procure, those I have seen appear to be too small for your purpose, perhaps they may be had in Baltimore if so, I will get one at that place. The 2 pole chain & 2 pair of fleecy socks have also been procured. I received your watch this morning from Mr. Voigt, who tells me shee is well regulated and in perfect order.[2] Mr. Whitney[3] has not yet repaired your sextant tho' it was put into his hands immediately on my arrival; he has promised however, after repeated applications, that it shall be ready tomorrow evening: he seemed unwilling to undertake the alteration you wished in the brass Sextant stand, I therefore declined having the alteration made; I was further induced to this resolution from the opinion of Mr. Ellicott, who thought that the ball and socket would be reather a disadvantage than otherwise, and that in every event he conceived the advantages of the ball & socket would not be equivalent to the expence attending the alteration.

[52]

I have writen again to Dr. Dickson at Nashville, (from whom I have not yet heard) on the subject of my boat and canoe. I have recieved an answer from Majr. Mac Rea, Comdt. at S.W. Point: his report is reather unfavorable to my wishes: he tells me that out of twenty men who have volunteered their services to accompany me, not more than three or four do by any means possess the necessary qualifications for this expedition, or who answer the discription which I had given him; this however I must endeavour to remedy by taking with me from that place a sufficient number of the best of them to man my boat, and if possible scelect others of a better discription as I pass the Garrisons of Massac, Kaskaskais & Illinois.

You will receive herewith inclosed some sketches taken from Vancouver's survey of the Western Coast of North America; they were taken in a haisty manner, but I believe they will be found sufficiently accurate to be of service in composing the map, which Mr. Gallatin was so good as to promise he would have projected and compleated for me. Will you be so obliging Sir, as to mention to Mr. Gallatin, that I have not been able to procure Danvill's map. The maps attatched to Vancouver's voyage cannot be procured seperately from that work, which is both too costly, and too weighty, for me either to purchase or carry. I have the honor to be with the most sincere esteem & attachment Your Obt. Servt.

MERIWETHER LEWIS

ALS, RC (DLC). Endorsed; received 4 June 1803.

1. Nicholas Gouin Dufief (d. 1834), bookseller, schoolmaster, and author; a native of France now living in Philadelphia.

2. Perhaps this is the silver watch listed on Voigt's bill of 10 June 1803 (under No. 55), which he cleaned for 62½ cents.

3. Thomas Whitney. He advertised in the *Federal Gazette* of 12 April 1798, from a location at 74 South Front Street in Philadelphia, and described himself as a Londoner. In the *Aurora* of 29 Nov. 1808 he advertised surveyors' compasses made by himself, for sale "Near the first gate on the Germantown road." In a letter to the editor of the *Aurora* 6 Jan. 1814 he signed himself a "mathematical instrument maker."

41. Lewis to William Linnard

Sir   June the 10th 1803

I called to see you with a view more fully to impress you with the necessity of providing a strong and effective team for the transportation of the public stores under my charge destined for Pittsburgh; the road mentioned in a former communication, and which from necessaty they must travel is by no means good, and I find that the

[53]

stores will weigh at least 35 Hundred. If a team could be provided with five horses perhaps it would be better. I expect every thing will be in readiness by tuesday or Wednesday next. Your Obt. & very Humble Sert.

MERIWETHER LEWIS
Capt. 1st. U.S. Regt. Infty.

ALS, RC (DNA, RG 92, Box 560A). Addressed, "Mr. Leonard"; endorsed, "Cap. Meriwether Lewis 10 June 1803 Respecting the proprity of procuring a team with five horses to transport the goods under his care from here to Pittsburg by the rout described in his former letter." Added in pencil, "Fredericktown." William Linnard (d. 1835), of Pennsylvania, was appointed military agent for the Middle Department 5 May 1802. He was instructed to "cause to be transported to their respective destinations, all Military, Medical and Hospital Stores, and all Indian goods intended as annuities, presents or as articles of commerce . . ." (DNA, RG 107, Letters Sent). His territory was to be the Atlantic coast from Norfolk to Portsmouth, and Fort McHenry, South West Point, Vincennes, Massac, Kaskaskia, Chickasaw Bluffs, Fort Adams, and Mobile. The title of assistant military agent was given to an officer at each post whose duty was to receive, account for, and dispense such stores as were sent him by the military agent.

42. Benjamin Rush to Jefferson

Dear Sir,   Philadelphia, June 11th, 1803
I have endeavored to fulfil your wishes by furnishing Mr. Lewis with some inquiries relative to the natural history of the Indians. The enclosed letter contains a few short directions for the preservation of his health, as well as the health of the persons under his command.

His mission is truly interesting. I shall wait with great solicitude for its issue. Mr. Lewis appears admirably qualified for it. May its advantages prove no less honorable to your administration than to the interests of science.

The enclosed letter from Mr. Sumpter contains some new views of the present military arrangements of France and Great Britain. You need not return it. From, dear sir, yours very respectfully and sincerely,

BENJN: RUSH

Printed, RUSH LETTERS, 2:868; original ALS in NjP. The enclosure mentioned is No. 43.

43. Benjamin Rush's Rules of Health

Dr. Rush to Capt. Lewis for preserving his health.   June 11. 1803.

1. When you feel the least indisposition, do not attempt to overcome it by labour or marching. *Rest* in a horizontal posture. Also

fasting and diluting drinks for a day or two will generally prevent an attack of fever. To these preventatives of disease may be added a gentle sweat obtained by warm drinks, or gently opening the bowels by means of one, two, or more of the purging pills.

2. Unusual costiveness is often a sign of approaching disease. When you feel it take one or more of the purging pills.

3. Want of appetite is likewise a sign of approaching indisposition. It should be obviated by the same remedy.

4. In difficult & laborious enterprises & marches, *eating sparingly* will enable you to bear them with less fatigue & less danger to your health.

5. Flannel should be worn constantly next to the skin, especially in wet weather.

6. The less spirit you use the better. After being *wetted* or *much* fatigued, or *long* exposed to the night air, it should be taken in an *undiluted* state. 3 tablespoonfuls taken in this way will be more useful in preventing sickness, than half a pint mixed with water.

7. Molasses or sugar & water with a few drops of the acid of vitriol will make a pleasant & wholsome drink with your meals.

8. After having had your feet much chilled, it will be useful to wash them with a little spirit.

9. Washing the feet every morning in *cold* water, will conduce very much to fortify them against the action of cold.

10. After long marches, or much fatigue from any cause, you will be more refreshed by *lying down* in a horizontal posture for two hours, than by resting a much longer time in any other position of the body.

11. Shoes made without heels, by affording *equal* action to all the muscles of the legs, will enable you to march with less fatigue, than shoes made in the ordinary way.

AD, in Jefferson's hand (DLC). Endorsed, "Health. Rush's rules for preserving." Rush's own copy is in his commonplace book (PPAmP), p. 268, and differs in some details. Rush struck from his copy this passage: "5. Where Salt cannot be had with your meat, steep it in Lye." It seems likely that Rush gave Lewis a copy of these rules personally; the present copy may be a transcript made by Jefferson for his own use. In RUSH LETTERS, 1:140, see Rush's "Directions for Preserving the Health of Soldiers," written in 1777, with predictable similarities.

44. Jefferson to James Cheetham

Sir   Washington June 17. 1803.

I have deferred answering your letter of May 30. until I could find the means of having paiment made in New York for the volume of the

Watch tower therein mentioned. Mr. Garnet tells me he has an account with Mr. Charles Ludlow of New York, on which some little balance will perhaps be due, and authorises me to say he will pay for that as well as what I am now to add. I have understood there is to be had in New York an 8vo edition of McKenzie's travels[1] with the same maps which are in the 4to edition: I will thank you to procure it for me. The American 8vo edition is defective in it's maps, and the English 4to edition is too large & cumbersome. I think I have seen advertised in some papers that an edition of Arrowsmith's map of the U.S. has been published at New York. I shall be glad to receive either that or the English [. . .] if to be had there. The latter would be preferred because I know the engraving is superiorly well done. Be so good as to deliver these articles to Mr. Ludlow who will pay for & forward them to me. Accept my best wishes.

TH: JEFFERSON

ALS, SC (DLC). James Cheetham (1772–1810), a bookseller and journalist, published a bi-weekly newspaper called the *Republican Watch-Tower* in New York.

1. Alexander MACKENZIE, *Voyages from Montreal, on the River St. Lawrence, through the continent of North America, to the frozen and Pacific Ocean; in the years 1789 and 1793* . . . (London, 1801). Since he wants a copy that is not "too large & cumbersome," Jefferson may be ordering the volume for Lewis. JACKSON (4) lists this work as one of several that the explorers may have carried witth them, and discusses further the sources of their book knowledge. Cheetham billed Jefferson $3.50 for a copy of Mackenzie on 22 June 1803 (DLC).

45. Robert Patterson to Jefferson

Sir   Philada. June 18th 1803.

I recommended to Capt. Lewis, the use of a *Statistical Table* in which to set down his astronomical observations, in the course of his intended expedition; as an expedient that would save a great deal of time, and be productive of many other obvious advantages. I had proposed to draw him out a sketch of such a table, but an unusual hurry of business prevented me, while he was in the city. I have now, however, fulfilled my promise and transmit the inclosed for his inspection.

I have sent it under cover to you, Sir, lest Capt. Lewis may have proceeded on his tour; in which case, if you shall judge it worth his notice, you will have the trouble of forwarding it to him. I am Sir with the highest respect & esteem Your Obedt. Servt.

R. PATTERSON

ALS, RC (DLC). Endorsed; received 21 June 1803.

46. Lewis to Clark

Dear Clark,   Washington June 19th 1803

Herewith inclosed you will receive the papers belonging to your brother Genl. Clark, which sometime since you requested me to procure and forward to you; pray excuse the delay which has taken place, it has really proceeded from causes which I could not control; Mr. Thompson Mason[1] the gentleman in whose possesion they were, is a member of the Virginia legislature, and was absent of course from his residence untill March, previous to his return I was compelled to leave this place on a matter of business, which has detained me in Lancaster & Philadelphia untill the day before yesterday and since my return haveing possessed myself of the papers I sieze the first moment to forward them to you: In this claim I wish you sucess most sincerely.

From the long and uninterupted friendship and confidence which has subsisted between us I feel no hesitation in making to you the following communication under the fulest impression that it will be held by you inviolably secret untill I see you, or you shall hear again from me.

During the last session of Congress a law was passed in conformity to a private message of the President of the United States, inti[t]led 'An Act making an appropriation for extending the external commerce of the United States." The object of this Act as understood by it's framers was to give the sanction of the government to exploreing the interior of the continent of North America, or that part of it bordering on the Missourie & Columbia Rivers. This enterprise has been confided to me by the President, and in consequence since the begining of March I have been engaged in making the necessary preparations for the tour, these arrangements being now nearly completed, I shall set out for Pittsburgh (the intended point of embarcation) about the last of this month, and as soon after as from the state of the water you can reasonably expect me I shall be with you, say about the 10th of August. To aid me in this enterprise I have the most ample and hearty support that the government can give in every possible shape. I am armed with the authority of the Government of the U. States for my protection, so far as its authority or influence extends; in addition to which, the further aid has been given me of liberal pasports from the Ministers both of France and England: I am instructed to select from any corps in the army a number of noncommissioned officers and privates not exceeding 12, who may be disposed voluntarily to enter into this service; and am also authorized to engage any other men not soldiers that I may think usefull in promoting the objects or success of this expedition. I am likewise furnished with letters of credit, and authorized to draw on the government for any sum necessary for the comfort of myself or party. To all the persons engaged in this service I am authorized to offer the following rewards by way of inducement—1st the bounty (if not a soldier) but in both cases six months pay in advance; 2dly to discharge them from the service if they wish it, immediately on their return from the expedition giving them their arrears of pay clothing &c. & 3dly to secure to them a portion of land equal to that given by the United States to the officers and soldiers who served in the revolutionary army. This is a sho[r]t view of means with which I am intrusted to carry this plan of the Government into effect. I will now give you a short sketch of my plan of operation: I shall embark at Pittsburgh with a party of recruits eight or nine in number, intended only to manage the boat and are not calculated on as a permanent part of my detatcment; when descending the Ohio it shall be my duty by enquiry to find out and engage some good hunters, stout, healthy, unmarried men, accustomed to the woods, and capable of bearing bodily fatigue in a pretty considerable degree: should any young men answering this discription be found in your neighborhood I would thank you to give information of them on my arivall at the falls of the Ohio; and if possible learn the probability of their engaging in this service, this may be done perhaps by holding out the idea that the direction of this expedition is up the Mississippi to its source, and thence to the lake of the Woods, stating the probable period of absence at about 18 months; if they would engage themselves in a service of this discription there would be but little doubt that they would engage in the real design when it became necessary to make it known to them, which I should take care to do before I finally engaged them: The soldiers that will most probably answer this expedition best will be found in some of the companies stationed at Massac, Kaskaskias & Illinois: pardon this digression from the discription of my plan: it is to descend the Ohio in a keeled boat of about ten tons burthen, from Pittsburgh to it's mouth, thence up the Mississippi to the mouth of the Missourie, and up that river as far as it's navigation is practicable with a boat of this discription, there to prepare canoes of bark or raw-hides, and proceed to it's source, and if practicable pass over to the waters of the Columbia or Origan River and by descending it reach the Western Ocean; the mouth of this river lies about one hundred and forty miles South of Nootka-

[58]

Sound, at which place there is a considerable European Tradeing establishment, and from which it will be easy to obtain a passage to the United States by way of the East-Indies in some of the trading vessels that visit Nootka Sound anually, provided it should be thought more expedient to do so, than to return by the rout I had pursued in my outward bound journey. The present season being already so far advanced, I do not calculate on geting further than two or three hundred miles up the Missourie before the commencement of the ensuing winter. At this point wherever it may be I shall make myself as comfortable as possible during the winter and resume my journey as early in the spring as the ice will permit: should nothing take place to defeat my progress altogether I feel confident that my passage to the Western Ocean can be effected by the end of the next Summer or the begining of Autumn. In order to subsist my party with some degree of comfort dureing the ensuing winter, I shall engage some French traders at Illinois to attend me to my wintering ground with a sufficient quantity of flour, pork, &c. to serve them plentifully during the winter, and thus be enabled to set out in the Spring with a healthy and vigorous party—so much for the great outlines of this scheem, permit me now to mention partially the objects which it has in view or those which it is desirable to effect through it's means, and then conclude this lengthy communication. You must know in the first place that very sanguine expectations are at this time formed by our Government that the whole of that immense country wartered by the Mississippi and it's tributary streams, Missourie inclusive, will be the property of the U. States in less than 12 Months from this date; but here let me again impress you with the necessity of keeping this matter a perfect secret—in such a state of things therefore as we have every reason to hope, you will readily concieve the importance to the U. States of an early friendly and intimate acquaintance with the tribes that inhabit that country, that they should be early impressed with a just idea of the rising importance of the U. States and of her friendly dispositions towards them, as also her desire to become useful to them by furnishing them through her citizens with such articles by way of barter as may be desired by them or usefull to them—the other objects of this mission are scientific, and of course not less interresting to the U. States than to the world generally, such is the ascertaining by celestial observation the geography of the country through which I shall pass; the names of the nations who inhabit it, the extent and limitts of their several possessions, their relation with other tribes and nations; their languages, traditions, and monuments;

[59]

their ordinary occupations in fishing, hunting, war, arts, and the implements for their food, clothing and domestic accomodation; the diseases prevalent among them and the remidies they use; the articles of commerce they may need, or furnish, and to what extent; the soil and face of the country; it's growth and vegetable productions, its animals; the miniral productions of every discription; and in short to collect the best possible information relative to whatever the country may afford as a tribute to general science.

My Instruments for celestial observation are an excellent set and my supply of Indian presents is sufficiently ample.

Thus my friend you have so far as leasure will at this time permit me to give it you, a summary view of the plan, the means and the objects of this expedition. If therefore there is anything under those circumstances, in this enterprise, which would induce you to participate with me in it's fatiegues, it's dangers and it's honors, believe me there is no man on earth with whom I should feel equal pleasure in sharing them as with yourself; I make this communication to you with the privity of the President, who expresses an anxious wish that you would consent to join me in this enterprise; he has authorized me to say that in the event of your accepting this proposition he will grant you a Captain's commission[2] which of course will intitle you to the pay and emoluments attached to that office and will equally with myself intitle you to such portion of land as was granted to officers of similar rank for their Revolutionary services; the commission with which he proposes to furnish you is not to be considered temporary but permanent if you wish it; your situation if joined with me in this mission will in all respects be precisely such as my own. Pray write to me on this subject as early as possible and direct to me at Pittsburgh. Should you feel disposed not to attatch yourself to this party in an official character, and at the same time feel a disposition to accompany me as a friend any part of the way up the Missouri I should be extremely happy in your company, and will furnish you with every aid for your return from any point you might wish it. With sincere and affectionate regard Your friend & Humble Sevt.

MERIWETHER LEWIS

ALS, RC (MoSHi). Reply is No. 74.

1. Stevens Thomson Mason (1760–1803), U.S. senator from Virginia.

2. Jefferson, of course, could only nominate officers for appointment; his selections had to be confirmed by the Senate. He routinely made these nominations on the recommendation of the Secretary of War. For a note on the red tape that thwarted Clark's appointment to a captaincy, see No. 110. For Clark's own reaction voiced many years later, see No. 345, in which he answers an inquiry put to him in No. 342 by Nicholas Biddle.

47. Jefferson's Instructions to Lewis

[20 June 1803]

To Captain Meriwether Lewis esq. Capt. of the 1st regimt. of Infantry of the U.S. of A.

Your situation as Secretary of the President of the U.S. has made you acquainted with the objects of my confidential message of Jan. 18, 1803 to the legislature; you have seen the act they passed, which, tho' expressed in general terms, was meant to sanction those objects, and you are appointed to carry them into execution.

Instruments for ascertaining, by celestial observations, the geography of the country through which you will pass, have been already provided. Light articles for barter and presents among the Indians, arms for your attendants, say for from 10. to 12. men, boats, tents, & other travelling apparatus, with ammunition, medecine, surgical instruments and provisions you will have prepared with such aids as the Secretary at War can yield in his department; & from him also you will recieve authority to engage among our troops, by voluntary agreement, the number of attendants above mentioned, over whom you, as their commanding officer, are invested with all the powers the laws give in such a case.

As your movements while within the limits of the U.S. will be better directed by occasional communications, adapted to circumstances as they arise, they will not be noticed here. What follows will respect your proceedings after your departure from the United states.

Your mission has been communicated to the ministers here from France, Spain & Great Britain, and through them to their governments; & such assurances given them as to it's objects, as we trust will satisfy them. The country <of Louisiana> having been ceded by Spain to France, <and possession by this time probably given,> the passport you have from the minister of France, the representative of the present sovereign of the country, will be a protection with all it's subjects; & that from the minister of England will entitle you to the friendly aid of any traders of that allegiance with whom you may happen to meet.

The object of your mission is to explore the Missouri river, & such principal stream of it, as, by it's course and communication with the waters of the Pacific ocean, whether the Columbia, Oregan, Colorado or any other river[1] may offer the most direct & practicable water communication across this continent for the purposes of commerce.

Beginning at the mouth of the Missouri, you will take <careful> observations of latitude & longitude, at all remarkeable points on the river, & especially at the mouths of rivers, at rapids, at islands, & other places & objects distinguished by such natural marks & characters of a durable kind, as that they may with certainty be recognised hereafter. The courses of the river between these points of observation may be supplied by the compass the log-line & by time, corrected by the observations themselves. The variations of the compass too, in different places, should be noticed.

The interesting points of the portage between the heads of the Missouri, & of the water offering the best communication with the Pacific ocean, should also be fixed by observation, & the course of that water to the ocean, in the same manner as that of the Missouri.

Your observations are to be taken with great pains & accuracy, to be entered distinctly & intelligibly for others as well as yourself, to comprehend all the elements necessary, with the aid of the usual tables, to fix the latitude and longitude of the places at which they were taken, and are to be rendered to the war-office, for the purpose of having the calculations made concurrently by proper persons within the U.S. Several copies of these as well as of your other notes should be made at leisure times, & put into the care of the most trust-worthy of your attendants, to guard, by multiplying them, against the accidental losses to which they will be exposed. A further guard would be that one of these copies be on the paper of the birch, as less liable to injury from damp than common paper.[2]

The commerce which may be carried on with the people inhabiting the line you will pursue, renders a knolege of those people important. You will therefore endeavor to make yourself acquainted, as far as a diligent pursuit of your journey shall admit, with the names of the nations & their numbers;

the extent & limits of their possessions;

their relations with other tribes of nations;

their language, traditions, monuments;

their ordinary occupations in agriculture, fishing, hunting, war, arts, & the implements for these;

their food, clothing, & domestic accomodations;

the diseases prevalent among them, & the remedies they use;

moral & physical circumstances which distinguish them from the tribes we know;

peculiarities in their laws, customs & dispositions;

and articles of commerce they may need or furnish, & to what extent.

And, considering the interest which every nation has in extending & strengthening the authority of reason & justice among the people around them, it will be useful to acquire what knolege you can of the

[62]

state of morality, religion, & information among them; as it may better enable those who may endeavor to civilize & instruct them, to adapt their measures to the existing notions & practices of those on whom they are to operate.

Other objects worthy of notice will be

the soil & face of the country, it's growth & vegetable productions, especially those not of the U.S.

the animals of the country generally, & especially those not known in the U.S.

the remains or accounts of any which may be deemed rare or extinct;

the mineral productions of every kind; but more particularly metals, limestone, pit coal, & saltpetre; salines & mineral waters, noting the temperature of the last, & such circumstances as may indicate their character;

volcanic appearances;

climate, as characterised by the thermometer, by the proportion of rainy, cloudy, & clear days, by lightning, hail, snow, ice, by the access & recess of frost, by the winds prevailing at different seasons, the dates at which particular plants put forth or lose their flower, or leaf, times of appearance of particular birds, reptiles or insects.

Altho' your route will be along the channel of the Missouri, yet you will endeavor to inform yourself, by enquiry, of the character & extent of the country watered by it's branches, & especially on it's Southern side. The North river or Rio Bravo which runs into the gulph of Mexico, and the North river, or Rio colorado which runs into the gulph of California, are understood to be the principal streams heading opposite to the waters of the Missouri, and running Southwardly. Whether the dividing grounds between the Missouri & them are mountains or flat lands, what are their distance from the Missouri, the character of the intermediate country, & the people inhabiting it, are worthy of particular enquiry. The Northern waters of the Missouri are less to be enquired after, becaue they have been ascertained to a considerable degree, & are still in a course of ascertainment by English traders, and travellers. But if you can learn any thing certain of the most Northern source of the Missisipi, & of it's position relatively to the lake of the woods, it will be interesting to us.

<*Two copies of your notes at least & as many more as leisure will admit, should be made & confided to the care of the most trusty individuals of your attendants.*> Some account too of the path of the Canadian traders from the Missisipi, at the mouth of the Ouisconsing

[63]

to where it strikes the Missouri, & of the soil and rivers in it's course, is desireable.

In all your intercourse with the natives, treat them in the most friendly & conciliatory manner which their own conduct will admit; allay all jealousies as to the object of your journey, satisfy them of it's innocence, make them acquainted with the position, extent, character, peaceable & commercial dispositions of the U.S.[,] of our wish to be neighborly, friendly & useful to them, & of our dispositions to a commercial intercourse with them; confer with them on the points most convenient as mutual emporiums, and the articles of most desireable interchange for them & us.[3] If a few of their influential chiefs, within practicable distance, wish to visit us, arrange such a visit with them, and furnish them with authority to call on our officers, on their entering the U.S. to have them conveyed to this place at the public expence. If any of them should wish to have some of their young people brought up with us, & taught such arts as may be useful to them, we will receive, instruct & take care of them. Such a mission, whether of influential chiefs or of young people, would give some security to your own party.[4] Carry with you some matter of the kine-pox; inform those of them with whom you may be, of it's efficacy as a preservative from the smallpox; & instruct & encourage them in the use of it. This may be especially done wherever you winter.

As it is impossible for us to foresee in what manner you will be recieved by those people, whether with hospitality or hostility, so is it impossible to prescribe the exact degree of perseverance with which you are to pursue your journey. We value too much the lives of citizens to offer them to probable destruction. Your numbers will be sufficient to secure you against the unauthorised opposition of individuals or of small parties: but if a superior force, authorised, or not authorised, by a nation, should be arrayed against your further passage, and inflexibly determined to arrest it, you must decline it's farther pursuit, and return. In the loss of yourselves, we should lose also the information you will have acquired. By returning safely with that, you may enable us to renew the essay with better calculated means. To your own discretion therefore must be left the degree of danger you may risk, and the point at which you should decline, only saying we wish you to err on the side of your safety, and to bring back your party safe even if it be with less information.

As far up the Missouri as the white settlements extend, an intercourse will probably be found to exist between them & the Spanish posts of St. Louis opposite Cahokia, or Ste. Genevieve opposite Kaskaskia. From still further up the river, the traders may furnish a

[64]

conveyance for letters. Beyond that, you may perhaps be able to engage Indians to bring letters for the government to Cahokia or Kaskaskia, on promising that they shall there recieve such special compensation as you shall have stipulated with them. Avail yourself of these means to communicate to us, at seasonable intervals, a copy of your journal, notes & observations, of every kind, putting into cypher[5] whatever might do injury if betrayed.

Should you reach the Pacific ocean inform yourself of the circumstances which may decide whether the furs of those parts may not be collected as advantageously at the head of the Missouri (convenient as is supposed to the waters of the Colorado & Oregan or Columbia) as at Nootka sound, or any other point of that coast; and that trade be consequently conducted through the Missouri & U.S. more beneficially than by the circumnavigation now practised.[6]

On your arrival on that coast endeavor to learn if there be any port within your reach frequented by the sea-vessels of any nation, & to send two of your trusty people back by sea, in such way as <*they shall judge*> shall appear practicable, with a copy of your notes: and should you be of opinion that the return of your party by the way they went will be eminently dangerous, then ship the whole, & return by sea, by the way either of cape Horn, or the cape of good Hope, as you shall be able. As you will be without money, clothes or provisions, you must endeavor to use the credit of the U.S. to obtain them, for which purpose open letters of credit[7] shall be furnished you, authorising you to draw upon the Executive of the U.S. or any of it's officers, in any part of the world, on which draughts can be disposed of, & to apply with our recommendations to the Consuls, agents, merchants, or citizens of any nation with which we have intercourse, assuring them, in our name, that any aids they may furnish you, shall be honorably repaid, and on demand. Our consuls Thomas Hewes at Batavia in Java, Wm. Buchanan in the Isles of France & Bourbon & John Elmslie at the Cape of good Hope will be able to supply your necessities by draughts on us.[8]

Should you find it safe to return by the way you go, after sending two of your party round by sea, or with your whole party, if no conveyance by sea can be found, do so; making such observations on your return, as may serve to supply, correct or confirm those made on your outward journey.

On re-entering the U.S. and reaching a place of safety, discharge any of your attendants who may desire & deserve it, procuring for them immediate paiment of all arrears of pay & cloathing which may have incurred since their departure, and assure them that they shall be

[65]

recommended to the liberality of the legislature for the grant of a souldier's portion of land each, as proposed in my message to Congress: & repair yourself with your papers to the seat of government <*to which I have only to add my sincere prayer for your safe return*>.

To provide, on the accident of your death, against anarchy, dispersion, & the consequent danger to your party, and total failure of the enterprize, you are hereby authorised, by any instrument signed & written in your own hand, to name the person among them who shall succeed to the command on your decease, and by like instruments to change the nomination from time to time as further experience of the characters accompanying you shall point out superior fitness: and all the powers and authorities given to yourself are, in the event of your death, transferred to, & vested in the successor so named, with further power to him, and his successors in like manner to name each his successor, who, on the death of his predecessor, shall be invested with all the powers & authorities given to yourself.

Given under my hand at the city of Washington this 20th day of June 1803.

TH: J. Pr. U.S. of A.

ADS, SC (DLC). This is a draft which Jefferson later incorporated into the draft of his memoir on Lewis (No. 362), and which is now filed with that document in DLC. A letterpress impression of the fair copy, in Jefferson's hand, is also in DLC.

1. The words "whether the Columbia, Oregan, Colorado or any other river" are omitted from the fair copy.

2. The last sentence in this paragraph appears in smaller letters, as if added later. A fragment of the text exists in Clark's hand, slightly abridged, on a two-page manuscript in MoSHi, extending from the beginning of this paragraph to superscript numeral 2.

3. End of version in Clark's hand (MoSHi).

4. This sentence is inserted in smaller letters, as if added later. Jefferson's reference to the security of the party may have given rise to the common belief that the group of Osages which left St. Louis for Washington in the spring of 1804 were "hostages" for the safety of the expedition. The sending back of Indian delegations was done for a much different reason, and even when there were reports that Lewis and Clark had been killed in the West, no one in Washington treated these delegations as hostages.

5. No enciphered messages from Lewis have been found.

6. This paragraph and the preceding one were written longitudinally in the right-hand margin, as insertions.

7. For the text of the letter of credit, see No. 67.

8. Thomas Hewes, consul for the port of Batavia, was appointed 24 Nov. 1801; William Buchanan of Maryland, commercial agent for the Isles of France and Bourbon, was appointed 9 July 1801; John Elmslie, Jr., consul at the Cape of Good Hope, was appointed 21 Feb. 1799.

48. Thomas H. Cushing to William A. Murray

Sir: Inspectors Office Fredk. Town (Md.) 20th June 1803.

You will please to select eight of the best and most sober of your party[1] for immediate Command to Pittsburgh. The one who appears to be the best qualified for the trust, will be considered as a lance Corporal, and to him you will give the charge of the party, with instructions to repair to Pittsburgh without loss of time and report to Lieut. Hooke. This party must be furnished with a Complete suit of Clothing each, including what they have already drawn, and with provisions to Pittsburgh, but they are to march without Arms.

A particular description of each man, and account of the articles receiv'd, must accompany the Party to Pittsburgh, and you will transmit a duplicate of said description and account to this Office, and let me know the name of the lance Corporal, and the day the party marches. I am Sir, Very Respectfully Your Obdt. Servt.

Lbk (DNA, RG 94, Letters Sent). Thomas Humphrey Cushing (d. 1822), of Massachusetts, was appointed lieutenant colonel in the Second Infantry in 1802, and served until 1807 as adjutant and inspector.

1. These men were all recruits for Capt. Henry Muhlenberg's company of artillerists, which was then at Fort Mifflin but was soon to be transferred to Fort Adams, Mississippi Territory. On a muster roll of this company for 28 Feb. 1803, Lt. Murray is listed as on recruiting duty (DNA, RG 94, Pay and Muster Rolls, Corps of Artillerists).

49. Lewis to Jefferson

[23 June 1803]

I promise to pay Thomas Jefferson his Heirs or Assigns, on demand, the sum of one hundred and three Dollars and ninety three Cents, for value received.

June 23rd 1803.   MERIWETHER LEWIS

$103.93

ADS, RC (MHi). Endorsed by Jefferson:

		D
Lewis Meriwether		
Note of hand		
1803. June 23		103.93
YMD		
1807. Aug. 1. 4–1–9		25.61
		129.54
by disbursments, for me		21.50
		108.04

A mention of this obligation appears in Jefferson's correspondence after Lewis's death (No. 323).

50. Jefferson to Benjamin Rush

Th: Jefferson to Dr. Rush   [24 June 1803]
  I am thankful to you for your attentions to Capt. Lewis while at Philadelphia and the useful counsels he received from you. He will set out in about 4. or 5. days, and expects to leave Kaskaskias about the 1st of September. He will have two travelling months which will probably carry him 7. or 800. miles up the river for his winter quarters, from whence he will communicate to us, in the course of the winter his observations so far. He tells me you wish to see the inclosed pamphlets on longevity by Sr. John Sinclair,[1] which you can return me at your leisure. Accept affectionate salutations.
June 24. 1803. Washington.

  AL, SC (DLC).
  1. Sir John Sinclair (1754–1835), Scottish agriculturist. His *An essay on longevity* (London, 1802) is a pamphlet of 15 leaves.

51. Henry Dearborn to the Army Paymaster

Paymaster of the Army   War Department June 29th 1803.
  You will please to pay Capt. Merewether Lewis Five hundred and fifty four dollars, being six Months pay for one Lieutenant, one Sergeant, one Corporal, and ten Privates; for which you will hold him accountable.

H. DEARBORN

  Lbk (DNA, RG 107, Letters Sent, 2:10).

52. Henry Dearborn to the Army Paymaster

Paymaster of the Army   [29 June 1803]
  The Paymaster of the Army is authorised to settle the Pay & subsistence due Capt. Meriwether Lewis to the 31st of Decr. next.
War Department   H. D.
June 29th 1803

  Lbk (DNA, RG 107, Letters Sent, 2:10).

EDITORIAL NOTE: Items 53 through 57 are grouped under one general heading, and the whole collection is assigned an arbitrary date of 30 June 1803 for convenience. Here are all the extant records showing Lewis's effort, during May and June 1803, to obtain an assortment of supplies and equipment that would see him through a two-year expedition. Much of this information is reproduced in the JOURNALS, 7:231–46, one notable exception being the vouchers from most of the individual suppliers under No. 55. Unless otherwise designated, all documents under Nos. 53–57 are in a single consolidated file at the National Archives, RG 92, Box 560A.

53. Lewis's List of Requirements

Mathematical Instruments

1   Hadley's Quadrant
1   Mariner's Compas & 2 pole chain
1   Sett of plotting instruments
3   Thermometers[1]
1   Cheap portable Microscope
1   Pocket Compass
1   brass Scale one foot in length
6   Magnetic needles in small straight silver or brass cases opening on the side with hinges.
1   Instrument for measuring made of tape with feet & inches mark'd on it, confined within a circular lethern box of sufficient thickness to admit the width of the tape which has one of its ends confined to an axis of metal passing through the center of the box, around which and within the box it is readily wound by means of a small crank on the outer side of the box which forms a part of the axis, the tape when necessary is drawn out with the same facility & ease with which it is wound up.
2   Hydrometers
1   Theodolite
1   Sett of planespheres
2   Artificial Horizons
1   Patent log
6   papers of Ink powder
4   Metal Pens brass or silver
1   Set of Small Slates & pencils

2 Creyons
Sealing wax *one bundle*[2]
1 Miller's edition of Lineus in 2 Vol: [3]
Books
Maps
Charts
Blank Vocabularies
Writing paper
1 Pair large brass money scales with two setts of weights the one of Troy the other of Averds.

Arms & Accoutrements

15 Rifles
15 Powder Horns & pouches complete
15 Pairs of Bullet Moulds
15 do. of Wipers or Gun worms
15 Ball Screws
24 Pipe Tomahawks
24 large knives
Extra parts of Locks & tools for repairing arms
15 Gun Slings
500 best Flints

Ammunition

200 lbs. Best rifle powder
400 lbs. Lead

Clothing

15 3 pt. Blankets
15 *Watch* Coats with Hoods & belts
15 Woolen Overalls
15 Rifle Frocks *of waterproof Cloth if possible*[4]
30 Pairs of Socks or half Stockings
20 Fatigue Frocks or hunting shirts
30 Shirts of Strong linnen
30 yds. Common flannel.

Camp Equipage

6 Copper kettles (1 of 5 Gallons, 1 of 3, 2 of 2, & 2 of 1)
25 falling Axes.
4 Drawing Knives, short & strong

[70]

2	Augers of the patent kind if they can be obtain'd with 6 bitts assorted, or otherwise 6 Augers of the common screw kind assorted
1	Small permanent Vice
1	Hand Vice
36	Gimblets assorted
24	Files do.
12	Chisels do.
10	Nails do.
2	Steel plate hand saws
2	Vials of Phosforus
1	do. of Phosforus made of allum & sugar
4	Groce fishing Hooks assorted
12	Bunches of Drum Line
2	Foot Adzes
12	Bunches of Small cord
2	Pick Axes
3	Coils of Rope
2	Spades
12	Bunches Small fishing line assorted
1	lb. Turkey or Oil Stone
1	Iron Mill for Grinding Corn
20	yds. Oil linnen for wrapping & securing Articles
10	yds do. do. of thicker quality for covering and lining boxes. &c
40	Yds Do. Do. To form two half faced Tents or Shelters contrived in such manner their parts may be taken to pieces & again connected at pleasure in order to answer the several purposes of Tents, covering to Boat or Canoe, or if necessary to be used as sails. The pieces when unconnected will be 5 feet in Width and rather more than 14 feet in length
4	Tin blowing Trumpets
2	hand or spiral spring Steelyards
20	yds Strong Oznaburgs
24	Iron Spoons
24	Pint Tin Cups (without handles)
30	Steels for striking or making fire
100	Flints for do. do. do.
2	Frows
6	Saddlers large Needles
6	Do. large Awls
	Muscatoe Curtains

        2   patent chamber lamps & wicks
       15   Oil Cloth Bags for securing provision
        1   Sea Grass Hammock

Provisions and Means of Subsistence

      150   lbs. Portable Soup.
        3   bushels of Allum or Rock Salt
            Spicies assorted
        6   Kegs of 5 Gallons each making 30 Gallons of rectified spirits
            such as is used for the Indian trade
        6   Kegs bound with iron Hoops

Indian Presents

        5   lbs. White Wampum
        5   lbs. White Glass Beads mostly small
       20   lbs. Red Do. Do. Assorted
        5   lbs. Yellow or Orange Do. Do. Assorted
       30   Calico Shirts
       12   Pieces of East India muslin Hanckerchiefs striped or check'd
            with brilliant Colours.
       12   Red Silk Hanckerchiefs
      144   Small cheap looking Glasses
      100   Burning Glasses
        4   Vials of Phosforus
      288   Steels for striking fire
      144   Small cheap Scizors
       20   Pair large Do.
       12   Groces Needles Assorted No. 1 to 8 Common points
       12   Groces Do. Assorted with points for sewing leather
      288   Common brass thimbles—part W. office
       10   lbs. Sewing Thread assorted
       24   Hanks Sewing Silk
        8   lbs. Red lead
        2   lbs. Vermillion—at War Office
      288   Knives Small such as are generally used for the Indian trade,
            with fix'd blades & handles inlaid with brass
       36   Large knives
       36   Pipe Tomahawks—*at H. Ferry*[5]
       12   lbs. Brass wire Assorted
       12   lbs. Iron do. do. generally large
        6   Belts of narrow Ribbons colours assorted
       50   lbs. Spun Tobacco.

[72]

20 Small falling axes *to be obtained in Tennessee*[6]
40 fish Giggs such as the Indians use with a single barbed point—
     at Harper's ferry[7]
 3 Groce fishing Hooks assorted
 4 Groce Mockerson awls assorted
50 lbs. Powder secured in a Keg covered with oil Cloth
24 Belts of Worsted feiret or Gartering Colours brilliant and
     Assorted
15 Sheets of Copper Cut into strips of an inch in width & a foot
     long
20 Sheets of Tin
12 lbs. Strips of Sheet iron 1 In. wide 1 foot long
 1 Pc. red Cloth second quality
 1 Nest of 8 or 9 small copper kettles
100 Block-tin rings cheap kind ornamented with Colour'd Glass
     or Mock-Stone
 2 Groces of brass Curtain Rings & sufficently large for the Finger
 1 Groce Cast Iron Combs
18 Cheap brass Combs
24 Blankets.
12 Arm Bands Silver at War Office
12 Wrist do. do. Do.
36 Ear Trinkets Do. part do.
36 Nose Do. Do.
 6 Groces Drops of Do. part Do.
 4 doz Rings for Fingers of do.
 4 Groces Broaches of do.
12 Small Medals Do.

Means of Transportation

 1 Keeled Boat light strong at least 60 feet in length her burthen
     equal to 8 Tons
 1 Iron frame of Canoe 40 feet long
 1 Large Wooden Canoe
12 Spikes for Setting-Poles
 4 Boat Hooks & points Complete
 2 Chains & Pad-Locks for confining the Boat & Canoes &c.

Medicine

15 lbs. best powder'd Bark
10 lbs. Epsom or Glauber Salts
 4 oz. Calomel

[73]

12 oz. Opium
½ oz. Tarter emetic
8 oz Borax
4 oz Powder'd Ipecacuana
8 oz Powder Jalap
8 oz Powdered Rhubarb
6 Best lancets
2 oz White Vitriol
4 oz Lacteaum Saturni
4 Pewter Penis Syringes
1 Flour of Sulphur
3 Clyster pipes
4 oz Turlingtons Balsam
2 lbs. Yellow Bascilicum
2 Sticks of Symple Diachylon
1 lb. Blistering Ointments
2 lbs. Nitre
2 lbs. Coperas

Materials for making up the Various Articles into portable Packs

30 Sheep skins taken off the Animal as perfectly whole as possible, without being split on the belly as usual and dress'd only with lime to free them from the wool; or otherwise about the same quantity of Oil Cloth bags well painted
Raw Hide for pack strings
Dress'd letter for Hoppus-Straps[8]
Other packing

----

1. Blue beads. This is a coarse cheap bead imported from China, & costing in England 13 d. the lbs. in strands. It is far more valued than the white beads of the same manufacture and answers all the purposes of money, being counted by the fathom.[9]
2. Common brass buttons more valued than any thing except beads.
3. Knives, with fixed wooden handles stained red, usually called red handled knives & such as are used by the N.W. Co. in their Indian trade.
4. Battle axes, and Tomahawks.
5. Saddlers seat awls, which answer for mockasin awls
6. Glove[r]'s Needles.
7. Cast Iron combs.

8. Nests of camp kettles: brass is much preferr'd to Iron, tho both are very useful to the Indians size from 1 to 4 gallons.

1. An undocumented family tradition, first related by DYE and renewed by MEANY, declares that St. Louis physician Antoine Saugrain made thermometers for Lewis and Clark by scraping the mercury off the back of his wife's mirror. Saugrain had social contacts with the explorers before and after the expedition, but it is not likely that he made thermometers for them. Lewis kept temperature records on his way down the Ohio in the summer of 1803. Clark continued the practice at the Wood River camp in the early months of 1804, and there is no reason to suppose that the thermometers obtained in Philadelphia were not used. The last one was broken in Sept. 1805 when it was accidentally struck against a tree (JOURNALS, 3:51, 6:197). The instruments must have been similar to that described by Jefferson in a request of 5 June 1804 to Isaac Briggs for two thermometers: "The kind preferred is that on a lackered plate slid into a mahogany case with a glass sliding cover, these being best on exposure to the weather" (DLC). I find no support for the statement of ROBINSON (1) that the explorers discovered, 14 Sept. 1804, a thermometer which had been lost since the start of the voyage, a loss which had prevented their taking temperature readings until then. Robinson also tells the story of the Saugrain mirror, quoting Mrs. Eva Emery Dye.

2. The words "one bundle" are in Lewis's hand. Except for the few other instances of Lewis's handwriting noted below, this document is in an unidentified hand. Perhaps it is the list Lewis speaks of in No. 28 when he tells Jefferson he has sent word to Gen. Irvine about the supplies he needs.

3. John Miller, *An illustration of the sexual system of Linnaeus,* vol. 1 (London, 1779), and *An illustration of the termini botanici of Linnaeus,* vol. 2 (London, 1789), a set intended to be used together although issued a decade apart.

4. The words "of waterproof Cloth if possible" are in Lewis's hand.

5. The words "at H. Ferry" are in Lewis's hand.

6. The words "to be obtained in Tennessee" are in Lewis's hand.

7. The words "at Harper's ferry" are in Lewis's hand.

8. CRISWELL, clxxxiv, 46, 48, notes this term and speculates on its origin, but is misled by Thwaites's transcription of the term as "hoppers-straps." The source of the term is not entirely clear; "hoppas" has been identified as an Indian term for knapsack.

9. Hence Lewis knew the greater value of blue beads in advance. But he underestimated the preference of the Indians for blue over white, took too few blue ones, and lamented the fact in his journal.

54. Orders from the War Department

Henry Dearborn to Joseph Perkins

Sir: 14th March 1803.

You will be pleased to make such arms & Iron work, as requested by the Bearer Captain Meriwether Lewis and to have them completed with the least possible delay. I am &c.

Lbk (DNA, RG 107, Order Book, 168–69). Perkins was superintendent of the arsenal at Harper's Ferry.

Joshua Wingate to Israel Whelan

Sir: War Department 14th March 1803.
You will be pleased to purchase when requested by the Bearer Captain Meriwether Lewis such articles as he may have occasion for, which he has not been able to obtain from the public Stores. By order of the Secretary of War.

J. WINGATE JUNR. C.C.

Lbk (DNA, RG 107, Order Book, 168–69); RC (PPAmP). Joshua Wingate was chief clerk of the War Department at this time. In 1806 Jefferson appointed him "Collector of the district and Inspector of revenue for the port of Bath in Massachusetts" (Jefferson to the U.S. Senate, 30 Jan. 1806, DLC). Israel Whelan served as purveyor of public supplies from 1800 to Aug. 1803.

Joshua Wingate to William Irvine

Sir: War Department 14th March 1803.
You will be pleased to furnish the Bearer Captain Meriwether Lewis with such Articles from the public Stores under your direction as he may have occasion for. By order of the Secretary of War.

J. WINGATE JUNR. C.C.

Lbk (DNA, RG 107, Order Book, 168–69).

Henry Dearborn to Israel Whelan

Sir,   War Department March 24th 1803
The Treasurer of the United States has been directed to transmit to you One Thousand dollars for the purpose of purchasing such Articles as you may be requested by Capt. Meriwether Lewis. I am respectfully your Huml. Servt.

H. DEARBORN

LS, RC (DNA, RG 92, Box 560A). Addressed; endorsed.

Lewis to Israel Whelan

Recieved Washington June 30th 1803 from Israel Whelen one thousand dollars remitted to him by the Secretary of War for the purpose of providing suitable stores for the expedition under my direction, for which I have signed duplicats.

$1000

MERIWETHER LEWIS
Capt. 1st. U.S. Regt. Infty.

ADS, RC (DNA, RG 92, Box 560A). P. Hagner, an official in the Army Accounting Office in Washington, wrote Whelan on 15 July 1803, asking for the vouchers for Lewis's expenditures and suspending Whelan's account for the quarter ending 31 March until the vouchers were received (DNA, RG 217, Accountant's letterbooks). On the same day, Whelan's office in Philadelphia sent the desired documents. Whelan's covering letter stated that the expenditures had all been made in May and June (DNA, RG 92, Purveyor's letterbooks).

Benjamin Mifflin to William Bass

Sir: Purveyor's Office 28 May 1803

By request of Captain Lewis the articles mention'd at foot are sent to be pack'd at the Arsenal in a suitable Cask, if the cask should contain more than those articles he wishes in such case (only) to have Twenty Pairs of shoes added to them. Fifteen Coatees will be sent out also when made up. Please to weigh the Calico & flannel shirts before they are pack'd & let us know their weight & the weight of the whole articles when pack'd. I am &c.

B. M.

1 Common Tent	20 frocks
15 Blankets	30 prs linen sheets
15 Watch Coats	45 Flannel shirts
15 Pr. Wool overalls (blue)	48 Calico shirts
30 Pairs stockgs.	

P. KELLY

Lbk (DNA, RG 92, Purveyor of Public Supplies). Benjamin Mifflin (d. 1812) was an assistant to Israel Whelan in the purveyor's office, and probably was the merchant of the same name who had an establishment at 22 North Eighth Street in Philadelphia in 1803. At the time of his death he was deputy commissary of the army, with headquarters in Philadelphia. William A. Bass was clerk to the superintendent of military stores. P. Kelly is unidentified.

55. Supplies from Private Vendors

Capt. Merewether Lewis   To Israel Whelen—Dr.

Paid

No.			
1	George Lawton	Fishg. tackle	25.37
2	Thos. Passmore	Tin	17.70
3	Nichs. Lloyd	Tomah[awks]	19.62
4	George Ludlam	Lead C[anisters]	26.33
5	Gillaspy & Strong	Med.	90.69
6	Francis Bellet	Soup	289.50
7	Pricilla Logan		3.80
8	Wm. Chancellor & Co.	Dry goods	119.01
9	Thomas Whitney	Inst.	162.20
10	Hervey & Worth	Ironm[onger]	102.46
11	Edwd. Shoemaker	do.	39.74
12	Thomas Leiper	Tobac[co]	14.25
13	Benj. Harbeson & Son	Copper Ket.	34.15
14	J. & C. J. Wister	Ind. Prest.	98.29
15	C. & Th. Dencla	Do.	151.49
16	Beck & Harvey	Powder	157.43
17	S. Williamson	Broaches &c.	68.07
			$1420.02
18	Matilda Chapman	makg. Shirts	142.14
19	Thomas Parker	Cron.	250.75
20	Francis Brown	Taylor	246.63
21	D. Jackson	Drugs	77.20
22	W. Chancellor		3.50
23	S. Wetherill & Son	Ver[milion]	4.22
24	Harvey & Worth	Pow.	15.67
			2160.13
25	Wm. Broome		8.00
26	Robt. C. Martin	Saddling	26.25
27	Richd. Wevill	Tents &c.	119.39
			2313.77
28	Robt. Barnhill		10.00
			2323.77

Dedt. Sundries chd. to Indian & Military
      Departments pr. accot.   462.67

        Balnce. due I. Whelen   1861.10

The Philadelphia merchants and artisans on this list are identified later, with their individual vouchers, except for one person whose voucher is

[78]

not present: Nicodemus Lloyd (No. 3 in the list above), a blacksmith doing business at Seventh and Sassafras Streets. My chief source of identification is James Robinson's *Philadelphia directory* for 1803, supplemented by information from Philadelphia newspaper advertisements.

Endorsements: "List of Bills for Capt. Lewis." "Recvd. June 30: 1803 of Capt. M. Lewis 1861.10 Drs. in full of the above balance. Signd. I. Whelen." "Withdrawn & chd. to other accounts No. 4. 5. 7. 26 & 27. Nos. 10. 13. 15. & 16. part of their amount are chd. only to this acct."

		Phila. May 18 1803
Mr. Israel Wheelen		Bt. of Geo. R. Lawton
70	Large hooks @ 30/ pr.[?]	$2.80
55	ditto @ 22/6 pr.[?]	[1.65]
1	donl. drum Lines	4.—
1	do. Rock ditto	2.50
1½	do India Lines $5	7.50
1	India Line	.42
2	Lines $1	2.—
Sportsman Flask		1.50
8	Stave reel	3.—
		$25.37

George R. Lawton, listed in the 1803 *Directory* as an auctioneer at 18 Dock Street, also was a dealer in fishing tackle. The bill he presented for the articles above is written on the back of a printed broadside announcing his wares. "Fishing Tackle of all Sorts, at the Old Experienced Tackle Shop kept by George R. Lawson, Successor to Edward Pole, No. 32, Great Dock-street, between Front and Second-streets, near the Drawbridge, Philadelphia. Where may be had a large complete and general assortment of all kinds of Fishing Tackle, for the use of either Sea or River. . . ."

Endorsements: "No. 1. G. Lawton." "Recd. Payt. Geo. R. Lawton." "Received the within articles. Meriwether Lewis. Capt. 1st. U.S. Regt. Infty." (On this endorsement and those that follow, signatures are present for the vendors or their representatives. All of Lewis's endorsements are in his own hand.)

		Phila. May 19th 1803
Isreal Whelen Esqr.		B. of Thomas Passmore
4 Tin horns	50 cts.	2.00
2 Lanthorns	1	2.00
2 Lamps	25	0.50
32 Canisters	25	8.00
1 Squar box		1.00
3 doz. pint Tumblers	1 40/100	4.20
		$17.70

[79]

Thomas Passmore made tinware at a manufactory on North Seventh between Market and Arch Streets, with a warehouse at 215 Market.

Endorsements: "No. 2. T. Passmore." "Recvd. of Isreal Whelen Esqr. the above amount in full. May 23d. 1803. Thomas Passmore." "Received the above articles. Meriwether Lewis. Capt. 1st. U.S. Regt. Infty."

Philad. May 25 1803

Israel Weeling Dr. to George Ludlam

To Making 52 lead Cannisters for Powder @ 50 Cents	$26.00
Porterage	0.33
	$26.33

George Ludlam was a plumber at 96 South Second and 47 South Wharves.

Endorsements: "No. 5. Geo. Ludlam $26.33. 27 May 1803. Expidn. to W.O. Ordnance Dept. Capt. Lewis. (Duplicate) Recieved the within articles. Meriwether Lewis. Capt. 1st. U.S. Regt. Infty." "Recd. 27 May 1803 of Israel Whelen twenty Six dollars 33 Cents in full of the above bill. George Ludlam."

Abbreviated statements such as "Expidn. to W.O." mean "expedition to the Western Ocean."

Israel Wheelen Purveyor   Bought of Gillaspy & Strong

the following articles for the use of M. Lewis Esquire on his tour up the Missisipi River, & supplied by his Order:—Viz

15 lb. Pulv. Cort. Peru	$30.00		4 oz. Laudanum				.50
½ " " Jalap	.67		2 lb. Ung. Basilic				
½ " " Rhei [rhubarb]	1.				Flav.	50	1.00
4 oz. " Ipecacuan.	1.25		1 " " [. . .] Cali-				
2 lb. " Crem. Tart.	.67				min	50	.50
2 oz. Gum Camphor	.40		1 " " Epispastric			1.	
1 lb. " Assafoetid.	1.		1 " " Mercuriale			1.25	
½ lb. " Opii Turk. opt.	2.50		1. Emplast. Diach. S.			.50	
¼ " " Tragacanth	.37		1. Set Pocket Insts. small			9.50	
6 lb. Sal Glauber	10	.60	1. " Teeth " "			2.25	
2 " " Nitri	33½	.67	1. Clyster Syringe			2.75	
2 " Copperas		.10	4. Penis do.			1.	
6 oz. Sacchar. Saturn. opt.		.37	3. Best Lancets		.80	2.40	
4 " Calomel		.75	1. Tourniquet			3.50	
1 " Tartar Emetic		.10	2. oz Patent Lint			.25	
4 " Vitriol Alb.		.12	50. doz. Bilious Pills to				
½ lb. Rad. Columbo		1.	Order of B. Rush.		10	5.00	
¼ " Elix. Vitriol		.25	6. Tin Canisters		25	1.50	

¼ " Ess. Menth. pip.	.50	3. 8 oz. Gd. Stopd.	
¼ " Bals. Copaiboe	.37	bottles 40	1.20
¼ " " Traumat.	.50	5 4 " Tinctures do	1.85
2 oz. Magnesia	.20	6 4 " Salt Mo.	2.22
¼ lb. Indian Ink	1.50	1. Walnut Chest	4.50
2 oz. Gum Elastic	.37	1. Pine do.	1.20
2 " Nutmegs	.75	Porterage	.30
2 " Cloves	.31		$90.69
4 " Cinnamon	.20		
	$46.52		

Phila. May 26, 1803

Gillaspy and Strong were druggists at 103 South Second and 243 High Streets. The proprietors were probably George Gillaspy, M.D., and Joseph Strong, M.D.

Endorsements: "No. 14. Gillaspy & Strong. Expedn. to W.O. $90.69. May 27. 1803. Say Hospital Dr." "Recd. May 27, 1803 of Israel Whelen Ninety Dollars & 69 cents in full—for Gillaspy & Strong. Thomas H. Dawson." "Duplicate. Received the within articles. Meriwether Lewis. Capt. 1st. U.S. Regt. Infty."

We have no other list of the medical supplies carried by Lewis and Clark. This is probably their main supply, supplemented by requisitions on the medical officers at Fort Massac, Kaskaskia, and—in the spring of 1804—St. Louis. It is less extensive than the standard list of medicines issued to military posts of the period, but contains most of the drugs then commonly used for the ailments to be expected among young, healthy soldiers. (See an estimate of medicines for eighty men for one year, DNA, RG 107, Letters Sent, 4:280–81.) The medical practice of Lewis and Clark has been the subject of several articles, most of which merely recount the illnesses of the party and the medications prescribed, usually by Clark; but the latest study, by WILL, is a more thorough evaluation. Earlier articles include BEARD, LARSELL, ROBINSON (2), and STANLEY. Beard believes that Lewis might have become a competent physician, "a most worthy successor of Benjamin Rush," had he been trained. "His rare powers of observation, his wide information and his capacity to recognize and to differentiate the various symptoms of disease would have made him one of the great diagnosticians of his day" (p. 520).

Israel Whelen for the United States   Bot. of Fras. Bellet
1803
May 30—193 lbs. of Portable Soup at 150 Cents $289.50

François Baillet was a cook at 21 North Ninth. The dried soup he prepared became important to the expedition in the fall of 1805; Lewis recorded in his journal for 18 Sept. (JOURNALS, 3:71) that the men had killed their last colt for food and had nothing left but a few canisters of the soup, some bear oil, and candles. Lewis wrote to Gen. Irvine 15 April 1803 about this soup, in a letter now owned by Mrs. Grace Lewis of St. Louis, not available for publication.

Endorsements: "No. 6. F. Bellet $289.50. Expidn. to W.O. May 30th 1803." "Recd. of Israel Whelen two hundred Eighty Nine dollars 50 Cents in full. $289 50/100. François Baillet." "Duplicates, Received the above articles. Meriwether Lewis. Capt. 1st. U.S. Regt. Infty."

Israel Whelen   Bot. of Pricilla Logan

1803

May 28. 2 lbs. Hyson Tea @ 12/6	£1.5
Cannister	3.6
	£1.8.6

Priscilla Logan or Login is not identified.

Endorsements: "No. ⟨7⟩ No. 15. ⟨Ordnance⟩ Hospital Dept. $3.50. May 31st. 1803." "Recd. payment in full three dollars & 80 Cents. $3.80. Duplicate. Priscilla Login. May 31st." "Duplicate. Received the within articles. Meriwether Lewis. Capt. 1st. U.S. Regt. Infty."

May 31th 1803   Mr. Israel Whelen Bot. of Thos. Whitney

	D	C
a Spirit level		4.—
Case of plotting Instruments		14.—
two pole Chain		2.—
Silver plated pocket Compass		5.—
Brass Boat Compass		1.50
3 Brass pocket Compasses	2.50	7.50
a Magnet		1.—
Tangent screw Quadrant		22.—
Metal Sextant		90.—
Making a Microscope and fixing Do. on the Index of the Sextant		7.—
Sett of Slates in a Case		4.—
log line, reel & log ship		1.95
parrallel glass for a horison		1.—
4 ounces of Talc		1.25
		$162.20

Whitney is identified under No. 40.

Endorsements: "No. 9. Thomas Whitney. Expedn. to W.O. $162.20. June 4th 1803. Recd. June 4th 1803. of Israel Whelen one hundred Sixty two dollars 20 Cents in full & Signed two rects. $162.20. Thomas Whitney." "Duplicate, Received the above articles. Meriwether Lewis. Capt. 1st. U.S. Regt. Infty."

[82]

Israel Wheelen Esqr.
Purveyor Public Supplies

2 lb. Brass wire No. 20	4/8	9 4
5 " " " ea. No. 21 4/10 & 23 5/		2 9 2
14 Knitting Pins	2/1	1 9 2
2 C Millinery Needles	1/4½	2 9
10 " Glovers "	1/3	12 6
1 " Yarn "	1/6	1 6
1 " Tabling "	5/	5
2 " Old work "	5/	10
3 M White Chapel "	13/9	2 1 3
2¹⁄₁₂ doz. Packing "	2/2	4 6¼
2 " Large Awls	2/	4
3 C Fish hooks 5	5/	15
5½ M " " ea. 12 7/6 11 8/9 9 15/		
8 18/9 6 40/		2 5
1 Gro. Iron Combs	21/	1 1
2 " Curtain Rings 263	3/3	6 6
1 " " " ea. 3/6 & 4/		7 6
1 " Brass Thimbles	8/	8
1 " Taylors "	16/3	16 3
1½ doz. Scissors 5109	7/	10 6
8½ " " 67	7/6	3 3 9
2 " " 8853	14/6	1 9
2 " Table Spoons	7/	14
6 " Knives 1	15/	4 10
2 " " 101	17/6	1 15
3 " " 104	21/3	3 3 9
⅓ " Drawing Knives	27/	9
2 " Gimblets	2/6	5
1 " Spike "	18/	18
½ " flat Files ea. 6 5/ 7 in. 6/3		5 7½
⅙ " " " 12 in.	21/6	3 7
½ " handsaw files	9/	4 6
⅙ " Rasps 8 in.	8/4	1 4½
¹⁄₁₂ " " 12	21/6	1 9½
1 Shoe Float	6 d	6
2 doz. Fish Lines	6/3	12 6
1¼ " Bed Laces	10/9	13 5
1 hand Vise	2/6	2 6
1 Bench "	10/	10
1 pair Bright Plyers	4/6	4 6

[83]

1 " Black "		2/9	2	9
1 Sawsett		9 d	9	
1 Socket Chessel ea. ½ 1/3 1½ 1/9			3	
2 " " ea. ¾ 1/4½ 1¾ 1/10½			6	6
2 Mortice " ¼ in.		1/3	2	6
1 " " ½ "		1/3	1	3
2 Adzes 1		4/6	9	
2 handsaws		11/6	1	3
1 Screw Auger ea. 2 1/2 5 2/11			4	
2 " " ea. 3 1/9 4 2/4			8	2
2 Shingling hatchets		3/1½		
1 Whetstone		3/6	3	6
6 lb. 8 d Cut Brads ⎱ 4 " 10 " " ⎰		9 d	3	6
2 pair Pocket Steelyards		1/9	3	6
			38 8	5½

Exd. B. M. $102 46/100

The firm of Harvy & Worth, merchants, 62 North Front Street, appears in the *Philadelphia directory* of 1803. The person who receipted the bill clearly wrote "Harvey & Worth."

Endorsements: "Recvd. June 6. 1803 of Israel Whelen One Hundred two Dollars & 46 Cts. in full. Harvey & Worth." "No. 10. Harvey & Worth. $102.46. Duplicate, Recieved the within articles. Meriwether Lewis. Capt. 1st U.S. Regt. Infty."

An accompanying note lists several items in the above bill, totaling $15.28, to be withdrawn from Lewis's account and charged to the Ordnance Department.

I interpret "Exd. B. M.," here and elsewhere, to mean "examined by Benjamin Mifflin."

                                        Philada. 18 May 1803
I. Whelen Esqr.   Bot. of E. Shoemaker & Co.

1 Corn Mill		9	
2 ditto	10	20	
1 Set Gold scales		2	33
1 Set Iron Wts			75
1 Rule			60
2 dn. Scissors	1/80	3	60
1 dn. Do.		1	60
2 pair large Shears	93	1	86
		$39	74

Edward Shoemaker and Company were hardware merchants at 127 High Street.

[84]

Endorsements: "No. 11. E. Shoemaker & Co. $39.74. June 6 1803. Recd. June 7 1803 of Israel Whelen Thirty nine Dolls. 74 cts. in full. Edward Shoemaker & Co." "Duplicate, Recieved the above articles. Meriwether Lewis. Capt. 1st U.S. Regt. Infty."

Mr. Israel Whelan   Philada. June 3d 1803

Bot of Thomas Leiper 130 Rolls pigtail Tobacco viz.

63 lbs. @ 1/8	5 5 0
Keg	1 10 1/2
	5 6 10 1/2
Exd. B. M.	$14 25/100

Thomas Leiper, Jr. (1745–1825), tobacconist at 274 Market Street.
Endorsements: "No. 12. T. Leiper. $14.25. June 6th 1803. Expidn. to W.O. Received June 6th 1803 of Israel Whelen Purveyor fourteen dollars 25 Cents in full of the within accot. $14.25. (Duplicate) Thomas Leiper." "Duplicate, Recieved the above articles. Meriwether Lewis. Capt. 1st. U.S. Regt. Infty."

Philada. May 19. 1803

Israel Wheelen   Bot. of Ben. Harberson & Sons

14 Brass Kettles 48 @ 4/	£9 12 0
48 Pieces Brass 12 @ 4/3	2 11 0
1 Black Tin Saucepan	11 3
Porterage	1 10½
	12 16 1½
Exd. B. M.	Drs. 34. 10/100

Benjamin Harberson & Sons were coppersmiths at 75 High Street.
Endorsements: "No. 13. Benj. Harberson & Sons. Expd. to W.O. $34.15. Brass Kettles of the within are charged to Indian Dept. amtg. to $15.18. Recvd. June 6 1803 of Israel Whelen Thirty four Dollars & 15 Cts. in full. Ben Harberson & Sons." "Recieved the above articles. Meriwether Lewis. Capt. 1st. U.S. Regt. Infty."

Philada. May 19. 1803

Israel Whelen Esqr.   Bot. of Jno. & Chas. J. Wister

1 pc. Scarlet Cloth No. 1518	22 y.	9/6	10 9 0
		Adv. 110 pct.	11 9 9
			£21 18 9
5 doz & 6 fancy hdfs. 2 29/ 3½ 26/		£ 7 9 0	
3 Gro. Br. Binding	13/6	2 0 6	
3 Gro. Scarlet do.	17/6	2 12 6	
2 Card Beads	15/	1 10 0	
		£13 12 0	
	Dist. 5 pct.	13 7	

[85]

		£34 17 2
4 dn. Butcher Knives	10/	2 0 0
		£36 17 2

Exd. B. M. $98.29

John Wister and Charles Jones Wister (1782–1865) were merchants at 143 High Street.

Endorsements: "No. 14. J. & C. J. Wister $98.29. Exdn. to W.O. Recvd. June 6. 1803 of Israel Whelen ninety eight Dollars & 29 cts. in full. $98.29. For John & Chas. J. Wister. M. Immel." "Duplicate, Received the within articles. Meriwether Lewis. Capt. 1st U.S. Regt. Infty."

		Philada. May 18 1803
Israel Wheelen Esqr.	Bot. of C. & Th. Denkla	
6½ D. pocket Looking Glasses	37 Cts.	$2.40
4 do.	40	1.60
1 do.		.86
½ do.	67	.33
8 burning Glasses	1½ Drs.	12.—
2 Nonsopretty	11/	2.94
2 Red Strip'd Tapes	10/6	2.80
72 Pc. Strip'd Silk Ribbon	55 Cts.	39.60
3 Dn. beads	67 Cts.	2.01
6 Paper Small bells	67 Cts.	4.02
1 box with 100 Larger do.		2.25
12 D. pewter Looking Glasses	35 Cts	3.—
3 do.	33	.99
6 bunches Red Garnet	10/	8.—
2 do. brown	40 & 60 Cts.	1.—
10 do. yellow ⎫ 25 do. white ⎬ beads	40 Cts.	14.—
10 do. blue ⎫ 10 do. yellow ⎬ do. smaller 10 do. white ⎭	60 Cts.	18.—
2 D. Tinzel Taizels	50 C	1.—
1 do.		1.50
½ do.	2.50	1.25
1 D. [. . .] Thread		1.50
1 D. Pin Cases		.30

1 " Lockets		1.—
¼ do.	125 Cts.	.31
1½ do.	150 Cts.	2.25
8½ D. Red beads	3 D.	25.50
2 D. Earings	50 Cts.	1.—
		$151.41

In a box.

Christian H. Denchla is listed as a merchant, 68 North Third Street, in the *Philadelphia directory* of 1803.

Endorsements: "No. 15. C. Th. Dencla. Expn. to W.O. Recd. June 6. 1803 of Israel Whelen One Hundred Fifty One Dollars & 41 Cts. in full. Chris & Th. Denckla." "Duplicate, Received the above articles. Meriwether Lewis. Capt. 1st U.S. Regt. Infty."

Philada. 28 May 1803

Israel Whelen Esquire Bot. of Beck & Harvey

123 lbs. English Cannister Powder at 90 cts pr. lb.	110.70
53 lbs. dbl. Seal Ditto in papers at 85 cts.	45.05
	155.75
17 6/12 lbs. Castile Soap	1.68
	157.43

Beck & Harvey were merchants at 11, 12, and 15 South Water Street.

Endorsements: "No. 16. Beck & Harvey. Recd. June 6. 1803 of Israel Whelen One Hundred fifty seven Dollars & 43 Cts. in full. $157.43. Beck & Harvey." "Duplicate, Received the above articles. Meriwether Lewis. Capt. 1st. U.S. Regt. Infty." "Of this Bill there are chd. to Ord. Dept. $155.75."

Philada. May 23rd 1803

Israel Whelen, Esqr. Bought of S. Williamson

	Drs. Cts.
Five hundred broaches	62. 7
Seventy two rings	6. –
	$68 7

Samuel Williamson was a goldsmith and silversmith at 118 South Front Street.

Endorsements: "No. 17. S. Williamson. Recvd. June 6th 1803 of Israel Whelen Sixty-Eight Dollars & 7 Cts. in full—for Saml. Williamson. Mary Williamson." "Duplicate, Recieved the above articles. Meriwether Lewis. Capt. 1st U.S. Regt. Infty."

[87]

Israel Whelen   June 3rd 1803
To Matilda Chapman Dr.
For 16 callico Ruffled Shirts @ 170 cts. $17.20
    32   do.   do.   137 "   43.84
    45 flannel Shirts with linnen collars &
       wrist bands   @ 158   77.10
                                                        $142.14

Matilda Chapman is not identified.
Endorsements: "No. 18. Matilda Chapman. Recd. June [*blank*] 1803 of
Israel Whelen one hundred forty two dollars 14 Cents in full. $142. 14/100.
Matilda Chapman." "Duplicate, Received the above articles. Meriwether
Lewis. Capt. 1st U.S. Regt. Infty."

                                           Phila. June 14th 1803.
Israel Whelen Esqr. Purveyor. Bot. of Willm. Irvine agt.
for Indian factories
    2 pcs. [. . .] Calico 56 Yds. @ 40 Cts. $22.40

Endorsements: "Recd. the above Amot. in full for Willm. Irvine
(Duplicate) Thos. Waterman." "No. 18. Chd. to Capt. Lewis's Expedition
in the Bill of M. Chapman."

                                           5 Mo. 19th 1803.
Israel Whelen Purveyor of Public Supplies. Bot. of Thos. Parker
    1 Gold Chronometer $250.
    Keys for do.   .75
                                           $250.75

Thomas Parker was a clockmaker and watchmaker at 13 South Third
Street.
Endorsements: "No. 19. Thos. Parker $250.75. June 6. 1803. Recd.
5 Mo. 19th 1803 of Israel Whelen Two Hundred & Fifty Dolls. 75 C. in
full. $250.75. Thos. Parker." "Duplicate, Received the above Chronometer
&c. Meriwether Lewis. Capt. 1st U.S. Regt. Infty."

Israel Whelan Esqr. for Cap. Lewis   Philada. June 1st 1803
Bot. of David Jackson
30 Gallons Strong Spt. Wine @ 233 1/3 $70.
 6 Iron Bound Kegs   1.20   7.20
                                           $77.20

David Jackson listed himself as a druggist, 26 South Third Street, in 1803.
In 1802 his *Aurora* advertisements were for Jackson and Betton, wholesale and

retail druggists at 129 Mulberry Street, and on 25 Nov. 1806 he advertised under the name of David & S. Jackson, Arch Street near Fourth Street.

Endorsements: "No. 21. David Jackson. $77.20. June 7. 1803. Recd. June 7. 1803. of Israel Whelen Seventy Seven Dollars & 20 C. in full. 77.20. David Jackson." "Duplicate, Received the above articles. Meriwether Lewis. Capt. 1st. U.S. Regt. Infty."

Israel Whelen	Philada. June 1 1803
Bot. of Wm. Chancellor & Co.	
1 Trunk (containing goods for Capt. Lewis)	£1 6 3

William Chancellor & Company were merchants at 105 High Street.

Endorsements: "No. 22. Wm. Chancellor $3.50. Recd. June 17. 1803 of Israel Whelen Three dollars 50 Cents in full of the above acct. $3 50/100. For Wm. Chancellor & Co. Wm. Andrews."

Philada. May 17. 1803

Israel Whelan Esqr.	Bot. of Saml. Wetherill & Son	
2 lb. Vermillion @ 12/6	1	5 –
8 lb. Red lead @ /8		6 8
	£1	11 8

Samuel Wetherill (1764–1829) and Son were at 65 North Front Street in 1803. RITTER says that Wetherill was a druggist, apothecary, and vendor of paints and colors.

Endorsements: "No. 23. S. Wetherill & Son. Ex. W.O. $4.22. Recd. June 7. 1803 of Israel Whelen Four Dollars & 22 Cts. in full. Duplicate. $4.22. for S. Witherill & Son. Saml. W. Bueld." "Duplicate, Recieved the above articles. Meriwether Lewis. Capt. 1st U.S. Regt. Infty."

Philada. 8th June 1803

Israel Whelen Esq. Purveyoir of Public Supplies
Bot. of Harvey & Worth

1 groce Seat Awls	12/6	12 6
7 " " "	15/	5 5 0
		5 17 6

$15. 67/100
Exd. B. M.

Endorsements: "No. 24. Harvey & Worth. $15.67. June 17. 1803. Recd. June 17. 1803 of Israel Whelen Fifteen dollars 67 Cents in full—duplicate. Harvey & Worth." "Duplicate, Recieved the above articles. Meriwether Lewis. Capt. 1st. U.S. Infty."

[89]

1803

Jin 9   Mr. Wheelin To Wm. Broome

To a painted Chest with [. . .] handles &c. Compt. for
Carying Instruments & packing up do. $8.00

William Broome was a carpenter at 24 North Fourth Street.

Endorsements: "No. 25. Wm. Broome $8 June 9. 1803, Expidn. to W.O."
"Recd. payment in full. Wm. Broome." "(Duplicate) Received the above
articles. Meriwether Lewis. Capt. 1st. U.S. Regt. Infty."

                                        Philadelphia June 16 1803

Israel Whelen Esqr. Prvyr. Genrl. U.S.

                                        To Robt C. Martin Dr.

To 15 rifle pouches @ 1 75/100 Ea. $26.25
The above fifteen Pouches were attached to a like number
of Powder Horns and delivered to Capt. M. Lewis on the
6th June 1803.
Exd. B. M.   TIMOTHY BANGER

A notice in the *Aurora* of 20 Sept. 1803 announced that the partnership
of Robert C. Martin and Abel Holmes was dissolved as of 24 March, and
that the saddling business would be continued at the old stand, 162
Market Street, by Martin.

Endorsements: "No. 19. Recd. June 18 1803 of I. Whelen Twenty Six
Dollars & 25 Cts. in full. $25.26. Robt. C. Martin." "United States Arsenal
July 20. 1803. Received the within specified Pouches. G. W. Ingels."

George W. Ingels was storekeeper for the War Department at the U.S.
arsenal in Philadelphia, appointed 2 April 1802. Timothy Banger was an
accountant, listed in the 1816 *Directory* as living at 15 North Twelfth
Street.

Mr. Israel Whelen   To Richd. Wevill Dr.
1803
June 15

To 107 yds of 7/8 brown Linen @ 1/6	21.40
To 46½ yds of 7/8 ⟨*Russia*⟩ Flanders Sheeting @ 2/5	14.49
To 10 yds of 7/8 Country Linen 3/	4.—
To making the brown Linen into 8 Tents, with	
Eyelet-holes, laps, &c. Thread &c.	16.—
To making the Russia Sheeting into 45	
Bags. Thread & cord. @ 1/6	9.—
To 2 Gross of Hooks & Eyes @ 3/9	1.—
To Oiling all the Linen & Sheeting—	
150 Square Yards @ 2/6	52.—
To numbering all the Bags & Tents	1.50
	$119.39

Richard Wevill was an upholsterer at 167 South Eighth Street.

Endorsements: "⟨No. 27⟩ No. 11. Richd. Wevill $199.39. June 18. 1803." "Recd. June 18 1803 of Israel Whelin One hundred Nineteen dollars 39 Cents in full & Signed Two Receipts. $119 39/100. Richard Wevill." "United States Arsenal July 20 1803. Received the above specified Tents & Bags. G. W. Ingels."

A note beside the second entry in the bill reads: "Shod. be 14.66 but no more pd. than 14.49."

Israel Whelen for Capt. Lewis   May 21st 1803
                                                    Bot. of Robt. Barnhill

1 Pair Pocket Pistols, Secret Triggers $10.

Robert Barnhill was a storekeeper at 63 North Second Street.

Endorsements: "Recvd. of Israel Whelen Ten Dollars in full of this Account. Robert Barnhill." "No. ⟨28⟩ 14. Robt. Barnhill. June 7. 1803. The within Pistols were delivered by me to Captn. Meriwether Lewis. Robt. Barnhill."

Mr. Israel Whelen   To Henry Voigt

1803		$	Ct.
June 10 To Cleaning a chronometer, & adjusting		2	
do.	To a new Box of Mohoconey Wood &c. paid for	2	25
do.	To a Universol choint	2	50
do.	To Cleaning a Silver Secont Watch	0	62 5
		$7	37 5

Henry Voigt has been identified earlier.

Endorsements: "No. 2. Henry Voight. $7.37. June 20th 1803." "Recd. June 20 1803 of Israel Whelen Seven dollars 37 Cents in full. John Hessler for Henry Voight. $7 37/100." "Received the within articles. Meriwether Lewis. Capt. 1st. U.S. Regt. Infty."

Mr. Israel Whelan   Bot. of David Lapsley

1803

May 19   32 Yards S fine Milled drab cloth @ $7 $225.75

David Lapsley sold carpets, carpeting, and dry goods at 18 South Second Street.

Endorsements: "No. 20. D. Lapsley. Mr. Israel Whelan's Bill." "Recieved payment in full. David Lapsley. 7th June 1803."

The U. States Military Dept.   To Joseph Thompson Dr.

1803

March 21–June 30

To 6	Packg.	Boxes	for Stationary &c. @ $2. ea.	$12.00
3	"	"	for Instruments	5.85
2	"	"	for Swords & Belts &c.	4.62½
1	"	"	for Horsemans Cloths	1.—
6	"	"	for Musk. Ball	3.25
1	"	"	for Slow Match	1.25
1	"	"	for Sundries	1.25
10	"	"	for Rifles	12.50
30				$41.72½

The *Philadelphia directory* for 1803 lists no Joseph Thompson.
Endorsements: "No. 13. Josh. Thompson 48 47/100. Ordnance Dept. June 30 1803." "U. States Arsenal July 1 1803 Received of Israel Whelen Esqr. the above specified Packg. Boxes. G. W. Ingels."
An addition to the bill, for five more boxes, adds $6.75 and brings the total to $48.47. Thompson has signed for the complete amount on the back of the bill. The boxes are described as being "for Capt. M. Lewis's Goods."

                                          Philada. 6 June 1803
          The United States   To Francis Brown Dr.

For 28 3/8 yds S. fine Mill'd drab Cloth @ $7	$198.63
24 doz. Large Buttons @ 13 Cts.	3.12
8 doz. Small do. @ 7	.56
Silk Twist & thread	4.32
Making 16 Coatees 2.50	40.—
	$246.63

Francis Brown was a tailor on Walnut above Eighth Street.
Endorsements: "No. 20. Francis Brown. Philada. 6 May 1803." "Recd. June 6 1803 of Israel Whelen Two Hundred forty Six Dolls. & 63 Cts. in full. Fras. Brown." "Recd. the above Sixteen Coatees—duplicate, Received the above articles. Meriwether Lewis. Capt. 1st U.S. Regt. Infty."

56. Memorandum on Packing

Capt. Lewis

Each article to be weighed separate, and the weight & price extended in the Invoice under the appropriate Head. In packing no regard need be had to the different divisions or classes as specified in the Invoice but pack'd indiscriminately as may be most advantageous, regard being paid to such articles as may be most likely to receive damage. The blankets may be used in the packing for the protection of the goods. Such articles as are taken from the Military stores are to be enter'd in the invoice under their proper heads with weight extend'd & without price.

Endorsement: "Memo Capt. Lewis. No. 19. 20. 22. 24. 25. 26. & 27. being copies of the Bills of Purchases for Capt. Lewis sent down to him, Copies of the other bills he took with him. June 20."

57. Summary of Purchases

Recapitulation of Purchases by The Purveyor
for Capt. Lewis

Mathematical Instruments	412.95
Arms, Ammunition & Accoutrements	182.08
Medicines &c.	94.49
Clothing	317.73
Provisions &c.	366.70
Indian Presents (see below)	669.50
Camp Equipage	116.68
	2160.14

Indian Presents

			Wt.						
12	Pipe Tomahawks	. . . . .	8¾		. . .		18	. .
6½	lbs. Strips Sheet Iron	. . .	6½		. . .		1	62
1	Ps. red flannel 47½ yds .	. . .	12¾	5	12	0	14	94
11	Ps. Hanckercheifs assd. .	. . .	13 lb	22	8	9	59	83
1	doz. Ivory Combs	. . . .	3 oz	1	5	0	3	33
½	Catty Inda. S. Silk .	. . . .	7 oz	1	8	1½	3	75
21	lbs. Tread assd.	. . . .	21 lbs	8	13	9	23	17
1	Ps. Scarlet Cloth 22 yds .	. . .	28¾	21	18	9	58	50
5½	doz fancy 1 Floss .	. . . 6¾		.	7	1	6	18	87
6	Gro. Binding .	. . . . 9¼		.	4	8	5	11	79
2	Cards Beads .	. . . . 1¾	26½	.	1	8	6	3	80
4	doz. Butcher Knives .	. . 8¾		.	2	0	0	5	33
12	doz. Pocket Looking Glasses	. .	12½ lb		. . .		5	19
15	doz. Pewter do. do. .	. . . .	3⁶⁄₁₆		. . .		3	99
8	doz. Burning do.	. . . . .	11¼		. . 12		12	. .

Indian Presents

		Wt.					
2	doz. Nonesopretty	3¼				2	94
2	doz. Red strip'd tapes	1½				2	80
72	ps. Strip'd silk ribbon	3¼				39	60
3	lbs. Beads	3 lb				2	01
6	Papers Small Bells	1¼				4	02
1	box with 100 larger do.	1³⁄₁₆				2	25
73	Bunches Beads assd.	20				41	..
3½	doz: Tinsel Bands assd.	9 oz				3	75
1	doz: Needle Cases	5½ oz					30
2¾	doz Lockets	3 oz				3	56
8½	lbs. Red Beads	8½				25	50
2	doz. Earings		4			1	..
8	Brass Kettles a 4/ Per lb.	20 lbs.				10	67
12	lbs. Brass Strips					6	80
500	Broaches	} 1½ lb.				62	07
72	Rings					6	00
2	Corn Mills	52¾				20	00
15	doz. Scissors	17¼				18	97
12	lbs. Brass Wire		2	18	6	7	80
14	lbs. Knitting Pins	14	1	9	2	3	89
4600	Needles assd.	2¼	3	13	.	9	73
2800	Fish Hooks assd.	6⅛	3	.	.	8	..
1	Gro. Iron Combs	8½	1	1	.	2	80
3	Gro. Curtain Rings	1¾	.	14	.	1	87
2	Gro. Thimbles assd.	2½	1	4	3	3	21
11	doz. Knives	37	9	8	9	25	17
10	lbs. Brads	16	7	6	.	1	00
8	lbs. Red lead	8					89
2	lbs. Vermillion	2		.	3	3	34
130	Rolls of Tobacco (pigtail)	63		.	14	14	25
48	Callico Ruffled Shirts					71	04
15	Blankets (from P. Store)						
1	Trunk to pack sundry Ind. Prests.					3	50
8	Groce Seat or Mockasin Awls					15	67
						669	50

From Public Store—vizt. 15 Blankets

Camp Equipage

Qty	Description	Wt.				$	¢
4	Tin Horns	1¾				2	..
2	" Lanthorns	1				2	..
2	" Lamps	½					50
32	" Cannisters of P. Soup	193				8	..
1	" Box sqr. of Small art.	1½				1	..
3	doz: Pint Tumblers	6½				4	20
125	Large fishg Hooks					4	45
	Fishg Lines assorted	10½				18	09
1	Stand of Fishg do. with hooks Complete					3	..
1	Sportsmans flaske					1	50
8	ps. Cat gut for Mosquito Curt.	11	5	16	3	15	50
6	Brass Kettles & Porterage 25 cts.	28				15	18
1	block tin Sauce pan	¾				1	50
1	Corn Mill	20				9	..
1	Set of Gold Scales & Wts.	¼				2	33
1	Rule	1 oz					60
1	Sett Iron Weights	4					75
2	pr. Large Shears	3½				1	86
4	doz: Packg. Needles & large Awls	1		8	6	1	13
2	doz: Table Spoons	3		14	.	1	87
4	drawing Knives	2½		9	.	1	20
3	doz: Gimblets	5¼ lbs	1	3	.	3	60
17	do. files & Rasps & 1 Shoe float	5	.	17	4	2	31
1¼	doz. Small cord	8½	13	5	5	1	79
2	Small Vices				6	1	67
2	pr. Plyers				3		97
1	Saw Sett	10		7	9		10
9	Chisels				3	1	77
2	Adzes	4		9	1	1	20
2	hand Saws	4½	1	3	.	3	06
6	Augers 6	3½		12	3	1	64
2	Hatchets			6	3		83
1	Wetstone	4½		3	6		47
2	p. Pocket steel yards			3	6		47
	Pkg 12 lbs Castile Soap	2				1	68
						117	67

From Public Store.

8 Receipt Books
48 ps. Tape
6 Brass Inkstands
6 Papers Ink Powder
1 Common Tent
1 lb. Sealing Wax
100 Quils
1 Packing Hogshead
    Bought by the Purveyor of Richd. Wevill

8 Tents
45 Bags
10 yd. Country Linnen ⎫
20 " Brown do.   ⎬ Oiled
                  ⎭

Mathematical Instruments

1 Spirit level	4 ..
1 Case platting Instruments	14 ..
1 Two pole chain	2 ..
1 Pocket Compas plated	5 ..
1 Brass Boat Compass	1 50
3 Brass Pocket Compasses	7 50
1 Magnet	1 ..
1 Hadleys Quadrant with Tangt Screw	22 ..
1 Metal Sextant	90 ..
Microscope to index of d	7 ..
Sett of Slates in a case	4 ..
4 oz of Talc	1 25
1 Surveying Compass with extra needles (P by L)	23 50
1 Circular protractor & index . . . do.	8 ..
1 Six In. Pocket Telescope . . . do.	7 ..
1 Nautical Ephemeris[1] . . . . do.	1 50
1 Requisite Tables[2] . . . . do.	2 50
Kirwan's Mineralogy[3] . . . . do.	5 ..
1 Chronometer & Keys	250 75
1 Copy Bartons Bottony[4] (pd. by C. L.)	6 ..
Kelleys Spherics[5] . . . . do.	3 ..
2 Nautical Ephemeris . . . . do.	4 ..
Log line reel & log ship	1 95
Parrellel Glass for a Horison	1 ..

Arms & Accoutrements & Ammn.

		lbs		
1	Pair Pocket pistols (P. by L.)	10	..	
176	lb. Gun powder	176	155	75
52	leaden Cannisters for Gunpowr	420	26	33
15	Powder Horns & Pouches		26	25

From Public Store

15 Powder Horns
18 Tomahaws
15 Scalpking Knives & Belts
15 Gun Slings
30 Brushes & Wires
15 Cartouch Boxes
15 painted Knapsacks
500 Rifle Flints
125 Musket do.
50 lb. best rifle Powder
1 pr. Horsemans Pistols
420 lbs. Sheet Lead

Medicines &c

1	Box	Wt.	} $90.69
1	do.	Wt.	
2	lbs. Tea & Cannister W. 2 lbs.		3.80
			94.49

Provisions &c

193	lbs. P. Soup	193	289	50
30	Galls. Spr. of Wine in 6 Kegs		77	20
			366	70

		Dolls.	Cts
45	Flannel Shirts	71	10
16	Coatees	246	63
		317	73

From Public Stores vizt.

15 Blankets
15 Match Coats
15 Ps. blue wool. overalls
36 pairs Stockgs.
20 Frocks
30 Pr. Shirts
20 Pr. Shoes

Invoice of Articles received from the Arsenal for the use of Capt Lewis May 18th. 1803[6]

Invoice of Articles to be Dld. Cap. Lewis—

A & A	15	Powder Horns	a & a	15	Painted Knapsacks
do.	18	Tomhawks	do.	500	Rifle flints
do.	15	Scalping Knives & Belts	do.	125	Musket do.
do.	15	Gun Slings	do.	50	lb. Best Rifle Powder
do.	30	Brushes & Wires	do.	1	P. Horsemans Pistols
do.	15	Cartouch Box Belts		420	lbs. Sheet lead
Camp	8	Rect. Books	Ind P	15	Blankets
do.	48	Pieces Tape	Camp	100	Quils
do.	6	Brass Ink Stands	Clothg.	20	Pr. Shoes
do.	6	Papers Ink Powder.	Camp	1	packg Hhd
do.	1	Common Tent			
Clothg.	15	Blankets 3 pt.			
do.	15	Match Coats			
do.	15	Priv. Wool Overalls (Blue)			
do.	36	Pair Stockings			
do.	20	Frocks			
do.	30	Priv Lin Shirts			
Camp	1	lb Sealg. Wax			

To be left at Mr. Whelens Office May 18″ 1803

List of Charges taken out of Cap Lewis's account to be charged to other accots. as specified

176 lbs. Gunpowder B. & H.		No. 16 ordnance		$155.75
Leaden Canesters for securing gunpowder			No. 4	26.33
	Ludlam			
15 Shot-pouches	Marten	Qr Mr.	26	26.25
1 Par of pistols	Barnhill	Ord		10...
6 Brass kettles from one to five gallons			No. 13	15.18

	Harbeson & Sons			
4 Drawing-knives	H & Worth		"	1.20
3 Doz. Gimblets assorted	Do.		"	3.6
2 Small vices	Do.		"	1.67
1 Saw-set	Do.		"	..10
9 Chissels assorted	Do.		"	1.77
2 Hand-saws	Do.	Ord. No. 10		3.6
6 Augers assorted	Do.		"	1.64
17 Files assorted	Do.		"	2.31

| 1 Whetstone | Do. | " | .47 |

1 Whetstone   Do.   "   .47

Medecine & Sergecal instruments Hospl.   "   94.49

No. 5 & 7—GOS & P. Logan

Oil-cloth tents & Baggs   Wevill—Qr Mr.   119.39

No. 27

Transportation of public stores from Philadelphia to Indian D. Pittsburgh

1 Boat and her caparison, including spiked poles, boat-hooks & toe line to be furnished at Pittsburgh

18 Small falling axes to be furnished at Do.   Indian D.

$462.67

Capt Lewis

This Box of Mathematical Instruments to be Sent for to Mr. Paterson's & well Secured with canvas—mark'd "This side up," on the top—& particular charge given to the waggoner respectg. it.

Some copies of Bills to be sent him.

weight of remaining articles to be sent him

a Strong Waggon. Wt. from here 2700—to be increased to 3500 or more.

If he has left any small bills unpaid requests Mr W. to pay them.

1. *The nautical almanac and astronomical ephemeris . . . published by order of the Commissioners of Longitude* (London, 1781–1804). This book gave the daily locations of the sun, moon, and planets in respect to the earth, for use in computing position. Lewis would require one ephemeris for every year of his expedition; three appear on this list.

2. Nevil Maskelyn, *Tables requisite to be used with the nautical ephemeris for finding the latitude and longitude at sea* (London, 1781). Lewis may have used the 1802 London reprint of this collection of tables required for computation of position. No American edition was available.

3. Richard Kirwan, *Elements of mineralogy* (London, 1784; 2nd ed., 1794).

4. Benjamin Smith Barton, *Elements of botany; or, outlines of the natural history of vegetables* (Philadelphia, 1803).

5. Patrick Kelly, *A practical introduction to spherics and nautical astronomy; being an attempt to simplify those . . . sciences. Containing . . . the discovery of a projection for clearing the lunar distances in order to find the longitude at sea.......*(London, 1796).

6. These entries are duplicated in DNA, RG 92, Journal of the Military Storekeeper at Philadelphia, Journal C, 6 June 1803. Also entered there under date of 12 Dec. 1803 is an item for 176 pounds of powder delivered to Lewis in the quarter ending 30 June 1803.

58. Lewis to Lucy Marks

Dear Mother,   Washington July 2nd 1803.

The day after tomorrow I shall set out for the Western Country; I had calculated on the pleasure of visiting you before my departure but circumstances have rendered this impossible; my absence will probably be equal to fifteen or eighteen months; the nature of this expedition is by no means dangerous, my rout will be altogether through tribes of Indians who are perfectly friendly to the United States, therefore consider the chances of life just as much in my favor on this trip as I should concieve them were I to remain at home for the same length of time; the charge of this expedition is honorable to myself, as it is important to my Country. For it's fatiegues I feel myself perfectly prepared, nor do I doubt my health and strength of constitution to bear me through it; I go with the most perfect preconviction in my own mind of returning safe and hope therefore that you will not suffer yourself to indulge any anxiety for my safety.

As John Marks has been with Mr. Colhoon[1] a considerable time I would not wish him to change his situation untill he is prepared for the C[o]llege of William & Mary at Williamsburgh, although he might be taught by Mr. Robertson[2] somewhat cheeper I do not think that the change would be advantageous. If no other means can be devised by which to get money to enable you to send John to Williamsburgh I must insist on his portion or half of the certificates being sold and appropriated to that purpose; I wish him to continue with Mr. Colhoon untill the 1st of October 1804 and then go on to Williamsburgh: the commencement takes place at that seminary on the 1st monday in October annually: I presume that from the progress that John will have made by the time mentioned that two years at the college will fit him for any professional study, and suppose that eight or nine hundred dollars will be adequate to this object, which sum will be not more than the one half of the Certificate to which he is intitled.

You will find thirty dollars inclosed which I wish you to give to Sister Anderson my love to her Edmund & the family; Reuben writes me that Sister Anderson has another son; remember me to Mary and Jack and tell them I hope the progress they will make in their studies will be equal to my wishes and that of their other friends. I shall write you again on my arrival at Pittsburgh. Adieu and believe me your affectionate Son,

MERIWETHER LEWIS

N.B. I send by Mr. Jefferson the patents belonging to P. & J. Marks for their Brush Creek lands.[3] M. LEWIS.

ALS, RC (MoSHi). Addressed. Lucy Marks, Lewis's mother, married John Marks after the death of her first husband, William Lewis. All the children of both marriages are mentioned by Lewis in the present letter. Reuben Lewis did not marry; Jane Lewis married Edmund Anderson. John Hastings Marks did not marry; Mary Garland Marks married William Moore. In his will, John Marks identifies his children as John Hastings Marks and Polly Garland Marks (transcript, MoSHi). I assume that Polly and Mary are the same person, and that the P. Marks in Lewis's postscript is also that person. The family genealogy by ANDERSON names Mary Garland Marks as the only daughter of John and Lucy; no Polly is mentioned.

1. I have not identified this tutor.

2. John Robertson, a Scottish tutor in Albemarle County, taught "a classical school on the east side of the South West Mountains" (WOODS, 86). He figured in the lives of many young men of the region, and appears in the study by DAVIS (2) of Francis Walker Gilmer. See the same work, p. 365, for Peachy Gilmer's physical description of his schoolmate Meriwether Lewis.

3. Lewis had been trying for some time to obtain patents on two tracts of land in Ohio, and once had turned to Clark for help. "Mr. Clark will be so good as to make application . . . for the plats and Certificates of two tracts of land surveyed . . . for John Marks on the waters of Ohio Brush-Creek. . . . Mr. Clark will oblige me by informing me as early as possible in what manner the business stands, and what he may judge to be the most expedient plan to pursue in order to obtain the necessary papers by which I should be enabled to obtain a patant" (27 June 1801, MoSHi). The tracts consisted of lands due John Marks as bounty for service in the Revolution, and were located on the east fork of Brush Creek and the Elk Run branch of the east fork of Brush Creek, possibly in Highland County, Ohio (memorandum in Lewis-Marks Papers, ViU).

59. Henry Dearborn to Moses Hooke

Sir,   War Department July 2d 1803.

You will give Capt. Lewis every aid in your power in the imbarkation of his Stores, &c. and for descen[d]ing the River, and you will see that the Contractors Agent has proper provisions put on board his Boat to carry him & his Men to Massac, and you will likewise furnish the Capt. with Eighteen light Axes. I am &c.

Lbk (DNA, RG 107, Letters Sent, 2:13). Lt. Moses Hooke had left Washington 16 Jan. 1803 to take command of Fort Fayette, succeeding Amos Stoddard, who was ordered west with his company (DNA, RG 94, AGO Lbk, 1:403–04). As collateral duty he served as assistant military agent. Hooke had joined the First Infantry as first lieutenant in 1799, and appears on a muster roll of Capt. Daniel Bissell's company of 1 Feb. 1801 (DNA, RG 94, Pay and Muster Rolls, First Infantry). When a tornado struck the cantonment at Wilkinsonville, Indiana Territory, 13 March 1801, he sustained serious injuries including a fractured leg (Frankfort, Ky., *Palladium*, 21 April 1801).

60. Henry Dearborn to William McRea

Sir, War Department July 2d 1803.

If you have been able to select a Sergeant and two or three men to accompany Capt. Lewis agreeably to his request, you will be pleased to send them without loss of time to Massac there to remain under the Command of Capt. Bissell and until the arrival of Capt. Lewis when they will be placed under his Command. I am &c.

Lbk (DNA, RG 107, Letters Sent, 2:14).

61. Henry Dearborn to the Army Paymaster

[2 July 1803]

The Paymaster of the Army is authorised to advance Capt. M: Lewis forty eight dollars for the recruiting service.

War Department H. D.
July 2d 1803

Lbk (DNA, RG 107, Letters Sent, 2:14).

62. Henry Dearborn to Lewis

Sir, War Department July 2d 1803

You will call on the Commanding Officers at Massac and Kaskaskais for such Non-commissioned Officers & privates as will be necessary to accompany you on your tour to the Westward. Directions have been given to the Commanding Officers of those Posts to furnish you with such Men as you may require from their respective Companies. You will in the mean time recruit such suitable Men as may be inclined to accompany you. The paymaster of the Army will be directed to furnish you with money for paying the Bounties to said Recruits. The whole number of non-commissioned officers and privates should not exceed twelve. You will also be furnished with a Blank Commission for a Lieutenant or Ensign, to be filled by you to your direction—And You are authorised to engage an Interpreter to accompany You whose compensation may be at the rate of three hundred dollars pr. Year. I am &c.

Lbk (DNA, RG 107, Letters Sent, 2:15).

63. Henry Dearborn to Russell Bissell, Amos Stoddard, and Daniel Bissell

Sir   War Department July 2d 1803
You will please to afford Capt. Meriwether Lewis all the aid in your power in selecting and engaging suitable men to accompany him on an expedition to the Westward. If any non-commissioned officer or private in your Company should be disposed to join Capt. Lewis, whose characters for sobriety, integrity and other necessary qualifications render them suitable for such service, you will detach them accordingly. I am &c.

Lbk (DNA, RG 107, Letters Sent, 2:12). The three officers named here were in command of the troops at Fort Massac on the lower Ohio, and Kaskaskia on the Mississippi above the mouth of the Ohio. The Bissells were brothers from Connecticut, both serving in the First Infantry, Capt. Russell Bissell (d. 1807) commanding at Kaskaskia and Capt. Daniel Bissell (1768–1833) at Massac. Capt. Amos Stoddard (1762–1813), lawyer and Revolutionary War soldier, now commanding a company of artillerists, would soon become the first civil and military commandant of Upper Louisiana. His mission in the West was to await completion of the Louisiana Purchase, then to establish U.S. headquarters at St. Louis. At this time he was under orders to erect a military post at Cahokia on the east bank of the Mississippi, opposite St. Louis, but the Secretary of War later canceled these instructions and ordered him to combine his company with Capt. Russell Bissell's at Kaskaskia (DNA, RG 107, Letters Sent, 19 July 1803).

64. Henry Dearborn to Russell Bissell and Amos Stoddard

Gentlemen.   War Department July 2d 1803
You will be pleased to furnish one Sergeant & Eight good Men who understand rowing a boat to go with Capt. Lewis as far up the River as they can go & return with certainty before the Ice will obstruct the passage of the river. They should be furnished with the best boat at the Post & take in provisions for Capt. Lewis's party & themselves. If an officer should be inclined to go with the boat, he should be

prefered. It would be desirable that the party should go voluntarily, if a sufficient number of suitable men should offer—they will have the usual allowance of Men on fatigue. I am &c.

Lbk (DNA, RG 107, Letters Sent, 2:12).

65. Blank Commission Form

Sir.   War Department July 2d 1803.
   The President of the United States has been pleased to appoint you
        in the Regiment of   in the service of the United
States, and should the Senate advise and consent thereto you will be commissioned accordingly.

You will please to signify your acceptance of this appointment to Capt. Meriwether Lewis of the 1st Regiment of Infantry, and place yourself under his orders, until otherwise instructed from this Department of the Commanding officer of your Corps. I am &c.

Lbk (DNA, RG 107, Letters Sent, 2:13). The blank commission is not intended for Clark, but for a substitute if Clark declines to accept. Later in the year, when Lewis had an opportunity to add a physician to his party, he explained that "I had a letter of appointment for a second lieut. which I could give him but did not feel myself altogether at liberty to use it as it was given me by the President to be used in the event of Mr. Clark's not consenting to go with me but as he had I could not use it without the previous consent of the President . . ." (Lewis's journal, 8 Sept. 1803, LEWIS & ORDWAY, 39). For more about this incident, see the note for No. 86.

66. Jefferson to Henri Peyroux

Dear Sir   Washington July 3. 1803.
   Since I had the pleasure of your acquaintance in Philadelphia in 1791. I had supposed you were returned to Europe. I have lately however been told that you preside at present at Ste. Genevieve & St. Louis. I cannot therefore omit the satisfaction of writing to you by Capt. Lewis, an officer in our army, & for some time past my Secretary. As our former acquaintance was a mixt one of science and business, so is the occasion of renewing it. You know that the geography of the Missouri and the most convenient water communication from the head of that to the Pacific ocean is a desideratum not yet satisfied. Since coming to the administration of the U.S. I have taken the earliest opportunity in my power to have that communication

explored, and Capt Lewis with a party of twelve or fifteen men is authorised to do it. His journey being merely literary, to inform us of the geography & natural history of the country, I have procured a passport for him & his party, from the Minister of France here, it being agreed between him & the Spanish minister, that the country having been ceded to France, her minister may most properly give the authority for the journey. This was the state of things when the passport was given, which was some time since. But before Capt Lewis's actual departure we learn through a channel of unquestionable information that France has ceded the whole country of Louisiana to the U.S. by a treaty concluded in the first days of May. But for an object as innocent & useful as this I am sure you will not be scrupulous as to the authorities on which this journey is undertaken; & that you will give all the protection you can to Capt. Lewis & his party in going & returning. I have no doubt you can be particularly useful to him, and it is to sollicit your patronage that I trouble you with the present letter, praying you at the same time to accept my friendly salutations and assurances of my high respect & consideration.

TH: JEFFERSON

ALS, SC (DLC). Transcript in Delassus to Salcedo and Casa Calvo, 9 Dec. 1803, reprinted in NASATIR (2), 2:721. Henri Peyroux de la Coudreniere was no longer in command at Ste. Genevieve and St. Louis, as Jefferson would learn from his long-delayed reply (No. 108). SOWERBY, 4:313, lists a tract by Peyroux, *System sur le soleil et les étoiles fixes,* included in Jefferson's catalog of his library but now lost. Another tract, *Mémoire sur les sept especes d'hommes,* is in the University of Michigan Library.

67. Jefferson to Lewis

Dear Sir   Washington. U.S. of America. July 4. 1803.

In the journey which you are about to undertake for the discovery of the course and source of the Missouri, and of the most convenient water communication from thence to the Pacific ocean, your party being small, it is to be expected that you will encounter considerable dangers from the Indian inhabitants. Should you escape those dangers and reach the Pacific ocean, you may find it imprudent to hazard a return the same way, and be forced to seek a passage round by sea, in such vessels as you may find on the Western coast. But you will be without money, without clothes, & other necessaries; as a sufficient supply cannot be carried with you from hence. Your resource in that case can only be in the credit ot the U.S. for which purpose I hereby authorise you to draw on the Secretaries of State, of the Treasury, of War & of the Navy of the U.S. according as you may find your draughts will be most negociable, for the purpose of obtaining money or necessaries for yourself & your men: and I solemnly pledge the faith of the United States that these draughts shall be paid punctually at the date they are made payable. I also ask of the Consuls, agents, merchants & citizens of any nation with which we have intercourse or amity to furnish you with those supplies which your necessities may call for, assuring them of honorable and prompt retribution. And our own Consuls in foreign parts where you may happen to be, are hereby instructed & required to be aiding & assisting to you in whatsoever may be necessary for procuring your return back to the United States. And to give more entire satisfaction & confidence to those who may be disposed to aid you, I Thomas Jefferson, President of the United States of America, have written this letter of general credit for you with my own hand, and signed it with my name.

TH: JEFFERSON

ALS, SC (DLC); RC (MoSHi, MtHi, NhD). An earlier draft in Jefferson's hand (DLC) contains minor variations that do not alter the meaning of the text. The MoSHi copy is addressed to Lewis. The day after this letter was written, Lewis set out for Pittsburgh and the West ("Capt. Lewis sets out on his journey to day," Jefferson to Thomas Mann Randolph, 5 July 1803, DLC).

68. Lewis to Jefferson

Dear Sir,   12. O,Clock. Harper's Ferry July 8th 1803.
    The waggon which was employed by Mr. Linnard the Military Agent at Philadelphia, to transport the articles forming my outfit, passed this place on the 28th Ulto. The waggoner determined that his team was not sufficiently strong to take the whole of the articles that had been prepared for me at this place and therefore took none of them; of course it became necessary to provide some other means of geting them forward; for this purpose on the evening of the 5th at Freder[i]cktown I engaged a person with a light two horse-waggon who promised to set out with them this morning, in this however he has disappointed me and I have been obliged to engage a second person who will be here this evening in time to load and will go on early in the morning: I shall set out myself in the course of an hour, taking the rout of Charlestown, Frankfort, Uniontown and Redstone old fort

PROPOSALS

By C. & A. CONRAD & Co.

FOR PUBLISHING

THE HISTORY

OF THE

Expedition of Captains Lewis and Clarke,

THROUGH

The Continent of North America.

Performed during the years 1804, 1805 and 1806, by order of the
Government of the United States.

THE appearance of this Work, which was announced for publication nearly three years ago,
has been retarded by a variety of causes, among
which the melancholy fate of Captain Lewis is
already known and lamented by the nation. This
delay, although it has disappointed the public expectation, and given rise to several imperfect accounts of the journey, may be the less regretted,

Nicholas Biddle prepared this brochure shortly after consenting to write a
narrative of the expedition in 1810.

William Clark (1770–1838), a portrait by Charles Willson Peale

Meriwether Lewis (1774–1809), a portrait by Charles Willson Peale

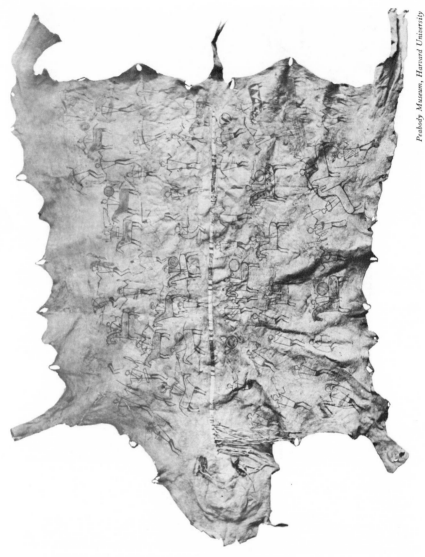

Buffalo skin with Indian battle scene, sent to Jefferson from Fort Mandan

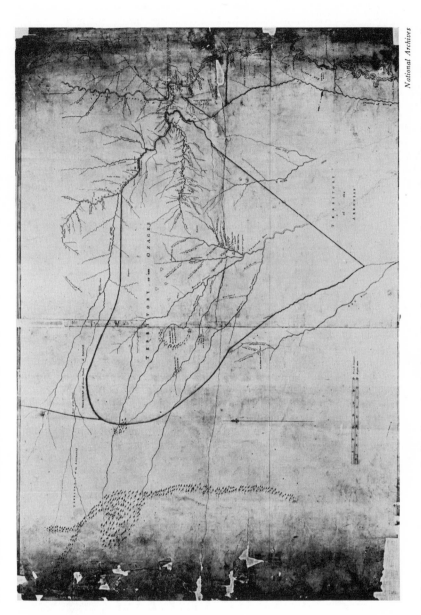

War Department copy of what is probably the earliest Lewis and Clark map, drawn in 1804. (See No. 122.)

Charles Willson Peale made these drawings of the mountain quail and Lewis' woodpecker from specimens sent by Lewis and Clark.

Among the many new plants collected by Lewis and Clark was the buffalo berry, obtained at the mouth of the Niobrara in Nebraska.

Copia

Moi soussigné chargé d'affaires de Sa Majesté Britannique près les États unis de l'amérique &c.

Certifie a tous ceux a qui viendront ces presentes, que le Porteur, Capitaine Merriwether Lewis Citoyen des États unis de l'amérique est envoyé (sous l'autorité desdits États unis) a la Découverte des Sources et des bords du Missoury et des parties occidentales du continent de l'amérique du Nord, et qu'il ne porte avec lui aucunes marchandises autres que celles qui lui sont nécessaires pour s'attirer un accueil favorable parmi les tribus sauvages, ou pour avancer les objets scientifiques et littéraires de son voyage. — En conséquence je prie tous ceux a qui viendront ces presentes, soit surintendants de Sa Majesté pour les affaires des Sauvages, soit quelques autres sujets de Sa Majesté qui font leur commerce avec les dites tribus, non seulement de permettre audit Capitaine Lewis de voyager sans aucun obstacle ni empêchement quelconque, mais aussi de lui fournir tous les secours et toute la protection qui dépendront d'eux, et enfin de faciliter et d'avancer de tout leur possible le but de son voyage, qu'il a entrepris par le seul motif de Science et dont la protection et l'accomplissement doivent intéresser également toutes les Nations civilisées.

Donné a la ville de Washington le vingt huit février 1803. = Edw.d Thornton

Copia
Delafu

Cuba, 2368

British passport issued to Meriwether Lewis. This copy is in French; no copy in English has been located. (See No. 14.)

Israel Whelen for
The United States ⅀ *Bo.t of Fra.s Baillet*

1803

May 30 = 193 ℔ Portable Soup at 150 Cents $289.50

Rec.d of Israel Whelen two hundred Eighty Nine
dollars 50 Cent in full —

$289 50/100 =) François Baillet

" — Duplicates, Received the above articles

Meriwether Lewis.
Capt. 1.st U.S. Reg.t Inf.y

Philadelphia cook François Baillet made 193 pounds of "portable soup" for the expedition. (See No. 55.)

Major Hooke.

Sir *War Department August 3.d 1803.*

40/43

Being informed by Capt. M. Lewis that
he and you have a mutual desire that you may
accompany him on his tour to the Westward, this is
to inform you that as soon as you can correctly arrange
Your accounts for settlement and deliver over the
public property to Capt. Reed who is requested to
receive and take charge of it until a successor to you
as assistant Military Agent shall be appointed,
You may at your own option with the concurrence
of Capt. Lewis proceed with him & consider your-
self under his immediate command. —

Sam De-

Had Clark not accepted the invitation, Lt. Moses Hooke would have accompanied Lewis on the "Lewis and Hooke Expedition." (See No. 79.)

Dear Sir   Washington. U.S. of America. July 4. 1803.

In the journey which you are about to undertake for the discovery of the course and source of the Missouri, and of the most convenient water communication from thence to the Pacific ocean, your party being small, it is to be expected that you will encounter considerable dangers from the Indian inhabitants. should you escape those dangers and reach the Pacific ocean, you may find it imprudent to hazard a return the same way, and be forced to seek a passage round by sea, in such vessels as you may find on the Western coast. but you will be without money, without clothes, & other necessaries; as a sufficient supply cannot be carried with you from hence. your resource in that case can only be in the credit of the U.S. for which purpose I hereby authorise you to draw on the Secretaries of State, of the Treasury, of War & of the Navy of the U.S. according as you may find your draughts will be most negociable, for the purpose of obtaining money or necessaries for yourself & your men: and I solemnly pledge the faith of the United States that these draughts shall be paid punctually at the date they are made payable. I also ask of the Consuls, agents, merchants & citizens of any nation with which we have intercourse or amity, to furnish you with those sup-plies which your necessities may call for, assuring them of honorable and prompt retribution. and our own Consuls in foreign parts where you may happen to be, are hereby instructed & required to be aiding & assisting to you in whatsoever may be necessary for procuring your return back to the United States. And to give more entire satisfaction & confidence to those who may be disposed to aid you, I Thomas Jefferson, President of the United States of America, have written this letter of general credit for you with my own hand, and signed it with my name.

Th: Jefferson

To Capt. Meriwether Lewis.

The letter of credit carried by the explorers. (See No. 67.)

Lewis acknowledges Clark's decision to join the expedition, and comments on the preparations.

Sir,

War Department
March 26th 1804

The peculiar situation, circumstances & organisation of the Corps of Engineers is such as would render the appointment of Mr. Clark a Captain in that Corps improper — and consequently no appointment above that of a Lieutenant in the Corps of Artillerists could with propriety be given him, which appointment he has rec.d & his Commission is herewith enclosed — his Military Grade will have no effect on his compensation for the service in which he is engaged — I hope by the time this reaches you all obstructions to your ascending the River will be removed & that you will be able to progress with facility & safety —

I am respectfully your
Humb.e Serv.t

H. Dearborn

Cap.t Meriwether Lewis

Clark had been promised a captain's rank, but the commission he finally received was that of lieutenant. Here the Secretary of War breaks the news. (See No. 110.)

St. Charles May 21st, 1804

Dear Sir

By Captain Lewis who arrived from St. Louis to day I had the pleasure of receiving your letter of the 2nd instant. and am happy to here of the recovery of your family & my Brother, whom I was much concerned about I am sorry to here that the negroes of the estate of Mr. Thruston hired so low, perhaps they may here for more the next year. My friend Capt Lewis expressed some sorrow that you happened not to be at home at the time he passed down, but hopes to see you on his return to the U. States, as to my self, I have, &c. and shall always have that Brotherly affection for you which you are well assured I always possessed; and hope that in less than two years to see you & that family yours whome I have every affection for, at your own house. My rout is uncertain I think it more than probable that Capt Lewis or my self will return by sea, the other by the same rout we proceed, the time is uncertain. all the alterations which I did not inform you of has been made since I saw you. and the law authorising the president to explore the Country &c. has just come to my knowledge.

I have been at this place five days waiting for Capt Lewis who had been detained at St. Louis to fix off the Osage Chiefs. he has just arrived and we shall leave this village immediately

The expedition had already begun when Clark sent this letter to his brother-in-law, William Croghan. (See No. 123.)

Fort mandan aprl 1st. 1805

Sir

[draft letter in Clark's and Lewis's hand, with numerous deletions and insertions]

... You will readily perceive in reading over those notes, that many parts are incorrect, owing to the variety information recieved at different times, I most sincerely wish that leasure had permited me to offer them in a more correct form. receive I pray you my unfained acknoledg=ments for your friendly recollection of me in your letters to my friend and companion Capt. Lewis. and be assured of the sincere regard with which I have the honor to be

Your most Obt. &

Humble Servt.—

D Sir:

I must request the favour of you to send by some safe conveyance a red box, to my brother ...as Directed on the top of the Box — R. Worvington the Bearer of this is entrusted with papers of considerable consequence which I wish lodged in the hands of my brother in Kentucky) be so good as to furnish this man with a publick horse, which may be returned to you by the post rider — I shall not enter into a detaile of occurrances as Capt Lewis has written you fully on those subjects. I send you

This draft of a letter from Clark to Jefferson was begun by Clark, then edited and completed by Lewis. The lines at the bottom are a draft of a letter from Clark to Amos Stoddard. (See Nos. 144, 145.)

St. Louis September 24 1806

Dear brother,

We arrived at this place on the 23 inst. from the pacific Ocean where we remained during the last winter near the entrance of the Columbia river. this station we left on the 23th of March last and should have reached St. Louis early in August had we not been detained by the snow which bared our passage across the Rocky mountains untill the 24th of June. in returning through those mountains we divided ourselves into several parties, digressing from the rout by which we went out in order the more effectually to explore the country, ~~the conjections of the principal branches of the Missouri and Columbia Rivers~~ and discover the most practicable road which does exist across the continent by way of the Missouri and Columbia rivers. in this we were completely successfull and have therefore no hesitation in declaring that such as nature

Lewis drafted this letter for Clark to sign, at the end of the expedition, for reasons explained in the notes. (See No. 209.)

Before Nicholas Biddle wrote his narrative of the expedition, he filled many notebook pages with information gathered during interviews with Clark. (See No. 326.)

to Pittsburgh, at which place I shall most probably arrive on the 15th.

Yesterday I shot my guns and examined the several articles which had been manufactered for me at this place; they appear to be well executed.

My complyments to Mr. Harvie, & accept the assureance of my sincere wishes for your health and happiness. Your friend & Obt. Servt.

MERIWETHER LEWIS.

ALS, RC (DLC). Endorsed; received 14 July 1803. Reply is No. 72.

69. Thomas H. Cushing to Lewis

Sir,   Inspectors Office Fredk. Town (Md.) 9th July 1803

I take the liberty of enclosing sundry letters for Officers to the Westward to which I request your attention, and also a descriptive list & account of the party[1] ordered to attend you from Pittsburgh.

Should any casualties happen in this party, I beg of you to note them on the list, and when you have done with the party, that you will order it to Fort Adams and send the necessary papers to the Commanding Officer of that post.

That your expedition may be pleasant to yourself and advantageous to our Country; and when its toils and dangers are over, that you may enjoy many years of happiness, prosperity and honor, is the sincere wish of Sir, Your most Obdt. Servt.

Lbk (DNA, RG 94, Letters Sent).
1. The detachment of soldiers accompanying Lewis down the Ohio may have rejoined Lt. Murray at Fort Massac and proceeded with him to Fort Adams. Cushing assumed they would in a letter of 12 July 1803 to Dearborn.

70. Jefferson to Lewis

Th: Jefferson to Capt. Lewis   [11 July 1803]

I inclose you your pocket book left here. If the dirk will appear passable by post, that shall also be sent, when received. Your bridle, left by the inattention of Joseph[1] in packing your saddle, is too bulky to go in that way. We have not received a word from Europe since you left us. Be so good as to keep me always advised how to direct to you. Accept my affectionate salutations & assurances of constant esteem.

Washington July 11. 03.

AL, SC (DLC). Reply is No. 75.

1. Joseph Dougherty. Dearborn refers to him as "one of your domestics" in a letter to Jefferson, and BETTS, 299, identifies him as Jefferson's business manager in Washington. He left Jefferson's employ when the second presidential term ended in 1809, but continued to correspond with him about the raising of sheep.

71. Caspar Wistar to Jefferson

Dear Sir [13 July 1803]

I beg leave to trouble you with the inclosed for Captain Lewis; they do not include many points, because his instructions have really anticipated every thing which occurred to me, & of course admitted of no additions but in detail. I have also avoided several subjects which I expected would be fully detailed by Dr. Barton, as being particularly within those departments of Science to which he has devoted himself.[1]

If the expedition should go on without any change in the original plan, in Consequence of the late happy events respecting Louisiana, might not Mr. Lewis derive some benefit from Monsieur Pirroux or Pierow,[2] a Gentleman who applied to you when Secretary of State respecting an Emigration which he wished to effect from Philada. to the Spanish Main. He had been Governor (under Spain) of a fort near the mouth of the Missouri & appeared to know more of the trade & navigation of that River than any person I have seen. He said (so long ago as 1792) that the Canada Traders supplied the Indians on the upper parts of the Missouri with goods. If you think it proper to write to him I believe the letter would be very useful to Mr. Lewis. What is the real direction of the Missouri? 'Till the publication of McKenzie's book I believed it to be nearly west, & if I am not mistaken M. Pirroux spoke of it in the Same way for 2000 miles of its extent. But McKenzies account is Confirmed by the Gentleman who gave the account of the Wild Sheep,[3] in his narrative he mentions the Missouri as existing no great distance from the Saskatchevine river. I shall write this day to Mr. Peter Pond [4] (who is mentioned by McKenzie) on the Subject, he lives in Connecticut & I believe will give any information in his power without any particular explanation respecting the reason for asking it.

I cannot conclude this letter without offering you my most sincere & cordial congratulations on the very happy acquisitions you have made for our Country on the Missisippi. Altho no one here appears to know the extent or price of the cession, it is generally considered as the most important & beneficial transaction which has occurred since the declaration of Independence, & next to it, most like to influence or regulate the destinies of our Country. I believe that allmost all impartial people here, who take the pains to think for themselves, consider the British reasons for the war as very slight. With the greatest respect I am your affectionate friend,

Philada. July 13th 1803   C. WISTAR Junr.

ALS, RC (DLC). Endorsed; received 18 July 1803.
1. Whatever Wistar enclosed for Lewis has not survived. He is clearly sending the list of subjects for inquiry that he promised while Lewis was in Philadelphia. If the material was received, and combined with that submitted by Benjamin Rush, it has perhaps survived in Clark's list (No. 101).
2. Henri Peyroux, obviously, but I have no information about the activities mentioned here or in Wistar's next letter to Jefferson (No. 91).
3. This can only be Duncan MC GILLIVRAY's "Account of the wild North-American sheep," *Medical Repository*, 6 (1803), 237–40. I cite it again in a note on the mountain sheep under No. 149.
4. Peter Pond (1740–1847), fur trader and explorer who presented a map of his travels to Congress about 1784.

72. Jefferson to Lewis

Dear Sir   Washington July 15. 1803.

I dropped you a line on the 11th inst.[1] and last night recieved yours of the 8th. Last night also we received the treaty from Paris ceding Louisiana according to the bounds to which France had a right. Price 11¼ millions of Dollars beside paying certain debts of France to our citizens which will be from 1. to 4. millions. I received also from Mr. La Cepede at Paris, to whom I had mentioned your intended expedition a letter[2] of which the following is an extract. 'Mr. Broughton, one of the companions of Captain Vancouver went up Columbia river 100. miles, in December 1792. He stopped at a point which he named Vancouver lat. 45° 27′ longitude 237° 50′ E. Here the river Columbia is still a quarter of a mile wide & from 12. to 36. feet deep. It is far then to it's head. From this point Mount Hood is seen 20. leagues distant, which is probably a dependence of the Stony mountains, of which Mr. Fiedler saw the beginning about lat. 40° and the source of the Missouri is probably in the Stony mountains. If your nation can establish an easy communication by rivers, canals, & short portages between N. York for example & the city [they were building] or [to be built] [for the badness of the writing renders it uncertain which is meant, but probably the last] at the mouth of the Columbia, what

[109]

a route for the commerce of Europe, Asia, & America.' Accept my affectionate salutations.

TH: JEFFERSON

ALS, SC (DLC). Reply is No. 75. The brackets are Jefferson's.
1. Not located.
2. Here Jefferson translates a portion of No. 35.

73. Lewis to Jefferson

Pittsburgh July 15th 1803.
Dear Sir,   3. O'Clock P.M.

I arrived here at 2 O'Clock, and learning that the mail closed at 5 this evening hasten to make this communication, tho' it can only contain the mere information of my arrival. No occurrence has taken place on my journey hither sufficiently interesting to be worthy of relation: the weather has been warm and dry; the roads in consequence extreemly dusty, yet I feel myself much benifitted by the exercise the journey has given me, and can with pleasure anounce, so far and *all is well.*

I have not yet seen Lieut. Hook nor made the enquiry relative to my boat, on the state of which, the time of my departu[r]e from hence must materially depend: the Ohio is quite low, but not so much so as to obstruct my passage altogether. Your Obt. Humble Sert.

MERIWETHER LEWIS.

ALS, RC (MHi). Endorsed; received 25 July 1803.

74. Clark to Lewis

Dear Lewis   Clarksville July 18th 1803

I received by yesterdays Mail, your letter of the 19th ulto. The Contents of which I recived with much pleasure. The enterprise &c. is Such as I have long anticipated and am much pleased with—and as my situation in life will admit of my absence the length of time necessary to accomplish such an undertaking I will chearfully join you in an "official Charrector" as mentioned in your letter,[1] and partake of the dangers, difficulties, and fatigues, and I anticipate the honors & rewards of the result of such an enterprise, should we be successful in accomplishing it. This is an undertaking fraited with many difeculties, but My friend I do assure you that no man lives whith whome I would perfur to undertake Such a Trip &c. as your self,[2] and I shall arrange my matters as well as I can against your arrival here.

It may be necessary that you inform the President of my acceding to the proposals, so that I may be furnished with such Credentials as the nature of the Toure may require, which I suppose had best be forwarded to Louisville. The Objcets of this Plan of Governments are Great and Worthey of that great Chaructor the Main Spring of its action. The Means with which we are furnished to carry it into effect, I think may be Sufficiently liberal. The plan of operation, as laid down by you (with a Small addition as to the outfit) I highly approve of.

I shall indeaver to engage (temporally) a fiew men, such as will best answer our purpose, holding out the Idea as stated in your letter —The subject of which has been mentioned in Louisville several weeks agoe.

Pray write to me by every post after recving this letter, I shall be exceedingly anxious to hear from you. With every sincerity & frendship Yr. Obt. Sevt.

WM. CLARK

Capt. Merriwether Lewis   Note this letter
at Washington City or on   forwarded to Pittsburgh.
his way to Pittsburgh.

ALS, RC (DLC). Addressed, "Captain Meriwether Lewis." Reply is No. 80. Clark's first draft is in MoSHi, with several false starts and minor changes in wording. Two such changes are noted below. The third page of the MoSHi version contains two drafts of Clark's letter of 24 July 1803 to Jefferson (No. 77).

1. Here, instead of "as mentioned in your letter," Clark first wrote "on equal footing &c."

2. In the first draft, Clark wrote here, "I reserve nothing from you that will add either to Yr. profit or satisfaction, and. . . ."

75. Lewis to Jefferson

Dear Sir,   Pittsburgh July 22nd 1803.

Yours of the 11th & 15th Inst. were duly recieved, the former on the 18th inst., the latter on this day. For my pocketbook I thank you: the dirk could not well come by post, nor is it of any moment to me, the knives that were made at Harper's ferry will answer my purposes equally as well and perhaps better; it can therefore be taken care of untill my return: the bridle is of no consequence at all. After the reciept of this letter I think it will be best to direct to me at Louisville Kentuckey.

The person who contracted to build my boat engaged to have it in readiness by the 20th inst.; in this however he has failed; he pleads his having been disappointed in procuring timber, but says he has now supplyed himself with the necessary materials, and that she shall be completed by the last of this month; however in this I am by no means sanguine, nor do I believe from the progress he makes that she will be ready before the 5th of August; I visit him every day, and endeavour by every means in my power to hasten the completion of the work: I have prevailed on him to engage more hands, and he tells me that two others will join him in the morning, if so, he may probably finish the boat by the time he mentioned: I shall embark immediately the boat is in readiness, there being no other consideration which at this moment detains me.

The Waggon from Harper's ferry arrived today, bringing every thing with which she was charged in good order.

The party of recruits that were ordered from Carlisle to this place with a view to descend the river with me, have arrived with the exception of one, who deserted on the march, his place however can be readily supplyed from the recruits at this place enlisted by Lieut. Hook.

The current of the Ohio is extreemly low and continues to decline, this may impede my progress but shall not prevent my proceeding, being dete[r]mined to get forward though I should not be able to make a greater distance than a mile pr. day. I am with the most sincere regard Your Obt. Servt.

MERIWETHER LEWIS.

ALS, RC (DLC). Received 1 Aug. 1803 according to Jefferson's index of letters.

76. Clark to Lewis

Dear Lewis   Louisville 24th July 1803

I wrote you in answer to your letter of the 19th ulto. by the last Mail, the contents of which as I before informed you were truely pleasing to me and such as I heartily join you in. I am arrangeing my matters so as to detain but a short time after your arrival here, well convinced of the necessity of getting as far as possible up the ———— this fall to accomplish the Object as laid down by yourself—and which I highly approve of. <My friend I join you with hand & Heart and anticipate advantages which will certainly derive from the accomplishment of so vast, Hazidous and fatiguing enterprize. You as doub[t]

[112]

will inform the president of my determination to join you in an "official Character" as mentioned in your letter. The Credentials necessary for me to be furnished with had best be forwarded to this place, and (if we set out before their arrival), to Kaskaskia.>

I have temperally engaged some men for the enterprise of a discription calculated to work & go thro' those labours & fatigues which will be necessary. Several young men (Gentlemens sons) have applyed to accompany us—as they are not accustomed to labour and as that is a verry assential part of the services required of the party, I am causious in giveing them any encouragement. The newspaper accounts seem to confirm the report of War in Europe & the session of Louisiana to the United States, and as I think it possible that a Confirmation of the session of Louisiana may have detained you at the City longer than you expected, I have inclosed a letter to you under cover to Mr. Jefferson. Pray let me here from you as often as possible. Yr.

W. C.

AL, SC (MoSHi). Reply is No. 80.

77. Clark to Jefferson

Sir   Clarksville 24th July 1803

I had the honor of receiving thro' Captain M. Lewis an assureance of your Approbation & wish that I would join him in a North Western enterprise. I will chearfully, and with great pleasure, join my friend Capt. Lewis in this Vast enterprise, and shall arrange my business so as to be in readiness to leave this soon after his arrival. May I request the favour of you to forward the inclosed letter to Capt. Lewis, should he not be with you. I have the honor to be with great respect your Mo. Ob. and Sincear

WM. CLARK

ALS, RC (DLC). Endorsed; received 6 Aug. 1803. Two earlier drafts of this letter appear on pp. 3 and 4 of Clark's draft of 18 July 1803 to Lewis (No. 74).

78. Lewis to Jefferson

Dear Sir,   Pittsburgh July 26th 1803.

I have recieved as yet no answer from Mr. Clark;[1] in the event of Mr. Clark's declining to accompany me Lieut. Hooke of this place has engaged to do so, if permitted; and I think from his disposition and qualifications that I might safely calculate on being as ably assisted by him in the execution of the objects of my mission, as I could wish, or would be, by any other officer in the Army. Lieut. Hooke is about 26 years of age, endowed with a good constitution, possessing a sensible well informed mind, is industrious, prudent and persevering, and withall intrepid and enterprising: he has acted as Military Agent at this place for a few months past, and of course will have some public accounts to adjust, tho' he tells me that he can settle those accounts, deliver the public stores to the person who may be directed to take charge of them, and prepare to go with me, at any time, within the course of a day or two. Should I recieve no answer from Mr. Clark previous to my leaving this place, or he decline going with me, I would be much gratifyed with being authorized to take Lieut. Hooke with me, first directing him to settle his public accounts, and make such disposition of the publick stores as the Secretary of War may think proper to direct. There is a Capt. Reed[2] of the Artly. here, who will probably not leave this place untill an answer can be recieved, or if he should, Majr. Craig[3] of Pittsburgh would take charge of the stores untill an officer could be ordered on for that purpose.

It is probable that you will have left Washington before this letter can reach that place, and if so, knowing the delay incident to a communication between yourself and the Secretary of War at such a distance, and conceiving that it would be necessary that he should decide whether from the nature of his arrangements Lieut. Hooke could leave his present station with propriety or not, or his place be supplyed without injury to the public service, I have thought it best to inclose this letter to him unsealed, with a request that should you be absent, he would read it and give me an answer on the subject of it as early as possible. It is most probable that I shall leave Pittsburgh before an answer can be returned to this letter, I take the liberty therefore to suggest, that the answer to me had better be inclosed to Lieut. Hooke, unsealed, with instructions to him that in the event of my absence, he should read it, and govern himself accordingly. If Lieut. Hooke sets out twenty days after me, by taking the rout of Limestone, Louisville and Vincennes he will reach the mouth of the Missourie as early as I shall. I am with the most sincere attachment Your Obt. Servt.

MERIWETHER LEWIS.

ALS, RC (DLC). Addressed; endorsed, "Lewis Meriwether. Pittsburg. July 25. 03. recd. Aug. 5." Jefferson dated the letter incorrectly in his endorsement and in his index of letters; it is apparently the letter he means in his of 22 Jan. 1804 to Lewis (No. 105) when he says he has received Lewis's of 25 July 1803. It is plainly the letter referred to by the Secretary of War in No. 81.

1. Three days later, Lewis had received Clark's acceptance. DNA, RG 107, Register of Letters Received, contains an entry numbered M-93, recording Lewis's letter of 29 July saying that Clark will "proceed with him on his tour."

2. Capt. James Read (d. 1813) was appointed captain of artillerists in 1802.

3. Maj. Isaac Craig (1741–1826), an Irish-born Revolutionary War soldier, prominent Pittsburgh merchant, serving as district paymaster for the army and assigned to pay the troops on the upper Ohio. In earlier years he had been a deputy quartermaster general in Pittsburgh.

79. Henry Dearborn to Moses Hooke

Sir   War Department August 3d 1803.

Being informed by Capt. M. Lewis that he and you have a mutual desire that you may accompany him on his tour to the Westward; this is to inform you that as soon as you can correctly arrange Your accounts for settlement and deliver over the public property to Capt. Reed who is requested to receive and take charge of it until a successor to you as assistant Military Agent shall be appointed,[1] You may at your own option with the concurrence of Capt. Lewis proceed with him & consider Yourself under his command. I am &c.

Lbk (DNA, RG 107, Letters Sent, 2:46).

1. In a letter of the same date to Read, Secretary Dearborn instructed him to receive the public property now in the care of Lt. Hooke until a successor could be appointed as assistant military agent (DNA, RG 107, Letters Sent, 2:46).

80. Lewis to Clark

Dear Clark.   Pittsburgh August 3rd 1803.

Yours of the 19th & 24th Ult. have been duly received, and be assured I feel myself much gratifyed with your decision; for I could neither hope, wish, or expect from a union with any man on earth, more perfect support or further aid in the discharge of the several duties of my mission, than that, which I am confident I shall derive from being associated with yourself.

The articles of every discription forming my outfit for this expedition have arrived in good order; my boat only detains me, she is not yet compleated tho' the work-man who contracted to build her promises that she shall be in readiness by the last of the next week.

[115]

The water is low, this may retard, but shall not totally obstruct my progress being determined to proceed though I should not be able to make greater speed than a boat's length pr. day.

I am pleased to heare that you have engaged some men for this service, your contract with them had better be with the condition of my approval, as by the time I shall arrive more will have offered themselves and a better scelection may of course be made; from the nature of this enterprise much must depend on a judicious scelection of our men; their qualifycations should be such as perfectly fit them for the service, outherwise they will reather clog than further the objects in view; on this principle I am well pleased that you have not admitted or encouraged the young gentlemen you mention, we must set our faces against all such applications and get rid of them on the best terms we can. They will not answer our purposes: if a good hunter or two could be conditionally engaged I would think them an acquisition, they must however understand that they will not be employed for the purposes of hunting exclusively but must bear a portion of the labour in common with the party.

Sometime in the month of February last a young man by the name of John Conner residing among the Delleware Indians on White River offered himself, by letter, to accompany me in the capacity of Interpreter; I wrote him in answer accepting his services and giving him some instructions relative to the points at which I wished him to join me as also to engage one or two indian hunters for the service— of this letter I forwarded triplicates by different routs but have never received an answer: I am personally acquainted with this man and think that we could not get a person better qualifyed in every respect than he is, and that it will be advisable to spare no pains to get him. If you can not learn that Conner has gone on to Massac Kaskaskais or Illinois, (which are the places I appointed for his joining me) I think it will be best for you to hire a man to go to the Delleware Town and enquire after him, you may offer him three hundred dollars a year and find him provisions and clothing. Should he be at the Deleware town and be willing to engage on these terms he had better com on immidiately and join us at Louisville. He is a trader among the Indians and I think he told me he lived on White river at the nearest Dellaware town to Fort Hamilton and distant from that place about 24 miles.

The session of Louisiana is now no s[ecret]; on the 14th of July the President recieved the treaty from Paris, by which France has ceded to the U. States, Louisiana according to the bounds to which she had a wright. Price 11¼ Millions of dollars, besides paying certan debts of

France to our Citizens which will be from one to four millions; the western people may now estimate the value of their possessions.

I have been detained much longer than I expected but shall be with you by the last of this month. Your sincere friend & Obt. Servt.

MERIWETHER LEWIS

[*In margin:*] Note—write & direct to me at Cincinnatti.

ALS, RC (MoSHi). Addressed. Reply is No. 82.

81. Henry Dearborn to Jefferson

Sir   Washington August 3d. 1803

I have the honour of enclosing a letter from Capt. Lewis which came open to me, I have given permission to Lt. Hook to accompany Capt. Lewis. With respectfull consideration, I am Sr Your Huml Servt,

H. DEARBORN

P.S. Your letter relative to Mr. Dupont has been duly recd. & attended to.

ALS, RC (DLC). Endorsed; received 5 Aug. 1803. In his reply, Jefferson wrote from Monticello 13 Aug. that "William Clarke accepts with great glee the office of going with Capt. Lewis up the Missouri" (DLC). Dearborn replied 28 Aug.: "Mr. W. Clark's having consented to accompany Capt. Lewis, is highly interesting, it adds very much to the ballance of chances in favour of ultimate success" (DLC).

82. Clark to Lewis

Dr. Lewis   Louisville August 21st 1803.

Yours of the 3d instant from <*Pittsburgh*> I received by yesterdays Mail. Am happy to find you are at Pittsburgh and that all the articles furnished yr. outfit have arrived at that place. The low water will retard your progress. If the water does not rise by the time you are ready to set out, the sholes & dificuelty in River will retard your progress greatly but I flatter my self the rains have been general at least as high as Pittsburgh and if so you must certainly have a rise of water from the smaller rivers as you Decend.

The young men that I have engaged or rather promised to take on this experdition are (four &c.) the best woodsmen & Hunters, of young men in this part of the Countrey, I have had many aplications from stout likely fellows but have refused to retain some & put others off with a promis of giveing "an answer after I see or hered from you." [1] A judicious choice of our party is of the greatest importance to the success of this vast enterprise, and as the best men may [be] got we should be much in our own [. . .] to take indifferent. I do not know exactly the prices allowed to hands have observed to those who wishes to ingage that the pay cloths & rations would exceed 10$ pr. month.

I <have never heard of a> Mr. J. Conner <being> residing at the <Delleware Town on White river> I have made some enquiry of a Boat just arrived <if such a man is at [. . .]> Masac for Mr. J. Conner (the man you mentioned), without hereing of him. I shall waite a fiew day for a party to come from Illinois to enquire if Conner is in that Country, in the time send out to a Dellaway Camp 15 or 20 miles from this place to make some for him, and if I do not here of his setting out to meet you at some one of those points you directed him to, I shall send a man to the Town on White river with a letter to him. I know one or two Dellaways prime hunters which might be got to go any other rout but doubt very much if they would go that, as this nation is going to war against the <Houzages> [. . .] or the [. . .]. I do not think we shall find much dificuelty in precureing the best Interpreters at St. Louey or Kohokoha as also prime water men if they should be necessary.

I am happy to here of the Session of Louisiana to the united States, this is an inestimable treasure to the Western People, who appear to feel its value. I shall write you next post &c.

W. C.

AL, SC (MoSHi). Reply is No. 89.
1. It is now possible to identify the "nine young men from Kentucky" who are mentioned in BIDDLE as the earliest recruits for the expedition. In the financial records (No. 277) appear the names of nine men, in one group, who received enlistment bounties in 1803. No other soldier members of the expedition would have had occasion to receive bounties in that year. The nine men must be those who were enlisted by Lewis and Clark at the Falls of the Ohio. Their names: Charles Floyd, Nathaniel Pryor, William Bratton, John Colter, Reuben Field, Joseph Field, George Gibson, George Shannon, and John Shields. In a note with No. 89 I explain that Shannon and Colter may already have been with Lewis when he reached the Falls.

83. Clark to John Conner

Sir   Falls Ohio [26 August 1803]
Some time in the month of February last you offered your self by letter to accompany Capt. Meriwether Lewis on an N. Western ex-

perdition <up the Mississippi &c.> in the capicity of an Interpreter;
and informed him that you resided among the Delleware Indians on
White River. Capt. Lewis wrote you in answer two letters & sent them
different routs accepting of yours services and in his letter gave instructions relative to the points at which he wished you to join him &c.
He has never received an answer from you on the subject, nor heard
of your being at the pointes at which he wished you to join him. I am
(one [of] the official characters for the Enterprise) equally anxious with
Capt. Lewis that you should become one of our party & in the event
of your <agreeing to> accompany[ing] us as an Interptr. we will
give you, 300$ a year and find you provisions & clothing. Should you
be willing to engage on those terms you had best come on emmediately
& join us at this place. Capt. Floyd [1] the gentlemen who will hand
you this letter has promised to enquire particularly after you. He is a
Gentlemen of Great integrity in whome you may put the most compleat Confidence. Yrs.

26th Augt. 1803   W. C.

AL, SC (MoSHi).
1. Perhaps Capt. Davis Floyd, who lived in Clarksville, Indiana Territory,
where he was a falls pilot and mail contractor. He later became a judge
and a commissioner to adjust land claims in Florida (HARRISON, 1:205n).
A less likely possibility is Capt. Charles Floyd (c.1753–1828), who had
soldiered with George Rogers Clark and was the father of Charles Floyd,
a member of the expedition.

84. Moses Hooke to William Linnard

Sir   Pittsburg Sept. 2nd 1803
    Your favors of the 23 & 26th Insts. with their encolsures have been
duly receved. Enclosed you have my receipts for three hundred
Dollars. I regrett very much that it was not in your power to send me a
larger supply, as my situation is very disagreeable, indeed I have once
been [?] I have been oblidged to use my own money and extend my
credit much further than I would have wished. Capt. Lewis embarked
yesterday;[1] but the river's so very low that I am fearfull he will
not be able to prossecute his voyge untill it rises, notwithstanding he
took the precaution to send two Waggon loads of his goods by land
to Wheelin. These Waggons I shall have to pay. I have also receiv'd
orders from the secretary of War to purchase several articles for the
garrison of St. Vincennes; but I cannot think of contracting new
debts, untill the present are paid. I am very respectfully Sir Your obt.
servt.

                                                       Ms. HOOKE

ALS, RC (DNA, RG 92, Box 560A). Addressed; endorsed.

1. Here Hooke seems to say that Lewis left Pittsburgh on 1 Sept. Lewis dates his first journal entry 30 Aug. (LEWIS & ORDWAY, 31), but that date appears to be an error for 31 Aug., the departure date he later reports to Jefferson in No. 86 and to Clark in No. 89.

85. John Ordway to Stephen Ordway

Sir,   Kaskaskias Indiana Territory 5 Sept. 1803.

Silence on your part and a desire to fulfill my engagement to you together with the call of duty and the promptitude of inclination induces me once more to Solicit you to inform me your reasons for your negligence in writing to me. Are you among the living or have you taken your departure for that "bourne from whence no traveller returns? Or have you never received any letters from me? For I have written time & again & weekly have I visited the Post Office but to my extreme mortification not a Syllable can I hear that breathes intelligence relative to any of my friends. Separated at least 1800 miles from you; the only consolation I have had Since I have been at this place is afforded me by a company of Troops from Portsmouth New hampshire with some of whoom I haveing been previously acquainted —their arrival gave fresh ardor to my desponding Spirits. In May 1802 I received a letter from Betsey Crosby; She informed me that my friends & relitives were well also that she was about offering hirself a Sacrifice at the Shrine of Hymen which information I wish to have corroborated. With respect to the flying report of a matrimonial engagement with Miss Nevens I have nothing further to add than that I positively deny the existence of even the Shadow of Such an engagement it having been an absolute Calumniatory falsehood; not that I wish Betsey to loose an oppertunity of enjoying connubial felicity by waiting for my return; but the probability is, that if She remains in a State of celibacy till my return I may perhaps join hands with hir yet. Please to give hir my Compliments & the rest of the family also, aspecialy to Jefrey. Give my love to my Parents & brethren & Compliments to all my acquaintances—I enjoy an uninterrupted State of health & retain my usual Spirits with an unusual degree of contentment & vivacity. I would particularly address a few lines to my mother for whoom I entertain the Most profound Veneration both respecting hir Solicitous & tender care of me & hir genuine advice to me which She may rest assured has been & will be Strictly attended to. I wish hir to give hirself no uneasiness on my account; as I have nothing to fear while I enjoy the common blessings of Divine Providence.

I would not have hir place too much dependence on Seeing me so soon as I have written for fear of accidence but if my life is Spared I Shall certainly Return the Same Season that I am discharged. Do not fail of taking pains to Send letters every oppertunity. Adieu. With every Sentiment of respectful esteem & affection I am realy Yours,

JOHN ORDWAY Searj in
Russell Bissells Compy 1st Regt.

P.S. Please to direct your letters to this place & I Shall be likely to get them. This is a very old Town with about 200 houses in it and the ruins of many more. We lie on the hill in Site of the Town within a quarter of a mile, and we have built a Garrison hear and will be likely to Stay here till my time will expire and I expect to receive a number of letters from you while I lie here &c. Adieu.

JOHN ORDWAY Seajt.

Transcript (OrHi); original not located. Addressed, "Mr. Stephen Ordway Hebron State of New Hampshire" with the added notation, "To be left at the P. Office in Concord N.H." Postmarked at Kaskaskia 23 Sept. 1803 and forwarded from Concord 2 Nov. 1803. The OrHi transcript was made about 1900 for Eva Emery DYE, who was writing a fictionalized account of the expedition for inclusion in her *The conquest* (Chicago, 1902). John Ordway was a member of the expedition whose name will appear throughout this volume; Stephen was his brother. I make no attempt to identify the other persons named in the letter.

86. Lewis to Jefferson

Dear Sir, Wheeling, September 8th 1803.

It was not untill 7 O'Clock on the morning of the 31st Ultmo. that my boat was completed, she was instantly loaded, and at 10. A.M. on the same day I left Pittsburgh, where I had been moste shamefully detained by the unpardonable negligence of my boat-builder. On my arrival at Pittsburgh, my calculation was that the boat would be in readiness by the 5th of August; this term however elapsed and the boat so far from being finished was only partially planked on one side. In this situation I had determined to abandon the boat, and to purchase two or three perogues and descend the river in them, and depend on purchasing a boat as I descended, there being none to be had at Pittsburgh; from this resolution I was dissuaded first by the representations of the best informed merchants at that place who assured me that the chances were much against my being able to procure a boat below; and secondly by the positive assureances given me by the boat-builder that she should be ready on the last of the

[121]

then ensuing week, (the 13th): however a few days after, according to his usual custom he got drunk, quarrelled with his workmen, and several of them left him, nor could they be prevailed on to return: I threatened him with the penalty of his contract, and exacted a promise of greater sobriety in future which, he took care to perform with as little good faith, as he had his previous promises with regard to the boat, continuing to be constantly either drunk or sick. I spent most of my time with the workmen, alternately presuading and threatening, but neither threats, presuasion or any other means which I could devise were sufficient to procure the completion of the work sooner than the 31st of August; by which time the water was so low that those who pretended to be acquainted with the navigation of the river declared it impracticable to descend it; however in conformity to my previous determineation I set out, having taken the precaution to send a part of my baggage by a waggon to this place, and also to procure a good pilot. My days journey have averaged about 12 miles, but in some instances, with every exertion I could make was unable to exceed 4½ & 5 miles pr. day. This place is one hundred miles distant from Pittsburgh by way of the river and about sixty five by land.

When the Ohio is in it's present state there are many obstructions to it's navigation, formed by bars of small stones, which in some instances are intermixed with, and partially cover large qu[a]ntities of drift-wood; these bars frequently extend themselves entirely across the bed of the river, over many of them I found it impossible to pass even with my em[p]ty boat, without geting into the water and lifting her over by hand; over others my force was even inadequate to enable me to pass in this manner, and I found myself compelled to hire horses or oxen from the neighbouring farms and drag her over them; in this way I have passed as many as five of those bars, (or as they are here called *riffles*) in a day, and to unload as many or more times. The river is lower than it has ever been known by the oldest settler in this country. I shall leave this place tomorrow morning,[1] and loose no time in geting on.

I have been compelled to purchase a perogue at this place in order to transport the baggage which was sent by land from Pittsburgh, and also to lighten the boat as much as possible. On many bars the water in the deepest part dose not exceed six inches. I have the honour to be with the most perfect regard and sincere attatchment Your Obt. Servt.

MERIWETHER LEWIS. Capt.
1st U.S. Regt. Infty.

[122]

ALS, RC (DLC). Addressed; endorsed; received 25 Sept. 1803.

1. He left on schedule, as verified by Thomas Rodney (1744–1811), who was at Wheeling en route to Mississippi Territory where he was to serve as territorial judge and land commissioner: "Captn. Lewis left here on Friday last [9 Sept.]—he had some trouble in coming from Pittsburg down here by having to unload and to have his Barge drawn by Oxen over several riffs or shoals. Before he left here he made his boat as light as possible by putting his lading in several canoes. We heard of him after he had passed 16 miles below this, when he had passed several of the worst riffs or shoals below this place without their stopping him and probably he will soon reach better water—yet as our Boat is much lighter than his we expect to overtake him before he gits out of the Ohio" (to Jefferson, 12 Sept. 1803, DLC). The date, and indeed the hour, of Lewis's departure from Wheeling was made notable by another occurrence—his refusal to wait for a physician whom he had invited to join the expedition. William Ewing Patterson, son of the professor who had counseled Lewis at Philadelphia in April and May, had expressed a desire to go along. Lewis agreed to take him to the winter quarters on the Mississippi, there to await permission from Jefferson to add a doctor to the party. But there was one stipulation: "I consented provided he could get ready by three the next evening. He thought he could and instantly set about it. . . ." But Patterson failed to meet the deadline and Lewis left Wheeling without him. "The Dr.," he wrote, "could not get ready" (LEWIS & ORDWAY, 39–40).

87. Clark to Lewis

Dr. Lewis   Near Louisville 11th Sept. 1803

I have not had the pleasure of receiving a letter from you since the one dated the 3rd of last month. Have heard of you as late as the 23rd by Mr. Campbell [1] who saw your Boat at Pittsburgh not quite Complete. Agreeable to your wish I sent an express to the Dellaware Towns on White River who has just returned. Connor has a verry large assortment of goods on hand and cant accompany us, he writes me that your letter to him of last Summer did not come to him untill the 17 July & you informed him that you would set out the 10 of June <he therefore Concluded you> the time was too short for him to arrange his business & join you." He Says that if he had "nothing to do at the prest. he would not oblege himself for the sum I offered him (300) pr. & should not think himself two much recompensed for 5000$ even if he was able to leave his home. As this man does not speake any of the languages to the Weste of the Mississippi, I do not think the falur in getting him is verry meterial. I still have apliciattions from young men to accompany us. Yrs. &c.

[123]

AL, SC (MoSHi). A draft written on the back of Clark's draft of 21 Aug. 1803 (No. 82) to Lewis. Reply is No. 89.

1. This cannot have been Lt. John Campbell, who would later be stationed in St. Louis, for he was on recruiting duty in Nashville. It may have been the man of the same name who arrived in St. Louis with White Matlack, from Philadelphia, with a stock of general merchandise "soon after the American occupation" (LEWIS (3), 362). Or it may have been the Scotch-Irish trader who was on the upper Mississippi as early as 1792, was met by Zebulon Pike in 1805, and was an Indian agent at Prairie du Chien until killed in a duel.

88. Lewis to Jefferson

On board my boat opposite Marietta

Dear Sir,   September 13th 1803.

I arrived here at 7. P.M. and shall pursue my journey early to-morrow. This place is one hundred miles distant from Wheeling, from whence in descending the water is reather more abundant than it is between that place and Pittsburgh, insomuch that I have been enabled to get on without the necessity employing oxen or horses to drag my boat over the ripples except in two instances; tho' I was obliged to cut a passage through four or five bars, and by that means past them: this last operation is much more readily performed than you would imagin; the gravel of which many of these bars are formed, being small and lying in a loose state is readily removed with a spade, or even with a wooden shovel and when set in motion the current drives it a considerable distance before it subsides or again settles at the bottom; in this manner I have cut a passage for my boat of 50 yards in length in the course of an hour; this method however is im-practicable when driftwood or clay in any quantity is intermixed with the gravel; in such cases Horses or oxen are the last resort: I find them the most efficient sailors in the present state of the naviga-tion of this river, altho' they may be considered somewhat clumsey. I have the honour to be with much respect Your Obt. Servt.

MERIWETHER LEWIS. Capt.

1st U.S. Regt. Infty.

ALS, RC (DLC). Endorsed; received 30 Sept. 1803.

89. Lewis to Clark

Dear Clark,   Cincinnati Sept. 28th 1803.

After the most tedious and laborious passage from Pittsburgh I have at length reached this place; it was not untill the 31st of August that I was enabled to take my departure from that place owing to the unpardonable negligence and inattention of the boat-builders who, unfortunately for me, were a set of most incorrigible drunkards, and with whom, neither threats, intreaties nor any other mode of treatment which I could devise had any effect; as an instance of their tardyness it may serfice to mention that they were twleve days in preparing my poles and oars.

I here had the pleasure of recieving yours of the 21st of August & the 11th of Septr. I am much pleased with the measures you have taken relative to the engaging the men you mention, as men of that discription only will answer our purposes; I scarcely suppose that such as you have conceived not fully qualifyed for this service will by any means meet my approbation; your ideas in the subject of a judicious scelection of our party perfectly comport with my own. I have two young men with me whom I have taken on trial and have not yet engaged them, but conditionally only, tho' I think they will answer tolerably well;[1] there are a party of soldiers, 6 or 8 in number, now at Massac waiting my arrival, they were scelected from the troops in the State of Tennessee by Majr. MacRea, perhaps most of these will answer; I am also authorized to scelect by voluntary engagement any men from the Company of Capts. Rl. and Dl. Bissel's and Stoddart's now occupying the posts of Massac & Kaskaskias; from these I think we shall be enabled to form our party without much difficulty; 4 or five french water-men I concieve will be esscential, this we can do I presume very readily at St. Louis.

The amount of the monthly compensation (or 10$) which you have mention to the men is precisely what I have calculated on; I shall cloth and subsist the men I have with me, these will of course form a proper charge against the U States and in addition to the monthly wages of a private will as estimated by the Secretary of War and myself amount to reather more than 10$ pr. month.

I do not much regret the loss of Mr. Connor for several reasons which I shall mention to you when we meet; he has decieved me very much.

It is probable before the reciept of this letter that I shall be with you; I shall leave this the day after tomorrow. Adieu and believe me your very sincere friend and associate,

MERIWETHER LEWIS.

ALS, RC (MoSHi). Addressed.

1. Perhaps John Colter (d. 1810) and George Shannon (1785–1836). DYE, 147, says that Shannon joined at Pittsburgh, and REID & GANNON, 57n, say that Colter joined at Limestone, now Maysville, Ky. If Shannon did not

join at Pittsburgh, at least he probably had joined by the time Lewis left Cincinnati. His family had been living in Pennsylvania at the time of his birth, but had moved to Belmont County, Ohio, in 1800 (BIOG. DIR.). Lewis's party experienced many changes in personnel on the trip from Pittsburgh to Cincinnati. Lewis left Pittsburgh with a party of eleven hands, including the seven soldiers of Lt. Murray, a pilot, and three young men on trial, "they having proposed to go with me throughout the voyage" (LEWIS & ORDWAY, 31). The pilot was T. Moore, who was paid $70 to guide Lewis to the Falls of the Ohio (DNA, RG 217, Records of the Army Accounting Office, Journal L, p. 5625). At McIntosh, Lewis discharged one of the hands, and at Georgetown hired another named Wilkinson to go with him as far as Wheeling. At Wheeling he bought a pirogue and hired Samuel Montgomery to work her; he also hired a young man who had "come on board and agreed to work his passage." At Marietta he dismissed both Wilkinson and Montgomery, and took on another crew member. Five days later his journal entries skip to 11 Nov. and we lose account of his hirings and firings.

90. Lewis to Jefferson

Dear Sir,   Cincinnati, October 3rd 1803.

I reached this place on the 28th Ult.; it being necessary to take in a further supply of provisions here, and finding my men much fatiegued with the labour to which they have been subjected in descending the river, I determined to recruit them by giving them a short respite of a few days,[1] having now obtained the distance of five hundred miles. On the evening of the 1st inst. I again dispatched my boat with orders to meet me at the Big Bone lick,[2] to which place I shall pass by land, it being distant from hence only seventeen miles while by water it is fifty three, a distance that will require my boat in the present state of the water near three days to attain.

The late reserches of Dr. William Goforth[3] of this plase at that Lick has made it a place of more interesting enquiry than formerly, I shall therefore seize the present moment to visit it, and set out early tomorrow morning for that purpose.

Dr. Goforth in the begining of May last with a view to obtain a complete skeleton of the Mammoth, sunk a pitt 30 feet square and eleven feet in debth in a moist part of the Big Bone Lick, from which he obtained a large number of specimens of the bones of this anamal, tho' generally in a very imperfect and mutilated state; he also obtained from the same pitt several grinders of the anamal generally supposed to be an Elephant from their affinity to the teeth of that anamal, these last are very perfect: a part of this collection of bones the Dr. has in his possession at this place and has been so obliging as to favour me with an examinetion of them; the other part of the Dr.'s collection is yet at the Lick, these he informs me are much more perfect than those he shewed me, particularly the *upper portion of a head,* and some other specimens which had been obtained from a small pitt, sunk in a dryer part of the Lick by a young man to whom, in his absence he had confided the prosecution of his researches; among these specimens the Dr. also mentioned a tusk of an immence size, the dementions of which he could not furnish me with, not having yet seen it, but from the information of his assistant, states it's weight at 180 lbs.; this tusk is said to be in a good state of preservation. The Dr. informed me that he had been interdicted by the Agent of Mr. David Ross[4] of Virginia, (the proprietor of the Lick) from removing these bones, as he was also from the further prosecution of his researches; he is much chagrined at this occurrence, and seems very anxious that some measures should be taken by which to induce Mr. Ross to suffer him to prosecute his enquiries. The Doctr. presented me with two handsome specimens, the one a grinder of the Elaphant, the other, that of the Mammoth, the former weighs ten and ½ pounds, the latter I have not weighed, from the circumstance of it's roots being attatched to a lump of clay, without seperating from which, it's weight could not be accurately ascertained; I concluded it would be better to forward it in it's present state, as the clay will not only guard this part of the tooth from injury in transporting it, but will at the same time furnish a good specimen of the earth of which the lick is formed. Dr. Goforth was so good as to grant me his permission to take from those bones now at the Lick the large tusk before noticed, and any other bones that are to be found among his collection at that place: Capt. Findley who accompanys me to the Lick says he is well acquainted with the Agent of Mr. Ross, and thinks that he can obtain his permission also for the same purpose; should I succeed you may expect to recieve through Mr. Trist,[5] this large tusk together with the two grinders before mentioned, and such other specimines as I may be enabled to procure, and which, I may think worthy your acceptance.[6]

All the bones, which I observed in the possession of Dr. Goforth appear to be those of the Mammoth, accept only the Elephant-like grin[d]ers; the most remarkable among them was a portion of the lower or larger part of a tusk; measuring one foot ten inches in circumpherence and five feet eight inches in length, the Dr. informed me when he first obtained it, it was upwards of six feet in length and weighed one hundred pounds; the greates[t] circumpherence of the tusks of Mr. Peale's skeleton I believe is not more than one foot six

½ inches. As the anatomy of the Mammoth has already been so well ascertained by the skeleton in the possession of Mr. Peal (the upper portion of the head excepted) I confined my enquiries mearly to a search for this part of the skeleton, and for such specimens of the tusks as would enable me to deside a question which appears not yet fully to have been satisfyed (viz) Whether the flated[?] or sythe-shaped tusks so frequently found in the same bed with the acknowledged tusks of the Mammoth, are the tusks of that anamal, or a different one?

With regard to the fi[r]st of these enquiries I was unsuccessfull, finding only one mutilated specimen of the upper portion of the head, the frontal bone of which had entirely decayed; I was therefore unable to form any just idea of it's shape; as to the second, I was more fortunate, obtaining many specimens of both the acknowledged Mammoth tusks, as well as those of the flat tusks, both in a sound and an imperfect state; these I compared with attention; but before I proceed to express an opinion with respect to the homogeniallogy of these tusks I will give a short description of those specimens, in order Sir, that you may from thence draw your own inferences, and make your own deduction.

The tusks of the Mammoth were conical, much Curved, and also spiral or twisted; the fragments of whatever portion of the tusk were homologus to the same part of a complete tusk; when by decay the end of a section of any large part of the tusk was observed, the ends of the broken lateral stratas of the lamina, formed a number of circular rings, each imbracing and inclosing the other from the center to the circumpherence of the tusk, these rings however, were of un-equal thickness; when perfe[c]t the lamina assumes a yellowish white or creem colour, in it's decayed state it resembles white chalk, both in colour and consistance (see No. 2. specn. inclosed); the surface of the tusk sometimes assumes partially a black colour, which from it's re-sembleance to the Buffaloe horn might on a slite examineation be taken for a similar substance, but on a more minute investigation it appears to be ivory, or the common lamina of the tusk, which, has acquired that colour from some cause, most probably, from the properties of the clay in which they had been so long deposited; this black Ivory (No. 2) is rarely more than two lines in thickness, gradually loosing it's hue inwards, untill it becomes the common colour of the tusk.

The flat or sythe-like tusks assumed a great variety of figures, tho' uniformly curved; one was flat on both sides near the large end of the tusk, where it was connected with the head; this was rendered con-spicuous from the conic concavity common to this part as well of the Mammoth, as these tusks at the larger end; and so much was it flated, that this end of the tusk was left in a forked shape, while the smaller end assumed the curved, and connic shape, and was also spiral, as is that of the Mammoth: several were flated unequally on both sides near the small extremity of the tusk, the larger end being conical, curved, and spiral; while others were flat on one side only throughout the whole extent of the tusk: the lamina of these tusks whether perfect, decayed, or assuming the horn-like appearance, is the same substance precisely of the Mammoth tusk: in every instance where the tusk is flatened, the circular rings of lamina are perfect when the diameter of those rings do not exceed the thickness of the tusk, which last I found unequal in the different specimens; and when the rings of lamina exceed the thickness of the tusk they are broken, but still we find the corrisponding parts of these broken rings, attatched to either side of the perfect one, and succeeding each other throughout the whole width of the tusk; thus presenting the exact figure of the Mammoth's tusk reduced to a flat surface on both sides by being grownd down.

I also observed that several bones that were in a good state of preservation, appeared to have been woarn away in the same manner, or from the same cause which had flattened the tusks, particularly a large grinder of the Mammoth which struck my attention, it was unconnected with the jaw bone; one third of the volume of this tooth seemed to have been woarn away, as if reduced on one side by being grown down to a plane surface; the enamel of the fractured edge appeared to have given way equally with the bone of the tooth and presented a smooth surface; no part of this tooth shewed any sharp fracture which, might induce a belief that it was reduced to it's p[r]esent shape by a violent or sudden stroke.

Finding that the upper part of a tusk was flattened, which shape it could not have acquired during the existence of the living anamal, it being that part of the tusk which by bone or cartilage must have been united with the head; that in every case where the same specimen united both the character of the Mammoth and flat tusk, that portion resembleing the Mammoth tusk was in all respects it's prototipe; that the tusk of the Mammoth is well defined, and that it's characteristics strongly mark it; that the lamina of both the flat and the conic tusks, are invariably the same in similar states of preservation; and that in all instances where the tusk is flattened the lateral lamina shews evedent marks of violence; I can therefore have no remaining doubt of these flat or sythe-like tusks being *the tusks of the Mammoth;* and from the appearance of the flatten[ed] grinder of the Mammoth before noticed, I am strongly disposed to believe that these flat tusks of the

[129]

Mammoth have acquired that shape in consequence of the sand and gravel passing over them for a great length of time caused by a runing stream or agitated water.

The Elephants teeth which I saw in the possession of Dr. Goforth weigh from four to eleven pounds, and appear to me precisely to resemble a specimen of these teeth which, I saw in the possession of Dr. Wister of Philadelphia; and which if my recollection serves me Dr. Wister informed me was found in S. Carolina: the Dr. has since assured me, that from a comparison of this specimen with the plates representing the teeth of the Asiatic Elepha[n]t contained in the late Vols. of the British philosophical transactions, that he is perfectly convinced that it is the tooth of the Asiatic Elephant or an anamal very much resembleing it. Relative to these teeth it may not be un-worthy of remark, that so far as I have been able to inform myself, they are never found adjacent to the bones of any anamal of their comparitive size, except those of the Mammoth; or such as from their affinity to the anatomy of that anamal, have always been admitted to be the bones of the Mammoth. These teeth are never found attatched to the bones of the jaw; and notwithstanding the high state of preservation in which those Elephant's teeth are found, that no other pa[r]t of it's fraim should yet have been discovered in America. From the shape and termination of both extremities of these grinders they each appear to have completely filled it's respective jaw bone.

Not any of the bones or tusks which I saw were petrifyed, either preserving their primitive states of bone or ivory; or when decayed, the former desolving into earth intermixed with scales of the header [harder] or more indissoluble parts of the bone, while the latter assumed the appearance of pure white chalk.

I would thank you for forward[ing] me some of the Vaxcine matter, as I have reason to believe from several experiments made with what I have, that it has lost it's virtue.

Conner, the interpretter I had calculated on engaging, has declined; however I do not feel much disappointment at this occurrence, being well assured that a suitable person of that discription can be procured at St. Louis.

So soon Sir, as you deem it expedient to promulge the late treaty, between the United States and France I would be much obliged by your directing an official copy of it to be furnished me, as I think it probable that the present inhabitants of Louisiana, from such an evidence of their having become the Citizens of the United States, would feel it their interest and would more readily yeald any informa-tion of which, they may be possessed relative to the country than they would be disposed to do, while there is any doubt remaining on that subject.

As this Session of Congress has commenced earlyer than usual, and as from a variety of incidental circumstances my progress has been unexpectedly delayed, and feeling as I do in the most anxious manner a wish to keep them in a good humour on the subject of the expedicion in which I am engaged, I have concluded to make a tour this winter on horseback of some hundred miles through the most interesting portion of the country adjoining my winter establishment; perhaps it may be up the Canceze River and towards Santafee, at all events it will bee on the South side of the Missouri. Should I find that Mr. Clark can with propiety also leave the party, I will prevail on him also to undertake a similar excurtion through some other portion of the country: by this means I hope and am pursuaded that by the middle of February or 1st of March I shall be enabled to procure and forward to you such information relative to that Country, which, if it dose not produce a conviction of the utility of this project, will at least procure the further toleration of the expedition.

It will be better to forward all letters and papers for me in future to *Cahokia*.

The water still continues lower in the Ohio than it was ever known. I am with every sentiment of gratitude and respect Your Obt. Servt.

MERIWETHER LEWIS. Capt.

1st. U.S. Regt. Infty.

ALS, RC (DLC). Endorsed. The date of receipt in Jefferson's endorsement is 25 Oct., but in his index of letters it is 26 Oct. 1803.

1. He was still in Cincinnati the next day, when he wrote to Thomas Rodney, introducing Thomas H. Williams who was on his way to Mississippi Territory (4 Oct. 1803, PHC).

2. Big Bone Lick was a deposit of fossil remains in Boone County, southwest of present Covington, Ky., which so interested Jefferson that he later engaged William Clark to supervise an excavation there. In 1807, when Clark was en route to St. Louis to become superintendent of Indian affairs, he paused at the Lick, hired workmen, and obtained a number of specimens for Jefferson. See Clark's eleven-page report to Jefferson of 10 Nov. 1807 (DLC) discussing this operation, and also Jefferson to Lacépède, 14 July 1808 (DLC). SIMPSON discusses the Big Bone Lick, Lewis and Clark, and early paleontology in general. Samuel George Morton, an early student of invertebrate fossils, reported that Lewis and Clark found "Baculites, Gryphaea and other marl fossils at the Great Bend of the Missouri River . . ." (MORTON, 25).

3. Goforth, a Cincinnati physician, had written Gen. Thomas Proctor in Philadelphia, 18 June 1803, revealing his discovery of mammoth remains and inquiring about the likelihood of his successfully exhibiting such objects in the U.S. or Europe. "I have the upper part of the head

and the under Jaws of the large Animal I have a large number of teeth from 19 or 20 pounds weight down to 4 or 5. One thigh bone weighing 31 pounds some ribs intire some broken the whole of the back bones one horn weighing about 100 pounds about twenty one Inches in Circumference & one horn about 5 feet long weighing 21 pounds and one other about seven feet long" (DLC). Proctor took the matter to Philadelphia artist and museum curator Charles Willson Peale (1741–1827), who had founded the Philadelphia Museum and was somewhat in competition with Goforth for the possession and display of fossil remains. Peale wrote of the matter rather delicately to Jefferson (18 July 1803, DLC), explaining that he already had a mammoth on display in his own museum, and declining to comment on Goforth's potential success. "I marval what are the teeth which he says weighs 19 or 20 pounds, can they be grinders[?]. The largest I have seen belongs to Doctr. Wistar, its weight 10 pounds."

4. David Ross (d. 1817), of Richmond, Va., was a large-scale speculator in lands of Kentucky and Ohio. He was representative from Fluvanna County in the Virginia House of Delegates for the sessions of 1782–83.

5. Hore Browse Trist (d. 1804) was at this time collector of revenue at Fort Adams on the lower Mississippi. On 11 Nov. he became collector for the Mississippi district, and by an act of 24 Feb. 1804 New Orleans became a part of this district and its sole port (TERR. PAPERS, 9:100n). Browse died while serving in New Orleans, and was succeeded by his deputy, William Brown.

6. The specimens went astray at Natchez and apparently were lost. Jefferson wrote to Gideon Fitz at Opelousas, La., 17 Sept. 1804, in reply to Fitz's message that some of the bones were recoverable and that he would undertake the task of saving them. "You will render me a very acceptable service if you will be so good as to do it, and send them to the care of Mr. Trist at N. Orleans to be forwarded to me to the care of Jefferson & Gibson in Richmond as they are intended to be brought to this place [Monticello]" (DLC). Fitz acknowledged the request from Washington, Mississippi Territory, 19 Oct. 1804, saying that he would proceed with the assignment but doubted if many could be recovered, as "it is said that some of them have been worked-up, and were very beautiful ivory" (DLC). I have found no record of Fitz's search, but the fate of the specimens is mentioned by Thomas Rodney in a letter of [?] Feb. 1806 to Peale: "The bones Collected by Capt. Lewis came down the River to Natchez the following Spring—1804. and unhappily the boat that brought them sunk at the Landing, and I understood that Most of them were lost, but one box being Saved, among them was a jaw bone and grinder of the wild Boar of our Country—but there being no person to take care of these Curiosities the box was thrown on the Shore, & broken open, by the Tennessee Militia, then at Natchez" (PPAmP). In an earlier draft of the letter, Rodney says that when he was going down the Mississippi in 1803 he "walked out six miles to the Big Bone Lick but Captn. Lewis had been there a little before me, on his way to the Missouri, and had taken off most of the bones that had been found there. . . ."

91. Caspar Wistar to Jefferson

Dear Sir   [6 October 1803]

Since my last, which inclosed a letter to Major Lewis, I have been informed that Monsieur Pieroux, while Commandant near the mouth of the Missouri, had sent a party of Indians up the river on a voyage of discovery, & that they returned after an absence of two years—this was communicated to me by Col: OHara[1] of Pittsburgh who saw Pieroux at Kaskaskias during the Revolution War. I believe that Pieroux is still in Louisiana, & that he is Proprietor of a Saline near St. Genevieve. I avail myself of this opportunity to state to the Major as a subject for enquiry, the trees on the Bark of which the Indians on the West Coast are said to subsist in times of scarcity. I have heard from persons who have been on that coast, that the natives are frequently forced to subsist in this way during winter—perhaps the information may be useful to the first settlers of that Country.

Here perhaps I ought to conclude, but I cannot refrain from mentioning to you a subject which has frequently occurred to me when thinking on the happy course of the events which relate to Louisiana. The seaport at the Mouth of the Missisippi will probably be a town of immense size & importance, but the situation of New Orleans seems every way unfit for such a town. If a place communicating more directly with the Sea & near the River could be found, (resembling the situation of Alexandria with respect to the Nile) would it not be proper to fix a town there—if such a thing is proper & practicable, ought it not to be attempted soon before N. Orleans increases so much as to prevent such a measure. I am not without apprehension that you will laugh at the scheme as impracticable, but I feel confident that your good nature will forgive the liberty I am taking.

Mr. Patterson has lately been informed by his Son that Major Lewis wished him to join the expedition as assistant Surgeon, & in consequence requested me to inform you what I knew of his qualifications. I therefore beg leave to say that he attended two courses of the Anatomical Lectures with diligence & assiduity, & appeared to devote himself with great industry to the study of Medicine, under the care of Dr. Church[2] a very respectable young Physician of this City, whose practice being very extensive among the poor, must have afforded him a great opportunity of improvement. He also appeared very correct & proper in his habits of Life.

To this miscellaneous letter I will only add the assurance of the sincere & affectionate regard of your friend & servant,

C. WISTAR JUNR.

Philada. Oct. 6. 1803.

[133]

My sister Mrs. Bache[3] is near the City, & in good health, having lately exhibited to us a second Daughter.

ALS, RC (DLC). Received 9 Oct. 1803 according to Jefferson's index of letters.

1. James O'Hara (d. 1819), quartermaster general of the army from 1792 to 1796 and later the business partner of Maj. Isaac Craig in Pittsburgh.

2. Dr. John Church, practicing at 266 South Second Street, Philadelphia.

3. Dr. William F. Bache (1773–1818), Benjamin Franklin's grandson, had arrived in New Orleans in March 1803—apparently to establish a seamen's hospital (Bache to Jefferson, 29 March 1803, DLC). In April 1804, Jefferson appointed him surveyor and inspector of the port of Philadelphia. He was married to Dr. Wistar's sister Catharine.

92. Tarleton Bates to Frederick Bates

Dear Frederick,   Pittsburg October 13 1803

Yours of the 22. Aug. & 21 Sep. have been received, the latter yesterday.

Conner never had in his offer the situation of *Companion* and Guide to Cap. Lewis. On the contrary Cap. Clark of Louisville goes in the former capacity, had the first offer, and the only one except to Hook conditionally, and the high preference. As to the guide, Mr. Lewis *had* engaged an indian interpreter from the interior of your territory, or the Ohio state, whose name I do not know. It may be Conner.

.   .   .   .

With esteem & regard—

TARLETON BATES.

ALS, RC (MoSHi). Addressed, "Frederic Bates Post-Master Detroit." Tarleton's brother Frederick (1777–1825) would become secretary of the Territory of Louisiana in 1807, and serve as acting governor in Lewis's absence. The animosity that developed between him and Lewis is not brought out in these letters, but can be traced in his published papers (BATES), his letterbooks and manuscripts (MoSHi), and in TERR. PAPERS, vol. 14. See also BAKELESS, 395–409, 426–27. To the unfruitful speculation about the causes of Bates's antagonism toward Lewis, I add one more crumb of evidence. A letter of 4 May [1801] from Thomas F. Bates to his son Frederick contains this statement: "A postscript to your letter, made by Tarleton 20th March, informs that a Capt. Lewis had received and accepted the appointment of private Secretary to the President, so that my golden dreams have been delusive" (MoSHi). This suggests that the elder Bates may have hoped that he or one of his sons might receive the appointment, a possible source of Frederick's resentment.

93. William Henry Harrison to Clark

My Dear Sir   Vincennes 13th Nov. 1803.

The map mentioned in your letter of the 5th Instant had been taken from me by Mr. Jones[1] who claimed it as the property of Mr. Hay[2] of Cahokia but as it was still in the possession of Mr. Jones I have had it copied & now send it to you by the Post rider—whom I have been obliged to detain for that purpose. I hope it will arrive safe.[3]

Your offer to let me hear from you occasionally I accept with a great deal of pleasure—& I beg of you to let me Know from Cahokia whether I can do any thing for you in yr. absence.

The mail of last night brought us the information that the Senate had advised the ratification of the French Treaty 24. to 7. There were 8 of the opposition present but Dayton voted with the Majority.

Give my respects to Captn. Lewis & ask him to spend a few days with me on his return. I am your friend,

WILLM. H. HARRISON

ALS, RC (MoSHi). Addressed in another hand, "Captain William Clark or Captain Meriwether Lewis on their way up the Mississippi supposed to be at Cahokia"; endorsed, "Govr. Harrison has sent by the post rider a map for Captn. Clark which Dr. Fisher will be so obliging as to forward to Cahokia with this letter." A notation on the addressed side, in Clark's hand, reads: "100 rations Bread & Med. 1050 Whiskey. 1 Barrel extra." William Henry Harrison (1773–1841) was at this time governor of Indiana Territory. Dr. George Fisher was a Kaskaskia physician, appointed sheriff of Randolph County 1 Aug. 1800 (HARRISON, 1:253n). He was also the postmaster at Kaskaskia and had the mail contract for the route between Vincennes, Kaskaskia, and Cahokia (DNA, RG 28, Postmaster General's letterbooks, M:213).

1. John Rice Jones (1759–1824), a lawyer of Vincennes and Kaskaskia, postmaster at Vincennes, and later a supreme court judge in Missouri.

2. John Hay (1769–1843), trader, merchant, and postmaster at Cahokia. His connection with Lewis and Clark is clarified in some of the letters that follow.

3. The cartography of Lewis and Clark is a specialized study which requires more attention than is appropriate to this volume. I hope that Herman Friis, chief archivist of the Technical Records Division of the National Archives, will someday give the problem sound treatment. A few comments, however, are necessary here. Some past conclusions about maps carried by the explorers have been flawed by the failure of historians to identify handwriting. For example: During World War I, a bundle of maps turned up in the Office of Indian Affairs, in Washington, which had been associated with Clark's superintendency in St. Louis. Among them was a map of the Missouri, from its mouth to the Mandan country, which Miss Annie Heloise ABEL made the subject of an article in the *Geographical*

Review. She believed that the map was one produced by John Evans and sent to Lewis by Jefferson with his letter of 13 Jan. 1804 (No. 103). Miss Abel was puzzled by the fact that most of the locations on the map were written in both French and English. "Both the English and the French appear to be the work of one draftsman," she said (p. 339n). On the contrary, while the French labels are the work of an unknown hand, the English translations are unmistakably in the hand of William Clark. (Three other maps in the bundle have not previously been identified as Clark's, I believe, although reprinted as recently as 1942 in an excellent work by TUCKER. They are rather unimportant sketch maps dating from Clark's superintendency, during the War of 1812 and shortly after. Miss Tucker, in reprinting them as plates 25, 36, and 39, pointed out that they seem to be in the same hand but she did not recognize the hand as Clark's.) For positive evidence of the manner in which the "Indian Office" map passed to Lewis and Clark, we have only to look at a notation on the back of the map. Miss Abel quoted and reproduced in facsimile an address from the back of the map which reads: "For Captn. William Clark or Captn. Meriwether Lewis on a voyage up the Mississippi." The passage is in the hand of Harrison, and the wording invites comparison with the similar phrase that serves as the address of the letter above. The map mentioned here by Harrison is obviously the "Indian Office" map. It reached Lewis in time for him to write Jefferson in late December (No. 100) that he already had "a map of the Missouri river, from it's mouth to the Mandane nation. . . ." Not until two weeks later does Jefferson send him the Evans map (No. 103). For convincing argument that the map is a copy of an original by James Mackay, and that the so-called Evans map appears in the JOURNALS, vol. 8, as Nos. 5–11 and 13, see DILLER (1). For an indication that the Mackay map (of which there are several versions) is also related to the one published by Perrin du Lac in 1805, and that Mackay is the "ancien traiteur" said to have accompanied Perrin du Lac, see TEGGART. For an indication that the trader was Jean Baptiste Truteau, see TRUTEAU.

94. Jefferson to Lewis

Dear Sir   Washington Nov. 16. 1803.

I have not written to you since the 11th & 15th of July, since which yours of July 15. 22. 25. Sep. 8. 13. & Oct. 3. have been recieved.[1] The present has been long delayed by an expectation daily of getting the inclosed 'account of Louisiana' through the press.[2] The materials are received from different persons, of good authority. I inclose you also copies of the Treaties for Louisiana, the act for taking possession, a letter from Dr. Wistar, & some information collected by myself from Truteau's journal[3] in MS. all of which may be useful to you. The act for taking possession passes with only some small verbal variations from that inclosed, of no consequence. Orders went from hence, signed by the King of Spain & the first Consul of France, so as to arrive at Natchez yesterday evening, and we expect the delivery of the province at New Orleans will take place about the close of the ensuing week, say about the 25th inst. Govr. Claiborne[4] is appointed to execute the powers of Commandant & Intendant, until a regular government shall be organized here. At the moment of delivering over the posts in the vicinity of N. Orleans, orders will be dispatched from thence to those in Upper Louisiana to evacuate & deliver them immediately. You can judge better than I can when they may be expected to arrive at these posts, considering how much you have been detained by low waters, how late it will be before you can leave Cahokia, how little progress up the Missouri you can make before the freezing of the river; that your winter might be passed in gaining much information by making Cahokia or Kaskaskia your head quarters, & going to St. Louis & the other Spanish posts that your stores &c. would thereby be spared for the winter, as your men would draw their military rations, all danger of Spanish opposition avoided. We are strongly of opinion here that you had better not enter the Missouri till the spring. But as you have a view of all circumstances on the spot, we do not pretend to enjoin it, but leave it to your own judgment in which we have entire confidence. One thing however we are decided in: that you must not undertake the winter excursion which you propose in yours of Oct. 3. Such an excursion will be more dangerous than the main expedition up the Missouri, & would, by an accident to you, hazard our main object, which, since the acquisition of Louisiana, interests every body in the highest degree. The object of your mission is single, the direct water communication from sea to sea formed by the bed of the Missouri & perhaps the Oregon. By having Mr. Clarke with you we consider the expedition double manned, & therefore the less liable to failure, for which reason neither of you should be exposed to risques by going off of your line. I have proposed in conversation, & it seems generally to be assented to, that Congress shall appropriate 10. or 12.000 D. for exploring the principal waters of the Missisipi & Missouri. In that case I should send a party up the Red river to it's head, then to cross over to the head of the Arcansa, & come down that. A 2d party for the Pani & Padouca rivers, & a 3d perhaps for the Moingona & St. Peters. As the boundaries of interior Louisiana are the *high lands inclosing all the waters which run into the Missisipi or Missouri directly or indirectly,* with a greater breadth on the gulph of Mexico, it becomes interesting to fix with precision by celestial observations the longitude & latitude of the sources of these rivers, and furnishing points in the contour of our new limits.

[137]

This will be attempted distinctly from your mission, which we consider as of major importance, & therefore not to be delayed or hazarded by any episodes whatever.

The votes of both houses on ratifying & carrying the treaties into execution have been precisely party votes, except that Genl. Dayton[5] has separated from his friends on these questions & voted for the treaties. I will direct the Aurora & National Intelligencer to be forwarded to you for 6. months at Cahokia or Kaskaskia, on the presumption you will be there. Your friends & acquaintances here & in Albemarle are all well as far as I have heard: and I recollect no other small news worth communicating; present my friendly salutations to Mr. Clarke, & accept them affectionately yourself.

Th: Jefferson

[Enclosure]

Extracts from the Journal of M. Truteau, Agent for the Illinois trading company, residing at the village of Ricara, up the Missouri.

This company was confirmed in 1795. with the exclusive right for 10. years to trade with all the nations above the Poncas, as well to the South, and the West, as to the North of the Missouri with a premium of 3000. prs. [piastres?] for the discovery of the South Sea: and a gratification of 10.000 prs. which the King of Spain is to pay for the support of a milice. The company however have [. . .]. In the Missouri river there is depth sufficient to carry a frigate as far up as it is known. It has no cataracts, no portages. The winds on it are so violent that the periogues are sometimes obliged to lie by one, two, three, or four days, and sometimes take as long time to descend as to ascend the river. The Canadians employed in the trading voyages on it have 250." to 300." for 18. months. and take it often in goods, on which the merchant gains half. The soil of the Missouri is the most fertile in the Universe. The rivers falling into it are all navigable more or less from 50. or 100. to 200. or 300. leagues.

The Ricaras, are a branch of the Panis, residing up the Missouri, about 430. leagues from the Illinois. There are 2. villages of them, half a league apart, the one 800. yds. from the river, the other 100. yards. They are a mild people, having about 300. warriors. There is no timber on the Missouri for 50. leagues above or below them.

The Crow nation inhabit near the Rocky mountain.

The Sioux inhabit the Northern part of the Missisipi, and are hostile to the Ricaras, Mendanes, big-bellies and others. Others of them live on the river St. Pierre. They have from 30. to 60.000[?] men, and abound in fire-arms. They are the greatest beaver hunters; and could furnish more beavers than all the nations besides, and could bring them to a depot on the Missouri, rather than to St. Pierre, or any other place. Their beaver is worth the double of the Canadian for the fineness of it's fur and parchment;

The Chayennes, Panis Mahas, Mendannes, Big bellies are in the neighborhood of the Ricaras.

The Pados are 80. leagues from the Ricaras, South, on a branch of the river.

The Cayoguas, Caminabiches and Pitapahatos are to the South and S.W. of the Ricaras, on a branch of the Missouri. They have had no communication with the Whites. This river is wide but too shallow for a periogue.

The Grand Osages are from 7. to 800. men. They furnish 20.000 skins of the small deer, and take 14. to 15. M. pcs. de Mes[?]. [qu. whether these character *pcs de Mes.* mean *pieces de Marchandis* or *piastres de Mexique?* [6]

The Petits Osages are 250. to 300. men. Furnish 7. to 8000. fine deer skins and take 4. to 5. M pcs. des Mes.

The Kansas, 250 to 300. men. Furnish and take the same as the Petits Osages.

With the three last nations the hunt continues to Oct. Nov. and even the middle of Dec. The hunters then meet, fix their prices, which are a blanket of 2½ points for 6. 7. or 8. deerskins. In 2 days the whole are sold, and, if the ice did not hinder, the traders could be returned by Christmas, whereas they do not return till April or May. These nations are very certain of the arrival of traders among them, but those above are often disappointed; because the merchants of St. Louis receive their goods from Mackinac, or Montreal, and they do not arrive at St. Louis early enough to reach the upper nations in time for the season. Through the Ohio the goods might be brought in time to reach the uppermost nations.

The Otoctatas take 2 M to 2.500. pcs. marchse. and furnish 3500. to 4000. fine peltries of Deer, and ¼ of that of beaver.

The Mahas are from 4. to 500. men. The Poncas 200. to 250. men. These two nations furnish and take each about the same as the Otoctatas, but more beaver. The English however drove them off by land to the river Moingona.

The Panis of the 2. villages are from 4. to 500. men. Take 2000. to 2500. pcs Marche. and furnish 4000 skins, robes and [. . .] of the 1st quality. Those of the Republic (Loups) are from 400 to 500. men. Take and furnish about half as much as the last. They are 50. or 100 leagues apart.

The Loups, which are Panis also are from 200. to 250. men.

[139]

ALS, SC (DLC). The letterpress copy is difficult to read, but a typed transcript is filed with the manuscript.

1. No letter from Lewis dated 25 July is found, but one dated 26 July is our No. 78, incorrectly dated 25 July in Jefferson's endorsement.

2. *An account of Louisiana, being an abstract of documents, in the offices of the Departments of State, and of the Treasury* (Washington, 1803). SOWERBY lists it as an 8vo with 26 leaves, the last blank, but her copy must lack the appendix. When it was reviewed in the *Medical Repository,* 2nd hexade, 1 (1804), 390–402, it was described as containing 48 pp. with an appendix of 90 pp. There was an edition by publisher William Duane and another by John Conrad, both of Philadelphia. The New York State Library, Albany, lists a copy which Clifford K. SHIPTON catalogs as a 12mo of 50 pp., dated Nov. 1800. His date cannot be correct. For an accessible version, see *American State Papers*, Misc., 10:344–56, containing the main account which was communicated to Congress 14 Nov. 1803, and 362–84 for the appendix communicated 29 Nov. The appendix includes census data and a digest of the laws of Louisiana. Many years later Jefferson wrote that the publication had resulted from inquiries he had sent to persons who might have the best information, and that "the originals, and their printed copy were probably burnt by the British . . ." (to Josiah Stoddard, 13 Feb. 1825, DLC).

3. Another version of these Truteau extracts, in Jefferson's hand, are with the Jefferson Papers and filed as 137:23685. It begins, "1795. Journal of Truteau the Agent of the Company of the haut Missouri, establd. at Illinois." In an unfortunate but understandable slip, Thwaites transcribed the phrase as "Printeau's journal." The letterpress copy is abominable; a copyist not expecting "Truteau" could easily have made such an error.

4. William Charles Cole Claiborne (1775–1817), governor of Mississippi Territory, appointed 1801, and one of the commissioners named in 1803 to take possession of Louisiana. He was governor of the Territory of Orleans from 1804 to 1812.

5. Jonathan Dayton (1760–1824), U.S. senator from New Jersey from 1799 to 1805, later arrested—but not tried—on a charge of conspiring with Aaron Burr.

6. The bracket at the beginning of this sentence is Jefferson's.

95. William Henry Harrison to Jefferson

Vincennes 26th Novr. 1803.

The Governor of the Indiana Territory presents his respectful compliments to the President of the United States and requests his acceptance of the enclosed map[1] which is a Copy of the manuscript map of Mr. Evans who ascended the Missouri River by order of the Spanish Government much further than any other person.

[*Enclosure*]
Refered to by the Map.[2]

No. 1 Plan. At about three hundred miles from the village of the great Ozages in a west direction, after having passed many branches of the River Arkansas, is found a low ground, surrounded with Hills of an immense extent, having a diameter of about fifteen Leagues. The soil is a black sand, very fine, & so hard, that Horses hardly leave their tracts upon it; in warm and dry weather, there is exhaled from that swamp, vapours, which being afterwards condensed, fall again upon the black sand and cover it with a bed of salt very white and very fine of the thickness of about half an inch. The rains distroy this kind of Phenomenon.

No. 2. Plan. At a distance of about fifteen Leagues, from the Swamp of which we have spoken, and in a South direction, there is a second mine of mineral salt of the same nature as the other, these two differing only in their colour, the first inclining to the white, and the second approaching to the red. Lastly much farther south, and always upon the branches of the Arkansas, there is a salt Spring which may be considered as one of the most interesting phenomenea of nature.

On the declivity of a little hill, there are five holes of about a foot and a half diameter, by two of depth always full, without ever overflowing a drop, very salt. If we take away this salt water, it fills immediately; and at about ten feet lower, there comes out of this same Hill, a Strong Spring of pure & Sweet water.

No. 3. Plan. At a distance of about 18 Miles from this low land are found mines of meneral Salt, almost at the surface of the Earth. The Savages who know it perfectly, are found to employ leavers to break it and get it out of the Ground.

AL, RC (DLC). Endorsed; received 20 Dec. 1803.

1. The enclosure bears no evidence that it is related to the letter, but is so identified by the Library of Congress. I present it here for that reason, but suspect that it belongs with Harrison's letter of 29 March 1805 to Jefferson, not located. In a letter to Harrison of 28 April 1805, Jefferson refers to the earlier message of Harrison's which he said enclosed "a map of the Arkansas" (DLC). Logan Esarey in HARRISON represents the document as an enclosure to a letter from Harrison to Jefferson, 24 June 1804, but this seems unlikely since that letter is concerned solely with the districting of Upper Louisiana and does not mention a map.

2. The "Evans map" again. Isaac Joslin Cox in 1917 believed that the Evans map reached Jefferson through Daniel Clarke of New Orleans (review in *Mississippi Valley Historical Review*, 4 (1917), 269). He was probably thinking of a letter from Clarke to Jefferson, 18 Aug. 1803, saying that Clarke had forwarded to the Secretary of State "as exact a Manuscript map as could be procured of this Country, on which the different Posts or Settlements are delineated . . ." (DLC). That map was sent in response to a questionnaire, and most likely would have portrayed only the lower portions of the territory.

96. Lewis's Receipt to Amos Stoddard

Decr. 1. 1803.

Received of Capt. Amos Stoddard, fifty pounds of public powder for the use of my command, bound to the western waters.

MERIWETHER LEWIS Capt.
1st U.S. Regt. Infty.

Recd. twenty five pounds of pow[d]er in addition to the above, as also one 100 lb. powder cask.

MERIWETHER LEWIS Capt.
1st U.S. Regt. Infty.

ADS, RC (MoSHi). Endorsed. The body of the receipt is in Stoddard's hand; the added notation and both signatures are by Lewis.

97. Carlos Dehault Delassus to Juan Manuel de Salcedo and the Marqués de Casa Calvo

No. 213   [St. Louis, 9 December 1803]

The 7th of this month[1] Mr. Merryweather Lewis, Captain of the United States army and former secretary of the President of them presented himself at this post.

He has given me a *carta avertoria* [sic] a copy of which I am enclosing telling me that the president thought that it was Captain Don Enrique Peyroux who commanded this Upper Louisiana but that he was presenting it to me so that I might become acquainted with it as well as with the passports, copies of which he also enclosed adding also that his intention was to continue his trip penetrating the Missouri in order to fulfill his mission of discoveries and observations. I have hinted to him that my orders did not permit me to consent to his passing to enter the Missouri River and that I was opposing it in the name of the King, my master.

He then told me my opinion sufficed and that from now he would not go to the said river, I having observed to him that he surprised me for not having provided himself with a passport from our Spanish Minister in Philadelphia; that if he had had a passport in the name of the King my master, he could have removed all difficulty. He answered me that when he left Philadelphia that it was already at the beginning of July, that he thought he would find here the French, that for that reason, he had not believed it necessary to

[142]

carry a passport from *Señor* Marqués de Yrujo; that he thought that then it would be useless, but that during his trip he had learned that even though the delivery to France had not been carried out, he well supposed that I would not allow him to continue on, and especially with the news of the day; and that in order not to lose any time and so that his men might hunt he would continue in the Mississippi maintaining himself on the American side.

And I have forewarned him that I was going to inform Your Excellencies of the matter and that before spring I would surely have an answer from Your Excellencies which would inform me if they determine who may pass. The said man with his committee, which according to the information he has given me consists of twenty five men (which truly cannot be less so as to be able to be somewhat secure among the nations and cannot be larger because of the difficulty of the provisions in such an expedition), in view of my proposition has agreed to wait for Your Excellencies' determination and he is going to spend the winter on the Dubois River.

Your Excellencies will determine what you think best.

I should inform Your Excellencies that according to advices, I believe that his mission has no other object than to discover the Pacific Ocean, following the Missouri, and to make intelligent observations, because he has the reputation of being a very well educated man and of many talents.

I have offered to serve him, in view of the cited letter, in all that I might be useful to him in so far as my orders did not oppose.

All of which I am informing Your Excellencies for your due knowledge.

May God keep Your Excellencies many years.

St. Louis, Illinois, December 9, 1803

CARLOS DEHAULT DELASSUS [rubric]

Señores Brigadiers of the Royal Armies
Don J. Manuel de Salcedo and Marqués de Casa Calvo.

Printed, NASATIR (2), 2:719–20. The Spanish original is in the Archivo General de Indias (Seville), Papeles de Cuba, legajo 2368. Delassus enclosed a copy in English of Jefferson's letter to Peyroux (No. 66) and copies in French of Lewis's two passports (Nos. 14, 15). Sebastian Calvo de la Puerta, Marqués de Casa Calvo, was military governor of Louisiana. Juan Manuel de Salcedo was a Spanish brigadier who, with the Marqués, had been commissioned to supervise the transfer of Louisiana to the French government.

1. In No. 99, Lewis says it was 8 Dec. 1803.

98. Lewis to Clark

Dear Captain,   Cahokia December 17th 1803.

Drewyer[1] arrived here last evening from Tennessee with eight men.[2] I do not know how they may answer on experiment but I am a little disappointed, in finding them not possessed of more of the requisite qualifications; there is not a hunter among them. I send you by Drewyer, your cloaths portmanteau and a letter which I recieved from St. Louis for you, and which did not reach me untill an hour after Floyd had set out. Drewyer and myself have made no positive bargain, I have offered him 25$ pr. Month so long as he may chuise to continue with us.[3] Among the party from Tennissee is a blacksmith and House-joiner—these may be of service in our present situation. If two men could be spared from building the hutts, would it not be better to set them at sawing of boards. Hennebury informed me that he would be at Morrison's farm[4] today or Tomorrow, and that he knew a person in the neighborhood who had a whip-saw, and that he would go with any person you might send to this gentleman, and prevail on him to let us have the uce of the saw. You can obtain corn for the horses by application to Hennebury or any person who has the care of Morrison's farm.

I shall be obliged to go by St. Louis but will be with you as soon as possible. Adieu, and believe sincerely Your friend & Obt. Servt.

M. LEWIS.

ALS, RC (MoSHi). Addressed, "Capt. William Clark   River Dubois."

1. George Drouillard. Lewis found him at Fort Massac and engaged him as an Indian interpreter, advancing him $30 on his pay of $25 a month (LEWIS & ORDWAY, 47).

2. Lewis had expected a detachment from South West Point, in Tennessee, to be waiting for him at Fort Massac. I surmise that these men were not present when he arrived at Massac, and that he sent Drouillard to get them. When the detachment reached Camp Dubois on 22 Dec. 1803, Clark wrote in his field notes (CtY) that they were not the kind of men he had been told were ready, in Tennessee, for his party.

3. Drouillard's engagement up to now had been tentative. Clark informed Lewis 23 Dec. that Drouillard had now agreed to go on with the party, and would first return to Massac to settle his affairs (Clark field notes, CtY).

4. Here I must identify Morrison first, then Heneberry. William Morrison (1763–1837), a prominent Kaskaskia merchant and landowner, was the partner of Guy Bryan in a merchandising operation which included a store at Cahokia. I am informed by John Tevebaugh, Morrison's biographer, that he had several commonfield tracts in the Cahokia area, and military and

donation rights in St. Clair County. There is no doubt that "Morrison's farm" was operated by this man. Patrick Heneberry was employed in various capacities by Morrison in the period 1799–1805. He had an acccount at the Bryan and Morrison store in Cahokia (Cahokia ledger B, fols. 30, 106, Morrison Business Records, IHi). His account was credited with $277.25 for hauling and other work done at Goshen, a community probably near present Collinsville, Ill., and for butchering beef at Cahokia (Cahokia daybook No. 7, fol. 107, same location). Sometime between 1805 and 1809 he disappeared, owing the Cahokia store $158.85.

99. Lewis to Jefferson

Dear Sir,   Cahokia, December 19th 1803

On my arrival at Kaskaskias, I made a selection of a sufficient number of men from the troops of that place to complete my party, and made a requisition on the Contractor to cause immediately an adequate deposit of provisions to be made at Cahokia subject to further orders or other destination should circumstances render it necessary. This done, it became important to learn as early as possible the ultimate decision of Colo. Charles Deheau de Lassuse (the Governor of Upper Louisiana) relative to my asscending the Missouri; it became the more necessary to learn his determination on this subject, as from the advanced state of the season it must in a good measure govern my arrangements for the present winter, and seeing also from the usual course of things, that the period was near at hand, when it was expected that the navigation of both the Mississippi & Missouri would be obstructed by the ice and of course some disposition necessarily made to protect my party from the inclemency of the season, I determined to loose no time in making this application; with a view therefore to greater expedition, I thought it best to travel by land to St. Louis (the residence of the Govr.) and accordingly set out from Kaskaskias on the evening of the 5th Inst. on horse-back, Capt. Clark having proceeded with the party by water the preceeding day. I arrived at Cahokia on the 7th and immediately took occasion to make myself acquainted with Mr. John Hay (the Post Master of this place) and a Mr. Jarrot,[1] in whom from previous information I had every confidence; both these Gentleman are well acquainted with the English & French Languages, a necessary qualification to enable them to be serviceable on the present occasion as the Spanish Commandant cannot speak the English Language, and I am unfortunately equally ignorant of that of the French—these gentlemen readily consented to accompany me, and the next day (the 8th) I set out in company with them to visit Colo. Lasuse; on our arrival at his quarters we were received with much politeness by him, and after a friendly interchange of the usual salutations, I proceeded to make him acquainted with the objects of my visit, handed him the Passports which I had received from the French & English Ministers, and your letter to Monsr. Peyroux, at the same time in a summary manner adding a few observations relative to those papers, the views of my government it [in?] fitting out this expedition, and my own wishes to proceed on my voyage; after perusing the papers he returned me an answer nearly to this effect, that he was sensible the objects of the Government of the U. States as well as my own were no other than those stated in my Passports or such as had been expressed by myself; that these in their execution, would not be injurious to his royal master, the King of Spain, nor would they in his opinion prove in any manner detrimental to his Majesty's subjects with whose interests he was at that moment particularly charged, that as an individual he viewed it as a hazardous enterprize, but wished it every success, nor would he from his personal inclinations obstruct it[s] progress a single moment; he then concluded by observing that whatever might be his feelings as a man, his duty as an Officer, and his orders as such, strengthened also by the undeviating policy of the Spanish Government, with the regard to the nonadmission of foreigners into the interior of their provinces, equally forbad his granting me permission at this time to asscend the Missouri river; however he would if permitted by me take a transcript of my Passports, and send them immediately by an express to New Orleans to the Govr. Genl. of the Province, and that he would with cheerfulness give the aid of his influence with that officer, to promote my wishes; and finally as a friend advised my remaining at Cahokia untill the next spring, alledging that by that time he had no doubt the Govrs. consent would be obtained, and that then all obstructions would be removed to my asscending the Missouri.

In return for this abundant politeness of the Colo. I granted him permission to take a transcript of the papers I had presented him, alledging that it was not the object of my Government to conceal any views which it entertained relative to my mission and that his government had already been advised of it through their minister resident in the U. States, that I did not doubt the sincerity of his good wishes for the success of the enterprize, and thanked him for the willingness he displayed in procuring from the Govr. Genl. the permission I had asked. I further observed, that it was not my intention at that

[146]

time, to question either the policy or the right of the Spanish Government to prohibit my passage up the Missouri, that the reasons he had given for his refusal of my application, were considered by me as furnishing an ample apology on his part as an Officer for his refusal, and that I should not attempt to asscend the Missouri this season. I concurred with him in the opinion, that by the ensuing spring *all obstructions would be removed to my asscending the Missouri:* this effect however I anticipated as eminating from a very different cause, than that which seemed to govern the predictions of the Commandant. I concluded by thanking him for the personal friendship he had evinced, in recommending to me a winter residence, which certainly in point of society or individual comfort must be considered as the most eligible of any in this quarter of the country, but that other considerations of more importance had induced me to assign myself a different position that I had selected for this purpose (provided it answered the description I had received of it, the mouth of a small river called Dubois on the E. side of the Mississippi opposite to the mouth of the Missouri. Thus defeated in my application, tho' not much disappointed nor at all diverted from my future views, I spent the evening with the Commandant and returned the next day to join Capt. Clark who had just arrived at Cahokia. On the evening of the 10th Inst. we left Cahokia, and continued our route up the Mississippi four miles, opposite to St. Louis where we remained for the night. Early the next morning Capt. Clark continuted his route with the party to the river Dubois (distant from St. Louis 18 Miles) in order to erect Cabins for our winter residence at that place (provided it answered the description we had received of it) or otherwise to establish himself on a more eligible one as near it as possible. I passed over to St. Louis with a view to obtain from the inhabitants such information as I might consider usefull to the Government, or such as might be usefull to me in my further prosecution of my voyage. I have the honor to be with much respect Your Obt. Servt.

MERIWETHER LEWIS Capt.

1st U.S. Regt. Infty.

Transcript (PHi). Entered in Jefferson's index of letters as received 27 Feb. 1804.

1. Nicholas Jarrot (d. 1823), a native of France, settled in Cahokia in 1794. He engaged in fur trading on the upper Mississippi as far north as Prairie du Chien, where Pike found him in 1806.

100. Lewis to Jefferson

Dear Sir,   Cahokia December 28th 1803.

On my arrival at St. Louis, the first object to which, I called my attention, was that of collecting such information as might be in some measure serviceable to you in forming your opinions, or shaping your arrangements to effect a certain point of policy, which you expressed to me while with you at Washington last Summer; I mean that of a wish you then entertained, if possible to induce the inhabitants of Louisiana to relinquish their landed possessions in that country, and removing with their families, accept of an equivalent portion of lands on the East side of the Mississippi, with a view more readily to induce the Indians on the East, to remove to the West side of the Mississippi, and dispose of their lands on the East side of that river to the U'States.[1] The advantages of such a policy has ever struck me as being of primary importance to the future prosperity of the Union, and therefore I gave it my earlyest and best attention. With a view to the main object I confined my enquiries to the following subjects—The population of Louisiana, The number of emigrants from the U'States within the last year, and the proportion which that disciption of people bear to the other free white population of Louisiana. The number of Slaves and other people of colour. The quantity of lands which have been granted to, or claimed by individuals; the species of rights or claims by which the present incumbents hold these lands; The wealth of the inhabitants, and the species of property which forms that wealth; The position and extent of the several settlements, the proportion of each that are thickly inhabited (admitting as the standard), one *family* to a *square mile*); the proportion which the remaining population of each settlement bears to the remaining quantity of square miles embraced by it. The state of agriculture, and the species and extent of the improvements made on the lands now inhabited.

Whatever I may say on these subjects, must be understood as applicable to Uper Louisiana; the distance we are removed from the capital and settlements of the lower portion of the Province, as well as the little inter[c]ourse, which takes place between the inhabitants of it's extreems at this season of the year, makes it as difficult to learn any thing in relation to Lower Louisiana as tho' I were in Washington.

With a view to obtain some information on these subjects, I found means to obtain an introduction to Monsr. Soulard,[2] the Surveyor Genl., and was recieved by him in a very friendly manner; he gave me many unqualifyed assurances of his willingness to serve me, and his readyness to give me any information of which, he was possessed, in relation to the province. Monsr. S. is a Frenchman, a man of good information, an active officer, and the particular friend and confident of Colo. Lassuse; but before I proceed, in order to shew you Sir, the *good faith* with which Monsr. S. complyed with his previous declirations, as also to shew the difficulty, which in the present state of things is attendant on the procureing any accurate information relative to the state of the Province, it will not perhaps be amiss to relate, some measure in detale, the occurrences which took place at this interview between Monsr. Soulard and myself.

In order to give as great latitude as possible to my inquiries, and at the same time to avoid being thought too importunate, I prefaced my enquiries by thanking Mr. S. for his friendly dispositions, and observed that it was to be expected, that in all newly settled countrys there were but few men of general information, and that a very small proportion even of that few, were in possession of such documents as would enable them to form an accurate opinion on many interesting subjects; and concluded by observing, that the policy of the government of the U'States did not in any manner prohibit her officers or citizens from giving strangers every informa- tion relative to the government itself or the country, if therefore, my habits as a citizen of such a government, should lead me in the course of my inquiries to ask questions, which the policy of his government forbid his giving, I should feel no mortification at his withholding it, and I hoped he would feel no compunction in doing so, if he concieved his duty as an officer, or the policy of his government required it. I then asked him if the census of Uper Louisiana had been recently taken? And if so, what was the state of the population? He told me, that an order had been lately issued for that purpose, but the returns had not yet been recieved from but few of the districts, but that he had a copy of the census taken in 1800, which he would shew me with pleasure; a few minutes after he handed me this statement, I asked his permission to take an extract of it, which was granted, he furnished me with pen, ink & paper, I set down, and had scarsely began the operation, when, (as I was afterwards informed by Mr. Hay the gentleman who acted as our mutual friend and interpreter) Monsr. Soulard exclaimed, "perhaps some person may come in," and taking hold of my hand with much apparent agitation, beged that I would desist, adding that when he had granted me permission to take an extract from that paper, the impropriety of such permission did not occur to him, he hoped I

[149]

would pardon his not permiting me to do so, alledging that the jealousy of his gouvernment was such, that if it were known that he had given me permission to copy an official paper, that it would injure him with his government, I instantly desisted of course, and assured him that it was by no means my wish, that he should in order to gratify me, in the slightest manner compromit himself in the good opinion of his government; that I considered him the sole judge of the propriety or impropriety of satisfying the inquiries I was making, and that while I should be thankful for such information as he could consistenly with his duty give me, I should not on the other hand feel any mortification in being refused such as he might consider improper to give. This appeared perfectly to satisfy him. He then told me he thought I might state the present population of Uper Louisiana in round numbers at 10,000 souls, 2,000 of whom were slaves & people of colour, and of the remaining 8,000, two thirds of them at least were emigrants from the U'States; that the remaining third, were either French or Canadian descendants, the Spaniards and their descendants being so few in number, that they deserved no particular notice as a class of people.

In consequence of the readiness with which Monsr. Soulard granted me permission to take a transcript of the statement of the census which he shewed me, I did not at first view, charge my memory with it's contents as I should have done, had he not so readily granted me that permission; tho' I think from the best of my recollection that the total exceeded 7,600, for the population in 1800.

When I extended my inquiries to the geography of the country, and asked for such information as he felt himself at liberty to give me on that subject, particularly of the interior of the country lying between the Missouri and New Mexico, he shewed me a manuscript map,[3] imbracing a portion of the Mississippi, the Missouri from it's junction with this river to the mouth of the Osages, and the last named river in it's whole extent; I asked permission to take a copy of it, he told me he had no objection on his part, but that he must first obtain the permission of the Merchant whose property it was, and also the permission of the Commandant; desirous of knowing how Colo. Lassuse would act in such a case, I told Monsr. S—— I would take upon myself to make the necessary application to the Commandant, if he would do me the favour to obtain the Merchant's permission for my copying it. This done, I asked Colo. Lassuse on the same evening, if he would be so good as to permit the Merchants of St. Louis to give me such information as they might be disposed to give relative to the geography of the country, the request was immediately granted, and the next day I called on Monsr. S—— who had been as good as his word with the merchant, whose permission he had obtained; notwithstanding the assureance which I gave Monsr. S——., that the Commandant's consent had been obtained, still he could not give me the map untill he had exacted a promise upon honour, that I would not let Colo. Lassuse know that I had such a map in my possession or from what quarter I had obtained it.

Thus it appears to me Sir, that these people are so much accustomed to elude the eye of dispotic power, that they can do no act but this principle seems in some measure to have interwoven itself with the actuating motive; it may however be affected in some degree, in order to inhance the obligation conferred, by inducing the person obliged, to believe, that in order to serve him they have themselves risked the displeasure of their government or the penalty of punishment; in short, whatever may be the prime spring of action among them, they move more as tho' the *fear of the Commandant,* than *that of god,* was before their eyes; Whenever information is asked from the most independant of them on any subject, the promiss to give it, is always qualifyed by, *so far as propyety will permit;* the measure of which *propryety* it must be understood *is the will of the Commandant.* Candure obliges me to acknowledge however, that they have some reason to fear Colo. Lassuse, he has been pretty tiranical with them. With regard to the more wealthy part of the community, the Colo. seems to have differed from his predecessors in office in respect to the policy he has observed towards them; formerly this class of people escaped punishment for almost every crime, but he has for very slight offences put some of the most wealthy among them into the Carraboose; this has produced a general dread of him among all classes of the people.

I have no doubt, as soon as the American government takes effect in Louisiana, that many of the best informed of it's inhabitants in order to make themselves known to it, will unsolicited come forward with much interesting information, till then, every thing must be obtained by stealth. I have been thus particular to shew you in the present state of things how difficult it is to acquire information on certain subjects, and the inacuracy which must necessarily attend even the little which may be obtained.

The census as given me by Monsr. Soulard, I think is more to be relyed on than any othe[r] information I have recieved on that subject. The census as known to the Spanish government itself can-

[151]

not for several reasons be very accurate, and in my opinion fall considerably short of the real population. The inaccuracy and inattention of many of their pette commandants, some of whom can neither read nor write; in many instances emigrants from the U'States pass the Mississippi, and without asking lands of the government, set themselves down and remain many months, perhaps a year, without the knowledge even of the Commandant in whose district they may be; the scattered population of a great portion of Uper Louisiana, as well as the frequent removals of the wandering emigrants from the U States, who now form a majority of the population; all form considerations which must in some degree contribute to the inaccuracy of the census.

I cannot learn that any of the commandants of districts keep an account of the number of persons who emigrate annually from the U'States to Louisiana, of course, what can be said on this head must of necessity be in a great measure conjectural; common opinion seems to fix the emigration of the last year at 100. families, but I believe it considerably more. I have learnt the population of the district of Cape Girardeau, for the present & some previous years with more precision than that of any other. This settlement was formed in 1795 by two families only, 45 miles above the mouth of the Ohio; taking the progressive increase of the population of this district for our data, we shal find, that by the census of 1801, they amounted to 705. souls, and in 1803 to 1,111. (This last number may be depended on for it's accuracy, I had it from the young gentleman who made out the report of the census of that district for Comdt. Lorimier[4] who can neither read nor write); from this it appears, that the population has increased within the 2 last years 406 souls; allowing 5 souls to a family, there will be 81 families for the emigration of the two last years, the half of which is 40½ for the emigration in the year 1803. It may be urged however, that in order to obtain the true annual increase of population by emigration only, there should be deducted from this sum, the probable excess of births over the deaths which have taken place in that period, but I think that a sufficient allowance for this, will be found in the annual progressive increase of emigration, added to the removals which take place from the older settlements, to those more recently formed, at the same time disposing of their rights to the soil, and their improvements to later adventurers, who more wealthy than themselves purchase from, and succeed them. I therefore think the increase of the district aluded to, may safely be stated at 40 families averaging 5 persons each, for the last 12 Months, ending the

31st of October; admitting this to be the case, when we take into consideration many other districts, equally with Cape Girardeau, rapidly increasing in population by emmigration from the U'States, as New Madrid, St. Genevieve, New Bourbon, St. Louis and the country on the Maremek river, St. Ferdinand, St. Charles and particularly St. Andrew and the country lying S. of the Missouri, and between it and the uper portions of the rivers Maremek and St. Francis—we would in such case have strong grounds to conjecture, that the emigration the last year from the U States to uper Louisiana was nearer 200 than 100, families; the emigration to Louisiana from any other quarter is so inconsiderable that it scarcely deserves notice. The emigration of the ensuing year may be expected to exceed that of the last at least a third, unless some measures are taken by the government to prevent it. Many persons from different parts of the U'States, particularly N. Carolina, have visited Louisiana since the cession of that country to the U'States has been made known; these persons were in serch of some eligible positions to form settlements as soon as the American government was in operation in that quarter; they appear generally pleased with the country, and will no doubt make a favourable report on their return.

I am fully persuaded, that your wishes to withdraw the inhabitants of Louisiana, may in every necessary degree be affected in the course of a few years, provided the gouvernment of the U. States is justly liberal in it's donations. The American emigrants will be much more readily prevailed on to come into this measure than the French, the French may be said almost exclusively to be the slave holder, they own at least five sixths of that property. I fear that the slaves will form a source of some unwillingness in the French to yeald to the wishes of the government. They appear to feel very sensibly a report which has been circulated among them on this subject, that *the Americans would emancipate their slaves immediately on taking possesion of the country,* this however false, is sufficient to show the Opinions and disposition of the people on that subject; there appears to be a general objection not only among the French, but even among the Americans not slave holders, to relinquish the right which they claim relative to slavery in it's present unqualifyed shape.

The Canadian French reside almost intirely in villages situated on the banks of the Mississippi and Missouri rivers; a few individuals among them only can be said to possess wealth, and such as do, obtained it by the Indian trade; the whole of them either directly, or indirectly look to this trade as the principal source of their maintenance; the proximity of their present situations to the trade

[153]

in which they are engaged, will of course produce a disposition to continue where they are; many of them are slave holders; slavery being prohibited in the Indianna Territory, (at least the further admission of any slaves), these proprietors of slaves will be compelled to deside, whether they will reside in an adjacent part of the Indianna Territory, enjoy the benefits of their indian trade, and sacrefice in some measure their slave property, or remove with these slaves to some part of the U'States where slavery is permitted, and sacrefice all prospects of their indian trade; thus the slaves appear to me in every view of this subject to be connected with the principal difficulties with which the government will have to contend in effecting this part of it's policy.

I know not what are the regulations, which have been, or are intended to be made by the government of the U'States in relation to the more permanent government of Uper Louisiana, but I trust I shall be pardoned for giving it as my opinion, (that of office-hunters to the contrary notwithstanding) that Uper Louisiana can be governed more for the happiness of, and justice to the people, with less expence to the mother government, and with better prospects of inforcing her future policy, by dividing it into about three counties, and incorporating it with the Indianna Territory, than by establishing it into a seperate territory, or continuing it as a part of the government of Lower Louisiana in any shape.

In pursuing my enquiries in relation to Louisiana, any information which I may recieve and which appears to me worthy of your attention shall be forwarded to you.

I have proposed many quiries under sundry heads to the best informed persons I have met with at St. Louis and within the vicinity of that place; these gentlemen have promised me answers in due time, but as every thing undergoes the examination of the Commandant, you may readily concieve the restraint which exists on many points.

Some of the traders of this country from their continual intercourse with the Indians, possess with more accuracy many interesting prarticulars in relation to that people, than persons in a higher sphere of life among them, yet they want both leasure and abilities to give this information in any satisfactory manner in detail; in order therefore to avail myself as far as possible of their information under these circumstances, I drew out a form on paper containing 13 or 14 columns, which I headed with such subjects as appeared to me most important to be known relative to the Indians; I have some of these in circulation; and expect to recieve one or more of them in a few days.[5]

[154]

I have obtained three maps; one of the Osages river, before mentioned, a general map of Uper Louisiana,[6] and a map of the Missouri river, from it's mouth to the Mandane nation;[7] these I shall retain for some time yet, in order to asscertain by further enquiries their accuracy or otherwise; I have also obtained Ivins's and Mac Kay's journal up the Missouri,[8] it is in French & is at present in the hands of Mr. Hay, who has promised to translate it for me; I am also promised by Mr. Hay a copy of his journal[9] from Michilimackinack to the Assinaboin river in the north, by way (on his autward bound journey), of the S. side of Lake Superior, the River St. Louis, the River of the sand lake branch of the Mississippi, a part of the last river downwards to the mouth of the crow-wing river or river L'aile dé curbeau, and with it to the Leaf river, thence up the Leaf river to the portage of the Otter-tale Lake, thence down the Red river to it's junction with the Assinaboin river (called improperly in Arrasmith's Map *Stone Indian river*), and up this river 80 leagues to his winter establishment; on his inward bound journey; by the Assinaboin river to Red river, thence down it 18 leagues to Lake Winnipeek, and through a part of it, the river Winnipeek, Lake of the Woods, the river of the rainy Lake, the rainy Lake, and the grand portage to Michilimackinack. These I shall forward to you as soon as they are recieved.

My best respects to your daughters, as also Messrs. T. Randolph, Eppes & Harvey,[10] and believe me with much sincere regard Your Most Obt. Servt.

MERIWETHER LEWIS. Capt.
1st. U.S. Regt. Infty.

ALS, RC (PHi). Endorsed; received 27 Feb. 1804.

1. Jefferson's consideration of a plan to remove the white population of Upper Louisiana across to the east side of the river is loosely consistent with his Indian policy. Unable to conceive of the speed with which the trans-Mississippi region would be engulfed by settlers, he thought of it as a kind of vast reservation where the tribes then living east of the river could retire for many years of unmolested prosperity. The best statement of Jefferson's Indian policy is in his letter to Harrison of 27 Feb. 1803 (DLC, and in HARRISON, 1:69–73). Here he expresses the hope that the Indians might "incorporate with us as citizens of the United States," or, failing this, "remove beyond the Mississippi."

2. Antoine Soulard (1766–1825), surveyor general of Upper Louisiana for the Spanish government, and continued in that post by the new American government.

3. This map not located, but probably was incorporated into the map sent to Jefferson in May 1804 and discussed under No. 122.

4. Louis Lorimier (1748–1812), commandant of the district of Cape Girardeau.

[155]

5. None located.

6. This may be the map reprinted in the JOURNALS, vol. 8, as No. 2—entitled, "A Topographical Sketch of the Missouri and Upper Mississippi; Exhibiting the various Nations and Tribes of Indians who inhabit the Country: Copied from the Original Spanish MS. Map." It bears annotations in Clark's hand, including a reference—obscured by a tear in the paper—to Mackenzie. DILLER (1) and (3) discusses this map of Soulard's, and in the latter article presents a reproduction of the French version. See also "Descriptive observations on certain parts of the country of Louisiana," *Medical Repository*, 2nd hexade, 2 (1805), 308–13, based on Soulard's letter of March 1805 to J. A. Chevallié, of Richmond, translated by Samuel Latham Mitchill and containing an extensive description of the Missouri. Mitchill (1764–1831), a New York physician who served both as U.S. senator and representative from that state, was founder of the *Medical Repository* and deeply interested in the West.

7. The so-called Mackay map, discussed under No. 93.

8. James Mackay (b. 1759), Scottish trader and explorer, had been with the Mandans on the upper Missouri in the 1780's and had traveled in the region of the Assiniboine and Mouse rivers in the Northwest. In 1795 he had left St. Louis on behalf of the Spanish-controlled Missouri Company and gone as far as the village of the Omaha tribe, six miles below present Omadi, Neb. From there he had sent his assistant, John Evans, in 1796 with instructions to try for the Pacific. Evans, a young Welshman who had come to America in the hope of discovering a fabled tribe of "Welsh Indians" (see No. 326, notes 39, 41), got no farther than the villages of the Mandans (NASATIR (2), 1:96–108). Evans died in 1798 but Mackay lived in the St. Charles district while Lewis and Clark were wintering at Wood River; a note by Clark, 10 Jan. 1804, mentions that Mackay had just come down the Missouri from a surveying trip (CtY). The present letter seems to verify what Quaife suspected when he edited the Mackay-Evans material in 1915: that the information had passed to Lewis and Clark directly from MACKAY. Hay provided some notes on the material which appear in the published version, but I am not aware that his work in translating the journals has been known before. First publication of the Mackay material occurred in 1807 when Mitchill ran in his *Medical Repository* an article entitled "Extract from the manuscript journal of James M'Kay," 2nd hexade, 4 (1807), 27–37. A manuscript version of the original is in PPAmP. I believe that this manuscript, and another by Mackay entitled "Notes on Indian Tribes" (MoSHi), were once carried together, folded lengthwise and bound with a paper band (also at MoSHi) which bears in Lewis's hand the words "Mr. Evin's sketches of the Missouri, present by Mr. MacKay." The manuscript on Indian tribes is unmistakably by Mackay, although the words "Evins notes" appear on the first page in Clark's hand.

9. No Hay journal has been found; perhaps Lewis refers only to Hay's notes on the Mackay-Evans journal. Lewis recorded in his own journals a table of distances "commencing at the discharge of the Ottertail Lake, which forms the source of the Red River, to his [Hay's] winter station on the Assinneboin River" (JOURNALS, 1:4–6). The assistance which Hay gave to Lewis and Clark, and the frequency of their contacts with him during the winter in the St. Louis area, led to a relationship that now appears to

have been substantial. The Clark notes (CtY) report that Lewis arrived at the winter camp with "Mr. J. Hay & Mr. Jo. Hays of Kohokia" on 30 Jan. 1804. (Hays was commissioned by Harrison as first sheriff of the Cape Girardeau district, and is addressed as such by Frederick Bates in a letter of 26 Jan. 1810 (BATES, 2:146). He is understandably confused with Hay by most historians.) The two men left camp 2 Feb. Hay returned on 26 April, and the next day Clark recorded the fact that they were "Preparing to pack up Indian goods." In an entry for 28 April he says, "Mr. Hay packing up." It appears that Hay, experienced at handling Indian goods, was help-ing Lewis and Clark with this chore. A baling invoice, showing how these goods were apportioned, is in JOURNALS, 6:270–73. Lewis's esteem for Hay was such that he recommended him for an Indian subagency, but the ap-pointment was not made (DNA, RG 107, Register of Letters Received, L-144, 4 April 1804). In a note under No. 210 I suggest Hay's relationship to a little-known Lewis letter. A biography of this man is overdue. I can only add the meager fact that he made out balance sheets and took in-ventory at the Cahokia store of Bryan and Morrison, in the period 1800–1810, and that his account at Cahokia was credited annually for "sundry court fees," "work done," etc. See Cahokia daybook No. 7, fols. 106–09, 186, 189 (IHi).

10. Thomas Mann Randolph (1768–1828), married to Jefferson's daughter Martha; John Wayles Eppes (1773–1823), married to his other daughter, Maria; and Lewis Harvie.

101. Clark's List of Questions

[1804]

Inquiries relitive to the *Indians* of Louisiania.

1st. *Physical History and Medicine*

What is their state of Life as to longivity?

At what age do both sexes usially marry?

How long do the Women usially succle their Children?

What is the diet of their Children after they wean them?

Is polygamy admited among them?

What is the state of the pulse in both sexes, Children, grown persons, and in old age, by feeling the Pulse Morning, Noon, & Night &c.?

What is their most general diet, manner of cooking, time and manner of eating; and how do they preserve their provisions?

What time do they generally consume in sleep?

What are their *acute* dis-eases?

Is rheumatism, Pluricy, or *bilious fevers* known among them? & does the latter ever terminate in a vomiting of *black matter*?

What are their chronic diseases—are palsy, apoplexy, Epilepsy, Madness, the goiture (or Swelled Neck) and the Venereal disease known among them?

What is their mode of treating the *Small pox* particularly?

Have they any other disease amongst them, and what are they?

What are their remidies for their different diseases?

Are artificial discharges of blood used among them?

In what manner do they generally induce evacuation?

Do they ever use Voluntary fasting?

What is the nature of their baths, and at what time of the day do they generally use them?

At what age do their women begin and cease to menstruate?

2nd. *Relative to Morrals*

What are the Vices most common among the Indians?

Do they ever resort to Suicide under the influence of their passions, particularly love?

Is murder common among them, and do their Laws punish it by Death?

Are the lives of the wife and Children subject to the Capprice of the husband, and father, and in case of the murder by him of either do their Laws punish the Culprit with Death?

Can the Crime of Murder be paliated by precuniary Considerations?

Do they use any liquor or Substitute to premote intoxication, besides ardent spirits?

Are they much attached to spiritous liquors, and is intoxication deemed a Crime among them?

Have they any and what are the *punishments* of which their usuages admit of—for either Crimes.

3rd. *Relative to Religion*

What affinity is there between their religious ceremonies and those of the ancient Jews?

Do they use animal sacrifises in their worship?

What are the principal objects of their worship?

Do they Consider *Mannatoe* or the *good Spirit* & *Michimannatoe* or the *bad Spirit* as two distinct powers, neither haveing the power of Controling the other?

Do they ever petition the *good Spirit* to interfere with his power to avert or relieve them from the evils which the *bad Spirit* meditates or is practicing against them.

Do they sacrifice to, or petition the *bad Spirit* in order to avert the pernicious design which they may conceive he has formed against them.

How do they dispose of their dead?

And with what ceremonies do they inter them?

Do they ever use human sacrifices in any case.

Do they Mourn for their disceased friends and what [is] their cerimony on such occasions.

4th. *Traditions or National History*

From what quarter of the earth did they emigrate as related to them by their ancisters.

What the cause of their removal and the circumstancies attending their peregrination.

With what savage nations have they formed strict allyance, or those of offensive and *Defensive* war.

Have they any *Monuments* to perpetuate national events or the memory of a distinguished Chief—and if so what are they?

5th. *Agriculture and Domestic economy*

Do they obtain by the Cultivation of the soil their principal mantainence?

What species of grain or pulse do they cultivate?

What are their implements of husbandry, and in what manner do they use them?

Have they any domestic anamals & what are they?

Do their men engage in agriculture or any other domestic employments.

How do they prepare their culinary and other domistic utensils and what are they?

At what time do they usually relinquish their hunt and return to their village?

What are the esculent plants, and how do they prepare them.

What are those that are Commonly used by them?

In what form and of what materials are their Lodges, or *Houses* usially built.

Of what does the furniture of those lodges Consist, for the accommidation of the necessary avocations of human life *eating Drinking & Sleeping.*

What materials compose, and in what form do they erect their temporary tents.

Do more that [than] one family inhabit the same lodge and in such case, is the furniture of the lodge considered as the common property of the inhabitants of it.

6th. *Fishing & Hunting*

Do those furnish their principal employment?

Do their [women?] participate in the fatigues of either?

How do they persue, and how take their game?

What are the employments used for those purposes—how prepare & in what manner do they use them?

[159]

How do they preserve, and how prepare the Skins & furs of their games when taken for raiment or for Market.

7th. *War*

What is the cerimony of declareing war, and making peace; or forming alliancies?

What the cerimony of setting out and the return of the war party?

Do their women ever accompany them on those th[e]ir hostile experditions.

At what season of the year do they usially go to war?

In what manner are those war parties organised?

What is their Disipline and the regulations by which they are governed?

Do they burn or torture their prisoners?

Do they eat the flesh of their prisoners?

Do they ever adopt their Prisoners as members of their Nation?

What are their implements of war, how do they prepare and how use them?

8th. *Amusements*

Have they any and what are they?

Do they with a view to amusement only make a feist.

Do they play at any games of risk, & what are they?

Have their women any games particularly to themselves, or do they ever engage in those common to the Men.

Do they ever dance and what is the cerimony of their Dance.

Have they any music, and what are their musical instruments.

9th. *Clothing Dress & Orniments*

What garments do their dress usially Consist, in both Sexes?

What are the shapes & materials of those garments?

In what manner are they worn?

What orniments do they use to decorate their person?

Do they use paints of Various Colours on the surface of their skins, and what are the most usial colours thus used?

Do they *tattoe* (or scarify) their bodys and on what parts?

Do they imprint with the aids of a sharp pointed instrument and som colouring matter any figures on their skins: and what are the part of the body on which they are usially imprinted.

Which are the usial figures?

Customs & Manners Generally

In what particularly do they differ from those nations in our neighbourhood.

Have they any & what are their festivals or feasts.

What is the cerimony of reciving a stranger at their Village?

When publickly recived at the Lodge of the Chief of the Village
is there any Cerimony afterwords necessary to your admission in
any other Lodge.

Any information of the Indians of Louisiania so far as you may
be inabled, at your Leasure dureing this winter either from Materials
which may be in your possession, or such as you may have it in your
power to acquire would be most sincerely acknowledged by me; the
Interest you feel for the extention of General Science would I have
no doubt more than any other consideration form your inducement
to comply with this request and [end of manuscript]

AD, in Clark's hand (MoSHi). The basis of this list is the one supplied
by Dr. Benjamin Rush (No. 38), perhaps with additional material from Dr.
Caspar Wistar and Dr. Benjamin Smith Barton. The letter of Wistar's enclosing his proposed subjects of inquiry was forwarded by Jefferson 16 Nov.
1803 (No. 94). One might be pardoned for suspecting that Dr. Barton
failed to submit such a list; he was a busy and a notoriously dilatory man,
often in ill health, always with more projects at hand than he could cope
with. His tendency to overestimate his output was well known to his
contemporaries: in a review of the Biddle edition in *Western Gleaner*, 1
(May 1814), 350–75, the reviewer declared that Barton was known to be a
writer who promised much and delivered little. However, he did prepare a
list of questions on the manners and language of the Indians for naturalist
Thomas Nuttall, when he financed an expedition by Nuttall in 1810 and
1811. See PENNELL (1), 7. A more sophisticated and detailed list of questions
was given to Maj. Stephen Long in 1819 by a committee of the American
Philosophical Society, whose members included Robert Patterson and Peter
S. Du Ponceau (Mss. Communicated, Philology and Literature, 2:41–47,
PPAmP).

102. Lewis to Auguste Chouteau

St. Louis, Jan'y 4, 1804.

Sir: I have taken the liberty to add to this, additional questions of
a mixed nature relating to Upper Louisiana, your answers to which
will be extremely gratifying, and very gratefully acknowledged.

Your friend and Ob't Servant,

MERIWETHER LEWIS,
Capt. 1st U.S. Regt. Infy.

Mr. Aug's. Chouteau.

Mixed questions relating to Upper Louisiana.

1. What is the present population?

2. What is the number of Emigrants from the United States into this country since the last year, ending Oct. 31, 1803, and what is the proportion of this kind of people, to the other free white population of Upper Louisiana?

3. What number of slaves and other people of colour?

4. What is the quantity of land granted, or which is claimed by individuals? The nature of the right, or pretensions by which the present possessors hold these lands? and the probable proportions of the whole amount which is separately held by these respective titles?

5. What is the condition of the inhabitants in general in regard to wealth? and what kind of property generally constitutes that wealth?

6. What is the situation and extent of the several settlements? and what is the prospect of each to become the most peopled? that is to say (allowing as a rule a family for each mile square) what proportion does the remaining population of each settlement bear to the remaining number of square miles she contains.

7. What is the condition of Agriculture? and what improvements, and to what extent, have been made on newly inhabited lands?

8. What is the probable amount in dollars of goods annually brought into Upper Louisiana? What proportion of them is intended for the consumption of her people, and what proportion for her Indian Trade? What proportion of all her entries arrives by way of Canada, New Orleans, or the United States?

9. What is the amount in dollars of the annual exports of Upper Louisiana? Of what articles do they consist in, and what proportion goes out by each of the routes, Canada, New Orleans, or the United States?

10. What are the names and nick-names of all the villages of Upper Louisiana? Where are they situated? When established, and the number of houses and people they contain at present?

11. What are your mines and minerals? Have you lead, iron, copper, pewter, gypsum, salts, salines, or other mineral waters, nitre, stone-coal, marble, lime-stone, or any other mineral substance? Where are they situated, and in what quantities found?

12. Which of those mines or salt springs are worked? and what quantity of metal or salt is annually produced?

13. What are the animals, birds and fish of Louisiana? and what their form, appearance, habits, dispositions, of those especially that are not abundant in the inhabited parts of the country.

M. L.

Printed, BILLON (2), 384–85. This is Billon's translation of what appears to have been a form letter. A manuscript version in French, in an unknown hand, signed by Lewis and dated 20 Jan. 1804, is in ICHi. It is not addressed and not all of the questions are present. René Auguste Chouteau (1749–1829), fur trader and merchant, was one of the founders of St. Louis. He and his brother, Jean Pierre, will later prove indispensible to Lewis and Clark in many ways.

103. Jefferson to Lewis

Dear Sir   Washington Jan. 13. 1804.
   I wrote you last on the 16th. of Nov. since which I have recieved no letter from you. The newspapers inform us you left Kaskaskia about the 8th. of December. I hope you will have recieved my letter by that day or very soon after; written in a belief it would be better that you should not enter the Missouri till the spring; yet not absolutely controuling your own judgment formed on the spot. We have not heard of the delivery of Louisiana to us as yet, tho' we have no doubt it took place about the 20th. of December, and that orders were at the same time expedited to evacuate the upper posts, troops of ours being in readiness & under orders to take possession. This change will probably have taken place before you recieve this letter, and facilitate your proceeding. I now inclose you a map[1] of the Missouri as far as the Mandans, 12. or 1500. miles I presume above it's mouth. It is said to be very accurate, having been done by a Mr. Evans by order of the Spanish government. But whether he corrected by astronomical observations or not we are not informed. I hope this will reach you before your final departure. The acquisition of the country through which you are to pass has inspired the public generally with a great deal of interest in your enterprize. The enquiries are perpetual as to your progress. The Feds. alone still treat it as philosophism, and would rejoice in it's failure.[2] Their bitterness increases with the diminution of their numbers and despair of a resurrection. I hope you will take care of yourself, and be the living witness of their malice and folly. Present my salutations to Mr. Clarke, assure all your party that we have our eyes turned on them with anxiety for their safety & the success of their enterprize. Accept yourself assurances of sincere esteem & attachment.

                                                   TH: JEFFERSON

ALS, SC (DLC).
   1. See No. 93, note 3, for my mention of this "Evans map" and its relationship to other maps carried by Lewis and Clark.
   2. The words "would rejoice in it's failure" are Jefferson's substitution for a heavily deleted passage which is not decipherable on this letterpress copy.

104. Clark to William Croghan

Dear Major   River a Dubois January 15th 1804

I have postponed writing to you untill this time with a view of haveing something worth informing you relitive to this Country, but have been disaptd. and this hasty scraul will do little more than inform you that I am in tolerable health. I have not been from Camp to any house since my arrival here. It is hourly expected that the American's will take possession of the other side of the Mississippi. All the Inhabitents appear anxious except the people of St. Louis, who are ingaged in the Indian Trade which they are doubtfull will be divided, amongst those whome will trade on the best terms. Capt. Amos Stoddard of the Corps of Artillirists, who is now stationed at Kaskaskia is appointed the Commandant of the Upper Louisiania, and to take possession of St. Louis with his Compy. as soon as orders arrive from New Orleans to the Spanish Lt. Govr. to give up possession which is hourly exptd. Capts. D. Bissell (at Massac) & Carmickle[1] to receve possession of the two Posts & Settlements below the mouth of the Ohio. From Sister Thrustons[2] letter of the 30th Novr. which is the only one I have recved, I find Nancy Croghan[3] was unwell, I hope she has recovered. I wish much to here whether she has or not.

My situation is as comfortable as could be expected in the woods, & on the frontiers; the Country back of me is butifull beyond discription; a rich bottom well timbered, from one to three mile wide, from the river to a Prarie; which runs nearly parrilal to the river from about three miles above me, to Kaskaskia and is from three to 7 miles wide, with gradual rises and several streams of runing water, and good Mill seats; This Prarie has settlements on its edges from Kahoka within three miles of this place. The Missouri which mouths imedeately opposet me <*is a large turbalent*> is the river we intend assending as soon as the weather will permit. This Great river which seems to dispute the preeminence with the Mississippi, coms in at right angles from the West, and forces its great sheets of muddy Ice (which is now running) against the Eastern bank. We are collecting what information we can of this river and its rises so as we may make just Calculations, before we set out.[4]

I shall be glad to here from you at all times. Please to present my best wishes to my sisters Lucy & Fanny & the Children, to them and your self I tender the assurances [of] sincear esteem & friendship.

WM. CLARK

ALS, SC (MoSHi). Maj. William C. Croghan, born in Ireland, had arrived in Louisville in 1784, married Clark's sister Lucy, and built an estate known as Locust Grove.

1. Capt. George Washington Carmichael, appointed to the Regiment of Artillerists in 1802.

2. Clark's sister Frances (Fanny) had lost her first husband, Dr. John O'Fallon, in 1793, and had married Charles M. Thruston in 1796. But at the time of this letter, he too had died and Frances would later marry Denis Fitzhugh.

3. Clark's niece.

4. The letters of Clark during this period do small justice to his role in gathering data and preparing the impedimenta of the expedition. His field notes (CtY) are a richer source of information. His work during these months is also summarized by John Louis Loos, both in an article and a very useful doctoral dissertation on Clark's career. See LOOS (1) and (2).

105. Jefferson to Lewis

Dear Sir   Washington Jan. 22. 1804.

My letters since your departure have been of July 11. & 15. Nov. 16. and Jan. 13. Yours recieved are of July 8. 15. 22. 25. Sep. 25. 30. & Oct. 3.[1] Since the date of the last we have no certain information of your movements. With mine of Nov. 16. I sent you some extracts made by myself from the journal of an agent of the trading company of St. Louis up the Missouri. I now inclose a translation of that journal in full for your information. In that of the 13th inst. I inclosed you the map[2] of a Mr. Evans, a Welshman, employed by the Spanish government for that purpose, but whose original object I believe had been to go in search of the Welsh Indians, said to be up the Missouri. On this subject a Mr. Rees[3] of the same nation, established in the Western parts of Pennsylvania, will write to you. N. Orleans was delivered to us on the 20th of Dec. and our garrisons & government established there. The order for the delivery of the Upper posts were to leave N. Orleans on the 28th and we presume all those posts will be occupied by our troops by the last day of the present month. When your instructions were penned, this new position was not so authentically known as to effect the complection of your instructions. Being now become sovereigns of the country, without however any diminution of the Indian rights of occupancy we are authorised to propose to them in direct terms the institution of commerce with them. It will now be proper you should inform those through whose country you will pass, or whom you may meet, that their late fathers the Spaniards have agreed to withdraw all their troops from all the waters & country of the Missisipi & Missouri, that they have surrendered to us all their subjects Spanish & French settled there, and all their posts & lands: that henceforward we become their fathers and friends, and that we shall endeavor that they shall have no cause to lament the change: that we have sent you to enquire into the nature of the country & the nations inhabiting it, to know at what places and times we must establish stores of goods among them, to exchange for their peltries: that as soon as you return with the necessary information we shall prepare supplies of goods and persons to carry them and make the proper establishments: that in the mean time, the same traders who reside among or visit them, and who now are a part of us, will continue to supply them as usual: that we shall endeavor to become acquainted with them as soon as possible, and that they will find in us faithful friends and protectors. Although you will pass through no settlements of the Sioux (except seceders) yet you will probably meet with parties of them. On that nation we wish most particularly to make a friendly impression, because of their immense power, and because we learn they are very desirous of being on the most friendly terms with us.

I inclose you a letter which I believe is from some one on the part of the Philosophical society.[4] They have made you a member, and your diploma is lodged with me; but I suppose it safest to keep it here & not to send it after you. Mr. Harvie departs tomorrow for France as the bearer of the Louisiana stock to Paris. Capt. William Brent takes his place with me. Congress will probably continue in session through the month of March. Your friends here & in Albemarle, as far as I recollect are well. Trist will be the Collector of N. Orleans, & his family will go to him in the spring. Dr. Bache is now in Philadelphia & probably will not return to N. Orleans. Accept my friendly salutations & assurances of affectionate esteem & respect.

TH: JEFFERSON

ALS, SC (DLC). A poor letterpress copy.

1. The Lewis letter which Jefferson dates 25 July is actually dated 26 July (our No. 78). The letters he dates 25 and 30 Sept. are Lewis's letters of 8 and 13 Sept. (our Nos. 86 and 88), erroneously listed here by date of endorsement.

2. Probably the one sent him by Harrison with No. 95.

3. Morgan John Rhys, founder of a Welsh settlement in western Pennsylvania and a supporter of John Evans in his search for the Welsh Indians of the Missouri. Thwaites identifies him incorrectly as Thomas Rees, a London bookseller. No letter from Morgan Rhys to Lewis has been found.

4. John Vaughan had written Jefferson 21 Nov., "Capt. Meriwether Lewis having been chosen a Member of the Society, I take the liberty of enclosing to you his Certificate of Election, & the letter advising of his Election, as the only Certain channel, by which the information can be Conveyed to him" (DLC).

106. [Governor of Louisiana?] to Carlos Dehault Delassus

[28 January 1804]

If upon the receipt of this Your Excellency finds himself commanding that post, without someone having presented himself, who would take charge in behalf of the United States, which took possession of this capital and province the 20th of December last: you will not put any obstacle to impede Capt. Merry Weather Lewis' entrance in the Missouri whenever he wishes; nevertheless Your Excellency did right in taking the dispositions of which your official letter no. 213 treats; since you had no order from your government.

Your Excellency should try to conform at the capital to the terms which have been prescribed to you by our order, which you should have received in duplicate, as soon as you will deliver your posts to the official or agent of the United States, who will present himself to that purpose.

God keep Your Excellency many years.

New Orleans, January 28, 1804

[draft]

Señor Don Carlos de Lassus

Printed, NASATIR (2), 2:725. The Spanish version is a draft in the Archivo General de Indias (Seville), Papeles de Cuba, legajo 141.

107. Lewis to Clark

Camp at River Dubois.
My Dear Friend,   Feby. 18th 1804.

Not any thing of moment has occurred since you left us, my detention has been caused by a visitation on the 13th & 14 insts. from a principal Chief of the Kickapoo nation, whom I have been anxious to see for some time past for several reasons, as also the arrival of the contractor[1] with whom some little arrangments were necessary; being disappointed in geting down to the ball on the 14th and finding more to do when I began to look about me than I had previously thought of I determined it would be as well to go to work and pospone my visit to Cahokia & St. Louis a few days.

If Mr. Manuel [2] will let us have the men you mention, pray engage them immediately, if you think from their appearance and characters they will answer the purpose.

My complyments to Mr. C. Chouteau[3] and inform him if you please that nothing has given me more pleasure than the proposition he has made to you on the subject of the Osages—that as he wishes, every circumstance in relation to this affair shall be kept a profound secret. I wish him not only to bring in some of those Chiefs (the number hereafter to be agreed on) but wish him to attend them to the seat of the government of the U'States provided he can make it convenient to do so; I presume the Chiefs would come more readily provided Mr. Chouteau would make them a promise to that effect; I am as anxious as Mr. C. can be that he should set out on this mission as early as possible, and shall therefore be with you the day after tomorrow for the purpose of conserting the necessary measures.

My complyments to the Govr. Lassuse and Monsr. Dabuke & Monsrs. Gratiott and A. Chouteau—not forgetting my most profound respects to *Mdam Manuel*.[4] I am with the most sincere respect Your friend,

M. Lewis. Capt. &c.

ALS, RC (MoSHi).

1. The contractor for army rations in the area for the period Oct. 1803 to Oct. 1804 was Elijah G. Galusha, and his agent was Maj. Nathan Rumsey. Galusha does not appear to have been present, but Rumsey is mentioned as a visitor to the Wood River camp several times (Clark field notes, CtY). Apparently Rumsey had been Galusha's predecessor as contractor, subletting from Matthew Lyon of Kentucky for the Oct. 1802 to Oct. 1803 period, and was now employed by Galusha. The relationship is implied but not specified in Lyon *vs.* Rumsey *et al.*, Randolph County, 1809–10, Misc. Kaskaskia Mss. and Papers, Bundle 29 (microfilm in IU-Hi). These papers also indicate that a man named Catlett was Galusha's partner in the army contract. He may be Hanson Catlett, who was surgeon's mate in Amos Stoddard's company at the St. Louis garrison in 1804. When Galusha submitted a proposal for supplying rations, 8 June 1803, his address was Middletown, Pa. (DNA, RG 107, Register of Letters Received), but by 1805, when he was awarded a mail contract, he was living in Eddyville, Ky. (DNA, RG 28, Postmaster General's letterbooks, N:311).

2. Manuel Lisa (1772–1820), merchant and fur trader, of Spanish descent.

3. He means Jean Pierre Chouteau (1758–1849), fur trader and Indian agent, commonly called Pierre. Lewis was now planning to send a delegation of Osage Indians to Washington in keeping with Jefferson's instructions.

4. Here, besides Carlos Dehault Delassus, Lewis mentions Julien Dubuque, a trader operating among the Indians near Prairie du Chien, with an interest in their lead mines; Charles Gratiot (1752–1817), Swiss-born trader and landowner, brother-in-law of the Chouteaus and the father of Charles Gratiot (1788–1855); Auguste Chouteau; and the wife of Manuel Lisa.

[168]

108. Henri Peyroux to Jefferson

Sir   [20 March 1804]

Before accepting the command of New Madrid, in 1798, I had the honor of writing to Your Excellency on some natural history subjects and on the origin of the habits, customs, and industry [industrie] of the American Indians. I was then in New Orleans, and I entrusted my letter to Monsieur Héraut[1] who promised to deliver it to you, when leaving for Philadelphia. That was the second letter I had had the honor of writing to you: but now I presume that they were not delivered.

Monsieur Menard,[2] Major of militia of the Cascakias, has informed me that several months ago Captain Luis, your nephew, and Captain Clarck were the bearers of a recommendation from Your Excellency addressed to me. Not having been commandant of the St. Geneviève District for the last ten years, and being in New Madrid, I was not able to see your nephew. All I have learned since is that Monsieur Lassus, formerly Lieutenant Governor of Upper Louisiana, has succeeded in obtaining a copy of that recommendation from Your Excellency and has sent it to the Spanish Government in the Capital, thinking to prove by this piece that I am engaged in a correspondence about this Province with foreign powers. That is what he and his father have never ceased saying, since my return from Philadelphia, to make me suspect: but I have always scorned their base and underhand maneuvers. I am very distressed not to have had the honor of seeing your nephew; I would have done my utmost to obtain for him at that post all the amenities which would have depended on me; likewise for his friends.

I leave in less than three days for New Orleans, where I expect to see Governor Claiborn. If Your Excellency would think it appropriate to address a reply to me in that town it would greatly flatter me. I have the honor to be very respectfully, Sir, Your Excellency's very humble and obedient servant,

New Madrid   HENRI PEYROUX
20 March 1804

ALS, RC (ViWC). This is a translation.
1. Not identified.
2. Pierre Menard (1766–1844), merchant, trader, and frontier political figure; first lieutenant governor of the state of Illinois.

109. Lewis to Jefferson

Dear Sir,   St. Louis March 26th 1804.

I send you herewith inclosed, some slips of the <great> Osages *Plums*, and *Apples*.[1] I fear the season is too far advanced for their success. Had I earlyer learnt that these fruits were in the neighbourhood, they would have been forwarded at a more proper time. I would thank you to send a part of them to Messrs. John Mason,[2] & William Hamilton.[3] Should they not succeed, Mr. Charles Gratiot, a gentleman of this place, has promised me that he would with pleasure attend to the orders of yourself, or any of my acquaintancies, who may think proper to write him on the subject. Mr. Gratiot can obtain the young plants at the proper season, and send them very readily to Mr. Trist if requested to do so. I obtained the cuttings, now sent you, from the garden of Mr. Peter Choteau, who resided the greater portion of his time for many years with the Osage nation. It is from this gentleman, that I obtained the information I possess with respect to these fruits.

The Osage's *Plum* appears to be a native of the country bordering on the vilages of that nation, situated on the Osage river, a south branch of the Missouri, about two hundred and sixty miles west from St. Louis. The shrub, which produces this fruit is remarkably small, seldom rising to a greater hight than five feet; it is much branced, and the smaller boughs are armed with long thorn-like or pinated twigs; in their native state they grow very thickly together, and I think from their appearance, might with a little attention, be made to form an ornimental and usefull hedg. They produce their fruit every year, and generally in great abundance. The fruit is a large oval plum, of a pale yellow colour and exquisite flavor. With other fruits of this family it's matrix is comparitively small; it comes to maturity about the begining of July, and continues to ripen in succession on the same plant untill the 20th or last of that month.

The *Osage Apple* is a native of the interior of the continent of North America, and is perhaps a nondiscript production; the information I have obtained with respect to it is not so minute as I could wish, nor such as will enable me to discribe it in a satisfactory manner. Mr. Peter Coteau, who first introduced this tree in the neighbourhood of St. Louis, about five years since, informed me, that he obtained the young plants at the great Osage vilage from an Indian of that nation, who said he procured them about three hundred miles west of that place. The general contour of this tree, is very much that of the *black haw*,[4] common to most parts of the

U. States, with these diferences however, that the bark is of a lighter colour, less branced, and arrives to a larger size, sometimes rising to the hight of thirty feet. It's smaller branches are armed with many single, long, & sharp, pinated thorns. The particular form of the leaf or flower I have been unable to learn. So much do the savages esteem the wood of this tree for the purpose of making their bows, that they travel many hundred miles in quest of it. The particulars with respect to the fruit, is taken principally from the Indian discription; my informant never having seen but one specimen of it, which was not fully ripe, and much shrivled and mutilated before he saw it. The Indians give an extravigant account of the exquisite odour of this fruit when it has obtained maturity, which takes place the latter end of summer, or the begining of Autumn. They state, that at this season they can always tell by the scent of the fruit when they arrive in the neighbourhood of the tree, and usually take advantage of this season to obtain the wood; as it appears not [to] be a very abundant growth, even in the country where it is to be found. An opinion prevails among the Osages, that the fruit is poisonous, tho' they acknowledge that they have never tasted it. They say that many anamals feed on it, and among others, a large species of *Hare*† which abounds in that country. This fruit is the size of the largest orange, of a globular form, and a fine orange colour. The pulp is contained in a number of conacal pustules, covered with a smooth membranous rind, having their smaller extremities attatched to the matrix, from which, they project in every direction, in such manner, as to form a compact <*globular*> figure. The form and consistancy of the *matrix* and *germ,* I have not been able to learn. The trees which are in the possession of Mr. Choteau have as yet produced neither flowers nor fruit.

† From the discription of this anamal,[5] it is in point of colour, figure, and habbits very much the same species with the European Hare, and is as large, if not larger than that anamal. This large hare of America, is found on the upper part of the Arkansas River, and in the country lying from thence South, and West, to the mountains which seperate us from New Mexico, it is said to be rema[r]kably fleet, and hard to be overtaken on horseback even in their open plains. I have the honour to be with sincere esteem Your Obt. Servt.

MERIWETHER LEWIS
Capt. 1st U.S. Infty.

ALS, RC (DLC). Endorsed; received 4 May 1804.
Between his letter of 28 Dec. 1803 and this one, Lewis dispatched four letters to Jefferson, according to the index of letters. They are: 10 Feb. 1804,

recd. 20 March; 25 Feb., recd. 4 May; 26 Feb., recd. 4 May; and 24 March, recd. 4 May. Jefferson's summary index also lists letters of Lewis dated 5 Jan. and 26 April, but they are not recorded in the index proper. Several other letters which Lewis wrote the Secretary of War during this period are missing, but are recorded in DNA, RG 107, Register of Letters Received. They include:

10 Feb., L-124. Regarding an appointment for Clark.

15 March, L-238. Copy of Lewis's speech to the Sauks and Foxes.

24 March, L-137. Regarding measures needed for the defense of Louisiana.

28 March, L-136. Recommending Charles Gratiot *fils,* Pierre Chouteau *fils,* and V. B. Lorimier for appointment to West Point.

4 April, L-144. Recommending John Hay for a subagency.

18 May, L-152. Regarding a deputation of Osage chiefs, and advising of drafts on their account totaling $3,000.

A few other letters to the Secretary of War in April and May were for the purpose of advising him of drafts or bills of exchange drawn on the War Department.

1. The wild plum, *Prunus* sp., and the Osage orange, *Maclura pomifera* (Raf.) C. K. Schneid.

2. John Mason, of Analostan Island in the Potomac, at Georgetown, D.C., was an attorney, banker, farmer, and later would become superintendent of Indian trade.

3. William Hamilton (1745–1813) was a wealthy devotee of landscape gardening, owner of an estate on the west side of the Schuylkill near Philadelphia called Woodlands (STETSON).

4. *Crataegus douglasii* Lindley.

5. The white-tailed jack rabbit, *Lepus townsendii campanius* Hollister.

110. Henry Dearborn to Lewis

Sir,   War Department 26th March 1804.

The peculiar situation, circumstances and organisation of the Corps of Engineers is such as would render the appointment of Mr. Clark a Captain in that Corps improper—and consequently no appointment above that of a Lieutenant in the Corps of Artillerists could with propriety be given him which appointment he has recd. and his Commission is herewith enclosed. His Military Grade will have no effect on his compensation for the service in which he is engaged. I hope by the time this reaches you, all obstructions to your ascending the River will be removed & that you will be able to progress with facility and safety. I am &c.

Lbk (DNA, RG 107, Letters Sent, 2:202); RC (MoSHi). Dearborn sent this letter to the commanding officer at Kaskaskia, asking him to forward it to Lewis by an express.

As the winter wore on and no commission for Clark was sent from Washington, Lewis wrote a reminder to Dearborn. It is missing, but in the

Register of Letters Received it is listed as L-124, 10 Feb. 1804, recd. 20 March, "relative to an appointment for Capt. Clark." Jefferson records a letter from Lewis written on the same day and also received 20 March; possibly Lewis was reminding the President, too, that Clark's commission had not been received. Dearborn sent a list of nominations to Jefferson on 24 March, including the name of William Clark of Kentucky, to be appointed second lieutenant in the Corps of Artillerists (DLC). On the same day, Jefferson routinely copied the recommendations and sent them to the Senate for confirmation. There is nothing to indicate that he protested the decision to make Clark a lieutenant. He offered no explanation to Lewis, and Lewis does not mention the matter in any extant letter to Jefferson. The nomination was approved by the Senate on 26 March, and on 30 March the Secretary of War notified the Adjutant and Inspector of the appointment, saying that Clark was to take rank from 26 March. Clark was thus not allowed the seniority that would have been his if the commission had been dated on the day of his decision to accompany the expedition, or even on the date of his joining Lewis at Louisville.

111. Marqués de Casa Calvo to Pedro Cevallos

No. 5 *Reservada*   [30 March 1804]
[Marginal note] The Brigadier of the Royal Army, Marqués de Casa Calvo, His Majesty's commissioner for the retrocession and limits of the province of Louisiana, communicates the steps that he has taken to detain the progress of the discoveries, that a subject sent by the president of the United States is making on the Missouri River towards the direction of the South Sea, where they are thinking of having a port within five years; writing to the Commandant-general of the *Provincias Internas* to arrest and detain him.

Received—July 18, 1804

Most Excellent Sir.

With the idea of detaining the hasty and gigantic steps which our neighbors are taking towards the South Sea, entering by way of the Missouri river and other rivers of the west bank of the Mississippi; furthering their discoveries in that district; I have written to the Commandant-General of the *Provincias Internas,* Brigadier Don Nemesio Salcedo[1] the letter, a copy of which is enclosed. I hope this step will merit the approbation of Your Excellency, with all the more reason in that it proceeds from the intimation made in [letter] number 13, that he believes and assures that it is of the greatest importance to restrain in that area the progress of the discoverers, who are directing towards that district all their views and voyages, not losing from sight the forming from the interior [*fondo*] of their states a chain of

[173]

establishments, making themselves masters of our rich possessions, which they desire.

It is painful to acknowledge it and to experience it, but it will be much more painful not to use all our forces, while there is still time to remedy it, even though it be at the cost of continual vigilance and no small expense.

The duty of a vassal zealous for the glory of the King and nation impels my pen with irresistible force to write and to assure that the moment is a critical one and it is best to take advantage of it, for otherwise the rich possessions of the Kingdom of New Spain remain exposed. Therefore I urgently beg Your Excellency to call the attention of His Majesty to these dominions if he does not wish to be a witness of their impending ruin and destruction.

May God Our Lord keep Your Excellency many years

New Orleans, March 30, 1804

Most Excellent Sir,

EL MARQUÉS DE CASA CALVO [rubric]

Most Excellent *Señor* Don Pedro Cavallos.

Most Excellent Sir:

I am sending to Your Excellency a copy of the official letter in which Brigadier Marqués de Casa Calvo advises me of Mr. Merry, Captain of the United States Army having presented himself in the establishments of Illinois, with the solicitation of penetrating the Missouri river in order to make observations and discoveries, so that with that object in mind, with the notices included in the letter and those included in my reply, a copy of which is also enclosed, Your Excellency may be able to make whatever use of them that you judge.

May God keep Your Excellency many years.

Chihuahua, May 3, 1804

Most Excellent Sir

NEMESIO SALCEDO [rubric]

Most Excellent *Señor* Don Joseph de Yturrigaray[2]

[Marginal note] acknowledge receipt and reply that His Excellency hopes that you will advise him of all results.

[draft of reply]
I have received Your Excellency's letter of May 3, last, the two copies

[174]

of which are enclosed in it relative to the intentions of Mr. Merry, Captain of the United States Army regarding penetrating the Missouri river for the purpose of making observations and discoveries. I am informed myself of all and hope Your Excellency will be pleased to give me advice of the results because of it being very important to the service of the King.

May God, etc.

June 2, 1804.

[draft]

Señor Don Nemesio de Salcedo.

Printed, NASATIR (2), 2:727–29. The covering letter, in Spanish, is in the Archivo Histórico Nacional (Madrid), Papeles de Estado, legajo 5542 (Nasatir also lists other copies); the enclosure is in the Archivo General de Mexico, Historia, vol. 200 (transcript in CU-B).

1. Nemesio Salcedo was commandant general of the Interior Provinces.
2. Joseph de Yturrigaray was viceroy of Mexico from 1803 to 1808.

112. Clark to Lewis

[April 1804]

Memorandom of Artecles which may be wanting

Not to be had Som red lead & oil Paints for the lockers on Deck &c.
200 sent " Nails 6d or 8d to put on Hinges
sent " red & blue Ribben (wide)
sent 2 Trumpits to be mended.

If 2 muskets were hung on Swivels in the Stern it would be well. *Do as you please on this subject.*

Perhaps if the Missouriis Indian was to be taken up by us, a favourable impression might be made, thro' him. *On inquiry he is not a character that can render us any service.* M. L.

I can't find Hair Pipes[1] purchased of Mr. Chouteau. Mr. Hays says they are necessary. *Perhaps you may since have found them. Those purchased are not to be found here.*

Jo. Whitehouse[2] says that Mr. Whitlock[3] has in his possession two months pay of his for the months of Feby. & March 1804. Mr. Pike gave a certificate to Mr. Whitlock to that amt.[4] *Mr. Whitlock says he cannot pay Whitehouse.*

2 *Sent.* Som raw hides are wanting.

Note if we have 47 men and have a Perogue sufficiently large

[175]

2000 lbs Pork   *sent 5 barrels*
2000 "   Flour ⌠ *do. 5 do.*
   5 Bar: Corn⌡ of Contr. to be furnished
   sent 25½ bushels of lyed corn

5 bar. whiskey ⎫ Woolford [5] has that qty. in store
                ⎭

Note—The Contractor will take Woodfords whiskey @ 1 Dol. pr.
Gal. I think we will find that we cannot take more provision than
the quantity sent. M. Lewis.

AD (MoSHi). The memorandum is in Clark's hand, with comments in
Lewis's hand which are here set in italics. The memorandum was returned
to Clark, at the Wood River camp, in Lewis's letter of 2 May (No. 115).
   1. The common term for a variety of tubular beads 1½ or more inches
in length, used by the Indians of the Eastern Woodlands and the Great
Plains. See EWERS (1).
   2. Joseph Whitehouse, a member of the expedition.
   3. Ambrose Whitlock (d. 1863) of Virginia, appointed second lieutenant
in the First Infantry in 1801. He was an assistant paymaster at this time, and
a district paymaster from 1805 to 1815.
   4. I do not understand this statement, unless Pike is serving as an assistant
paymaster. Whitehouse had probably been transferred to Lewis from Capt.
Daniel Bissell's company at Fort Massac; his name appears on the pay and
muster rolls of that company, with enlistments of 14 May 1798 and 14
May 1803 (DNA, RG 94, Pay and Muster Rolls, First Infantry).
   5. No doubt the same as Adam Wolford in No. 217. Except that he
operated a boat between Louisville and St. Louis, I know nothing else about
him. John H. Marks spells the name "A. Woolfort" in a letter to Clark of
20 June 1810 (Lewis-Marks Papers, ViU).

113. John Ordway to His Parents

Honored Parence.   Camp River Dubois April the 8th 1804
   I now embrace this oppertunity of writing to you once more to
let you know where I am and where I am going. I am well thank God,
and in high Spirits. I am now on an expidition to the westward, with
Capt. Lewis and Capt. Clark, who are appointed by the President
of the united States to go on an expidition through the interior
parts of North America. We are to ascend the Missouri River with a
boat as far as it is navigable and then to go by land, to the western
ocean, if nothing prevents, &c.
   This party consists of 25 picked Men of the armey & country likewise and I am So happy as to be one of them pick'd Men from the
armey, and I and all the party are if we live to Return, to Receive
our Discharge when ever we return again to the united States if we

chuse it. This place is on the Mississippi River oppisite to the Mouth of the Missouri River and we are to Start in ten days up the Missouri River. This has been our winter quarters. We expect to be gone 18 months or two years. We are to Receive a great Reward for this expidition, when we Return. I am to Receive 15 dollars pr. month and at least 400 ackers of first Rate land, and if we make Great Discoveries as we expect, the united States, has promised to make us Great Rewards more than we are promised, &c. For fear of exidants I wish to inform you that I left 200 dollars in cash, at Kaskaskias. Put it on interest with a Substantial man by the name of Charles Smith &c. pertnership which were three[?] more Substantial men binding with him and Capt. Clark is bound to See me paid at the time and place where I receive my discharge and if I Should not live to return my heirs can git that and all the pay Due me from the U.S. by applying to the Seat of Government. I have Recd. no letters Since Betseys yet, but will write next winter if I have a chance. Yours, &c.

JOHN ORDWAY Sergt.

Photostat of ALS, RC (OrHi); original not found. As published in the *Oregon Historical Quarterly*, 23 (1922), 268–69, the letter was addressed to "Stephen Ordway, Hebron, New Hampshire," and was postmarked at Cahokia on 14 April 1804.

114. Lewis to Clark

Dear friend— St. Louis May 2nd 1804.

I cannot hear of or find the *hair pipes*. The articles you sent by Sergt. Floyd wer duly recieved. The mail has not arrived. The Osages will set out about the 10th. I return you the memorandom you inclosed me with remarks on several particulars therein contained. I send you 19 small flaggs, sixteen Musquitoe nets and our shirts— pray send down as soon as possible thirteen ells of the brown linin purchased of Morrison to replace that quantity borrowed of Mr. Gratiot, also the case with the Maps, and the specimines of salt which you will find in my writing desk, on the shelves where our books are, or in the drawer of the Instrument case.

The pay of the men will commence from the dates of their last inlistments and will be made up to the last of November 1804. at the regular wages of soldiers & Sergts. &c.—including the bounty of such as are intitled to it, which is not the case with those whose former inlistments do not expire before the said 31st of November. Other receipt rolls will be made out for five dollars pr. month as an advance

on the score of Cloathing and provisions not furnished by the government—this to commence with those inlisted in Kentuckey from the
dates of their inlistments, all others from the 1st of January 1804.
Mr. Choteau has procured seven engages to go as far as the Mandanes
—but they will not agree to go further, and I found it impossible to
reduce them to any other engagement than that usually made with
those people. Your sincere friend,

M. LEWIS.—in haist

ALS, RC (DLC). Clark sent two men down with this letter, and the
items it mentions, on 4 May (Clark field notes, CtY).

115. Clark to William Croghan

Dear Sir   Camp Mouth of Missouri May the 2d 1804
 This will be handed you by Mr. Peter Choteau, an inhabitant of St.
Louis, a gentleman deservedly esteemed among the most respectable
and influential citizens of upper Louisiana. Mr. Choteau's zeal to
promote the public welfar has induced him, at the instance of our
government to visit the Osage Nation since the session of this
Country to the united States. He has brought with him the great Chief
of that Nation, and many other Chiefs of the first consideration and
respectability among them, and is now on his rout to the City of
Washington in charge of those Chiefs, with a view to effect a treaty
between the united States and that Nation. The promptitude and
fidelity with which Mr. Choteau has fulfilled the wishes of the
government on this ocasion, as also the personal dangers to which he
has been exposed in the course of this transaction, intitle him in an
emenant degree to the particular attention and best services, not
only of yourself but of his fellow Citizens generally. Besides Mr.
Choteaus personal merits and his claims to the attention of his
fellow citizens, he has still a stronger claim upon my particular
friends; arrissing from the mark[ed] politeness and attention displayed by himself, his Lady and family towards Capt. Lewis and my
self during our residence in this Countrey. On our several visits to
St. Louis, in the course of the Winter and Spring, we have made the
house of this gentleman our home.
 Any Services therefore which you may have in your power to render
Mr. Choteau, or those of his Party, I now beg leave to claim. Your
Sincere friend,

WM. CLARK

ALS, RC (MoSHi). No one familiar with Clark's straightforward prose
style would expect him to say "promptitude and fidelity" or to describe

Chouteau as "a gentleman deservedly esteemed." The letter is phrased in the more ornate language of Lewis, and is nearly identical to the one sent by Lewis to Capt. William Preston (No. 116).

116. Lewis to William Preston

Sir,   St. Louis 3d May 1804

This will be handed you by my Friend Mr. Peter Choteau, an Inhabitant of this Place, a Gentleman deservedly Considered, among the most respectable and influential Citizens of Upper Louisiana. Since the Cession of this Country to the U State, Mr. Choteau's zeal to promote the public Welfare, has induced him at the Instance of our Government, to visit the Osage Nation with a view to prevail on some of their most Important Chiefs, to accompany him to the Seat of Government, in order to form a Treaty of Alliance with the U States; in this Mission Mr. Choteau has been completely successful, and is now on his rout to the City of Washington in Charge of the Deputation from that Nation, consisting of their King and a Number of their Chiefs of the first respectability and Consideration.

The promptitude and Fidelity with which Mr. Choteau has executed the wishes of the Government on this occasion, as also the personal Danger to which he has been exposed in the course of this Transaction, entitles him in an eminent Degree to the particular Attention and best Services, not only of yourself, but of his fellow Citizens generally. Therefore any Services which you may have in your Power to render him, either in his private or public Capacity, will be gratefully acknowledged by, Your sincere friend and Obedt. Servt.

MERIWETHER LEWIS, Capt.
1st. U.S. Regt. Infty.

Typed copy of LS (ViU). William Preston had served with Gen. Anthony Wayne on the western frontier, becoming a captain 4 March 1792 and resigning 31 July 1798.

117. Lewis to Clark

My dear friend,   St. Louis May 6th 1804.

I send you herewith inclosed your commission accompanyed by the Secretary of War's letter; it is not such as I wished, or had reason to expect; but so it is—a further explaneation when I join you. I think it will be best to let none of our party or any other persons know any thing about the grade, you will observe that the grade has no effect upon your compensation, which by G———d, shall be equal to my own.

[179]

Pray send down the small perogue on Monday; I think she had better have *way*-strips put along her gunwals—I send you by Colter and Reed [1] 200 lbs. of tallow which you will be so good as to have melted with 50 lbs. of hog's lard, cooled in small vessels and put into some of those small Keggs which wer intended for whiskey. Not a kegg can be obtained in St. Louis nor are they to be expected from Mr. *Contractor* we must therefore do the best we can. The French hands eight in number are all engaged; they will go up in the Perogue on Tuesday or Wednesday next; by which time I hope all matters will be in readiness for my departure from this place. Damn Manuel and triply Damn Mr. B.[2] They give me more vexation and trouble than their lives are worth. I have dealt very plainly with these gentlemen, in short I have come to an open rupture with them; I think them both great scoundrels, and they have given me abundant proofs of their unfrendly dispositions towards our government and it's measures. These <*gentlemen*> (no I will scratch it out) these puppies, are not unacquainted with my opinions; and I am well informed that they have engaged some hireling writer to draught a petition and remonstrance to Govr. Claibourne against me; strange indeed, that men to appearance in their senses, will <*show*> manifest such strong sumptoms of insanity, as to be *wheting knives to cut their own throats.*

I have determined to take two horses on with me, the one which is at Camp and the one the men now bring you. Adieu it is late. Your sincer friend,

M. LEWIS

ALS, RC (MoSHi).
1. Moses B. Reed, a member of the expedition until expelled from the party for attempted desertion.
2. Manuel Lisa and his partner in the fur trade, Francis Marie Benoit, Sr. (1768–1819). Lewis and Lisa wasted no affection upon each other; when Lisa met Thomas Nuttall in Pittsburgh a few years later, he described Lewis as "fond of exaggerating everything relative to his expedition, & . . . a very headstrong, & in many instances an imprudent man" (Nuttall to Benjamin Smith Barton, 22 April 1810, transcript in the Academy of Natural Sciences, Philadelphia).

118. Lewis's Notes on Salines and Proposed Districts

May 6th 1804.
Information recieved from Monsr. *Etiene Cadron*[1] at St. Louis relative to the saline on the Ar[k]ansas River most generally known by the name of the pot saline.

This saline I visited last winter; when I observed it's situation particularly as also every circumstance in relation to it's peculiarity —it is situated on the East side of the first of what are usually called the t[h]ree forks of the Arcansas River, within a quarter of a league of that stream; this junction called the three forks of the Arcansas is estimated at two hundred and forty leagues from it's junction with the Mississippi.

Description—

At the mouth of the small stream which discharges itself from this saline there is a thick wood which continues on both sides of the same within a small distance of the saline. Near this place are several remarkable salines, one of which in particular contains about 4 acres. It contains a variety of springs, which boil from the ground, and hence they have obtained among the Indians [the name of] *the Pots*. So strong is the water, that the salt concretes as it courses from the ground, and forms a kind of rim around the fissures.

Great Saline to the westward of the main branch of the Arkansas —From the Osage town on the Osage river 11 days travel to the Great Saline.

From St. Louis to the Osage Vilage t[h]ence West 120 leagues to the Great saline situated on a Southern branch of the river Arkansas, called niscue and by the French the river of the grand saline which after pursuing a course of about 40 leagues discharges itself into the Arkansas. About 30 leagues due west from the Great saline and situated on the S.W. side of a considerable Southern branch of the Arkansas stands the saline which produces the purest rock salt it is of white or clear colour. This stream is called by the Osages the *Na-ches, ri-tchin-gar.* 30 leagues below this saline and on the same side of that stream is situated the Red saline so named from the colour of the salt it Lys S.W. 20 leagues from the Great Saline. This stream discharges itself into the Arcansaw about 20 leagues above the three forks of that river—after traversing the country for about 60 leages after it passes the red saline.

The Pot saline situated on the Eastern bank of the most Easterly of the three forks of the Arcansas River about 10 leagues from it's mouth this stream is navigable, [to] the saline and many miles above it for perogues or light boats. Two other salines of inferior note are found West from the Osage Vilage, the first 55 leagues W. near the head of the middle fork of the Arkansas, called *Vai-ce-ton-hand-hos* —the other bearing a little south of West from the same and distant from it about 30 leagues; the last is near the main river Arkansas, on it's North side.

[181]

I.J.K. denotes the vilages of the Snake Lizard and Squirel.[2]

In the Panis Country at the head of the river Cansies is a large saline of the same nature of the Great saline of the Osages.

The narrowest part of the Osage country is 300 Miles bordering on the Missouri.

Districts proposed—[3]

1st. St. Louis—from the mouth of R. de Platin to it's source thence with that stream to it's source, thence West to the Renaud a fork of the Maremeg river thence down the same to the mouth of the said fork, thence with the main river to interseect a line drawn N. 15 W. from the source of the St. Francis River to the Gasconade, thence with this line untill it arrives at the Gasconade, thence down the Gasconade to the Missouri, thence down the Missouri and with it to the Mississippi, thence down the Mississippi to the beginning—it is to be understood that this district includes the Settlements between the Missouri and Mississippi.

2nd. St. Genavive District. Begining at the mouth of Apple Creek &c. and runing with the dotted red line as pr. Map.

3rd. Cape Gerardeau begining at the southeren extremity of the grand bend and with a due West line to the St. Francis, and thence with the dotted line as aforesaid.

4th. Begining on the lower side at the Beyou which discharges itself into the St. Francis river and leaving the Mississippi oposite to the Beyou River following the same untill it interseects the St. Francis thence up the St. Francis untill it reaches the line which devides it from the District of Cape Gerardeau.

AD, SC (MoSHi). In Lewis's hand. This document must be considered together with No. 122. It appears to be a draft of information Lewis was preparing to send to Jefferson in care of Pierre Chouteau. The portion headed "Districts proposed" links it with the map described in No. 122, and so does the cryptic line about prairie-dog villages. The information on salines is recapitulated by Clark in the JOURNALS, 6:267.

1. A French waterman and fur trader. He was *patron* of a party granted a license to hunt on the Missouri no higher than Fort Osage in 1808, and in 1812 was an *engagé* with Manuel Lisa's expedition up that river.

2. A reference to four circles on the map described in No. 122, denoting prairie-dog villages. It was the belief of Indians and early settlers that the prairie dog, the horned toad, and the rattlesnake all occupied the same burrows. Lewis and Clark at first accepted this legend but later doubted it. In his journal entry of 7 Sept. 1804, Clark wrote of finding a village of prairie dogs, which he and Lewis often called "barking squirrels," and added, "it is Said that a kind of Lizard also a Snake reside with those animals." But after the expedition, when the Biddle narrative was being prepared, either Clark or Biddle wrote after this statement in the manuscript,

[182]

"did not find this correct" (JOURNALS, 1:142). For another note on the prairie dog, see No. 149, note 31.

3. To provide a government for the new Louisiana Purchase, Congress approved an act of 26 March 1804 which divided the area into two districts. The upper one, consisting of the portion lying above the southern boundary of present Arkansas, was termed the District of Louisiana, and for governmental purposes was made a part of Indiana Territory (STATUTES, 2:287). Dissatisfaction with this arrangement caused Congress a year later to form a separate territorial government, establishing the Territory of Louisiana (STATUTES, 2:331–32). Immediately after the District of Louisiana was formed in 1804, it became necessary to divide it into subdivisions (*also* to be called districts), and Jefferson wrote to Harrison for advice. "As something to begin upon I will barely mention that on the imperfect information I have, I suppose we may throw the settlements together so as to make three or four districts, something like our frontier counties in Virginia. But to decide on this further information is necessary, and this I shall hope to receive from you" (HARRISON, 1:94). Harrison solicited the counsel of Amos Stoddard in St. Louis, then sent to Jefferson a proposal that exactly duplicated Stoddard's. It did not vary markedly from that presented here by Lewis, except for the addition of a fifth district, Arkansas, to provide for the settlements on the Arkansas River which were not contiguous with the other settled areas. After comparing the suggestions of Harrison and Lewis, Jefferson decided to adopt the divisions which had existed under the Spanish government. He therefore provided a separate district of St. Charles for the area lying north of the Missouri, which neither Lewis nor Harrison had proposed, and he failed to make a new district for the Arkansas settlements—combining them instead with the New Madrid district. The districts finally decided upon were St. Charles, St. Louis, St. Genevieve, Cape Girardeau, and New Madrid.

119. Nemesio Salcedo to Pedro Cevallos

No. 4   [8 May 1804]
[Marginal notation] The commandant-general of the *Provincias Internas* of New Spain relates that the governor of Louisiana has notified him that Captain Merry, commissioned by the United States for the purpose of making observations and discoveries, presented himself in Illinois. He also states what he answered to the said governor concerning the matter.

Most Excellent Sir:
I am remitting to Your Excellency under number one a copy of an official letter in which the Marqués de Casa Calvo notified me of Captain Merry having presented himself in Illinois soliciting to penetrate the Missouri River in order to carry out the commission which has been conferred upon him by the United States of America concerning observations and discoveries; and likewise is enclosed under

number two a copy of the answer which I have given to the referred to Marqués concerning the matter.

By both papers Your Excellency will recognize that that expedition is directed to territories under my command and that it is a step of the said United States which indicates its ambitious views in the same act of taking possession of the province of Louisiana. I am unable to dictate any other precautionary step than the orders already communicated to the governors of Texas and New Mexico relative to their preventing the introduction of foreigners in the districts of both provinces, and to their refusing permission to such foreigners, and relative to their not allowing the boundaries of Louisiana to be marked out [set up] along their frontiers [borders of Texas and New Mexico], as I informed Your Excellency in my letter number three of October 4, last.

Even though these steps taken with all anticipation and the charge which the principal Indian nations have of giving advice of any news which they learn are the only ones in this case and for which cause I now repeat their observance to the cited governors, it has seemed to me well to augment those relative to New Mexico in the terms verified in copy number three.

I am informing you in it that in the present circumstances the limited forces of that province should be used to restrain one of the barbarous nations which has become restless [getting out of hand]. I sent a party of Comanche Indians or others of those who are affected to us to reconnoitre the country as far as the banks of the Missouri river in order to examine if the expedition of Merry has penetrated into these territories, to acquire all possible knowledge of its progress, and even to stop them, making efforts to apprehend it.

Notwithstanding, as I have insinuated to the Marqués de Casa Calvo, I judge that through the Chief of Louisiana, you may have called the attention of the governor of the United States to this suspicious conduct. I am sending an official letter to the Minister of the King in Philadelphia instructing him of the present case for the conduct of the better service, and thus I hope it may please Your Excellency to inform His Majesty of it for his sovereign intelligence.

May God keep Your Excellency many years.

Chihuahua, 8 May, 1804

Most Excellent Sir

NEMESIO SALCEDO [rubric]

Most Excellent *Señor* Don Pedro Ceballos

[*Enclosures with dispatch no. 4*]

[184]

No. 1 Colonel Don Carlos Dehault Delassus, Lieutenant-Governor of the establishment of Illinois gave information under date of December 9 of last year that on the seventh of the same month Mr. Merry Weather Lewis, Captain of the Army of the United States and former secretary of the president of those states, presented himself in that post, intending to penetrate the Missouri River in order to fulfill the commission which he has of making discoveries and observations. The same commandant advises that he was opposed to his entrance until receiving the corresponding permission from the general government.

This step on the part of the United States at the same time that it took possession of the province of Louisiana; its haste to instruct itself and to explore the course of the Missouri whose origin they claim belongs to them, extending their designs as far as the South Sea, forces us necessarily to become active and to hasten our steps in order to cut off the gigantic steps of our neighbors if we wish, as it is our duty, to preserve undamaged [intact] the dominions of the King and to prevent ruin and destruction of the *Provincias Internas* and of the Kingdom of New Spain.

The only means which presents itself is to arrest Captain Merry Weather and his party, which cannot help but pass through the nations neighboring New Mexico, its presidios or *rancherías*.

A decisive and vigorous blow will prevent immense expenditures and even countless disagreeable replies which must originate between the respective governments, and immediately we are impelled to act out of the necessity of the moment. The public claims which they manifest concerning the extensions of the province of Louisiana which the French Republic has sold to them dictate it. No less do they claim as their western limits than the mouth of the Rio Bravo up to 30 degrees north latitude, and from there the line of demarcation penetrates [undetermined] far to the north west as well as to the north, until it loses itself in the immense forests and wilderness, even though they are not [as yet] inhabited by Europeans.

What other end can the repeated designs and incursions of the Americans have, designs seen even earlier in the unfortunate one, for them, of Philip Nolan.

We must not lose time, and the slightest omission can be of great consequence for the orders and confidential instruction with which I find myself. The greatest responsibility would fall upon us if we should not take, without losing a moment, steps to put a stop to these dispositions and give time for measures to be taken so that the limits of Louisiana may be arranged without compromising the interest of Spain or endangering its vast and rich possessions.

In view of what has been said above I do not doubt that Your Excellency will give orders that the most efficacious steps be taken to arrest the referred to Captain Merry and his followers, who, according to notices, number twenty-five men, and to seize their papers and instruments that may be found on them. This action may be based upon the fact that without permission of the Spanish government they have entered its territory. Since the line of demarcation has not been determined as yet, they cannot infer that it already belongs to the United States. It is fitting to the confidential intentions of the ministry, by which I am instructed to stop the progress of these investigations, that although there be no motive or pretext whatsoever, nevertheless it is absolutely necessary for reasons of state to carry out the arrest of the said captain, and in order to exonerate Your Excellency of whatever responsibility I am immediately giving an account of it to the Court including a copy of this official letter.

May God keep Your Excellency many years.

New Orleans, March 5, 1804, El Marqués de Casa Calvo [and Manuel de Salcedo] to *Señor* Don Nemesio Salcedo.

This is a copy. Chihuahua, May 8, 1804

Francisco Xavr. de Truxillo [rubric]

No. 2 I received today Your Excellency's official letter of March 5, last, in which you inform me of the Lieutenant-Governor of Illinois having informed you under date of December 9, last, that Mr. Merry, Captain of the United States Army, presented himself to him requesting permission to penetrate the Missouri river in order to carry out the commission which he has to make discoveries and observations.

With this motive Your Excellency reflects upon the ambitious views of the said United States, and in justification, your view concerning how important it will be to prevent Mr. Merry from carrying out his commission. But the *noticias* of the situation of demarcations which Your Excellency includes in your official letter, not agreeing completely with the only maps of the territories to which they relate and which I have before me, and noting among other things that since the date of the dispatch of the Lieutenant of Illinois five months have elapsed, I am notifying you regretfully that this concurrence of circumstances makes it difficult for me to take the steps, the success of which will be as fortunate as I desire.

Eight months ago I communicated to the governors of the border provinces of your province the orders that I judged opportune not only to excite their care and vigilance but also for the purpose of forewarning their dispositions in every event, and they being quite opportune even in the very case that Your Excellency speaks of, I see with satisfaction that until I receive more exact news, the notices that I now have will suffice and I am protecting myself by repeating to you the punctual observance of my cited orders.

As concerning the expedition of Merry it is customary that Your Excellency might have called the attention of the United States by means of the chief or general who commands that province, I must commend your zeal, which may please you to communicate to me the reply which you must have received, for you must know already how useful must be any constancy of the manner of thinking of the referred to government in the present circumstances.

Likewise I ask Your Excellency that when you retire from that province to please give me knowledge of some person of confidence who resides in it with whom I may correspond in order to acquire the news which is necessary for the best service.

I am sending this official letter to Your Excellency by way of Havana, considering that course more convenient and secure on account of the delay to Your Excellency's letter to which I am answering, for having taken eight days from Texas to this residence, it took fifty-one in the remainder of the trip. Moreover, the direction by the indicated route of important letters prevents the inevitable contingencies of sending by land from your capital.

> May God keep Your Excellency many years.

Chihuahua, May 3, 1804,

> Nemesio Salcedo [to] *Señor* Marques de Casa Calbo,

This is a copy, Chihuahua, May 8, 1804

> FRANCISCO XAVR. DE TRUXILLO [rubric]

No. 3

The Brigadier, Marqués de Casa Calvo, commissioned for the delivery of the province of Louisiana has sent me by extraordinary [express] the official letter a copy of which is enclosed, including the notice that on Demember 7, last, Mr. Merry, Captain in the United States army, presented himself in Illinois with a solicitude to penetrate the Missouri river in order to make some discoveries and observations.

As the views of this expedition may be directed to the ends which the said Marqués affirms, it is very prudent and necessary that on our part they may be impeded and [if] it may not be possible, either on account of the weather which they have had since the cited

[187]

date, or on account of the considerable distances, let us take at least some knowledge of its progress and state of being.

To this end, it is important under the circumstances that the force of that province occupy itself in continuing to punish the barbarous Navajo nation; that Your Excellency, making use of the friendship and difference towards us in which the other gentile nations find themselves, come to an agreement with the chief of the Comanches or with the Chief of any other [nation] which you judge more à propos, [to] send a party of individuals which you may collect to reconnoitre the country which lies between those villages as far as the right bank of the Missouri, with instructions and necessary provitions so that they examine if there are traces or other vestiges of the expedition of Merry and so that they acquaint themselves with the direction that it has taken and of their operations upon the territory, if they do not succeed in finding any other Indian village which may have seen it and may be able to give these notices.

If it appears to you opportune to give to the Indians that Your Excellency destines to such an important service one or two soldier-interpreters, [you may do so for] I am leaving to your judgment to order it, as likewise that Your Excellency inform Don Pedro Vial of the object of this voyage in case he may desire to join the expedition, as he is the most experienced in those territories, and in this case you may provide him with whatever may be necesesary for his maintenance, forewarning him that he must keep an exact diary which he must present to Your Excellency upon his return.

Nothing would be more useful than the apprehension of Merry, and even though I realize it is not an easy undertaking, chance might proportion things in such a way that it might be successful, for which reason it will not be superfluous for Your Excellency to give notice of this matter to the Indians, interesting their friendship and notions of generosity, telling them that they will be well compensated.

May God keep Your Excellency many years.

Chihuahua, May 3, 1804

Nemesio Salcedo [to] *Señor Gobernado*
of New Mexico

This is a copy. Chihuahua, May 8, 1804.

Francisco Xavr. de Truxillo [rubric]

To Don Nemesio Salcedo, San Ildefonso, September 24, 1804.

I have given account to the King of the contents of Your Excellency's letter No. 4 in which you give an account that the Governor of Louisiana had given notice, etc. and informed of all this His Majesty has given his royal approbation to Your Excellency's reply.

Printed, NASATIR (2), 2:729–35. The Spanish original is in the Archivo Histórico Nacional (Madrid), Papeles de Estado, legajo 5542, expediente 2. All enclosures except the last are in the Archivo General de Mexico, Historia, vol. 200 (transcript in CU-B). The original of enclosure No. 2 is in the Archivo General de Indias (Seville), Papeles de Cuba, legajo 2368.

120. Charles Gratiot to William Morrison

Kaskaskias Mr. Wm. Morrison   St. Louis the 12th May 1804
   Mr. Pike will deliver you three Bills of exchange with the letter of advice on each, which I have endorsed to Messrs. Guy Bryan & Wm. Morrison; Those Bills are drawn by Capt. Meriwether Lewis on the Secretary at War, they are by first and second, all here enclosed. The first

No. 42 his of the Sum of	$477.25	
The second No. 43 his of	72.51 2/3	
The third No. 44—of	950.23 1/3	

Amounting to the sum of fifteen hundred dollars, for which I beg you will give your receipt in deduction of a Sum of the Money I owe you on a bound I have past to your house in Philadelphia the 7th of July Eighteen hundred and two.

.   .   .   .

SC (MoSHi—Gratiot letterbook, 1798–1816). The remainder of the letter is not pertinent, except for the statement that Gratiot's son Charles is accompanying the Osage delegation soon to leave for Washington under the supervision of Pierre Chouteau.

121. Lewis to Amos Stoddard

Sir: [16 May 1804]
   In virtue of the authority vested in me by the President of the United States, I do constitute and appoint you my sole Agent to do and perform all and singularly the duties hereafter expressed, and in order to furnish you with the means of executing promptly those duties, I do by the authority aforesaid authorize you in my behalf to draw bills of exchange on the Secretary of War to any amount, which the nature of the service, whether required or performed, may in

your judgment and at your discretion be deemed necessary—provided nevertheless that in all cases where the compensation has been fixed by myself for the services of any person or persons, and of which you are or shall be informed, your bills in such cases must not exceed the sum stipulated. The duties hereby requested and required are

First, That at all times when any party of Indian chiefs should present themselves at St. Louis, with sufficient evidence of my having invited them to that place with a view of their being sent on to the City of Washington, you will please to provide them with the means of their going forward in a comfortable manner by the route prescribed in the memorandum with which I have furnished you: You will employ a suitable person to conduct such parties, and provide such interpreters to accompany them as may enable them to communicate their wishes to our Government in the English language: You will furnish them with no presents in merchandize, except such articles as you may deem necessary for their comfort and protection on their route. A deputation from a large band of the Sioux and Ayawăs nations, residing on the river Demoin, may be shortly expected to arrive here with this view; they have been invited to this place by me thro' the Agency of Mr. Crawford [1] for the purpose of going on to the seat of the General Government; they will therefore be received and furnished accordingly. I limited Mr. Crawford to the number of twelve from both nations inclusive; it is my wish therefore that this number may not be augmented, unless there does appear an absolute necessity for such an augmentation.

Secondly—On the return of the French Engagees, whom I have employed to accompany me to the Mandanes, you will settle with and pay them such ballances as may be due them agreeably to our contract for their services—which sums so due them will be stated by me, and forwarded to you by them on their return.

Thirdly—On a written notification from me of any engagement, which I may make with any individual after my departure from hence, for the payment of any sum of money, or the furnishing of any particular articles of merchandize, you will be pleased immediately on the receipt of such notification to fulfill my engagements, and as soon thereafter as possible to inform the Secretary of war of the same.

Fourthly—That should any letters arrive for me by the mail, other than such as the Government may order to be forwarded by Express to me, you will be so good as to put them under cover, and address them to the President of the United States: You will make the above disposition of all letters or other papers, which may be addressed to me at this place from whatever quarter they may come. Should any occurrence make it necessary that you should remove or be absent from this place, it is my wish that you should in such case transfer these my instructions, with all and completely the powers thereby given, together with the injunctions therein contained, to Mr. Charles Gratiot of this place, who is hereby requested to accept the same, and discharge the duties incident to the said Agent as herein before expressed: Should you have occasion to make this transfer, be pleased to notify the Secretary of war of the same. These instructions to continue in full force untill my return, unless otherwise directed by the Executive of the United States.

MERIWETHER LEWIS Capt.
1st U.S. Regt. Infty.

Signed Duplicates—
Signed and delivered to
Captain Amos Stoddard of the
U. States Artillerists at
St. Louis, the 16th day of
May 1804, in the presence of

Clarence Mulford [2] Lieut.
S. Worrell [3] Lt.

As it is possible that I may be absent for some time, I hereby transfer the above instructions to Charles Gratiot, Esq. with all and compleatly the powers thereby given, together with the injunctions therein contained agreably to the request of Capt. Lewis; reserving, however the right of receiving them again myself at pleasure.[4] Given under my hand at St. Louis the twenty [. . .] of April 1805.

AMOS STODDARD, Capt. of
corps of Artillerists.

ALS, RC (MoSHi).

1. Lewis Crawford, a trader who later became a member of the North West Company. For his role in the War of 1812, see *Wisconsin Historical Collections*, 19 (1910), 342n.

2. Clarence Mulford, first lieutenant of artillerists as of 1 April 1802, was assistant military agent for the St. Louis garrison under Stoddard's command. He had just joined Stoddard as a transfer from Capt. John McClallen's company, according to notations in Stoddard's company book (MoSHi).

3. Stephen Worrell, first lieutenant of artillerists as of 1 April 1802.

4. Evidence that Gratiot used his power of attorney for a short time in 1805, before transferring it to Pierre Chouteau, may be found in the financial records (No. 277). Two entries in DNA, RG 107, Register of Letters Sent, are pertinent: G-159, 25 May 1805, Gratiot to the Secretary, stating that he has forwarded two tin cases sent by Lewis, and that he is enclosing a copy of his power of attorney to act for Lewis; G-161, 1 June 1805, Gratiot

to the Secretary, stating that he has delivered to Chouteau all papers, etc.,
relating to his agency and has accepted a receipt. He encloses copies of the
receipt and of drafts executed by Lewis.

122. Lewis to Jefferson

Sir,   Saint Louis, May 18 1804.
     The following is a list of Articles forwarded you by Mr. Peter
Chouteau.

Minerals

No. 1. A specimen of Silver Oar from Mexico
No. 2. ditto of lead, supposed to contain a considerable quantity of Silver, from Mexico.
No. 3. An elegant Specimen of Rock Chrystal, also from Mexico.

> These were presented me by Mr. Peter Chouteau, who received them from the Osage Indians. They having collected them in some of their War excursions into that Country.

Nos. 4 & 5. Specimens of led oar from the Bed of the Osage River.
Nos. 6, 7–8–9–10–11–12 14–& 15. Specimens of led oar from the Mine of Berton, situate on the Marimec River, now more extensively wrought than any other led Mine in <*Upper*> Louisiana.

> Presented by Mr. Boilevin[1] and Mr. Peter Chouteau.

Miscellanious Articles

No. 13. Taken from the Stomach of a Buffaloe, which I suppose has been formed by the Animal's licking itself and thus collecting and swallowing the hair of its old coat, which from the motion, warmth and moisture of the Stomach has been reduced to the shape and consistance of the sample.

> Presented by Doctr. Anthony Sograine.[2]

A horned Lizzard,[3] a native of the Osage Plains, on the Waters of the Arkansas River, from five to six hundred miles West of Saint Louis, in a small Trunk.

> Presented by Mr. Charles Gratiott.

A specimen of Salt formed by concretion, procured at the great Saline of the Osage Nation, situate on a Southern branch of the Arkansas River, about six hundred Miles West of St. Louis. } Presented by Mr. August Chouteau.

Maps &c.

A Chart of the Mississippi, from the Mouth of the Missouri, to New Orleans compiled from the observations of Mr. August Chouteau, made with a Marinors Compass, distance being computed by his own estimate and that of many other French traders, accustomed to ascend and descend this River, the same being drawn by Mr. Soulard, late Surveyor General of Upper Louisiana. } Presented by Mr. August Chouteau.

A Map[4] of a part of Upper Louisiana, compiled from the best information that Capt. Clark and myself could collect, from the Inhabitants of Saint Louis, haistily corrected by the information obtained from the[5] Osage Indians lately arrived at this place. The Country claimed by the Osage Nation is designated on this Map, by lines doted with red ink. The Country lying between those lands claimed by the Osage Nation, and the Mississippi, imbraces all the Settlements at present established in Upper-Louisiana, except the Settlement near the Mouth of the Arkansas and those below it—there are no set-

[193]

tlement beyond the St. Francis river and I think it would be good policy to prohibit any settlement being made beyond it; the country between this river and White river which lies West of it, is said to be a delightful tract of land, and there appears to be no Indian claim to it.[6]

I have designated by lines doted with red ink, the manner in which I concieve it would be most proper to district Upper Louisiana for governmental purposes. This map has but small claims to correctnes, but I hope it will furnish some general ideas of the country which may be servicable.

M. LEWIS

Continued

Two plans of the town of St. Louis, you'l find on examination that they do not perfectly correspond—the small one is that which I believe to be correct—the deviation from which, observable in the large one may properly in my opinion, be attributed to the late unauthorised Sales of land in this quarter.

The smallest of these was drawn and presented by Mr. Soulard—the largest was more recently drawn in part by the same Gentleman, and completed by Capt. Clark.

ALS, RC (DLC, MHi). In Clark's hand except passages by Lewis noted below. Endorsed, "Lewis Meriwether." Endorsed by Lewis, "A List of Articles forwarded by Mr. Peter Chouteau."

This letter of four pages originally consisted of a sheet folded into two leaves. The manuscript is separated into three parts which are lodged in two different archives. The parts are as follows: (a) The upper three-quarters of the first leaf, including all text through the first twenty-one words of the paragraph headed "Maps &c." with the exception noted below. This is the fragment reprinted by Thwaites in the JOURNALS, 7:300, and is the portion in the Jefferson Papers (DLC). (b) The lower quarter of the first leaf. On the recto side is the paragraph headed "No. 13," and on the verso the rest of the first paragraph under "Maps &c." This portion is in MHi. (c) Also in MHi but detached from the other piece is the second complete leaf, containing the remainder of the text. When I first published this letter in JACKSON (6), I assumed that it had come apart as the result of time and wear. Since then, Dr. Julian P. Boyd has suggested to me that the letter may have been cut apart—perhaps by Jefferson himself. The fact that Jefferson's endorsement is on what was originally p. 2, rather than p. 4 where it would normally appear, supports this conjecture.

1. Nicholas Boilvin (1761–1827), French-Canadian trader, interpreter, and Indian subagent.

2. Antoine François Saugrain (1763–1820), French scientist and physician, had come to St. Louis in 1800 after spending several years in the eastern U.S.

3. The horned toad, *Phrynosoma douglassi* (Bell). For a note on this species, and Jefferson's interest in it, see No. 185, note 2.

4. This map, which I have called the first cartographic product of the expedition, was not positively identified until the fragments of Lewis's letter were brought together and considered in connection with his "notes on salines" (No. 118). The map which has survived as IR 20 in the Cartographic Records Branch of the National Archives is not the original, produced by the explorers, but a draftsman's copy done for the War Department soon after Chouteau's arrival in Washington. In JACKSON (6) this map is reproduced and discussed.

5. The words "haistily corrected by the information obtained from the" were added by Lewis.

6. The next paragraph and signature are in Lewis's hand. The word "Continued" and the paragraph which follows it are added by Clark.

123. Clark to William Croghan

Dear Sir   St. Charles May 21st 1804

By Captain Lewis who arrived from St. Louis today I had the pleasure of receiving your letter of the 2nd instant and am happy to here of the recovery of your family & my Brother, whom I was much concerned about. I am sorry to here that the negrows of the estate of Mr. Thruston[1] hired so low, perhaps they may hire for more the next year. My friend Capt. Lewis expressed some sorrow that you happened not to be at home at the time he passed down, but hopes to see you on his return to the U. States, as to my self, I *have, do,* and *shall* [al]ways have that Brotherly effection for you which you are well assured I always possessed, and hope that in less than two years to see you & that family (yours) whome I have every effection for, at your own house. My rout is uncertain. I think it more than probable that Capt. Lewis or my self will return by sea, the other by the same rout we proceed, the time is uncertain. All the other alterations which I did not inform you of has been made since I saw you. And the law authorising the president to explore the Countrey &c. has just come to my knowledge.

I have been at the [this] place five days waiting for Capt. Lewis who had been detained at St. Louis to fix off the Osage Chiefs. He has just arrived and we shall leave this Village immediately & proceed on our journey. We have had a great Deel of rain thunder lightning with wind for several days past, which dis-commodes me a little in sitting out.

The politeness of the gentlemen of this place and about twelve or fifteen who came from S. Louis to see us set out and are constantly with us, prevents me giving you, at this time, a description of the Countrey, river, or the accurrences which have or may happen.

Capt. Lewis joins me in the most sincere wish for your my sister and the families helth & happiness for many years. With every sentiment your sincere friend,

WM. CLARK

ALS, SC (MoSHi).
1. Charles M. Thruston, Clark's late brother-in-law.

124. Amos Stoddard to Henry Dearborn

St. Louis June 3d 1804.

I have the pleasure to inform you, that Captain Lewis, with his party, began to ascend the Missouri from the village of St. Charles on the 21 Ultimo. I accompanied him to that village; and he was also attended by most of the principal Gentlemen in this place and vicinity. [He] began his expedition with a Barge of 18 oars, attended by two large perogues; all of which were deeply laden, and well manned. I have heard from him about 60 miles on his route, and it appears, that he proceeds about 15 miles per day—a celerity seldom witnessed on the Missouri; and this is the more extraordinary as the time required to ascertain the courses of the river and to make other necessary observations, must considerably retard his progress. *His men possess great resolution and they [are in the best] health and spirits.*

A few weeks before he left this, he intrusted an Indian trader by the name of Crawford with a parole and speech[1] addressed to the Ayowas and Scioux, who dwell on the banks of the river Demoine. The effects of that parole may be known by a letter from Mr. Crawford to his partners in this place—a copy of which I enclose you.

The Demoine is an extensive river. It joins the Missisippi from the west about 240 miles above this. It is navigable for light craft to some distance above the falls of St. Anthony; and the distance from

[196]

the head of navigation on this river to the Missisippi is usually travelled in two days. The Sioux inhabit the upper parts of the Demoine, and the Ayowas the lower part of it. These two nations are generally at peace with each other, and speak nearly the same language. [The b]ands on the Demoine are inferior to none in this quarter, if the trader may be believed.

I presume that Capt. Lewis has mentioned to you the fate of some Osage Indians, who were on their way to this place in a boat belonging to Messrs. Mannuel & Benoit. The boat was fired on by the Saucks and some of the Osages killed, and the others made prisoners. The Saucks were headed by the *Paux blanche*,[2] a chief of bad fame, who was on his way to intercept the Osage chiefs under the care of Mr. Chouteau, and accidentally fell in with the boat already mentioned. The Saucks are the implacable enemies of the Osages, and I suspect it will be difficult to reconcile them. They certainly do not pay that respect to the United States which is entertained by the other Indians—and in some instances they have assumed a pretty elevated tone. At this time most of them, together with the Reynards or Foxes reside on the west side of the Missisippi.

I believe an opinion has generally prevailed that the Saucks mostly resided on the East side of the Missisippi—whereas the contrary appears to be the fact. A trader who has resided among them for upwards of 20 years, lately informed me, that he now resides among them on the west side of that river—and that they can raise 3000 warriors from some villages contiguous to each other. He further states that they have only a few straggling villages in Indiana, and no chiefs of any consequence. I do not implicitly credit this account—but I give it as I receive it.[3]

· · · ·

AL, SC (MoSHi). Endorsed.

1. Not found. On 15 March, Lewis had sent a similar speech to the truculent Sauks and Foxes. "It was forwarded by a Sauck chief, and interpreted by an English trader, and not much to the advantage of the United States" (Stoddard to Dearborn, 22 June 1804, MoSHi). Stoddard sent his own interpreter later to repeat the message to the Indians.

2. Peau Blanche or White Skin, a principal Fox chief. He visited Washington in 1810 and may have died before 1813, as there are references to him as "former chief" in that year; but a man of this name, whose Indian name was Wapasai, signed the Fox treaty of 14 Sept. 1815 at St. Louis (STATUTES, 7:136).

3. The American government was just getting to know the Sauks and Foxes, a loosely confederated tribe living on both sides of the Mississippi above and below the mouth of the Des Moines, and about the mouth of the Rock River. In this period the Americans did not seem to know of the

confederation, and spoke only of the Sauks. These two tribes were the cause of much tension and bloodshed later, after Harrison induced a small delegation of their chiefs to sell their lands in the treaty of Nov. 1804. See HAGAN, JACKSON (1), and TERR. PAPERS, vols. 13, 14. Stoddard's statement points up the difficulty of learning about these outlying tribes: they shifted their villages often, and the white men who traded with them were not always reliable informants. In a letter written less than three weeks after this one, Stoddard tells Dearborn (22 June 1804, MoSHi) that a trader named Louis Tesson Honoré now describes the Sauks as inhabiting "a large Island formed by a lake on the *west* side of that river just above the mouth of the Demoine," and that their three villages contain 2,100 warriors. These population figures are much higher than those given later by responsible observers. In the summer of 1813, when Clark asked three of his agents to estimate the number of men in these tribes, Nicholas Boilvin reported 750 Sauks, 500 Foxes; John Johnson reported 700 Sauks, 400 Foxes; Maurice Blondeau reported 650 Sauks, 500 Foxes (Clark letterbooks, KHi). Nothing had happened between 1804 and 1813 to decimate these tribes. As for the location of their villages, nearly all the land the Sauks and Foxes later ceded to the Americans lay on the east side of the Mississippi. Although in winter they hunted on Wyaconda Prairie, west of the river and a good deal farther downstream, and although they ordinarily maintained two or three villages in the vicinity of the Des Moines on the west side, the biggest habitation was Saukenuk, a Sauk village near the mouth of the Rock and lying on the east side of the Mississippi. I cannot identify the lake mentioned by Honoré. Pierre Chouteau mentions a "Lake la Pensee" as the site of a Sauk village, but his information almost certainly comes from Honoré, too (Chouteau to Harrison, 14 May 1805, MoSHi).

125. Henry Dearborn to Thomas H. Cushing

War Department
Sir.   July 9th 1804

Should a deputation of Osage Indians under the direction of Mr. Chouteau have arrived at Fredericktown, I will thank you to inform Mr. Chouteau, that as the President of the United States will leave this place very soon, for his seat in Virginia, and as I wish to set out as early in the present Month as possible for New England it is very desirable that he should arrive here without delay. And if they shall not have arrived at Fredricktown when this reaches you, I will thank you to send Lt. Clyma[1] on the road to Harpers Ferry and from thence by Shepherds town to Winchester if he should not meet them sooner, for the purpose of hastening them on as soon as possible. Mr. Chouteau is a man of respectability and should be treated as such.

Mr. Clyma's expences will be paid. Yours—

Lbk (DNA, RG 107, Letters Sent, 2:253).
1. William P. Clyma, of Virginia, a lieutenant in the Second Infantry.

126. Jefferson to the Osages

[12 July 1804]

My Children. White hairs, Chiefs & Warriors of the Osage Nation.

I recieve you with great pleasure at the seat of the govmt. of the 17. United nations, and tender you a sincere welcome. I thank the Great Spirit who has inspired you with a desire to visit your new friends, & who has conducted you in safety to take us this day by the hand. The journey you have come is long, the weather has been warm & wet, & I fear you have suffered on the road, notwithstanding our endeavors for your accomodation. But you have come through a land of friends, all of whom I hope have looked on you kindly, & been ready to give you every aid and comfort by the way.

You are as yet fatigued with your journey. But you are under the roof of your fathers and best friends, who will spare nothing for your refreshment and comfort. Repose yourselves therefore, and recruit your health and strength, and when you are rested we will open the bottoms of our hearts more fully to one another. In the mean time we will be considering how we may best secure everlasting peace, friendship & commerce between the Osage nation, and the 17. United nations in whose name I speak to you, and take you by the hand.

TH: JEFFERSON
July 12. 1804.

ADS, SC (DLC). These remarks were preliminary; Jefferson reserved his formal message until later (No. 127). Filed after this document in DLC are two pages of notes in Jefferson's hand on the speech made by Chief White Hair. The notes appear to have been made hurriedly, perhaps as the interpreter repeated the speech to the President. White Hair said he had come on the recommendation of Capt. Lewis, had always wanted to meet the greatest chief, was glad he had come, etc. Cheveux Blancs or White Hair (more literally White Hairs) was a principal chief of the Great Osages, whose main village was on the Osage River in present Vernon County, Mo., a few miles from the village of the Little Osages. He was the signer for the Great Osages in the treaty of 18 Oct. 1805 (TERR. PAPERS, 13:245–47). For a biographical sketch see HODGE, 2:944, but note that this man, who was dead by 1811, is confused with his son who died in 1825.

The delegation had arrived on the preceding day. "They are twelve men & two boys, and certainly the most gigantic men we have ever seen," Jefferson wrote to Gallatin (12 July 1804, DLC). His admiration for these people shows most clearly in his letter to Secretary of the Navy Robert Smith the next day (13 July, DLC): "They are the finest men we have ever seen. They have not yet learnt the use of spirituous liquors. We shall endeavor to impress them strongly not only with our justice & liberality, but with our power. . . ."

Jefferson then summed up the American attitude toward the stronger western tribes, revealing in a few words the justification for the expense, the anxiety, and the elaborate detail with which he and Dearborn had arranged for Lewis to send back these delegations. "The truth is," he said, "they are the great nation South of the Missouri, their possession extending from thence to the Red river, as the Sioux are great North of that river. With these two powerful nations we must stand well, because in their quarter we are miserably weak."

127. Jefferson to the Osages

[16 July 1804]

My children. White-hairs, Chiefs & Warriors of the Osage nation.

I repeat to you assurances of the satisfaction it has given me to recieve you here. Besides the labour of such a journey, the confidence you have shown in the honor & friendship of my countrymen is peculiarly gratifying and I hope you have seen that your confidence was justly placed, that you have found yourselves, since you crossed the Missisipi, among brothers & friends, with whom you were as safe as at home.

My children. I sincerely weep with you over the graves of your chiefs & friends, who fell by the hands of their enemies lately descending the Osage river.[1] Had they been prisoners, & living, we would have recovered them: but no voice can awake the dead; no power undo what is done. On this side the Missisipi where our government has been long established, and our authority organised our friends visiting us are safe. We hope it will not be long before our voice will be heard and our arm respected, by those who meditate to injure our friends, on the other side of that river. In the mean time Governor Harrison will be directed to take proper measures to enquire into the circumstances of the transaction, to report them to us for consideration, and for the further measures they may require.

My children. By late arrangements with France & Spain, we now take their place as your neighbors, friends and fathers: and we hope you will have no cause to regret the change. It is so long since our forefathers came from beyond the great water, that we have lost the memory of it, and seem to have grown out of this land, as you have done. Never more will you have occasion to change your fathers. We are all now of one family, born in the same land, & bound to live as brothers; & the strangers from beyond the great water are gone from among us. The great Spirit has

[200]

given you strength, and has given us strength; not that we might hurt one another, but to do each other all the good in our power. Our dwellings indeed are very far apart; but not too far to carry on commerce & useful intercourse. You have furs and peltries which we want, and we have clothes and other useful things which you want. Let us employ ourselves then in mutually accomodating each other. To begin this on our part it was necessary to know what nations inhabited the great country called Louisiana, which embraces all the waters of the Missisipi and Missouri, what number of peltries they could furnish, what quantities & kinds of merchandize they would require, where would be the deposits most convenient for them, and to make an exact map of all those waters. For this purpose I sent a beloved man, Capt. Lewis, one of my own household to learn something of the people with whom we are now united, to let you know we were your friends, to invite you to come and see us, and to tell us how we can be useful to you. I thank you for the readiness with which you have listened to his voice, and for the favor you shewed him in his passage up the Missouri. I hope your countrymen will favor and protect him as far as they extend. On his return we shall hear what he has seen & learnt, & proceed to establish trading houses where our red brethren shall think best, & to exchange commodities with them on terms with which they will be satisfied.

With the same views I had prepared another party to go up the Red river to it's source, thence to the source of the Arkansa, & down it to it's mouth. But I will now give orders that they shall only go a small distance up the red river this season, and return to tell us what they have seen, and that they shall not set out for the head of that river till the ensuing spring, when you will be at home, and will I hope guide and guard them in their journey.[2] I also propose the next year to send another small party up the river of the Kansas to it's source, thence to the head of the river of the Panis, and down to it's mouth; and others up the rivers on the North side of the Missouri. For guides along these rivers we must make arrangements with the nations inhabiting them.

My children. I was sorry to learn that a schism had taken place in your nation, and that a part of your people had withdrawn with the Great-track, to the Arkansa river. We will send an Agent to them and will use our best offices to prevail on them to return, and to live in union with you. We wish to make them also our friends, and to make that friendship, and the weight it may give us with them, useful to you and them.

[201]

We propose, my children, immediately to establish an Agent to reside with you, who will speak to you our words, and convey yours to us: who will be the guardian of our peace and friendship, convey truths from the one to the other, dissipate all falsehoods which might tend to alienate and divide us, and maintain a good understanding & friendship between us. As the distance is too great for you to come often and tell us your wants, you will tell them to him on the spot, and he will convey them to us in writing, so that we shall be sure that they come from you. Through the intervention of such an Agent we shall hope that our friendship will forever be preserved. No wrong will ever be done you by our nation, and we trust that yours will do none to us: and should ungovernable individuals commit unauthorised outrage on either side, let them be duly punished; or if they escape, let us make to each other the best satisfaction the case admits, and not let our peace be broken by bad men. For all people have some bad men among them whom no laws can restrain.

As you have taken so long a journey to see your fathers, we wish you not to return till you shall have visited our country & towns towards the sea coast. This will be new and satisfactory to you, and it will give you the same knowledge of the country on this side the Missisipi, which we are endeavoring to acquire of that on the other side, by sending trusty persons to explore them. We propose to do in your country only what we are desirous you should do in ours. We will provide accomodations for your journey, for your comfort while engaged in it, and for your return in safety to your own country, carrying with you those proofs of esteem with which we distinguish our friends, and shall particularly distinguish you. On your return tell your people that I take them all by the hand; that I become their father hereafter, that they shall know our nation only as friends and benefactors; that we have no views upon them but to carry on a commerce useful to them and us; to keep them in peace with their neighbors, that their children may multiply, may grow up & live to a good old age, and their women no longer fear the tomahawk of any enemy.

My children. These are my words. Carry them to your nation. Keep them in your memories, and our friendship in your hearts. And may the Great Spirit look down upon us, & cover us with the mantle of his love.

Th: Jefferson
July 16. 04.

[202]

ADS, SC (DLC). There are also a French version of the document, in Jefferson's hand; Jefferson's notes on White Hair's reply; and a speech in French and English to le Soldat du Chien, or the Dog Soldier, a chief of the Little Osages.

1. Referring to an attack by the Sauks, mentioned by Stoddard in No. 124.

2. Dearborn to Pierre Chouteau, 12 July 1804 (DNA, RG 75, Letters Sent, Bk. B): "You will take the necessary measures for obtaining permission of the Big-track and his party for the safe passage of any party which may be sent by the President of the United States to explore the sources of the Arkansas river and the interior country generally bordering on the waters of the Red River. . . ."

128. Henry Dearborn to Moses Hooke

War Department
Sir   July 18th 1804

You will procure a light Boat to be built, capable of carrying fifteen men with their baggage, and to draw but very little water. It must be ready by the 20th of next August.

You will receive the public horses which the Osage Indians under the care of Capt. Chouteau will ride to Pittsburg, and have them sold as soon as recruited, you will afford every aid in your power to Capt. Chouteau and the people with him. You will furnish suitable quarters for them while at Pittsburg and assist in procuring provisions for their voyage down the river—And you will write by Capt. Chouteau to the Commanding Officer at Massac requesting him to treat the party with the greatest attention and to furnish them with an escort from the Garrison to Kaskaskia and with provisions for their journey. You will send six sober men with a noncommissioned Officer with the party down the river to Massac. If you have not men sufficient you will write immediately to Capt. McClallan at Carlisle and inform him that I request him to furnish a sober careful noncommissioned Officer and six good sober privates to be immediately sent to Pittsburg for the purpose above mentioned. Yours &c.

Lbk (DNA, RG 107, Letters Sent, 2:255).

129. Lewis and Clark to the Oto Indians

[4 August 1804]

To the Petit Voleur, or Wear-ruge-nor, the great Chief of the Ottoes, to the Chiefs and Warriors of the Ottoes, and the Chiefs and Warriors of the Missouri nation residing with the Ottoes—

[203]

Children. Convene from among you the old men of experience; the men, on the wisdom of whose judgement you are willing to risk the future happiness of your nations; and the warriors, to the strength of whose arms you have been taught to look for protection in the days of danger. When in Council tranquilly assembled, reflect on the time past, and that to come; do not deceive yourselves, nor suffer others to deceive you; but like men and warriors devoted to the real interests of their nation, seek those truths; which can alone perpetuate its happiness.

Children. Commissioned and sent by the great Chief of the Seventeen great nations of America, we have come to inform you, as we go also to inform all the nations of red men who inhabit the borders of the Missouri, that a great council was lately held between this great chief of the Seventeen great nations of America, and your old fathers the french and Spaniards; and that in this great council it was agreed that all the white men of Louisiana, inhabiting the waters of the Missouri and Mississippi should obey the commands of this great chief; he has accordingly adopted them as his children and they now form one common family with us: your old traders are of this description; they are no longer the subjects of France or Spain, but have become the Citizens of the Seventeen great nations of america, and are bound to obey the commands of their great Chief the President who is now your only great father.

Children. This council being concluded between your old fathers the french and Spaniards, and your great father the Chief of the Seventeen great nations of America, your old fathers the French and Spaniards in complyance with their engagements made in that council, have withdrawn all their troops from all their military posts on the waters of the Mississippi and missouri, and have Surrendered to our great cheif all their fortifications and lands in this country, together with the mouths of all the rivers through which the traders bring goods to the red men on the troubled waters. These arangements being made, your old fathers the french and Spaniards have gone beyond the great lake towards the rising Sun, from whence they never intend returning to visit their former red-children in this quarter; nor will they, or any other nation of white men, ever again display their flag on the troubled waters; because the mouths of all those rivers are in the possession of the great Chief of the Seventeen great nations of America, who will command his war chiefs to suffer no vessel to pass—but those which sail under the protection of his flag, and who acknowledge his Supreme authority.

Children. From what has been said, you will readily perceive, that the great chief of the Seventeen great nations of America, has become your only father; he is the only father; he is the only friend to whom you can now look for protection, or from whom you can ask favours, or receive good councils, and he will take care that you shall have no just cause to regret this change; he will serve you, & not deceive you.

Children. The great chief of the Seventeen great nations of America, impelled by his parental regard for his newly adopted children on the troubled waters, has sent us out to clear the road, remove every obstruction, and to make it the road of peace between himself and his red children residing there; to enquire into the Nature of their wants, and on our return to inform Him of them, in order that he may make the necessary arrangements for their relief, he has sent by us, one of his flags, a medal and some cloathes, such as he dresses his war chiefs with, which he directed should be given to the great chief of the Ottoe nation, to be kept by him, as a pledge of the sincerity with which he now offers you the hand of friendship.

Children. Know that the great chief who has thus offered you the hand of unalterable friendship, is the great Chief of the Seventeen great Nations of America, whose cities are as numerous as the stars of the heavens, and whose people like the grass of your plains, cover with their Cultivated fields and wigwams, the wide Extended country, reaching from the western borders of the Mississippi, to the great lakes of the East, where the land ends and the Sun rises from the face of the great waters.

Children. Know that this great chief, as powerfull as he is just, and as beneficient as he is wise, always entertaining a sincere and friendly disposition towards the red people of America, has commanded us his war chiefs to undertake this long journey, which we have so far accomplished with great labour & much expence, in order to council with yourselves and his other red-children on the troubled waters, to give you his good advice; to point out to you the road in which you must walk to obtain happiness. He has further commanded us to tell you that when you accept his flag and medal, you accept therewith his hand of friendship, which will never be withdrawn from your nation as long as you continue to follow the councils which he may command his chiefs to give you, and shut your ears to the councils of Bad birds.

Children. The road in which your great father and friend, has commanded us to tell you and your nation that you must walk in order to enjoy the benefit of his friendship, is, that you are to live

[205]

in peace with all the *white men*, for they are his children; neither wage war against the *red men* your neighbours, for they are equally his children and he is bound to protect them. Injure not the persons of any traders who may come among you, neither destroy nor take their property from them by force; more particularly those traders who visit you under the protection of your great fathers flag. Do not obstruct the passage of any boat, pirogue, or other vessel, which may be ascending or decending the Missouri River, more especially such as may be under cover of your great fathers flag neither injure any red or white man on board such vessels as may possess the flag, for by that signal you may know them to be good men, and that they do not intend to injure you; they are therefore to be treated as friends, and as the common children of one great father, (the great chief of the Seventeen great nations of America.

Children. Do these things which your great father advises and be happy. Avoid the councils of bad birds; turn on your heel from them as you would from the precipice of an high rock, whose summit reached the Clouds, and whose base was washed by the gulph of human woes; lest by one false step you should bring upon your nation the displeasure of your great father, the great chief of the Seventeen great nations of America, who could consume you as the fire consumes the grass of the plains. The mouths of all the rivers through which the traders bring goods to you are in his possession, and if you displease him he could at pleasure shut them up and prevent his traders from coming among you; and this would of course bring all the Calamities of want upon you; but it is not the wish of your great father to injure you, on the contrary he is now pursuing the measures best Calculated to insure your happiness.

Children. If you open your ears to the councils of your great father, the great chief of the Seventeen great nations of America, & strictly pursue the advice which he has now given you through us, he will as soon as possible after our return, send a store of goods to the mouth of the river Platte to trade with you for your pelteries and furs; these goods will be furnished you annually in a regular manner, and in such quantities as will be equal to your necessities. You will then obtain goods on much better terms than you have ever received them heretofore.

Children. As it will necessarily take some time before we can return, and your great father send and establish this store of goods; he will permit your old traders who reside among you, or who annually visit you, to continue to trade with you, provided they give you good Council.

[206]

Children. We are now on a long journey to the head of the Missouri; the length of this journey compelled us to load our boat and perogues with provisions, we have therefore brought but very few goods as presents for yourselves or any other nations which we may meet on our way. We are no traders, but have come to consult you on the subject of your trade; to open the road and prepare the way, in order that your nation may hereafter receive a regular and plentifull supply of goods.

Children. We are sorry that your absence from your town prevented our seeing your great chief and yourselves; it would have given us much pleasure to have spoken to you personnally; but as the cold season is fast advancing, and we have a long distance to travel, we could not wait your return.

Children. If your great Chief wishes to see your great father and speak with him, he can readily do so. Let your chief engage some trader who may reside with you the ensuing winter, to take him and four of his principal chiefs or warriors with him to St. Louis when he returns thither on the ensuing spring; your great chief may take with him also an interpreter of his own choice, who shall be well paid for his services by your great father's Chiefs; the trader will also be well paid for his services by the Commandant at St. Louis. The commandant at St. Louis will furnish you with the necessary number of horses, and all other means to make your journey from thence to your great father's town Comfortable and safe.

Children. In order that the Commandant at St. Louis, as well as your great father, and all his chiefs may know you, you must take with you, the flag, the medal and this parole which we now send you. When your great father and his chiefs see those things, they will know that you have opened your ears to your great father's voice, and have come to hear his good Councils.

Our oldest son the Wear-ruge-nor. If the situation of your nation is such that you cannot with propriety leave them, you may send some of your principal men not exceeding five, to see your great father and hear his words. You must give them authority to act for you and your Nation. Your great father will receive them as his children, give them his good councils, and send them back loaded with presents for their nation; your nation would then see that all we have told you is true, and that the great chief of the Seventeen great nations of America never sends his red children from him to return with empty hands to their village.

Our oldest son the Wear-ruge-nor. Whomsoever you send to your great father must carry the flag and this parole, in order that your great father and his chiefs may know that they have come to see them by our invitation. Send by them also all the flags and medals which you may have received from your old fathers the French and Spaniards, or from any other nation whatever, your father will give you new flags and new medals of his own in exchange for those which you send him. It is not proper since you have become the children of the great chief of the Seventeen great nations of America, that you should wear or keep those emblems of attachment to any other great father but himself, nor will it be pleasing to him if you continue to do so.

Children. We hope that the great Spirit will open your ears to our councils, and dispose your minds to their observance. Follow these councils and you will have nothing to fear, because the great Spirit will smile upon your nation, and in future ages will make you to outnumber the trees of the forest.

Signed and sealed this 4th day of August 1804 at the council Bluff, by us, the friends of all the red-men, and the war chiefs of the great chief of the Seventeen great nations of America.

MERIWETHER LEWIS Captn.

1st U.S. Regt. Infantry.

WILLIAM CLARK

Capt. on the Missouri Expedition

Transcript (DNA, RG 107, W-491). Endorsed in James Wilkinson's hand, "Talk of Capt. Lewis to the Oto Nation &c.," and sent by Wilkinson to the War Department in Aug. 1805. The phrase after Clark's name is in Wilkinson's hand.

Upon receiving Lewis's speech, the Petit Voleur or Little Thief overtook the explorers on 18 Aug.—hoping to enlist their aid in bringing about a truce with the Omahas. Lewis explained that he could mediate no peace because the Omahas were away, but he repeated his invitation to Little Thief to visit Washington. The chief went down to St. Louis in the spring of 1805 with two other Oto men, three Republican Pawnees, and a Missouri, intent on visiting the President. But when the delegation finally left St. Louis in the fall, Little Thief could not go; he had become ill and was asking to be taken back to his village. He died on the river while returning home. For a longer discussion of this episode, see JACKSON (5).

130. Hezekiah Rogers to Jefferson

Sir,   Philadelphia 21. August 1804.

I have the honor to inform you that this day Capt. Chouteau with the Chiefs of the Osage nation of Indians took their departure from this city for Pittsburgh, on their way to their own country.[1]

We proceeded on our tour as far North as the city of New York, where we continued eight days.

During our journey the party enjoyed perfect health, and no untoward circumstance occurred to mar the pleasure of the natives, or to fustrate the object contemplated by government.

The principal villages and cities through which we passed, and individual citizens vied with each other in acts of hospitality and kindness, and I am persuaded the impressions which have been made on the minds of the Indians are most favorable to the views and wishes of the Executive.

In executing the trust committed to me I have assiduously endeavored to effect the object intended, with as much frugality in my expenditures, as circumstances and the nature of that object would permit; and if, Sir, my well-intentioned exertions shall meet your approbation it will amply compensate me for the trouble and fatigue which I have experienced.

Tomorrow I purpose leaving this city for Washington. I am, Sir, with very sincere Respect, Yr. Obt. Servant,

HEZ. ROGERS.

ALS, RC (ViWC). Endorsed; received 28 Aug. 1804. Hezekiah Rogers (d. 1811) was a former Revolutionary War officer, former military storekeeper, and now successor to Joshua Wingate as chief clerk in the War Department.

1. Chouteau arrived home in St. Louis with his charges 3 Oct. 1804, according to his letter to Dearborn of 12 Oct. (DNA, RG 107, Register of Letters Received). Before leaving Washington he had been sized up by Albert Gallatin: "I had two conversations with Chotteau. He seems well disposed, but what he wants is power and money. He proposed that he should have a negative on all the Indian trading licenses and the direction & all the profits of the trade carried on by Government with all the Indians of Louisiana replacing only the capital. I told him this was inadmissable, and his last demand was the exclusive trade with the Osages. . . . As he may be either useful or dangerous I gave no flat denial to his last request but told him to modify it in the least objectionable shape and to write to Gen. Dearborn from St. Louis which he said he would do" (to Jefferson, 20 Aug. 1804, DLC).

131. Parole to War Char Pa

[31 August 1804]

THOMAS JEFFERSON, PRESIDENT OF THE UNITED STATES OF AMERICA.

From the powers vested in us by the above authority: To all who shall see these presents, Greeting: KNOW YE, that from the special confidence reposed by us in the sincere and unalterable attachment of *War char pa the Sticker a Warrier* of the *Soues* Nation to the UNITED STATES; as also from the abundant proofs given by him of his amicable disposition to cultivate peace, harmony, and good neighbourhood with the said States, and the citizens of the same; we do by the authority vested in us, require and charge, all citizens of the United States, all Indian Nations, in treaty with the same, and all other persons whomsoever, to *receive* acknowledge, and treat the said *War Char Pa the Sticker* in the most friendly manner, declaring him to be the friend and ally of the said States: the government of which will at all times be extended to his protection, so long as he dos acknowledge the authority of the same. Having signed with our hands and affixed our seals this *Thirty first* day of *August* 180 *four*.

M. Lewis Capt.
1st. U.S. Regt. Infty.

Wm. Clark Captn. on
an Expdn. for N. W. Descy.

DS (CSmH). A printed form, filled in by Lewis. Italicized words are in Lewis's hand. Five blank forms like this one have survived, one in the Yale University Library and four, with ribbon and wax seals affixed, in the holdings of the Missouri Historical Society. When painter William Dunlap visited the Arikara chief in Washington in 1806, the old man produced a "certificate & recommendation from Genl. Clark & Capt. Merriweather Lewis" which he carried under his belt or in a pouch suspended from it (DUNLAP, 2:390). A photographic copy of the present version is reproduced in BAKELESS, opposite p. 83.

132. [Marqués de Casa Calvo] to Pedro Cevallos

September 15, 1804
No. 41 To His Most Excellent *Señor*, Pedro Cevallos
I am enclosing to Your Excellency a copy of the answer of the *Comandante-General* of the *Provincias Internas*, dated May 3rd, which is in reply to my letter of March 5th. With it I also enclose my intention to record that my message's only object was the reconnaissance which the American Captain Merry Whether was going to make of the origin and course of the Missouri, recalling to mind the pretensions of the French over the limits of this Province, which the Colonial Prefect manifested, and in which I had no other object than to hasten with doubled fears the news and excite the

dispositions which must be taken to contain the ambitious designs and extraordinary intentions of our neighbors.

In these parallel documents Your Excellency will surely observe the indifference with which so important a message has been treated and therefore since there will have remained obscure in their meaning the efficacious and prompt measures which might have been followed upon receipt of my letter in order to compensate for the time and distance. I say to compensate for time and distance because, the notice being from the Lieutenant Governor of Illinois, in the month of December on the 20th of which month the Americans took possession of the province. Since that time Merry has had time to undertake and to advance his expedition, and the *Comandante-General* is unable to know the district in which the expedition is at present, due to Spain's not having establishments on the Upper Missouri. Consequently I think that before writing the second paragraph of his answer, he should have [had] examined and inquired all that was possible about the immediate roads, [surrounding passage-ways] in order to see if he could acquire news as to his stopping place, not having had notice of his stopping place at the time he was writing because the expedition was enroute to the Upper Missouri. This having been done there would have been left no object which would delay another message as long as five months.

It is impossible for me to procure any news as to the course of the voyage since I have no plans [*planos*] of the upper part of that river, since we only calculate its proximity to the New Kingdom of Mexico from the news of travelers, from the voyages recently made, from what the Indians tell us, and from the landmarks and the signs which are observed among the Indians of the Upper Missouri, which manifest clearly their traffic with Spaniards. From a summing up of these facts the writers have decided that the origin of that river is to the northwest. This in the general plan of the maps should bring it very near to the capital of the afore-mentioned Kingdom of New Mexico.

I cannot understand the idea of the *Comandante-General,* nor on what basis he can uphold himself, nor to what expression of my letter he is making allusion when he says that the notices of the demarcation survey which I include, in my official letter are the only maps of the territory in my possession [to which they relate], but they are not satisfactory. I have tormented my spirit, but have not been able to find a single phrase in all my letter which gives rise to such a slighting statement as announced. What limits are outlined in it? If the prefect himself of whose proposition I made

[211]

literal use when treating of the pretensions of France, only speaks indeterminately, who fixed them and how can it be imputed that I have pointed them out?

These I find extraordinary as I have already mentioned that the *Comandante-General* has not taken more active measures because of an erroneous confidence, and I fear that this same confidence will injure the promptness of the dispositions which should be taken to stop the progress of Merry. And thus it has appeared to me proper to my duty to inform Your Excellency, so that instructed of everything, it may please you to take the steps which may be best.

God, etc., Sept. 15, 1804

[unsigned]

Most Excellent *Señor,* Don Pedro Ceballos.

Don Pedro Cevallos to *Señor* Marqués de Casa Calvo

The King has been kind enough to approve the official letters sent by Your Excellency to Don Nemesio Salcedo, *Comandante-general* of the *Provincias Internas* for the purpose of stopping [detaining] the expedition of the American Captain Merry Weather directed to reconnoitre the territory which belongs to His Majesty, and with this motive [and in] replying to Your Excellency's official letter number 41 I am informing you that His Majesty has ordered me to instruct his Minister Plenipotentiary in the United States that he complain to that government against so manifest an offense against the sovereignty of the King.

May God keep Your Excellency many years.

January 17, 1805—

PEDRO CEVALLOS [rubric]

Señor Marqués de Casa Calvo.

Printed, NASATIR (2), 2:750–52. A draft of the Casa Calvo letter, in Spanish, is in the Archivo General de Indias (Seville), Papeles de Cuba, legajo 2368. The original of Cevallos' reply is in the same file, legajo 176B.

133. Amos Stoddard to Jefferson

Sir,   St. Louis 29th Octr. 1804.

Captain Lewis, before he left this, engaged a trader on the River Desmoine to procure vocabularies of the Ayowais and Sioux lan-

[212]

guages.[1] The trader has obtained that of the former, which I do myself the honor to enclose: That of the latter will be furnished sometime next spring, when it will be transmitted to you, agreeably to the request of Capt. Lewis. I am, Sir, with sentiments of high respect, Your very humb. Servt.

AMOS STODDARD, Capt.
Corps of Artillerists.

ALS, RC (DLC). Endorsed; received 29 Nov. 1804.

1. These vocabularies collected by Lewis Crawford probably were lost when Jefferson's entire collection was pillaged and destroyed (No. 399).

134. Lewis and Clark to Charles Chaboillez

Upper Mandane Village, Oct. 31, 1804.

To Charles Chaboiller, Esq. of the N.W. Co.

Sir: on our arrival at this Mandane Village, the 26th instant, we met with Mr. Hugh McCrachen,[1] who informed us that he was in some measure employed by you in behalf of the North West Company, to traffic with the natives of this quarter; the return of the man to your parts affords us the means of making, thus early, the present communication; the contents of which we would thank you to make known, as early as possible, to those engaged, and traders immediately under your direction, as also, if convenient, to the principal representatives of any other company of his Britannic Majesty's subjects, who may reside or trade in this quarter.

We have been commissioned and sent by the government of the United States for the purpose of exploring the river Missouri, and the western parts of the continent of North America, with a view to the promotion of general science. Your government have been advised of the voyage and its objects, as the enclosed copy of a passport, granted by Mr. Edward Thornton, his Britannic Majesty's charge d'affaires to the United States, will evidence.

The cold season, having now nearly arrived, we have determined to fortify ourselves, and remain the ensuing winter, in the neighbourhood of this place. During our residence here, or future progress on our voyage, we calculate that the injunctions contained in the passport before mentioned will, with respect to ourselves, govern the conduct of such of his Brintannic Majesty's subjects as may be within communicative reach of us. As individuals, we feel every disposition to cultivate the friendship of all well-disposed persons; and all that we have at this moment to ask of them, is a mutual

[213]

exchange of good offices. We shall, at all times, extend our protection as well to British subjects as American citizens, who may visit the Indians of our neighbourhood, provided they are well-disposed; this we are disposed to do, as well from the pleasure we feel in becoming serviceable to good men, as from a conviction that it is consonant with the liberal policy of our government, not only to admit within her territory the free egress and regress of all citizens and subjects of foreign powers with which she is in amity, but also to extend to them her protection, while within limits of her jurisdiction.

If, sir, in the course of the winter, you have it in your power to furnish us with any hints in relation to the geography of the country, its productions, either mineral, animal, or vegetable, or any other information which you might conceive of utility to mankind, or which might be serviceable to us in the prosecution of our voyage, we should feel ourselves extremely obliged by your furnishing us with it. We are, with much respect, Your ob't. serv'ts.

MERIWETHER LEWIS, Capt. 1st U.S.R. Inf.
WILLIAM CLARK, Capt.

Printed, JOURNALS, 7:307–08, from the version in *Port-Folio, 7* (May 1812), 448–49. Jason Chamberlain, of the University of Vermont, received the original from Canadian sources and sent it on to the magazine. Charles Jean Baptiste Chaboillez (1742–1809) had been on the Red and Assiniboine rivers since 1796, and in the winter of 1804–05 was in charge of the Department of the Assiniboine for the North West Company.

1. Lewis and Clark met Hugh McCracken and one other British trader on 26 Oct. The day after this letter was written, McCracken set out for the fort on the Assiniboine. Chaboillez sent another employee, Hugh Heney, with a reply to the letter on 16 Dec., and "in his letter expressed a great anxiety to Serve us in any thing in his power" (JOURNALS, 1:238). Further contact with the North West Company resulted from the arrival of a party under François-Antoine Larocque in Nov. 1804. Both Larocque and Charles McKenzie, a member of his group, left journal records of their meeting with Lewis and Clark, reprinted by MASSON. Larocque says that he "was very politely received by Captains Lewis and Clarke and passed the night with them. Just as I arrived, they were dispatching a man for me, having heard that I intended giving flags and medals to the Indians, which they forbid me from giving in the name of the United States, saying that the government looked upon those things as the sacred emblems of the attachment of the Indians to their country. As I had neither flags nor medals, I ran no risk of disobeying those orders, of which I assured them" (1:304). McKenzie, an assistant clerk who visited the expedition headquarters several times during the winter, thought he sensed in Lewis a strain of anglophobia: "It is true, Captain Lewis could not make himself agreeable to us. He could speak fluently and learnedly on all subjects, but his inveterate disposition against the British stained, at least in our eyes, all his eloquence" (1:336).

[214]

135. James Bruff to James Wilkinson

Sir.   St. Louis—U. Louisiana. November 5. 1804.

. . . .

The Osage chiefs left this a few days after the arrival of the Gouvenour for their nation, loaded with valuable presents & puffed up with ideas of their great superiority to other nations—on account of the distinction paid them by our government; But this has excited the jealousy & hatred of the other nations to such a degree that I am apprehensive of the consequence if as large presents are not made them also. Indeed the Saukies own'd it was on that account *principally* that their young men committed the murders.[1] They seem to think we give them the most, we fear the most—those who are the most daring and desperate.

No news since the 4. August from Capts. Lewis & Clark—they were then at the mouth of the river Platt where two of their boatmen deserted: and it is reported by several Canadians who happened there at that time, that the others were much dissatisfied & complained of too regid a discipline. I am not, however, disposed to give *full* credit to their story, as they report other unfavourable circumstances that cannot be true:—Such as a difference between the Captains &c.[2]

. . . .

With Great respect—I have the honour to be Your Very Obedient Servant

J. BRUFF Majr. Arty.

Col. Lassuss with the Spanish troops, arty. & stores are on the point of departure—his boats are loaded &c.

ALS, RC (DNA, RG 107, Letters Received). Enclosed in Wilkinson to Dearborn, 13 Dec. 1804. James Bruff of Maryland became a major of artillerists and engineers in 1803, and was sent in the spring of 1804 to be commandant of the Department of Upper Louisiana—replacing Amos Stoddard. In the early part of the period, Stoddard retained the duties of civil commandant while Bruff served only as military comandant (Dearborn to Stoddard, 16 May 1804, DNA, RG 107, Letters Sent, 2:236).

1. Pierre Chouteau corroborated Bruff's statement about the jealousy of other tribes toward the Osages, but said that white men were behind it (to Dearborn, 11 March 1805, Chouteau letterbook, MoSHi). The murders were committed by a small party of Sauks in early Sept. 1804; they attacked three American settlers on the Cuivre River above St. Louis. The crime alarmed Gen. James Wilkinson for the safety of Lewis and Clark. He told Dearborn that he would warn the explorers if it were practicable, "for the manner[?] bespeaks premeditated general Hostility from some Nation" (26 Oct. 1804, DNA, RG 107, W-353). Actually the murders bespoke no such thing; but they

did alarm the Sauks and Foxes—so much that the villages at the mouth of the Des Moines, where the attackers lived, broke up and moved north (Bruff to Wilkinson, 29 Sept. 1804, TERR. PAPERS, 13:56). As a result of parleys between the tribal leaders and American officials, a hostage was chosen from among the killers and put in prison. And as a surprise result of one such meeting, a party of five Sauk and Fox chiefs went home from St. Louis to tell their tribesmen that they had ceded to the U.S. every square mile of their homeland. Jefferson finally pardoned the Sauk hostage, saying that "we ought to commence our intercourse with the Indians in Louisiana in such a manner as to show not only our regard for justice, but our benevolent and tender feelings for the unhappy . . ." (quoted in Dearborn to Harrison, 12 Feb. 1805, DNA, RG 107, Letters Sent). But it was too late; the man had been shot by a sentinel while attempting to escape.

2. For my comment on this information, which was already in Jefferson's hands, see No. 136.

136. Jefferson to Reuben Lewis

Dear Sir   Washington Nov. 6. 04.
I inclose you a letter directed to your brother which came to me under cover a few days ago. I have the pleasure also to inform you that we have lately received thro a channel meriting entire confidence, advice that on the 4th of Aug. he was at the mouth of the river Plate, 600 miles up the Missouri, where he had met a great council of the Missouris, Panis & Ottos, at their invitation, and had also on their request appointed among them three grand chiefs. Two of his men had deserted from him. He had with him 2. boats and about 48 men. He was then setting out up the river. One of his boats & half the men would return from his winter quarters. In the Spring he would leave about a fourth where he wintered to make corn for his return, & would proceed with the other fourth. All accounts concur in the entire friendly dispositions of the Indians and that he will be through his whole course as safe as at home.[1] Believing that this information would be acceptable to your self, his mother & friends, I communicate it with pleasure and with it tender my salutations & best wishes.

TH: JEFFERSON

ALS, SC (CSmH).
1. Note that Jefferson already had heard the news of Lewis and Clark, and had a somewhat straighter story, before Bruff transmitted his report to Wilkinson. Although much of the information is garbled, there is enough solid fact in it to assure us that someone saw and talked with the explorers at about the time they were holding their first council with the Oto party on 3 Aug. They were past the mouth of the Platte but not far past. None of the

journals mentions the appearance of a trader's boat which might have carried the news down the river. Perhaps the informant was Mr. Fairfong, identified only as interpreter for the Oto tribe, who was present at the council. The name "Fairfong" is one of Clark's ingenious phonetic atrocities, and no one has ever suggested a plausible identification for the man. Clark also calls him Faufon and Faufonn.

137. Charles Gratiot to Lewis

Dear Sir   St. Louis the 13th Novr. 1804.

I take the favourable opportunity of Mr. Augte. Chouteau my brother in law, who is the bearer of the petition of the inhabitants of the district of Louisiana to Congress, to transmit according to your directions all the informations I possibly could Collect respecting this Country;[1] I am sorry that it has not been in my power to comply with your request in a more general Manner, but I kno that Capt. Amos Stoddard & the bearer Mr. Chouteau will supply to my difficiency; I have made several applications to sundry Gentlmn. in the different districts of whom I have not received yett any answer, except from Mr. Cousin[2] at *Cape Girardeau,* which I take the liberty to enclose herewith with his letter to me, because his statement can be depended upon for his correctness. I shall be very happy to here of Your safe return after your toilsome journey up the Missoury, and from thence down the Colombia river throw the Pacific Ocean, you arrive at the Federal City with every success which you so well deserve, at whatever time these lines may reach you, believe me to be with a saincere respect Dear Sir your most obedt. friend,

CH. GRATIOT

ALS, RC (DLC). Endorsed by Jefferson, "Gratiot Ch. to Capt. Meriwether Lewis."

1. Not found.

2. Barthelemi Cousin (1767–1824), surveyor, interpreter, and secretary to the commandant at Cape Girardeau. His letter to Gratiot of 24 Aug. 1804, answering questions about the Cape Girardeau district, is filed in the Jefferson Papers as fols. 24792–95.

138. C. S. Rafinesque to Jefferson

Sir   [27 November 1804]

· · · ·

The Western parts of the U.S. are as yet very little known, I intend to go and explore part of Kentucky & Ohio next Spring:

I wish I could go still farther and across the Mississipi into the unexplored region of Louisiana, but it is a mere impossiblity in my private Capacity to visit such unsettled and as yet very wild Country. I wonder the American Governt. have not sent some Botanist there along with Messrs. Lewis & Hunter;[1] a Country containing perhaps a great number of the valuable vegetables of Mexico is worth and deserves highly to be fully explored; If it ever seems worthwhile to you, to send a Botanist in Company with the parties you propose to make visit the A[r]kansas or other Rivers, I can not forbear Mentioning that I would think myself highly honored with the choice of in being selected to make known the Veget[abl]e and Animal riches of such a New Country and would think that Glory fully adequate to compensate the dangers and difficulties to encounter. I remain respectfully Sir Yr. most obedt. Servt.

Philad. 27th 9bre 1804   C. S. RAFINESQUE

ALS, RC (ViWC). Endorsed, "Rafinesque. C. S. Phila. Nov. 27. 04. recd. Dec. 1. His address is Mr. C. S. Rafinesque to the care of Mr. Thos. Clifford. Phila." Constantine Samuel Rafinesque (1783–1840), a naturalist, was at this time only visiting in the U.S. but later settled permanently and joined the faculty of Transylvania University, Lexington, Ky.

1. Jefferson made the right decision in not sending a trained botanist with Lewis and Clark. If a botanist, why not also a zoologist and perhaps a geologist? Later the government could send out such specialists; now the problem was to get a few men to the Pacific and back, encumbered no more than necessary by equipment, and intelligent enough to recognize and collect—but not necessarily to evaluate—the natural resources of the region. This distinction has not always been appreciated, even by modern observers. One writer, in a brief evaluation of the zoological contributions of the expedition, refers to Lewis and Clark as engineers (SETZER). Another pair, writing a monograph purporting to deal with the study of natural history in the early West, devotes less than a page to the expedition. "Little need be said here concerning the famous Lewis and Clark expedition of 1804, since no trained naturalist was included in the party" (ALDEN & IFFT). The man whom Rafinesque mentions above is Dr. George Hunter, of Philadelphia, who was exploring the Red River and the Washita with William Dunbar.

139. Jefferson to Reuben Lewis

Dear Sir   Washington Jan. 4. 05.

I recieved last night the inclosed letter for Capt. Lewis; and at the same time information[1] from St. Louis that on the 19th of August he was 850. miles up the Missouri. No accident had happened & he had been well received by all the Indians on his way. It was expected he would winter with the Mandans, 1300 miles up the river, about Lat.

48°, from whence he would have about 1000. miles to the mouth of the Oregan river on the South sea. It is believed he may the ensuing summer reach that & return to winter again with the mandans. If so we may expect to see him in the fall of 1806. Accept my salutations & best wishes.

Th: Jefferson

ALS, SC (DLC).

1. Jefferson had received a letter of 20 Nov. 1804 from Auguste Chouteau, saying, "Par des nouvelles certaine, j'ai appris que le Capt. Lewis etoit arrivé sans aucun accident a Huit cent cinquante mille de l'ambouchure du Missoury a l'epoque du 19 D'aoust dernier, que les sauvages l'avoyent parfaitemente reçus; et je presume qu'il passera la saison de l'hivers chez les Mendanes, à environ 1300 Miles d'ici" (DLC). Again, the informant may be Fairfong. On 19 Aug. he interpreted once more for the Oto chiefs, when the second delegation overtook the exploring party. The next day, Lewis and Clark set off after giving Fairfong a few presents and the Indians a canister of whiskey. Had they delayed for a few hours, Fairfong might have been the bearer of sadder news—the death of Sgt. Charles Floyd. He died of "Biliose Chorlick" later in the day.

140. John Hay to Jefferson

Sir,   [12 February 1805]

Being fully persuaded that any information given you of Capt. Lewis, will be acceptable, I take the Liberty to announce You, that I have lately learnt, that a Letter has come to hand at St. Charles, from his Sioux Interpreter one *Dorion*[1] to his son, letting him Know, that they wintered fifty Leagues above the Mandanes; as the persons who acquainted me of this are very respectable men, I do not doubt of its being a true Report. If Capt. Lewis has wintered there, he will I presume get to his Journey's End, by July, as I am certain the Missoury will break up at furthest, at the End of April. I shall nevertheless do my Endeavours to find out, if the Report, is a fact or not. I remain Sir, With perfect Respect Your most obdt. And humble Servt.

Cahokia 12th Feby. 1805   John Hay

ALS, RC (PHi). Jefferson forwarded this letter to Dearborn 3 April 1805, saying that he was also sending one written by Chouteau (DLC). No doubt he referred to Pierre Chouteau's letter of 13 Jan., stating that hearsay reports from the Indians had placed the expedition fifty leagues above the Mandans. Chouteau confirmed the report in a letter of [2] March: "Un negociant de cette ville qui a hiverné au Village des Mahas a ecrit par un expres que M. Le Captaine Lewis etoit arrivé avant les glaces et sans aucun

accident facheux a environ cinquante Lieues au dessus des Mananes"
(MoSHi).

1. Pierre Dorion (c.1750–1810), trader, interpreter, and Indian agent.
Lewis and Clark met him as he was coming down the river on a raft, and
hired him to return upstream with them as an interpreter. At that time he
was serving as subagent for the Indians of the Missouri, appointed by
Wilkinson. In a letter to Dearborn, 19 Nov. 1807 (DNA, RG 107, D-208), he
was still trying to collect his expenses of $748.26⅔ for the trip up the river
—an amount that covered his assignment for Wilkinson as well as his work
for Lewis and Clark. I date his death from a letter of Clark's, 12 Sept. 1810:
"P. Dorion the Sac Sub Agent is dead" (TERR. PAPERS, 14:414).

141. Lewis to Jefferson

Fort Mandan March 5. 1805

This specimen of a plant[1] common to the praries in this quarter
was presented to me by Mr. Hugh heney[2] a gentleman of rispectability
and information who has resided many years among the natives of this
country from whom he obtained the knowledge of it's virtues. Mr.
Heney informed me that he had used the root of this plant frequently
with the most happy effect in cases of the bite of the mad wolf
or dog and also for the bite of the rattle snake.[3] He assured me that
he had made a great number of experiments on various subjects
of men horses and dogs particularly in the case of madness, where
the symptoms were in some instances far advanced and had never
witnessed it's failing to produce the desired effect. The method of
using it is by external application, to half an ounce of the root
finely pulverized, add as much water as is necessary to reduce
it to the consistency of a common poltice and apply it to the
bitten part, renewing the dressing once in twelve hours. In cases
of the bite of the mad dog where the wound has healed before the
symptoms of madness appear, the bitten part must be lacerated or
sca[r]efyed before the application is made. The application had
always better be made as early as possible after the injury has been
sustained.

I have sent herewith a few pounds of this root, in order that
experiments may be made by some skilfull person under the direction
of the pilosophical society of Philadelphia. I have the honor to be
with much rispect Your Obt. Servt.

MERIWETHER LEWIS.

ALS (PPAmP—Donation Book). The donation book is a blank book into
which John Vaughan copied the identifications of certain natural history
specimens sent back by Lewis and Clark. The entries are dated 16 Nov.

1805, and many of them are coded with a mark resembling the letter *H* —possibly to designate that the specimen mentioned was present. The above letter bears this mark. The book contains a listing of botanical specimens in Vaughan's hand, and a listing of mineralogical specimens in his hand with added comments in the hand of Adam Seybert. These two lists are reprinted in the JOURNALS, 6:152–64. Other unrelated sections of the book include a list of copper coins in Vaughan's hand and a record of books borrowed by members of the Society—mainly in Vaughan's hand but with a few signatures of book borrowers.

1. The heading and the words "This specimen of a plant" are in the hand of John Vaughan. Curiously, the remainder is in the hand of Lewis himself. Since this letter appears at the very end of the entries, we can surmise that Vaughan was interrupted as he began to copy it, and that Lewis —during one of his several visits to the quarters of the Society in the spring and summer of 1807—noticed the incomplete entry and finished copying it into the donation book.

2. Hugh Heney, a former Montreal innkeeper who became a trader with the Sioux, then joined the North West Company in 1804. He is the man that Elliott Coues called Alexander Henry, Jr., throughout his edition of the Biddle narrative, but correctly identified in a subsequent edition of Henry's journal (COUES (2), 1:424–25). Heney visited the Lewis and Clark camp twice during the winter of 1804–05, then sent two messengers down with this plant specimen 28 Feb. 1805.

3. Coues, who was a pretty good amateur botanist but who relied on a consultant for identification of the plants in the Biddle narrative, presents a note that helps but little (BIDDLE-COUES, 1:238–39), and suggests *Astragalus* sp. Explorer Stephen Long understood that the Indians used *Gerardia* sp. as a snake-bite remedy (KEATING, 1:347–48). Trader Antoine Tabeau, whose narrative was edited by Annie Heloise Abel, mentions an occasion on which Henry himself administered the remedy, dressing a wolf-bite wound "by chewing a root known by the name of white wood of the prairie and very common in the Illinois" (TABEAU, 80–81).

142. Amos Stoddard to Jefferson

Sir,   St. Louis, 24th March 1805.

I have the honor to forward you the enclosed Vocabulary of the Scioux language, furnished me by Mr. Crawford, at the request of Capt. Lewis.

Such information as I have received of Capt. Lewis, I transmitted to the Secretary of war by the last mail. Permit me to add here, that the Scioux Chiefs from the River Demoine, invited to the seat of Government by him, have just arrived. Their intention was to join those expected from the Missouri—but as the latter will not probably reach this place till about the middle of May, the former have resolved to return home. I have favored this resolution, because part of them belong to the same nation, and because I conceived the visitors would be more numerous than the policy of the Government dictated. Any arrangements made with those from the Missouri, will be considered as obligatory on those from the Demoine. I am, Sir, with sentiments of high respect, your very huml. Servant,

AMOS STODDARD, Capt.
& Agt. for Capt. Lewis.

ALS, RC (DLC). Endorsed; received 10 May 1805.

143. Lewis to Lucy Marks

Fort Mandan, 1609 miles above the
entrance of the Missouri, March 31st 1805.

Dear Mother.

I arrived at this place on the 27th of October last with the party under my command, destined to the Pacific Ocean, by way of the Missouri and Columbia rivers. The near approach of winter, the low state of the water, and the known scarcity of timber which exists on the Missouri for many hundred Miles above the Mandans, together with many other considerations equally important, determined my friend and companion Capt. Clark and myself, to fortify ourselves and remain for the winter in the neighbourhood of the Mandans Minetares[1] and Ahwahharways,[2] who are the most friendly and well disposed savages that we have yet met with. Accordingly we saught and found a convenient situation for our purposes a few miles below the villages of these people on the North side of the river in an extensive and well timbered bottom, where we commenced the erection of our houses on the 2nd of November, and completed them so far as to put ourselves under shelter on the 21st of the same Month, by which time, the season wore the aspect of winter. Having completed our fortifi[cation] early in December, we called it *Fort Mandan,* in honour of our friendly neighbours. So far, we have experienced more difficulty from the navigation of the Missouri, than danger from the Savages. The difficulties which oppose themselves to the navigation of this immence river, arise from the rapidity of it's current, it's falling banks, sandbars, and timber which remains wholy, or partially concealed in it's bed, usually called by the navigators of the Missouri and Mississippi Sawyers or planters. One of those difficulties, the navigator never ceases to contend with, from the entrance of the Missouri to this place; and in innumerable instances most of those obstructions are at the sam[e] instant combined to oppose his progress, or threaten his distruction. To these we may also add a fifth and not much less inconsiderable difficulty, the turbed quality of the water, which renders it impracticable to discover any obstruction even to the debth of a single inch. Such is the velocity of the current at all seasons of the year, from the entrance of the Missouri, to the mouth of the great river Platte, that it is impossible to resist it's force by means of oars or poles in the main channel of the river; the eddies therefore which generally exist one side or the other of the river, are saught by the navigator; but these are almost universally incumbered with concealed timber, or within the reach of the falling banks, but notwithstanding are usually preferable to that of passing along the edges of the sand bars, over which, the water tho' shallow runs with such violence, that if your vessel happens to touch the sand, or is by any accedent turned sidewise to the current it is driven on the bar, and overset in an instant, generally distroyed, and always attended with the loss of the cargo. The base of the river banks being composed of a fine light sand, is easily removed by the water, it hapens that when this capricious and violent current, sets against it's banks, which are usually covered with heavy timber, it quickly undermines them, sometimes to the debth of 40 or 50 paces, and several miles in length. The banks being unable to support themselves longer, tumble into the river with tremendious force, distroying every thing within their reach. The timber thus precipitated into the water with large masses of earth about their roots, are seen drifting with the stream, their points above the water, while the roots more heavy are draged along the bottom untill they become firmly fixed in the quicksands which form the bed of the river, where they remain for many years, forming an irregular, tho' dangerous chevauxdefrise to oppose the navigator.

This immence river so far as we have yet ascended, waters one of the fairest portions of the globe, nor do I believe that there is in the universe a similar extent of country, equally fertile, well watered, and intersected by such a number of navigable streams. The country as high up this river as the Mouth of the river Platte, a distance of 630 miles is generallly well timbered; at some little distance above this river the open or prarie country commences. With respect this open country I have been agreeably disappointed. From previous information I had been led to believe, that it was barren, steril and sandy; but on the contrary I found it fertile in the extreem, the soil being from one to 20 feet in debth, consisting of a fine black loam, intermixed with a sufficient quantity of sand only to induce a luxuriant growth of grass and other vegitable

[223]

productions, particularly such as are not liable to be much injured, or wholy distroyed by the ravages of the fire. It is also generally level yet well watered; in short there can exist no other objection to it except that of the want of timber, which is truly a very serious one. This want of timber is by no means attributeable to a deficiency in the soil to produce it, but ows it's orrigine to the ravages of the fires, which the natives kindle in these plains at all seasons of the year. The country on both sides of the river, except some of it's bottom lands, for an immence distance is one continued open plain, in which no timber is to be seen, except a few detatched and scattered copse, and clumps of trees, which from their moist situations, or the steep declivities of hills ar[e] sheltered from the effects of fire. The general aspect of the country is level so far as the perception of the spectator will enable him to determine, but from the rapidity of the Missoury, it must be considerably elevated as it passes to the N. West; it is broken only on the borders of the watercourses.

Game is very abundant, and seems to increase as we progress; our prospect for starving is therefore consequently small. On the lower portion of the Missouri, from it's junction with the Mississippi, to the entrance of the Osage river, we met with some deer, bear, and turkies; from thence to the Kancez river, the deer were more abundant, a great number of black bear, some turkies, geese, swan and ducks; from thence to the mouth of the Great river Platte, an immence quantity of deer, some bear, Elk, turkies, geese, swan, and ducks. From thence to the river Sioux, some deer, a great number of Elk, the bear disappeared almost entirely, some turkies, geese swan and ducks; from thence to the mouth of white river, vast herds of Buffaloe, Elk, and some deer and a greater quantity of turkies than we had before seen; a circumstance which I did not much expect, in a country so destitute of timber. From hence to Fort Mandan, the Buffaloe, Elk and deer increase in quantity, with the addition of the Cabrí[3] as they are generally called by the French engages, but which is [a creature], abot the size of a small deer, it's flesh is delic[iously fla]voured.

[T]he ice in the Missouri has now nearly dissapea[red.] I shal set out on my voyage in the course of a few [days.] I can foresee no material obstruction to our progress, and [I] feel the most perfect confidence that we shall reach [the Pa]cific Ocean this sum[mer.] For myself individually I [enjoy] better health than I [have] since I commenced my [voyage. The] party are now in [good] health and excellent sperits, [are at]tatched to the enterp[rise and] anxious to proceed; not a whisper of discontent or murmur is to be heared among them, but all act in unison, and with the most perfect harmony. With such men, I feel every confidence necessary to insure success. The party with Capt. Clark and myself, consists of thirty one white persons, one negroe man, and two Indians.

The Indians in this neighbourhood inform us, that the Missouri is navigable nearly to it's source, and that from a navigable part of the river, at a distance not exceeding half a days march, there is a large river runing from South to North, along the Western base of the Rocky mountains; but as their war excurtions have never extended far beyond this point, they can give no account of the discharge or source of this river. We believe this stream to be the principal South fork of the Columbia river, and if so we shall probably find but little difficulty in passing to the Ocean. We have subsisted this winter on meat principally, with which, our guns have furnished us an ample supply, and have by that means reserved a sufficient stock of the provisions which we brought with us from the Illinois, to guard us against accedental wants, during the voyage of the present year. You may expect me in Albemarle about the last of next September twelve months. I request that you will give yourself no uneasiness with rispect to my fate, for I assure you that I feel myself perfectly as safe as I should do in Albemarle; and the only difference between 3 or 4 thousand miles and 130, is that I can not have the pleasure of seeing you as often as I did while at Washington.

I must request of you before I conclude this letter, to send John Markes to the College at Williamsburgh, as soon as it shall be thought that his education has been sufficiently advanced to fit him for that ceminary; for you may rest assured that as you reguard his future prosperity you had better make any sacrefice of his property than suffer his education to be neglected or remain incomple[te]. Give my love to my brothers and sisters, and all my neighbours and friends, and rest assured yourself of the most devoted filial affection of Yours,

MERIWETHER LEWIS

ALS, RC (MoSHi). Addressed, "Mrs. Lucy Markes Charlottesville Virginia."

1. The Minitari, now called the Hidatsa Indians.

2. Ahwahaway, Ahwahharway, Wattasoon, Wettersoon, are Lewis's and Clark's names for a division of the Hidatsa Indians.

3. *Antilocapra americana americana* (Ord). The pronghorn, commonly called the pronghorn antelope. Probably from *cabril,* the French word for this animal. The French of the region applied the same term to the goat, and the Spanish word for goat is *cabra.* Lewis and Clark variously called this species the cabrie, cabbra, etc. MATHEWS lists *cabree* as an Americanism. For fuller comment on the animal, see No. 149, note 10.

144. Clark to Jefferson

Sir   Fort Mandan April 1st 1805

<*As Capt. Lewis has not Leasure to Send*> <*write*> <*a correct Coppy journal of our proceedings &c.*> It being the wish of Capt. Lewis I take the liberty <*by the request of Captain Lewis to send you*> to send you for your own <*perusal*> perusal, the notes which I have taken in the form of a journal in their original state. You will readily perceive in reading over those notes, that many parts are incorrect, <*principally*> owing to the variety [of] information recived at different times, I most sincerely wish that leasure had permited me to offer them in a more correct form. Receive I pray you my unfained acknoledgements for your friendly recollection of me in your letters to my friend and companion Capt. Lewis, and be assured of the sincere regard with which I have the honor to be Your most Obt. & Humble Servt.

AL, SC (MoSHi). A draft of No. 148. The opening phrase, "It being the wish of Capt. Lewis," and the entire last portion of the letter beginning with "I most sincerely wish" are in Lewis's hand. Endorsed by Clark, "Copy to the Presdt."

The change of meaning that Lewis introduces is pertinent to an unanswered question: has he kept a journal to this point in the expedition? Perhaps he has one in incomplete form; perhaps he expects to write one from his field notes later. At any rate, he wants Clark's statement to Jefferson to be completely noncommittal. No Lewis journal for the first leg of the expedition (as far as Fort Mandan) has been found, but there are fragments which suggest that he kept one. And there certainly is ample evidence that he gathered a great amount of information, whether or not it was in journal form.

145. Clark to [Amos Stoddard?]

Dr. Sir.   [1 April 1805]

I must request the favour of you to send by some safe conveyance as early as possible a red box containing some specimens & papers of consequence[?] to my brother Genl. Jonathin Clark,[1] of Kentuckey as Directed on the top of the Box. R. Worvington[2] the Bearer of this is intrusted with duplicates & papers of considerable consequence which I wish lodged in the hands of my brother <*in Kentucky*> be so good as to furnish this man with a publick horse if you have one which may be returned to you by the post rider. I do not think it worth while to enter into a detaill of occurences as Capt. Lewis has written you fully <*on that subject Yrs. &c.*> I send you [*In margin:*] accept the assurance of my sincer rispect

AL, SC (MoSHi). A draft, on the same sheet as No. 144. Accordingly I give it the same date and assume that it goes to Stoddard. Stoddard is Lewis's agent, the only person empowered to disburse money, forward shipments of specimens, and handle the mail of the expedition. Before all this material from Fort Mandan can reach him, he will have transferred his agency to Charles Gratiot.

1. Jonathan Clark (1750–1816), William's oldest brother. He held the rank of major general awarded by the state of Virginia. In the Clark field notes (CtY) is a sheet of paper with these words written across it diagonally in the manner of an address: "Genl. Jonathan Clark Near Louisville Kentuckey." In one corner of the sheet are the words "Notes at Wood River in 1803–4." Journal entries for 30 Nov. and 1 Dec. 1804, on the back of the sheet, indicate that it was used by Clark at Fort Mandan. This suggests that the red box Clark is sending to his brother contains the journal he kept at the Wood River camp.

2. Corp. Richard Warfington, originally transferred from Capt. John Campbell's company and placed in charge of the detachment of soldiers scheduled to go only as far as Fort Mandan. See No. 149.

146. Clark to William Henry Harrison

Fort Mandan, 1609 Miles up the Missouri,
Dear Sir,   lat. 47 21 47, long. 101 25, W. April 2d, 1805

By the return of a party which we send from this place with dispatches, I do myself the pleasure of giving you a summary view of the Missouri, &c.

In ascending as high as the Kanzas river, which is 334 miles up the Missouri on the S.W. side, we met a strong current, which runs from five to seven miles an hour, the bottoms extensive, and covered with timber; the high country is interspersed with rich handsome prairies; well watered, and abounds in dear and bear. In ascending as high as the river Plate, we met a current less rapid, not exceeding 6 miles an hour; in this distance we pass several small rivers on each side which water some fine diversified country principally prairie as between the Vincennes and Illinois, the bottomed continued wide, and covered with timber, this river is about 600 yards wide, at the mouth, not navigable, it heads the rocky mountains, with the North River, and Yellow Stone River, and passes through an open country; 15 leagues up this river the Ottoes, and thirty Missouries live in one village, and can raise 200 men, 15 leagues h[i]gher up the Paneas and Penea republicans live in one village, and can raise 700 men; up the Wolf Fork of this river, the Pania Lousis live in one village, and can raise 280 men. The Indians have partial rupture frequently. River Plate is 630 miles up the Missouri, on the south west side: Here we find the antelope or goat. The next river of size ascending, is the Stone river, commonly called by the Indians, little River Desioux: it takes its rise in lake Despice, 15 miles from the river Demoir, and is 64 yards wide. Here commences the Sioux country. The next river of note is the Big Sioux river, which heads with St. Peters and waters of lake Winnepic, in some high wooded country. About 90 miles higher up, the river Jaque falls on the same side, and about one hundred yards wide. This river heads with the waters of lake Winnepic, at no great distance east from this place. The head of the River Demon is in Pilican lake, between the Sioux rivers and the St. Peters. The country on both sides of the Missouri, from the river Plate to that place, has very much the same appearance: extensive fertile plains, with but very little timber, and that little principally confined to the river bottoms and streams. The country east of this place, and off from the Missouri as low as Stone river, contains a number of small lakes, many of which are said to be so much impregnated with glauber salts, as to produce all its effects; certain it is, that the water in the small streams from the hills below, on the south west side, possess this quality. About the river Jacque, Bruffala county [country?] contains great quantities of mineral, cobalt, cinnebar, alum, copperas, and several other things; the stone coal which is on the Missouri is very indifferent. Ascending 52 miles above the Jacque, the river Quicum falls in on the south west side. This river is, 1026 miles up, 150 yards wide, not navigable; it heads in the black mountains, which run nearly parallel to the Missouri, from about the head of the Kanzas river, and end S.W. of this place. Quicum waters a broken country, 122 miles by water higher. White river falls in on the south west side, and is 300 yards wide, and navigable, as all the other streams are, which are not particularly mentioned. This river heads in some small lakes short of the black mountains. The Mahan and Poncan nations rove on the heads of this river and the Quicum and Can raise 250 men, they were very numerous a few years ago, but the small-pox and the Sioux have reduced them to their present state—the Sioux possess the south west of the Missouri, above White river; 132 miles higher, and on the west side.—Teton river falls into it, it is small, and heads in the open plains; here we met a large band of Sioux. and the second which we had seen called Tetons, those are great rascals, and may be justly termed the pirates of the Missouri; they made two attemps to stop us; they are subdivided and stretched on the river to near this place, having reduced the Ruaras and Mandans, and drove them from the country they now occupy, the Sioux bands rove in the country to the Mississippi. About 47 miles above the Teton river, the Chyenne river falls in from the south west, 400 yards wide, and navigable to the Black mountains, in which it takes its rise, in the 3d range. Several bands of Indians but little known, rove on the heads of this and the river Plate, and are stated to be as follows; Chayenne, 300 men, Staetan 100 men; Canenaviech, 400 men; Cavanwa and Wetabato, 200 men; Catoha, 70 men; Detain, 30 men: Memetoon, 50 men; Castah na, 1300 men; it is probable that some of these bands are the remains of the Paducar nation; at 1440 miles up the Missouri, (and a short distance above two handsome rivers which take their rise in the Black mountains) the Rickaras live in three villages, and are the remains of ten different tribes of Paneas, who have been reduced and drove from their country lower down, by the Sioux, their number is about 500 men, they raise corn, beans &c. and appear friendly and well disposed, they were at war with the nations of this neighborhood, we have brought about a peace between the Recars and this place, two rivers fall in on the south west, and one on the north east, not very long, and take their rise in the open country; this country abounds in a great variety of wild animals but a few of which the Indians take, many of those animals are uncommon in the U. States, such as white, red and grey bears, long ear'd male or black tailed deer (black at the end of the tail only) large hare, antelope or goat, the red fox, the ground prairie dog, (burrows in the ground) the braroca, which has a head like a dog, and the size of a small dog, the white brant, magpye, calumet eagle, &c and many other are said to inhabit the rocky mountains.

I have collected the following account of the rivers and country in advance of this, to wit: at two days march in advance of this the Little Missouri, falls in on the side and heads in at the north extremity of the Black mountains; six days further a large river joins the Missouri, affording as much water as the main river, this river is rapid, without a fall, and navagable to the Rocky mountains; its branches head with the waters of the river Plate; the country in advance is said to be broken.

The trade of the nations at this place is from the N.W. and Hudsons bay establishments on the Assinneboin river, distant about 150 miles; those traders are nearly at open war with each other, and better calculated to destroy then promote the happiness of those na-

[229]

tions to whom they have latterly extended their trade, and intend to form an establishment near this place in the course of this year. Your most obdt. servt.

WM. CLARK

Printed, JOURNALS, 7:314–16, from the Baltimore *Telegraphe and Daily Advertiser,* 25 July 1805. Clark's spelling obviously has been modified, and many words and passages have been garbled.

147. Clark to William Croghan

Fort Mandan in Lat. 47° 21′ 47″ N. Long. 101° 25′ W
Dear Major   April the 2nd 1805.

By the return of a party of Soldiars and french men who accompanied us to this place for the purpose of assisting in transporting provisions &c. I have the pleasure of sending you this hasty scrawl which will do little more than inform you where I am. My time being entirely taken up in preparing information for our government and attending to those duties which is absolutely necessary for the promotion of our enterprise and attending to Indians deprives me the satisfaction of giveing you a satisfactory detail of this Countrey. I must therefore take the liberty of refuring you to my brother to whome I have inclosed a Map and some sketches relative to the Indians. Our party has enjoyed a great share of health and are in high spirits. We shall leave this place in two days on our journey. Country and River above this is but little Known. Our information is altogether from Indians collected at different times and entitled to some credit. My return will not be so soon as I expected, I fear not sooner than about June or July 1806. Every exertion will be made to accomplish this enterprise in a shorter period, please to present me most respectfully to my Sister Lucy & the family and accept the assurance of my sincere affections &c.

WM. CLARK

I send my sister Croghan some seed of several Kinds of Grapes.

ALS, RC (WHi—Draper Coll., 12J4).

148. Clark to Jefferson

Sir   Fort Mandan April the 3rd 1805.

It being the wish of Captain Lewis, I take the liberty to send you for your own perusal the notes which I have taken in the form of a journal in their original state. You will readily perceive in reading over those notes, that many parts are incorrect, owing to the variety of information received at different times, I most sincerely wish that leasure had permited me to offer them in a more correct form.

Receive I pray you my unfained acknowledgments for your friendly recollection of me in your letters to my friend and companion Captn. Lewis. And be assured of the sincere regard with which I have the honor to be Your most obedient and Humble Servent,

WM. CLARK

ALS, RC (DLC). Endorsed; received 13 July 1805. The fair copy of No. 144.

149. Lewis to Jefferson

Dear Sir.   Fort Mandan, April 7th 1805.

Herewith inclosed you will receive an invoice of certain articles, which I have forwarded to you from this place. Among other articles, you will observe by reference to the invoice, 67. specimens of earths, salts and minerals; and 60 specimens of plants; these are accompanyed by their rispective labels expressing the days on which obtained, places where found, and also their virtues and properties when known. By means of these labels, reference may be made to the Chart of the Missouri forwarded to the Secretary at War, on which, the encampment of each day has been carefully marked; thus the places at which these specimens have been obtained may be easily pointed out, or again found, should any of them prove valuable to the community on further investegation. These have been forwarded with a view of their being presented to the Philosophical society of Philadelphia, in order that they may under their direction be examined or analyzed. After examining these specimens yourself, I would thank you to have a copy of their labels made out, and retained untill my return. The other articles are intended particularly for yourself, to be retained, or disposed off as you may think proper.

You will also receive herewith inclosed a part of Capt. Clark's private journal, the other part you will find inclosed in a seperate tin box. This journal is in it's original state, and of course incorrect, but it will serve to give you the daily detales of our progress, and transactions. Capt. Clark dose not wish this journal exposed in it's present state, but has no objection, that one or more copies of it be made by some confidential person under your direction, correcting it's gramatical errors &c. Indeed it is the wish of both of us, that two of those copies should be made, if convenient, and retained untill our return; in this state there is no objection to your submitting them to the perusal of the heads of the departments, or such others as you may think proper. A copy of this journal will assist me in compiling my own for publication after my return. I shall dispatch a canoe[1] with three, perhaps four persons, from the extreem navigable point of the Missouri, or the portage betwen this river, and the Columbia river, as either may first happen; by the return of this canoe, I shal send you my journal, and some one or two of the best of those kept by my men. I have sent a journal kept by one of the Sergeants,[2] to Capt. Stoddard, my agent at St. Louis, in order as much as possible to multiply the chances of saving something. We have encouraged our men to keep journals, and seven of them do so, to whom in this respect we give every assistance in our power.

I have transmitted to the Secretary at War, every information relative to the geography of the country which we possess, together with a view of the Indian nations,[3] containing information relative to them, on those points with which, I conceived it important that the government should be informed. If it could be done with propriety and convenience, I should feel myself much obliged by your having a copy taken of my dispatches to the Secretary at War, on those subjects, retaining them for me untill my return. By reference to the Muster-rolls[4] forwarded to the War Department, you will see the state of the party; in addition to which, we have two Interpreters, one negroe man, servant to Capt. Clark, one Indian woman, wife to one of the interpreters, and a Mandan man, whom we take with a view to restore peace between the Snake Indians, and those in this neighbourhood amounting in total with ourselves to 33 persons. By means of the Interpreters and Indians, we shall be enabled to converse with all the Indians that we shall probably meet with on the Missouri.

I have forwarded to the Secretary at War, my public Accounts[5] rendered up to the present day. They have been much longer delayed than I had any idea that they would have been, when we departed from the Illinois, but this delay, under the circumstances which I was compelled to act, has been unavoidable. The provision perogue and her crew, could not have been dismissed in time to have returned to St. Louis last fall without evedently in my opinion, hazarding the fate of the enterprise in which I am engaged, and I therefore did not hesitate to prefer the sensure that I may have incurred by the detention of these papers, to that of risking in any degree the success of the expedition. To me, the detention of those papers have formed a serious source of disquiet and anxiety; and the recollection of your particular charge to me on this subject, has made it still more poignant. I am fully aware of the inconvenience which must have arrisen to the War Department, from the want of these vouchers, previous to the last session of Congress, but how to divert[6] it was out of my power to devise.

From this plase we shall send the barge and crew early tomorrow morning with orders to proceed as expeditiauly as possible to St. Louis, by her we send our dispatches, which I trust will get safe to hand. Her crew consists of ten ablebodied men[7] well armed and provided with a sufficient stock of provision to last them to St. Louis. I have but little doubt but they will be fired on by the Siouxs; but they have pledged themselves to us that they will not yeald while there is a man of them living.

Our baggage is all embarked on board six small canoes and two perogues; we shall set out at the same moment that we dispatch the barge. One or perhaps both of these perogues we shall leave at the falls of the Missouri, from whence we intend continuing our voyage in the canoes and a perogue of skins, the frame of which was prepared at Harper's ferry. This perogue is now in a situation which will enable us to prepare it in the course of a few hours. As our vessels are now small and the current of the river much more moderate, we calculate on traveling at the rate of 20 or 25 miles pr. day as far as the falls of the Missouri. Beyond this point, or the first range of rocky Mountains situated about 100 miles further, any calculation with rispect to our daily progress, can be little more than bare conjecture. The circumstance of the Snake Indians possessing large quantities of horses, is much in our favour, as by means of horses, the transportation of our baggage will be rendered easy and expeditious over land, from the Missouri, to the Columbia river. Should this river not prove navigable where we first meet with it, our present intention is, to continue our march by land down the river untill it becomes so, or to the Pacific Ocean. The map,[8] which has been forwarded to the Secretary at War, will give you the idea we entertain of the connection of these rivers, which has been formed from the corresponding testimony of a number of Indians who have visited the country, and who have been seperately and carefully examined on that subject, and we therefore think it entitled to some degree of confidence.

Since our arrival at this place we have subsisted principally on meat, with which our guns have supplyed us amply, and have thus been enabled to reserve the parched meal, portable soup, and a con-

[233]

siderable proportion of pork and flour, which we had intended for the more difficult parts of our voyage. If Indian information can be credited, the vast quantity of game with which the country abounds through which we are to pass leaves us but little to apprehend from the want of food.

We do not calculate on completeing our voyage within the present year, but expect to reach the Pacific Ocean, and return, as far as the head of the Missouri, or perhaps to this place before winter. You may therefore expect me to meet you at Montachello in September 1806.

On our return we shal probably pass down the yellow stone river, which from Indian informations, waters one of the fairest portions of this continent.

I can foresee no material or probable obstruction to our progress, and entertain therefore the most sanguine hopes of complete success. As to myself individually I never enjoyed a more perfect state of good health, than I have since we commenced our voyage. My inestimable friend and companion Capt. Clark has also enjoyed good health generally. At this moment, every individual of the party are in good health, and excellent sperits; zealously attatched to the enterprise, and anxious to proceed; not a whisper of discontent or murmur is to be heard among them; but all in unison, act with the most perfect harmoney. With such men I have every thing to hope, and but little to fear.

Be so good as to present my most affectionate regard to all my friends, and be assured of the sincere and unalterable attachment of Your most Obt. Servt.

MERIWETHER LEWIS Capt.
1st. U.S. Regt. Infty.

[Enclosure]

Invoice of articles[9] forwarded from Fort Mandan to the President of the United States through Captn. Stoddard at St. Louis and Mr. H. B. Trist the Collector of the Port of New Orleans.

No.	Package	Contents
1	Box	Skins of the Male and female Antelope,[10] with their skeletons. [came. P.]
"	do	2 Horns and ears, of the Black tail, or Mule Deer.[11] [came]
"	"	A Martin[12] skin [came] containing the skin of a weasel[13] [came. P.] and three small squirels[14] of the Rocky Mountains & the tail of a Mule deer fully grown. [came.]

[234]

"	"	Skeletons of the small, or burrowing wolf [15] of the Praries, the skin haveing been lost by accedent. [some skeletons came, not distinguishable. sent to P.]
"	"	2 skeletons of the White Hare.[16] [as above. P.]
"	"	A Mandan bow with a quiver of arrows [came] the quiver containing some seed of the Mandan tobacco.[17] [came]
"	"	A carrot[18] of Ricara tobacco. [came.]
2	Box	4 Buffalow robes, [came] and an *ear* of Mandan corn.[19]
3	Box	Skins of the Male and female Antelope, with their skeletons [undistinguishable. P.] and the skin of a brown, or yellow Bear.[20]
4	Box	Specimens of earths, salts, and minerals, numbered from 1. to 67. [came]
"	"	Specimens of plants[21] numbered from 1 to 60. [came.] [A. Ph. Society.]
"	"	1 earthen pot,[22] such as the Mandans manufacture, and use for culinary purposes. [came]
"	"	1 tin box containing insects, mice &c.
"	"	a specimen of the fur of the Antilope.
"	"	a specimen of a plant, and a parsel of its roots, highly prized by the natives as an efficatious remidy in the cure of the bite of the rattle snake, or mad dog.[23]
	in a Large Trunk	Skin of a Male and female Braro, or burrowing Dog of the Praries,[24] with the skeleton of the female. [came. P.]
"	in a large Trunk	1 skin of a red fox[25] containing a Magpie.[26] [came.]
"	"	2 cased skins of the white hare. [came. P.]
"	"	1 Minetarre Buffalow robe, [came] containing some articles of Indian dress. [came]
"	"	1 Mandan Buffalow robe, [came] containing a dressed skin of the Lousivire[27] [came] and two cased skins of the burrowing squirels of the praries. [came P.]
"	"	13 red fox skins [came.]
"	"	4 horns of the mountain ram, or *big horn*.[28] [came.]
"	"	1 Buffalow robe[29] painted by a Mandan man representing a battle which was faught 8 years since,

[235]

		by the Sioux & Ricaras, against the Mandans, Minitarras & Ahwahharways. [came.]
6	Cage	Containing four liveing Magpies.[30] [1. came P.]
7	do.	Containing a liveing burrowing squirel of the praries.[31] [came. P.]
9	do.	Containing one liveing hen of the Prarie.[32]
10	————	1 large par of Elk's horns connected by the frontal bone.[33]

ALS, RC (DLC). Endorsed; received 13 July 1805. Enclosure in Clark's hand. In the enclosure the words in brackets, in Jefferson's hand, show whether the materials were sent to Charles Willson Peale or to the American Philosophical Society. Those marked only "came" probably were retained by Jefferson. A penciled notation at the head of the letter, in the hand of Elliott Coues, reads: "This letter was originally printed, *revised*, with Jeff's. Message to Congr. of Feb. 19 1806, and afterwards in many other places, always misdated 'April 17th.'" Another annotation by Coues, at the end of the enclosure, reads: "above is original of the invoice of presents etc. to Mr. Jefferson, shipped by the Barge from Fort Mandan April 7th 1804. Coues." For more about Coues's habit of writing on valuable manuscripts, see Appendix II.

Jefferson's index of letters records a letter from Lewis dated 30 March 1805, received 13 July. Perhaps that communication (not found) was his personal report to the President, and this one was written with a view to publication. It first appeared in JEFFERSON's *Message from the President of the United States communicating discoveries made in exploring the Missouri, Red River and Washita, by Captains Lewis and Clark, Doctor Sibley, and Mr. Dunbar* (Washington, 1806), issued to accompany Jefferson's message to Congress (No. 193). Among the other works in which it may be found is *American State Papers*, Indian Affairs, 1:706–07.

1. Not done. No more was heard of the expedition, except sketchy and unfounded Indian reports, until it returned to St. Louis in Sept. 1806.

2. Probably the journal of the late Sgt. Floyd.

3. This is a large table in Clark's hand, now at the American Philosophical Society. From it Jefferson prepared as part of his *Message from the President* a section entitled "A statistical view of the Indian nations inhabiting the Territory of Louisiana and the countries adjacent to its northern and western boundaries."

4. None found. The muster rolls of the regular army for this period are not very numerous; those which have survived are soon to be made available as a microfilm publication of the National Archives.

5. Not found, but reflected in the statement of Lewis's account now presented as No. 277. Two entries in DNA, RG 107, Register of Letters Received, are pertinent: L-267, Fort Mandan, 6 April 1805, enclosing Lewis's accounts for 1805; and L-291, Fort Mandan, 6 April 1805, advising of his draft in favor of "Rani Jessome" for $220. These and other items are doubtless the ones mentioned by Charles Gratiot on 1 June 1805 when he told Dearborn he was forwarding "copies of drafts of Capt. Lewis" (G-161).

6. The word "divert" altered in pencil to "avert," in the hand of Coues.

7. Plus two Frenchmen and a lame Arikara who wish to go only as far as the Arikara village. At that village the boat will be boarded by trader Antoine Tabeau and an Arikara chief who has consented to go to Washington. The permanent crew as the boat leaves Fort Mandan consists of these persons: (a) Corp. Richard Warfington, in charge of boat and crew. (b) Joseph Gravelines, interpreter. An assistant to Tabeau, he knows the Arikara language and will later conduct the Arikara chief to Washington. (c) Six army privates. Of these, two are men expelled from the permanent party and four are members of the crew of the white pirogue on the upstream voyage, never considered part of the permanent party. John Newman had been expelled for mutinous expressions and Moses B. Reed for desertion. John Boley was probably from Capt. Russell Bissell's company. On his return from Fort Mandan he was a member of the detachment from the companies of Daniel and Russell Bissell which Pike commanded on his voyage up the Mississippi in 1805, and to the West in 1806. On the muster roll which Pike submitted upon returning from his western expedition, Boley's date of enlistment is 27 Oct. 1803 (DNA, RG 94, Pay and Muster Rolls, First Infantry). The other three men are all members of Capt. Amos Stoddard's company. They are entered in Stoddard's company book (MoSHi) with brief descriptions which I summarize here. John Dame, age seventeen upon enlistment 20 Aug. 1801; five feet nine inches, blue eyes, light hair, fair complexion; born Pallingham, N.H.; occupation, laborer. Ebenezer Tuttle, age twenty-nine upon enlistment 1 Jan. 1803; five feet seven inches, blue eyes, brown hair, fair complexion; born New Haven, Conn.; occupation, farmer. Isaac White, age twenty-six upon enlistment 13 Feb. 1801; five feet seven and one-half inches, blue eyes, sandy hair, light complexion; born Holliston, Mass.; occupation, laborer. (d) Two Frenchmen. There are also two other Frenchmen in a small pirogue accompanying the boat, identified by Clark (JOURNALS, 1:283) as *engagés* who had been with the expedition coming upstream. I cannot say which of these were in the boat crew and which in the pirogue; perhaps all are among the five Frenchmen who were paid back wages by Lewis's agent in St. Louis in 1805 after their return. The five, as listed in the financial records, include Baptiste Des-champs, who was *patron* on the upstream voyage, Jean Baptiste Lajeunesse, Etienne Malboeuf, Charles Pineau (Peter Pinaut in Clark's listing, JOURNALS, 1:31), and François Rivet.

8. Original not found, but the War Department copy is in the Carto-graphic Records Branch of the National Archives, entitled: "A Map of part of the Continent of North America, Between the 35th. and 51st. degrees of North Latitude, and extending from 89 Degrees of West Longitude to the Pacific Ocean. Compiled from the Authorities of the best informed travellers, by M. Lewis. . . . Copied by Nicholas King, 1806." It was first reproduced, though not as a facsimile, by HAGUE in 1887; then Coues included a full-size version in vol. 4 of his edition of the Biddle narrative. More recently the map has been reproduced as plate 31 in TUCKER and has been discussed by DOUGLAS. A later manuscript copy in the library of the Boston Athenaeum, also by the hand of Nicholas King, is reproduced in vol. 2 of WHEAT. Samuel L. Mitchill saw the map when it reached Washington

but declined to publish it in his *Medical Repository,* declaring that the privilege should be reserved for Lewis. But see his commentary in MITCHILL.

9. "I think I sent you Capt. Lewis's original catalogue of the articles he had forwarded to me. I retained no copy of it, & having occasion to turn to it, would thank you for it" (Jefferson to Peale, 1 Jan. 1806, DLC). For the duplicate invoice that Clark included in his journal, see JOURNALS, 1:280–82.

10. The pronghorn. Lewis and Clark were the first to put specimens and a detailed, firsthand description into the hands of scientists, although the existence of the animal had long been known. Benjamin Smith Barton, in his *Philadelphia Medical and Physical Journal,* supp. 2 (1807), 194, reported that the animal had been known for more than 150 years; that a drawing of its horns had been published by Dutch naturalist Albertus SEBA in his *Locupletissimi rerum naturalium thesauri accurata description . . . per universam physices historiam* (Amsterdam, 1734–65); and that a tolerably good figure of the animal had been published as early as 1651. HARLAN, 251, believed it was the species described and badly figured by Francisco HERNANDEZ under the name of *"Mazame seu Ceruis"* in his *Nova plantarum, animalum et mineralum Mexicanorum historia . . .* (Rome, 1651). I assume that Barton also was referring to this drawing. Jefferson had heard of the pronghorn through the Osages, and he discusses it in a letter to naturalist William Bartram, 7 April 1805: "I dare say you know that Westward of the Misipi there is an animal of the Capra kind; & tho by some it is called a deer, & by some a goat that would not authorise us to call it the Cervicapra of the East. . . . The Osage Indians shewed me a specimen of it's leather, superior to any thing of the kind I ever saw. Their manner of dressing the leather too receives enquiry, as it receives no injury from being wet. I count on special information as to this animal from Capt. Lewis, and that he will enrich us with other articles of Zoology, in which he is more skilled than in botany" (DLC).

11. *Odocoileus hemionus* (Raf.). See another note under No. 192.

12. *Martes americana americana* (Turton).

13. The long-tailed weasel, *Mustela frenata longicauda* Bonaparte.

14. The red squirrel, perhaps either *Tamiasciurus hudsonicus fremonti* (Audubon and Bachman) or *Tamiasciurus hudsonicus richardsoni* (Bachman). Such common names as "Fremont's squirrel" and "Richardson's red squirrel" have been discarded by mammalogists, who now designate all such subspecies by one common name, "red squirrel."

15. The coyote, *Canis latrans latrans* Say.

16. The white-tailed jack rabbit, *Lepus townsendii campanius* Hollister, first mentioned by Lewis in No. 109.

17. *Nicotiana quadrivolvus* Pursh. Lewis and Clark observed a difference between Arikara and Mandan tobacco, and sent back specimens of what they thought were two species of Arikara tobacco, differing mainly in size of leaf and flower. For Lewis's description of both species and the manner of cultivation, see the JOURNALS, 6:150–51. A sample of tobacco that Jefferson sent to Philadelphia tobacconist Thomas Leiper may have been brought back by the explorers, or even grown by Jefferson from the seed mentioned here. Leiper reported to Jefferson 20 Aug. 1807: "I returned you by Major

[238]

Lewis Two Bundles of segars manufactured from the Tobacco you sent me by him. From the manner the Tobacco was packed it was not possible it could retain much of its original flavour. From the smalness of the sample I had it not in my power to manufacture it into any thing else but segars and I believe it to be the kind of tobacco that the very fine segars are made of for it has as little substance as the Kitefoot owing no doubt to its being top't high . . ." (DLC).

18. A length of tobacco leaves twisted together, roughly resembling a carrot.

19. Maize or Indian corn, *Zea mays* L. Seed collected by Lewis and Clark was said by PURSH, 1:46, to produce "as excellent ears as any sort I know." Jefferson experimented with two varieties sent back by the explorers, the Mandan and the Pawnee [Arikara], and took special pains to compare them with some European corn sent him by his old friend André Thoüin (b. 1747), chief of the Jardin des Plantes in Paris. Hence this entry in Jefferson's weather memorandum book, quoted by BETTS, 336: "Aug. 11 [1807]. my Quarentine corn planted May 1 gave rosten ears in the last week of June. Being about 8. weeks. It is now dry enough to grind, to wit 3½ months. My Pani corn planted the same day was a week or fortnight later. But Shoemaker [a tenant] planted Pani corn about the 2d. week of May, & had rosten ears the last week of June. . . ." By quarantine corn, Jefferson seems to mean corn that matures in about forty days—from the original meaning of the word. This is conjecture, but I find some support in BURTT-DAVY, 346, in a reference to "Six Weeks, or Quarantino" corn. Jefferson was still raising the Pawnee or Arikara variety some years later. An entry of 9 April 1811 in his garden book reads: "Planted Pani corn in the middle part of grounds below Bailey's alley. Come to table July 18" (BETTS, 446). English botanist John Bradbury wrote William Roscoe, of the Liverpool Botanic Garden, 12 Aug. 1809, that Jefferson planned to send to England "a New Variety of Zea Maize which was brought by Capn. Lewis from . . . a Tribe of Cultivating Indians in Latitude 49° and a Country so much elevated as to render it almost a Greenland climate." On 10 May 1809, Bradbury wrote Roscoe that he had planted the corn in his own St. Louis garden. "I have no doubt of its doing very well in England & it will be an immense National benefit. . . ." In the fall he sent some seed to Roscoe. "I send you herewith some varieties of Maize amongst which are two kinds which will I think succeed in England as they will frequently come to maturity here in 10 or 11 weeks whereas the common variety requires the whole summer . . ." (RICKETT, 59–89). For further comments on Mandan, Arikara, and other Indian corn varieties, see ATKINSON & WILKINSON.

20. My note on bears, particularly the grizzly, is with No. 194.

21. These plants and the geological specimens reached Philadelphia in the fall, and were the subject of this entry in the minutes of the American Philosophical Society, 15 Nov. 1805:

"The following donations were received. . . . A box containing various specimens of plants, earths and minerals collected by Captn. Merewether Lewis and by him presented to the Society.

"These articles were forwarded by the President who desires that the seeds may be sent to Mr. Hamilton.

[239]

"Mr. Vaughan and Dr. Seybert are appointed a committee to examine the different Earths and Minerals and make a list of the same.

"Resolved that the seeds transmitted by the President be referred to Mr. Wm. Hamilton with a request that he plant them in due season and report as soon as may be to the Society the nature of the plants produced by them with such descriptions & specimens as may serve for the information of the Society or the Public, and that the Secretaries be enjoined to give him due information of this resolution.

"The Hortus siccus is referred to Dr. Barton who is to examine the same and report to the Society. He is at the same time requested to reserve the seeds which are to be transmitted to Mr. Hamilton" (PPAmP).

These donations were then entered into the Society's donation book as noted under No. 141. Adam Seybert (1773–1825), physician, scientist, and later congressman from Pennsylvania, made some tentative identifications of the geologcial specimens, which he wrote into the book, but he later resigned from his committee assignment before he had "arranged" these specimens.

22. In an article on pottery vessels of the upper Missouri, WEDEL discusses and illustrates two fragmentary vessels said to be Mandan pots from the Lewis and Clark Expedition. They are at the University Museum in Philadelphia, on deposit from the American Philosophical Society and the Academy of Natural Sciences of Philadelphia.

23. See No. 141.

24. The American badger, *Taxidea taxus taxus* (Schreber). "Braro" is Clark's version of the French *blaireau*.

25. *Vulpes fulva regalis* Merriam.

26. The black-billed magpie, *Pica pica hudsonia* (Sabine).

27. *Lynx canadensis canadensis* Kerr. For Clark's "Lousivire" read the French *loup-cervier*.

28. The Audubon mountain sheep, *Ovis canadensis auduboni* Merriam. This is the species which Lewis and Clark called the ibex or argali, as well as the bighorn, and which early naturalists thought of in connection with the *Ovis ammon* or Siberian argali of Cuvier. Its existence came as no surprise to Lewis and Clark; the animal was known in St. Louis, and word of it had passed to American settlers east of the Mississippi, as shown in a letter written by George Turner, territorial judge in Kaskaskia, 1794–95: "[Mr. Chouteau] tells me that at a great distance up that River [the Missouri], you will meet with some new—animals—animals unknown in our Natural History: particularly one, of the size and nearly the colour of the elk, but with much longer hair. Under this hair, he is clothed with a fine and very long fur. He has two large horns—which, issuing from behind the ears and turning backwards in a circle, terminate in two points projecting before the head, in a horizontal direction" (to John Evans, 10 March 1795, Archivo General de Indias (Seville), Papeles de Cuba, legajo 213, printed by NASATIR (2) and DILLER (2)). Diller believes that Turner also wrote an account of the Missouri, mentioning the mountain sheep, which Samuel L. Mitchill published in his *Medical Repository*, 2nd hexade, 1 (April 1804), 412–14. It is possible that Lewis and Clark already knew of the mountain sheep before coming to the West. In a note on the animal, Barton said that its existence had been known to Spanish historians before 1633 (*Philadelphia Medical and Physical Journal*,

supp. 2 (1807), 193–94). Mitchill, in an introduction to an article by Duncan McGillivray (d. 1808) in the *Repository* (MC GILLIVRAY, 237), asserted that Father Picolo, a Spanish missionary in California, had reported in 1697 having seen such animals and eaten their flesh. Mitchill probably was referring to an account by Francis Maria PICOLO, published in 1708. Miguel VENEGAS described and illustrated the mountain sheep in 1:36 of his *Natural and civil history of California* (London, 1759), which was the English edition of his *Noticia de la California . . .* (Madrid [1757]). Thomas PENNANT followed Picolo's account in his *Arctic zoology* (London, 1784–87). McGillivray collected a specimen while traveling in the fall of 1800 with explorer David Thompson in the Rockies, between the Saskatchewan and Missouri rivers; he included a woodcut with his published description. The drawing of the animal in DOUGHTY, 1:193, was done partly from the male and female specimens in Peale's museum, presented by Lewis and Clark. Lewis left a slip of paper among his effects, upon his death, reading "History of quadrupeds published by A. Anderson N. York Page 526—the american Argali discribed—copy of this work in the possession of the A. P. Socyety—Philadelphia" (MoSHi). He was referring to the first American edition of Thomas Bewick's *A general history of quadrupeds* (New York, 1804), issued by engraver Alexander Anderson with an appendix containing descriptions of some American animals. After the expedition, Lewis asked Manuel Lisa to try raising some of the young sheep, but lack of milk was a handicap. Lisa told Thomas Nuttall in 1810 that he was still trying to raise some, using tame goat's milk (Nuttall to Barton, 22 April 1810, transcript in the Philadelphia Academy of Natural Sciences).

29. This robe survived the dissolution of Peale's museum and is now at the Peabody Museum, Harvard University. For a description, see WILLOUGHBY, 638; for an illustration, see the section of illustrations in this volume after p. 106.

30. One survived the long voyage down to New Orleans, up the coast by sea to Baltimore, overland to Washington, and on to Peale's museum in Philadelphia. Its itinerary can be traced in several letters below. The bird served as model for ornithologist Alexander WILSON when he produced his *American ornithology* (Philadelphia, 1808–14), and in describing it in 4:75 he explains: "The drawing was taken from a very beautiful specimen, sent from the Mandan nation, on the Missouri, to Mr. Jefferson, and by that gentleman to Mr. Peale of this city, in whose museum it lived for several months."

31. The black-tailed prairie dog, *Cynomys ludovicianus ludovicianus* (Ord). It was new to science when the specimens and a living animal came down from Fort Mandan. Barton surmised that it was perhaps the earless marmot of Pennant or the *Arctomys citillus* of Peter Pallas (*Philadelphia Medical and Physical Journal*, 2 (1806), 159). The first allusion to this animal in the papers of the expedition is Lewis's reference, in No. 118, to the "vilages of the Snake Lizard and Squirel." Probably the first published reference is in Clark's letter to Harrison (No. 142). The next mention in print occurs in GASS, followed by PIKE.

32. The sharp-tailed grouse, *Pedioecetes phasianellus jamesi* Lincoln. This bird reached St. Louis alive but failed to arrive at New Orleans.

33. The wapiti, *Cervus canadensis canadensis* Erxleben. A pair of horns

[241]

like these now hang inside the main entrance of Jefferson's home at Monticello, together with those of a moose, and both are labeled as having been presented by Lewis and Clark. The wapiti is, of course, the species known also as the elk though it is not a true elk. Barton first proposed the specific name "wapiti" in 1806, "which is the name by which it is known among the Shawnees or Shawnese Indian" (INGERSOLL, 162).

150. Pierre Chouteau to William Henry Harrison

Sir   St. Louis le [22] May 1805

The barge of Capn. Lewis arrived the day before yesterday[1] he has sent by this opportunity 45 chiefs or *considerés* of the nations Ricaras, poncas, Sioux of the tribes on the Missoury, Mahas, ottos & missouris in order that they may be conducted from here to the federal city. I send you an express to give you notice of their arrival, they unanimously wish to undertake this Journey, but as my instructions whereof you have a perfect knowledge do not permitt the departure of any Indians for the seat of government without a special permission I think it is my Duty to wait your answer before I give them mine and I hope that in the shortest possible you will transmit to me your orders and will direct my conduct in this occasion as minutely as possible.

I Will observe to you that I am ever in the same opinion that the Warm Season is very dangerous for these Indians of whom perhaps a great number will fall victims to so long and penible Journey in a climate so different from their own, and I think that the automn and Winter are the only proper season to undertake with security that trip, if you were of the same opinion, it would be convenient, I Believe, to Kept them here till next fall, and to send them from time to time in hunting party in the District.[2] What ever may be your decision I think that it will be necessary to call for some chiefs and considerès of the nations Sakias and foxes who are already called by the government, which is already known to them as the expences of the voyage will be proportion to the number of the Indians which will amount to 60 at least. Perhaps you will find convenient to send back to theyr nations some of them to bring the news of the departure of the others. Finally I pray you to give me particular instructions on every article being very desirous that my conduct may be approved. Fix if you please to the certain epoch of the departure the number of the Indians to be conducted, the road to be taken, and authorises me to expend which sums you will

[242]

judge necessary. I am ready to start with the Indians in all season and if I propose you some objections on the time it is only in order to avoid any reproach from the government and from the Indians in the supposition that some unhappy event would arrive.

Mr. Wm. Ewing[3] will start in a few days. I remain, Sir, with the greatest consideration Sir &c. &c.

SC (MoSHi—Pierre Chouteau letterbook). Reply is No. 153. Although Chouteau normally corresponded in French, this letter is in English.

1. Maj. James Bruff, military commandant at St. Louis, sent Warfington's barge to meet a part of the command of James Wilkinson, who was coming to assume the governorship of Louisiana Territory. See Wilkinson to Dearborn, 15 June 1805, with its enclosure of 28 May 1805, Bruff to Wilkinson, in TERR. PAPERS, 13:135-38. At least two of the soldiers who came down from Fort Mandan were with the barge when it reached Wilkinson at Fort Massac, and Wilkinson obtained from them some information which he sent on to officials in Washington.

2. Harrison agreed with Chouteau that the journey should be postponed until autumn (No. 153). Chouteau wrote him again on 31 May, "Conformement a votre justes observations les circonstances ne permiettent guere de conduire presentement les sauvages a federal city." He said that many of the Indians already had colds brought on by the change of climate, and that it would be difficult to find horses for an early journey. For their hunting parties in the St. Louis area, he planned to outfit a wagon. Several other letters in Chouteau's letterbook reflect his activity in arranging the journey and also his attitude toward it. On 2 March he had written Dearborn about Lewis's plan to send the delegation of Sioux to Washington, expressing a belief that representatives of several tribes ought to be sent to avoid jealousies—and hoping that the journey might be put off until fall. He feared that mishaps to the delegates might cancel all the advantages of the tour. On 9 March he wrote Harrison that nine Sioux chiefs already had arrived, and on 11 March he reminded Dearborn that Lewis's decision in the spring of 1804 to send only an Osage delegation had excited blind jealousies among other tribes. On 20 April he told Dearborn he had sent the Sioux chiefs home, with presents, content to wait until fall to make the trip. These Indians, escorted by trader Lewis Crawford, probably were the Sioux of the Des Moines River. Next in sequence comes Chouteau's letter to Harrison presented above. Then, on 12 June, he told Harrison that some of the Indians who had come down on Lewis's barge already were anxious to go home, and that some already had departed. A few of those remaining in St. Louis were ill with dysentery. One Omaha chief was so ill that he had to be sent on a horse to his village. Only the delegates from the Oto, Missouri, Arikara, and Sioux tribes remained, and Chouteau was sending the Sioux to a village on the Des Moines to wait until autumn. On 1 Dec. 1805, after the delegation had left for Washington, Chouteau warned Dearborn that he must expect to be continually importuned by demands from the Indians, but that most of these demands would be suggested to the savages by their interpreters. "Vous pouvez justement juger de ces interpretes par celui que vous aves connu et les ranger tout dans la même classe."

[243]

3. Meaning that William Ewing, a young Pennsylvania farmer sent by Dearborn to teach agriculture to the Sauks and Foxes, was ready to ascend the Mississippi to the Indian villages above the mouth of the Des Moines. For an account of his poor luck there, see JACKSON (2).

151. Jefferson to William Dunbar

Dear Sir   Washington May 25. 1805.

. . . .

While Capt. Lewis's mission was preparing,[1] as it was understood that his reliance for his longitudes must be on the Lunar observations taken, as at sea, with the aid of a timekeeper, and I knew that a thousand accidents might happen to that in such a journey as his, & thus deprive us of the principal object of the expedition, to wit, the ascertaining the geography of that river, I sat myself to consider whether in making observations at land, that furnishes no resource which may dispense with the timekeeper, so necessary at sea, it occurred to me that as we can always have a meridian at land, that would furnish what the want of it at sea obliges us to supply by the time-keeper. Supposing Capt. Lewis then furnished with a meridian, & having the requisite tables & Nautical Almanac with him, 1. he might find the right ascension of the moon when on the meridian of Greenwich on any given day, then find by observation; when the moon should attain that right ascension (by the aid of a known star) & measure her distance in that moment from his meridian. This distance would be the difference of longitude between Greenwich & the place of observation. Or 2dly. observe the moon's passage over his meridian & her right ascencion at that moment, see by the tables the time at Greenwich when she had that right ascencion: that gives her distance from the meridian of Greenwich when she was on his meridian. Or 3dly. observe the moon's distance from his meridian at any moment, & her right ascension at that moment, & find from the tables her distance from the meridian of Greenwich when she had that right ascension, which will give the distance of the two meridians. This last process will be simplified by taking for the moment of observation that of an appulse of the moon and a known star, or when the moon & a known star are in the same vertical. I suggested this to Mr. Briggs,[2] who considered it as correct & practicable and proposed communicating it to the Phil. society, but I observed that it was too obvious not to have been thought of before, and supposed it had not been adopted in practice because of no use

[244]

at sea where a meridian cannot be had, and where alone the nations of Europe had occasion for it. Before his confirmation of the idea however, Capt. Lewis was gone. In conversation afterwards with Baron Humboldt, he observed that the idea was correct, but not new & that I would find it in the 3d vol. of Delalande.[3] I recieved two days ago the 3d & 4th vols. of Montucla's hist. of Mathematics,[4] finished & edited by Delalande; and find in fact that Morin & Van-langren[5] in the 17th. century proposed observations of the moon on the meridian, but it does not appear whether they meant to dispense with the time keeper: but a meridian at sea being too impracticable, their idea was not pursued. The purpose of troubling you with these details is to submit to your consideration and decision whether any use can be made of them advantageously in our future expeditions, & particularly that up the Red river.

. . . .

The work we are now doing, is, I trust, done for posterity, in such a way that they need not repeat it. For this we are much indebted to you not only for the labour & time you have devoted to it, but for the excellent method of which you have set the example, and which I hope will be the model to be followed by others. We shall delineate with correctness the great arteries of this great country: those who come after us will extend the ramifications as they become acquainted with them, and fill up the canvas we begin. With my acknolegements for your zealous aid in this business, accept my friendly salutations & assurances of great esteem & respect.

TH: JEFFERSON

ALS, SC (DLC). Reply is No. 157. The omitted portion of the letter concerns Dunbar's four-month expedition up the Red and Washita rivers, starting in Oct. 1804, an account of which JEFFERSON included in his *Message from the President*. Pending John Francis McDermott's detailed study, the most reliable treatment of this expedition is in cox.

1. Jefferson's determination to solve the problem of finding longitude without a chronometer led him to query several experts. Dunbar answered in a letter of 8 Oct. (No. 157) and finally sent Jefferson his own method of finding longitude by a single observer, without a timepiece, in a letter of 12 Dec. 1805 (DLC). The enclosure, describing his procedure, is filed separately as 137:23735-36. Dunbar wrote, "As it is probable that this method will be found chiefly useful to Scientific Gentlemen traveling by land, who are unprovided with a Chronometer & without the aid of an assistant or second observer, it is presumable that such persons will find no difficulty in making these calculations." Dunbar's letter to Jefferson, 18 March 1806 (DLC), is also on this subject. His interest led him to submit a paper to the American Philosophical Society, published as "On finding the longitude from the moon's meridian altitude," *Transactions of the*

American Philosophical Society, 6 (1809), 277–82. Jefferson also had outlined his own method to William Lambert, of Washington, D.C., in a letter of 22 Dec. 1804: "When contemplating the mission of Capt. Lewis and others to procure us the geography of the rivers of Louisiana, a sense of the importance of some method of finding longitudes without the aid of any time piece, and by measuring angles alone with an accurate instrument, led me to reflections on the subject which suggested to me the following method" (DLC). His procedure is then outlined. See also Joshua Moore's method, dated 7 Sept. 1805 (DLC) and endorsed by Jefferson, "Moore's method of Longitude," filed out of order as fol. 22488. Jefferson promised to forward Moore's nine-page manuscript to Dunbar. See also No. 180, below.

2. "Agreeably to my promise, I have investigated thy Problem for finding the longitude by lunar observation" (Briggs to Jefferson, 1 March 1805, DLC). Briggs's own two-page system follows.

3. Joseph Jérôme le Français de Lalande. The first edition of his *Astronomie* had appeared in 1782.

4. Jean-Etienne Montucla (1725–99), French mathematician. The third and last volume of his *Histoire des mathematiques* was completed after his death by Lalande.

5. Jean Baptiste Morin (1583–1656), French astronomer; Michael Floris van Langeren (d. 1675), Flemish mathematician and cartographer.

152. William Henry Harrison to Henry Dearborn

Sir: Vincennes 27th May 1805

The enclosed letter[1] from M. Choteau I received this day by a special messenger and have returned him an answer of which the enclosed is a copy (No. 2). If the Indians should now go forward to the seat of Government I will dispatch them as quickly as possible. On their arrival at this place I will have them innoculated with the vaccine disease that they may avoid the small pox which is at this time in Kentucky. I have directed Mr. Choteau to go on with them because he is better acquainted with their manners and their wants than any other person that could be procured. A party of the Sioux of the Mississippi have lately visited St. Louis for the purpose of delivering up one of their warriors who had killed two Canadians, the Servants of a trader in their country, but upon examination it appeared that the Indian killed them in his own defence and that they were the aggressors. He was accordingly permitted to return with his friends upon condition of his being delivered up at any time hereafter when he should be demanded. Inclosed (No. 3)[2] is a letter from a friend of mine on spot which gives a particular account of the transaction. The respect which has been manifested towards the United States by this numerous and warlike tribe and the favourable reception which Captains Lewis and Clark have met with from the

Tribes of the Missouri augers well to our affairs in that quarter and forms a striking contrast to the conduct of some of the more neighboring Tribes which have been treated by our government with the utmost tenderness and indulgence. . . .

. . . .

I received by the express from St. Louis a long letter[3] from Capt. Clark the companion of Capt. Lewis. The dispatches for the President and for your department were not sent on which will delay their arrival at Washington nearly a fortnight. They passed the Winter with the Mandans 1609 miles up the Missouri in latitude 47° 21′ 47″ N. Longitude 101° 25′ and had met with no material accident.

Your letter of the ——— Febry.[4] covering the President's Pardon of the Sac Indian confined at St. Louis did not reach me until nearly two months after its date. It was immediately forwarded to St. Louis but unfortunately it did not arrive until the Indian had effected his escape from the guard house. He was fired on by the sentinel and the body of an Indian has lately been found near St. Louis with the marks of the buck shot in his head which is supposed to be the prisoner.[5] I have the honor to be with the greatest respect and consideration Sir your humble servt.

WILL HENRY HARRISON

Printed, HARRISON, 1:132–34.

1. Chouteau to Harrison, [22] May 1805 (No. 150).

2. Apparently Benjamin Parke to Harrison, 25 May 1805 (HARRISON, 1:131–32). Parke (1777–1835) was a delegate to Congress from the Territory of Indiana.

3. Clark to Harrison, 2 April 1805 (No. 146).

4. Given as 12 Feb. 1805 in a letter of Wilkinson to Dearborn, 27 July 1805 (TERR. PAPERS, 13:164).

5. This hapless Sauk had surrendered himself as a hostage for the murder of three American settlers near the mouth of the Cuivre in Sept. 1804. The killings occurred just before Harrison's visit to St. Louis to organize the Louisiana Territory, and in the ensuing series of councils Harrison was able to obtain a substantial land cession. For the details of the controversial treaty of Nov. 1804 with the Sauks and Foxes, which led to the Black Hawk War of 1832, see TERR. PAPERS, vol. 13. The treaty itself is in STATUTES, 7:84–87, KAPPLER, 2:54–56, and JACKSON (1), 183–86. For the land cession, see ROYCE.

153. William Henry Harrison to Pierre Chouteau

Sir: Vincennes 27th May 1805

I have this moment received your favour of the 22nd instant. The arrival of the Indians from the upper parts of the Missouri at this particular time is certainly an unfortunate circumstance. After as full a consideration of the affair as the time will allow I have determined as follows: You will please to state to the Indians the inconveniences that will attend their going on at present and explain to them your arrangement for their spending the summer in the neighborhood of St. Louis. If they should readily agree to it that plan will be adopted. If on the contrary they should express a wish to go on you will proceed immediately to make the necessary arrangements and set out for this place with all the expedition in your power—expedition is the more necessary as the President and the Heads of Departments will be absent from the seat of Government after the month of June. It is impossible for me at this distance to prescribe to you in the detail the arrangements necessary for your outfit in this Trip. I must therefore leave it entirely to yourself relying upon your judgment and economy that no expenses will be gone into but such as the due execution of the object requires. I therefore hereby authorize you to draw upon the Secretary of War for such sums as may be required for the purchase of Horses and other necessaries for the Trip. On your arrival at this place you will receive more particular instructions. If any engagement for interpreters has been made and no particular objection can be made to their integrity or capacity you will please to employ them. An English Interpreter will also be necessary. You will also please to apply to Major Bruff for an escort as far as this place where you will be furnished with one to take you to the Ohio. I wish very much to send on a few of the Sioux, of the Demoin, and some of Sacs and Foxes if you can get them ready to go on with the others do so. Every exertion in your power must be made to diminish the number by sending back as many of those that have come down the Missouri as you can get to go back. Give them a few articles that will be acceptable to them and send them with a speech to their nation informing them of the departure of their friends for the seat of Government. I am very Respectfully Your Humble Servant,

[WM. HENRY HARRISON]

Printed, HARRISON, 1:135-36.

154. Pierre Chouteau to William Claiborne

Mr   St. Louis 15 Juin 1805

Capn. Lewis having sent by his barge from the Missoury river two trunks, two cages or boxes with some birds and one Ditto with a

[248]

prairy Dog, which are to be send according to his instructions, to the President of the United States, I send them to you by Mr. Mallock according to his receipt here annexed, as the only proper opportunity to take them with safety to Washington city. I beg you will give me notice of theyr safe arrival at new Orleans. I am Sir very respectfully &c. &c.

SC (MoSHi—Pierre Chouteau letterbook). In a letter of 12 June to Jefferson, Chouteau mentioned that this shipment was on the way. A payment of $5 to Henry K. Mullin for keeping four magpies, a prairie hen, and a prairie dog appears in DNA, RG 217, Records of the Army Accounting Office, Journal M, p. 6306. A soldier named Henry Kd. [Kincaid?] Mullin appears in Amos Stoddard's company book (MoSHi) as a sergeant, age twenty-four at enlistment 1 Feb. 1803; born in Virginia; occupation, printer.

155. Jefferson to William Eustis

Dear Sir   Washington June 25. 05.

.   .   .   .

I have the pleasure to inform you that one of Capt. Lewis's barges, returned to St. Louis brings us certain information from him. He wintered with the Mandanes, 1609. miles up the Missouri, Lat. 47. Long. 101° with some additional minutes to both numbers, all well, and peculiarly cherished by all the Indian nations. He has sent in his barge 45. deputies from 6. of the principal nations in that quarter who will be joined at St. Louis by those of 3. or 4. nations between the Missouri & Missisipi, and will come on here. Whether before our departure or after our return we do not yet know.[1] We shall endeavor to get them to go on as far North as Boston, being desirous of impressing them correctly as to our strength & resources. This with kind usage, and a commerce advantageous to them, & not losing to us, will better secure their & our peace & friendship than an army of thousands. . . . Accept my friendly salutations, & assurances of great esteem & respect.

TH: JEFFERSON

ALS, SC (DLC).
1. "We are still uninformed whether the Indians from Capt. Lewis will agree to stay at St. Louis till autumn. Should they do so, I see nothing else which will prevent my leaving this [for Monticello] on the 15th of July" (Jefferson to Thomas Mann Randolph, 26 June 1805, DLC).

156. William Claiborne to Jefferson

Dear Sir,   New Orleans July 6th 1805

I have this day received from on Board a Barge several Trunks and Boxes directed to you, one Cage with four Birds, and a small living animal somewhat resembling our common Grey Squirrel. They were sent by Captain Lewis to Mr. Chanteau of St. Louis, and by him transmitted to me. Finding that some of the Trunks and Boxes contained Peltry of various kinds, I had the same opened. The Skins had been wet and were a little injured, but by being carefully dryed in the sun, cleansed and put up in Barrells, I am advised that they may be preserved. I received no particular Memorandum of the contents of the Boxes, but I find that many of the skins are numbered, and of course I conclude, that Mr. Lewis's communications relating thereto has been forwarded to you, from St. Louis.

The little Animal seems to be sick & I fear will not live.[1] The Birds are well, and have excellent appetites; I shall be very careful of them, and propose forwarding the whole to Baltimore by the Ship Comet that will probably sail for that Port in fifteen days. I am D. Sir with great respect Your faithful friend,

WILLIAM C. C. CLAIBORNE

Printed, CLAIBORNE, 3:116–17; original in MsAr; RC (DLC).

1. In another letter on 8 July, Claiborne told Jefferson, "The little animal mentioned in my Letter of the 6th is now much better in health, & I hope will live. The Peltry has been aired, cleansed, & will on this Day be repacked" (DLC).

157. William Dunbar to Jefferson

Dear Sir   Natchez 9th July 1805

.   .   .

I have considered the methods you propose for ascertaining the Longitude in the event of derangement to the time-keepers. There can be no doubt as to the principle, but it seems to me that the execution will involve some new difficulties. There must be at least two good observers and a nice instrument different from the Sextant: it is at all times a curious operation to form a meridian sufficiently correct for the purpose of being applied to the ascertainment of the Longitude, and in order to measure the moon's distance from any meridian, we must have an instrument similar to the Astronomical Circles of Troughton, to give us the true azimuth of that planet, for the sextant would be there of no use, & this azimuth must be referred by Calculation to the pole to give us what we are in pursuit of. To find the moon's distance from a known star when she is on the meridian of Greenwich is easily ascertained, but in order to watch & observe this distance, we must previously calculate what ought to be the moon's apparent distance from the star as seen from our Latitude & longitude (a very intricate calculation) & supposes the longitude nearly known, which may not be the Case: moreover the moon being on the meridian of Greenwich, will be to us always under the horizon with south declination & at all times too low for good observation: if we take the moon's distance from a star when the former is upon our own meridian, a good observer must be at the transit instrument to give notice of the moons passage, and as we have no knowledge of the apparent time to enable us to calculate the true and apparent altitudes of the moon & star or sun, those must both be taken by two additional observers: upon the whole the best remedy seems to be to have two good observers (three would be better) with excellent instruments & to chuse that time of the day when the Sun or star is at a sufficient distance from the meridian, so that taking the altitude of either will give the apparent time at the moment of taking the distance between the moon and either of those: in this case it will be found always preferable to use the Sun, because it is extremely difficult for inexperienced observers (& for others) to take double altitudes of a star with the artificial horizon on several accounts.

One other method of a very simple nature I will mention in a subsequent letter, fearing that the mail may depart too speedily to allow time at present. With the highest respect and attachment, I have the honor to be Your most Obedt. Servant,

WILLIAM DUNBAR

ALS, RC (DLC). Endorsed; received 16 Aug. 1805. Reply is No. 190.

158. Jefferson to Reuben Lewis

Dear Sir   Washington July 10. 05

I have not yet received the dispatches from Capt. Lewis which we know to have arrived at St. Louis. It is probable they are coming on by a special messenger who travels slow. In the mean time I inclose you a newspaper account which is probably authentic, as it is understood to come from Capt. Clarke. In the Aurora you will see another account containing some additional particulars. As you will recieve that paper as soon as this letter I say nothing of it. I shall be in Albemarle this day sennight so presume the dispatches will find me there. Accept my salutations & best wishes.

TH: JEFFERSON

ALS, SC (CSmH).

159. Jefferson to Henry Dearborn

Th: J. to Genl. Dearborn   [14 July 1805]

I have left Lewis's large map with a servt. to be carried to your office tomorrow morning. It is the 29. half sheets which contain very accurately his survey of the river & no more. Mr. King being with me this morning I gave them to him to be reduced to a scale of 20. miles to the inch for engraving.

. . . .

Sunday July 14. 05.

AL, SC (DLC).

160. Jefferson to William Claiborne

Dear Sir   Washington July 14. 05.

In the moment of my departure for Monticello I recieve letters from Capt. Lewis by which I percieve he has sent about 6. or 8. packages, filled with very curious subjects from the upper country of the Missouri, to St. Louis, from whence they will be embarked for N. Orleans to your care, to be forwarded to me. Altho' I know you will give them all possible attention, yet I could not avoid recommending them particularly to you. The best port they could come to would be Richmond. Next to that this place. But as I presume you have not so much intercourse with us as to have always a choice of ports, be so good as to commit them by a safe vessel bound to any port of Virginia or of the states North of that, from which I can have them readily brought here. Colo. Tousard is arrived at Philadelphia. I am told he is the Consul of France for New-Orleans. Accept my friendly salutations & assurances of great esteem & respect.

TH: JEFFERSON

ALS, SC (DLC). Claiborne acknowledged this letter 11 Sept., after travel and illness had intervened. He assured Jefferson that the specimens had been shipped to Baltimore, and added: "To preserve the Skins, it became necessary to repack them; this may have deranged their numbers, but I persuade myself, no material inconvenience has ensued" (DLC).

161. William Claiborne to the Collector at Baltimore

(Private)
Sir,   New Orleans July 23rd 1805
   I have taken the Liberty to address to your care one Hoggshead three Boxes and two Cases directed to the President of the United States and which were this day put on Board the Ship Comet Captain McNeal bound for Baltimore. The Hoggshead & Boxes Contain curiosities which were collected by Captain Lewis in his Voyage up the Missouri: in one case is a living animal called the wild dog of the Prairie, and in the other are four Birds, called the Missouri Magpies. I hope they may reach you in safety, and I must ask the favour of you to forward them by Land, to the City of Washington. I have the Honor to be Sir very Respectfully Your Hbl. Sevt.

                                        WM. C. C. CLAIBORNE

   Printed, CLAIBORNE, 3:132–33; original in MsAr.

162. William Claiborne to Jefferson

Dear Sir   New-Orleans August 3rd 1805.
   The Articles sent you by Captain Lewis, left this City some Days ago, and were put on board the Ship Comet; they were addressed to the care of the Collector at Baltimore, and he was requested to forward them by Land to the City of Washington.
   The Skins were carefully repacked, and the necessary measures taken to preserve them. The little Animal and the Birds were all well, and I sincerely hope may reach you in Safety. By Captain Cormick of the Marine Corps, who sailed two Days since, from this Port for Washington, I forwarded you, a *Mandine Pot,* being the only species of Culinary Instruments used by the Mandine Indians; *It* came in a Boat, from the Illinois, and is supposed to have been transmitted by Captain Lewis. I have the honor to be Sir, with great respect, Your faithful friend

                                        WM. C. C. CLAIBORNE

   ALS, RC (DLC). Out of sequence, fol. 31750. Endorsed; received 13 Sept. 1805.

163. Etienne Lemaire to Jefferson

Sir   Washington City 12 August 1805
   I take the liberty of presenting my respects to you. This is to inform you that I have just received by Baltimore a barrel and 4 boxes,

and a kind of cage in which there is a little animal very much resembling the squirrel, and in the other a bird resembling the magpie of Europe. Sir, I have the honor to advise you also that the work on the interior and exterior of the House is going very smoothly and I really think that what is most essential may be finished for your return to Washington; I have not yet received the order from Marseille. Sir, I hope with all my heart that you are enjoying perfect health, and all your honorable family. I close while awaiting the honor of receiving your orders. I am with all the deepest respect, your very humble and very obedient Servant,

ETIENNE LEMAIRE

All the family is well.

ALS, RC (MHi). Endorsed; received 16 Aug. 1805. Reply is No. 165. This letter and No. 166 are in very poor French; no attempt has been made to preserve the flavor in translation. Lemaire was Jefferson's maître d'hôtel or "purveyor of the household" in Washington.

164. Henry Dearborn to Jefferson

Sir,   Washington August 15th 1805

The various articles sent by Capt. Lewis by the way of New Orlians arrived yesterday at your house from Baltimore. Suspecting that vermin had made their way into the packages, I took the liberty of requesting your Steward to have the boxes opened, in which there were great numbers of vermin. I then had the cask opened in which the Buffalo Robes & other dressed skins were packed, all which were in good order, no vermin having found their way into the cask, but as the robes & other skins appeared a little damp, I advised Le Mare to have them exposed to a dry air for twenty four hours & then after sprinkling them with snuff, to have them seperately covered with linnen & put into trunks or boxes, and within three or four weeks to have them examined and aired if necessary.[1] The undressed skins, the skeletons, horns, &c. &c., I directed to be cleand from vermin, and after being exposed to the air for one day, to be put into boxes. The box containing, as I presumed, minerals & earths, was not opened. One magpie and the little burrowing dog or squirrel, are alive & appear healthy, the latter is undoubtedly of the family of what we call woodchucks, or ground hoggs. The Buffalo robes are good skins, well dressed, and highly embellished with

Indian finery. Some of the undressed skins are considerably injured, but I hope they will receive no further injury.

I believe the Frigate went down river yesterday. With sentiments of respectful esteem I am Sir Your Huml. Sevt.

H. DEABORN

ALS, RC (DLC). Endorsed; received 19 Aug. 1805.

1. If Lewis and Clark did not know, they would surely have been told by their experienced *engagés* that animal skins could never reach the East in good condition unless they were beaten every few weeks to flail away the moth larvae. Had this been done in St. Louis, the shipment might have reached Claiborne, and later Jefferson, in better condition. Fur shippers were plagued not only by moths but by the effects of improper skinning. Workers in the fur trade, unpacking the tightly pressed bales, often found pates, shanks, hooves, and even heads in the fetid packs. Rotting was the inevitable result. A common deterrent to vermin was to sprinkle turpentine among the furs. Some of the traders' packing and preserving methods are treated in PEAKE.

165. Jefferson to Etienne Lemaire

Dear Sir Monticello Aug. 17. 05

The barrel, boxes, & cases from Baltimore mentioned in your letter contain skins, furs, horns, bones, seeds, vases, & some other articles. Being apprehensive that the skins & furs may be suffering I would wish you to take them out, have them well dried & brushed, and then done up close in strong linen to keep the worm-fly out. As I do not know in which packages they are, it will be necessary for you to open them all, & take out the skins & furs, leaving every thing else in their cases. The cases had better first be placed in my cabinet where they will remain safe without being nailed up again, if merely closed so as to keep out rats & mice. The things from Marseilles are at New York and may soon be expected at Washington. Be so good as to have particular care taken of the squirrel & pie which came with the things from Baltimore that I may see them alive at my return. Should any accident happen to the squirrel his skin & skeleton must be preserved. Tell Joseph the first box of ornaments is safety arrived, & that I shall hope soon to recieve the second order. We are all in good health here, and I am glad to learn that the family at Washington is well. I salute you with my friendly & best wishes.

TH: JEFFERSON

ALS, SC (DLC). Endorsed.

166. Etienne Lemaire to Jefferson

Sir   Washington City 20 August 1805

Having received the honor of your letter I take the liberty of re-plying immediately, to inform you that I have opened the boxes and the barrel on the orders of General Dearborn [General g'ner Borde]. There were many insects, especially in the skins of the wild goat and in their bones. As for the small one, it is not so much damaged, and that of the buffalo [Boeuf Saûvage] is in good condition. We have beaten them all well and put them in the sun for 4 days. I have had some sacks made and we have put them in in pairs and rolled with leaf tobacco, and the bones separately in another box left open so that I may have them put in the way you intend, and the whole is in the [granié d'ans le n'ouveau Stor]. If, Sir, you find it appropriate to have them put below in the Cabinet I will have them taken down immediately. The magpie and the kind of squirrel are very well; they are in the room where Monsieur receives his callers; if, Sir, you have any orders to give me, I beg you to command me, Sir; I close with all the devotion possible. Your humble and obedient Servant,

E. LEMAIRE

ALS, RC (MHi). Endorsed; received 23 Aug. 1805. This is a translation.

167. James Wilkinson to the Officials of Louisiana

Gentlemen,   St. Louis Augt. 22nd 1805

I take the liberty to solicit your opinions on a subject novel, delicate, and in my conception, highly interresting to the united States.

The trade of the Missouri River anterior to the purchase of Louisiana, was confined to a few licensed Spanish Subjects, whose enterprise had not penetrated, far beyond the vicinity of the river Plate; but among the first measures of the President, subsequent to this acquisition, we perceive a plan for exploring this majestic stream to its source, as well to discover its extent and direction, as to con-ciliate the numerous tribes of Indians who inhabit its banks.

The Party employed on this interesting, perilous and expensive expedition, have not yet completed their work, but still remain within the power even of those nations whom they have passed, yet the re-sults of their inquiries so far as they have transpired are flattering, in as much as, it appears that the various nations with whom they have held intercourse (one only excepted) have not been prejudiced by foreign attachments, and are well disposed to receive the controul of the United States, whose policy and interest it evidently is to cherish these dispositions, in order to preserve Peace, to facilitate convenient alliances, to accelerate our possession of the interior of the Country by Military Posts, and to extend our legitimate commerce.

In this state of things, I am advised that extensive arrangements have been taken on the side of Canada, to commence, pending the present season, a general trade with the Indians of the Missouri, and we observe several Batteaux charged with merchandise, and navigated by the subjects of a foreign power, have already descended the Mississippi; these circumstances having excited doubts in my mind, relative to the effects of such intercourse, on the temper, dispositions, and attachments of the Indians, when conducted by Aliens, their Agents or dependents, whose interest and perhaps duty it may be, to thwart the Politics of the United States; I am inclined to believe the Prohibition, may at the present moment be salutary, but as this measure must prove detrimental to the Individual adventurers, I am desirous to avail myself of your judgement in aid of my own, on the following specific points, Viz—

1st. Shall goods and merchandise imported from Canada, be suffered to enter the Missouri?

2nd. Shall fire arms under the existing circumstances of our exploring party and our unsettled limits with Spain, be carried into the same river?

3rd. Shall the Citizens or subjects of any foreign power, be suffered to enter the said river in company with boats of trade, destined to the Indian nations, in any capacity whatever.

I Beg you Gentlemen to pardon me for the trouble I offer you, and that you may be assured of the high consideration & respect with which I am, Your Most Obdt. Servt.

JA: WILKINSON

To the Honorable
The Judges, The Secretary
and the Cols. Commandant Hammond and Scott.
Territory of Louisiana.

LS, RC (DNA, RG 107, W-499). Wilkinson received a reply 24 Aug. 1805, endorsing his measures, signed by Rufus Easton, John B. C. Lucas, Joseph Browne, Samuel Hammond, and John B. Scott. But on the same day he received a letter from the merchants of St. Louis, led by Auguste Chouteau, protesting that to deprive the Indians of firearms would make it impossible for them to collect furs for trade. Accordingly, when Wilkinson issued a proclamation on 26 Aug. forbidding foreign traders to enter the Missouri, he omitted the stricture against firearms. The letter from the officials, the letter from the merchants, and the proclamation are in TERR. PAPERS, 13:200–205, but the letter reproduced here is not.

168. Jefferson to David Robinson

Sir   Monticello Aug. 26. 05

I have read with satisfaction the account of the Missouri which you have been so kind as to send me and have recieved from it an addition to the stock of information which I have been endeavoring to acquire from various sources respecting that country. I thank you therefore for the communication of it. Possessing, as we now do, an accurate map of the Missouri to the Mandan towns, which before winter will be extended to the falls, if not the source of the river, by actual admeasurement, corrected by celestial observation, by Capt. Lewis, together with a minute account of the country, it's soil, pro-ductions, animals, waters, climate &c., it will be for yourself to decide whether the printing of yours will repay it's cost; and as the copy inclosed to me seems to be the one you intended for the press, I return it to you, for your own determination, and to do in it what you shall think best. I pray you to accept my salutations & best wishes.

TH: JEFFERSON

ALS, SC (DLC). This is a reply to Robinson's letter of 22 June 1805 from Kanawha County, Va. (MHi): "I have taken Some pains to keep a Journal of my travils thro the Louisiana and think a Copie of it is my Duty to present you with. I have it in Contemplation to pay another visit to it Next September and perhaps will penitrate farther into the Country and bring an accurate account of the Salt Mountain and Volcano and make a Return of my Journals to you." Robinson had three sons on the frontier at this time: Robert was an attorney in Kaskaskia; David C. was a surveyor in Kaskaskia; and Dr. John H. Robinson was a physician who would later travel west with Pike and publish in 1819 a map of his own, "A map of Mexico, Louisiana and Missouri Territory. . . ."

169. Jefferson to Samuel L. Mitchill

[8 September 1805]

Th: Jefferson presents his compliments to Dr. Mitchell and his thanks for the pamphlets he was so kind as to send him & which he com-municated to Mr. Randolph. He expects on his return to Washington (which will be in 3. weeks from this time) to find there a great collec-tion of the chemical subjects of Louisiana, which Capt. Lewis has sent, with a desire to forward them to the Phil. society at Philadelphia: from whom we are to hope to learn their contents. He tenders to Dr. Mitchell his friendly salutations & assurances of great respect. Monticello Sep. 8. 05.

AL, SC (DLC). Endorsed.

170. James Wilkinson to Henry Dearborn

Sir,   St. Louis Septr. 22nd 1805.

.   .   .   .   .

The two grand sources of our present expenses [for Indian affairs], are the Visits of the Indians to this place and to the Seat of Government; the first cannot be regulated with precision, before We have introduced Factors and Agents into the interior, and it may be politic to increase the latter for a year or two, i.e. until the deputies of the most respectable nations, have had opportunities to examine our population and improvements, after which these visitations may be safely discontinued, unless when they may be deemed essential to some particular end.

Henceforward I shall adopt measures, to prevent unlicensed visits to this place, and to contract every space of expense, of which strict accounts shall be rendered, and I do flatter myself that the result, will prove beneficial to the United States, and satisfactory to you.

I shall endeavour to limit the depending visit of the Missouri and Mississippi Chiefs, who have been invited by Capt. Lewis, to twenty, this deputation will consist of Riccara's, Otto's Missouris', Scioux, Sacques, Ayowas and Reynards, for whose departure, about the 1st of next month, I am now preparing on the most reasonable terms possible. Captain Stoddard will accompany the Indians, as he has long since requested a furlough, and if Cadet Chouteau can be prevailed on to abandon his wish to go in, without hazarding such disgusts as may impair his Zeal, and finally oblige us to turn him off, the Captain will have charge of them.

If these Visitants could have been assembled at an earlier period, they might have ascended to Pittsburgh in a Barge with a Military Crew, which would have saved several hundred Dollars, but the arrangement for their departure hence, was made before my arrival here. I could not purchase horses, for them under 1500 Dollars, and these Personages will not walk on an Embassy to their Father, I have therefore adopted the plan of hiring, and shall be able to drop them at Louisville for $400, including horse hire, equipments and every

[259]

other expense of transport, from whence should the season be favorable, they will ascend by water to Wheeling and there take the stage by squads—otherwise they will proceed by land to Pittsburgh, which may cost about $300 more, and will there take the stage. By this mode when we take into view the cost of horses, their equipments with saddles and Bridles and the expense of forage, we shall save at least $1200, allowing the horses all to live through the Journey, and to sell for half their cost, which would not be a warrantable calculation. The Chiefs will be equipt each with a course Capot, two shirts, a Hat, leggins & Clout, a blanket, handkerchief for the head, and mocassins, on the cheapest terms of the place.

. . . .

At this moment Mr. Chouteau arrived from the Osages, where he fortunately met a Deputation from the Republican Panis, who live high up on a North West Branch of the Kan, or Kances River, and with extrem difficulty has prevailed on a deputation of seven Chiefs from this party, to accompany him to this place and to proceed from hence to visit the President. Mr. Chouteau has descended in light canoes, the water of the Osage River being too low for the descent of our Barge. He is attended by twenty Chiefs (Osages) with White hair at their head, whose visit is for the purpose of holding the proposed conference with the hostile Nations. This addition of the Panis to the visiting Corps, will increase our expences unavoidably. . . . With perfect respect I am Sir Yr. Ob. Servt.

JA: WILKINSON

ALS, RC (DNA, RG 107, W-508). Endorsed; received 26 Oct. 1805.

171. Jefferson to Charles Willson Peale

Dear Sir   Washington Oct. 6. 05.

. . . .

I arrived here two days ago, & found the articles which had been forwarded by Capt. Lewis. There is a box of minerals which he particularly desired should go to the Philosophical society. There are some articles which I shall keep for an Indian Hall I am forming at Monticello, e.g. horns, dressed skins, utensils &c., and I am now packing up for you the following articles

2. skins of the white hare

2. skeletons of do.

A skeleton of the small or burrowing wolf of the prairies

A male & female Blaireau or burrowing dog of the prairies with the skeleton of the female

13. red fox skins

Skins of the male & female antilope with their skeletons.

2. skins of the burrowing squirrel of the prairies

A living burrowing squirrel of the prairies.

A living magpie

A dead one preserved. These are the descriptive words of Capt. Lewis. The Blaireau is the badger. It is the first time it has been found out of Europe. The burrowing squirrel is a species of Marmotte.

I have some doubts whether Capt. Lewis has not mistaken the Roe for the Antelope, because I have recieved from him a pair of horns which I am confident are of the Roe (tho' I never before supposed that animal to be in America) and no Antelope horns came. These you know are hollow, annulated & single. Those of the Roe are horny, solid, & branching. I hope you will have the skeletons well examined to settle this point. You will recieve them in great disorder as they came here, having been unpacked in several places on the road, & unpacked again here before I returned, so that they have probably got mixed. Capt. Cormack[1] who sets out for Philadelphia 3. or 4. days hence will take charge of the bag of skins & the Marmot. I am much afraid of the season of torpidity coming on him before you get him. He is a most harmless & tame creature. You will do well to watch Capt. Cormack's arrival at the stage office, that no risks from curiosity may happen to him between his arrival & your getting him. The other articles shall all go by Capt. Elwood.[2] Accept affectionate salutations.

TH: JEFFERSON

ALS, SC (DLC). Reply is No. 177.

1. Capt. Daniel Carmick, of the U.S. Marine Corps (Muster roll of the officers at headquarters [Washington]), Oct. 1807, fol. 30380, DLC.

2. John Ellwood, captain of the sloop *Harmony.*

172. James Wilkinson to Henry Dearborn

Sir   St. Louis Octo. 8th 1805

. . . .

Fortunately in point of expense, but unfortunately perhaps in point of policy, the Riccari & Otto' Chiefs have been dangerously ill & remain so feeble, as not to be able to accompany the deputation Destined to the City of Washington, and have become impatient to be returned to their respective Nations, with an Escort for their protection without which they dare not move, on Account of the Hostility of the Scioux. Their safe return is deemed an Object of great Magnitude, not only to the safe return of Capt. Lewis, but to our future negotiations among the distant nations of the Missouri; I should not therefore hesitate to indulge them, did no other consideration offer to recommend the expediency, of our seizing the occasion, to make an Establishment on the River plate at the Otto or Panis Towns, but this measure is rendered expedient, to prevent the machinations of the Spaniards & the sinister intrigues of the traders, and to confirm & secure the friendly dispositions of these Nations to our Government. I shall therefore dispatch immediately two subalterns & thirty Men, properly Equipt & provided, to accompany the returning Chiefs, and with their consent to take post at the Otto Towns on the Plate River, about fifteen Leagues from its Mouth, under such Instructions as may secure a sound discretion, should an Interview Ensue with the Spaniards, of which I have no expectation. This movement with the accommodation which the Natives will derive, from a Black Smith, a Cooper, & a Taylor, must increase our friends & extend our influence, and at the same time obstruct the plots of our Enemies. It will be made at a trifling expense & may lead to important discoveries, and therefore I hope it will meet your approbation. Mr. P. Chouteau tho much disappointed, has acquiesced with a good grace, in the disposition made for sending on, the Indian deputation to the seat of Government. . . .

. . .

I am assailed too by one Interpreter[1] only Commissioned by Capts. Lewis & Clark, for more than 1100$ due to Him as he asserts agreably to the Accounts in due cause—and to the Instructions of Capt. Lewis of which you have a Copy inclosed. In this case I feel much perplexity, because I believe the Accounts for necessaries furnished the Indians are iniquitous, yet this Man seems to hold too much importance among the Scioux to be disobliged, for at this moment several British traders are endeavouring to engage Him in their Service; I shall endeavour to retain Him in our service, & if possible to wave a settlement, until I hear from you respecting the payment of his Accounts. . . .

I recollect nothing further to add at this time & am most respectfully Sir Your Obedt. Servt.

JA: WILKINSON

ALS, RC (DNA, RG 107, W-508). Addressed; endorsed; received 9 Nov. 1805.
1. Pierre Dorion is the interpreter. The copy of his instructions is not present.

173. Jefferson to Charles Willson Peale

Dear Sir   Washington Oct. 9. 05

Capt. Cormack's departure is deferred, and Capt. Elwood not yet arrived. Of course I cannot yet announce to you the departure of any of the objects destined for you. By the former will go the Marmotte & a bag of skins. By the latter a large box of skins, skeletons & horns for you, a small box of minerals for the P. Society, a cage with a magpie & a box with the Polygraph. When I wrote you on the 6th I had not examined the box containing the skins & skeletons of the Antilope, which was then in a situation difficult to come at, and having seen no Antilope horns I had too hastily supposed those of the roe belonged to the skins & skeletons called Antilopes. On examining these I found the bony prominence to the cranium on which the horn is fixed, & afterwards 2. pr. of the horns themselves. These sufficiently prove that the animal is of the Antilope family & of the Chamois branch of it. This is strengthened by the dressed skin which is softer, & stronger in it's texture than any Chamois I have seen. I have put a pair of horns into the box for you. I have also put into it a pair of the horns of the unknown ram. Judging from these alone I should suppose the animal to be a variety of the Ovis Ammon of Linnaeus the Moufflon of the French. The pair of horns which I retain have the bony prominence of the skull left in them. With this they weigh each 6½ lb. The new animals[1] therefore for which we are already indebted to Capt. Lewis are 1. the Ovis Ammon. 2. the black-tailed deer. 3. the Roe. 4. the badger. 5. the marmotte. 6. the red fox qu? 7. the white weasel qu? 8. the magpie. 9. the Prairie hen. This last did not come. I am told it resembles the Guinea hen. He speaks also of a burrowing wolf, a brown or yellow bear, a Loup-cervier the skins of which not having come, we know not what they are. Accept affectionate salutations.

Th: Jefferson

ALS, SC (DLC). Reply is No. 177.
1. For a discussion of those Lewis and Clark species which actually were new, see a note under No. 192.

174. Jefferson to Charles Willson Peale

Dear Sir   Washington Oct. 21. 05

The day before yesterday I sent to Alexandria

1. a large box containing skins, skeletons & horns

1. small box containing the Polygraph

1. do. with minerals for the Phil. society to be presented in Capt. Lewis's name.

a cage with a living magpie.

These were delivered to Capt. Elwood as you will see by the inclosed reciept & the freight paid. He promised he would sail yesterday & I hope you will recieve them in good order. The undressed skins arrived here full of worms. I fear you will be puzzled to put them into form. Accept friendly salutations.

TH: JEFFERSON

ALS, SC (DLC). Endorsed.

175. James Wilkinson to Amos Stoddard

Sir,   St. Louis Octr. 21st 1805

You are to proceed tomorrow morning[1] with the Indian Deputation destined to visit the President at the City of Washington, by St. Vincennes and Louisville to Frankfort, where it may be found most expedient to take the Stage but of this you are to be the judge, after having examined and weighed well the most economical mode of transport.

It will occur to you, that the comfort and accommodation of our red Bretheren must be consulted, but at the same time, it is no less interresting to the Public, than to your own Character, that every unnecessary expense should be carefully avoided. You must guard against Tavern rates, by the purchase of your provision or [. . .] by encamping and cooking, and by every other means in your power.

You will be pleased to advise the Secretary of War of your approach from time to time, and if the bills which I have drawn on him in your favor for $1450, should fall short of your expenses, and I have no doubt they will, you are hereby authorised to draw on him at ten days sight, for such sums as you may find necessary, giving him previous advice of your intentions.

[264]

I shall be glad to hear from you on your route and after your arrival. I wish you an agreeable journey and am with unfeigned sentiments of Friendship and respect, Sir Your Obdt. Servt.

JN: WILKINSON

LS, RC (DNA, RG 107, W-515).

1. Here begins the second trek of Indian delegates sent to Washington by Meriwether Lewis. Stoddard, in a work called *Sketches historical and descriptive of Louisiana*, wrote that these hearty travelers consumed nearly twelve pounds of beef a day during the journey (STODDARD, 429). Later the Indians expressed dissatisfaction with his stewardship (No. 188). As usual when western Indians ventured eastward, illness and death plagued the group. JANSON, 220–33, describes the fate of one chief who died in bed after a night of heavy drinking and a vigorous dance performed on the stage of a Washington theater. In Kentucky an Ioway chief gave away his tobacco pouch made of shell, and then said, "I have given away my tobacco shell, and this circumstance puts me in mind that I shall die in a few days." Four days later he died (STODDARD, 425). For accounts of the visit to Washington, see JANSON, SMITH (2), 400–403, and the *National Intelligencer*, 27 and 30 Dec. 1805. Augustus John Foster wrote to his mother: "Deputies from Eight Nations behond the Metchiseppi are arrived. They passed on Horseback by my Windows a few Days ago, in arriving. . . . Two of them were naked to the waist, their Heads shaved to the Crown, faces red, Ears green & Feathers & bills of Birds stuck all over them. Others had their faces shaded with black & streaks of Black painted from the Crown to the Chin, with Sack loads of Feathers & Quills tied to their Hair behind. They are 21 in all generally tall stout men but not so much so as I expected to find them" (27 Dec. 1805, Foster Papers, DLC). Foster, an Englishman serving as secretary of the British legation, has more to say of the Indians' visit in DAVIS (2).

176. James Wilkinson to Henry Dearborn

Sir   St. Louis October 22nd 1805

The Kickapoos deputation did not arrive here untill the evening of the 14th Instant, and we commenced our conference the next day and finished it the 18th, as you will perceive from Governor Harrisons [. . .] of the 19th, which accompanies this—

The Deputation destined to visit the President, will commence their journey this day under the conduct of Captn. Stoddard, and will consist of twenty six persons from eleven Nations, (to wit) The Ottos Missouri, Panis, Canzès, Osage, Sacque, Reynard, Ayoua, Kickapoo, Pottowattomee, and Miamis, eight of these nations are strangers to us, and the seven last embrace the belligerents among whom we have been making Peace—The Panis Chief could not be prevailed on to make the visit, but [he] deputised [three of] his [young men] one of whom communicates, in osage to the Interpreter of that Nation, and appears to be intelligent. A third of this deputation, as you will perceive from the inclosed list, consists of Sacques and Renards, whose wishes have been undulged in consideration of our very delicate standing with those Nations, and the Osages consist of the head Chief of the little Towns and four of his select men—indeed our very critical situation, with the Machinations of the British on one side and the Spaniards on the other, and the apparently encreasing jealousies of the Indians, recommended to us to swell the Deputation to its present extent. Two Scioux from the River du moine attended the conference, but could not be prevailed on to accompany the Deputation, by presents or persuasions. It is much to be regreted that the Ricari and principal Otto Chiefs could not proceed, but their health made it impossible, and their impatience to get home forbade the proposition, they return however under every profession of perfect content, and left this place, the day before yesterday, accompanied by Lt. Wilkinson[1] and a Detachment of twenty five men, properly equipt to make a Post at the Otto Towns, or the mouth of the River Plate, should the nations be disposed to permit it.

T[he annuities] of [the] visiting Deputation and expenses of their journey—the sum necessary to supply the Sacques and Renards annuity, and the presents to the Chiefs of the Distant Nations, who have attended the conference and are about to return home, may I fear encrease the necessary disbursements beyond your calculations; I shall however in every instance, regulate my conduct by the advice of Governor Harrison who is better acquainted with the habits of the Country than I can be, and you may be assured a single Cent shall not with my approbation be unnecessarily expended.

I have given Capt. Stoddert Bills on you for $1450, agreeably to his receipt under [cover] for account of the expenses of his Journey [with the] Indian Deputation, and have authorised him to draw on you for any further sum which he may find necessary for which he is to be held accountable. With perfect respect I am Sir Your Obedient Servt.

[JA: WILKINSON]

N.B. Since closing this letter, one of the Scioux Chiefs, has agreed to accompany the deputation. W.

LS, RC (DNA, RG 107, W-515). Endorsed; received 16 Nov. 1805. The manuscript is quite tattered, and the version printed here is based partly upon one found in TERR. PAPERS, 13:243. For Stoddard's instructions see No. 175. Enclosed with this bundle of letters are the 18 Oct. report of

Harrison and Wilkinson on their conference with the Indians; a copy of the treaty of 18 Oct. signed by several western tribes; and a "List of a Deputation of Indians destined to the Seat of Government" enumerating twenty-seven men from twelve tribes.

1. James Biddle Wilkinson (d. 1813), Gen. Wilkinson's son, had been appointed second lieutenant in the Second Infantry in 1803.

177. Charles Willson Peale to Jefferson

Dear Sir   Museum Octr. 22d 1805.

I have just returned from the Country, where my young family was during the late fever, and found with my son Rubens here your favors of the 6th and 9th Instant. With latter he received the Fox Skins and the living Marmotte, it is a handsome little Animal, smaller and much more gentle than our Monax & I expect like it will not eat during the Winter, for this eats but little at present. It shall be kept in a Warm Room for tryal.

I am surprised to see the Magpie so correctly like that of Europe, for I have always found some difference in the Birds which has been discribed as belonging to both continants. It is interresting to get the living one in good condition, for a better comparison and also to give it a place near one I have from Great Britain handsomely mounted.

I am very thankful for these additions to the Museum,[1] every thing that comes from Louisiana must be interresting to the Public.

. . . . .

I am dear Sir with much esteem your friend,

C. W. PEALE

ALS, RC (DLC). Endorsed; received 25 Oct. 1805.
1. Peale entered these items in his "Memoranda of the Philadelphia Museum," 17 Oct. 1805: "A living marmotte, from up the Osage Country, Pr. Thos. Jefferson. A Bag of Skins, Foxes, marmotts, White weasel, White Hair, and a Ferrett. The above were brought from Washington by Capt. Cormack—pr. Thos. Jefferson" (PHi).

178. Charles Willson Peale to Jefferson

Dear Sir   Museum Novr. 3d 1805.

. . . . .

The Magpye is in good health,[1] It is surprising to me to see so exact a likeness of it to the European species. I have commonly found some difference of the plumage of our birds from those of Europe even where Authors have called them common to both Countries. It may be well to inquire whether this breed of the Magpye has not origionally been from Europe.

The Badger appears to be different, at least in Buffons plate, I have not had time to examine Pennant [2] and some other Authors who say it belongs to America, but is a scarce Animal every where. Turtons translation[3] of Linn:s says one variety of it at New York, "White with reddish yellow and brown Spots." This can scarcely be said to have brown spots. I much doubt whether it has ever been described.

The Antelope appears to be a fine Animal, the hair considerably more like that of the Deer, than I find on the Antelopes in the Museum. The branched horns perhapes makes it a singular Animal, I dont yet see any of such discription. After I have mounted these several Skins, I may be able to say more on them—they are a valuable addition to the Museum, altho' some parts of them are in bad condition owing to the Moth & Dermest [4] having made great havock.

The Skeletons are much broken and I fear some of the bones are lost at the places where they have been opened. I can mend the broken bones but cannot make good the deficiency of lost bones, being mixed togather is of no great consequence, as every bone must find its fellow bone. Whether I can get an intire Skeleton from all this mass of bones, I cannot yet determine, it will be a work of time and the exercise of much patience, this I shall not reguard provided the object is accomplished & the loss of bones will be my only obstacle in the work. I wish the Skeletons had not been mixed with the Skins, for the uncleaned bones bred the Insects which afterwards fed on the Skins and has entirely destroyed some of them. If I can mount one of the Antilopes to be decent, it will be a valuable addition to my Antilopes. I am very much obliged to Capt. Lewis for his endeavors to increase our knowledge of the Animals of that new acquired Territory. I wish I could get one of the sheep that carry such large horns as those you have done me the favor of sending. It is more important to have this Museum supplied with the American Animals than those of other Countryes, yet for a comparative view it ought to possess those of every part of the Globe!

.   .   .   .

I am with all due respect your friend,

C. W. PEALE

[268]

ALS, RC (DLC). Endorsed; received 6 Nov. 1805.

1. "The Marmot sleeps, and the Magpie chatters a great deal" (Peale to Jefferson, 12 Jan. 1806, DLC).

2. Thomas Pennant, *History of quadrupeds* (London, 1781) and *Arctic zoology* (London, 1784–87).

3. William Turton, *A general system of nature, through the three grand kingdoms of animals, vegetables, and minerals . . .* (London, 1802–06).

4. Small beetles of the family Dermestidae, the larvae of which attack meats, skins, and furs.

179. Jefferson to William Hamilton

Dear Sir   Washington Nov. 6. 05

Your nephew delivered safely to me the plant of the Chinese silk tree in perfect good order, and I shall nurse it with care until it shall be in a condition to be planted at Monticello. Mr. Madison mentioned to me your wish to recieve any seeds which should be sent me by Capt. Lewis or from any other quarter of plants which are rare. I lately forwarded to Mr. Peal for the Philosophical society a box containing minerals & seeds from Capt. Lewis, which I did not open, and I am persuaded the society will be pleased to dispose of them so well as into your hands. Mr. Peale would readily ask this. I happen to have two papers of seeds which Capt. Lewis enclosed to me in a letter, and which I gladly consign over to you, as I shall any thing else which may fall into my hands & be worthy your acceptance. One of these is of the Mandan tobacco, a very singular species, uncommonly weak & probably suitable for segars. The other had no ticket but I believe it is a plant used by the Indians with extraordinary success for curing the bite of the rattle snake & other venomous animals. I send also some seeds of the Winter melon which I recieved from Malta. Some were planted here the last season, but too early. They were so ripe before the time of gathering (before the first frost) that all rotted but one which is still sound & firm & we hope will keep some time. Experience alone will fix the time of planting them in our climate, so that a little before frost they may not be so ripe as to rot, & still ripe enough to advance after gathering in the process of maturation or mellowing as fruit does. I hope you will find it worthy a place in your kitchen garden. Mr. Madison had flattered us with a hope of seeing you here at the races. I should have been happy to have seen you, as I shall be with

[269]

every opportunity of testifying to you my esteem & respect & tendering you my friendly salutations.

TH: JEFFERSON

ALS, SC (DLC).

180. Jefferson to Robert Patterson

Dear Sir   Washington Nov. 16. 05

When Capt. Lewis's mission was under contemplation, and it's principal object the obtaining a correct map of the Missouri, I recommended to him the making himself thoroughly acquainted with the practice of the Lunar observations for the longitude. But fearful that the loss or derangement of his watch on which these were to depend, might lose us this great object of his journey, I endeavored to devise some method of ascertaining the longitude by the moon's motion without a time piece. I thought that a meridian, always to be had at land, tho' not at sea, might supply the want of the time piece, and proposed a method of determining by the aid of a meridian. Having never been a practical astronomer, and a life far otherwise spent having even rendered me unfamiliar with the detailed theory of the lunar observations, I suggested my idea to Mr. Ellicot by Capt. Lewis who was going on to him to take some lessons. However he never communicated to me what he thought of my suggestion. I have since mentioned it to Mr. Briggs, Mr. Dunbar & some others, and I am led by them to believe that the calculations would be very complicated & liable to error. Mr. Freeman[1] told me he had put my paper into your hands, and as you have taken the trouble to think of it I will ask the favor of your information as to it's practicability.[2] Mr. Dunbar promises to send me another method of attaining the same object without a time piece. Mr. Moore of this place has proposed one to me which I now inclose for your consideration & opinion, the paper to be returned as I retain no copy. I persevere on this enquiry because we have a mission now preparing for the Red river, in which Mr. Freeman goes, and shall send others up other rivers hereafter. Will you be so good as to give the inclosed letter to Mr. Freeman who was to set out this morning and will call on you. Accept my friendly salutations & assurances of great esteem & respect.

TH: JEFFERSON

[270]

ALS, SC (DLC).

1. Thomas Freeman (d. 1821), a civil engineer and astronomer, was preparing an expedition up the Red River under the direction of William Dunbar. Starting in April 1806 from Fort Adams, he traveled—in company with botanist Peter Custis and others—about 600 miles up the river before his party was turned back by the Spanish. This expedition, like Dunbar's in 1804–05, was instigated by Jefferson as part of his plan to explore as much of Louisiana as possible; the two voyages were the southern counterparts of the Lewis and Clark Expedition, though less extensive. For the official account, see FREEMAN & CUSTIS. For a modern account, see COX.

2. Patterson replied 23 Nov. 1805 (DLC) with extensive comments on Jefferson's method. Jefferson acknowledged the letter 29 Dec. and made some additional remarks.

181. Benjamin Smith Barton to Jefferson

Sir, [17 November 1805]

. . . .

I have seen, but have not yet had time to examine with sufficient attention, the animals collected by Capt. Lewis. The bird is, unquestionably, Corvus Pica, which I find inhabits Hudson's-Bay. I take the Marmot to be the Arctomys Citillus, common in the north of Asia, never known, before, to be a native of our Western cont. I long to see the large horns of a species of *Sheep*. I doubt not, this will prove to be the Taye of California, described and figured by Venegas,[1] in 1757. With great respect, I remain, Sir, Your very obedient and humble servant, &c.

Philadelphia, B. S. BARTON
17th of November, 1805.

ALS, RC (DLC). Endorsed; received 19 Nov. 1805.
1. VENEGAS, 1:86. He attributes the word "taye" to the Monqui Indians.

182. Jefferson to Benjamin Smith Barton

Dear [Sir] Washington Nov. 21. 05.

. . . .

Mr. Peale informs me that the Missouri magpie is precisely the same with the European. I had not expected this, tho' I never had observed the magpie of Europe, because the descriptions speak of the blue & red hues of the wings & tail, which, I had not observed on the

Missouri magpie. The Marmotte may very possibly be the Arctomys Citallus. But, from what I observed in Europe both of animals & vegetables, natives, I am apt in all cases to expect a sufficient permanent difference to authorize the considering them as specifically different. I shall be happy however to learn the ultimate result of your examination of all the subjects which I sent to Mr. Peale. Accept my friendly salutations & assurances of great esteem & respect.

TH: JEFFERSON

ALS, SC (DLC); RC (PHi).

183. Jefferson to Benjamin Smith Barton

Dear Sir   Washington Dec. 22. 05

Under another cover I send you drawings & specimens of the seed, cotton, & leaf of the cotton tree of the Western country, received from Genl. Wilkinson at St. Louis. To these I must add that it appears from the journals of Lewis & Clarke that the boughs of this tree are the sole food of the horses up the Missouri during winter. Their horses having on a particular occasion gone through extraordinary fatigue, bran of the maïs was ordered for them, which they refused, preferring their ordinary food the boughs of this tree, a few of which are chopped off from the tree with a hatchet every evening & thrown into their pen. Accept affectionate salutations & assurances of great esteem & respect.

TH: JEFFERSON

ALS, SC (DLC); RC (PHi). Reply is No. 185.

184. James Wilkinson to Jefferson

Sir   St. Louis: Decr. 23rd 1805

The opposition of a party of Kances Indians, to a small detachment destined up the Missouri, for the purpose of returning to their respective Nations, the Riccari & Otto Chiefs, sent down last Spring by Captain Lewis, puts it in my Power to introduce the former[1] to you.

From observation & the limited Enquiry to which I am confined by an illiterate Interpreter, I think you may be able to derive a fund of correct Information from this Chief, relative to the region Watered by the South Western Branches of the Missouri & its Inhabitants: I understand Him to be a great traveller, a warrior & Geographer, and He is certainly a *learned* Savage, because He not only speaks Eleven different Languages, but is Master of the *Language* of Arms, Hands & Fingers,[2] the only practicable mode of Communication (he informs me), at the Annual Grand Councils of twelve or fifteen Nations of his Acquaintance. He has Himself been so much in the Habit of Dumb Expression, that in conveying his Ideas, you will perceive He is more indebted to His Fingers than His Tongue. I was first apprized of this mode of mute *Conversation*, by my Unfortunate protegé Nolan,[3] who had acquired a perfect knowledge of it among the Commanches, (or Ya-i-tans) & drew from De Valny[4] the exclamation that "it was the language of Nature." The Subject of this Paragraph yesterday answered me, that He "could find no more difficulty in *speaking* with the Hand & Fingers than the Tongue, because they were moved with Equal Ease & Velocity"— you have under cover a list[5] of the Tribes & population of his own Nation, of the Mandanes the Gros Ventres, the Corbeau, & ten other Nations who speak different Languages, the last nine of whom are Erratic & appear to be confederated; of these the Too-pa-cas present a singular species to us, born with White Hair—a Red-haired family of Choctaws, which I have seen & examined, excited my surprize, but this is more extraordinary.

The bold adventure, long absence & observation of this Chief, during his travels in the United States, and his presumed knowledge and influence over the Nations of the Upper Missouri, may I think enable us to convert Him into an important Instrument of Humanity & of Policy. He should in my Judgement be returned as early as possible, without regard to the other Deputies, & sent up to his Nation by a Military Escort loaded with presents.

He is able to correct many parts of the Leathern Chart which I sent you by Capt. Stoddard, & will recognize several Interesting points of it—particularly the Aquatic horned Animal,[6] & the drum-beating Fish. He has seen & can locate a volcano also.

Should the Intercourse Law with the Indians be modified, It seems necessary in order to meet every emergency which may occur, that you should be authorized, to prevent Aliens & suspicious Characters from mingling with the Natives, & to suspend all Commerce with them at Your discretion, but in aid of the exercise of such discretion, certain Barriers should be erected on the side of Canada, & two or three Posts on the Missouri.

The Lead mineral of this Country is inexhaustible, for it is found scattered over hundreds of Leagues in immense Bodies, & no Vein has ever yet been sought for. Copper & other Metals more precious yet less useful, may also be found within our Limits.

The transfer of the Inhabitants from the lower settlements of this Territory, to any other quarter within our Limits, will be opposed by many busy short-sighted politicians in & out of Power, yet I do believe that a dead silence relative to the sales of Land within the Territory & Legislative Lures to a removal from it, may accomplish your views on this Subject, which I shall continue to promote without regard to personal consequences.

I send you by the Bearer Lt. Clemson,[7] who accompanies the Riccari Chief & is a Young Man of modesty & worth, a light stoney substance[8] taken from the Beach of the Missouri an hundred Leagues from its confluence with the Mississippi, which has Evidently undergone the operation of Fire—also a bit of Lead ore which from its weight & aspect promises a portion of Silver, and a specimen of native nitrate of Pot Ash found in abundance in the Caverns of the Country, with a small sample of veritable plumbago.

These details have doubtless occupied Capt. Lewis' attention, but the repetition will do no harm I hope. With perfect respect I am sir your Obliged & faithful

JA: WILKINSON

N.B. The speedy return of the Riccari to His Nation, may prove Interesting to Capt. Lewis, by whose persuasion He visits us, contrary to the will of his whole People.

ALS, RC (DLC). Endorsed; received 13 Feb. 1806.

1. This is the Arikara chief who had come down the river with Warfington, and whose death in 1806 will cause much unpleasantness in relations between the Arikara tribe and the white men on the river. Wilkinson wrote Dearborn 29 Oct. that the chief was returning to his home, after an illness, without visiting Washington; but on 10 Dec. he further advised that the chief's party had been turned back by the hostile Kansas Indians about twenty leagues below the mouth of the Kansas River, and that he would now proceed to Washington (TERR. PAPERS, 13:247, 298). Painter William Dunlap visited the Arikara chief in Washington, in Feb. 1806, accompanied by Samuel L. Mitchill. The chief was "seated cross-legg'd on a mattrass scraping & cutting Guinea-hen feathers. . . . His dress was a second hand blue, military coat, without facings, but with two large gold epaulets, a flannel shirt, dirty light colored pantaloons & shoes covered with mud of many days standing. He had rings in his ears & a blue cotton handkerchief, tied about his head in the French manner with a buckle disposed in the front. He is a large old man & nearly as dark as an American born negroe, but with light hazle colored [eyes]" (DUNLAP, 2:389).

2. William Dunlap was intrigued by the man's ability to make himself understood by signs. "He traced his rout to the place where he met Capn. Lewis. Then he told us that he guided him westward & returned again with him. His sign for speaking truth & the contrary is very expressive, he draws a

[274]

line with his finger from his heart to his mouth & thence straight to the auditor or spectator; for falsehood the line comes crooked from any part of the Abdomen & on issuing from the lips, splits, diverges & crosses in every direction" (DUNLAP, 2:389).

3. Philip Nolan (c.1771–1803), contraband trader, friend and protégé of Wilkinson, was killed by the Spanish near present Waco, Tex.

4. Constantin François Chasseboeuf, Comte de Volney, had traveled in America in the 1790's and had published *Tableau du climat et du sol des Etats-Unis d'Amèrique . . .* (Paris, 1803). See also No. 192.

5. "An Enumeration of Some of the Indian Nations South West of the Missouri River," 146:25409 (DLC). A note at the bottom of this chart says, "The above Enumeration has been given by the Riccari Chief but Indian calculations are always uncertain & capricious, & they seldom make the same report." Although the DLC copy is dated [1804], I take it to be the document mentioned here.

6. The chief showed Dunlap and Mitchill a map on which he traced his route and pointed out "a lake in which a monstrous amphibious animal resides, with horns like a Cow &c." (DUNLAP, 2:392).

7. Lt. Eli B. Clemson of the First Infantry, from Pennsylvania, commissioned in 1800 and made a captain in 1807. He was the first commander of Fort Osage, which he and Clark built on the Missouri, not far from present Kansas City, Mo., in the summer of 1808.

8. It was commonly believed, by travelers on the Missouri, that the pumice-like substance which floated downstream came from active volcanoes or subterranean fires. Samuel L. Mitchill quoted the journal of Stephen Ayres, who had traveled in the Mississippi and Missouri river regions, as saying that this material commonly floated on the Missouri. "Pieces of this pumice-stone which are in our possession," Mitchill wrote, "and which now readily swim in the water, were taken up fifty miles above the mouth of that river, and lead to a conviction of the existence of volcanoes, in the neighborhood of its superior streams. These probably issue from that chain of mountains which stretching N. and N.W. from the Cordelieras in South America, form the insurmountable barrier of Darien, and . . . in the higher latitudes . . . constitute the immense and unexplored mountains which may be called the 'Northern Andes'" (*Medical Repository*, 1st hexade, 4 (1801), 304). It is difficult to say what substance Mitchill and his contemporaries were discussing. It could have been genuine pumice, of igneous origin; it could have been scoriaceous material from fields of burning lignite. See Lewis's description of the substance, and Adam Seybert's identification, in the JOURNALS, 6:163, 164. For an expert opinion in 1823, see JAMES (2).

185. Benjamin Smith Barton to Jefferson

Sir, [27 December 1805]

I am greatly obliged to you for the drawing and specimens, which you have forwarded to me. The Cotton-tree is, no doubt, the Populus deltoides of Bartram and Marshall. I am not certain that it is noticed in any of the systematic books on Botany. It seems, however, to have been known to Charlevoix, who mentions it (English translation) by the name of Cotton-tree. He even tells us, that it extends as far north as lake Ontario. Any additional information concerning this tree will be highly acceptable to me.[1]

The lizard[2] has come safe to the Phil. Society, and is alive, in my possession. This singular animal, of which I am preparing a description, with a drawing, for the Society, was known to Hernandez, who figures it, pretty well, and calls it *Tapayaxin*,[3] or lacertus orbicularis. "Viuit (he says) in montibus frigidarum regionum, ubi passim offenditur." p. 327, 328. Clavigero[4] also figures it. Linnaeus has named it Lacerta orbicularis, but does not appear to have seen it. Of late, it has been badly figured by Dr. Shaw.[5] A new account of it is wanted. To complete this, perhaps some information may be gathered from the Indians now in Washington, as they reside in the country of this animal. May I request you, then, to desire some person, at Washington, to institute the inquiry? I ought not to think of thus troubling you, knowing how much you must be engaged with more important business.

In the box of plants transmitted by Capt. Lewis, there are two specimens of an extremely minute quadruped, of the genus Sorex, or Shrew. It turns out to be the Sorex exilis of Gmelin, discovered by Pallas in Siberia, and, until now, unknown as a native of America.[6] The asiatic animal weighs only xxx grains: ours could not, I think, have weighed more.

The *Tucan* of Hernandez I lately received from Georgia. It is a most singular quadruped,[7] of which systematic naturalists know nothing sure.

We are made uneasy here by a report, that Capt. Lewis and his party have been cut off. I hope this is not true.[8]

I am truly sorry, to have given you any trouble concerning the printed paper on manures. It was, however, put into the post-office, at the time I mentioned; about the 16th of June last. The loss of the paper is a matter of no consequence: but I regret that any packages transmitted to you should be lost, as it gives room to suspect, that papers of more consequence may have met with a similar fate. With very high respects, I remain, Dear Sir, Your obedient, humble Servant, &c.,

December 27th, 1805.   B. S. BARTON

ALS, RC (DLC). Endorsed; received 31 Dec. 1805. Reply is No. 189.
1. Depending upon the location, it is the eastern cottonwood, *Populus deltoides* Bartram, or the narrowleaf cottonwood, *P. angustifolia* James. Barton mentions two American botanists, John Bartram, author of *A*

[276]

description of East-Florida, with a journal (London, 1769), and Humphrey Marshall, author of *Arbustrum Americanum* (Philadelphia, 1785). Marshall's first name is usually given as "Humphry," but EWAN finds no basis for this spelling. The citation Barton makes to Jesuit traveler Pierre François Xavier de Charlevoix is probably in *Histoire et description générale de la nouvelle France* (Paris, 1744; English translation, London, 1761). Barton inserted a note on the cottonwood in his *Philadelphia Medical and Physical Journal*, explaining that Jefferson had sent him a colored drawing and specimens. "Whether it is capable of being employed, in any case, as a substitute for the real cotton . . . remains to be ascertained" (supp. 1 (1806), 71).

2. This living horned toad may be the one presented to Jefferson by Chouteau in 1804, but I am inclined to suppose it was brought by the second delegation of Indians, under Capt. Stoddard. Jefferson wrote Caspar Wistar 15 Dec. 1805: "By Mr. Wingate who goes on in a few days he [Jefferson] shall send for the society addressed to Mr. Peale a horned or rather thorny lizard, living. It comes nearer to the Lacerta amphibia of Linnaeus than any thing else. It differs materially in the tail, which is conical & shorter than the body" (DLC). A reply came from John Vaughan, 21 Jan. 1806: "The Lacerta recd. by Mr. Wingate is in Dr. Bartons hands for description—it is yet alive—Mr. Ancora is employed to draw it" (DLC). Pietro Ancora was a painter and drawing master who had come to Philadelphia in 1800.

3. In the *Philadelphia Medical and Physical Journal,* supp. 1 (1806), 68, Barton proposed to name the species *Lacerta tapajaxin.* Ord in GUTHRIE gave it the name "horned lizard," and retained the latin name *Lacerta orbicularis* assigned by Linnaeus. For Lewis's own description of the horned toad, see the JOURNALS, 5:80–81.

4. Francisco Clavijero was the author of *The history of Mexico* (London, 1787) translated from the Italian, and *Storia della California* (Venice, 1789).

5. George Shaw, *General zoology* (London, 1800–1812), 8 vols.

6. Almost surely speaking of this specimen, Barton later wrote in the *Philadelphia Medical and Physical Journal,* supp. 1 (1806), 71: "The Sorex minutissimus of Zimmerman has been discovered in the *trans*-Mississippi part of the United-States, in the country that is watered by the Missouri." He added that it was common to Asia and North America, and was an argument for the land bridge that was once thought to exist between the two continents. Ord in GUTHRIE, in 1815, probably was referring to this specimen when he listed the pygmy shrew, *Sorex exilis,* as a native of North America. The men Barton names include Samuel Gottlieb Gmelin (1744–74), botanist and explorer of southeastern Russia; Peter Simon Pallas (1741–1811), naturalist who also traveled in Russia; and perhaps Johann Georg von Zimmerman (1728–95), noted Swiss physician.

7. A kind of mole, discussed by HERNANDEZ, 7, under the heading, "De Tucan, seu Talparum Indicarum quondam genere."

8. Not true, and source of the rumor not known.

186. James Wilkinson to Henry Dearborn

Sir   St. Louis Decr. 30th 1805

It was with sensible concern I received on the 25th Inst. your Letter of the 20th Ultmo,[1] because it has been written evidently under impressions extremely unfavourable to me, which must have originated in misapprehension, or been excited by misrepresentation.

For your satisfaction & my own exculpation, I am obliged to call your attention to sundry details, which may cost more time & trouble perhaps than the subject is worth, but when charged it becomes my Duty to explain & to defend my Conduct.

On my Arrival at this place I found here, One Chief of the Riccari & another of the Otto Nations, (both of high repute) who had been sent down the Missouri last Spring by Capt. Lewis, at an expense of many hundreds of Dollars, for the purpose of visiting the President, but were stopt here by the Agent of Indian Affairs under your Orders.

In the Month of September these Men fell sick & were so sorely afflicted, that their Lives were despaired of. They had acquired a state of feeble convalescence, when the deputation attended by Capt. Stoddard was preparing to March, yet they were not only too weak to sit on Horseback, but yielding to the prejudices of superstition, they charged their afflictions to their abandonment of their Country, and clamoured loudly & incessantly to be sent back agreably to the promose of Capt. Lewis made to them; a Conference of many Nations was then impending at this place, & I was advised by several persons long conversant with the Indians of the Missouri, that should these Chiefs be detained here contrary to their will, & the Engagements of Capt. Lewis, information theirof might be conveyed to their Nations, either by our Traders or some of the tribes who attended the conference, and the Jealousies which would ensue might prove fatal to Capt. Lewis, should He attempt to return by the Missouri.

Under such circumstances it was my own opinion we were bound, not only by motives of Policy but by Obligations of good faith, to comply with the reiterated demands of these Chiefs, pressed upon me from several Quarters, and on this Ground a Boat was suitably equipt & manned, with orders to the Officer Commanding to ascend to the River plate, there to land the Otto Chief at his Village, & from thence to send the Riccari to his Nation, eight or Nine hundred Miles higher Up the Missouri, accompanied by two Soldiers & his interpreter, which arrangement was deemed indispensable to his

[278]

safety against the Scioux, & it was necessarily followed that the residue of the Detachment, must wait the return of the Men, to be sent with the Riccari, at the River plate, and of course Winter there.

Such were the substantial motives, on which the light movement up the Missouri was projected, and they may I hope justify it on the Grounds of expediency, Policy & good faith; I will however freely acknowledge that I considered the occasion, propitious to other Objects of serious import to the United States, under our then very critical standing with the Court of Spain, & the measures I had been apprized the Mexican Government was pursuing, with the Indians who live on the River plate, and therefore I determined to give to the small mission, all the Effect of which it was susceptible, to defeat the hostile Intrigues of the Spaniards, to restrain the machinations of the Traders, and to conciliate & attach the Natives to the United States, agreably to my Instructions of the 19th of April last, in which I am advised that "To conciliate the Friendship and Esteem of the Indians generally of that extensive Country, and to produce peace & Harmony, as well among the several Nations & Tribes as between them & the white Inhabitants, is too important an Object to escape your notice." To accomplish these Objects the exercise of a sound discretion was implied, & I did beleive that the lattitude of my Instructions warranted it, but if my Zeal has cheated my Judgement, & carried me beyond the Limits of prudence or propriety, I sincerely regret it; yet I must declare, that the Establishment near the Mouth of the plate, was intended for the safety & comfort of the party, sent up with the Indian Chiefs, pending the Winter, to be confirmed or removed in the Spring at the discretion of the executive, as will fully appear from the following extract of my Letter to you bearing date the 26th Ultmo "I have a Letter from Lt. Wilkinson dated at Grand River the 13th Inst: his Crew in Health & the Riccari Chief so far well pleased. It is doubtful whether this party will reach the River plate before the Winter Obstructs them, in which case they will proceed in the Spring, deliver the Chief take Post & wait Orders, which I must beg you may be so good as to forward me in Season, to be sent up the Moment the frosts cease. If the post is to be maintained it should be strengthened, otherwise the party can descend in ten Days." Whatever may have been the Ardor of my Enterprize, whatever my solicitudes on this occasion, to extend & confirm our influence at a critical point, where it had become at least doubtful, or to explore the interior, and however strong the language in which I may

[279]

have expressed my views & intentions, I flatter myself the preceeding paragraph may acquit me of any intentional Usurpation of Power. If respect is to be attached to the Mission of Capt. Lewis, or to the Engagements he may have made.—If the successful Issue of the gallant Enterprize in which He is engaged, is considered of national importance, or if we are bound to regard his personal safety as an Object of public Interest, then I trust I have barely done my duty, in attempting to convey the Otto & Riccari Chiefs to their respective Nations; But if I have done wrong by designing at the same time, to make a small provisional depot (on the principles expressly declared in my communications) of which Government might or might not avail itself. Then I cannot sufficiently express my sorrow, & I hope my Conduct may be ascribed to my Zeal for the promotion of a Step, which I considered deeply Interesting to the United States.

. . . .

I beg Sir that this explanation of my Conduct may be submited to the eye of the President, & I hope it may give Satisfaction to you & to him. With perfect respect I am Sir Your Obedt. Sevt.[2]

JA: WILKINSON

ALS, RC (DNA, RG 107, W-508). Endorsed; received 6 Feb. 1806.
1. Apparently Wilkinson is referring to Dearborn's letter of 21 Nov. 1805 (TERR. PAPERS, 13:290), in which Dearborn reprimands him for ordering a detachment to the Platte without permission, "especially with a view of establishing a Military Post." TERR. PAPERS, 13:325n, cites Dearborn's letter of 20 Nov. 1805, Wilkinson Papers, Chicago Historical Society; but the only letter of this date in the Chicago collection is a copy of Dearborn's to the commanding officer at Natchitoches.
2. One copy of this letter, signed by Wilkinson, bears the endorsement "no answer." But on 10 Feb. 1806 Dearborn wrote: "I do not perfectly comprehend your former and present reasoning relative to the establishment of a post on the River Plat;—and that of the mere conveyance of one or two Indian Chiefs to their homes;—but as the thing has *ended* it requires no further notice" (TERR. PAPERS, 13:442).

187. Jefferson to the Indian Delegation

[4 January 1806]

My friends & children, Chiefs of the Osages, Missouris, Kanzas, Ottos, Panis, Ayowas, & Sioux.

I take you by the hand of friendship and give you a hearty welcome to the seat of the govmt. of the U.S. The journey which you have taken to visit your fathers on this side of our island is a long one, and your having undertaken it is a proof that you desired to become acquainted with us. I thank the great spirit that he has protected you through the journey and brought you safely to the residence of your friends, and I hope he will have you constantly in his safekeeping and restore you in good health to your nations and families.

My friends & children. We are descended from the old nations which live beyond the great water: but we & our forefathers have been so long here that we seem like you to have grown out of this land: we consider ourselves no longer as of the old nations beyond the great water, but as united in one family with our red brethren here. The French, the English, the Spaniards, have now agreed with us to retire from all the country which you & we hold between Canada & Mexico, and never more to return to it. And remember the words I now speak to you my children, they are never to return again. We are become as numerous as the leaves of the trees, and, tho' we do not boast, we do not fear any nation. We are now your fathers; and you shall not lose by the change. As soon as Spain had agreed to withdraw from all the waters of the Missouri & Missisipi, I felt the desire of becoming acquainted with all my red children beyond the Missipi, and of uniting them with us, as we have done those on this side of that river in the bonds of peace & friendship. I wished to learn what we could do to benefit them by furnishing them the necessaries they want in exchange for their furs & peltries. I therefore sent our beloved man Capt. Lewis one of my own family, to go up the Missouri river, to get acquainted with all the Indian nations in it's neighborhood, to take them by the hand, deliver my talks to them, and to inform us in what way we could be useful to them. Some of you who are here have seen him & heard his words. You have taken him by the hand, and been friendly to him. My children I thank you for the services you rendered him, and for your attention to his words. When he returns he will tell us where we should establish factories to be convenient to you all, and what we must send to them. In establishing a trade with you we desire to make no profit. We shall ask from you only what every thing costs us, and give you for your furs & pelts whatever we can get for them again. Be assured you shall find your advantage in this change of your friends. It will take us some time to be in readiness to supply your wants, but in the mean while & till Capt. Lewis returns, the traders who have heretofore furnished you will continue to do so.

My friends & children. I have now an important advice to give you. I have already told you that you are all my children, and I wish you to live in peace & friendship with one another as brethren of the same family ought to do. How much better is it for neighbors to help than to hurt one another, how much happier must it make them. If you will cease to make war on one another, if you will live in friendship with all mankind, you can employ all your time in providing food & clothing for yourselves and your families. Your men will not be destroyed in war and your women & children will lie down to sleep in their cabins without fear of being surprised by their enemies & killed or carried away. Your numbers will be increased, instead of diminishing, and you will live in plenty & in quiet. My children, I have given this advice to all your red brethren on this side of the Missipi, they are following it, they are increasing in their numbers, are learning to clothe & provide for their families as we do, and you see the proofs of it in such of them as you happened to find here. My children, we are strong, we are numerous as the stars in the heavens, & we are all gun-men. Yet we live in peace with all nations; and all nations esteem & honour us because we are peaceable & just. Then let my red children then be peaceable & just also; take each other by the hand, and hold it fast. If ever bad men among your neighbors should do you wrong, and their nation refuse you justice, apply to the beloved man whom we shall place nearest to you; he will go to the offending nation, & endeavor to obtain right, & preserve peace. If ever bad men among yourselves injure your neighbors, be always ready to do justice. It is always honorable in those who have done wrong to acknolege & make amends for it; and it is the only way in which peace can be maintained among men. Remember then my advice, my children, carry it home to your people, and tell them that from the day that they have become all the same family, from the day that we became father to them all, we wish as a true father should do, that we may all live together as one household, and that before they strike one another, they should come to their father & let him endeavor to make up the quarrel.

My children. You are come from the other side of our great island, from where the sun sets to see your new friends at the sun rising. You have now arrived where the waters are constantly rising & falling every day, but you are still distant from the sea. I very much desire that you should not stop here, but go on and see your brethren as far as the edge of the great water. I am persuaded you have so far seen that every man by the way has recieved you as his brothers, and has been ready to do you all the kindnesses in his power. You will see the same thing quite to the sea shore; and I wish you therefore to go and visit our great cities in that quarter, & to see how many friends & brothers you have here. You will then have travelled a long line from West to East, and if you had time to go from North to South, from Canada to Florida, you would find it as long in that direction, & all the people as sincerely your friends. I wish you, my children to see all you can and to tell your people all you see; because I am sure the more they know of us, the more they will be our hearty friends. I invite you therefore to pay a visit to Baltimore, Philadelphia, New York, & the cities still beyond that if you should be willing to go further. We will provide carriages to convey you, & a person to go with you to see that you want for nothing. By the time you come back, the snows will be melted on the mountains, ice in the rivers broken up and you will be wishing to set out on your return home.

My children, I have long desired to see you. I have now opened my heart to you; let my words sink into your hearts & never be forgotten. If ever lying people or bad spirits should raise up clouds between us: let us come together as friends & explain to each other what is misrepresented or misunderstood. The clouds will fly away like the morning fog and the sun of friendship appear, & shine for ever bright & clear between us.

My children, it may happen that while you are here, occasion may arise to talk about many things which I do not now particularly mention. The Secretary at War will always be ready to talk with you: and you are to consider whatever he says as said by myself. He will also take care of you & see that you are furnished with all comforts here.

TH: JEFFERSON
Jan. 4. 1806.

ADS, SC (DLC). A draft with many deletions and interlineations. Bracketed lower-case letters inserted in the text (not shown here), which Jefferson keyed to similar letters in the margin, denote passages he borrowed for his speech of 6 Jan. 1806 to the Sauks, Foxes, and Potawatomis. The latter speech also is present in French and English, and is similar in vein. When the delegation left Washington for the West, 11 April 1806, Jefferson addressed the members again, expressing sorrow that several of their chiefs had died. "Accident & the change in their diet & manner of living has probably occasioned this & the will of the great spirit to which we must all submit. Man must die at home or abroad" (DLC).

[283]

188. Indian Speech to Jefferson and the Secretary of War

[4 January 1806]
Speech of the Osages, Missouri, Otos, Panis, Cansas, Ayowais & Sioux Nations to the president of the U.S. & to the Secretary at War.

My Grandfather & My Father

It is with an open heart that we recieve your hands, friendship streches ours in yours & unites them together.

fathers

We feel entirely our happiness at this Day, since you tell us that we are wellcome in the Grand lodge of prosperity. We percieve that we are numbered among your Most Cherished Children.

fathers

You observe that we have undertaken a very long journey in order to see our fathers & Brethren; it is Most true: but fathers, we will tell you that we Did not look back for to measure the road, & our Sight streching to the rising Sun, discovered every New day the pleasure Rising with him, as we were reflecting our daily approach, our hearts were overjoy'd, for we were Soon to See our New good fathers who wish to pity us.

Fathers

There is a long While that we wish to be acquiainted with our fathers & Brothers of the rising Sun & we hope that, when w'ill return back, where the sun sets, we will Dispell all the thick Clouds whose Darkness obscures the Light of the Day.

Fathers

That Great Spirit who disposes of every thing, & fixes into our Bosom the ardent Desire of seeing you, we thank him & we will thank him more when w'ill be at home amongst our Wives & children, for, then, our eyes Will be satisfied, our ears full with your words, & our hearts with joy.

But, fathers, we have to thank our interpreters who advis'd us to strengthen our hearts, & listen not to the sense of those men who wanted to prevent us from Coming to see you, alledging that we would be unwellcome & all of us should die. Our interpreters told us that our fathers were good & would pity us, that they wanted to be acquainted with their new red Children; & that we ought not to listen to the Crowing of Bad Birds.

fathers

You do not know yet your new red Children, & we see that you are as much worthy of pity as we are; flatterers Came Before you, made vast promises, but when far away, they Constitute themselves masters, decieve you & your Children Suffer.

fathers

Do pity your Children who wish to do Good & Behave well, if you say it [is] in their power, but, fathers trust them we know: we know them who love your new red Children who wish them to be happy, who hear your word, fill up our ears with it insinuate it in our hearts & spread it all over our fields; & fathers, that Spirit who took Care of us in Coming hither, here he is! He alone Can Carry your words together with us, to our Warriors wives & Children & they all will Call you then their fathers.

Fathers

We Believe that you wish to pity us & to prevent our wants by sending us supplies of goods, but look sharp & tell to your men to take not too much fur for a little of goods, should they act in that way we would not be better off than we are now with our actual traders.

Fathers

We have Seen the belov'd Man, we shook hands with him & we heard the words you put in his mouth. We wish him well, where he is, we have him in our hearts, & when he will return we believe that he will take Care of us prevent our wants & make us happy: he told us you wished us to Come to see you & our Brethren of the rising Sun: here we are: we are happy to see you & glad to hear the words of good fathers.

Fathers

You tell us to be in peace & amity with our Brethren: we wish to be So: Misunderstanding Sometimes Breaks Peace & Amity, because we listen too much to those men who live yet amongst us & who do not belong to your family, but when we will have but your own Children with us, then it will be easy for you to maintain the peace of your red children & we will all acknowledge that we have good fathers.

Fathers

Meditate what you say, you tell us that your children of this side of the Mississipi hear your Word, you are Mistaken, Since every day

[285]

they Rise their tomahawks Over our heads, but we believe it be Contrary to your orders & inclination, & that, before long, should they be deaf to your voice, you will chastise them.

Fathers

Though your forefathers were inhabiting the other side of the Big lake, we Consider you as ourselves, since, like us, you spring out of our land, for the Same reason, we believe you Consider us to be your Children, that you pity us & wish to make us happy should we follow your advices.

Fathers

You say that the french, English & Spanish nations have left the waters of the Missouri & Missisipi, we are all glad of it, & we believe that the day they will leave us the weather will be Clear, the paths Clean, & our ears will be no more affected with the disagreable sounds of the bad Birds who wish us to relinquish the words of our Good fathers whose words we keep in our hearts.

Although fathers

Do not believe that the number of our new Brethren would be able to frighten us, were we not inclined to acknowledge you for our fathers; but we wish to live like you & to be Men like you; we hope you will protect us from the wicked, you will punish them who wont hear your word, open their ears, & lead them in the good path.

Fathers

Since you wish to be acquainted with your new children of the other Side of the mississipi, you may Believe that they have the same desire, but if we Contempt your word as they do on this side of that River you will soon be Compell'd to Chastise the wicked, but, fathers, we shall not do as they do, for we wish to be numbered among your best Children, & we will try only to punish the wicked.

Fathers

You say that you are as numerous as the stars in the skies, & as strong as numerous. So much the better, fathers, tho', if you are so, we will see you ere long punishing all the wicked Red skins that you'll find amongst us, & you may tell to your white Children on our lands, to follow your orders, & to do not as they please, for they do not keep your word. Our Brothers who Came here before told us you had ordered good things to be done & sent to our villages, but we have seen nothing, & your waged Men think that truth will not reach your ears, but we are Conscious that we must speak the truth, truth must be spoken to the ears of our fathers, & our fathers must open their ears to truth to get in.

Fathers

You tell us to Complain to the beloved man, should any one Commit injury & decline Compensation, but you Know fathers that the beloved man is gone far away, that he Can not do the justice which you want him to do; while he is absent we do better to Complain to his fathers, & when he will arrive we will Complain to him, then he will have justice done to the injured man & if he loves his fathers he will chastise the one who Broke the peace which our good fathers told us to make together & to maintain.

Fathers

We hear your word, we will Carry it into our villages, & spread it all over our fields, we will tell to our warriors, wives & Children that, ever since you became the fathers of all the red skins, like good fathers, you wish us to live like Children of but one family who have but one father, & that before we should go at war we have to take the advice of our good fathers & then we shall know what these latter will tell us.

Fathers

Our hearts are good, though we are powerfull & strong, & we know how to fight, we do not wish to fight but shut the mouth of your Children who speak war, stop the arm of those who rise the tomahawk over our heads & Crush those who strike first, then we will Confess that we have good fathers who wish to make their red Children happy & peace maintained among them. For when we are at peace we hunt freely, our wives & Children Do not stand in want, we smoke & sleep easy.

Fathers

We left the place where the sun sets in order to see & hear you, fathers we see & hear you & we are happy; the skies are Clear where our fathers breathe & we wish it may be so where the sun sets. We wish our wives & children may be joy full when they think that we breathe where our fathers Breathe, for we are wellcome to Breathe with you, fathers.

fathers

Pity your own new Children, they wish to follow your advice, tell them what you wish them to do, they will do any thing that you wish them to do, they do not Belong any more to themselves but they are your own property, dispose of them as you please.

[287]

Fathers

As you spoke that we had brethren inhabiting the shores of the big Lake & that you offered us to visit them, we do wish to be acquainted with them, to shake hands with them & to tell them that we are their Brothers & if they are good Children we will tell them that we are so, for you know fathers we acknoledge you for our fathers.

Fathers

After shaking hands with all our new Brothers, being acquainted with them all, then we will tell to our warriors, our wives, our Children how many things we have seen, they all will listen to our sayings, they will gather around us, hear the words of their new fathers & Brethren, love them all & wonder at all things; yes fathers, we will speak the truth, you know the truth must Come out of the mouth of a father.

Fathers

We hope the more we will See our new Brethren the More we will love them for we hope they will wellcome us & recieve us as their Brethren.

Fathers

We wish to have this, your Warrior (major Rodger) for our leader in the Journey that we will undertake to visit our Brethren: he will take good Care of us, for he does love us, he will hold the weather Clear, Clean & smooth the paths of his red Brethren. Our Brother (Capt. Stoddert) is a good man, but he is not acquainted with his Brethren, the red Skins, he can not take good Care of them for he is always Sick & leaves them to the Care of Careless people who are not acquainted with your new Children the red Skins.

Fathers

You Say, that, when we will Come back the ice will be broken, the snow Melted, & then we will return into our Villages:—yes, fathers, when we will see our Warriors, when we will see our Wives, when we will see our Children, our hearts will be overjoy'd, their hearts will be overjoyed they will hear the word you put in our Mouth, we will Carry it to them Deeply engraved in our hearts. Our Warriors will bury the tomahawk, the wicked will be good, when ever they will hear the word of their fathers & know them to be good to all the red Skins.

Fathers

We will keep your Word in our Bosom; the stinking Cloud may Rise, it will melt away when We will remember the Word of our fathers, the bad birds may fly over our heads, & Crow Mischief, their flesh will be poor, their voice weak, they will hush & fly away when hearing the word of our fathers; we will be happy with your word, fathers, & never part with it.

Fathers

It is most true, there is some people amongst us, who wish us to be deaf to your word, they have a smooth lying tongue but they Can't be your Children, because a Child allways says the word of his father. They are unhappy for we will not listen to them, your sun will give them light, & shine heretofore over all your Children.

Grandfather (the President)

You told us to go now & then to see our father the great chief of War (the secretary at war), that he would Communicate your word to us, we have visited him & have been wellcome. We hope that he does love your new Children Worthy of pity, & Consider us as Your white Children.

fathers

We give you again the hand of friendship.

DS, RC (PHi). Written by a clerk and signed by fourteen representatives of the tribes involved. Endorsed. A French version is present.

189. Jefferson to Benjamin Smith Barton

Dear Sir   Washington Jan. 11. 06

In answer to your letter of Dec. 27. I snatch a moment from incessant business & interruption to inform you that the Missouri & Missisipi chiefs will set out in a few days to go as far as New York & perhaps Boston, and consequently will give you an opportunity at Philada. of making all the enquiries you desire & more satisfactorily by yourself than by another.[1] There are 4. Little Osages, 2 Missouris, 1 Kanza, 1 Otto, 2 Panis, 2 Ayowas, 1 Sioux, 2 Renards, 5 Sacs, 1 Poutewatami, with 2 interpreters who serve for the whole. Accept affectionate salutations.

TH: JEFFERSON

ALS, SC (DLC); RC (PHi).

1. In his interviews with the Indians, Barton found the language of the Osages to be "a dialect of the language of the Naudowessie, or Sious. . . . Its relation to the Finnic, both of Europe and of Asia, is very striking" (*Philadelphia Medical and Physical Journal,* 2 (1806), 190). Charles Willson Peale sent Jefferson profiles of some of these Indians and of the two interpreters, whom he identified as Paul Chouteau and Joseph Baume (8 Feb. 1806, DLC).

190. Jefferson to William Dunbar

Dear Sir   Washington. Jan. 12. 06

· · · ·

We have Capt. Lewis's notes of the Missouri to his wintering place at
Fort Mandan, and a map of the whole country watered by the
Missouri & Columbia composed by himself last winter on very
extensive informaton from Indians & traders, in which he expresses
a good deal of confidence. You will have percieved that my suggestion
of a method of finding the longitude at land without a time piece
was that of a theorist only, not a practical astronomer. It was founded
too in the use of the Equatorial the only instrument with which
I have any familiarity. I never used the Quadrant at all; and had
thought of importing three or four Equatorials for the use of those
parties. They get over all difficulty in finding a meridian. The
suggestion however of my imperfect method has had the good effect
of producing those less so. Your own, founded in practical skill
will doubtless answer it's end. I inclose you a method devised by
Mr. Joshua Moore of this place. Colo. Freeman will communicate
to you one of Mr. Patterson's. He will have an opportunity of
deciding from experience which is preferable of the whole. We have
no certain information of Capt. Lewis since he left Fort Mandan.
But we have through Indians an account of his having entered on
the passage over the high lands dividing the Missouri from the
waters of the Pacific. Accept my friendly salutations & assurances of
great esteem & respect.

TH: JEFFERSON

ALS, SC (DLC).

191. Jefferson to Reuben Lewis

Dear Sir   Washington Jan 13. 06.
   A letter from our Indian Agent [1] at St. Louis informs me that
some Osage chiefs had just arrived there who assured him that
just as they were leaving their nation two Ottos arrived there with
a pretty direct account that Capt. Lewis & his party had reached
that part of the Missouri near the mountains where the Indian
tract leads across (in 8. days march) to the Columbia, that he had
there procured horses and had, with his whole party entered on the
tract. In this case I do not expect we shall again hear from him or of

him until he gets back to St. Louis, because when he begins to re-
descend the Missouri, he will travel as fast as the news could come
by any other conveyance. Knowing the anxiety of a mother in such
a case, I mention this information praying you to present her my
respects, & to aceppt yourself my friendly salutations.

TH: JEFFERSON

ALS, SC (MoSHi). Endorsed.

1. Pierre Chouteau had sent Jefferson a report, obviously spurious, that
had come secondhand from two Oto Indians. They said they had accompanied Lewis "jusqu'a peu de distance de la Mer du Sud," and that they had
reached a white settlement. Lewis, they declared, had obtained horses with
which to continue his journey (1 Dec. 1805, MoSHi).

192. Jefferson to C. F. C. Volney

Dear Sir   Washington Feb. 11. 1806.

.   .   .   .

Our last news of Captn. Lewis was that he had reached the upper
part of the Missouri and had taken horses to cross the highlands
to the Columbia river. He passed the last winter among the Mandans
1610 miles above the mouth of the river. So far he had delineated it
with as great accuracy as will probably be ever applied to it, as his
courses & distances by mensuration were corrected by almost daily
observations of Latitude & Longitude. With his map he sent us
specimens or information of the following animals not before known
to the Northern continent of America. 1. The horns of what is
perhaps a species of the Ovis Ammon. 2. A new variety of the deer
having a black tail. 3. An antelope. 4. The badger, not before known
out of Europe. 5. A new species of Marmotte. 6. A white weasel.
7. The magpie. 8. The Prairie hen, said to resemble the Guinea-hen
(Peintade). 9. A prickly Lizard. To these are added a considerable
collection of minerals, not yet analysed. He wintered in Lat. 47° 20′
and found the Maximum of cold 43° below the zero of Farenheit.
We expect he has reached the Pacific, & is now wintering on the
head of the Missouri, & will be here next autumn.

.   .   .   .

TH: JEFFERSON

ALS, SC (DLC). "Nous sommes aux grandes scènes de l'histoire. Quoique
ma part ne soit pas mauvaise, j'aimerais autant être de l'expédition des voyageurs à l'Ouest" (Volney to Jefferson, 7 May 1804, CHINARD, 166–67).

It is difficult to know exactly what species of birds and animals Lewis and Clark may be credited with discovering. The two men were not equipped to make the kind of disciplined observations required by science, and Benjamin Smith Barton, who was to have organized their notes, failed to do so. The Biddle narrative was weak in natural history, was never intended to be a scientific treatise, and after its appearance Jefferson realized that "the papers respecting natural history & geography of the country" still required publication (No. 377). Sending back specimens and general descriptions of a new species was one thing; describing it formally in a scientific publication was quite another. While Lewis still lived, his trained contemporaries refrained from publishing his discoveries. After his death the various species were named and renamed, as teams of naturalists worked their way westward. One of the men best qualified to know which discoveries might properly be credited to Lewis and Clark was George Ord (1781–1866), a Philadelphia naturalist and philologist who had access to the specimens in Peale's museum. When he wrote the zoological section for the 1815 edition of William GUTHRIE's *A new geographical, historical, and commercial grammar,* he appeared to attribute the following mammals to Lewis and Clark. The common and scientific names are retained as Ord presented them.

Large Prairie Wolf, *Canis* ———.
Small Prairie Wolf, *Canis* ———.
Large Red Fox, *Canis* ———.
Small Red Fox, *Canis* ———.
Varied Fox, *Canis alopex?*
Ash-coloured Rat, *Mus cinereus.*
Columbia Gray Squirrel, *Sciurus* ———.
Red-breasted Squirrel, *Sciurus* ———.
Rocky-mountain Ground Squirrel, *Sciurus* ———.
Brown Squirrel, *Sciurus* ———.
White Weasel, *Viverra albus.*
American or Prong horned Antelope, *Antilope americanus.*
Rocky-mountain Sheep, *Ovis montanus.*
Mule Deer, *Cervus* ———.
Long-tailed Fallow Deer, *Cervus* ———.
Black-tailed Fallow Deer, *Cervus* ———.

Ord quotes descriptions by Lewis and Clark for the following mammals, but does not specifically credit the explorers with priority:

Grizzly Bear, *Ursus horribilis.*
Big-horned Sheep or Argali, *Ovis ammon.*
Louisiana Marmot or Prairie-dog, *Arctomys Ludoviciana.*

The birds which he associates with the expedition, without clearly assigning priority, are these:

Columbia Vulture, *Vultur Columbianus.*
Rocky-mountain Woodpecker, *Picus montanus.*
Columbia Pheasant, *Phasianus Columbianus.*
Sharp-tailed Grous[e], *Tetrao phasianellus?*
Brown Grous[e], *T. Fusca.*
Whistling Swan, *Anas Columbianus.*

The next serious student of the zoology of the expedition was Elliott Coues, a very competent naturalist. Coues first devoted a few pages to zoology when he issued an account of the various Lewis and Clark publications (COUES (1)). Later he incorporated these into the remarkable set of notes he wrote for his edition of the Biddle narrative. Any extended study of the birds and animals observed by Lewis and Clark must start with Coues, particularly with his annotation of Biddle's chapter on natural history (BIDDLE-COUES, 3:821–900).

What follows is not an attempt to improve upon Coues, but to do the one thing I wish that he had done. Although he comments upon the new species as they occur in the narrative, his discussion is scattered throughout the footnotes of three volumes; nowhere does he set forth plainly and in one list the mammals and birds which he considers attributable to Lewis and Clark. With Coues as a basis, supplemented by other sources, I undertake here a trial list of those species, presented with several disclaimers and qualifications. These are the species and subspecies which can be identified, by the explorers' descriptions and the known extent of the range, and which were new to science at the time of the expedition. In no instance are Lewis and Clark the recognized or "official" discoverers, for reasons already set forth. Some of the species were first described by GASS in 1807, others by BIDDLE in 1814, and some did not appear in print as Lewis and Clark described them until the appearance of the JOURNALS in 1904–05. My task has been made easier by the work of CRISWELL, who ferreted out for a different reason all of the Lewis and Clark references to zoological and botanical species. REID & GANNON also was a useful aid. A work by Raymond Darwin Burroughs, *The natural history of the Lewis and Clark Expedition* (East Lansing, Mich., 1960), was not published until after the following material had been prepared. Burroughs lists the birds and animals mentioned by the explorers, with quotations from the journals and with additional annotation. His debt to Coues, like mine, is substantial.

MAMMALS

Current scientific and vernacular names are from Gerrit S. MILLER, Jr., and Remington KELLOGG, "List of North American recent mammals," U.S. National Museum Bulletin 205 (Washington, 1955), supplemented by E. Raymond HALL and Keith R. KELSON, *The mammals of North America* (New York, 1959). I retain the sequence of species generally adopted by zoologists for taxonomic works.

SHORT-TAILED SHREW, *Blarina brevicauda brevicauda* (Say) or *Cryptotis parva parva* (Say). The shrew is not mentioned in the journals, but a specimen came back in a box of plant specimens and was commented upon by Barton (No. 185). Both species listed here were collected by Thomas Say of the Long expedition, on the west bank of the Missouri near present Blair, Neb., and first described in the account of that expedition (JAMES (1), 1:164). They are the *Sorex brevicaudus* and the *Sorex parvus* of Say.

TOWNSEND'S MOLE, *Scapanus townsendii* (Bachman). This species inhabits the coastal area of Oregon and Washington and is no doubt the mole seen at Fort Clatsop (JOURNALS, 4:113).

WHITE-TAILED JACK RABBIT, *Lepus townsendii campanius* Hollister. Specimens collected between St. Louis and Fort Mandan were sent back in April 1805, and on the basis of these Benjamin Smith Barton assumed that the animal was the American varying hare, *Lepus americanus americanus* Erxleben; he so reported in the *Philadelphia Medical and Physical Journal*, 2 (1806), 159. Ord failed to identify the species with the expedition; HARLAN, 310, treated it as a variety of the varying hare; and it was not set apart as a distinct species until 1837 when John Bachman gave it the name *Lepus campestris*. Farther west, Lewis and Clark would also have encountered another subspecies of Bachman's, *Lepus townsendii townsendii* Bachman.

DESERT COTTONTAIL, *Sylvilagus auduboni baileyi* (Merriam). Lewis and Clark did not differentiate between this species and the common cottontail they had known back home. "The rabbit is the same with those of our own country; it is found indifferently, either in the prairies or the woodlands, but is not very abundant" (BIDDLE-COUES, 3:866).

MOUNTAIN BEAVER, *Apoldontia rufa rufa* (Raf.). Lewis and Clark did not see this remarkable little animal, which they called the "sewellel," but described it from the robes made of its skin by the Indians. Coues credits Clark with the original description, having overlooked Lewis's of the same date, 26 Feb. 1806. Ord does not seem to have mentioned the species. Rafinesque named it *Anisonyx rufa* in 1817.

YELLOW-BELLIED MARMOT, *Marmota flaviventris flaviventris* (Audubon and Bachman). The explorers called it simply a monax or marmot, but from the range it probably is this species, not *Marmota monax canadensis* (Erxleben), the woodchuck. See the JOURNALS, 2:376, 4:320.

BLACK-TAILED PRAIRIE DOG, *Cynomys ludovicianus ludovicianus* (Ord). Coues says it was "then unknown to science, and not technically named till 1815," when Ord listed it in GUTHRIE.

COLUMBIAN GROUND SQUIRREL, *Spermophilus columbianus columbianus* (Ord). "There is also a species of squirrel, evidently distinct, which we have denominated the burrowing squirrel. He inhabits these plains, and somewhat resembles those found on the Missouri" (BIDDLE, 2:174). Ord named it *Arctomys Columbianus* under the impression that it was a marmot, and it was not recognized as a spermophile until J. A. Allen changed its name to *Spermophilus empetra erythrogluteia* in 1877.

THIRTEEN-LINED GROUND SQUIRREL, *Spermophilus tridecemlineatus pallidus* J. A. Allen. "A find of remarkable interest, which nobody has noticed all these years, because the text gives no clew" (BIDDLE-COUES, 2:405n). He adds: "The curious point is that here we have the pale Western variety described before the stock species to which it belongs had a name" (since Mitchill did not describe the basic species in the *Medical Repository* until 1821).

TOWNSEND'S CHIPMUNK, *Eutamias townsendii townsendii* (Bachman). See the JOURNALS, 4:105.

WESTERN GRAY SQUIRREL, *Sciurus griseus griseus* Ord. It was listed by Ord in 1815 but not given a specific name by him until 1818. It was also assigned names by Rafinesque, Harlan, and finally by Titian R. Peale in 1848.

RED SQUIRREL, *Tamiasciurus hudsonicus richardsoni* (Bachman) and *Tamiasciurus hudsonicus fremonti* (Audubon and Bachman). Two members of the red squirrel group almost certainly observed by Lewis and Clark. Coues assumes that the species mentioned in the narrative in 3:855 is *T. h. richardsoni*.

DOUGLAS' SQUIRREL, *Tamiasciurus douglasii douglasii* (Bachman). Another of the red squirrel group, but a distinct form. Ord listed it as a brown

[294]

squirrel and gave it no specific name. After 1838 it received four different names from various authors, beginning with John Bachman's *Sciurus douglassii* in 1838. See BIDDLE-COUES, 3:858.

NORTHERN POCKET GOPHER, *Thomomys talpoides talpoides* (Richardson). There are many subspecies. See the JOURNALS, 1:289, 4:368.

EASTERN WOOD RAT, *Neotoma floridana floridana* (Ord). "It was unknown to science when thus discovered by Lewis and Clark" (BIDDLE-COUES, 1:40n). It was found by Thomas Say, of Long's party, along the Mississippi in 1819. Ord had named it *Mus floridanus* in 1818, and in 1825 Say and Ord made this species the type of their new genus, *Neotoma*. It is cited by GASS, 20.

BUSHY-TAILED WOOD RAT, *Neotoma cinerea cinerea* (Ord). The well-known Rocky Mountain pack rat was then new to science, and was not technically named until Ord in 1815 called it *Mus cinereus*. See BIDDLE-COUES, 2:400.

COYOTE, *Canis latrans latrans* Say. Lewis and Clark have doubtful priority here. The coyote was mentioned by VENEGAS, 1:37, as "a peculiar species of wild dog, in particulars resembling the foxes of Spain, especially in their arts and stratagems. . . ." But Lewis and Clark were the first to bring it to the attention of contemporary scientists, and it was not technically named until 1823 when Say, after Long's expedition, called it *Canis latrans*.

GRAY WOLF, *Canis lupus nubilis* Say, probably now extinct. Lewis and Clark were probably the first to see and refer to this subspecies, not technically named until Long's expedition. Other subspecies whose ranges lay across the trail of Lewis and Clark were *C. l. fuscus* Richardson and *C. l. irremotus* Goldman, both differing from the common gray wolf of the eastern states, *C. l. lycaon* Schreber.

SWIFT FOX, *Vulpes velox velox* (Say). Called by Coues "one of our authors' discoveries." It may be only subspecifically different from *V. macrotis*, the kit fox—slightly larger, shorter ears, etc.

GRIZZLY BEAR, *Ursus horribilis horribilis* Ord. This subspecies is now probably extinct, but three others are listed by MILLER & KELLOGG. The story of the grizzly demonstrates the fact that a species may be known to many men, including scientists, and still be "unknown to science." The species was not named and described until 1815, when Ord presented it in GUTHRIE on the basis of the Lewis and Clark specimens and descriptions. On the evidence which follows here, it is difficult to understand why it remained unknown for so long.

Perhaps the first white man to report the grizzly was Henry Kelsey, while exploring for the Hudson's Bay Company on the Canadian prairies in the summer of 1691. He wrote in his journal, "this plain affords Nothing but short Round sticky grass & Buffillo & a great s[ort] of a Bear w[hi]ch is Bigger then any white Bear & is Neither White nor Black But silver hair'd like our English Rabbitt . . ." (DOUGHTY & MARTIN, 12–13). It is not clear whether he was reporting from hearsay or actual sightings. Another early report, not necessarily an eyewitness account, was given by John Long in a summary of his travels in the years 1768–88 (LONG, 78). He mentioned the grizzly and explained how the Indians customarily killed the animal.

Sir Alexander Mackenzie saw the grizzly in 1793. "We this day saw two grisly and hideous bears" (MACKENZIE, 2:164). And on 8 June 1805, Charles Willson Peale wrote in his museum memoranda (PHi), "a Claw of the Grisly Bear brought from the interior of America by Alexr. McKenzie. . . ."

William Henry Harrison reported to Jefferson that he was sending him what may have been a grizzly in 1803. "The Lieut. Governor [of Upper Louisiana] was so obliging as to give me one of two bears that were brought from a great distance up the Missouri & is of a kind not hitherto described that I know of. This shall be sent with the other articles as soon as I get some one to take them" (29 Oct. 1803, DLC). I find no further record of this specimen.

The first opportunity for eastern scientists to see the bear may have come in the summer of 1803, when Peale had one on display. As Peale told the story to Jefferson: "A french-man; an Indian trader from new Orleans, brought here in the sickly season last summer a Grisley-bear to exhibit. Enclosed is one of his Bills—he expected to make a fortune by the Animal, but he was disappointed, altho' it differed considerably from the common, yet nevertheless it was a Bear, & as such did not excite much curiosity." Peale said he bought the bear and kept it until early March 1804, when it broke loose and had to be shot. "Please to accept a hind quarter which I have sent by the Mail stage, directed for you." And he added: "I much suspect that this species of Bear has not been described and therefore I shall shortly write some observations & give a drawing of it, which I mean to send to you" (Peale to Jefferson, 18 March 1804, DLC).

A handbill which Peale enclosed with the letter reads in part: "THE FAMOUS GRISLY BEAR, hitherto unseen in the inhabited countries, and entirely unknown untill the celebrated A. Mackenzie gave some account of that extraordinary animal, having met him in the neighbourhood of the Rocky Mountains. . . . This animal was born in the spring of the year 1802 not far from the sources of the river Missory, about 4500 miles from Philadelphia, in a country inhabited by an indian nation called the Cattanahowes. He is the first of his specie that ever was seen, and seems to be a separate class of White Bear, which differs from those known to and described by the naturalists, as well in point of colour, as in point of inclinations. His hair is a kind of straw colour or light sorrel, neither hard nor stiff, but somewhat like wool. . . . By the size of this one, who has hardly attained the third part of his bigness, by the length of his claws, when yet so young, one may form an idea of the powerful strength of that dangerous animal. . . ."

Lewis probably missed seeing this animal, since he had left Philadelphia in 1803 before the "sickly season," but he was familiar with Mackenzie's *Voyages* and could not have failed to learn of the grizzly before the start of his expedition. It has been mistakenly supposed that the species was new to Lewis and Clark, and that they devised the name "grizzly" themselves. "Lewis gave it the name 'grizzly,' which means having a grizzled coat" (INGERSOLL, 159). And in CRISWELL, 13: "The long endeavors to name would indicate that Lewis and Clark did not know the term *grizzly* previous to the expedition. . . ." It is more likely that their indecisiveness in applying the name arose from their inability to determine immediately, considering the color variants they found, whether they had actually encountered Mackenzie's "grisly and hideous" bear.

For a note on Zebulon Pike's two live grizzlies, which were on display in Philadelphia in 1808 and thus available for description by scientists, see No. 281.

LONG-TAILED WEASEL, *Mustela frenata longicauda* Bonaparte. See BIDDLE-COUES, 1:91.

BOBCAT, *Lynx rufus fasciatus* Raf. A subspecies of *Lynx rufus* (Schreber) which Lewis and Clark discovered in the Pacific Northwest.

BLACK-TAILED DEER, *Odocoileus hemionus hemionus* (Raf.). Cited by Ord in GUTHRIE but not named until 1923 when Say called it *Cervus macrotis* (JAMES (1), 2:88). "Yet another discovery of Lewis and Clark," said Coues. The explorers first encountered this species in what is now South Dakota, in Sept. 1804. "Colter Killed . . . a curious kind of Deer of a Dark gray Colr. more so than common, hair long & fine, the ears large & long . . . the Taile about the length of Common Deer, round (like a Cow) a tuft of black hair about the end" (JOURNALS, 1:152). Later they discovered another sub-species in the Northwest, *O. h. columbiana* (Richardson).

PRONGHORN, *Antilocapra americana americana* (Ord). See a note under No. 149. The first published mention of this animal in English may be Clark's reference in his letter to Harrison (No. 146), followed by the one in Lewis's "Statistical view," published in 1806 as a part of JEFFERSON.

MOUNTAIN GOAT, *Oreamnos americanus americanus* (Blainville). Ord named it *Ovis montanus* in 1815 under the impression that it belonged to the sheep genus, and two years later published a brief paper on the species—calling attention to Lewis's description and skin specimens (ORD). Neither of the two explorers ever saw a live animal or whole specimen. The description which Lewis entered in his journal for 22 Feb. 1806 (JOURNALS, 4:95–96) was based upon Indian information and on the observation of skins.

BIRDS

Current scientific and vernacular names are from the *Check-list* of the American Ornithologists' Union, 5th ed., 1957. I have listed the species in order and assigned the useful check-list numbers of the A.O.U.

WESTERN GREBE, *Aechmophorus occidentalis* (Lawrence), A.O.U. 1. "This is the original and an easily recognizable description of this bird, which was not formally characterized till many years afterward . . ." (BIDDLE-COUES, 3:882n).

RING-NECKED DUCK, *Aythya collaris* (Donovan), A.O.U. 150. "L. and C. are again discoverers of a new species; for this duck was unknown to science in 1806" (BIDDLE-COUES, 3:880n).

MOUNTAIN QUAIL, *Oreortyx pictus pictus* (Douglas), A.O.U. 292a. The bird is not described in the Biddle narrative, but appears in the journals of 7 April 1806.

BLUE GROUSE, *Dendragapus obscurus richardsonii* (Douglas), A.O.U. 297b. The northern dusky grouse of BIDDLE-COUES, 2:453.

SPRUCE GROUSE, *Canachites canadensis franklinii* (Douglas), A.O.U. 299. "As it now stands, amended, we clearly recognize another discovery made by Lewis and Clark" (BIDDLE-COUES, 3:870n).

OREGON RUFFED GROUSE, *Bonasa umbelus sabini* (Douglas), A.O.U. 300c. "Lewis and Clark are the discoverers and first describers of the Oregon ruffed grouse; and on the present paragraph was exclusively based the *Tetrao fusca* of Ord" (BIDDLE-COUES, 3:872n).

SHARP-TAILED GROUSE, *Pedioecetes phasianellus columbianus* (Ord), A.O.U. 308a. This is Ord's *Phasianus Columbianus,* which he based on the prairie hen, of the great plains of the Columbia, described by Lewis and Clark.

SAGE GROUSE, *Centrocercus urophasianus urophasianus* (Bonaparte), A.O.U. 309. "Another notable discovery of Lewis and Clark" (BIDDLE-COUES, 3:868n).

MONTANA HORNED OWL, *Bubo virginianus occidentalis* Stone, A.O.U. 375j. "One of the party killed a large hooting owl; I observed no difference between this bird and those of the same family common to the U. States, except that this appeared to be more booted and more thickly clad with feathers" (Lewis, 14 April 1805, in the JOURNALS, 1:308).

LEWIS' WOODPECKER, *Asyndesmus lewis* (Gray), A.O.U. 408. Alexander Wilson named this bird *Picus torquatus* in 1811, basing his description on GASS, 224: "They are about the size of a common red-headed woodpecker; but are all black except the belly and neck, where the ends of the feathers are tipped with a deep red," etc. Lewis's own description did not appear until the Biddle edition of 1814.

POOR-WILL, *Phalaenoptilus nuttallii nuttallii* (Audubon), A.O.U. 418. The Biddle text (1:111) says, "We caught a whippoorwill of a small and uncommon kind." This is the bird named and described by Audubon in 1839 as Nuttall's whippoorwill, *Caprimulgus nuttallii*.

BROAD-TAILED HUMMINGBIRD, *Selasphorus platycercus platycercus* (Swainson), A.O.U. 432. "Credit Lewis and Clark with the discovery of this species, which was unknown to science until described . . . by Swainson . . . in 1827" (BIDDLE-COUES, 3:1044n).

BLACK-BILLED MAGPIE, *Pica pica hudsonia* (Sabine), A.O.U. 427. Not new to science, but unknown in North America until Lewis and Clark sent back descriptions and living specimens. It is the *Corvus pica* of Linnaeus.

GRAY JAY, *Perisoreus canadensis capitalis* Ridgway, A.O.U. 484a, and *P. c. obscurus* Ridgway, A.O.U. 485, both varieties of the gray jay.

PIÑON JAY, *Gymnorhinus cyanocephala* Wied, A.O.U. 491. According to BIDDLE-COUES, 2:454n: "here first discovered and described, but not for years afterward scientifically named. . . ."

CLARK'S NUTCRACKER, *Nucifraga columbiana* (Wilson), A.O.U. 491. WILSON named this bird in Clark's honor and pictured it as plate 29 in the first edition of his work. The first brief description is in Lewis's journal entry for 22 Aug. 1805: "I saw today a speceis of woodpecker, which fed on the seeds of the pine. It's beak and tail were white, it's wings were black, and every other part of a dark brown. It was about the size of a robin." Lewis presents a much fuller description in his entry for 28 May 1806.

WESTERN TANAGER, *Piranga ludoviciana* (Wilson), A.O.U. 607. "The earliest description of the Louisiana tanager . . . ever penned is in [the journals] June 6th 1806" (BIDDLE-COUES, 3:1035n).

193. Jefferson to the Senate and House of Representatives

[19 February 1806]

In pursuance of a measure proposed to Congress by a message of Jan. 18. 1803. and sanctioned by their appropriation for carrying it into execution, Capt. Meriwether Lewis, of the 1st regiment of infantry was appointed with a party of men, to explore the river

Missouri from it's mouth to it's source, and, crossing the highlands by the shortest portage, to seek the best water communication thence to the Pacific ocean; and Lieut. Clarke was appointed second in command. They were to enter into conference with the Indian nations on their route, with a view to the establishment of commerce with them. They entered the Missouri May 14. 1804. and on the 1st of Nov. took up their winter quarters near the Mandan towns, 1609 miles above the mouth of the river, in Lat. 47° 21′ 47″ N. and Long. 99° 24′ 45″ W. from Greenwich. On the 8th of April 1805. they proceeded up the river in pursuance of the objects prescribed to them. A letter of the preceding day, Apr. 7. from Capt. Lewis is herewith communicated. During his stay among the Mandans, he had been able to lay down the Missouri according to courses & distances taken on his passage up it, corrected by frequent observations of longitude & latitude; & to add to the actual survey of this portion of the river, a general map of the country between the Missisipi and Pacific, from the 34th to the 54th degrees of Latitude. These additions are from information collected from Indians with whom he had opportunities of communicating during his journey & residence with them. Copies of this map are now presented to both houses of Congress. With these I communicate also a statistical view, procured & forwarded by him, of the Indian nations inhabiting the territory of Louisiana & the countries adjacent to it's Northern & Western borders, of their commerce, & of other interesting circumstances respecting them.

In order to render the statement as compleat as may be of the Indians inhabiting the country West of the Missisipi, I add Dr. Sibley's account of those residing in, & adjacent to the territory of Orleans.

I communicate also from the same person an account of the Red river, according to the best information he had been able to collect.

Having been disappointed, after considerable preparations, in the purpose of sending an exploring party up that river in the summer of 1804. it was thought best to employ the autumn of that year in procuring a knowledge of an interesting branch of the river called the Washita. This was undertaken under the direction of Mr. Dunbar of Natchez, a citizen of distinguished science, who had aided & continues to aid us with his disinterested & valuable services, in the prosecution of these enterprizes. He ascended the river to the remarkeable Hot springs near it in Latitude 34° 31′ 4.16″ & Longitude 92° 50′ 45″ W. from Greenwich, taking it's courses and distances, & correcting them by frequent celestial observations. Extracts from his observations, & copies of his map of the river from it's mouth to the Hot springs, make part of the present communications. The examination of the Red river itself is but now commencing.

TH: JEFFERSON

Feb. 19. 1806.

ADS, SC (DLC); RC (DNA, Senate Papers, RG 46). Markings on the National Archives manuscript indicate that it was used as printer's copy for the published version (JEFFERSON). The message and its accompanying documents also appear in *American State Papers*, Indian Affairs, 1:705–43. Jefferson sent a copy of the printed version to John Vaughan at the American Philosophical Society, 25 March 1806 (DLC).

194. Fort Clatsop Memorandum

[18 March 1806]

The object of this list is, that through the medium of some civilized person who may see the same, it may be made known to the informed world, that the party consisting of the persons whose names are hereunto annexed, and who were sent out by the government of the U'States in May 1804. to explore the interior of the Continent of North America, did penetrate the same by way of the Missouri and Columbia Rivers, to the discharge of the latter into the Pacific Ocean, where they arrived on the 14th of November 1805, and from whence they departed the [*blank*] day of March 1806 on their return to the United States by the same rout they had come out.

Printed, JOURNALS, 4:180–81, and in BIDDLE, 2:204, with date of 23 March supplied in the blank. Lewis's explanation: "These lists of our names we have given to several of the natives and also paisted up a copy in our room [Fort Clatsop]. The object of these lists we stated in the preamble. . . . On the back of some of these lists we added a sketch of the connection of the upper branches of the Missouri with those of the Columbia, particularly of it's main S.E. branch, on which we also deliniated the track we had come and that we meant to pursue on our return where the same happened to vary" (JOURNALS, 4:180–81). Biddle adds: "By a singular casualty, this note fell into the possession of Captain Hill, who, while on the coast of the Pacific, procured it from the natives. This note accompanied him on his voyage to Canton, from whence it arrived in the United States." Biddle includes an extract from the letter, dated "Canton, January, 1807," omitting names of sender and recipient.

A sailor named John Rodgers JEWITT later claimed to have been aboard a brig out of Boston when, in the fall of 1805 and again in the spring of 1806, it lay to in the estuary of the Columbia. On the second visit, said Jewitt, crew members were told by Indians that Lewis and Clark had been in the area a fortnight earlier. To prove their story the natives showed the seamen several medals left by the explorers.

195. Charles Willson Peale to Jefferson

Dear Sir   Museum [Philadelphia] April 5th 1806.

The Skins of the several Antilopes was so badly managed in the Skinning, and also so much eaten by Dermests, that it was with much difficulty I could mount one of them, but being so interesting an Animal, I conceived it was better to have one even in bad condition, than to let it be wanting in the Museum, and should no description and plate have yet been made of this American Antilope, it may be acceptable to the public to give one in the American Philosophical transactions, I have therefore made the enclosed drawing.[1] It is done with a pen the better to aid an Engraver should you think it deserving publication, could I hope to see a better subject I should prefer giving a better drawing, however in this I have endeavored to give a general Idea of the Animal, and the imperfections will only be known to those who possess anatomical knowledge, but I must leave it to your better judgement whether to give it for publication or not, and to make such alterations and amendments as you chuse in the few remarks I shall make on the Animal by way of discription. I have not found it described in any author, except in Seba, and he only gives the horns and says it belongs to an American Antilope. It is an approaching link to our Elk; by the white patch on the Rump, but the tail is longer than the elks. The hair is more like the Deer than that of any Antilope I have seen. The Eye is placed very far back, and the forehead has a considerable elevation, so much so as to render that part a striking trait. The horns are very flat, and somewhat warty amidst the furrows near the bottom. They are hollow, and have each a prong, or branch, of 2 Inches long, which is also flat; it projects forward, and above this the horn begins to take a round form, and is round & smooth at the point, which curves back and also inward. The horns are strewed with hairs as high as the prong; that is 6 Inches from the base. The general colour of the Animal is a russet brown and white; the belly and half way up the sides are white, a patch of white from the throat on each side of the neck, and on the cheeks. A stif & long white maine on the back of the head extending a little distance down the neck. The hair divides on the heals more in this Animal than on the Elk, or other Deer, (this mark is more conspicuous in my Elks than the common Deer) ?It is a query whether this Antilope had a sack larger than what I found in the heals of our Common deer, containing a waxy substance of a very strong odour? I cannot at this moment recollect making any observation about this part of the Elk when I made a discection of it.

Dimentions: 5 feet from the nose along the neck and back to the insersion of the Tail, the tail 4 Inches long. The heigth is 2 f 10 Inches. The head 11 Inches long, and the Horns are each one foot in length, 6 Inches from the bottom projects a prong 2 Inches long. The width of the flat of the Horns in widest part is 2⅛ Inches. As a comparative I send the dementions of the *Common Antilope (C. Cervicapra)* in the Museum: heigth 2 feet 3 Inches. Length from the nose to the insertion of the tail 4 feet 4 Inches. Tail 7 Inches. I also send you inclosed some of the hair of both these Antilopes, as by a comparison of them, the hair of ours is seen to approach much nearer to that of Deers—and as you observed to me you thought it a Deer untill you saw the hollow horns. I have endeavored to imbrace all the essential parts, yet I have not attended to the teeth, and examining them since I wrote the foregoing, I find in the under jaw 8 front teeth nearly of equal size, and in the *Cervicapra* the two middle ones are considerably larger than the others. Amongst the Bones sent, I find an under jaw that is smaller than those belonging to the Antilopes, which I judge belonged to a Skin without the upper head, (for which reason I cannot mount that Skin) and this jaw has the two middle teeth larger than the others, I wish I could know more of this Animal, it may be a small Elk, as the rump is white— or a small species of Deer, having no Scull we cannot determine what the horns might have been, whether hollow or solid. Linneus gives to Deer and also to Antilopes the character of 8 front under teeth, but no mention of a difference in the size of them, whether they have been found to vary in the different Animals & therefore not made a part of the description, I cannot determine, no doubt so accurate an observer has not neglected any essential description, and if any doubts has arisen it was sufficient for that great Naturalist to reject it. For I find by my observation that many Authors attemptg. to refine on his Classification & description of Characters, that they all refine away the easy mode of knowing Animals, and thus renders the science of nature more difficult to be remembered and understood. I will attemp a description of the Marmot accompanied with a drawing of it, when it becomes more animated, as it must be soon, as the spring becomes warmer, at present it stirs but little. It is a pleasing little Animal, and not in the least dangerous to handle like our Ground Hog. Doctr. Barton is about a description of the Lizard, and says that I shall have the preserved Animal? This I have understood was your intention when you sent it to the Philosophical society, but which was not mentioned in your letter to me, when you sent that Animal.

. . . .

I have intruded on you a long letter in a time that I expect you have your mind fully engaged with public affairs. Accept my best wishes for your health & beleive me your friend,

C. W. PEALE

ALS, RC (DLC). Endorsed; received 9 April 1806.

1. The drawing has not been found. (There is an excellent water color of the pronghorn, done by Peale's son Titian during the Stephen Long expedition, in the library of the American Philosophical Society.) Peale submitted his drawing and description to the Society, and it was recommended for publication in the *Transactions* by a committee of which Benjamin Smith Barton was chairman (printed, A.P.S., 19 Sept. 1806). But when Lewis met with the Society on 19 June 1807 and asked for the use of some specimens that he had submitted, Peale withdrew his own material in favor of Lewis's expected publication (17 June in manuscript minutes of the Society, 19 June in PPAmP).

196. Henry Dearborn to James Wilkinson

Sir,   War Deptmt. Ap. 9. 1806.

The Missouri and Mississippi Indian Chiefs, will leave this place tomorrow for Pittsburg, from whence they will descend the River & proceed on to St. Louis. Several have died; but what is more especially to be regretted is the death of the very respectable & amiable Ricara Chief,[1] which happened on the 7th Instant.

It has been considered expedient, to have the interpreter, Gravline, and one of the Panas, who speak the Ricara language, sent, in a light boat, with a sober, discreet Sergeant & four faithful sober soldiers, up to the Ricara Nation, as soon as you can make the necessary arrangements. We shall forward the Big Medal, clothes, trinkets &c. &c. of the Old Chief, to his favorite son, together with something like a commission to him of a Chief. And it is thought advisable to send presents to his wives and children, to the amount of, from two to three hundred Dollars, which you will please to have selected from the Factory Goods. Mr. Tillier will be written to on the subject. It will likewise be proper to furnish Gravline with 100 lbs. of Powder and a corresponding quantity of Lead, to be distributed to the Chiefs of the Ricaras and Mandanes &c.

The escort, which ascends the River, will return in the Autumn, if it arrives at the place of its destination in Season; if not, it must

Winter with the Ricaras and return in the Spring. There should be no unnecessary delay in their departure; and they should be as little encumbered with baggage as the nature of the voyage will permit. If Gravline should wish to carry a few hundred dollars worth of Goods, he may be allowed the privilege. I shall agree with him what his compensation is to be.

If a present of four or five hundred Dollars, in such articles as can be procured at the Factory, will serve to wipe away the tears, in any considerable degree, from the eyes of the unfortunate Osages, whose connections have been killed, or held in captivity by the faithless Puttawattamies, you will please to have the same delivered into the hands of the Principal Osage Chiefs, to be by them distributed among the unfortunate families. But the Osages should be informed that their depredations on the Caddos, on the waters of Red River, are known by the President; and unless they take effectual measures for preventing any further hostilities on our particular friends, the Caddos, they will forfeit the good opinion and friendship of their father the President.

I have taken every means in my power, to impress the minds of the Osages, who are here, with the necessity of their being at peace with our Red friends, and especially with the Caddos. I have likewise made strong Talks to the Puttawattamies, and other Mississippi Chiefs, as well as the Upper Missouri Chiefs, on the Subject of general peace and friendship among those Nations, whom we consider as our friends.

We shall settle with and pay the several interpreters, with an allowance of one dollar per day until they arrive at St. Louis, computing the length of the journey to be two months, from hence to that place.

It has been thought advisable to appoint Boilvin[2] an Assistant Agent at a salary of Five hundred Dollars, and one hundred and fifty dollars for subsistence, annually, to reside at the Rapids above the River Lamoin at the Sacque Village. You will please to give him such instructions from time to time as he may require.

I have agreed with Gravline, to request you to assign a building, at the Cantonement, left by the Troops, for his family to reside in during his absence, with the privilege of a piece of Ground for a garden. I will thank you to give directions accordingly. I have not only paid Gravline for his time until he arrives at St. Louis, but for three months in advance, beyond that period, for his voyage up the River;—and have consented to give him the pay of Three hundred and sixty five dollars a year after his voyage ends, as an Interpreter &c. for the Upper Missouri Indians; where he may, if he please, reside

[304]

and carry on some trade with the Ricaras and Mandanes. We have made young Paul Chouteau,[3] a chief of the Little Osages.

In addition to the other presents, for the family of the Old Ricara Chief, you will please to send nine muskets for his sons, to be put into the hands of their uncles, for them as they become able to use them. I am very resp. &c.

Lbk (DNA, RG 75, Letters Sent, B:192–94).

1. Three weeks earlier, Dearborn had written Wilkinson that the band of chiefs were now returning from Boston to Washington and would meet the Arikara chief in Philadelphia. "The Ricardi Chief is an interesting character;—and we shall not fail of sending him away particularly satisfied. I most ardently hope, he will return home in safety." Dearborn added that he had been overwhelmed by Indian delegations lately, and that in the future they must come to Washington only when Congress was not in session (DNA, RG 107, Letters Sent, Bk. 2). Lewis and Clark were to learn of the death of this influential chief before they returned from the West. Descending the Missouri 21 Aug. 1806, they were given the news by François Rivet and a man they identify as Greinyea (probably Grenier; see TABEAU, 168). They met Gravelines 12 Sept. and heard the full story (JOURNALS, 5:382–83). For another comment on the chief's death, see FOSTER (2), 42–43.

2. Sending Boilvin up the Mississippi was the first concrete action taken by Dearborn to provide an agent and a factory for the Sauks, Foxes, and other tribes in the upper river valley, after the establishment at Belle Fontaine proved to be poorly located. Dearborn was not eager to make this move. Wilkinson had suggested a post at the mouth of the Des Moines in the preceding fall, but Dearborn had advised against it "until the subject shall have been more fully considered" (16 Oct. 1805, TERR. PAPERS, 13:239). Perhaps it was at the prompting of Quashquame, one of the principal Sauk chiefs in the delegation, that he decided to send Boilvin up to the Des Moines. The Sauks had never considered the establishment of the factory at Belle Fontaine a suitable compliance with their treaty of 1804 (which Quashquame had signed), because of its poor location. Not until the fall of 1808 would a fully equipped factory be sent to the Sauks and Foxes. For a summary history of Fort Madison and the factory that was built with it, see JACKSON (3). For Boilvin, see the biographical details in SCANLAN.

3. Paul Loise or Louis, also called Paul Chouteau, was from all indications an Osage half-breed. Lewis describes him in 1808 as "resident Interpreter of the Osage Nations" (TERR. PAPERS, 14:231). One of the Chouteaus may have been his father, but he is not Paul Liguest Chouteau (1792–1851), the son of Pierre.

197. Henry Dearborn to Jefferson

Sir   [c. 10 April 1806]

The name of the Ricara Chief, as well as I could make it out from the three Interpreters, was Ankedoucharo. According to Gravelins pronounciation the letters would be thus divided: Ank.e.douch.a.ro. but I doubt whether they are correct. Yours,

H. DEARBORN

I think it not improbable, that insted of Ank.e. it should be Inca. as we find that the Peruvian term, Inca, for Chief, is known and continued among some of the Tribes in Lousiana. H. D.

ALS, RC (DLC). Endorsed; received 10 April 1806.

198. Jefferson to the Arikaras

My friends & children of the Ricara nation   [11 April 1806]

It gave me a great pleasure to see your beloved chief* arrive here on a visit to his white brothers of the United States of America. I took him by the hand with affection, I considered him as bringing to me the assurances of your friendship and that you were willing to become of one family with us. Wishing to see as much as he could of his new brethren he consented to go towards the sea as far as Baltimore & Philadelphia. He found nothing but kindness & good will wherever he passed. On his return to this place he was taken sick; every thing we could do to help him was done; but it pleased the great Spirit to take him from among us. We buried him among our own deceased friends & relatives, we shed many tears over his grave, and we now mingle our afflictions with yours on the loss of this beloved chief. But death must happen to all men; and his time was come.

Here follows select parts of the first speech made to the Osages Missouris &c. on their arrival.[1]

* Leave a blank for the name of the deceased chief, which is not known as yet.[2]

AD, SC (DLC). Undated, but obviously prepared for the departure of the delegation, and so dated above.

1. This passage is an instruction to the clerk who will prepare the final text. Jefferson is referring to No. 187.

2. The fair text (not located) probably read "your beloved chief Arketarnawhar." At the head of the present text, Jefferson first wrote "Piaketo" and then above it the English version, "Eagle's feather." He then struck out this combination and wrote "Toone," with the English version, "Whippoorwill," above. Finally he struck that out, writing "Arketarnawhar" and "chief of the town" above that. There is no deleting line through this last combination.

199. Jefferson to the Mandans

To the chiefs & people of the Mandane nation.

My friends & children   [11 April 1806]

I should have recieved with great satisfaction at the seat of our govmt. some of your chiefs, with those of the Osages, Ricaras, Missouris, Panis & others who have lately visited us. They would have seen with their own eyes proofs of the friendship which myself and all their white brethren of these United states bear them, of our desire to live in peace with them, & to render them all the services in our power. But the journey is long, liable to many accidents and therefore not to be insisted on between friends. At some future time perhaps I shall have the pleasure of seeing some of you here. I consider you as the first nation beyond the Missisipi which we became acquainted with through our beloved man Capt. Lewis, who passed a winter with you. You recieved him as a friend, were kind to him, and I now thank you for all the services you rendered him and his people.

My friends and children. We are descended &c. as in the Message to the Ricaras, being those parts of the speech made to the Osages &c. on their arrival as are applicable to the Mandanes.

TH: J.
Apr. 11. 1806.

AD, SC (DLC). A copy in DNA, RG 75, Letters Sent, Bk. B, is dated 19 April 1806. The message was sent to Wilkinson in two versions, French and English, for delivery to Gravelines on his arrival in St. Louis—and for subsequent transmission to the Mandans (Dearborn to Wilkinson, 16 April 1806, DNA, RG 107, Letters Sent, 2:449).

200. Henry Dearborn to James S. Swearingen

Sir,   War Deptmt. Ap: 30. 1806.

By some mistake the direction for procuring suitable Boats for the Indians to descend the Ohio, and ascend the Mississippi, has taken a wrong direction. You will, with as little delay as practicable, furnish two suitable Keel Boats for the Indians who are now at Pittsburg— and you will furnish them with provisions suitable for their voyage.

You will please to inform the Osage Chiefs, that their friend, left sick here, is alive, and that I have hopes of his recovery.[1]

You will select for each of the Chiefs at Pittsburg, a musket, in

[307]

good repair, and deliver each one pound of powder & forty balls, with three flints. I am &c. &c. &c.

Lbk (DNA, RG 107, Letters Sent, 2:462). Lt. James Strode Swearingen, of Virginia, was appointed to the Corps of Artillerists in 1803 and became assistant military agent at Fort Fayette, Pittsburgh, in Aug. 1805.
1. Not identified.

201. Henry Dearborn to James S. Swearingen

Sir   War Deptmt. May 9. 1806.

Mr. Morin,[1] the bearer of this, has been sent to Pittsburg with an Osage Cheif who was left sick at this place, when the other Chiefs set out for home. You will take particular care of the Osage; he is a sober, honest man, in a low state of health. You will procure a passage for him to Massac, in some boat, where he will be taken good care of & decently treated. You will furnish him with a good musket, one pound of powder and forty balls & some flints; & also with a sufficient supply of provisions for his passage, & two bottles of Wine. You will write to the Commanding Officer at Massac, & request him to recieve the Osage Chief, take good care of him, & send him, by the first conveyance, to St. Louis to the care of Mr. Peter Chouteau, the Indian Agent.

You will furnish the Osage with Eight Dollars to purchase such small articles on his passage as he may stand in need of. I am &c. &c.

Lbk (DNA, RG 107, Letters Sent, 3:12).
1. Not identified.

202. Charles Willson Peale to Jefferson

Dear Sir   Museum [Philadelphia] July 4th 1806.

I presented to the Philosophical Society at their last setting, the drawing of the Antilope with a short description of it, "done from a specimen in my Museum, which was sent from the interior of Louisiana by Captn. Lewis, and presented to the Museum by the President in Octr. 1805." A member demanded of me, what name I gave it? To which, after a few moments reflection, I replyed The *forked Horned Antilope*. But Sir that is not a scientific name. It is not a Lattin name but one most descriptive of the Animal, since we know of no Antilope besides having forked Horns. This was admitted as true. As men pretending to a knowledge must be humoured with

the high sounding names made from the dead Languages, I most
humbly request of you my dear Sir, to give me a Name for this
American Antilope, perhaps the Indian name, if it could be had
would be a proper one, however I leave it to your superior judgement,
and shall only say that whatever you think proper to give it, will
be placed in print on the Animal in the Museum, and given to the
Society, as of your choise or not as you may please to direct. I shall
be glad to hear that you have got the machinery to moove the Ink
pots to your small Polygraph without much difficulty, and to satisfaction. I have heard of a proposal by Mr. Joel Barlow,[1] to form
a National Institute at Washington, I have not seen the Pamphlet,
and therefore dont know whether my Museum might not be im-
braced amongst the first of its establishments. At my time of Life I
cannot help feeling some anxiety to know the fate of my labours.
Every thing I do is with a view to a permancy, yet at my death there
is a danger of its being divided or lost to my Country. Accept the
respects of

C. W. Peale

ALS, RC (DLC). Endorsed; received 11 Aug. 1806.
   1. Barlow (1754–1812) was a poet and diplomat. See No. 234 and the accompanying note.

203. Clark to Hugh Heney

Sir

Camp on the River Rochejhone East of the Rocky
Mountains July 20th 1806—a Copy

   In the winter of 1805, you were so obliging as to express a disposition to assist us in the execution of any measure relitive to the
Savages with whome you were conversant, or that you would lend your
aid in furthering the friendly views of our government in relation
to the same. No object as we then informed you did at that time
present itself to our view, which we conceived worthy of your attention. At present we have a commission to charge you with, which
if executed, we have no doubt will tend to advance your private
interest, while it will also promote those of the U. States in relation to
the intercourse of her citizens with the Indian nations in the interior
of North America. It is that of provailing on some of the most in-
fluensial Chiefs of those bands of Sioux who usially resort the borders
of the Missouri to visit the Seat of our Government, and to accompany
them there yourself with us. The Tetons of the burnt woods, Teton
Ockandandas, and other bands of Tetons, Cisitons, and yanktons of

the Plains are the objects of our attention on this occasion, Particularly the Bands of Tetons; those untill some effectual measures be taken to render them pacific, will always prove a serious source of inconveniance to the free navigation of the Missouri, or at least to it's upper branches, from whence the richest portion of it's fur trade is to be derived.

The ardent wish of our government has ever been to conciliate the esteem and secure the friendship of all the Savage nations within their territory by the exercise of every consistent and pacific measure in her power, applying those of coercion only in the last resort; certain we are that her disposition towards the native inhabitants of her newly acquired Territory of Louisiana is not less friendly; but we are also positive that she will not long suffer her citizens to be deprived of the free navigation of the Missouri by a fiew comparitively feeble bands of Savages who may be so illy advised as to refuse her proffered friendship and continue their depridation on her citizens who may in future assend or decend that river.

We believe that the surest guarantee of savage fidility to any nation is a thorough conviction on their minds that their government possesses the power of punishing promptly every act of aggression committed on their part against the person or property of their citizens; to produce this conviction without the use of violence, is the wish of our government; and to effect it, we cannot devise a more expedient method than that of takeing some of the best informed and most influential Chiefs with us to the U. States, where they will have an ample view of our population and resourses, become convinced themselves, and on their return convince their nations of the futility of an attempt to oppose the will of our government, particularly when they shall find, that their acquiescence will be productive of greater advantages to their nation than their most sanguine hopes could lead them to expect from oppersition.

We have before mentioned to you the intention of our government to form trading establishments on the Missouri with a view to secure the attatchments of the nativs and emeliorate their sufferings by furnishing them with such articles as are necessary for their comfort on the most moderate terms in exchange for their peltries and furs. Forming those establishments will most probably be delayed untill our return for the want of sufficient information relitive to the state of the country. We have recommended a position in the neighbourhood of the enterance of the Chyenne river as an eligible situation for one of those establishments principally with a view to the accomodation of the *Sioux*. An Indian *Agent* will of course be necessary at that

[310]

post. Your long acquaintance and influence with those people necessar[il]y places your protentions to that appointment on the fairest ground, and should you think proper to undertake the commission now proposed, it will still further advance those pretentions. If you wish such an office you may rest assured of our wormest intersessions in your behalf with our government. The emoluments attatched to the office of an Indian Agent in our service is 75$ pr. month and six rations pr. day, which last at so distant a post might safely be calculated at 20 cts. pr. ration or one Dollar & 20 cents pr. day in addition to the Monthly pay makeing a total of 111$ pr. month.

Under this view of the Subject should you think proper to engage in the business proposed, we promise you in behalf of our governmt. one dollar pr. day while you are employed in that service whether you succeed or not, recconing from the date at which you receive this letter. All necessary expences incedent to traveling, hireing guides, expresses &c. which may accur in the course of your transactions will also be allowed. In order the better to ensure you success, you are at liberty to take with you on this occasion any amount in merchandize not exceeding 200$ which you may conceive necessary by way of presents to those people. As horses will also be necessary for your journey you are at liberty to take any three of those which the men who hand you this, may bring with them to the establishments on the Assinniboin river or to the Mandans. We have directed Sergt. Pryor to take 12 horses to the Establishments on the Assinniboin for the several purposes of exchangeing for a fiew articles which are necessary to the comfort of our party, to furnish you with as maney as will be necessary for your journey, and to pay the amount of the merchindize which we have instructed you to take on that occasion. Should the Merchents not be disposed to barter for the horses and prefur Bills on our Government or furs at the Mandans, either of the latter will be delivered them imediately on our arival. In all pecuniary transactions where the case will permit it, you will take bills of particulars and receipts as vouchers in the settlement of your public accounts.

Haveing accomplished our voyage to the Pacific Ocian by way of the Missouri and Columbia rivers we are now on our return to the United States where we must arive if possible in the course of this season. We shall spend a fiew weeks in exploring the country on the River Rochejhone and a large northerly branch of the Missouri dischargeing itself 50 miles below the Great falls of that river to which we have given the name of Maria's river. In order that no time shall be lost, we have in the interim dispatched a party over land from the upper part of the Rochejhone or Yellow Stone river to the Mandans and thence to your establishment on the assinniboin, with a view to give you as much time as possible to collect the Sioux Chiefs at some convenient part of the Missouri against our arival, that we may not experience any detention. We shall in all probability arrive at the Mandans about the beginning of September, perhaps earlyer; at all events we wish you to lose no time in collecting the chiefs and repairing to the Missouri where you will wait our arrival, informing us if possible of your position. Perhaps the Ricaras Village, if they have not removed will be an eligible place of rendezvous, but in this respect we shall not pretend to controal you, as you will be on the ground and can better judge of the most expedient position for this purpose. It may possibly so happen that you will be absent from the Missouri at the time of our arrival at the Mandans and Ricaras, and as some communication may be necessary between us in such case, we wish you to concert a plan with Sergt. Pryor for that purpose. Should you not suceed in prevailing on the chiefs to go on with us as early as we wish, if you will meat us yourself on the Missouri we will make some other arrangement by which you will be enabled perhaps to bring them on afterwards yourself; but it would be preferable in every point of view that they should go on with us. The number of chiefs and their attendance must not exceed 12 persons, as we cannot possibly accommodate more.

In your communication with the *Sioux,* in addition to other considerations which may suggest themselves to your mind, you will be pleased to assure them of the friendly views of our government towards them, their power and resourses, their intention of establishing trading houses in their neighbourhood and the objects of those establishments. Inform them that the mouth of all the rivers through [which] traders convey Merchindize to their country are now in the possession of the United States, who can at pleasure cut off all communication between themselves and their accustomed traders, and consiquently the interest they have in cultivateing our friendship. You may also promis them in the event of their going on with us, that they shall receive from our government a considerable preasent in Merchindize, which will be conveyed at the public expence with them to their nation on their return. Urge them also to go imediately, on the ground, that their doing so will haisten the establishment of the tradeing house in contemplation.

You no doubt are acquainted with the influence which Mr. Cammaron[1] and other traders of the River St. Peters possess over those people, the implicit confidence which they place in the power and resourses of those traders, the hitherto unfriendly dispositions of those men in relation to the trade of the Missouri, and thence the aggressions practised by the Sieoux on the traders of that river. Their long established prejudices in favour of the Traders of the river St. Peters will probably prove a serious bar to your present negociations, unless our government has taken some measures on this subject in consequence of the representation which we made them in the Spring [of] 1805. If so, and those traders have been prevented from bringing out their merchindize this spring as they were accustomed to do, the Indians will most probably not long hesitate in complying with our wishes; however be this as it may, the most perfect reliance is placed in your exertions by Your friends and obedient Servents,

W. CLARK Capt. &c.

Mr. Hugh Heney
at the N. W. Co. Establishment
on the Assinniboin river

ALS, SC (MoSHi). This manuscript is in Clark's hand and is signed by him, but it cannot be his letter. The ideas are typically Lewis's and so is the prose style. It was written about 1 July, before Lewis and Clark parted to make separate explorations on their homeward course. In his journal entry of 1 July, Lewis speaks of "a letter which we have written for the purpose to engage Mr. H. Haney" (JOURNALS, 5:179). By 20 July, the date of the letter, the two men were far apart—Clark on the Yellowstone and Lewis on the Marias River. I take the present document to be Clark's retained copy, made before he sent the original off with Pryor, and I assume that the original was signed by both Lewis and Clark. It has been commonly accepted as Clark's, as in this passage: "It was, however, Clark who finally made advances to Heney with the idea of profiting from his acquaintance with and influence over the Sioux" (TABEAU, 88n).

1. Murdoch Cameron (d. 1811), trader on the St. Peter's or Minnesota River. For Pike's encounter with him on the Mississippi, and an editorial note, see PIKE, 1:66.

204. Clark to Nathaniel Pryor

Camp on the River Rochejhone 115 Miles
Sir   below the Rocky Mountains July 25th [23rd] 1806
You will with George Shannon, George Gibson & Richard Windser take the horses which we have brought with us to the Mandans Village on the Missouri. When you arrive at the Mandans, you will enquire of Mr. Jussomme[1] and any british Traders who may be in neighbourhood of this place for Mr. Hugh Heney. If you are informed,

or have reasons to believe that he still remains at the establishments on the Assinniboin River, you will hire a pilot to conduct you and proceed on to those establishments and deliver Mr. Heney the letter which is directed to him. You will take with you to the Establishments on the Assinniboin River 12 or 14 horses, 3 of which Mr. Heney is to have choise if he agrees to engage in the Mission preposed to him. As maney of the remaining horses as may be necessary you will barter with the traders for such articles as we may stand in need of such as *Flints* three or 4 Doz. *Knives,* a fiew lbs. of *Paint,* some *Pepper, Sugar* & *Coffee* or *Tea,* 2 doz. Cors *Handkerchiefs,* 2 small Kegs of *Sperits,* 2 *Cappoes,* a <*hat for Sergt. Ordway*> *Tobacco* sufficient, *Glaubr. Salts,* and such curious species of *fur* as you may see. Or such of those articles as you may be enabled to get and we are most in want of viz. Tobacco Knives & Flints &c. The horses which you do not take with you from the Mandans you will leave in the care of the *Black Cat*[2] Grand Chief of that nation untill we arive. They together with those you may not dispose of as before directed is to pay for $200 of Merchendize to be put in the hands of Mr. Heney as presents for the Soux chiefs as an inducement for them to accompany us to the Seat of our Government, and to purchase cors robes and such other articles as the party may stand in need of. Should Mr. Heney not be at the Establishments on the Assinniboin River or at the Mandans, you will remain with the Mandans untill our arival at that place. Should Mr. Heney agree to under take the Mission preposed in the letter you are to agre with him upon some plan by which means we may hear from him in the event that he should not suckceed with the Sioux chiefs as soon as he expects; or what point he will meet us at on the Missouri.[3] Haveing the fullest confidence of your exertions on this enterprise, health hapiness and a safe journey is the sincere wish of your Frend,

W. CLARK Capt. &c.

ALS, SC (MoSHi). Endorsed, "a Copy of Sergt. Pryors Orders." Although Clark dated the letter 25 July, he wrote in his journal for 23 July: "I gave Sergt. Pryor his instructions and a letter to Mr. Haney . . ." (JOURNALS, 5:281).

1. René Jusseaume or Jussome, a Canadian who may have been with the Mandans as an independent trader as early as 1791. He was with the North West Company on the Red River in 1793 and with David Thompson on his voyage of 1797. Lewis and Clark first met him 27 Oct. 1804 at the Mandan towns, and hired him temporarily as an interpreter.

2. Black Cat or Posecopsahe, the principal Mandan chief, who had visited the explorers' camp frequently during the winter of 1804–05.

3. The failure of Pryor's mission is recorded by Lewis, who learned in a

note from Clark "that Sergt. Pryor having been robed of all his horses had decended the Yelowstone river in skin canoes and had overtaken him. . . . This I fear puts an end to our prospects of obtaining the Sioux Cheifs to accompany us as we have not now leasure to send and engage Mr. Heney on this service . . ." (11 Aug. 1806, JOURNALS, 5:242).

205. Clark to Toussaint Charbonneau

Charbono On Board the Perogue Near the Ricara Village
Sir August 20th 1806

Your present situation with the Indians givs me some concern. I wish now that I had advised you to come on with me to the Illinois where it most probably would be in my power to put you in some way to do something for your self. I was so engaged after the *Big White*[1] had concluded to go down with Jessomme as his Interpreter, that I had not time to talk with you as much as I intended to have done. You have been a long time with me and have conducted your Self in Such a manner as to gain my friendship, your woman who accompanied you that long dangerous and fatigueing rout to the Pacific Ocian and back diserved a greater reward for her attention and services on that rout than we had in our power to give her at the Mandans. As to your little Son (my boy *Pomp*)[2] you well know my fondness for him and my anxiety to take and raise him as my own child. I once more tell you if you will bring your son Baptiest to me I will educate him and treat him as my own child. I do not forgit the promis which I made to you and shall now repeat them that you may be certain. Charbono, if you wish to live with the white people, and will come to me I will give you a piece of land and furnish you with horses cows & hogs. If you wish to visit your friends in *Montrall* I will let you have a horse, and your family shall be taken care of untill your return. If you wish to return as an Interpreter for the Menetarras when the troops come up to form the establishment, you will be with me ready and I will precure you the place—or if you wish to return to trade with the indians and will leave your little *Son Pomp* with me, I will assist you with merchendize for that purpose from time [to time] and become my self conserned with you in trade on a Small scale that is to say not exceeding a perogue load at one time. If you are desposed to accept either of my offers to you and will bring down your *Son* your famn Janey[3] had best come along with you to take care of the boy untill I get him. Let me advise you to keep your Bill of Exchange and what furs and pelteries you have in possession, and get as much more as you can—and get as maney robes, and big horn and Cabbra Skins as you can collect in the course of this winter and take them down to St. Louis as early as possible in the Spring. When you get to St. Louis enquire of the Govorner of that place for a letter which I shall leave with him for you. In the letter which I shall leave with the governer I shall inform you what you had best do with your firs pelteries and robes &c. and derect you where to find me. If you should meet with any misfortune on the river &c. when you get to St. Louis write a letter to me by the post and let me know your situation. If you do not intend to go down either this fall or in the Spring, write a letter to me by the first oppirtunity and inform me what you intend to do that I may know if I may expect you or not. If you ever intend to come down this fall or the next Spring will be the best time. This fall would be best if you could get down before the winter. I shall be found either in St. Louis or in Clarksville at the Falls of the Ohio.

Wishing you and your family great suckcess & with anxious expectations of seeing my little danceing boy Baptiest I shall remain your Friend,

WILLIAM CLARK

Keep this letter and let not more than one or 2 persons see it, and when you write to me seal your letter. I think you best not deturmin which of my offers to accept untill you See me. Come prepared to accept of either which you may chuse after you get down.

Mr. Teousant Charbono
Minetarras Village

ALS, SC (MoSHi).
Here Clark shows concern for the future of the most mismated couple in all of American history: the inept and lazy Charbonneau, and the young Shoshoni slave girl Sacagawea. It is perhaps unfair to expect Charbonneau to perform as a hero simply because he was hired out to a heroic troupe. And when in 1839 he limps into the Indian Affairs office in St. Louis, penniless and "tottering under the infirmities of 80 winters" (No. 409), he becomes a sympathetic character at last. For biographical sketches of the man, see LUTTIG, 135–40, and CHARDON, 276–82.

As for Sacagawea, I follow BAKELESS in adopting the Bureau of American Ethnology spelling, realizing that it is more frequently found as "Sacajawea" or "Sakakawea." It may mean "bird woman" or may mean "boat launcher," depending on whether it is a Shoshoni or Hidatsa word. REES, who lived among the Shoshonis and knew the language, has attempted to explain the word. He says that the girl was not called Sacagawea until the exploring party met the Shoshonis, at which time she was given that name, on the spot, by her people. It means, Rees says, "travels with the boat that is pulled." Before this she had been called *Wadze-wipe*. The trouble with his explanation is that Ordway calls her "Sah-cah-gah" before the Shoshoni tribe has been encountered, in his journal entry of 10 June 1805. (Clark calls her "Sah-kah-gar we â" as early as the winter days at Fort Mandan, but his and Lewis's journals show evidence of revision with some altering of dates. I am assuming that Ordway actually wrote his 10 June 1805 entry on that day.)

Of Sacagawea's valor and stolid determination there can be no doubt. but her contribution to the expedition is often magnified by her biographers. For a detached appraisal of her usefulness as a guide to Lewis and Clark, see KINGSTON. See also a brief and objective biography by CRAWFORD, especially the editorial note explaining why—for linguistic reasons—the word should be spelled "Sakakawea." For a note on her death, see under No. 404a.

1. Sheheke or the Big White, a Mandan chief who had agreed to descend the river with the expedition and visit Washington.

2. Jean Baptiste Charbonneau, born 11 Feb. 1805 at Fort Mandan.

3. For "your famn Janey" read "your *femme* Sacagawea." It is tempting to suppose that Clark may have written "Jawey," but the original is clearly Janey.

206. Lewis to Jefferson

Sir,   St. Louis September 21st 1806

Having acquired information & provisions of the Mandans on the evening of the 7th of Apl. 1805 we embarked with our baggage on board 2 large perogues and six small canoes at Fort Mandan on a Voyage of Discovery to the Pacific Ocean. The party consisted of the following persons my friend and Colleague Capt. Wm. Clark, Interpreters George Drewyer and Tuasant Charbono, Sergts. John Ordway Nathanial Pryor and Patric Gass, privates John Sheilds &c. a Shoshone Woman and child wife and Infant of Toust. Charbono and York[1] a black man servant to Capt Clark making a total with myself of 33 persons. A Man of the Mandan nation also set out with us under promis to accompany us to the Rocky Mountains with a view to reestablish peace between the Minnetares & Ahwahaways and the Shoshones and others at the head of the Missouri, but becoming very early tired of his mission he abandoned us on the 8th and returned to his village. The river was full and the water excessively cold the ice which confined it from the [*blank*]th[2] of November 1804 had departed only within a few days previously. In this navigating we employed the oar cord and sail the water being too high to permit the uce of the seting pole which in the latter part of summer and autumn may be employed to great advantage on a large proportion of every part of the Missouri, (and when the state of the river is such as to permit the uce of the pole it is always to be prefered to the oar in resisting the forse of it's currant). We ascended with as little difficulty as we had previously met with, found the river equally wide deep and navigable as below fort Mandan.

* It may not be amis to premise that the distances herein stated are those from the confluence of the Missouri and Mississippi from which you will recollect that Fort Mandan is 1609 miles distant. We have through the whole course of the voyage taken a chart of the several rivers which we have navigated on a large scale as well as delineated our several tracts by land marking our dayly encampments the entrance of watercourses points of celestial observation and all other places and objects worthy of notice.[3]

* At the distance of 1699 miles from the confluence of the Missouri and Mississippi we arrived on the 13th[4] of Apl. at the entrance of the little Missouri a handsom river of [blank] yds[5] in width discharging itself on the S. side, navigable for canoes [blank] ms.[6] Here we remained untill the 15th.[7] In pursuing our rout we passed the entrance of the white earth river[8] on the [blank] Apr. at 1[blank] ms. This river discharged itself on the N.E. side is [blank] yds in width and appears as if it might be navigated with small canoes many miles. It's course is due north through an open level plain. A small party of whitemen, residing with the Mandans, had ascended the Missouri within [blank] miles of the entrance of this river about 4 years before but we have no certain account of any white persons reaching its entrance previous to ourselves. From hence therefore our footsteps were on unkn. ground. Here the beaver become very abundant on the R. At the distance of 1888 miles we reached the entrance of the Yellow Rock river on the 27th of Apl.[9] This noble branch of the Missouri discharges itself on the S.W. side. It is nearly as wide as the Missouri has from 6 to 8 feet water with an even gentle currant. It discharges much more water than any other branch of the Missouri, at least twice as much at many seasons of the year as the great river Platte which has been hitherto considered the most conspicuous among the branches of the Missouri. We examined the country minutely in the vicinity of the entrance of the River Rochejone[10] and found it possessed of every natural advantage necessary for an establishment, it's position in a geographical point of view has destined it for one of the most important establishments both as it reguards the fur trade and the government of the natives in that quarter of the continent. Having made the necessary observations at this place we left it on the [blank] of Apr.[11] determined to explore this river on our return. Still ascending we passed the entrances of two handsome rivers on the N.E. side the 1st at 1944 ms. to which we gave the name of Marthy's river the 2d at 53 miles further which we called Porcupine river,[12] the

1st is 50 yds. wide and the 2d 112, both discharge considerable quantities of water; the latter we believe to be navigable many miles for canoes the latter not so far. On the [*blank*] of May we arrived at the entrance of a bold river on the N.E. side 150 yds. wide which from the colour of it's water we called milk river.[13] The currant is gentle stream deep and is probably navigable for large perogues or boats for 150 miles, that is judging from streams of similar size which like it pass through an open country. It's course as far as we could discover it from an eminence of about 30 Ms. was due north and I am [*end of manuscript*]

AL, SC (PPAmP). An incomplete draft, in Codex S of the manuscript journals. This letter is commonly assumed to be for Jefferson, and Thwaites conjectures that it might be a draft of the letter Lewis promised the President in No. 207. If Lewis actually wrote it on this date, he probably penned it on the boat—as the poor quality of the hand indicates—during a forty-eight-mile run down to St. Charles. There would have been no time for writing in the evening after arrival, as the party found the townsfolk "excessively polite" and eager to entertain.

1. A slave bequeathed to Clark by his father, John Clark, in a will dated 24 July 1799 (MoSHi).
2. 29 Nov. (JOURNALS, 1:228).
3. In the manuscript this paragraph appears midway in the following one, with asterisks to indicate that it belongs here instead.
4. They actually arrived 12 April.
5. Given as 134 yards in Clark's journal entry for 12 April.
6. Clark wrote, "one of our men Baptiest [Lepage] who came down this river in a canoe informs me that it is not navagable, he was 45 days descending" (JOURNALS, 1:300).
7. Not so. They left 13 April (JOURNALS, 1:301).
8. Little Muddy River in Buford County, N.D., reached 21 April, described by Lewis as being not more than ten yards wide at the mouth but widening to sixty yards upstream (JOURNALS, 1:326).
9. They reached the Yellowstone on 26 April. Apparently Lewis is guessing at some dates, omitting others, intending to verify them when he writes his fair copy.
10. Also the Yellowstone. From the French *roche jaune*.
11. They stayed only a day, setting out on the 27th.
12. Martha's River, named by Clark "in honour to the Selebrated M. F.," is now the Big Muddy in Montana, and the Porcupine is now the Poplar.
13. The Milk River, largest of the Missouri's northern tributaries, was reached 8 May.

207. Lewis to Jefferson

Sir,   St. Louis September 23rd 1806.

It is with pleasure that I anounce to you the safe arrival of myself and party at 12 OClk. today at this place with our papers and baggage. In obedience to your orders we have penitrated the Continent of North America to the Pacific Ocean, and sufficiently explored the interior of the country to affirm with confidence that we have discovered the most practicable rout[1] which dose exist across the continent by means of the navigable branches of the Missouri and Columbia Rivers. Such is that by way of the Missouri to the foot of the rapids five miles below the great falls of that river a distance of 2575 miles, thence by land passing the Rocky Mountains to a navigable part of the Kooskooske[2] 340; with the Kooskooske 73 mls. a South Easterly branch[3] of the Columbia 154 miles and the latter river 413 mls. to the Pacific Ocean; making the total distance from the confluence of the Missouri and Mississippi to the discharge of the Columbia into the Pacific Ocean 3555 miles. The navigation of the Missouri may be deemed safe and good; it's difficulties arrise from it's falling banks, timber imbeded in the mud of it's channel, it's sand bars and steady rapidity of it's current, all which may be overcome with a great degree of certainty by taking the necessary precautions. The passage by land of 340 miles from the Missouri to the Kooskooske is the most formidable part of the tract proposed across the Continent; of this distance 200 miles is along a good road, and 140 over tremendious mountains which for 60 mls. are covered with eternal snows; however a passage over these mountains is practicable from the latter part of June to the last of September, and the cheep rate at which horses are to be obtained from the Indians of the Rocky Mountains and West of them, reduces the expences of transportation over this portage to a mere trifle. The navigation of the Kooskooske, the South East branch of the Columbia itself is safe and good from the 1st of April to the middle of August, by making three portages on the latter; the first of which in decending is that of 1200 paces at the great falls of the Columbia, 261 mls. from the Ocean, the second of two miles at the long narrows six miles below the falls, and the 3rd also of 2 miles at the great rapids 65 miles still lower down. The tides flow up the Columbia 183 miles, or within seven miles of the great rapids, thus far large sloops might ascend in safety, and vessels of 300 tons burthen could with equal safety reach the entrance of the river Multnomah,[4] a large Southern branch of the Columbia, which taking it's rise on the confines of Mexico with the Callarado and Apostles[5] river, discharges itself into the Columbia 125 miles from it's mouth. From the head of tide water to the foot of the long narrows the Columbia could be most advantageously navigated with large batteauxs, and from thence upwards by perogues. The Missouri possesses sufficient debth of water as far as is specifyed for boats of 15 tons burthen, but those of smaller capacity are to be prefered.

We view this passage across the Continent as affording immence advantages to the fur trade, but fear that the advantages which it offers as a communication for the productions of the Eeast Indies to the United States and thence to Europe will never be found equal on an extensive scale to that by way of the Cape of Good hope; still we believe that many articles not bulky brittle nor of a very perishable nature may be conveyed to the United States by this rout with more facility and at less expence than by that at present practiced.

The Missouri and all it's branches from the Chyenne upwards abound more in beaver and Common Otter, than any other streams on earth, particularly that proportion of them lying within the Rocky Mountains. The furs of all this immence tract of country including such as may be collected on the upper portion of the River St. Peters, Red river and the Assinniboin with the immence country watered by the Columbia, may be conveyed to the mouth of the Columbia by the 1st of August in each year and from thence be shiped to, and arrive in Canton earlier than the furs at present shiped from Montreal annually arrive in London. The British N. West Company of Canada were they permitted by the United States might also convey their furs collected in the Athabaske, on the Saskashawan, and South and West of Lake Winnipic by that rout within the period before mentioned. Thus the productions [of] nine tenths of the most valuable fur country of America could be conveyed by the rout proposed to the East Indies.

In the infancy of the trade across the continent, or during the period that the trading establishments shall be confined to the Missouri and it's branches, the men employed in this trade will be compelled to convey the furs collected in that quarter as low on the Columbia as tide water, in which case they could not return to the falls of the Missouri untill about the 1st of October, which would be so late in the season that there would be considerable danger of the river being obstructed by ice before they could reach this place and consequently that the comodites brought from the East indies would be detained untill the following spring; but this difficulty will at once vanish when establishments are also made on the Columbia, and a sufficient number of men employed at them to convey annually the productions of the East indies to the upper establishment on the Kooskooske, and there exchange them with the men of the Missouri for their furs, in the begining of July. By this means the furs not only of the Missouri but those also of the Columbia may be shiped to the East indies by the season before mentioned, and the comodities of the East indies arrive at St. Louis or the mouth of the Ohio by the last of September in each year.

Although the Columbia dose not as much as the Missouri abound in beaver and Otter, yet it is by no means despicable in this rispect, and would furnish a valuable fur trade distinct from any other consideration in addition to the otter and beaver which it could furnish. There might be collected considerable quantities of the skins of three speceis of bear affording a great variety of colours and of superior delicacy, those also of the tyger cat, several species of fox, martin and several others of an inferior class of furs, besides the valuable Sea Otter of the coast.

If the government will only aid, even in a very limited manner, the enterprize of her Citizens I am fully convinced that we shal shortly derive the benifits of a most lucrative trade from this source, and that in the course of ten or twelve years a tour across the Continent by the rout mentioned will be undertaken by individuals with as little concern as a voyage across the Atlantic is at present.

The British N. West Company of Canada has for several years, carried on a partial trade with the Minnetares Ahwayhaways and Mandans on the Missouri from their establishments on the Assinniboin at the entrance of Mouse river; at present I have good reason for beleiving that they intend shortly to form an establishment near those nations with a view to engroce the fur trade of the Missouri. The known enterprize and resources of this Company, latterly strengthened by an union with their powerfull rival the X. Y. Company renders them formidable in that distant part of the continent to all other traders; and in my opinion if we are to regard the trade of the Missouri as an object of importance to the United States; the strides of this Company towards the Missouri cannot be too vigilantly watched nor too firmly and speedily opposed by our government. The embarrasments under which the navigation of the Missouri at present labours from the unfriendly dispositions of the Kancez, the several bands of Tetons, Assinniboins and those tribes that resort to the British establishments on the Saskashawan is also a subject which requires the earliest attention of our government. As I shall shortly be with you I have deemed it unnecessary here to detail the several ideas which have presented themselves to my mind on those subjects, more especially when I consider that a thorough knowledge of the geography of the country is absolutely necessary to their being unde[r]stood, and leasure has not yet permitted us to make but one

[322]

general map of the country which I am unwilling to wrisk by the Mail.

As a sketch of the most prominent features of our perigrination since we left the Mandans may not be uninteresting, I shall indeavour to give it to you by way of letter from this place, where I shall necessarily be detained several days in order to settle with and discharge the men who accompanyed me on the voyage as well as to prepare for my rout to the City of Washington.

We left Fort Clatsop where we wintered near the entrance of the Columbia on the 27th of March last, and arrived at the foot of the Rocky mountains on the 10th of May where we were detained untill the 24th of June in consequence of the snow which rendered a passage over the those Mountains impracticable untill that moment; had it not been for this detention I should ere this have joined you at Montichello. In my last communication to you from the Mandans I mentioned my intention of sending back a canoe with a small party from the Rocky Mountains; but on our arrival at the great falls of the Missouri on the 14th of June 1805, in view of that formidable snowey barrier, the discourageing difficulties which we had to encounter in making a portage of eighteen miles of our canoes and baggage around those falls were such that my friend Capt. Clark and myself conceived it inexpedient to reduce the party, lest by doing so we should lessen the ardor of those who remained and thus hazard the fate of the expedition, and therefore declined that measure, thinking it better that the government as well as our friends should for a moment feel some anxiety for our fate than to wrisk so much; experience has since proved the justice of our dicision, for we have more than once owed our lives and the fate of the expedition to our number which consisted of 31 men.

I have brought with me several skins of the Sea Otter,[6] two skins of the native sheep of America, five skins and skelitons complete of the Bighorn or mountain ram, and a skin of the Mule deer beside the skins of several other quadrupeds and birds natives of the countries through which we have passed. I have also preserved a pretty extensive collection of plants, and collected nine other vocabularies.

I have prevailed on the great Cheif of the Mandan nation to accompany me to Washington;[7] he is now with my frind and colligue Capt. Clark at this place, in good health and sperits, and very anxious to proceede.

With rispect to the exertions and services rendered by that esteemable man Capt. William Clark in the course of late voyage I cannot say too much; if sir any credit be due for the success of that arduous enterprize in which we have been mutually engaged, he is equally with myself entitled to your consideration and that of our common country.

The anxiety which I feel in returning once more to the bosom of my friends is a sufficient guarantee that no time will be unnecessarily expended in this quarter.

I have detained the post several hours for the purpose of making you this haisty communication. I hope that while I am pardoned for this detention of the mail, the situation in which I have been compelled to write will sufficiently apologize for having been this laconic.

The rout by which I purpose traveling from hence to Washington is by way of Cahokia, Vincennes, Louisvill Ky., the Crab orchard, Abington, Fincastle, Stanton and Charlottsville. Any letters directed to me at Louisville ten days after the receipt of this will most probably meet me at that place. I am very anxious to learn the state of my friends in Albemarle particularly whether my mother is yet living. I am with every sentiment of esteem Your Obt. and very Humble servent.

MERIWETHER LEWIS Capt.
1st. U.S. Regt. Infty.

N.B. The whole of the party who accompanyed me from the Mandans have returned in good health, which is not, I assure you, to me one of the least pleasing considerations of the Voyage.

M. L.

ALS, RC (DLC); SC (PPAmP). Endorsed; received 24 Oct. 1806. Reply is No. 220. The copy in PPAmP is a draft in Codex S, seemingly written before the arrival of the party in St. Louis. In that copy the day of the month, in the date, appears to have been added later. The first sentence reads, "It is with pleasure that I announce to you the safe arrival of myself and party at this place on the [blank] inst. with our papers and baggage." It is written in a shaky and uneven hand, like No. 206, as if produced on a moving boat. The draft contains many small variations from the present text, but no substantial differences.

1. An anonymous reviewer of the Biddle narrative, in the *Western Gleaner*, 1 (May 1814), 350–75, deplores the choice of route across the mountains. Quoting H. M. Brackenridge's *Views of Louisiana* (Pittsburgh, 1814), he says that a partner of the Missouri Fur Company discovered several passes across the Rockies south of Jefferson's River which were less difficult than those of the Alleghenies. The informant, Andrew Henry, thought that horses or even wagons might pass in six or seven days from a navigable part of the Columbia to a navigable part of the Missouri. "Had the party selected this route," said the reviewer, "one of the principal objects of the expedi-

tion would have been satisfactorily accomplished." This review, signed only "B," may have been written by Brackenridge himself. The *Gleaner* was published by Cramer, Spear and Eichbaum, the house which had issued Brackenridge's *Views* a few weeks earlier.

2. The Clearwater River.

3. The Snake River, called Lewis's River by the explorers.

4. The Willamette River.

5. The Nicholas King map of 1806 shows the Colorado and the "R. des los Apostolos" both flowing into the Gulf of California.

6. *Enhydra lutris lutris* (L.).

7. When Lewis and his party left St. Louis in October, en route to Washington, the group included Clark, York, Ordway, Francis Labiche, Pierre Chouteau and a delegation of Osage chiefs under his direction, the Mandan chief Sheheke and his wife and son, and interpreter René Jusseaume with his wife and two children. The group may also have included Pierre Provenchere, of St. Louis; he was present at a Washington dinner in Lewis's honor in Jan. 1807. Apparently the party did not travel together. Lewis passed through Frankfort, Ky., in mid-November while Chouteau shepherded his Indians through Lexington and arrived in Washington first. According to the diary of Augustus John Foster (Foster Papers, DLC), Lewis reached Washington on the evening of 28 Dec. Entries in the records of the General Accounting Office support the presence of Ordway and Labiche. There is a notice of $112.00 due to Ordway, "being the amount of his account for a Horse, Saddle, Bridle &c. employed in the public Service from St. Louis to Washington City under the direction of Capt. Meriwr. Lewis" (DNA, RG 217, Report Book E, 142). An entry on p. 146 of the same document records the sum of $49.00 due him for pay as an assistant to Lewis in escorting the Mandans and pack horses from 11 Oct. 1806 to 19 Jan. 1807. An entry on p. 150 reports $23.50 due to Labiche for pay as an assistant, interpreter, and pack horseman from 21 Oct. to 20 Jan.

Jefferson welcomed Sheheke in a speech dated 30 Dec. and the Osages in another dated 31 Dec. (DLC). Except for a few particulars, these messages were adapted from earlier ones; no doubt Sheheke could have observed that the words of the Great Father were very similar to those he had sent up the river to the Mandans earlier in the year. The long effort to get Sheheke and his family back to his village is chronicled in later letters. The date of his death is cited in F. A. Chardon's journal as 7 Jan. 1832 (CHARDON, 20). For biographical sketches, see JAMES (4), 248n, and *North Dakota Historical Collections,* 2:470.

208. Clark to [George Rogers Clark?]

Dear Brother   St. Louis 23rd September 1806

We arrived at this place at 12 oClock today[1] from the Pacific Ocian where we remained dureing the last winter near the entrance of the Columbia river. This station we left on the 27th of March last and should have reached St. Louis early in August had we not been detained by the snow which bared our passage across the Rocky Mountains untill the 24th of June. In returning through those mountains we devided ourselves into several parties, disgressing from the rout by which we went out in order the more effectually to explore the Country and discover the most practicable rout which does exist across the Continent by way of the Missouri and Columbia rivers, in this we were completely successfull and have therefore no hesitation in declaring that such as nature has permited it we have discovered the best rout which does exist across the continent of North America in that direction. Such is that, by way of the Missouri to the foot of the rapids below the great falls of that river a distance of 2575 miles thence by land passing the Rocky Mountains to a navagable part of the Kooskooske 340. and with the Kooskooske 73 miles Lewis's river 154 miles and the Columbia 413 miles to the Pacific Ocian makeing the total distance from the confluence of the Missouri and Mississippi to the discharge of the Columbia into the Pacific Ocian 3555 miles. The navegation of the Missouri may be deemed good; it's dificulties arise from it's falling banks, timber embeded in the mud of it's channel, it's sand-bars and steady rapidity of it's current all which may be over come with a great degree of certainty by useing the necessary precauitions. The passage by land of 340 miles from the Falls of the Missouri to the Kooskooske is the most formadable part of the tract proposed across the continent. Of this distance 200 miles is along a good road, and 140 miles over tremendious Mountains which for 60 miles are covered with eternal snows. A passage over those mountains is however practicable from the latter part of June to the last of September and the cheap rate at which horses are to be obtained from the Indians of the Rocky Mountains and west of them reduce the expences of transportation over this portage to a mere trifle. The navagation of the Kooskooske Lewis's river and the Columbia is safe and good from the 1st of April to the middle of August by makeing these portages on the latter river. The first of which in decending is 1200 paces at the Falls of the Columbia 261 miles up that river, the second of 2 miles at the long narrows 6 miles below the falls and a third also of 2 miles at the Great Rapids 65 miles still lower down. The tide flows up the Columbia 183 miles and within 7 miles of the great rapids. Large Sloops may with safty ascend as high as tide water and Vessels of 300 Tons burthen reach the entrance of the Multnomah River a large Southern branch of the Columbia which takes it's rise on the confines of New Mexico with the Callarado and Apostles rivers dischargeing itself into the Columbia 125 miles from it's entrance into the Pacific Ocian. I consider this tract across the continant of

[326]

emence advantage to the fur trade, as all the furs collected in 9/10ths of the most valuable furr country in America may be conveyed to the mouth of the Columbia and shiped from thence to East indias by the 1st of august in each year, and will of course reach Canton earlier than the furs which are annually exported from Montrall arive in Great Britain.

In our outward bound voyage we ascended to the foot of the rapids below the great falls of the Missouri where we arived on the 14th of June 1805. Not haveing met with any of the nativs of the Rocky Mountains we were of course ignorant of the passes by land which existed through those mountains to the Columbia river, and had we even known the rout we were destitute of horses which would have been indispensibly necessary to enable us to transport the requisit quantity of amunition and other stores to ensure the success of the remaining part of our voyage down the Columbia; we therefore deturmined to navigate the Missouri as far as it was practicable, or unless we met with some of the nativs from whom we could obtain horses and information of the Country. Accordingly we undertook a most laborious portage at the falls of the Missouri of 18 miles which we effected with our Canoes and baggage by the 3rd of July. From hence ascending the Missouri we penetrated the Rocky Mountain at the distance of 71 miles above the upper part of the portage and penetrated as far as the three forks of that river a distance of 181 miles further; here the Missouri devides into three nearly equal branches at the Same point. The two largest branches are so nearly of the same dignity that we did not conceive that either of them could with propriety retain the name of the Missouri and therefore called these three streems Jefferson's Madisons and Gallitin's rivers. The confluence of those rivers is 2848 miles from the mouth of the Missouri by the meanders of that river. We arived at the three forks of the Missouri the 27th of July. Not haveing yet been so fortunate as to meet with the nativs altho' I had previously made several excurtions for that purpose, we were compelled still to continue our rout by water. The most northerly of the three forks, that to which we had given the name of Jeffersons river was deemed the most proper for our purpose and we accordingly ascended it 248 miles to the upper forks and it's extreem navigable point, makeing the total distance to which we had navigated the waters of the Missouri 3096 miles of which 429 lay within the Rocky Mountains. On the morning of the 17th of August 1805 I arrived at the forks of Jeffersons river where I met Capt. Lewis who had previously penitrated with a party of three men to

the waters of the Columbia discovered a band of the Shoshone Nation
and had found means to induce thirty five of their chiefs and
warriors to accompany him to that place. From these people we
learned that the river on which they resided was not navagable and
that a passage through the mountains in that direction was impracticable; being unwilling to confide in the unfavorable account of the
natives it was concerted between Capt. Lewis and myself that one
of us should go forward immediately with a small party and explore
the river while the other in the intirem would lay up the Canoes at
that place and engage the nativs with their horses to assist in
transporting our stores and baggage to their camp. Accordingly I
set out the next day passed the deviding mountains between the
waters of the Missouri and Columbia and decended the river which
I since call the East fork of Lewis's river about 70 miles. Finding that
the Indians account of the country in the direction of this river
was correct I returned and joined Capt. Lewis on the 29th of
August at the Shoshone camp excessively fatigued as you may suppose,
haveing passed mountains almost inexcessable and compelled to
subsist on berries dureing the greater part of my rout. We now
purchased 27 horses of these indians and hired a guide who assured
us that he could in 15 days take us to a large river in an open
country west of these mountains by a rout some Distance to the
North of the river on which they lived, and that by which the
nativs west of the mountains visited the plains of the Missouri for
the purpose of hunting the buffalow. Every preperation being made
we set forward with our guide on the 31st of August through those
tremendious mountains, in which we continued untill the 22nd of
September before we reached the lower country beyond them; on
our way we met with the Ootelachshoot a band of the Tuchapahs[2]
from whome we obtained axcession of seven horses and exchanged
eight or ten others. This proved of infinite service to us as we
were compelled to subsist on horse beef about Eight days before we
reached the Kooskooske. Dureing our passage over those mountains
we suffered every thing which hunger cold and fatigue could impose;
nor did our difficulties with respect to provision cease on our arival
at the Kooskooske for although the Pallotepallors[3] a noumerous
nation inhabiting that country were extremely hospitable and for
a fiew trifling articles furnished us with an abundance of roots and
dryed salmon the food to which they were accustomed we found that
we could not subsist on those articles and almost all of us grew sick
on eating them. We were obliged therefore to have recourse to the
flesh of horses and dogs as food to supply the dificiency of our guns

which produced but little meat as game was scarce in the vicinity of our camp on the Kooskooske where we were compelled to remain in order to construct our perogues to decend the river. At this season the salmon are m[e]agre and form but indifferent food. While we remained here I was my self sick for several days and my friend Capt. Lewis suffered a serious indesposition. Haveing completed four Perogues and a small canoe we gave our horses in charge to the Pallotepallors untill we returned and on the 7th of October reimbarked for the Pacific Ocian. We decended by the rout I have already mentioned. The water of the river being low at this season we experienced much dificuelty in decending, we found it obstructed by a great number of dificuelt and dangerous rapids in passing of which our perogues several times filled and the men escaped narrowly with there lives. However the dificuelty does not exist in high water which happens within the period which I have previously mentioned. We found the nativs extreemly noumerous and generally friendly though we have on several occasions owed our lives and the fate of the expedition to our number which consisted of 31 men. On the 17th of November we reached the Ocian where various considerations induced us to spend the winter. We therefore searched for an eligible situation for that purpose and selected a spot on the South side of a little river called by the nativs the *Netul*[4] which discharges itself at a small bar on the South Side of the Columbia and 14 miles within point Adams. Here we constructed some log houses and defended them with a common stockade work; this place we called Fort Clatsop after a nation of that name who were our nearest neighbours. In this country we found an abundance of Elk on which we subsisted principally during the last winter. We left Fort Clatsop on the 27th of March. On our homeward bound voyage being much better acquainted with the Country we were enabled to take such precautions as in a great measure secured us from the want of provision at any time, and greatly lessoned our fatiegues, when compared with those to which we were compelled to submit, in our Outward bound journey. We have not lost a man since we left the Mandans a circumstance which I assure you is a pleasing consideration to me. As I shall shortly be with you and the post is now waiting I deem it unnecessary here to attempt minutely to detail the Occurencies of the last 18 month. I am &c. Yr. affectunate brother,

WM. CLARK

ALS, RC (KyLoF). Historians have always supposed that this letter was addressed to George Rogers Clark. When it first appeared in the Frankfort,

Ky., *Palladium* for 9 Oct. 1806, an editorial note explained: "By the mail of this morning we have received from an obliging friend, the following letter from captain Clark to his brother gen. Clark, near Louisville. Captain Clark did not, perhaps, intend it for publication; but to gratify, in some measure, the impatient wishes of his countrymen, the general was prevailed upon to permit its appearance in our paper of to-day." Indeed, the editor could have been referring to George Rogers Clark, who was living at Clarksville, Indiana Territory, across the river from Louisville; but he may also have meant another brother, Jonathan, who also was a general and who also was living near Louisville. When William had wished to send important papers home from Fort Mandan in April 1805, it was to Jonathan that he sent them, not to George Rogers. The question is academic, anyway, because the letter was written for publication; its nominal addressee did not matter.

The initial fame of the expedition rests largely upon this communication, which spread throughout the country as rapidly as the means of the day would allow. The only publication in Louisville at this time, the *Farmers Library, or Ohio Intelligencer,* was not a regular newspaper; the nearest newspaper was in Frankfort, where the *Palladium* and *Western World* were being produced in the same shop but under different ownership. The *Western World* ran the letter 11 Oct., together with an account from a St. Louis correspondent describing the arrival of the expedition; the Pittsburgh *Gazette* ran the letter 28 Oct., the *National Intelligencer* 3 Nov., and soon it had been reprinted scores of times. I comment on the purpose of the letter, and its origin, in a note under the next item, No. 209.

1. The phrase "at 12 oClock today" appears to have been written over an erasure.

2. The Tushepaws of Lewis and Clark may have been Kutenai. See HODGE, 1:740.

3. The Palouse, a tribe related to the Nez Percé Indians, which Lewis and Clark found on the Clearwater in Idaho.

4. The Lewis and Clark River.

209. Lewis's Draft of the Clark Letter

Dear brother,   St. Louis September 24[1] 1806

We arrived at this place on the 23 inst. from the pacific Ocean where we remained during the last winter near the entrance of the Columbia river. This station we left on the 23rd [2] of March last and should have reached St. Louis early in August had we not been detained by the snow which bared our passage across the Rocky mountains untill the 24th of June. In returning through those mountains we divided ourselves into several parties, digressing from the rout by which we went out in order the more effectually to explore <*the* [. . .] *connections of the principal branches of the Missouri and Columbia Rivers*> the country and discover the most

[330]

practicable rout which dose exist across the continent by way of the Missouri and Columbia rivers. In this we were completely successfull and have therefore no hesitation in declaring that such as nature has permited it we have discovered the best rout which dose exist across the Continent of North America in that direction. Such is that by way of the Missouri to the foot of the rapids below the great falls of that <*Missouri*> River a distance of 2575 miles thence by land passing the Rocky Mountains to a navigable part of the Kooskee 340. and with the Kooskooskee 73 miles Lewis's river 154 miles and the Columbia 413 miles to the Pacific Ocean making the total distance from the confluence of the Missouri and Mississippi to the discharge of the columbia into the Pacific Ocean 3555. miles. The navigation of the Missouri may be deemed good; it's difficulties arise from it's falling banks, timber embeded in the mud of it's channel, it's sandbars and steady rapidity of it's current all which may be overcome with a great degree of certainty by using the necessary precautions. The passage by land of 340 miles from the Missouri to the Kooskooske is the most formidable part of the tract proposed across the continent. Of this distance 200 miles is along a good road, and 140 over tremendious mountains which for 60 miles are covered with eternal snows. A passage over these mountains is however practicable from the latter part of June to the last of September and the cheep rate at which horses are to be obtained from the indians of the Rocky mountains and west of them reduces the expences of transportation over this portage to a mere trifle. The navigation of the Kooskooske Lewis's R. and the Columbia is safe and good from the 1st of april to the middle of August <*with the exception of*> by making 3 portages on the latter river. The first of which in decending is <*one of*> 1200 paces at the falls of the Columbia, 261 mil[e]s up that river, the second of 2 miles at the long narrows 6 miles below the falls and a third also of 2 ms. at the great rapids 65 miles still lower down. The tide flows up the Columbia 183 miles and within 7 miles of the great rapids. Large sloops may with safety ascend as high as tide water and vessels of 300 tons burthen may reach the entrance of the Multnomah R. a large Southern branch of the Columbia which taking it's rise on the confines of Mexico with the Callarado and Apostles rivers discharges itself into the Columbia 125 miles from it's mouth. I consider this tract across the continent of imence advantage to the fur trade, as all the furs collected in <*much the largest*> <*¾ths*> 9/10ths of the most valuable fur country in America may be conveyed to the mouth of the Columbia and shiped from thence

[331]

to the East Indies by the 1st of August in each year. And will of course reach Canton earlyer than the furs which are annually exported from Montreal arrive in great Britain.

In our outward bound <passage> voyage we ascended to the foot of the rapids below the great falls of the Missouri, <here we made> where we arrived on the 14th of June 1805. <Here we made a portage> Not having met with any of the natives <from whom we could learn the> of the Rocky mountains we were of course ignorant of the passes by land which existed through that <rocky Mountains> country to the Columbia River, and had we even known the rout we were destitute of horses which would have been indispensibly necessary to enable us to transport the requisite quantity of amunition and other stores to ensure the success of the remaining part of our voyage down the Columbia; we therefore determined to navigate the Missouri as far as it was practicable or untill we met with some of the natives from whom we could obtain horses and information of the country. Accordingly we undertook a most laborious <and [. . .]> portage at the falls of the Missouri of 18 miles which we effected with our canoes and baggage by the 3rd of july. From hence ascending the Missouri we <entered> penetrated the Rocky mountains at the distance of 71³ miles above the upper part of the portage and penetrated as far as the three forks of that river a distance of 181 miles further; here the Missouri divides itself into three nearly equal branches at the same point. The two <of them> largest branches are so nearly of the same dignity that we did not conceive that either of them could with propryety retain the Name of the Missouri and therefore called the three streams Jefferson's Madisons and Gallitin's rivers. The confluence of these rivers is 2848 miles from the mouth of the Missouri by the meanders of that river. We arrived at the 3 forks of the Missouri 27th of July. Not having yet been so fortunate as to meet with the natives although I had previously made several excurtions for that purpose, we were compelled still to continue our rout by water. The most Northwardly of the three forks, that to which we had given the name of Jefferson's river was deemed the most proper for our purposes and we accordingly ascended <248 miles> it 248 miles to the upper forks and it's extreem navigable point; <being 248 miles> making the total distance to which we had navigated the waters of the Missouri 3096 miles of which 429 lay within the Rocky Mountains. On the morning of the 17th of August 1805 I arrived at the forks of Jefferson's river where I met Capt. Lewis who had previously penitrated with a party of three men to the waters of the columbia <and had brought with him> discovered a band of the Shoshones and had found means to induce thirty five of their chiefs and warriors to accompany him to that place. From these people we learned that the river on which they resided was not navigable and that a passage through the Mountains in <the> that direction <of that river> was impracticable; <however> being unwilling to confide in this unfavourable account of the natives it was conscerted between Capt. Lewis and myself that I should go forward immediately with a small party and explore the river while he in the interim would lay up the canoes at that place and engage the natives with their horses to assist in transporting our stores and baggage to their camp <on the East fork of Lewis's river.> Accordingly I set out the next day passed the dividing mountain between the waters of the Missouri and Columbia and decended the river which I have since called the East fork of Lewis's R. about 70 miles. Finding that the Indian account of the country in the derection of this river was correct I returned and joined Capt. Lewis on the 29th of August at the Shoshone Camp excessively fatiegued having been compelled to subsist <principally> on berries during the greater part of my rout. We now purchased 27 horses of these indians and hired a guide who assured us that he could in 15 days take us to a large river in an open country west of these mountains by a rout some distance to the North of the river on which they lived and that by which the nations west of the Mountains visited the plains of the Missouri for the purpose of hunting buffaloe. <All necessary> Every preparation being made we set forward with our guide on the 31st of <September> August[4] through those tremendious mountains, in which we continued untill the 22nd of September before we reached the level country beyond them; on our way we met with the Ootslashshoot a band of the Tushepahs from whom we obtained an accession of seven horses and exchanged eight or ten others this proved of infinite service to us as we were compelled to <kill> subsist on horse beef about eight days before we reached the Kooskooskie. During our passage over these mountains we suffered every thing which hunger cold and fatigue could impose; nor did our difficulties with rispect to provision cease on our arrival at the Kooskooske for although the Pallotepailers a numerous nation inhabiting that country were extremly hospitable and for a few trifling articles furnished us with an abundance of roots and dryed salmon the food to which they were accustomed we found that we could not subsist on <it> those articles and almost all of us grew sick on eating them. We were obliged therefore to have recourse to the flesh of horses and dogs as food to supply the deficiency of our guns which produced but little meat as game was scarce in the vicinity of our camp on the Kooskooske where we were compelled to remain in order to construct our perogues to decend the river. At this season the salmon are me[a]gre and form but indifferent food. While we remained here I was myself sick for several days and my friend Capt. Lewis suffered a severe indisposition. Having completed 4 large perogues and a small canoe we <left> gave our horses in charge <of> to the Pallotepallers untill we returned and on the 7 of <September> Octr.⁵ reimbarked for the Pacific Ocean. We decended by the rout which I have already mentioned. The water of the rivers being low at this season we experienced much difficulty in decending, we found them obstructed by a great number of difficult and dangerous rapids in passing of which our perogues several times filled and the men escaped narrowly with their lives. However this difficulty dose not exist in high water which happens within the period which I have previously mentioned. <On the 14th of November we reached the ocean.> We found the natives extreemly numerous and generally <respect-> friendly though we have <in more than> on several occasions owed our lives and the fate of the expedicion to <the strength of> our number which consisted of 31 men. On the <14th> 17th⁶ of November we reached the Ocean where various considerations induced us to spend the winter we therefore surched for an eligible situation for that purpose and <found> scelected a spot on the S. side of a little river called by the <Clatsops and> natives the Netul <river> which discharges itself into a small bay on the S.E. side of the Columbia and[?] 14 miles within point Adams. Here we <fortifyed ourselves and built comfortable quarters> constructed some log houses and defended them with a common stoccade work; this place we <named after> called Fort Clatsop after <our near nei> a nation of that name who were our nearest neighbours. In this country we found an abundance of Elk on which we subsisted principally during the last winter. *On our homeward bound voyage being much better acquainted with the country we were enabled to take such precautions as have in a great measure secured us from the want of provision at any time, and greatly lessened our fatiegues when compared with those to which we were compelled to submit in our outward bound Journey. *We left Fort Clatsop on the 23th of March.⁷ We have not lost a man since we left the Mandans a circumstance which I assure you is a pleasing consideration to me. As I shall shortly be with you I deem it unnecessary to <be minute>

[334]

here to <*detail*> attempt minutely <*every*> to detail the occurances of the last eighteen months. Adieu &c.

AL, SC (MoSHi). In Lewis's hand, although drafted as if written by Clark. Clark wrote on the back:

> on our return Seperated at Travellers rest
> a breif account of our rout
> the Country abounding in Beaver &c.
> The great numbers of Indians & their conduct
> Productions of the Country
> open plains to Rocky Mts.

Lewis and Clark were well aware that publication of letters from the frontiers was a common journalistic practice. Some of the letters they had sent down from Fort Mandan in 1805 were surely intended for public consumption. In descending the lower reaches of the Missouri, at the end of their voyage, they could not have failed to learn—from men such as Robert McClellan and John McClallen, whom they met on the river—that those Fort Mandan letters had been widely circulated. Now they were confronted by a problem which, between two men of lesser stature, might have been a delicate one. Clark's talents as a prose stylist were limited, yet his letters home to Kentucky would reach the newspapers long before Lewis's, since Lewis's mail would have to go all the way to Virginia. As usual, they did the practical thing. Lewis wrote Clark's letter for him; Clark copied it and sent it off to Jonathan or George Rogers Clark for transmission to the press.

1. This date, and the "23" in the next line, appear to have been written in at a different time—possibly by Clark. I have no foolproof explanation of why this draft is dated a day later than Clark's fair copy.

2. Altered from "27th" by Lewis. But in his own copy, Clark restored the original date.

3. This number and "181" in the same sentence are corrected figures; the original figures are illegible.

4. A correction in Clark's hand. He must have made the change while copying the letter, for in his own version he started to write "September," then noticed the error and changed the word to "August."

5. A correction apparently in Clark's hand.

6. A correction apparently in Clark's hand.

7. The asterisks at the beginning of this sentence and the preceding one indicate that Lewis or Clark intended the sentences to be transposed.

210. Lewis to an Unknown Correspondent

Sketch of Captn. Lewis's Voyage to the Pacific Ocean by the Missesourii & Columbia Rivers from the States of America

Dear Sir,

Annexed is the sketch I mentioned to you in my last of the 7th inst. I will give it you verbatim.

Cahokia 14th Oct. 1806

Dear Sir,   St. Louis 29th Sept. 1806

I arrived here the 23rd instant from the Pacific Ocean where I remained during the last winter, near the entrance of the Columbia River—This Station we left the 23rd March last and should have reached St. Louis early in August had we not been detained by the snows which buried the passage of the Rocky Mountains until the 26th June, even at this late season, strange as it may appear to an inhabitant of the southern States, we were compelled to travel over snows from 4 to 6 feet for the distance of 60 miles—In returning thro' the Rocky Mountains, we divided ourselves into several parties digressing from the Route by which we went out with a view more effectually to explore the Country, and discover the most practicable Route which existed across the continent by way of the Missesouris & Columbia Rivers: in this we have been completely successful. Therefore have no hesitation to say & declare, that such as Nature has permitted we have discovered the most practicable Route which does exist across the Continent of North America in that direction; such is that by way of the Missesourii to the foot of the Rapids below the great Falls of that River a distance of 2575 miles, thence by land passing the Rocky Mountains to a navigable part of the Kooskooskee 320 M. & the Kooskooskee 73 M. Lewis River 152 M. & the Columbia 413 M. to the Pacific Ocean making the total Distance from the confluence of the Missesourii & Mississippi to the discharge of the Columbia into the Pacific Ocean 3555 miles.—The navigation of the Missesourii may be deemed good, it's difficulties arise from it's falling Banks, Timbers imbedded in the Mud of it's channels, it's sand Bars, & steady rapidity of it's Current, all which may be overcome with a great degree of certainty by taking the necessary precautions—The Passage of 320 M. from the Missesourii to the Kooskooskee is the most formidable part of the Track proposed across the Continent, of this distance 200 M. is along a good Road and 140 M. over tremendous Mountains, which for 60 miles are covered with eternal Snows; however a passage over those Mountains is practicable from the latter part of June to the last of September. The cheap rate at which Horses are to be obtained from the Indians of the Rocky Mountains & west of them, reduces the Expences of Transportation over this Passage to a mere Trifle. The Navigation of the Kooskooskee, Louise Rivers & Columbia safe and good from the 9th April to the middle of August, by making three Portages in the Columbia; the first of which in descending that River is of 1200

Paces at the Falls of that River 261 Miles from the Ocean. The second of 2 miles at the long Narrows, 6 M. below the Falls, the third also of 2 Miles 65 Miles still lower down. The Tides flow up the Columbia 183 Miles, thus far large Sloops might ascend in safety & vessels of 300 Tons could with equal safety reach the Entrance of Multnomack River, a large southern Branch of the Columbia, which taking it's rise on the confines of Mexico with the Collarado & Apostles River discharges itself into the Columbia 25 M. from it's Mouth.—I consider this Track across the Continent as presenting immense advantages to the Fur Trade—as all the Furs collected in 9/10 of the valuable Fur Country of America may be conveyed to the Mouth of the Columbia & shipped from thence for the East Indies by the 1st of August in each year, & will of course reach Canton earlier than the Furs which are annually exported from Montreal reach Great Britain.

In our outward bound Voyage we ascended the Missesourii to the Foot of the Rapids 5 Miles below the great Falls, where we arrived the 14th June 1805 not having then met with any of the Natives of the Rocky Mountains, we were of course ignorant of the passes by Land across these Mountains, & even had we known them, we were destitute of Horses; which were absolutely necessary to enable us to transport the requisite quantity of ammunition & other stores to insure the success of the remaining part of the Voyage down the Columbia, we therefore determined to navigate the Missesourii as far as it was practicable, or until we met some of the Natives from whom we could obtain Horses & the requisite Information with respect to the Country; accordingly we undertook a most laborious Portage of our Canoes & Baggage, around the Falls of the Missesourii of 16 Miles which we finally effected the 3rd July, from hence ascending the Missesourii, we entered the Rocky Mountains at the distance of 71 Miles farther, here the Missesourii divides itself into 3 nearly equal Branches. At the same point, the two largest Branches are so nearly of the same dignity that we did not conceive that either of them could with propriety retain the name of Missesourii, & therefore we called them, Jefferson's, Maddison's & Gallatin's Rivers; the confluence of these Rivers may properly be deemed the Head of that majestic River the Missesourii & to it's Forks is 2848 Miles from it's Junction with the Mississippi. We arrived at the Head of the Missesourii the 27 July 1805 not having yet been so fortunate as to meet with the Natives altho' Capt. Clark had previously made several excursions since we had entered the Mountains for that Purpose—We were compelled still to continue our Route by water. The most northward of the 3 Forks, that which we had given the name Jefferson's River was deemed the most proper for our purpose accordingly we ascended it 248 Miles to it's upper Forks, being it's extreme navigable Point making the distance to which we had navigated the waters of the Missesourii 3096 Miles of which 429 lay within the Mountains. On the evening of 16th August at the upper Forks of Jefferson's River having previously with a Party of 3 men ascended the main Fork of Jefferson's River to it's extreme Fountain, passed the Rocky Mountains to the Natives of the Columbia, discovered a Band of Shoshones, who were in Possession of an abundance of Horses, & found means to prevail on 34 of their principal Chiefs & Warriors to accompany me to that place; here I was joined early in the morning of the 17th by Capt. Clark & Party with our Canoes & Baggage. From the Natives we now learned that the River on which they reside was not navigable, & that a Passage thro' the Mountains in that direction was impracticable; being unwilling to confide implicitly in this unfavourable account of the Natives, it was concerted between Capt. Clark & myself that he should go forward immediately with a small party and explore the River, while I in the interim would lay up the Canoes at that place & engage the Shoshones with their Horses to assist in transporting our Baggage over the Mountains to their Camp, a distance of 45 Miles, accordingly he set out early next morning, passed the dividing Mountains between the waters of the Missesourii & Columbia Rivers, & descended that Branch of the little River about 70 Miles; finding the indian account of the Country in the direction of that River correct, he returned & joined me at the Shoshones Camp on the 27th August excessively fatigued, having been compelled to subsist on Berries during the greater part of his Route; we now purchased 27 Horses of these Indians, and engaged a Guide to conduct us. The Guide informed us he would in 15 days take us to a large River in an open level Country, west of these Mountains by a Route some distance to the north of the River on which they lived & that by which the Natives west of the Mountains visited the Plains of the Missesourii for the purpose of hunting the Buffalo, pleased with this Information, after doubting from our observations as well as the corroborating testimony of many Indians that a passage was practicable thro' those Mountains to the west, we hastened the preparations for our departure & set forward with our Guide 31st August depending principally for subsistance on our pack Horses already heavily laden with Ammunition & other Stores necessary to the successful prosecution of our voyage beyond the Montains, which of course we should have been compelled to deposit as we killed the Horses that transported them. Thus situated we attempted with success those unknown formidable snow clad Mountains on the bare word of a Savage, while 99/100th of his Countrymen assured us that a passage was impracticable, most fortunately on our way within the Mountains we met with a travelling Band of the Tushopahs going to the Plains of the Missesourii in quest of Buffaloe & obtained from them an accession of 7 Horses to our former Stock exchanging at the same time 10 or 12 to great advantage; this ultimately proved of infinite Service to us as we were compelled to subsist on Horse Beef & Dogs previous to our arrival in the navigable [part?] of the Kooskooskee. I have not leisure at this moment to state all those difficulties which we encountered in our Passage over these Mountains—suffice it to say we suffered everything Cold, Hunger & Fatigue could impart, or the Keenest Anxiety excited for the fate of Expedition in which our whole Souls were embarked. Our difficulties with respect to Provisions did not cease on our arrival at the Kooskooskee 24th Sept. 1805 altho' the Pallotepalless a numerous People enhabiting that Country, extremely friendly & for a few paltry articles furnished us with an abundance of Provisions such as they were accustomed to themselves, consisting of dried Salmon & Roots; we found in experiment that we could not subsist on it, and grew sick on eating those Articles & we were obliged to have recourse to the Flesh of Horses, Dogs & to supply the deficiency of our Guns, which produced but little meat as Game was scarce in the vicinity of our Camp on the Kooskooskee, where we were compelled to remain in order to construct Pirogues for the purpose of descending the River. At this season the Salmon altho' abundant are so meagre that they are unfit for use in great measure—During our residence at this compound we were all Sick—for my own part I suffered a severe Indisposition for 10 or 12 days, thus sick feeble & emaciated, we commenced & continued the operation of building four large Pirogues & a small Canoe, which we finally completed on the 6th October— The next day we delivered our Horses in charge to the Pallotepalless until our Return, & embarked ourselves & Baggage aboard our Pirogues & Canoe for the Pacific Ocean, descending by that Route already mentioned; the water of the River being low at this season we experienced much difficulty in descending—we found the Channels obstructed by a great number of dangerous rapids in passing across which our Pirogues several times foundered on the Rocks the Crew narrowly escaped with their Lives; this difficulty however does not exist in the high Water which happens within the Period previously mentioned; in this State the Current is not so great as that of the Missesourii in the Spring Tides—On this portion of our Route we found the Natives extremely numerous & generally friendly, tho' we have on several occasions owed our Lives & consequently the final success of the Expedition to our Number which consisted of 31 Men—On the 17th November we reached the Pacific Ocean where various considerations induced us to spend the last Winter; we therefore searched for an eligible situation for that purpose & slected a Spit on the south Shore of a little River called by the Natives Netit which discharges itself into a small Bay S.E. side of the Columbia 14 miles within point Adams. Here we constructed some Log Houses & defended them by a common Stockade Work, this Place we called Fort Clatsop after a Nation of that Name, who were our nearest neighbors, it is 7 miles distant from the Ocean on a direct Line, & 3 Miles from the discharge of the Netit near Fort Clatsop—We found an abundance of Elk on which we subsisted principally during the Winter at the Ocean. We made a sufficient quantity of Salt to supply our wants until our return to our deposit of that Article on the Missesourii—During our residence at this place we saw no trading vessels, but we had abundant Proofs there are 11 or 12 vessels which annually enter the River for the purpose of trading with the Natives.—These people gave us the Names of 12 Commanders of Vessels 11 of whom they informed us, visited them once & sometimes twice a year all these names are English or American as Haley, More, Davidsons. The Natives never attempted to speak the Language of any other civilized Nation except that of the English—many words of which they pronounce distinctly—I believe these Traders to be for the most part Americans, if not exclusively so—We learned nothing of the state of the Settlement of Nootka Sound. On our homeward bound Journey, being much better acquainted with the Country we were enabled to take such precautions as did in a great Measure secure us from the want of Provisions, & lessens our fatigues infinitely when compared to those to which we were exposed when we went out—Within the Rocky Mountains Capt. Clark & myself separated, he travelled in the first Instance to the Forts [forks] of Jefferson's River where we had laid up the Canoes in August 1805, & myself directly to the Falls of Missesourii, both without Guides & by Routes which we had never previously travelled & yet we both succeeded beyond our Expectations & reached our place of destination without any difficulty of consequence—Capt. Clark having descended Jefferson's River to it's confluence with Maddison's & Gallatin's Rivers dispatched the Canoes with a Party under the command of Serjeant John Otway [Ordway] to the entrance of the River Maria a large northern branch of the Missesourii which taking it's rise in the Rocky Mountains adjacent to the Saskatchewan River, discharges itself [   ] Miles below the Falls of the Missessourii, to the Yellowstone River a distance of 48 Miles, where that River issues from the Mountains, & from whence it is navigable to the Missesourii 817 Miles, not finding Timber in the Yellowstone River of sufficient Size to construct Canoes—Capt. Clark & Party travelled down it by land 115 Miles when finding Timber proper for his purpose he built 2 small Canoes & descended without difficulty to the Missessourii from the point at which Capt. Clark constructed those Canoes.—He dispatched Serjeant Nat Pryer with 3 men & Horses by Land to the Mandans in order to carry into execution certain arrangements which we had made in relation to Sicoux's but unfortunately the second evening after Serjeant Pryer had separated from Capt. Clark on the 25 July last the Natives stole his Horses & he was compelled to return with his small Party to the Yellowstone River where he formed Canoes of Skins of Buffaloes, descended the River & overtook Capt. Clark on the Missesourii the 8th August.—In the meantime I had passed with the remainder of the party to the upper part of the Portage near the great Falls of the Missesourii & explored the Medicine River from the Rocky Mountains to it's discharge in the Missesourii on the north side near that place.

I had now in conformity to my plan to undertake another enterprise which was to explore the River Maria completely with a view to establish, provided it so existed that some of it's Branches extended so far north as Lat 49° 37′ N on the same parallel of Lat with the N W extremity of the Lake of the Woods. The entrance of the River Maria I had previously ascertained to be 27° 25′ 17″ N & from the rise of that River as well as the direction it first takes, there were good grounds to hope that it extended to Lat 49° 37′ N believing it of the highest national importance as it respects our Treaty of 1783 with Great Britain. To establish that, I determined to execute it at every hazard & for that purpose I had brought with me a set of excellent Horses from the Plains of the Columbia west of the Rocky Mountains—I was well apprised that the Country thro' which it became necessary for me to pass was inhabited by several large & roving Bands of the Minnitares & Black Foot Indians, who trade at the British Settlements on the Saskoohawan, & from whom should I meet them I could have but little to hope from their friendship— unfortunately for me on the 11 July the day of my arrival at the

[341]

upper part of the Portage on Missesourii, the Indians, believed to be the Tushopahs stole 7 of my best Horses, this accident compelled me not only to take my Route to the River Maria on inferior Horses, but also to reduce my Escort from 6 to 3 only—having left Serjeant Pat Glass [Gass] with 5 Men & 4 Horses at the Portage to make necessary preparations in order to facilitate the transportation of the Canoes & Baggage overland when they should arrive—I selected Geo Droulliard, Ruben & Jos Fields to accompany me, these were three of the most active resolute young Men which I had & the best marksmen—with these Men I quitted my Station at the Portage of the Missesourii on the 17th July & explored, with all it's Branches to the Rocky Mountains, being fully satisfied that no branch of this River extended so far North as Lat. 49. 37—I set out on my return on the 20th of the same Month met with a party of Minnitaries, these people appeared extremely friendly on our first interview & insisted on remaining with us all that night to which I consented. Early in the morning of the 27th they treacherously seized on & made themselves masters of all our Guns—in which Situation we engaged them with our Knives & our Pistol recovered our Guns & killed 2 of them & put the others to flight, pursued them retook our Horses, excepting 2 which they had attempted to carry off & took from them 15 Horses, a Gun and Several Bows & Quivers of Arrows, Shields & all their Baggage—fearing pursuit from 2 large Bands whom the Indians had informed us on the evening before were in our neighborhood, we hastened to the confluence of the Rivers Maria & Missesourii where I had appointed the Canoes & Party to meet me—at 8 o'clock on the 28th I arrived on the Bank of the Missesourii about 15 Miles above it's Junction with the River Maria & met accidently with the Canoes & Party descending. I now dismissed my Horses & embarked having travelled from 6 o'clock in the morning of the 27th to the time I met the Canoes 142 Miles—We now continued our Route down the Missesourii without interruption or material accident until the 11th August, when going in there with one of my Hunters to kill some Elk he mistook me from the colour of my Dress which was leather from an Elk fired on me & hit me thro' the upper part of my thigh fortunately the Ball missed the bone & being in a good State of Health I recovered rapidly & by the 7 Sept. was able to walk with tolerable convenience, having since fully recovered.—On the 12 August I overtook Capt. Clark & Party on the Missesourii 130 Miles above the Mandans, here we found ourselves once more all together and descended in safety to this Place, where we arrived as has been before mentioned on the 23rd Instant in perfect Health.

Printed, "David Thompson and the Lewis and Clark Expedition," Vancouver Public Library, Vancouver, B.C., 1959, from a transcript in the hand of David Thompson (1770–1857). The original is in a seventy-page Thompson manuscript acquired in 1927 by the Vancouver Public Library and also containing an account of explorer Thompson's first attempt to cross the Rockies in 1801 and some extracts from George Vancouver's narrative of his voyages.

In a brief introduction to the printed version, Peter Grossman says, "There can be no doubt that the letter was written by Lewis and probably the covering note as well." I agree that the letter is Lewis's, but I conclude that the covering note is *not* his, and that it provides a clue to the means by which Thompson received the letter.

Jefferson can be eliminated as an addressee. The material in the letter repeats too much of what Lewis had already told him, and Jefferson's reliable index of letters shows nothing from Lewis of this date. But early in the narrative, Lewis speaks of the deep snows he has traversed, "strange as it may appear to an inhabitant of the southern States." The point is debatable, but I assume he means that the addressee himself lives in the southern states. I find no closer identification of the addressee.

It is quite possible that Lewis was in Cahokia on 14 Oct., and that he penned the covering note. But the note says, "I will give it you verbatim." Those are the words of a man who is copying someone else's text. So we must look for a man in Cahokia who would have had enough interest in these matters to make a copy and send it on, and would have had Lewis's permission to do so. The best candidate is John Hay, a friend of Lewis's, vitally concerned with any new information from the Northwest, who had himself journeyed and traded in the region. He is likely to have had business or personal contacts with whom he exchanged such information.

One bothersome factor is the spirit of the times. There was much anti-British feeling on the frontier. The Missouri had been closed to alien traders since Aug. 1805, and Lewis himself was unfriendly toward the British. It is improbable that he would have let Hay or anyone else copy his letter for the express purpose of conveying it to an English subject. The garbled condition of the letter suggests that it may have been copied several times before it finally reached Thompson.

Dale L. Morgan has suggested to me that the letter may have been written to William Henry Harrison. Lewis assumes the recipient has already received a report on the first leg of the expedition (as Harrison has, No. 146), and so he begins his narrative with the departure of the party from Fort Mandan.

211. Joseph Whitehouse's Bond to Convey Land Warrant

[29 September 1806]

All men are to know by these presents that I Joseph Whitehouse of the county of Fairfax state of Virginia, being one of those who accompanyed Captains Lewis & Clark as a private in an expedition up the Missouri river and to the Pacific Ocean, do hereby for and in consideration of the sum of Two hundred and eighty dollars to me in hand paid (the receipt of which I do hereby acknowledge) Bargain sell release and Convey unto George Drewyer of the District of Cape Girardeaux in the Territory of Louisiana all the right title interest, claim and property to all that tract or parcel of land, to which I may hereafter be entitled for my services as a private in the aforesaid expedition, by any act of Congress or governmental provision which may hereafter be made on this subject and for this purpose. And I do hereby for and in consideration of the sum of money aforesaid bind and oblige myself, legally to empower Captain Meriwether Lewis for me and in my name to apply at any office or other place which for this purpose may be established, for such Warrant, order of survey or other evidence of claim as I may be entitled to in manner and form as aforesaid, and then as my lawfull attorney for me and in my name to assign transfer, make over and Convey all my right title interest claim and property therein to the aforesaid George Drewyer to the end that a title in form may be executed therefor to him. But it is to be understood that if the government should not grant or conceed to me any land in consideration of my services in the Trip or voyage aforesaid, he the said George is not to have any recourse to me. Hereby Warranting and defending the said Tract or parcel of land, to which I am entitled in expectancy as aforesaid, to him the said George his heirs & assigns from me my heirs executors administrators & assigns forever.

In Testimony of which I have hereunto set my hand & affixed my seal, this twenty ninth day of September one thousand eight hundred and Six.

Signed Sealed & Delivered   JOSEPH WHITEHOUSE
in the presence of
John Ordway
Will C. Carr[1]

District of St. Louis Ss. Before the subscriber one of the Justices of the court of Common Pleas for the district aforesaid came the within named Joseph Whitehouse and acknowledged the within as his proper act and Deed for the purposes therein mentioned. Given under my hand & seal this 29th day of September 1806.

District of St. Louis Ss   WM. CHRISTY J.P.[2]

Recorded Book A. Pages 350 & following this 29th day of September A.D. 1806

                                  M. P. LEDUC[3]
                                    Recorder

DS (MoSHi). Endorsed, "Joseph Whitehouse to George Drewyer. Bond to Convey land Warrant." Also present is an identical document signed by John Collins, of the expedition, cconveying his anticipated land warrant to Drouillard. Collins listed himself as residing in Frederick County, Md., and signed the document with his mark. Other documents present:

30 April 1807, Drouillard conveys his own warrant and the two he has purchased to Thomas F. Riddick and Alexander McNair for $1,300. Riddick (1781–1830) was a Virginian who had come to St. Louis in 1804. He served as assessor of rates and levies; clerk of the courts of common pleas, quarter sessions, oyer and terminer; justice of the peace; and deputy recorder of deeds. McNair (1776–1826) was a St. Louis merchant, later to become the first governor of the state of Missouri.

23 Jan. 1808. McNair conveys his half of the property to Frederick Bates for $550.

17 May 1808. Riddick conveys his half to Bates for $550.

1. William C. Carr (1783–1851) was a St. Louis attorney and later a judge.

2. Maj. William Christie (1764–1837) established a public house at Main and Walnut in St. Louis in 1806, and in the same year became a justice of the court of quarter sessions.

3. Marie Philip Le Duc, notary public and first clerk and recorder of St. Louis.

212. The Robert Frazer Prospectus

[October 1806]

Proposals for Publishing by Subscription
Robert Frazers Journal
From St. Louis in Louisiana to the Pacific Ocean
Containing

An accurate description of the Missouri and its several branches; of the mountains seperating the Eastern from the Western waters; of the Columbia river and the Bay it forms on the Pacific Ocean; of the face of the Country in general; of the several Tribes of Indians on the Missouri and Columbia rivers; of the vegetable, animal and [mineral] productions discovered in those Extensive regions. The Latitudes and Longitudes of some of the most remarkable places—

Together with

a variety of Curious and interesting occurrences during a voyage of two years four months and nine days; conducted by Captns. Lewis & Clarke—

Published by Permission of
Captn. Meriwether Lewis—

This work will be contained in about four Hundred pages Octavo

[345]

and will be put to the press so soon as there shall be a sufficient subscription to defray the expenses.
Price to subscribers three Dollars.

AD (WHi), not in Frazer's hand. Pvt. Robert Frazer was the first member
of the expedition to announce plans for publication of a journal, followed
by Sgt. Patrick Gass (No. 259), then by Lewis (No. 262a). The present document marks, then, the beginning of the acrimonious exchange that occurred
when Lewis attempted to discredit the competing journals. See also JACKSON
(7).
  The only surviving portion of Frazer's journal which we know is a manuscript map in the Library of Congress, with a legend reading: "A Map
of the discoveries of Capt. Lewis & Clark from the Rockey mountain and
the River Lewis to the Cap of Disappointement Or the Coloumbia River
At the North Pacific Ocean By observation Of Robert Frazer." For
a discussion of the map, see WHEAT, 2:46–48, and for a reproduction, pp. 50–
51. Because Frazer was an articulate man, his journal might have been a
major contribution to our knowledge of the expedition. Decades later, it
was mentioned by John R. McBride, who said that Frazer's record "was
in many respects more interesting than that of his commanders," and that
Frazer had been a frequent visitor to the McBride home in Franklin, Mo.
(MC BRIDE, 316).
  This copy of the prospectus was deposited with the State Historical Society
of Wisconsin by James D. Butler in 1893. In an accompanying note (21 Dec.
1893) he states that when John Butler saw Frazer in St. Louis, in Sept. 1806,
he recognized him as a former fencing master from Rutland, Vt. Frazer
handed him copies of the prospectus, and the present copy was found in a
bundle of John Butler's letters. WAGNER-CAMP, No. 5a, has a note about a
broadside version of the prospectus. It also appeared in various newspapers,
including the Philadelphia Aurora of 13 Dec. 1806 and 6 Jan. 1807.

213. Bond to Joseph Whitehouse

St. Louis October 8th 1806
Whereas we the undersigned having on the 1st of Jany. 1804. engaged
Joseph Whitehouse to accompany us on a Voyage of Discovery
through the Continent of North America to the Pacific Ocean did
then in behalf of the United States bind ourselves to allow the said
Whitehouse for his services on that expedition a compensation in
Lands equal to that granted by the said States to a Soldier of the
Revolutionary Army—Now Know ye that the said Whitehouse having faithfully complied with the several stipulations of his engagement, the undersigned in their said capacity do hold themselves
bound to the said Whitehouse his heirs or assigns for the quantity of

Lands above stipulated. Given under our hands & seals the day & date above mentioned.

MERIWETHER LEWIS Capt.

1st. U.S. Regt. Infty.

WILLIAM CLARK

ADS, RC (MoSHi). Endorsed, "October 10th 1806 I assign the within to George Drewyer. Joseph Whitehouse." The endorsement is in Lewis's hand, and signed by Whitehouse. Also present is a bond of the same date to Robert Frazer, in Lewis's hand, unsigned. The wording is the same except that Frazer's date of engagement is 1 Oct. 1804.

214. Clark to Henry Dearborn

Sir   St. Louis 10th October 1806

The inclosed commission haveing answered the purpose for which it was intended, I take the liberty of returning it to you.

I have the honor to be with every Sentiment of the highest respect Your Most Obedient and Very humble Sevent,

WILLIAM CLARK

ALS, SC (MoSHi). Endorsed by Clark, "a Copy to Genl. Dearborn Secretary of War." Clark may have intended this as a resignation. If so, it was not accepted until 27 Feb. 1807 (HEITMAN). But it is primarily a gesture of retaliation from the triumphant Clark, who felt that he was wronged by Dearborn when he failed to receive a captain's commission, and who now has reason to believe that he will receive a civil or military appointment of far greater importance.

215. William Bratton's Discharge

To all whom it may concern   St. Louis October 10th 1806

Know ye, that the bearer hereof William Bratton, private in a corps distined for the discovery of the interior of the continent of North America, having faithfully discharged his duty in said capacity so long as his services have been necessary to complete the objects of a Voyage to the Pacific Ocean, is in virtue of the authority vested in me by the President of the United States hereby discharged from the military service of the said States; and as a tribute justly due the merits of the said Willm. Bratton, I with cheerfullness declare that the ample support which he gave me under every difficulty, the manly firmness which he evinced on every necessary occation, and the fortitude with which he boar the fatugues and painfull sufferings incident to that long Voyage, entitled him to my highest confidence and sincere

[347]

thanks; while it eminently recommends him to the consideration and rispect of his fellow Citizens.

MERIWETHER LEWIS Capt.
1st U.S. Regt. Infty.

I certify that the within named Wm. Bratton has received from me all the arrears of pay cloathing and rations due him by the United States from the date of his enlistment to the present date.

October 10th 1806   MERIWETHER LEWIS Capt.
1st U.S. Regt. Infty.

ADS, RC (Ia-HA). The endorsement regarding pay and allowances is on the back of the document.

216. Lewis to Henry Dearborn

Sir   Saint Louis October 11th 1806

My Bill of Exchange No. 72 of this date in favor of Thomas P. Howard or order for one hundred Dollars —— Cents is for that sum due him in part, on final Settlement for his Services as a Private on an expedition lately Conducted under the auspices of the Goverment through the interior of the Continent of North America to the Pacific Ocean. I have the honor to be with due Consideration Your obt. Servt.

MERIWETHER LEWIS Capt.
1st U.S. Regt. Infty.

LS, RC (DNA, RG 107, L-Misc.). A form letter, filled in and signed by Lewis and addressed in his hand to the Secretary of War. Also present are the following similar letters, some dated 11 Oct. 1806 and some with the day of the month omitted; presumably all were done on 11 Oct.:

> No. 74, Joseph Field, $266.93
> No. 75, John Shields, $180.07
> No. 76, George Shannon, $70.00
> No. 77, Richard Windsor, $100.33
> No. 80, John Potts, $400.00
> No. 83, Alexander Willard, $100.22
> No. 84, John Collins, $100.00

Windsor's letter is endorsed: "For value Received I assign the within to Alexander Crump. St. Louis 4th Novr. 1806. Richard Windsor his mark." Witnessed by Wm. Russell.

217. Lewis to Henry Dearborn

Sir   Saint Louis October 12th 1806

My Bill of Exchange No. 88 of this date in favor of John Bustard or order, for the Sum of one hundred Dollars —— Cents is on account of that sum delivered me in Specie, and which when paid will be charged to me on the faith of my final settlement with the party who accompanied me to the Pacific Ocean. I have the honor to be with due Consideration Your obt. Servt.

MERIWETHER LEWIS Capt.
1st U.S. Regt. Infty.

LS, RC (DNA, RG 107, L-Misc.). Addressed to Dearborn in Lewis's hand; postmarked, "Louisville K. Nov. 12th"; endorsed by Bustard; and, by the War Department, "Capt. Lewis Advising a draft No. 88 in favor of John Bustard $100. 12 Oct. 1806." I have not identified Bustard. The document is a form letter with date, name, and sum filled in by Lewis. Also present are the following letters using the same basic form:

13 Oct. 1806. Bill of exchange No. 95 in favor of James Martin or order, $309.00. Martin is unidentified.

13 Oct. 1806. Bill of exchange No. 97 in favor of Thomas F. Reddick [Riddick], $72.73. Riddick has been already identified.

14 Oct. 1806. Bill of exchange No. 104 in favor of Adam Wolford, $35.00. This name occurs elsewhere as Woolford, Wolfort, etc.; I have not identified him.

14 Oct. 1806. Bill of exchange No. 105 in favor of Wilkinson and Price, $615.36. Benjamin Wilkinson and Risdon H. Price were St. Louis merchants.

14 Oct. 1806. Bill of exchange No. 107 in favor of Calvin Adams, $101.00. BILLON (2), 11, lists him as a tavernkeeper in 1805, and says elsewhere, (1), 401, that he came to St. Louis from Connecticut at the close of the eighteenth century.

17 Oct. 1806. Bill of exchange No. 109 in favor of John Bustard, $100.00.

17 Oct. 1806. Bill of exchange No. 110 in favor of George Ming, $55.40. Ming is unidentified.

17 Oct. 1806. Bill of exchange No. 111 in favor of William Christy [Christie], $19.50. Christie has been identified earlier.

The Missouri Historical Society has an ALS copy of this form, not executed. Lewis's notification of Bill of exchange No. 113, of 30 Oct. 1806 in favor of George Wallace, Jr., for $500.00, written at Vincennes, is in the Montana Historical Society library. Wallace (d. 1826), son-in-law of Gen. John Gibson, was a merchant in Vincennes and a contractor for army rations. After the death of his father, George Wallace, Sr., in 1812, he returned to his home in Braddock's Field, Pa. I am grateful to Miss Caroline Dunn, librarian of the Indiana Historical Society, for helping me to straighten out the two Wallaces.

In DNA, RG 107, Register of Letters Received, vol. 3, I find these additional records of Lewis's expenditures during his first days in St. Louis after the expedition:

L-72. 27 Sept. 1806. Lewis advises the Secretary of a bill for $300.00 in favor of Wilson P. Hunt and John Hankinson, St. Louis merchants.

L-73. 4 Oct. 1806. Notification of a bill for $49.67 in favor of Corp. Richard Warfington.

L-74. 27 Sept. 1806. Notification of a draft for $220.00 in favor of P. Falconer and John G. Comegys, St. Genevieve merchants after 1806. The firm was a branch of the establishment of C. and John G. Comegys, Baltimore.

L-75. 27 Sept. 1806. Another draft on Falconer and Comegys for $300.00.

L-79. 24 Sept. 1806. Notification of a draft for $272.00 in favor of Samuel Smith. I have not identified this man (he was from Pittsburgh) nor the Meriwether Smith to whom Lewis paid $67.00 on 20 May 1804 "on account of his pay" (DNA, RG 217, Records of the Army Accounting Office, Journal L, p. 6002).

218. Lewis to Henry Dearborn

Sir,   St. Louis October 17th 1806

My Bill of exchange No. 112 of this date in favor of Charles Gratiot or order fo[r] the sum of two hundred and sixty dollars is for four horses purchased by me of the said Gratiott for the public service, and which when paid will be charged to me accordingly. I am with due consideration and rispect Your Obt. Sevt.

MERIWETHER LEWIS Capt.
1st U.S. Regt. Infty.

ALS, RC (DNA, RG 107, L-Misc.).

219. Jefferson to Reuben Lewis

Sir   Washington Oct. 26. 06.

If Capt. Lewis be not already with you, I have the pleasure to inform you of his safe arrival at St. Louis, & that you may expect every hour to see him in Albemarle. In this confidence I take the liberty of putting a letter to him under cover & salute you with esteem & respect.

TH: JEFFERSON

ALS, SC (MoSHi). Endorsed. Jefferson also wrote Thomas Mann Randolph on 3 Nov.: "Yesterday was sennight I wrote to Reuben Lewis, informing him he might hourly expect his brother there. I meant the next day which was the post day, to have written it to you also, but was in the intervening evening taken with the autumnal fever so as to be unable to write" (DLC).

220. Jefferson to Lewis

Washington Oct. 26. 06

I recieved, my dear Sir, with unspeakable joy your letter of Sep. 23 announcing the return of yourself, Capt. Clarke & your party in good health to St. Louis. The unknown scenes in which you were engaged,

& the length of time without hearing of you had begun to be felt awfully. Your letter having been 31. days coming, this cannot find you at Louisville, & I therefore think it safest to lodge it at Charlottesville. It's only object is to assure you of what you already know, my constant affection for you & the joy with which all your friends here will recieve you.[1] Tell my friend of Mandane also that I have already opened my arms to recieve him. Perhaps while in our neighborhood, it may be gratifying to him, & not otherwise to yourself to take a ride to Monticello and see in what manner I have arranged the tokens of friendship I have recieved from his country particularly as well as from other Indian friends: that I am in fact preparing a kind of Indian hall. Mr. Dinsmore,[2] my principal workman will shew you every thing there. Had you not better bring him by Richmond, Fredericksburg, & Alexandria? He will thus see what none of the others have visited, & the convenience of the public stages will facilitate your taking that route. I salute you with sincere affection.

TH: JEFFERSON

ALS, SC (DLC). Endorsed. Printed versions of this letter invariably are dated 20 Oct., because the upper portion of the 6 is missing in Jefferson's date at the head of the letter; his polygraph pen appears to have skipped. But Jefferson's own endorsement on the back, and his listing in the index of letters, make it 26 Oct. It could not have been written before 24 Oct. in any case, since that is the day on which Jefferson received Lewis's notice of his return (No. 207). This is undoubtedly the letter for Lewis that Jefferson mentions in his note to Reuben (No. 219).

1. By this time Jefferson already was thinking of appointing Lewis to the post of governor of Louisiana Territory, as shown in this comment by Albert Gallatin: "If you select him for Governor, ought not provision to be made for the contingency of his leaving that place for Washington before the arrival of a commission? And does not that render the appointment of a Secretary who may govern in the interim still more important?" (25 Oct. 1806, DLC).

2. James Dinsmore, Jefferson's carpenter since 1798, "an excellent young man from Philadelphia who has lived in my family as a house joiner 5 or 6 years" (Jefferson to Isaac Briggs, 20 April 1803, DLC).

221. Lewis to Henry Dearborn

Sir,   Louisville November 9th 1806.

My bill of Exchange no. 117 in favor of Thomas Prathor or order for *four hundred Dollars* is for that sum advanced me in specie; and which when paid will be charged to me on account of expences incident to the conveying certain Indians to the seat of the general government, and for other public purposes. I have the honor to be with due consideration Your Obt. Servt.

MERIWETHER LEWIS Capt.
1st. U.S. Regt. Infty.

ALS, RC (DLC—Hart Coll., photostat). Thomas Prather was a Louisville merchant.

222. Jefferson's Annual Message to Congress

[2 December 1806]
[Extract from first draft]

The expedition of Messrs. Lewis and Clarke for exploring the river Missouri, & the best communication from that to the Pacific ocean, has had all the success which could have been expected. They traced the Missouri nearly to it's source, traversed the high mountains dividing it from the Columbia, descended that river to the Pacific ocean, where they passed a winter of five months, & returned to St. Louis on the Missisipi two years & an half after their departure from it, with the loss of one of their party only, who died on the way. In the course of their journey they acquired a knolege of numerous tribes of Indians hitherto unknown; they informed themselves of the trade which may be carried on with them, the best channels & positions for it, & they are enabled to give with accuracy the geography of the line they pursued, fixing it in all it's parts by observations of latitude & longitude. The desideratum therefore of the interior of our continent along this important channel of communication with the Pacific, is now obtained, & it is but justice to say that Messrs. Lewis & Clarke, & their brave companions, have, by this arduous service, deserved well of their country, *<& merit from it's rulers their honorable approbation>*.

[Extract from revised draft]

The expedition of Messrs. Lewis & Clarke, for exploring the river Missouri, and the best communication from that to the Pacific ocean, has had all the success which could have been expected. They have traced the Missouri nearly to it's source, descended the Columbia to the Pacific ocean, ascertained with accuracy the geography of that interesting communication across our continent, learnt the character of the country, of it's commerce & inhabitants, and it is but justice to say that Messrs. Lewis and Clarke, & their brave companions, have, by this arduous service, deserved well of their country.

[352]

ADS, SC (DLC). The revised draft is dated by Jefferson; the first is not. Changes made in the revised version are indicated in the margins of the first.

223. Jefferson to Caspar Wistar

[8 December 1806]

Th: Jefferson presents his salutations to Dr. Wistar; & incloses him Mr. Stuart's letter which gives the only information he possesses respecting the squirrel's head. Capt. Lewis's rout will probably, as soon as he arrives here, be engraved. A copy shall be sent to the society, as also of Lt. Pike's survey of the Misipi & Freeman's of the Red river.

Washington Dec. 8. 06.

ALS, SC (DLC). Endorsed. Wistar had asked in a letter of 5 Dec. for "the general course of the Missouri, or the latitude & longitude of the falls" (DLC). The squirrel's head was a specimen sent to Wistar for identification—not collected by Lewis and Clark.

224. Lewis to Henry Dearborn

Sir,   Staunton December 11th 1806

My bill of exchange No. 119 for two hundred Dollars in favour of Heiskell & Sowers is for that sum delivered me in specie, and which when paid will be charged to me on account of traveling and other necessary expences incured on a tour from St. Louis to the City of Washington in charge of certain Mandan Indians. I am with due consideration Your Obt. Servt.

MERIWETHER LEWIS Capt.
1st U.S. Regt. Infty.

ALS, RC (DNA, RG 107, L-Misc.). Addressed; endorsed. Heiskell & Sowers appears to have been a firm of Staunton, Va., merchants.

225. Michael Leib to Jefferson

Sir,   Lancaster Decr. 22nd 1806

My friend Dr. Muhlenberg[1] of this place, whose reputation as a botanist you are not unacquainted with, is very desirous of possessing the seed of any rare plants that Captain Lewis may have brought with

[353]

him. As you will be in possession of them, I have taken the liberty of requesting a specimen of any that you may have to spare, for my friend the Doctor. As you have always evinced the strongest desire to promote science of every kind, and to give every encouragement in your power to men of science, I shall make no apology for the freedom of this request. Permit me to tender to you the homage of my sincere respect and regard.

M. LEIB

ALS, RC (DLC). Endorsed, "Leib Matthew. Lancaster Dec. 22. 06. recd. Dec. 23." Jefferson wrote "Matthew" but the letter is in the hand of Michael Leib (1760–1822), a physician and U.S. representative from Pennsylvania.

1. Henry Muhlenberg (1753–1815), Lutheran clergyman and Pennsylvania botanist, author of *Catalogus plantarum Americae septentrionalis . . . or, a catalogue of the hitherto known native and naturalized plants of North America* (Lancaster, Pa., 1813). His attempts to obtain botanical specimens from the expedition were nearly futile. He wrote to Stephen Elliott, 8 Nov. 1809: "I have received from Mr. Lewis only 6 different seeds and they are all valuable Plants—I will not publish anything about them untill his work has been published." He also made the curious statement, "Dr. Barton speaks rather too hard of Lewis's Discoveries" (Arnold Arboretum Library quoted by EWAN, 612n). A couple of years later he was still trying. Writing to William Baldwin, he said: "Pray have you specimens of any of Lewis's plants? I have tried every method to get a sight of them,—but in vain. My friends in Philadelphia have denied me the pleasure of seeing them in flower. I would wish to add them to my catalogue, without any description;—leaving that to the compiler of Lewis's work. I am afraid the description will be made in England, and Lewis's work will come too late. Perhaps you can get the specimens from Mr. M'Mahon, or Dr. Barton." To this Baldwin replied, "I have no specimens of Lewis's plants; but will most cheerfully use my endeavors to obtain them" (BALDWIN, 34, 35). Baldwin (1779–1819) was a botanist and naval surgeon. I take Muhlenberg's references to a possible English publication to mean that he knows of Frederick Pursh's intentions—or at least suspects. See No. 263.

226. Bernard McMahon to Jefferson

Dear Sir   Philadelphia Decr. 26th 1806

It is painful to me to trouble you at this period, when you are so much occupied with the important affairs of the Nation; but your goodness I hope will excuse my anxiety to procure some seeds[1] of the indigenous plants of the western parts of America, if you received such from Capt. Lewis on his return. A small portion of every kind you could conveniently spare, would greatly oblige me and perhaps, render me essential service; and it would be of some importance to get them as soon as you could make it convenient to have them forwarded, that each kind might be treated according to its apparent nature, and different methods tried to effect its successful propagation with the greater degree of certainty, especially, the nondescripts, if any.

Of the Cucurbita[2] you were so kind as to send me, some grew to the length of five feet five inches. I have one of them now in my shop window, perfectly dry, which is five feet one inch long, perfectly straight and in every part about four inches in diameter: they are excellent to use, as squashes while young.

The quarantine Corn, was with me fit for the table, in fifty days after sowing; our last summer was colder than usual, or it, probably, would have been fit for use in forty days; however, it is a great acquisition and highly deserving of cultivation for the early part of the season. I have the happiness of being, with great respect and esteem, Sir, Your sincere wellwisher,

BERND. MCMAHON

ALS, RC (DLC). Endorsed; received 30 Dec. 1806. Reply is No. 228. Bernard McMahon (c.1775–1816), a Philadelphia botanist and gardener, had come to the U.S. from Ireland in 1796 and had recently published one of the earliest American works on horticulture, *The American gardener's calendar* (Philadelphia, 1806). According to his advertisements in the *Aurora* of 1807, he was operating from an "Agricultural, Horticultural and Botanical Book-store, and Grass and Garden Seed Ware House," at 39 South Second Street.

The exchange of correspondence that begins here between Jefferson and McMahon is noteworthy for two reasons. It reveals the eagerness with which the botanists of the eastern states awaited the botanical discoveries of Lewis and Clark, and the care with which McMahon nurtured the several new species he was able to propagate; and it provides an ample view of Jefferson the botanist, the flower lover, the farmer, the scientific observer. "Planting is one of my great amusements," he wrote Dr. Samuel Brown a few years later, "and even of those things which can only be for posterity. For a Septuaginary has no right to count on any thing but annuals" (17 April 1813, DLC).

Unfortunately, the botanical aspects of the Lewis and Clark Expedition cannot be understood from correspondence alone. The plants named in the letters are but a fraction of those collected by the explorers. A student of Lewis and Clark botanizing must turn first to the JOURNALS, and to the annotation provided there by Reuben G. Thwaites and his consultants, supplementing this information with the notes in the BIDDLE-COUES edition. He also must see the surviving herbarium specimens in the Academy of Natural Sciences of Philadelphia—those in the Lambert herbarium, and those in the Barton herbarium, which is on loan from the American Philosophical Society. Then he may turn to a number of books and journal articles which I now discuss.

Frederick Pursh was the first to publish on the botanical specimens of the expedition, in his *Flora Americae septentrionalis* (London, 1814). How he achieved prior publication of more than a hundred Lewis and Clark species is not entirely clear; see my note on his accomplishment under No. 263. Dendrologist Charles Sprague SARGENT, in discussing the trees described in the Biddle-Coues account, is mainly interested in correcting some of the identifications made for Coues by Dr. Frank Hall Knowlton, who did not have access to specimens. Thomas MEEHAN undertakes to identify all the plant specimens, and his paper is stiffly criticized by COUES (3). Coues claimed to know little botany but he knew the route of the expedition thoroughly, and he disliked the vague localities assigned by Meehan to plant specimens; he assigns precise localities where possible from the available data. No zoologist, he says in a typical Couesian mood, would be content with a locality as general as "on the banks of the Missouri."

The raising and distribution of the plants grown from seeds and cuttings is treated by Rodney TRUE, in an article based chiefly on the correspondence between Jefferson and McMahon. Francis PENNELL (2) and RUDD make further comment on the specimens collected. Less helpful in regard to Lewis and Clark, but important for an over-all view of early western botanizing, is MC KELVEY.

1. McMahon had tried earlier to obtain some of the seeds sent down from Fort Mandan (all of which had gone to William Hamilton). Jefferson wrote him 25 April 1806 that they had all been sent to the American Philosophical Society for assignment (DLC).

2. Gourds.

227. [Canceled.]

228. Jefferson to Bernard McMahon

Sir   Washington Jan. 6. 07

I recieved in due time your letter of Dec. 26. but it has been impossible for me to answer it sooner. Capt. Lewis has brought a considerable number of seeds[1] of plants peculiar to the countries he has visited. I have recommended to him to confide principal shares of them to Mr. Hamilton of the Woodlands & yourself, as the persons most likely to take care of them, which he will accordingly do. He will carry them on to Philadelphia himself.

The tulip roots you were so kind as to send me, I planted at Monticello last autumn. I intend to go there the first week in March in order to commence planting out some things to be in readiness for my kitchen & flower gardens two years hence.[2] A small cart will come here for such articles as I collect here, chiefly trees. But there are several articles for the selection of which I would rather ask the assistance of your judgment than that of any other. I note them at the foot of my letter. If you could be so good as to furnish me with them you would greatly oblige me. Seeds & bulbs can be so packed as to come with perfect safety by the stage, the best conveyance to this place because we can command it at all times. Whether tuberous & fibrous roots can come succesfully in moss or any thing else not too bulky, you are the best judge. To give them the better chance they will be safest with you till about the 25th of February. Your bill for their amount shall be immediately provided for by remittance. Accept my salutations & best wishes.

TH: JEFFERSON

best Globe artichoke.	Anemone.	Marigold.
Antwerp raspberry.	Auricula.	Saffron.
Alpine strawberry.	Ranunculus.	
Lillies of a few of the best kinds.	Hyacinths.	
Tuberose.	Sweet William	
Crown Imperials.	(Divers Hues)	
	Wall flower.	

ALS, SC (DLC). Endorsed. McMahon replied to this letter 25 Feb., saying that he had been able to send most of the plants Jefferson had asked for, and adding: "I am extremely obliged to you for your kindness in speaking to Capt. Lewis about the seeds; I anxiously wish for his arrival in this City, fearing to lose the advantage of early sowing for some articles which might require it" (DLC).

1. This undated document in Clark's hand (MoSHi) lists at least a part of the seeds brought back by the expedition:

A list of Seed
The flesh coloured Flower
Wild Parsnip
Wild Plumb
Peas, common to the Columbian Plains
Flowers from Clarks River
[. . .] Species of Sun Flower
Shallon Cherry
Honey Succle
Black Currant
Purple Currant
Yellow Currant
Sarvice Berry
Ricara Currant
Red Currant
Rocky Mountain Cherry
[. . .] Cherry of the River Rochejhone
Egg Plant
Wild Flax
large species of Tobacco

2. Jefferson was looking forward to retirement at the expiration of his second term of office as President, in 1809. According to a memorandum

[357]

dated 7 Jan. (MHi), he was sending the following to Monticello for the forthcoming planting season:

> Missouri hominy corn
> soft corn
> Pani [Pawnee] 6. weeks corn
> 9. nuts from Missouri
> 2. boxes do. from Roanoke

See a note under No. 149 for his luck with the corn, and a comparison with the quarantine corn of France.

229. Citizens of Fincastle to Lewis and Clark

An Address from the Citizens of Fincastle & its vicinity to Captains Meriwether Lewis & William Clarke.

Gentlemen   8th of January 1807

Sentiments of esteem and gratitude induce us to offer you our sincere congratulations, upon your safe return to the bosom of your country. During your absence upon a perilous & laborious service, we have reflected with the deepest solicitude, on the dangers which you must necessarily encounter; our anxiety for your safety, and that of the party under your command, is now happily terminated. Your prudence, courage and good conduct have afforded us an oppertunety of yielding, without restraint to those emotions of Joy so natural to the mind, after having experienced a painful suspense. To those who have acted so distinguished & honorable a part on the theatre of human affairs, future life can not but afford the most soothing recollections. In whatever situation it may hereafter please the Supreme Being to place you, it will be a source of unmixed gratification to remember that in order to meet the just expectations, which your appointment by Government had excited, you have navigated bold & unknown rivers, traversed Mountains, which had never before been impressed with the footsteps of civilized man, and surmounted every obstacle, which climate, Nature, or ferocious Savages could throw in your way. You have the further satisfaction to reflect that, you have extended the knowledge of the Geography of your country; in other respects enriched Science; and opened to the United States a source of inexhaustible wealth, no event, which occurred during the expedition, can, in the smallest degree, impair the force of those solacing reflections. You have uniformly respected the rights of humanity, actuated by principles of genuine philanthropy, you have not sprinkled your path with the blood of unoffending savages. Your fame will be as pure and unsullied, as of that great man to whom Europe is indebted for a knowledge of our continent; the extent and importance of which, it has been reserved for you to disclose to the world.

We concieve it to be a signal proof of the wisdom and attention with which you have conducted the expedition, that but one man has been lost to your country. This fact will afford to future travellers the most salutary instruction. It will teach them, that, discoveries (apparently the most difficult) may be effected without the effusion of human blood.

You will, Gentlemen, indulge us in declaring it as our opinion, that the rewards, which a grateful country may think proper to bestow, ought not to be apportioned to common merit or services; but that the recompence to yourselves and to each individual under your command should be such as, in some measure, to atone for past perils, difficulties and privations. With great respect we are Gentn. your Humble Servts.

PAT LOCKHART, Chairman,
By order & on behalf of the Citizens
of Fincastle &c.

LS, RC (MoSHi). Addressed, "Captains Meriwether Lewis and William Clarke." Reply is No. 230.

230. Clark to the Citizens of Fincastle

Gentlemen   [after 8 January 1807]

Those sentiments of esteem and solicitude for our personal safty expressed in your affectionate address has excited in me the livelyest sencibility. To meet with the approbation of our country for the attempt which has been made to render services to the government by Capt. Lewis Myself and the party that accompanied us, is a source of the highest gratification. It will be a pleaseing reflection in future life to find that the expedition has been productive of those advantages to our country, Geography, and science that you are willing to imagine. To respect the rights of humanity has and ever will be the leading principal of my life, and no reflection is more pleasing to me than that of effecting the objects we had in view with the effusion of so small a portion of human blood.

Gentlemen we ought to assign the general safty of the party to a singular interposition of providence, and not to the wisdom of those who commanded the expedition. Your anxiety that our country should reward our services with liberality, produces in me those immotions natural to the mind, at the same time acknowledging our uniform confidence not only in the justice but the liberality of our Country.

[359]

The friendly attention manifasted towards us by many of our fellow citizens is highly flattering, but the distinguished attention shewn to me by the Citizens of Fincastle & it's vicinity produces those emmotions which I am unable to discribe, I will do my self the Honor to hand Capt. Lewis and make known to the faithfull party that accompanied us, your friendly address, which I will undertake to say for them will be justly appreciated. You will please Gentlemen except of the best wishes of your most obedient Humble Servant,

WM. CLARK

To the Citizens of Fincastle and it's vicinity

ALS, SC (MoSHi).

231. James L. Donaldson to Jefferson

Sir—   New York. January 11th 1807.

I lose no time in forwarding to the Seat of Government the enclosed Dispatches from Genl. Wilkinson, and agreeably to his instructions shall follow them to Washington, as early as a short but necessary delay here will permit.

I have in my charge three boxes directed to the President of the United States, which had been forwarded from St. Louis to New Orleans by Capt. Lewis. These packages I shall if a good opportunity offer during the few days I shall remain here, either forward to Baltimore, Alexandria, or if possible Georgetown, or Washington. If an opportunity to one or other of these Ports do not present itself, I shall leave the Packages in the Public Stores under the care of the Collector of this Port. I have the honor to be with respect Your obt. hble. Servt.

JAS. L. DONALDSON.

ALS, RC (DLC). Endorsed; received 14 Jan. 1807. James Lowry Donaldson, a Baltimore attorney, had been appointed recorder of land titles for Louisiana Territory in 1805, and in 1806 had become attorney general for the territory. At the time of this letter he had returned to visit his family in the East.

232. Jefferson to Jonathan Williams and Charles Willson Peale

Gentlemen   Washington Jan. 12. 07.

I am again to return the tribute of my thanks for the continued proofs of favor from the American Philosophical society; and I ever do it with sincere gratitude, sensible it is the effect of their good will, and not of any services I have it in my power to render them. I pray you to convey to them these expressions of my dutiful acknolegements, and to accept yourselves thanks for the favorable terms in which your letter of the 2d inst. announces the suffrage of the society.

I am happy at the same time to greet them on the safe return of a valuable member of our fraternity from a journey of uncommon length & peril. He will ere long be with them, & present them with the additions he brings to our knolege of the geography & natural history of our country, from the Missisipi to the Pacific.

Tendering them my humble respects, permit me to add for yourselves my friendly salutations & assurances of high consideration.

TH: JEFFERSON

ALS, SC (DLC). Col. Jonathan Williams (1750–1815) was the first superintendent of the U.S. Military Academy. He served as chief engineer of the army in 1802–03, and was founder of the Military Philosophical Society.

233. Willis Alston to Henry Dearborn

Sir: Committee Room, January 12, 1807.

The committee to whom has been referred a resolution of the House of Representatives, to enquire what compensation ought to be made to Messrs. Lewis and Clarke, and their brave companions for their late service in exploring the western waters, have instructed me to request that you will furnish them with such information in the possession of the Department of War as you may deem necessary to guide the committee in establishing their rate of compensation; also a list of the names of the officers, and their respective grades, and the names of the soldiars under their command. I am your most obedient servant,

WILLIS ALSTON, JUNR.

ALS, RC (DNA, RG 107, A-52). Reply is No. 235. Willis Alston, Jr. (1769–1837), was a representative from North Carolina. He was chairman of a committee which the House had named 2 Jan. "to inquire what compensation ought to be made to Messrs. Lewis, and Clarke, and their brave companions . . . to report by bill or otherwise" (*Annals of the Congress of the United States*, 16:246).

234. Joel Barlow to Jefferson

Dear Sir   Washington 13 Jany. 1807

Is there any cogent reason for continuing to call the Columbia

[361]

River by that name? If not I should propose to name it Lewis, & one of its principal branches Clarke.

We have so many towns, districts & counties, & I believe some smaller streams, called Columbia, besides its being the general name of the Continent, that it will tend to run our geography into some confusion, which may as well be avoided.[1]

Should this suggestion meet your approbation & that of the two houses of Congress, would it not be proper that they should so establish these names in the same act by which they grant a reward to these meritorious discoverers; a measure which I understand is now in contemplation.

You will perceive I had the thing in view, with regard to Lewis, when I wrote the verses of which I enclose you a copy.[2]

The world has justly given the name of MacKensie to the great river of the north for the same obvious reason, the merit of discovery. The names of these western rivers & their branches will probably be unchangeably fixt in Captain Lewis's map; and nothing short of some public authorization will reconcile it with his modesty to give his own name to so great a river. Your very obet. Sevt.

JOEL BARLOW

ALS, RC (DLC). Endorsed; received 13 Jan. 1807.

1. No doubt Jefferson told him that there was indeed a cogent reason for retaining the original name of the Columbia River. It had been so named by Capt. Robert Gray, who discovered it in 1792, in honor of his ship *Columbia*. It is curious that Barlow was getting tired of the word, for at this time he was expanding his own poem, *The vision of Columbus*, into an epic work of 8,350 lines which he would call *The Columbiad*.

2. Barlow had composed a poem to be read at a testimonial dinner for Lewis and Clark. After several postponements while the sponsors waited for Clark to arrive from Virginia, the dinner was held without him on 14 Jan. 1807. Mayor Robert Brent presided, and the guests from the frontier included Lewis, Pierre Chouteau, Pierre Provenchere, and the Mandan chief Sheheke. The *National Intelligencer* for 16 Jan. reported that the party drank several "volunteers," including Lewis's own: "May works be a test of patriotism, as they ought of right to be that of religion." The Barlow poem, read by a Mr. Beckley, ran like this:

On the Discoveries of Captain Lewis

Let the Nile cloak his head in the clouds, and defy
The researches of science and time;
Let the Niger escape the keen traveller's eye,
By plunging, or changing his clime.

Columbus, not so shall thy boundless domain
Defraud thy brave sons of their right;

[362]

Streams, midlands, and shorelands illude us in vain,
We shall drag their dark regions to light.

[*and six more stanzas*]

A parody of this eulogium quickly followed in the *Monthly Anthology*
for March 1807, by an anonymous writer who went unidentified for more
than a century until named by HOWE in 1910. John Quincy Adams was the
perpetrator of the work, which began:

Good people, listen to my tale,
'Tis nothing but what true is;
I'll tell you of the mighty deeds
Achieved by Captain Lewis—
How starting from the Atlantick shore
By fair and easy motion,
He journied, *all the way by land,*
Until he met the ocean.

235. Henry Dearborn to Willis Alston

Sir: War Department, January 14, 1807.

Agreeably to the request of the committee, as expressed in your
letter of the 12th inst., I herewith transmit a list of the officers, non-
commissioned officers, and privates, who formed the party recently
returned from an enterprise, which they commenced and prosecuted
with a degree of boldness, perseverance, and judgment, and success,
that has rarely, if ever, occurred, in this or any other country.

The officers and soldiers will receive their usual compensations
from this Department, up to the time of their return to St. Louis.

The quantum of gratuity, either in land or money, or in both, to
which such meritorious and unusual services may be entitled, on the
score of national justice, or on the principles of sound policy and
national liberality, being principally a matter of opinion, it is with
diffidence I take the liberty of proposing, for the consideration of the
committee, a grant to each non-commissioned officer and private, of
320 acres of land; to Lieut. Clarke, of 1000; and to Captain Lewis, of
1,500; with the addition of double pay to each while engaged in the
enterprise; and that each one should have permission to locate his
grant on any lands that have been surveyed, and are now for sale by
the United States.

It may be proper for me to remark, that, in a conversation with
Captain Lewis, he observed, that whatever grant of land Congress
might think proper to make, to himself and Lieutenant Clarke, it was
his wish there should be no distinction of rank so noticed as to make

a difference in the quantity granted to each; and that he would prefer an equal division of whatever quantity might be granted to them.

I also transmit, herewith, the letter from Captain Lewis to the Secretary of War, which accompanied said list. I have the honor to be, very respectfully, sir, your obedient servant,

H. DEARBORN.

Printed, *American State Papers,* Military Affairs, 1:207–09. Although this letter is dated 14 Jan., the letter by Lewis which it enclosed (No. 236) is dated 15 Jan.

236. Lewis to Henry Dearborn

Sir,   City of Washington January 15th 1807.

Herewith inclosed I transmit you the roll of the men who accompanied me on my late tour to the Pacific Ocean, through the interior of the continent of North America.

In addition to the men whose names are entered on this roll, there are two others who have some claims to a gratuity as connected with the expedition, but as I cannot consider them in all respects as of the permanent party I have thought their pretentions more properly the subjects of this detached communication than of the roll which accompanys it.

Richard Warfington was a Corporal in the Infantry of the U. States army whom I had occasion to take with me on my voyage as far as the Mandan nation. His term of service expired on the 4th of August within nearly three months previous to my arrival at that fort, and knowing, that it would become necessary for me to send back my boat in the spring 1805 with a party of soldiers whose terms of service had not expired; that it was of some importance that the government should receive in safety the dispatches which I was about to transmit from thence; that there was not one of the party destined to be returned from thence in whom I could place the least confidence except himself, and that if he was discharged at the moment of the expiration of his term of service that he would necessarily loose his military standing and thereby lessen the efficiency of his command among the soldiery; I was induced under these considerations to make an arrangement with him by which it was agreed between us that he should not receive his discharge from the military service untill his return to St. Louis, and that he should in the interim retain his rank

[364]

and receive only for his services the accustomed compensation. Accordingly he remained with me during the winter, and was the next spring in conformity to my plan placed in command of the boat and charged with my dispatches to the government. The duties assigned him on this occasion were performed with a punctuality which uniformly characterized his conduct while under my command. Taking into view the cheerfulness with which he continued in the service after every obligation had ceased to exist, from the exposures, the fatigues, labour and dangers incident to that service, and above all the fidelity with which he discharged this duty, it would seem that when rewards are about to be distributed among those of the party who were engaged in the enterprise that his claim to something more than his pay of seven dollars pr. month as corporal cannot be considered unreasonable.

John Newman was a private in the Infantry of the U'States army who joined me as a volunteer and entered into an enlistment in common with others by which he was held and mustered as one of the permanent party. In the course of the expedition, or shortly before we arrived at the Mandan Villages he committed himself by using certain mutinous expressions which caused me to arrest him and to have him tryed by a Court Martial formed of his peers; they finding him guilty sentenced him to receive seventy-five lashes and to be discharged from the permanent party, this sentence was enforced by me, and the punishment took place. The conduct of this man previous to this period had been generally correct, and the zeal he afterwards displayed for the benefit of the service was highly meritorious. In the course of the winter while at Fort Mandan, from an ardent wish to attone for the crime which he had committed at an unguarded moment, he exerted himself on every occasion to become usefull. This disposition induced him to expose himself too much to the intense cold of that climate, and on a hunting excurtion he had his hands and feet severely frozen with which he suffered extreme pain for some weeks. Having recovered from this accident by the 1st of April 1805, he asked forgivness for what had passed, and beged that I would permit him to continue with me through the voyage, but deeming it impolitic to relax from the sentence, altho' he stood acquitted in my mind, I determined to send him back, which was accordingly done. Since my return I have been informed that he was extremely serviceable as a hunter on the voyage to St. Louis and that the boat on several occasions owed her safety in a great measure to his personal exertions, being a man of uncommon activity and bodily strength. If under these circumstances it should be thought proper to give Newman the remaining third which will be deducted from the gratuity awarded Paptiest La Page who occupied his station in the after part of the voyage I should feel myself much gratifyed. I have the honor to be with due consideration and much respect Your Obt. Servt.

MERIWETHER LEWIS Capt.
1st U.S. Regt. Infty.

[*Enclosure*]

A Roll of the men who accompanyed Captains Lewis and Clark on their late tour to the Pacific Ocean through the interior of the continent of North America, showing their rank with some remarks on their rispective merits and services.

No.	Names.	Rank.	Remarks
1	John Ordway	Sergeant	
2	Nathaniel Pryor	ditto.	
3	Charles Floyd	ditto.	Deceased the 20th of August 1804. A young man of much merit. His father, who now resides in Kentucky, is a man much rispected, tho' possessed of but moderate wealth. As the son has lost his life while on this service, I consider his father entitled to some gratuity, in consideration of his loss, and also, that the deceased being noticed in this way, will be a tribute but justly due to his merit.
4	Patric Gass	ditto.	Promoted to sergeant, 20th of August, 1804, in the place of Charles Floyd, deceased; in which capacity he continued until discharged at St. Louis, November 10, 1806.
5	William Bratton	Private	
6	John Collins	ditto.	
7	John Colter	ditto.	
8	Pier Cruzatte	ditto.	

No.	Names.	Rank.	Remarks
9	Joseph Field	ditto.	Two of the most active and enterprising young men who accompanied us. It was their peculiar fate to have been engaged in all the most dangerous and difficult scenes of the voyage, in which they uniformly acquited themselves with much honor.
10	Reuben Field	ditto.	
11	Robert Frazier	ditto.	
12	Silas Goodrich	ditto.	
13	George Gibson	ditto.	
14	Thomas P. Howard	ditto.	
15	Hugh Hall	ditto.	
16	Francis Labuiche	ditto.	He has received the pay only of a private, though, besides the duties performed as such, he has rendered me very essential services as a French and English interpreter; therefore, I should think it only just that some small addition to his pay, as a private, should be added, tho' no such addition has at any time been promised by me.
17	Hugh McNeal	ditto.	
18	John Sheilds	ditto.	Has received the pay only of a private. Nothing was more peculiarly useful to us, in various situations, than the skill and ingenuity of this man as an artist, in repairing our guns, accoutrements, &c. and should it be thought proper to allow him something as an artificer, he has well deserved it.
19	George Shannon	ditto.	
20	John Potts	ditto.	

No.	Names.	Rank.	Remarks
21	John Baptiest La Page	ditto.	Entitled to no peculiar merit. Was enlisted at Fort Mandan, on the 2d of November 1804 in order to supply the deficiency in my permanent party occasioned by the discharge of John Newman. He performed the tour to the Pacific Ocean and returned to St. Louis, where he was discharged in common with others, on the 10th of November last. As he did not perform the labors incident to the summer of 1804, it would be proper to give him the gratuity only of two-thirds as much as is given to others of his rank.
22	John B. Thompson	ditto.	
23	William Werner	ditto.	
24	Richard Windsor	ditto.	
25	Peter Wiser	ditto.	
26	Alexander Willard	ditto.	
27	Joseph Whitehouse	ditto.	
28	George Drulyard	Interpreter.	A man of much merit; he has been peculiarly usefull from his knowledge of the common language of gesticulation, and his uncommon skill as a hunter and woodsman; those several duties he performed in good faith, and with an ardor which deserves the highest commendation. It was his fate also to have encountered, on various occasions, with either Captain Clark or myself, all the most dangerous and trying scenes of the voyage, in which he uniformly acquited himself with honor. He has served the

No.	Names.	Rank.	Remarks
			complete term of the whole tour and received only 25 dollars pr. month, and one ration pr. day, while I am informed that it is not unusual for individuals, in similar employments, to receive 30 dollars per month.
29	Touisant Charbono	ditto.	A man of no peculiar merit; was useful as an interpreter only, in which capacity he discharged his duties with good faith, from the moment of our departure from the Mandans, on the 7th of April 1805 until our return to that place in August last and received as a compensation 25 dollars pr. month while in service.

General Remark.

With rispect to all those persons whose names are entered on this roll, I feel a peculiar pleasure in declaring, that the Ample support which they gave me under every difficulty; the manly firmness which they evinced on every necessary occasion; and the patience and fortitude with which they submitted to, and bore, the fatigues and painful sufferings incident to my late tour to the Pacific Ocean, entitles them to my warmest approbation and thanks; nor will I suppress the expression of a hope, that the recollection of services thus faithfully performed will meet a just reward in an ample remuneration on the part of our Government.

City of Washington   MERIWETHER LEWIS
January 15th 1807.   Captain 1st U.S. Regt. Infty.

ALS with ADS enclosed, RC (DNA, RG 107, L-100). Endorsed; received 16 Jan. 1807. The original letter and its enclosure are in such poor condition that they can no longer be accurately transcribed. I have relied partially on a typewritten copy of the letter and a longhand copy of the roll, which are filed with the originals, and have checked these against the originals as closely as possible.

Since Lewis's roster of his party is the only document in this collection in which he names all his men, I use it as a vehicle for some biographical details. My intention is to limit these notes to information which is new or at least recent. I shall not repeat the standard sketches of these men which appear in works such as BIDDLE-COUES, WHEELER, and the JOURNALS. Only a few of the participants left fairly full records of their lives; the others sank early into obscurity. I fear that much of the interest the world has shown in these people borders on antiquarianism; our understanding of the expedition is increased little by the scanty biographical facts that history has preserved. Still, I make no apology for adding what follows here. The index to this volume should be consulted for additional references. I follow Lewis's numbering.

1. John Ordway (c.1775–c.1817), from Capt. Russell Bissell's company, First Infantry, Kaskaskia. No new information except that found elsewhere in this volume.

2. Nathaniel Pryor, one of the enlistees from Kentucky. For new information see No. 405 and the accompanying notes.

3. Charles Floyd (1782–1804), an enlistee from Kentucky and the cousin of Sgt. Pryor. A few additional details about his illness and death on the expedition are to be found in the Clark field notes (CtY). A letter not often quoted, which was at one time in the possession of the Floyd Memorial Association in Sioux City, Iowa, is this brief fragment from Charles's younger brother Nathaniel to his sister Nancy: "Our dear Charles died on the voyage of colic. He was well cared for as Clark was there, my heart is too full to say more [*several words illegible*]. I will see you soon, your brother Nat" (HOLMAN & MARKS).

4. Patrick Gass (1771–1870), from Capt. Russell Bissell's company, First Infantry, Kaskaskia. I believe that he and John Colter are the only enlisted members of the expedition about which books have been written. See the biography of Gass by JACOB, and articles by FORREST, MC GIRR, and SMITH (1). His correspondence while obtaining and defending his pension has provided a substantial amount of hitherto unused biographical data (see Nos. 408, 410, 411). On the publication of his journal, see No. 264.

5. William Bratton (1778–1841), an enlistee from Kentucky. No new information.

6. John Collins, army unit unknown. In No. 211 he lists himself as residing in Frederick County, Md. After his name, on some rough notes made at the Wood River camp, Clark wrote "Blackguard" (CtY)—but he seems to have conducted himself acceptably, if not commendably, on the expedition, after some early misbehavior for which he was flogged. Collins, like several other members of the expedition, cannot be traced back to the company from which he was detached. It is likely that all such men were from the company of Capt. Russell Bissell. Those who came from John Campbell's company at South West Point I have identified through Campbell's company book. The same is true for those from Amos Stoddard's company of artillerists at St. Louis (Stoddard furnished only one man to the permanent party, but also supplied others to go as far as the Mandans). The "nine young men from Kentucky" enlisted for the expedition and can be identified through the financial records. I have seen the muster rolls for Daniel Bissell's company and obtained from them only the name of Joseph Whitehouse (John Newman is also credited to Daniel Bissell, but through another source). This leaves Russell Bissell's company, and unfortunately the only muster rolls of this company I have found in the National Archives are those for Lt. Zebulon Pike's detachment—from the

companies of both Daniel and Russell Bissell—in connection with his western exploration.

7. John Colter (c.1775–1813), an enlistee from Kentucky and the subject of two books, VINTON and HARRIS. A manuscript biography by W. H. Ghent, unpublished in 1953 and not available to Harris, is listed by WAGNER-CAMP, No. 14. Colter's fame rests more upon his travels in the Yellowstone region than his work with Lewis and Clark.

8. Pierre Cruzatte, an enlistee from St. Louis whose mother was an Omaha Indian. No new information.

9. Joseph Field, an enlistee from Kentucky. No new information.

10. Reuben Field, an enlistee from Kentucky. He was recommended for a lieutenancy in a letter from Clark to Dearborn, 26 Nov. 1807, "if the army should be augmented" (DNA, RG 107, Register of Letters Received, C-375). At the same time, Clark recommended a man named R. C. Floyd— possibly a relative of Sgt. Floyd—for a captaincy.

11. Robert Frazer, army unit unknown. No. 266 is an unpublished letter of his, and he is mentioned elsewhere in connection with his proposed journal. In the period 1825–28 he was living on the Gasconade in Missouri.

12. Silas Goodrich, army unit unknown. No new information.

13. George Gibson, an enlistee from Kentucky. No new information.

14. Thomas Procter Howard, from Capt. John Campbell's company, Second Infantry. He was from Brimfield, Mass., enlisted 1 April 1801, twenty-two years of age, no height given, hair and complexion fair, eyes blue. Listed in Capt. Campbell's company book as being on command with Capt. Lewis 24 Nov. 1803 (DNA, RG 94, Post-Revolutionary Records, No. 104). A private named Thomas Howard, serving as a boatman, left Fort Adams in May 1808 attached to the command of Capt. Horatio Stark, First Infantry. He reached Fort Madison in August and served at that post for an undetermined period (see DNA, RG 94, Muster, Pay, and Recruiting Rolls, First Infantry).

15. Hugh Hall, from Capt. John Campbell's company, Second Infantry. He was from Carlisle, Pa., enlisted 13 Dec. 1798, twenty-six years of age, five feet eight inches, fair hair, sandy complexion, gray eyes. Re-enlisted 1 Oct. 1803. On command with Capt. Lewis 24 Nov. 1803, according to his commanding officer's company book. Hall was still in the St. Louis area in 1809; on 11 April of that year Lewis lent him $2 (Lewis's account book, MoSHi).

16. Francis Labiche, an enlistee from St. Louis. No new information.

17. Hugh McNeal, army unit unknown. A private of this name was with Ninian Pinkney's company, First Infantry, when it left Cantonment Belle Fontaine and went up the Mississippi in Aug. 1803 to establish Fort Madison. He appears on the muster rolls as late as Sept. 1811. Although the company was Pinkney's, it was commanded by Lt. Alpha Kingsley.

18. John Shields, an enlistee from Kentucky. No new information.

19. George Shannon, an enlistee, probably from Ohio. There is new information on Shannon in this volume; see the index.

20. John Potts, from Capt. John Campbell's company, Second Infantry. A native of Dillenburg, Germany, enlisted 22 July 1800, twenty-four years of age, black hair, fair complexion, blue eyes. Occupation, miller. He had served in Capt. Robert Purdy's company at South West Point, and went on command with Capt. Lewis 24 Nov. 1803.

21. Jean Baptiste Lepage, enlisted at Fort Mandan. No new information.
22. John B. Thompson, army unit unknown. No new information.
23. William Werner, army unit unknown. No new information.
24. Richard Windsor, army unit unknown. In the 1825–28 period he was living along the Sangamon in Illinois.
25. Peter Wiser, army unit unknown. He was involved in fur-trading activities out of St. Louis in the years following the expedition, and is mentioned here and there in the Clark Papers (MoSHi).
26. Alexander Willard (1777–1865), from Capt. Amos Stoddard's company, Corps of Artillerists. Born in Charleston, N.H., enlisted 9 June 1800, twenty-one years of age, five feet ten inches, dark eyes, brown hair, dark complexion. Occupation, blacksmith. Stoddard's company book (MoSHi) shows him "Transferd to Captain Lewis. 1804." Lewis hired him as a blacksmith for the Sauks and Foxes 16 March 1808 (BATES, 1:310–11). Since this was before the establishment of Fort Madison, he probably lived in or near Quashquame's village at present Montrose, Iowa, or across the river at William Ewing's place at present Nauvoo, Ill. But by 1 July 1809, Clark had listed him as blacksmith for the Shawnees and Delawares (TERR. PAPERS, 14:289). When news of the Battle of Tippecanoe reached St. Louis late in 1811, Willard was sent as an express to carry the news up the Mississippi; but he arrived at the lead mines below Prairie du Chien too late to alert the white men there, including Nathaniel Pryor, and they were plundered by hostile Indians (see No. 405).
27. Joseph Whitehouse, from Capt. Daniel Bissell's company, First Infantry (see note under No. 112). In No. 211 he lists himself as being from Fairfax County, Va. At one place in the Wood River field notes, Clark calls him a corporal (26 Dec. 1803, CtY), but during the expedition he was a private.
28. George Drouillard, a civilian employee. No new information except that given elsewhere in this volume.
29. Toussaint Charbonneau, a civilian employee. See No. 205.

Two men are named in the body of Lewis's letter but not in the roster. They are Corp. Richard Warfington and Pvt. John Newman. Warfington was from Capt. John Campbell's company, Second Infantry. He was from Louisburg, N.C., enlisted 4 Aug. 1799, twenty-two years of age, five feet ten inches, brown hair, fair complexion, black eyes. On command with Capt. Lewis 24 Nov. 1803. After his return from Fort Mandan he went back to his company. An entry in the company book for 19 June 1805 shows that he drew from Lt. John Brahan at Fort Massac some articles of uniform clothing, and a later undated entry marks him "Discharged, time expired" (DNA, RG 94, Post-Revolutionary Records, No. 104).

John Newman was from Capt. Russell Bissell's company, First Infantry (see financial records, No. 277). He was trading on the Missouri in the 1830's and is frequently mentioned in the journal of F. A. CHARDON. In annotating that journal, Annie Heloise Abel conjectures that he may have been the person named in the Roman Catholic records of Pennsylvania, son of Walter Newman and Catherine Zimmerman, who married Olympia Dubreuil in July 1832.

Two men who were with the party at Wood River did not continue with the expedition. A man named Leakins was present 31 Dec. 1803 but was discharged for theft 4 Feb. 1804, according to Clark's field notes (CtY). The other man is called "Corpl. Robertson" in Clark's entry for 26 Dec. I have found no soldier of this name in the area, but suggest that it might have been Corp. John Robinson, from Stoddard's company, listed in the company book as being from New Hampshire, enlisted 1 Oct. 1803 at Kaskaskia, twenty-three years of age; occupation, shoemaker.

Another class of men must be considered: the ones who claimed to have been with the expedition but were not. Two examples will be cited here. An article in the Columbia City, Ind., *Commercial-Mail*, 5 March 1960, about Samuel Wilson (1778–1878), a centenarian who had claimed to be the original Uncle Sam: "When they were young men, Samuel and Nathaniel [Wilson] accompanied the Lewis-Clark expedition as far north as the place where Mandan, North Dakota is now located. They spent the winter there and returned to St. Louis in the spring." Another claimant was Alexander Carson. CLARKE, 295, quotes a letter of T. J. Hubbard to James W. Nesmith, 24 Sept. 1858 (OrHi), saying that Carson had come out to the mountains [Mandans?] with Lewis and Clark and later was with Wilson P. Hunt in 1811, finally settling in Oregon. A man of this name was in the St. Louis area in Dec. 1805 (TERR. PAPERS, 13:344), but I find no evidence that he was ever with Lewis and Clark. Thwaites left room for speculation when he failed to comment adequately on an unclear name that Clark put into the JOURNALS, 1:109. The name appears as "Carrn" and Thwaites adds "[Carson?—Ed.]." I have checked the word in the manuscript journals, and like Thwaites I get nothing from it but "Carrn." But I still believe that Carson, had he been with the expedition, would have been mentioned in the rosters and journal entries.

237. Charles Willson Peale to Jefferson

Dear Sir   Museum [Philadelphia] Feby. 10th 1807.

In conversation with a *friend* this morning as the Indians were leaving this City, he said they were sadly deseased; they had been with the women of bad fame in the lower part of the town and contracted the venerial disease. I have had no opportunity to enquire for the facts of this report, however think it my duty to give you this notice, with the Idea that you will give orders for their cure before their departure, if such is realy their situation. I remember that when I was at Washington you desired me to enquire if I could precure some small Inkholders on my return either at Baltimore or in Philada. and that then, I could not find them after diligent search. A Stationer here has imported some very small; ¾ In. square, and one Inch square. If you have occasion at present for such be so obliging as to give me early notice that I may purchase for you. I long to see Captain Lewis. I wish to possess his portrait for the Museum.[1] With much esteem I am Dr. Sir your friend,

C. W. PEALE

P.S. When I reflect with what freedom I dictate my letters to you, they may be thought by those who do not know me, presumptive and deficient of respect, very wide this is from my feelings. I have long been accustomed to address you with the freedom of a friend, that has always sought occasions to serve me. C. P.

If it is known to those who have had the care of these Indians that I have given you this notice they may be offended with me, and my situation require me to make freinds.

ALS, RC (DLC). Endorsed; received 12 Feb. 1807. Reply is No. 238.
   1. "Mr. Lewis is richly entitled to a place amongst the Portraits of the Museum, and I hope he will do me the favor of sitting as soon as he arrives here" (Peale to Jefferson, 24 Dec. 1806, DLC).

238. Jefferson to Charles Willson Peale

Dear Sir   Washington Feb. 13. 07.
   Nothing would be wanting to fill up the measure of dissatisfaction with my present situation, but to see my friends adopt a stile of formality & distance towards me. Be assured that your communications are always welcome, & the more so when the most frank. I shall make a proper use of that in your letter recieved last night. I will thank you to procure for me a pair of the inkholders of ¾ I. square & another of those of 1. inch square which you are so kind as to mention as now to be had in Philadelphia, and note their cost, which I will find the means of replacing. I presume Capt. Lewis will leave this about the close of the session of Congress. Accept my friendly salutations and assurances of great esteem & respect.

                                        TH: JEFFERSON

ALS, SC (DLC). Endorsed.

239. Jefferson to Henry Dearborn

[14 February 1807]
   Th: Jefferson salutes Genl. Dearborne with friendship and communicates the following information from Capt. Lewis, which may be useful to Colo. Freeman and our future explorers, and indeed may enable us understandingly to do acceptable things to our Louisiana neighbors when we wish to gratify them. He says the following are the articles in highest value with them.

1. *Blue* beads. This is a coarse cheap bead imported from China, & costing in England 13d. the lb. in strands. It is far more valued by the Indians than the *white* beads of the same manufacture, & answers all the purposes of money, being counted by the fathom. He says that were his journey to be performed again, one half or ⅔ of his stores *in value,* should be of these.

2. Common brass buttons, more valued than any thing except beads.

3. Knives.

4. Battle axes & tomahawks.

5. Sadler's seat awls, which answer for mockasin awls.

6. Some glover's needles.

7. Some iron combs.

8. Some nests of camp kettles. Brass is much preferred to iron, tho both are very useful to the indians.

Feb. 14. 07.

Arrow points should have been added.

AL, SC (DLC).

240. Henry Dearborn to Jefferson

Sir   War Department Feby. 24. 1807
    I have the honor of proposing for your approbation first Lieutenant William Clark[1] of the Regiment of Artillerists to be promoted to the Rank of Lieut. Colonel in the second Regiment of Infantry, vice Thomas H. Cushing promoted to the rank of Colonel. Accept Sir assurances of my high respect & consideration.

H. DEARBORN.

LS, RC (DLC); SC (PHi).
1. Clark had been routinely promoted to the rank of first lieutenant 31 Jan. 1806, while wintering at Fort Mandan.

241. Henry Dearborn to Jefferson

Sir   [c. 25 February 1807]
    The name & proposed promotion of Capt. Clark has been left out of the list by a misunderstanding of my directions. Yours.

H. DEARBORN

ALS, RC (DLC). Addressed; endorsed; received 25 Feb. 1807.

242. Jefferson to the Senate

To the Senate of the United States [28 February 1807]

I nominate Meriwether Lewis of Virginia to be Governor of the territory of Louisiana.

William Clarke of Indiana, now a 1st Lieut. of the regiment of artillerists to be promoted to the rank of Lieutenant Colonel in the 2d regiment of infantry v. Thos. Cushing promoted.

Thomas Todd of Kentucky to be an associate justice of the Supreme court of the United States.

James Tremble of Tennessee to be attorney for the U.S. in the district of East Tennessee.

Levi Barber of Ohio to be Reciever of public monies at Marietta.

Edmund H. Taylor of Kentucky to be Reciever of the public monies at Detroit.

TH: JEFFERSON
Feb. 28. 1807.

ADS, SC (DLC). Lewis's nomination was approved, but Clark's failed. Apparently some senators did not wish to advance Clark over the heads of other officers with greater seniority. For an editorial comment on the incident, see the *National Intelligencer*, 20 April 1807. Clark did not seem very disappointed by the outcome. He wrote his brother Edmund on 5 March: "The President thought proper to nomonate me as Lt. Col. to one of the regiments which was rejected by the Senate on the Grounds of braking through a Principal. I am truly gratified to find that in this decission of the Senate they as I am told unanimussly agreed that they would confirm any other nomonation in the gift of the government" (WHi). When Clark wrote these lines he almost surely knew that he was going to be appointed superintendent of Indian affairs for Louisiana Territory, an appointment which came through on 9 March. And on 12 March, Dearborn successfully nominated him to become brigadier-general of militia for the territory (SC, PHi).

243. Lewis to Henry Dearborn

Sir, City of Washington March 2nd 1807.

I request your acceptance of this my resignation of the Military appointment which I have had the honor to bear in the Army of the United States; in doing this Sir, I beg leave to express the pleasure I feel in acknowledging the justice propriety and confidence which has ever been evinced towards me by your department. I am with due consideration and rispect Your most Obt. Servt.

MERIWETHER LEWIS Capt.
1st U.S. Regt. Infty.

ALS, RC (DNA, RG 107, L-124).

244. The Act Compensating Lewis and Clark

[3 March 1807]

An Act making compensation to Messrs. Lewis and Clarke, and their companions.

Be it enacted, &c., That the Secretary of War be, and he is hereby, directed to issue land warrants to Meriwether Lewis and William Clarke, for one thousand six hundred acres each; to John Ordway, Nathaniel Prior, the heirs or legal representatives of Charles Floyd, (deceased,) Patrick Gass, William Bratton, John Collins, John Colter, Pier Cruzatte, Joseph Field, Reuben Field, Robert Frazier, Silas Goodrich, George Gibson, Thomas P. Howard, Hugh Hall, Francis Labuiche, High M'Neal, John Shields, George Shannon, John Potts, John Baptiste Le Page, John B. Thompson, William Werner, Richard Windsor, Peter Wiser, Alexander Willard, Joseph Whitehouse, George Grulyard, Tousaint Charbono, Richard Worfengton, and John Newman, for three hundred and twenty acres each: which several warrants may, at the option of the holder or possessor, be located with any register or registers of the land offices, subsequent to the public sales in such office, on any of the public lands of the United States, lying on the west side of the Mississippi, then and there offered for sale, or may be received at the rate of two dollars per acre, in payment of any such public lands.

Sec. 2. *And be it further enacted,* That double pay shall be allowed, by the Secretary of War, to each of the before named persons, agreeably to the time he or they may have served in the late enterprise to the Pacific Ocean, conducted by Messrs. Lewis and Clarke, and that the sum of eleven thousand dollars be and the same hereby is appropriated to discharge the same, out of any moneys in the Treasury not otherwise appropriated.

Approved, March 3, 1807.

Printed, STATUTES, 6:65–66. After Chairman Alston presented his bill for the compensation of Lewis and Clark on 23 Jan., it survived considerable debate and a proposed amendment to include the names of William Eaton, Presley Neville O'Bannon, and George Washington Mann, who had lately been involved in the war with the Barbary pirates. Then some representatives contended that the grant was extravagant and beyond precedent. "It was the equivalent to taking more than $60,000 out of the Treasury, and might be perhaps three or four times that sum, as the grantees might go over all the Western country and locate their warrants on the best land, in 160 acre lots" (*Annals of the Congress of the United States,* 15:591). The bill passed the House by a vote of 62 to 23 on 28 Feb. and went to the Senate the same day. It was passed in the Senate without amendment and with little debate.

A list of the land warrants issued pursuant to the act will be found under No. 246. The following summary of the extra pay due the men is from a roster in Clark's hand (CtY), headed, "We the Subscribers do acknowledge to have received of [blank] the several Sums set opposite to our Names, the Same being due us from the War department pursuant to an Act of Congress bearing date March the 3rd 1807. entitled 'an Act makeing compensation to Messrs. Lewis & Clark and their companions'—Signed Duplicates." The rank of each man, and total time served, is omitted here. On the original form, space is provided for the signatures of the men and their witnesses, but no signatures are present.

Name	Period of Service	Monthly Rate	Amount
John Ordway	1 Jan. 1804 to 10 Oct. 1806	$ 8	$266.66⅔
Nathaniel Pryor	20 Oct. 1803 to 10 Oct. 1806	5 & 8	278.50
Charles Floyd	1 Aug. 1803 to 20 Aug. 1804	5 & 8	86.33⅓
Patrick Gass	1 Jan. 1804 to 10 Oct. 1806	5 & 8	243.66⅔
William Bratton	20 Oct. 1803 to 10 Oct. 1806	5	178.33⅓
John Collins	1 Jan. 1804 to 10 Oct. 1806	5	166.66⅔
John Colter	15 Oct. 1803 to 10 Oct. 1806	5	179.33⅓
Pierre Cruzatte	16 May 1804 to 10 Oct. 1806	5	144.16⅔
Joseph Field	1 Aug. 1803 to 10 Oct. 1806	5	191.66⅔
Reuben Field	1 Aug. 1803 to 10 Oct. 1806	5	191.66⅔
Robert Frazer	1 Jan. 1804 to 10 Oct. 1806	5	166.66⅔
Silas Goodrich	1 Jan. 1804 to 10 Oct. 1806	5	166.66⅔
George Gibson	19 Oct. 1803 to 10 Oct. 1806	5	178.50
Thomas P. Howard	1 Jan. 1804 to 10 Oct. 1806	5	166.66⅔
Hugh Hall	1 Jan. 1804 to 10 Oct. 1806	5	166.66⅔
Francis Labiche	16 May 1804 to 10 Oct. 1806	5	144.66⅔
Hugh McNeal	1 Jan. 1804 to 10 Oct. 1806	5	166.66⅔
John Shields	19 Oct. 1803 to 10 Oct. 1806	5	178.50
George Shannon	19 Oct. 1803 to 10 Oct. 1806	5	178.50
John Potts	1 Jan. 1804 to 10 Oct. 1806	5	166.66⅔
Jean Baptiste Lepage	2 Nov. 1804 to 10 Oct. 1806	5	111.50
John B. Thompson	1 Jan. 1804 to 10 Oct. 1806	5	166.66⅔
William Werner	1 Jan. 1804 to 10 Oct. 1806	5	166.66⅔
Richard Windsor	1 Jan. 1804 to 10 Oct. 1806	5	166.66⅔
Peter Wiser	1 Jan. 1804 to 10 Oct. 1806	5	166.66⅔
Alexander Willard	1 Jan. 1804 to 10 Oct. 1806	5	166.66⅔
Joseph Whitehouse	1 Jan. 1804 to 10 Oct. 1806	5	166.66⅔
Richard Warfington	14 May 1804 to 1 June 1805	7	99.96⅔
John Newman	14 May 1804 to 1 June 1805	5	62.83⅓
George Drouillard	1 Jan. 1804 to 10 Oct. 1806	25	833.33⅓
Toussaint Charbonneau	7 April 1805 to 17 Aug. 1806	25	409.16⅔

245. Petition to the Senate and House

[after 3 March 1807]

To the Senate & House of Representatives in Congress assembled.
The Petition of the undersigned being a part of those who ac-

companied, the expedition of Captains Lewis & Clark to the Pacific Ocean respectfully sheweth—

That your petitioners without presuming to call in question the liberality & justice of Congress in the provisions which they have already made for the followers of the aforsd. expedition, beg leave to express their desire that further measures may be adopted by Congress, in order that they may derive to themselves the full benefit of those Provisions.

Many of your Petitioners are poor & earnestly solicit that whatever price their country may set upon their toilsome & perilous services may not be withheld from them. Having abandoned their ordinary pursuits & establishments, at the time they embarked under the auspices of the aforesaid expedition the[y] are confident of finding in your wisdom & liberality an admission of those difficulties they would have to encounter in regaining their former situations, or in again betaking themselves (with little to commence with, to those occupations which would afford them the necessaries, if not the comforts of life.

Your petitioners would beg leave to represent, that many of them have married since their return & are generally residents of the Territory of Louisiana or Indiana—where they have settled themselves; not doubting, but that it would be found equally expedient to lay off their lands within the limits of one of the said Territories, as within the boundaries of any more distant Country. It may not perhaps be unnecessary for your petitioners to observe, that should they be compelled to Travel to any land office, situate at a great distance from their place of residence, for the purpose of obtaining & completing their title, the trouble and expence would be more than an equivalent for the value of the lands.

They would therefore respectfully submit their desire that some portion of the public land within one of the above mentioned Territories, where it is their wish to settle themselves may be designated for the purpose of *immediately locating* the respective quantities of land to which by the act of the last Session of Congress, they may be entitled—& your petitioners as in duty bound will ever pray—

JOHN B. THOMPSON
HUGH HALL
SILAS GOODRICH
GEORGE GIBSON
ALEXANDER WILLARD
PATK. GASS
REUBEN FIELD
JOSEPH FIELD

DS, RC (MoSHi). In the hand of Frederick Bates. The signatures are on the back of the sheet. Although I date this petition "after 3 March 1807" to give it a position among related documents, no actual date can be determined. It could not have been written until news of the compensation act had reached St. Louis.

246. "Messrs. Lewis & Clarke's Donation Lands"

No. 1   [6 March 1807]

Pursuant to an act of congress passed on the 3d day of March, 1807, entitled "An act making compensation to messieurs Lewis and Clarke and their companions," *Meriwether Lewis* is entitled to *one thousand, six hundred acres of land* to be located agreeably to said act, at the option of the holder or possessor, "with any register or registers of the land offices, subsequent to the public sales in such office, on any of the public lands lying on the west side of the Mississippi, then and there offered for sale, or may be received at the rate of two dollars per acre, in payment of any such lands." Given at the War-office this *6th* day of *march* in the year one thousand eight hundred and seven.

Registered.   Secretary of war.

(DNA, RG 15). A bound book labeled "Messrs. Lewis & Clarke's Donation Lands," containing both blank and executed forms, with stubs indicating that similar forms have been torn out. The stubs represent warrants of which the remaining executed forms are duplicates. In the example above, italicized words are those written into the printed form.

Forms and matching stubs are present for members of the expedition named in the Act of 3 March (No. 244). All executed forms are endorsed on the back: "March 6th, 1807, Received the warrant of which the within is a record." The endorsements are signed by Lewis except those for Clark, the Floyd heirs, Drouillard, Charbonneau, Warfington, and Newman, which are signed by Clark. Lewis lists himself "attorney in fact" for all the men he signed for, except John Colter. Clark lists himself "attorney in fact" for the heirs and legal representatives of Floyd, and in all other instances merely engages to deliver the warrants to the recipients. Clark's warrant, like Lewis's, is for 1,600 acres; the others are for 320 acres each.

The warrants are listed below according to their original numbers. When I have additional information I add it after the name. Unless noted otherwise, the information—highly variable in form and completeness—comes from a consolidated file in DNA, RG 49, called "Special acts, Box 1," where all available data on these warrants has been assembled.

1. Meriwether Lewis. The warrant is present and is the only one known to be extant. It is endorsed: "A part of the within warrant has been received as Cash, to the amount of two hundred and twenty two dollars and forty seven and a half cents from William Moore, in payment of land. W. Noland,

Receiver, Batesville [Ark.], Nov. 30, 1826." Lewis left his mother, Lucy Marks, all his property including the warrant. She gave a portion, not in acres but to the value of $500, to Reuben Lewis; then she sold the rest of it on 24 May 1824 to William Moore, her son-in-law, for $1,000. The following transcript (MoSHi) of an assignment from Reuben Lewis to William Moore indicates that Moore bought Reuben's interest in the warrant. The assignment was not made until 1829, but from the context of the documents with it I gather that it was drawn retroactively to comply with a legal requirement. "For value Received I hereby assign unto William Moore of Madison County Alabama all my right and claim in and to a Land Warrant No. 1 granted per Act of Congress of 3d March 1807 . . . in which 1600 Acres of Land was granted to Meriwether Lewis."

2. William Clark.

3. John Ordway.

4. Nathaniel Pryor.

5. Heirs of Charles Floyd. Floyd's sister, Mary L. Walton, sold the warrant to John G. Berry and John T. Winn for $640, in Adams County, Miss., 1 Nov. 1839.

6. Patrick Gass. For other warrants received by Gass, in payment for services in the War of 1812 and as additional compensation for his role in the expedition, see a note under No. 411.

7. William Bratton. He assigned the warrant to Samuel Barclay, 8 Oct. 1816.

8. John Collins.

9. John Colter. He assigned to John G. Comegys 20 Aug. 1810[?], and the warrant was surrendered at St. Louis for land in 1824.

10. Pierre Cruzatte.

11. Joseph Field. By 7 March 1822 his warrant had been accepted by the Receiver of Public Monies at Franklin, Mo., in payment for land.

12. Reuben Field. By 7 March 1822 his warrant had been accepted by the Receiver of Public Monies at Franklin, Mo., in payment for land.

13. Robert Frazer. Surrendered in payment for land by John Vivian, at Franklin, Mo., in 1821.

14. Silas Goodrich. Assigned to John Ordway 29 Sept. 1806 and surrendered in payment for land at Jackson, Mo., by an unknown person in 1822.

15. George Gibson.

16. Thomas P. Howard. An act of Congress authorized the Secretary of War to issue another warrant to Robert Haile in lieu of No. 16, which had been lost. Date of new warrant not given.

17. Hugh Hall.

18. Francis Labiche.

19. Hugh McNeal.

20. John Shields. By 7 March 1822 his warrant had been accepted by the Receiver of Public Monies at Franklin, Mo., in payment for land.

21. George Shannon. He petitioned successfully for renewal of his warrant, 16 April 1814, then sold it to Henry Clay.

22. John Potts. He still held this warrant at the time of his death in 1810 (he was killed by the Blackfeet in the West), when it was valued at $450 by a board of appraisers headed by his administrator, Rufus Easton. The appraisal of 4 Aug. 1810 is in the Lewis Papers (MoSHi). The warrant was sold at auction later in the year.

23. Jean Baptiste Lepage. Warrant assigned to Ordway 20 Oct. 1806.
24. John B. Thompson.
25. William Werner. Warrant assigned to Ordway 29 Oct. 1806.
26. Richard Windsor. By 7 March 1822 his warrant had been accepted by the Receiver of Public Monies at Franklin, Mo., in payment for land.
27. Peter Wiser.
28. Alexander Willard.
29. Joseph Whitehouse.
30. George Drouillard.
31. Toussaint Charbonneau.
32. Richard Warfington.
33. John Newman.

247. Henry Dearborn to Clark

Wm. Clark   War Department March 9. 1807

Sir, On your arrival at St. Louis you will please to take measures for sending the Mandan Chief and his famely to his Nation by as safe and Speedy conveyance as practicable.

You will with this receive an order on Colo. Hunt[1] for a Sergeant and ten Men, to be placed under the command of Ensign Pryor, who will be ordered to take charge of the party, and receive directions from you for the government of his conduct.

You are authorized to draw on this Department, for four hundred dollars, to be laid out in suitable articles to be sent with the party, as presents to the Mandan Nation, to be distributed under the directions of the principal Chiefs: you will likewise draw on this Department for such Sum as may be found indispensibly neccessary in fitting out the party for the Voyage.

If Ensign Pryor can recruit from two to six Men of suitable characters for Soldiers, and for the proposed voyage; such recruits may be added to the above mentioned party.

Should any merchants or traders be found disposed to send goods as high up the Missouri as the Mandan Towns, and will, without delay take measures for dispatching a suitable number of men with such goods so that they may be associated in the voyage with Ensign Pryor and his party, you will afford them encouragement, by granting them licenses to trade with the Indians generally on the Missouri from the Ricaras upward: and engage that, for two years at least, no other persons will be licensed to trade with those Indians. And if necessary, you may furnish, each man, who may accompany such traders and their goods, with amunition for the voyage up the river at the expense of the United States: say two pounds of powder, and lead or ball in proportion, to each man.

You will please to send orders to Ensign Pryor to be in readiness without delay, and to recruit as many suitable men as he can, to be enlisted for five years as Soldiers.

Your compensation as Agent of Indian Affairs in the Territory of Louisiana will be fifteen hundred dollars a year commencing on this day. I am respectfully &c.[2]

Lbk (DNA, RG 75, Letters Sent, B:287–88).
1. Col. Thomas Hunt (d. 1808), commandant of the First Infantry Regiment, and at this time commanding Cantonment Belle Fontaine.
2. Enclosed with this letter was Clark's commission as "Agent of Indian Affairs to the Several Nations of Indians within the Territory of Louisiana excepting the Great and little Osages and their several divisions, and detachments." The Osages had been assigned to Pierre Chouteau.

248. Clark's Receipt for Land Warrants

D. Copy.   [9 March 1807]
Received of Meriwether Lewis the land warrants severally issued and granted at the War-office by virtue of an act of Congress entitled "An act making compensation for Messieurs Lewis & Clarke and their companions" in favor of the following persons (to wit) Nathaniel Pryor, Patrick Gass, William Bratton, John Collins, John Colter, Pierre Cruzatte, Joseph Field, Reuben Field, Robert Frazier, George Gibson, Thomas P. Howard, Hugh Hall, Francis Labuiche, Hugh McNeal, John Shields, George Shannon, John Potts, John B. Thompson, Richard Windsor, Peter Wi[ser, Alexa]nder Willard, & Joseph Whitehouse, which said warrants I promise and engage to deliver to the several proprietors of the same on application.
March 9th 1807.   W. C.

Test:

Hezekiah Rogers
C. Swan[1]

Transcript (MoSHi). A copy in an unknown hand. Clark's initials are deleted.
1. Caleb Swan (d. 1809), paymaster of the army.

249. Henry Dearborn to Nathaniel Pryor

Sir   War Department March 9. 1807
You will receive orders and directions, from Capt. Wm. Clark

[383]

Principal Agent for Indian affairs in the Territory of Louisiana, for ascending the Missouri as far as the Mandan Towns; and you will act in strict conformity to such orders and directions. I am respectfully &c.

Lbk (DNA, RG 107, Letters Sent, 3:139).

250. Henry Dearborn to Thomas Hunt

Sir,   War Department March 9. 1807.
   You will please to detach a careful sober serjeant, and ten sober good privates to be put under the Command of Ensign Pryor to ascend the Missouri under the direction of Wm. Clark Esqr., who is principal Indian Agent in the Louisiana Territory. The detachment should be furnished with such provisions and ammunition for the Voyage as Mr. Clark may judge necessary. I am respectfully &c.

Lbk (DNA, RG 107, Letters Sent, 3:140).

251. Clark's Receipt to Lewis

                                        City of Washington March 10th 1807.
Received of Meriwether Lewis the sum of six thousand eight hundred and ninty six dollars and thirty four cents, the same being in full of the sum of one thousand two hundred and twenty eight dollars and six cents granted me by an act of congress bearing date the 3rd of March 1807 and including also the gratuitous donations under the said act to all the men who were with us on our late expedition to the Pacific Ocean except John Ordway and John Colter, which several gratuities I promise to pay to the said individuals and transmit their receipts for the same to Meriwether Lewis or to the department of war within one year from this date or sooner if I am enabled to obtain such receipts, having signed this receipt in addition to the regular receipt rolls.

$6,896.34   WM. CLARK
Delivered up the Vouchers 20 Augt. to Gov. Lewis for all except LePage and his I paid Cash back to Gov. M. Lewis.[1]

DS, RC (MoSHi). Endorsed, "Receipt to Govr. Lewis paid up." The signature has been heavily deleted with ink. The body of the document is in Lewis's hand. Another copy present is in Clark's hand, bearing his initials, and endorsed by him, "a Copy for a receipt to Capt. Lewis."

[384]

1. Lewis still owed Lepage $116.33 at the time of his death, according to a note by John Hastings Marks headed "Statement of the Situation of the Estate of M. Lewis" (Lewis-Marks Papers, ViU).

252. Lewis to Clark

My Dear Friend,   City of Washington March 11th 1807.

I took some pills last evening after your departure from which I have found considerable relief, and have no doubt of recovering my health perfectly in the course of a few days.

We were in such haste yesterday in arranging our accounts for settlement with our men that I entirely neglected to deduct from Werner's pay the advances which I have made him; the inclosed receipts will shew the amount. Should you learn that he has sold or gambled away the horse saddle &c. with which I intrusted him you will deduct $44.50 cts. on that account in addition to 30 Dols. 75 cts. the sum advanced him in cash, but if the horse died not through his negligence then I do not wish any deduction to be made on that account; the money which may thus fall into your hands you may transmit me by mail to Washington.

I have written duplicates of this letter and directed one to Staunton and the other to Findcastle in order to insure the receipt of one or the other. Your sincer friend,

MERIWETHER LEWIS

ALS, RC (MoSHi). Addressed, "Capt. William Clark   Findcastle Virginia." On the back is an undated draft of Clark's reply, printed below as No. 255.

253. Lewis to the Public

City of Washington
March 14th, 1807.

Having been informed that there were several unauthorised and probably some spurious publications now preparing for the press, on the subject of my late tour to the Pacific Ocean by individuals entirely unknown to me, I have considered it a duty which I owe the public, as well as myself to put them on their guard with respect to such publications, lest from the practice of such impositions they may be taught to depreciate the worth of the work which I am myself preparing for publication before it can possibly appear, as much time, labor, and expense are absolutely necessary in order to do

[385]

justice to the several subjects which it will embrace: With a view therefore to prevent the practice of those deceptions the public are informed that the lists for subscriptions which have been promulgated by myself are headed with the subjoined Prospectus, and that those who wish to possess the genuine work, may obtain it by entering their names on those lists. The Prospectus will serve to shew the distribution and contents of the work.

The map will most probably be published by the latter end of October next, and the first volume of the work about the 1st of January 1808; the two remaining volumes will follow in succession as early as they can possibly be prepared for publication.

As early as a just estimate of the price of the several parts of this work can be formed, public notice will be given of the same through the medium of the Press.

To Robert Frazier only has permission been given either by Gen. William Clark or myself, to publish any thing in relation to our late voyage. When the proposals were first drawn in October last for the publication of the journal of that man, they were submitted to me for correction; I then expunged the promise which had been made, that the work should contain certain information in relation to the natural history of the country through which we had passed and cautioned the persons concerned in the publication not to promise the world any thing with which they had not the means of complying; but as the hope of gain seems to have outstripped their good faith to the public in this respect; I think it my duty to declare that Robert Frazier, who was only a private on this expedition, is entirely unacquainted with celestial observations, mineralogy, botany, or zoology, and therefore cannot possibly give any accurate information on those subjects, nor on that of geography, and that the whole which can be expected from his Journal is merely a limited detail of our daily transactions. With respect to all unauthorised publications relative to this voyage, I presume that they cannot have stronger pretensions to accuracy of information than that of Robert Frazier.

MERIWETHER LEWIS.

Printed, *National Intelligencer,* 18 March 1807. A prospectus similar to No. 262a follows the letter, concluding with the note: "Editors of Public Prints in the United States, disposed to aid the publication of this work, are requested to give the foregoing a few insertions." The *National Intelligencer* ran the prospectus without the letter in its issue of 23 March, then used both together in the issues of 25, 27, 30 March, and 1 April. The *Aurora* ran letter and prospectus 23 March. This letter provoked a stinging reply from David McKeehan (No. 264).

254. Lewis to Clark

My Dear friend,   City of Washington March 15th 1807.
This will be handed you by Frazier, whose receipt you will find inclosed for $50. which be pleased to deduct from the monies of his in your hands and transmit it to me by the mail.

Frazier will deliver you your commission as a Brigadier General of the Militia of Louisiana together with a letter to Mr. Bates. The letter to Mr. Bates has been left unsealed in order that you may read it's contents; you will be pleased to seal it before you deliver it. Frazier has been bound in a recognisance of several hundred dollars to appear as a witness against Waistcoat[1] and others who have been apprehended as the associates of Colo. Burr in his treasonable practices, and who are to be tryed about the begining of May next. Dispatch is therefore necessary on the part of Frazier, and if you cannot proceed as rapidly as it is necessary he should it would be well to seal my letter to Mr. Bates and forward it to him by Frazier; it might be well also to write to Mr. Bates yourself, as he may probably have it in his power to expedite some parts of the preparations for the departure of the Mandan chief. Your friend,

M. LEWIS

ALS, RC (MoSHi).
1. Frazer was scheduled to testify at the fall 1807 term of the general court of Louisiana Territory against Robert Wescott, who was accused of conspiring with Aaron Burr. Wescott's role in the episode is set forth by CARTER, in an article on the Burr-Wilkinson intrigue in St. Louis.

255. [Clark to Lewis]

[after 15 March 1807]
The post brought 3 letters to me from you dureing the time I delayed at near Fincastle 2 of them by Charlotsville and one directed to me at Fincastle which contained 2 receipts from Werner amounting to 30.75. This sum and $50 which I deducted from Frazier I here enclose to you in a Check on the bank the safest way &c. I met with Werner at Charlottsville and paid him 100 Dollars, and promised to pay the ballance at Fincastle to which place he intended to come in the stage. He did not arrive dureing my delay at Fincastle. I therefore left the ballance of his pay after directing the 30$ 75 cents to be paid to him on his arrival. I can get no proof that he sold your horse. He said that your horse died and he then purchased one which he sold on the way at Mad. Courthouse. I enquired in that neighbour-

hood and hird of him selling a Bay horse. Frazier says he heard the same. I fear you will be obliged to lose the horse, altho I think it probable that he swoped & then sold but I have no proof & he positively denies. I have requested a gentleman and negh. of mine to whome I have given the ballance of his money to investigate W. Privately on the subject of the horse and save what he can. I wrote to you a hasty letter on this subject from Col. Lewis. I also requested you to mention to the Secy. of War to send me at St. L. 2 large & 1 small Medals inclosed.

Frazier overtook me at Col. H.[1] with a letter from you to me one to Mr. Bates, and a commission of B G of the Milita of Louisiana. Your letter to Mr. Bates I sealed and sent on by Frazier and wrote one myself &c. As the appointment is not accompanied by any instructions from the Departmt. of War I shall proceed without delay to St. Louis and shall assist Bates in every thing I can respecting the Milita of that Teritory, or any thing else which I can do. It would be well to get some powder allowed for Exercise as well as a Deposit in case of an imergency.

I have made an attacked most vigorously, we have come to terms, and a delivery is to be made first of January [. . .] when I shall be in possession highly pleasing to my self.[2] I shall return at that time eagerly to be in possession of what I have never yet experienced. I hope my absence from the Louisiana will not be displeasing to the govermt. You can hint a little on that subject if you think proper and let me know. My F. your choice is one I highly approve, but should the thing not take to your wish I have discovered a most lovly girl Butiful rich possessing those accomplishments which is calculated to make a man hapy—inferior to you—but to few others the Daughter of C—His politicks is in opposition to yours. I understand the father of my ——— is also a Fed which I did not know untill the other day. I took him to be a good plain republican. At all events I will hope to introduce some substantial sincere republicanism into some branch of the family about January.

AL, SC (MoSHi). A penciled draft on the back of Lewis's letter, No. 252.
1. Col. George Hancock, father of Julia.
2. A reference to Clark's engagement to Julia Hancock.

256. Jefferson to Bernard McMahon

Sir   Washington Mar. 20. 07.

I am in hopes I am more fortunate in the seeds I now send you than the effete roots before sent. The inclosed seeds are given me by

Capt. Lewis for my own garden; but as I am not in a situation to do them justice, I am more anxious they should be saved in any way than merely to see them in my own possession, I forward them to you who can give them their best chance. It will give you too an opportunity of committing them earlier to the ground than those you will recieve from Capt. Lewis for yourself, as it may yet be some time before he is with you. Perhaps you may as well say nothing of your recieving this, lest it might lessen the portion he will be disposed to give you; and believing myself they will be best in your hands, I wish to increase the portion deposited with you. Accept my salutations & respects.

TH: JEFFERSON

ALS, SC (DLC). Endorsed.

257. Jefferson to William Hamilton

Dear Sir   Washington Mar. 22. 07.

It is with great pleasure that, at the request of Governor Lewis, I send you the seeds now inclosed, being part of the Botanical fruits of his journey across the continent. I cannot but hope that some of them will be found to add useful or agreeable varieties to what we now possess. These, with the descriptions of plants, which, not being in seed at the time, he could not bring, will add considerably to our Botanical possessions. He will equally add to the Natural history of our country. On the whole, the result confirms me in my first opinion that he was the fittest person in the world for such an expedition. He will be with you shortly at Philadelphia, where I have no doubt you will be so kind as to shew him those civilities which you so readily bestow on worth. I send a similar packet to Mr. McMahon, to take the chance of a double treatment in confiding these public deposits to your & his hands, I am sure I make the best possible disposition of them. Accept my friendly salutations & assurances of great esteem & respect.

TH: JEFFERSON

ALS, SC (DLC). Endorsed. Hamilton was less successful than McMahon in raising plants from Lewis's seeds. Nearly a year later he wrote to Jefferson, "Mr. Lewis's seeds have not yet vegetated freely, more however may come up this spring. I have nevertheless obtained plants, of the yellow wood, or *Osage apple*, seven or eight sorts of *gooseberries* & *currants* & one of his kind of aricarara tobacco, have flowered so well as to afford me an elegant drawing from it" (5 Feb. 1808, DLC).

258. Jefferson to Bernard McMahon

Sir   Washington Mar. 22. 07.

Governor Lewis's journey to Philadelphia being delayed longer than
was expected, and the season advancing, we have thought it best to
forward to you by post the packet of seeds destined for you. They
are the fruits of his journey across the continent, & will I trust add
some useful or agreeable varieties to what we now possess. I send a
similar packet to Mr. Hamilton of the Woodlands. In making him &
yourself the depositories of these public treasures, I am sure we take
the best measures possible to ensure them from beng lost. I sent you
a small packet a few days ago which he had destined for myself: but
I am in too indifferent a situation to take the care of them which
they merit. Accept my salutations & best wishes.

TH: JEFFERSON

ALS, SC (DLC). Endorsed. Reply is No. 260.

259. The Patrick Gass Prospectus

[23 March 1807]

PROPOSALS for publishing by subscription, By David M'Keehan,[1]
Bookseller, a Journal of the Voyages & Travels of a Corps of Discovery, under the command of Captain Lewis and Captain Clarke of
the Army of the United States, from the mouth of the river Missouri
through the interior parts of North America to the Pacific Ocean,
during the years 1804, 1805 & 1806. Containing An authentic relation of the most interesting transactions during the expedition;—A
description of the country, and an account of its inhabitants, soil,
climate, curiosities, & vegetable and animal productions. By Patrick
Gass, one of the persons employed in the expedition: with geographical & explanatory notes, by the Publisher.

To recommend the correctness of this work, the publisher begs leave
to state, that at the different resting places during the expedition, the
several journals were brought together, compared, corrected, and the
blanks, which had been unavoidably left, filled up; and that, since he
became the proprietor, in order to render it more useful and acceptable, he has undertaken and completed the labourious task of
arranging and transcribing the whole of it. To this he will add, the
following extract from a certificate delivered by Captain Lewis to Mr.
Gass, dated St. Louis, 10th Oct. 1806.

"As a tribute justly due to the merits of the said *Patrick Gass*, I with chearfulness declare, that the ample support, which he gave me, under every difficulty; the manly firmness, which he evinced on every occasion; and the fortitude with which he bore the fatigues and painful sufferings incident to that long voyage, intitles him to my highest confidence and sincere thanks, while it eminently recommends him to the consideration and respect of his fellow citizens.[2]

CONDITIONS.

I. This work will be published in one volume duodecimo; and is expected to contain near 300 pages.

II. The price to subscribers will be one dollar, handsomely bound in boards. As the expence, however, of publishing an edition sufficiently large to meet the demands for this work, including the original purchase money, will be very considerable; those who pay in advance, will be intitled to a discount of 12½ per cent.

III. Those who obtain ten subscribers and become responsible for the payment of the subscription money shall receive one copy gratis.

The work will be ready for delivery in two months from this date.

Subscriptions will be received at the Store of the publisher, and at the Office of the Pittsburgh Gazette.

Pittsburgh, March 23d, 1807.

Printed, Pittsburgh *Gazette,* 24 March 1807 and later issues.

1. McKeehan was a bookseller who ran a "Book and Stationary Store, in front of the Court House," in Pittsburgh. His name appears as signer of advertisements from the Pittsburgh land office, appearing in the *Gazette* in 1807; he may have been the register of that office. He may also be the David McKeehan who was graduated from Dickinson College in 1787 and admitted to the Pennsylvania bar in 1792. Perhaps he had lived at one time in Wellsburg, W. Va.; Gass's biographer JACOB associates him with that place.

2. Lewis wrote similar testimonials for all his men. Bratton's has survived as No. 215.

260. Bernard McMahon to Jefferson

Sir.   Philadelphia March 27th 1807

I duly received the roots and seeds you were so good as to send me, for which I return you and Governor Lewis my hearty thanks. I have no doubt but I will be able to give a good account of the produce, for I never saw seeds in a better state of preservation, and their having reached me in good time will be a considerable advantage. I have already sowed several kinds, will treat the whole with very particular care, and have no doubt but I will be able to send you in due time, plants *of every kind* committed to my care.[1]

[391]

I request the favour of your informing Governor Lewis that I wish him to accept from me, a collection of seeds of culinary & ornamental plants, to take with him when going to the territory over which he is to preside; they shall be ready for him whenever he pleases.

The dwarf Cedar[2] of the plains of Missouri, I take, from the seed, to be a species of Juniperus; the *Shallan*[3] of the Clatsops, a Vaccinium; and the flowering Pea[4] of the plains of Arkansas, a Lupinus. I shall from time to time report to you or to Governor Lewis the progress of this precious collection, and of any other articles with which I may be favoured.

Mr. Duane[5] intends to leave this City for Washington on tuesday next; by him I will send the Antwerp Raspberries. Accept Sir My most grateful thanks, and sincere good wishes,

BERND. McMAHON.

ALS, RC (DLC). Endorsed; received 29 March 1807.

1. A few days later, when sending some plants to Jefferson, McMahon wrote, "I have fine crops already up of the Aricara Tobacco, and perennial flax [*Linum* sp.], and expect numbers of the others up in a few days" (2 April 1807, DLC). Later he said, "I have several sorts growing of the seeds you were pleased to send me, among which are four varieties of Currants [*Ribes* sp.], and I am confident that I shall have plants from every kind I received" (10 April 1807, DLC).

2. *Juniperus horizontalis* Moench.

3. *Gualtheria shallon* Pursh, known as the salalberry. McMahon mistakes it for *Vaccinium*. Coues does mention "a cranberry of the low and viny kind" which his botanical consultant, F. H. Knowlton, identifies as *V. macrocarpon* (BIDDLE-COUES, 2:826).

4. *Vicia americana* Muhlenberg.

5. William Duane, publisher of the Philadelphia *Aurora*.

261. Conrad's Estimate of Publishing Costs

[c. April 1807]

Composition of 90 forms 8000 ems each @ 50 cts.		$358
Press Work—90 forms 16 Tokens each 50 cts. pr. Token		$720
	Printing	1078
420 Reams paper at 42 dolls. pr. ream		1890
	Say	2968
Map		400
Four Plans		100
Two Views	$150	300
Mouth of Columbia R.		30
		3798

Putting in boards @ 17 1/2   500

4298

Copper	100
Contingent expenses 5 pc.	102

$4500

each in boards 112 1/2 cts.

AD (MoSHi). In publisher John Conrad's hand; probably his preliminary estimate of the cost of producing the Lewis and Clark work he had undertaken. For a note on Conrad, see No. 262.

262. John Conrad to Lewis

Dear Sir   [c. 1 April 1807]

Inclosed I hand you a proof of the prospectus, if it is as you wish it it may be printed immediately & put in circulation. If you can suggest any alteration or make any additions that you think will be serviceable they can be made without any inconvenience to the printer. In two or three days I will beg leave to shew you a proof of it printed as a pamphlet which I think will be more convenient to send to distant places. Very respectfully &c.

JOHN CONRAD

ALS, RC (MoSHi). Addressed, "Captn. M. Lewis at Mrs. Woods." On the back of the sheet, in Lewis's hand:

5 Handkerchiefs
1 pr. socks
1 pr. nankeen briches
3 Cravats
2 shirts
1 flannl. do.

While in Philadelphia, Lewis stayed at the boardinghouse operated by Mrs. Wood. She was either Eliza Wood, listed in the 1816 *Philadelphia directory* as operating a boardinghouse at Cherry near Tenth, or Sarah Wood, listed in the *New trade directory* of 1800 as operating one in Mifflin's Court. A listing in the *Directory* of 1803 for "Wood, Widow," with a boardinghouse at 159 North Front, might apply either to Sarah or Eliza. Entries in Lewis's account book (MoSHi) for payments to Mrs. Wood are these: 20 April 1807, he gave her $5.00 to purchase "a douzen of porter"; 5 May, $10.00 for a dozen of ale; 8 May, he lent her $40.00; 29 May, he paid her $50.00 "for board, &c."; 21 June, he lent her, on account of board, $20.00; and on 8 July he paid her in full, $28.58.

John Conrad was in business as a Philadelphia printer as early as 1795 (BROWN). In the *Aurora* for 30 Aug. 1800 he announced, "John Conrad & Co. have succeeded the late Robert Campbell in the Bookselling and

Stationary Business, and will use every endeavor to give satisfaction to those who favor them with their custom. . . ." He operated under this name at 30 Chestnut Street until the early months of 1807, when the name began to appear as C. and A. Conrad and Co., meaning that brothers Cornelius and Andrew had come into the firm (a bill to Jefferson in 1812 is signed by still another member of the family, Samuel Conrad). The failure of the company, which was to occur before the Lewis and Clark volumes could be produced, came in 1812. A notice in the *Aurora* of 6 June declared that John Conrad had, on 30 May, assigned his property "in trust for the benefit of all his creditors" to Samuel F. Bradford, Robert Taylor, and John Morgan, assignees. His book stock was offered for sale beginning 7 July, according to an *Aurora* advertisement of 3 July. But a year later he was back in the publishing business at the same location, announcing in the *Aurora* of 23 June 1813 the issuance of *The military laws, and rules and regulations for the armies of the United States.*

262a. The Conrad Prospectus

[c. 1 April 1807]

PROSPECTUS

OF

LEWIS AND CLARK'S TOUR

TO THE

PACIFIC OCEAN

THROUGH

THE INTERIOR OF THE CONTINENT OF NORTH AMERICA

Performed by order of the Government of the United States,

during the Years 1804, 1805, & 1806.

This work will be prepared by Captain Meriwether Lewis, and will be divided into two parts, the whole comprized in three volumes octavo, containing from four to five hundred pages, each, printed on good paper, and a fair Pica type. The several volumes in succession will be put to press at as early periods as the avocations of the author will permit him to prepare them for publication.

· PART THE FIRST—IN TWO VOLUMES.

VOLUME FIRST—

WILL contain a narrative of the voyage, with a description of some of the most remarkable places in those hitherto unknown wilds of

America, accompanied by a Map of good size, and embellished with a view of the great cataract of the Missouri,—the plan, on a large scale, of the connected falls of that river, as also of those of the falls, narrows, and great rapids of the Columbia, with their several portages. For the information of future voyagers there will be added in the sequel of this volume, some observations and remarks on the navigation of the Missouri and Columbia rivers, pointing out the precautions which must necessarily be taken, in order to ensure success, together with an itinerary of the most direct and practicable rout across the continent of North America, from the confluence of the Missouri and Mississippi rivers to the discharge of the Columbia into the Pacific Ocean.

VOLUME SECOND—

WHATEVER properly appertains to geography, embracing a description of the rivers, mountains, climate, soil and face of the country; a view of the Indian nations distributed over that vast region, shewing their traditions, habits, manners, customs, national characters, stature, complexions, dress, dwellings, arms, and domestic utensils, with many other interesting particulars in relation to them: Also observations and reflections on the subjects of civilizing, governing and maintaining a friendly intercourse with those nations. A view of the fur trade of North America, setting forth a plan for its extension, and shewing the immense advantages which would accrue to the Mercantile interests of the United States, by combining the same with a direct trade to the East Indies through the continent of North America. This volume will be embellished with a number of plates illustrative of the dress and general appearance of such Indian nations as differ materially from each other: of their habitations; their weapons and habiliments used in war; their hunting and fishing apparatus; domestic utensils, &c. In an appendix there will also be given a diary of the weather, kept with great attention thoughout the whole of the voyage, shewing also the daily rise and fall of the principal watercourses which were navigated in the course of the same.

PART THE SECOND—IN ONE VOLUME—

THIS part of the work will be confined exclusively to scientific research, and principally to the natural history of those hitherto unknown regions. It will contain a full dissertation on such subjects as have fallen within the notice of the author, and which may properly be distributed under the heads of Botany, Mineralogy, and Zoology, together with some strictures on the origin of Prairies, the cause of the muddiness of the Missouri, of volcanic appearances, and other natural phenomena which were met with in the course of this interesting tour.

This volume will also contain a comparative view of twenty-three vocabularies of distinct Indian languages, procured by Captains Lewis and Clark on the voyage, and will be ornamented and embellished with a much greater number of plates than will be bestowed on the first part of the work, as it is intended that every subject of natural history which is entirely new, and of which there are a considerable number, shall be accompanied by an appropriate engraving illustrative of it.

THIS distribution of the work has been made with a view to the accommodation of every description of readers, and is here offered to the patronage of the public in such shape, that all persons wishing to become subscribers, may accommodate themselves with either of the parts, or the entire work, as it shall be most convenient to themselves.

DETACHED from this work, there will be published on a large scale, as soon as a sufficient number of subscribers be obtained to defray the expence,

LEWIS & CLARK's MAP OF NORTH AMERICA,

From longitude 9 deg. west to the Pacific Ocean, and between
36 deg. and 52 deg. north latitude,

Embracing all their late discoveries, and that part of the continent heretofore the least known. This map will be compiled from the best maps now extant, as well published as in manuscript, from the collective information of the best informed travellers through the various portions of that region, and corrected by a series of several hundred celestial observations, made by Captain Lewis during his late tour.

FOR the convenience of subscribers, these several works will be delivered at the most respectable commercial towns, and at the seats of government of the respective states and territories within the Union: no advance is required, nor will payment de demanded until such delivery is made.

KNOWING that a very considerable proportion of the expence of such publications depends on the engravings which embellish or form them, and that the precise number of such engravings, particularly as it regards the second part of the work, have not yet been settled, it is difficult for the author at this moment to fix a price on them; he therefore declares to the public, that his late voyage was not undertaken with a view to pecuniary advantages, and pledges himself that the estimate which he will in this instance set on his literary labours shall be of the most moderate description;

his principal reason indeed for proposing a subscription at all, is that he may be enabled to form some estimate of the number of copies to be struck off.

Printed copy (MoSHi). Although a version appeared with Lewis's letter in the *National Intelligencer* of 14 March 1807 (No. 253), this separately printed form must date after Conrad's note to Lewis (No. 262).

As first issued by Conrad, the prospectus exists in at least three forms. For a later version probably written by Nicholas Biddle, see No. 327a. Of the present version, the three forms are:

(a) A single folio sheet of 10¼ by 16¾ inches, printed on both sides, with text as above. The St. Louis copy contains the names of two subscribers, John Chandler, of Monmouth, Me., and Peter Norton, of Readfield, Me., both of whom ordered one copy each of the two volumes and the map.

(b) An 8vo version printed in the JOURNALS, 7:363–66, by Thwaites, of which I have located no original copy. In a footnote Thwaites reports three extant copies as of 1904, all of which were then in the possession of Mrs. Julia Clark Voorhis and Miss Eleanor Glasgow Voorhis. He identifies these as consisting of one 8vo and two folio versions. My only clue to the fact that the version he prints is the 8vo consists of a single line which differs from the other two texts; in describing the map, the writer has included the dimensions "five feet eight inches by three feet ten inches." This version and the one to be listed below as (c) both differ from (a) in two principal details. The price of the work is given—$10 for the first part, $11 for the second, $10 for the map—and the prospectus is dated 3 June 1807. The name of the publisher, C. and A. Conrad and Co., also is included.

(c) A folio sheet, folded to 11½ by 17⅝ inches, with text on pp. 1 and 3. The only copy I have seen is at MoSHi, and like (a) it was once owned by the Voorhis family. Although the two sheets have become separated, and the second one reduced to a fragment, it is clear that they once were joined.

A note in Clark's hand on the verso of the second sheet may mean that he carried this copy with him when he went to Philadelphia, in 1810, to continue plans for publication of the work. It reads:

> C. & A. Conrad
> Bernd. McMahon 39 S. Second
> John Conrad 161 Walnut
> Charles W. Peale Museum 5 below Ches.
> John F. Miflin Con. [counselor] at law 5 & 9 Union
> Dr. Bj. Sm. Barton 241 Chesnot
> [. . .] Dr. Rush 96 S. 4th
> Dr. Wistar corner Prune & 4th
> Tench Coxe perveyor of Pu. Supplies 196 Spruce

All of these men have been identified in earlier notes except John Francis Mifflin, an attorney (mentioned as Peale's attorney in SELLERS), and Tench Coxe (1755–1824), purveyor of public supplies in Jefferson's administration.

A blank form at the end of the prospectus provides space for subscribers to write their names, addresses, and number of copies desired.

263. Bernard McMahon to Lewis

Sir.   Philadelphia April 5th 1807
   I duly received through the kindness of the President U.S. the
very valuable parcel of seeds you were so good as to destine for me,
and for which I am extremely obliged to you. I sowed some of each
sort, and have seven kinds up and in a growing state already. I
never saw seeds in a better state of preservation, and there is no
doubt, but I will have plants from every species and variety. If
you have yet any kinds different from those you were pleased to
send me, I would think it a great and additional favour to get a
small portion of each, and you may rest assured that they shall be
taken good care of, and that I shall duly report their progress to you,
with such observations as I may deem useful.
   I have heard that, in your tour, you had collected a number of
specimens of new and curious plants, and that you intend to bring
some of them to this City for examination; if so, I would wish you
to be here before the 20th inst. as there is at present a young man[1]
boarding in my house, who, in my opinion, is better acquainted
with plants, in general, than any man I ever conversed with on the
subject; he was regularly bred to the business in Saxony, lived with
Wm. Hamilton Esqr. two years, who, *between you and me*, did not
use him well; he was employed for these last twelve months collecting,
to the southward, specimens for Doctor Barton, and arranging
them; for whom he is to depart, to the northward, on similar
business, about the 20th inst. He is a very intelligent and practical
Botanist, would be well inclined to render you any service in his
power, and I am confident would defer his intended journey, to the
first of May to oblige you.
   I solicit the favour of your acceptance of a box of seeds from me,
to produce you esculent vegetables &c. at the seat of your new Government, and of your considering me, Sir, Your sincere Wellwisher,
                                            BERND. MCMAHON.

ALS, RC (MoSHi). Addressed, "Governor M. Lewis Washington City."
The letter was forwarded 10 April 1807 to Philadelphia.
   1. Frederick Pursh (1774–1820), born in Saxony, came to the U.S. in
1799 to work as a botanist. He may have served for a time with Humphrey
Marshall (EWAN, 602–03), after which he became William Hamilton's gardener
in 1803. Benjamin Smith Barton became his patron in 1806 and sent him
on a botanizing tour of western Maryland and adjacent regions. His
second tour for Barton, mentioned above, was to northern Pennsylvania and
central New York. The letters in the present volume dealing with his
work for Lewis are Nos. 309, 314, and 316, with some notes on payment

[398]

in No. 295. The best account of his career, and particularly his connection with the Lewis and Clark plants, is in EWAN. But TRUE also should be consulted. Apparently this letter from McMahon to Lewis was not available to either of those authors, and Ewan states that Pursh took up lodging with McMahon "to work on the Lewis and Clark collections." The letter makes it clear, first, that Pursh was associated with McMahon before his assignment to the Lewis and Clark plants, and, second, that McMahon was instrumental in bringing Pursh's abilities to the attention of Lewis.

Pursh left McMahon in April 1809 to work in the botanical garden of Dr. David Hosack in New York City; made a trip to the West Indies in the winter of 1810–11; went to England the following winter; and in 1814 published his well-known *Flora* in London. Still unsolved is the question of how and why he was able to include in his work a large number of the new species collected by Lewis and Clark, and how his own use of the material was related to the plans of Dr. Barton. His own account of his association with Lewis, in the preface of his work, is not helpful. He says he turned all his drawings over to Clark (they have not been located), and occasionally he refers to particular drawings, such as those of *Fritillaria lanceolata* (1:230) and *Bartonia ornata* (1:327). Perhaps he did surrender the drawings after being paid by Clark (No. 316); but he took with him to London a collection of the specimens from which he was able to publish descriptions, some with figures, in his *Flora*. Many of these specimens were later returned to the U.S. from the herbarium of A. B. Lambert, and forty-six have been located in the herbarium of the Academy of Natural Sciences of Philadelphia (EWAN, 611). Ewan suggests that Pursh may have selected duplicates from Barton's collection, divided specimens into two portions, or simply pulled specimen sheets out of Barton's collection. He notes that some of the sheets in the Lambert collection are those missing from the series in the Barton herbarium (PPAmP, on deposit with the Academy). Pursh named two of the new plants in honor of the explorers: *Lewisia rediviva*, the root of which grew and produced flowers when removed from the collection of dried specimens, and *Clarckia pulchella*, a purple or rose-colored flower collected along the Clearwater.

264. [David McKeehan] to Lewis

[7 April 1807]

To his Excellency Meriwether Lewis, Esquire, Governor of Upper Louisiana.

Sir,

Your publication in the National Intelligencer,[1] dated the 14th of last month, has forced into notice an obscure individual, who, of course, has had the misfortune of being "entirely unknown to you," to defend his character and his rights. However unpleasant it may be to his feelings to appear before the public in his own defence;

and however he may regret the necessity of drawing their attention to the remarks he may offer, it is some consolation that the conduct of his antagonist claims of him no scrupulous adherence to the rules of formality, or of punctilious delicacy; and that to meet Your Excellency on the subject of your publication requires to *you* no apology. Your rapid advancement to power and wealth seems to have changed the polite, humble and respectful language of a *Sir Clement* into that of him who commands and dispenses favours; even your subscription lists, when you offer your learned works for publication must be *"promulgated."*

As your notice may not be favored with a general insertion in the newspapers, it may be an act of candour towards Your Excellency, before I proceed in my principal remarks relative to it, to give, as far as necessary, a statement of its contents.

Your Excellency is pleased to observe,—"Having been informed that there *were* several unauthorized and probably some spurious publications *now* preparing for the press, on the subject of *my* late tour to the Pacific Ocean, by individuals entirely unknown to me, I have considered it a duty which I owe to the public, as well as myself to put them on their guard against such impositions, lest from the practice of such impositions they may be taught to depreciate the worth of the work which I am myself preparing for publication before it can possibly appear, as much time, labour and expense are absolutely necessary in order to do justice to the several subjects which it will embrace."—The public are then referred to the lists for subscriptions which have been *promulgated* by yourself, and the prospectus with which they are headed; and obligingly informed, "that those who wish to possess the genuine work, may obtain it by entering their names on those lists." But, as an inducement perhaps to make the entries, we are told that the price of this "genuine work" is to be fixed at a future day; that the map *will most probably* be published the latter end of October next; the first volume of the work *about* the first of January, 1808; and that the two remaining volumes will follow in succession as early *as they possibly can be prepared for publication;* or (as it stated in the proposals) *at as early periods as the avocations of the author will permit.* Next you tell the public that to Robert Frazer only permission has been given to publish any thing relative to your late voyage. But even the *proposals* of Frazer must feel the effect of your expunging fingers: what amputations and mutilations his journal itself has suffered, you do not think proper to communicate; but it is reasonable to suppose that all those parts were *expunged* which might *depreciate the worth of the work,* which you are preparing for publication. Do you yet stop here? No, but in order to defeat the ostensible object of your own permission, and to deprive poor Frazer, or those who may have purchased from him, of all benefit arising from his publication, you attack his capacity, and "declare that Robert Frazer, *who was only a private on this expedition,* is entirely unacquainted with *celestial observations, mineralogy, botany,* or *zoology,* and therefore cannot possibly give any accurate information on *those subjects,* nor on that of geography, and that the whole which can be expected from his journal is merely *a limited detail* of our daily transactions." Limited perhaps in proportion to your expunging operations! Having thus attempted to expose Frazer and his work, you conclude your notice with the following sweeping clause intended to affect all other persons interested in any of the journals; "With respect to all unauthorised publications relative to this voyage, I presume that they cannot have stronger pretensions to accuracy or information than that of Robert Frazer."

Having given this exposition of your note, it may perhaps be agreeable to Your Excellency to know the reasons of my interfereing in this affair of the journals of what you very modestly call *your* late tour. You will therefore please to understand, that, without soliciting either your permission or authority, I have purchased the journal of one of the persons engaged in the late expedition from the mouth of the Missouri to the Pacific ocean, "performed by order of the government;" that I have arranged and transcribed it for the press, supplying such geographical notes and other observations, as I supposed would render it more useful and satisfactory to the reader; that a large edition of it is now printing is this place, and will be published and ready for delivery (unless some unforeseen circumstances occur to prevent it) the latter end of next month; according to the proposals inserted in this paper.[2]

After having furnished Your Excellency with this information, I must be permitted to make some short observations, which I think necessary, on a few points in order to render the subject in discussion between us fairly understood.

With respect to the hazardous nature of the enterprize and the courage necessary for undertaking it, candour compels me to say, that public opinion has placed them on too high ground. Mr. M'Kenzie[3] with a party consisting of about one fourth part of the number under your command, with means which will not bear a comparison with those furnished you, and without the *authority,*

[401]

the *flags,* or *medals* of his government, crossed the Rocky mountains several degrees north of your rout, and for the *first time* penetrated to the Pacific Ocean. You had the advantage of the information contained in his journal, and could in some degree estimate and guard against the dangers and difficulties you were to meet; and I have no doubt that, had government given an invitation, hundreds as daring, enterprising and capable as your Excellency, would have offered to engage in the expedition, and for compensations much smaller than were received by yourself and the other persons composing the corps actually engaged in it.

Having mentioned compensations; with your Excellency's leave, I will next notice that received by you. What compensations did your Excellency receive? By an act of congress passed the 3d of last month, double pay was allowed you as captain of infantry, during the expedition, and also a grant of 1600 acres of land; to these may be added the value of your rations and your pay as private secretary or master of ceremonies to the president, the latter of which it is alledged and believed you pocketed though you could perform no part of the duties or ceremonies attached to the office.[4] Have we got through the items of the account? No. To these perquisites the executive adds the honorable and lucrative office of Governor of Upper Louisiana! Why, sir, these grants and rewards savour more of the splendid munificence of a Prince than the economy of a republican government. It ought not to escape notice that the land is to be located within your own government, where your influence and means of information may render the value of the grant incalculable. There is besides a good deal of tinsel thrown into the scale with these solid considerations; such as the praises of the president (for a hobby horse as well as another will sometimes run away with his rider); the honor of leading such an expedition; of knighting or making chiefs (an act perhaps not strictly constitutional) of the poor savages of the west; of immortalizing your name and those of your friends by giving them to the mighty streams which flow from the Rocky mountains; and what I had almost forgot, the warblings of the Muses, who have been celebrating the *"Young Hero's name."* Who could have thought that after so much liberality shewn by the country, your Excellency would have been found contending with the poor fellows, who for their small pittance were equally exposed with yourself to the toils and dangers attending the expedition, about the publication of their journals, which cost them so much trouble and anxiety to keep and preserve! I am afraid Captain Clarke, who appears to have acted during the whole of the tour with the greatest prudence, firmness and courage, will be forced to blush for the man he has called his friend.

Solomon says, "There are three things which are never satisfied, yea, four things say not, *It is enough*." Had your Excellency lived in the days of Solomon, and been as near his court, as you have lately been to that of the United States, the wise and discerning monarch would easily have found a *fifth thing* which would say not, *It is enough*.

By way of interlude in this exhibition of curious things, let me put a question to Your Excellency. Where was your journal during the session of Congress? Snug, eh! No notice is given in the government paper of an intention to publish it;—No warnings against impositions;—only a few proposals circulated among book-sellers at a distance! Some of the members begin to wince, complain that they are called upon to legislate in the dark, that no journal of the expedition was laid before them; others boldly assert that the grants they are asked for are extravagant—that double pay is a sufficient compensation; and that to get rid of importunate applicants, and to be allowed to attend to the important business of the session, they are obliged to consent to grants which they know to be unreasonable and unjust. This was the time to keep the journal out of view; and to be silent about the fortune to be made out of the *three* volumes and a map. "I'll squeeze, (says His Excellency in embrio) "I'll squeeze the nation first, and then raise a heavy contribution on the citizens individually: I'll cry down these *one-*volume journals, and frighten the publishers; and no man, woman, or child shall read a word about *my* tour, unless they enter their names on *my* lists, and pay what price I shall afterwards fix on my *three* volumes and map." Without thinking it worth while to ask by what right you call this tour, which you acknowledge was "performed by order of the government," *your* tour, let me enquire by what high grant or privilege you claim the right of authorizing, licensing or suppressing journals or other publications concerning it? Every man of sense must agree that these journals are either *private* property of the individuals who took them, or *public* property; for none but an ideot could for a moment suppose, that any officer upon the expedition could have a property in any but his own. If therefore they are the private property of the individuals severally who kept them, there is an end to the question. Are they public property and has the government done any act either to manifest or relinquish its claim? In my opinion there may be cases where the journals, maps, surveys, and all other documents

[403]

taken during a military expedition, especially where policy and the interest of the country requires secrecy, ought to be considered the property of the public and delivered up to the government; but where no such policy, interest or secrecy exist; and where it is for the public advantage that the information collected shall be diffused as widely as possible; where the government never calls for any documents for their inspection but those taken by the commanding officers; where other persons belonging to the expedition, who had taken journals or other documents, were discharged from public service with these journals and documents in their hands, and no claim made of them as public property when other public property in their possession was delivered up; where the commanding officers have been allowed by the government to publish their journals, maps and other documents for their private emolument; will it be said that in a country governed by equal laws, and where equal rights and privileges are secured to all the citizens, these persons who have been so discharged from public service and become private citizens, have not also a right to publish the documents they have taken and preserved? Why, sir, scorn itself would hardly deign to point its finger at the administration, which would attempt to suppress them and prevent their publication; and despotism would blush at the deed, even to advance its favorites and sycophants. The fact is, sir, that these journals were considered as unnecessary (those of the commanding officers being preserved) for the information of the government, and all claim relinquished to them by the act of discharge, without a demand, when the persons who had taken them were retiring from public service, to private life. These journals, when first ordered to be taken were intended to be made use of only conditionally, and therefore more of the nature of private property than the others. The object of multiplying journals of the tour was that, in case of defeat or other misfortune affecting the safety of those taken by the commanding officers, the chances of preserving information with respect to the country through which the expedition was to pass might also be multiplied. Connected with this part of the investigation, is another point (and a material one) on which I must ask a question or two, and say a few words: this respects the credit due to these journals and their claim to correctness. Was it not a part of your duty to see that these journals were regularly kept, and, if necessary, to supply from your journal, any defects or omissions? Were not all the journals belonging to the corps brought together at certain resting places, examined, compared and corrected? If Mr. Gass (from whom I purchased) "is unacquainted with celestial

[404]

observations" (which I will grant) was it not your duty, and did you not supply him with the result of those made by yourself? How else did Mr. Gass find out the latitude of certain places where your observations were taken to the exactness of minutes, seconds and tenths of seconds? Without information from Captain Clarke or yourself, how did he ascertain the distances of places, the breadth of rivers and bays, height of falls and length of portages? But it is unnecessary to multiply questions: you know that these journals will furnish the necessary information relative to the tour; and that the publication of them will *depreciate the worth of the work you are preparing for publication.* This is what alarms your insatiable avarice. If there were not some consequence connected with these journals, why all this uneasiness about them? Why purchase them at high prices in order to have them supressed? Did you not lately purchase the journal of sergeant Prior or Sergeant Ordway,[5] for that purpose? I will next grant that Mr. Gass is not acquainted with mineralogy, botany or zoology, that his geographical knowledge is neither extensive nor correct, "and (to use your own words) that the whole which can be expected from his journal is merely a limited detail of your daily transactions," and yet strange as it may appear to such a phenomenon in literature as Your Excellency, I am of opinion it will be more interesting and useful to readers generally than the volume of your work, which is to be "confined exclusively to scientific research." He may in some respects be considered as having the advantage; for while your Excellency was star-gazing, and taking celestial observations, he was taking observations in the world below. If Mr. Gass and the publisher of his journal can lead their readers along the rout of the expedition and make them acquainted with those things which were the objects of the external senses, and as they appeared to those senses, the greater number will willingly dispense with "scientific research." Of what consequence is it to the generality of readers to know how a plant has been classed, to what order, genus or species it has been confined by Botanists? And as to zoology and mineralogy similar questions might be asked with equal propriety. Who is not pleased with M'Kenzie's journal? And what does he say of himself? Does he pretend to be either a mineralogist, a botanist or zoologist? "I do not possess," says he, "the science of the naturalist; and even if the qualifications of that character had been attained by me, its curious spirit had not been gratified. I could not stop to dig into the earth, over whose surface I was compelled to pass with rapid steps; nor could I turn aside to collect the plants which nature might

[405]

have scattered on the way, when my thoughts were anxiously imployed in making provision for the day that was passing over me." Yet he "flatters himself" that his "work will be found to excite an interest, and conciliate a regard, in the minds of those who peruse it." What! without "scientific research!" Unacquainted with "mineralogy, botany and zoology!" What a presumptuous fellow!

To shew the public that Mr. Gass has some talents and merit, I will introduce the following extract from a paper delivered to him under your own signature.

"As a tribute justly due the merits of the said Patrick Gass, I with cheerfulness declare that the ample support, which he gave me under every difficulty; the manly firmness, which he evinced on every necessary occasion; and the fortitude with which he bore (boar, in the original) the fatigues and painful sufferings incident to that long voyage, entitles him to my highest confidence and sincere thanks, while it eminently recommends him to the consideration and respect of his fellow citizens."

This certificate does you honor, and it is to be regretted that the wealth and honours heaped upon you so soon rendered your heart callous towards the companions of your "fatigues and painful sufferings." Perhaps I ought to beg pardon for using the word *companions,* as it has been thought proper at the seat of government to degrade them to mere *"Followers."*

The publication of the journal of Mr. Gass I expect will have the following good effects; first, It may save many the trouble of purchasing your *three volumes* and map, by affording them at a cheap rate, a plain and satisfactory account of the tour; in the second place, it will so *depreciate the worth of your work* that there may be a chance of getting it at a reasonable price; and in the third place, as it will contain plain matter of fact, it may deter you from swelling your work with such *tales of wonder* as have sometimes issued from the *Ten-mile-square.*

But, by the bye, did your Excellency never attend to the advice given to those who have glass houses? Were you not afraid that some persons affected by your publication, might inform the public that you were not a man of science, that you were not a man of letters, and that you were not qualified for scientific research. The length of the observations already made prevent me from giving even a *limited detail* of my information upon this point.

I, however, assure you that I shall wait with some impatience for your voluminous work; and shall willingly subscribe for it, when a reasonable price is fixed; but hope you will be cautious in magnifying trifles; and in giving too long and learned dissertations with respect to the *"Origin of Prairies,"* and "the cause of the muddiness of the Missouri." With respect to the latter, which you make one of your great points of investigation, Mr. Gass, who does not speak scientifically, only says, "At two, we proceeded again on our voyage, and passed a long chain of Bluffs on the north side, of a dark colour. From these and others of the same kind the Missouri gets its muddy colour. The earth of which they are composed dissolves like sugar; every rain washes down great quantities of it, and the rapidity of the stream keeps it mixing and afloat in the water until it reaches the mouth of the Mississippi." Now who can relish this homespun account without a spice of "scientific research!"

I must pass over the unhappy affair with the Indians on the plains of Maria's river,[6] also that very affecting one of your own posteriors,[7] and conclude with congratulating you that Mr. Gass's Journal did not fall into the hands of some wag, who might have insinuated that your wound was not accidental, but that it was the consequence of design,—that the *young hero* might not return without more scars (if not *honorable,* near the *place of honour*) to excite the curiosity and compassion of some favorite widow Wadman, who might have been languishing during his absence. In what a ludicrous situation he might have placed the *young hero* with his *point of honour* just past the *point of a rock,* with Crusatte taking aim!— perhaps there will be a representation in the plates embellishing your second volume!

Pittsburgh, 7th April, 1807.   The Editor of Gass's Journal

The Publisher of Gass's Journal will return his grateful thanks to those Editors of public papers who will please to insert the foregoing;[8] and to those gentlemen in every part of the Union who will promote and encourage the circulation of the work itself.

Printed, Pittsburgh *Gazette,* 14 April 1807, occupying all of p. 2.

1. See No. 253.

2. McKeehan inserted a notice in the *Gazette* of 16 June that his edition of Gass's journal would be ready late that month. He asked that all subscription papers be forwarded to him, and explained that the delay had been due to heavy rains which had prevented deliveries of paper. He added: "It is not yet clearly ascertained how far the illiberal and indelicate notice of Captain Lewis has been injurious. In a few instances it has had a good effect; while in some parts of the country, there is no doubt, it has occasioned a temporary deception, which will vanish on correct information, and when the *price* of his work is made known. What price will finally be fixed on this large work, which is to consist of three octavo volumes and a map, it is impossible for a stranger unacquainted with captain Lewis's

opinions and views to estimate. The only sum mentioned in this country with any appearance of authority, is fifty dollars; but this is so extravagant a computation that it would seem to deserve no credit. But should the work, as set forth in the prospectus be properly executed, a copy cannot be expected under fifteen or twenty dollars. . . . The rapidity with which the subscription papers have been filled, and his prospects of being able in a short time to dispose of the whole of his large edition of 5000 copies, leave the Publisher no grounds of complaint; unless, indeed, they may be found in the conduct of those Editors of newspapers, who declined to publish his observations on captain Lewis's Notice,—especially of such as had given place to that Notice. . . ." When McKeehan finally learned the proposed selling price of Lewis's work—$31 for two volumes and a map—he ran a half-column announcement in the *Gazette* of 30 June to compare his own publication with Lewis's, to repeat that his price was only a dollar, and to say that "instead of binding in boards, which was at first intended, it will appear in a handsome marble paper with red and green leather backs; and will be cut, coloured, filleted and lettered; so that it will be elegantly and substantially half bound." McKeehan had copies ready for distribution by 7 July.

3. Sir Alexander Mackenzie.

4. Almost certainly untrue. There is no record that Jefferson kept Lewis on his payroll; that money would have been earmarked for his successor, Lewis Harvie.

5. Nathaniel Pryor may have kept a journal, but it has never come to light. The supposition that he kept one is based upon the instructions given all the sergeants to "keep a seperate journal from day to day of all passing occurences" (JOURNALS, 1:33), and upon a later statement that they were doing so. Ordway's journal has been mentioned earlier, and the record of its purchase by Lewis and Clark is in No. 295.

6. An encounter with a small band of Piegans, on Lewis's reconnaissance of the Marias River, during which Reuben Field killed one Indian with a knife and Lewis wounded another by gunfire. The Indians had attempted to steal guns and horses from the party (JOURNALS, 5:218–28). Lewis identified the Indians as "Minnetares of Fort de Prarie," that is, Gros Ventres; but John C. Ewers believes they were Piegans and cites supporting documents (EWERS (2), 48).

7. The gunshot wound accidentally inflicted by Pierre Cruzatte, which Lewis mentions in No. 210.

8. I have not found this letter reprinted in any other contemporary newspaper. McKeehan's failure to obtain circulation has kept the letter relatively unknown to students of the expedition.

265. William Simmons to Lewis

Sir,   15 April 1807
Upon examining your several Drafts which have been paid at this office, I find the following among the number; and which upon referring to your Accounts, I cannot discover that you have ever brought to your debit—vizt:

No. 65 dated St. Louis 24th Septr. 1806 drawn in favor of
Saml. Smith of Pittsburg for . . . . Drs. 272.
No. 66 dated St. Louis 27th Septr. 1806 in favor of
Falconer & Comegys for . . . . 220.
No. 67 same date with the foregoing & in favor of
the same men for . . . . 300.
No. 68 same date with the foregoing in favor of
Hunt and Hankinson for . . . . 300.
No. 69 dated St. Louis Octor. 3rd 1806 in favor of
Bradhurst & Field for . . . . 300.
No. 70 same date with the favor of
Thomas Oliver for . . . . 287.

No. 64, which it also appears you have omitted to credit, has not
yet been presented for payment—of course if such a number was
drawn by you I cannot ascertain the amount of it at present. Should
you have any claims to oppose to the above-mentioned Bills, or
explanation to give, I beg you will have the goodness to state the
same as early as convenient. I am &c.

W. S.

Lbk (DNA, RG 217, Accountant's letterbooks). William Simmons was the
accountant of the War Department. Notification of the first four drafts
were received and entered in the War Department register. The two bills
of exchange in favor of Falconer and Comegys and the one in favor
of Hunt and Hankinson were paid by warrants entered in the Army
Accounting Office Journal M, p. 6507. The last two have not come to my
attention. Bradhurst and Field probably were St. Louis merchants; Thomas
Oliver, a Virginian, was prothonotary and clerk of sessions for the district of
Ste. Genevieve, Louisiana Territory, in 1806 (TERR. PAPERS, 13:546).

266. Robert Frazer to Jefferson

Sir   Henderson County (Ken.) April 16th 1807
I this day arrived at Genl. Hopkins's[1] and found himself and
family well, and possessing the same patriotic sentiments as when
I left him on my way to Washington. At Breckinridge court house
I was informed of a number of inquiries that some of the party
(dispached to overtake & wrest from me my papers) had been making
relative to my business at Washington. I shall take proper measures
to bring these sub-traitors if not to condign punishment, at least to
a full exposure at the tribunal of my country. I also learned from
a gentleman of high respectability, directly from St. Louis that
Colo. John Smith (T)[2] will not suffer himself to be taken by the

civil authority; but has threatened and reviled me with the harshest and most bitter epithets.

From this man's character as a desperado & from the servility of a vile and desperate junto of which he is the head, I really think I am in no small danger of assassination, or some other means of taking me off. If they would face me fairly and openly, I would boldly confront them, and set them at defiance; but this is not their method of attack. I advised with several gentlemen on the subject of my personal safety before I arrived here, whom I knew were friends to the government, and who referred me to Gen. Hopkins. He advises me to travel by way of Vincennes; there being but few houses between thence and St. Louis and the country chiefly prairé. That it is the safest I have not a doubt & have consequently adopted it.

I delivered the commission with which I was charged to Genl. Clark at Fincastle in Virginia. He could not travel as fast as I did and therefore advised me to proceed as quick as possible. Whatever may be the fate I shall meet with, I have the [. . .] consolation to know that I have been [. . .] and true to my country. And whatever may be the temptation I trust I shall perish sooner than prove otherwise.

With the most grateful acknowledgements for the honour done me in your kindness—I have the pleasure to subscribe myself Yr. Mo. Ob. Huml. Servt.

ROBERT FRAZER

ALS, RC (DLC). Addressed; endorsed; received 19 May 1807.

1. Samuel Hopkins (1753–1819), a lawyer originally from Albemarle County, Va., was a member of the Kentucky House of Representatives from 1803 to 1806. He later commanded the western frontier in the War of 1812, and became U.S. representative from Kentucky in 1813.

2. John Smith T, a supporter of Aaron Burr who added the "T" to his name to distinguish himself from other John Smiths. He was a notorious duelist and was said to carry two pistols in his belt, two in his pockets, and a dirk in his bosom. Frederick Bates removed him 1 May 1807 from his positions as lieutenant colonel of militia, justice of the general quarter sessions and common pleas, and member of the Commission of Rates and Levies for the district of Ste. Genevieve (BATES, 1:98n, 320). For his activities with Burr, see CARTER.

267. Charles Willson Peale to John Hawkins

Dear Hawkins, Museum. May 5th 1807 Philada.

. . . . . .

I mentioned in my last that I had resumed my pensil and I have lately painted the Portraits of Mr. Barton, Mr. Fulton and lastly

[410]

one of Govr. Lewis (late Captain on an expedition up the Missouri) he is the first Person who has crossed to the Pacific Ocean. McKinsey only went to a River which ran into the South Sea. But M[ess]rs. Lewis and Clark have actually visited the sea shore, and I have animals brought from the sea coast, also some parts of the dress &c of the Natives of Columbia River, [and] have some animals totally unknown before the presentation to Naturalists, which we are now mounting to put into the Museum. The drawings for Governor Lewis's Journal I mean to draw myself to be engraved for the work.[1] It is a work that seems to excite much attention, & will I hope have a great sale & give considerable profit to this bold adventurer.

Mrs. Peale joins me in respect to Mrs. Hawkins. Your friend,

C. W. PEALE.

AL, SC (PPAmP). John I. Hawkins was living in 1803 at 14 South Fifth Street. His advertisements in the *Aurora* of 1802 offered patent portable grand pianos invented by himself, and on 15 June he announced that he would present a concert on the claviol. He also was the inventor of the physiognotrace, a device used by portrait artists for tracing profiles.

1. Peale wrote his son Raphael, 6 June 1806, that he had completed three drawings for Lewis which were "much to his satisfaction" (PPAmP). The Titian R. Peale sketchbook (PPAmP) also contains a drawing of the horned toad, not signed by Peale but labeled "Drawn by C. W. Peale from a specimen brought by Lewis & Clark." But this drawing may be by Pietro Ancora; see a note under No. 185. Lewis also arranged for some drawings to be made by C. B. J. Fevret de Saint Memin (1770–1852), a Philadelphia artist who used Hawkins' physiognotrace. An entry in Lewis's account book reads: "To this sum paid St. Memin for likenesses of the indians &c. necessary to my publication to be charged to the expences of that work. $83.50" (MoSHi). Perhaps some or all of the Saint Memin crayon drawings and water colors of the Osage and Mandan Indians, published in WOLLON & KINARD, were commissioned by Lewis. Saint Memin apparently made these likenesses, as well as a crayon drawing of Lewis, in the spring of 1807. The drawings are all of Osage men except one of the Mandan chief and another of his wife, identified as a "Mandan queen."

268. Clark to Henry Dearborn

Sir   St. Louis May 18th 1807.

Since my arrival at this place arrangemts. have been made to send the Mandan Chief to his Town in safty, he will set out this evening. The party will concist of Ensign Pryor and 14 soldiers, & young Choteau[1] with 22 men with promition to trade at the Mandans. Two large Companies of Traders and Trappers set out from this place

[411]

about the first of the month intending to assend the Missouri to the Rocky Mountains, and remain in that Country two or three years— One other party set out from this place in March—one small party set early in the Spring from the Mahars Nation, and I am informed a party of British Traders have passed over by land from the North, all aiming for the same point the head of the Missouri.

. . . .

A fiew days ago *fifteen* Sieoux Indians arived at this place with a Mr. Pierr Durion Sub:Agent (appointed by Genl. Wilkinson for the Missouri) as they are Cheifs and Warriours of Considerable note and the representativs of several of the most noumerous and vicious Bands of that nation inhabiting the Missouri, who had been invited to visit the President of the U. States through this special mesinger Mr. Durion, I offered to send them to see their great father the President, which they declined after three days delibration. They delivered several short speeches which I shall send you with my answer next mail.

As I have no instructions to Send Indians to the Government from this Country; and takeing into Consideration, the trouble, difficuelty and expence which such a measure would incur to the Government; I have not thought it prudent to solicit those Sieoux to proceed on, at this time.

. . . .

With the highest respect I have the honor to be your most Obedient Hle. Sevt.

WM. CLARK. Bgdr. Genl. & Indn. Agent Louisana

ALS, RC (DNA, RG 107, C-280). Endorsed; received 29 June 1807.
1. Auguste Pierre Chouteau (1786–1838), son of Pierre.

269. Michel Amoureux to Lewis

Sir   New Madrid May 31st 1807.
   In the public prints, just come to hand, I have seen the Prospectus of a work, to be published under the title of "Messrs. Lewis & Clark's Tour to the Pacific Ocean &c. in the years 1804, 1805 & 1806. The work to be divided in two Parts, and to be delivered at the Seat of Government of the respective States & Territories &c."
   I am desirous to become a Subscriber to that useful work; but as the Prospectus does not mention any Special person, with whom

the Subscribers Should enter their names or engagements, I have taken the liberty of applying to you, and to request that you will be so obliging as to cause my name and engagement of Subscription to the First Part to be entered for one Copy, agreeably to the terms in Said Prospectus.

I had wished that my pecuniary means would have allowed me to subscribe also to the Second Part, the various Subjects of which will be very interesting indeed; but that I must Submit to my present Circumstances. If this direct application Should be deemed not proper, I beg, Sir, that you will excuse it, for the reasons above cited, to which may be added the difficulties, under which we labour here, with regard to direct communications with any part of the Union, occasioned by the frequent irregularities of the Mails &c.

Some of my neighbours & fellow farmers have testified a wish to become Subscribers also: upon your favouring me with an answer, I will then be able to inform them where they are to apply for that purpose.

I avail my self of this opportunity to express the Satisfaction I feel, in common with all the Louisianians, by the choice made of your Person to govern over this Territory: Thanks be given to the wise and virtuous Magistrate, who presides over the Union!

I hope, nay I have not the least doubt but the Louisianians will Shew them Selves worthy of your paternal Care, and that those Kinds of factions, which have existed throughout this territory, as they have originated in the unruly and misguided ambition only of a few men, will vanish, or at least be Silenced effectually by the well disposed citizens uniting cordially with their Chief Magistrate, and by their clinging with firmness to those principles, which are the foundation of equal rights, and equal laws, and are best Calculated to insure happiness to reasonable men. I beg you will forgive this digression to an old man, whose most favorite wish has constantly been to See his fellow creatures happy, and who views with a deep regret some of them active in operating their own miseries, by deviating from the right path. I have the honor to be with a high respect Sir Your obedt. Servant,

MEL. AMOUREUX

ALS, RC (MoSHi). Mathurin Michel Amoureux (c.1748–1832), a French revolutionist, came to America in 1793 and moved to Louisiana Territory in 1803. During 1805 and 1806 he was one of the judges of the court of common pleas for the district of New Madrid, and in 1808 was a probate judge.

270. Clark to Henry Dearborn

Sir   Saint Louis June 1st 1807.

In my letter to you of the 18th Ulto. I inform'd you that a deputation from several bands of the Sieoux Nation had arrived at this place with Mr. Dorion &c. Those Indians set out on their return a fiew days past highly pleased with the presents & treatment which they have received. Colonel Hunt furnished a Lieut. seven Men and a Boat to escort those people to their Country in safty. By the request of the Mandan Chief, I have suffered him to delay and go in Company with the Sieoux. The party accompanying those Indians consists of 1 Lieut. 1 Ensign 1 Sergt. 1 Corpl. 18 Privates, 1 hunter & 3 hired boat men. Young Chouteau (late an Officer) has a Boat and perogue and 32 men (for the Mandan Trade). Young Dorion[1] has a Boat and 10 men (For the Sieoux Trade). Those together with the 2 interpreters makes a total of 70 men; exclusive of the 18 Indian men 8 womin and 6 children. After Lieut. Kimble's[2] return which will be from the Sieoux Country, Ensign Pryors Party will consist of 48 men which will be fully sufficient to pass any hostile band which he may probably meet with. I am informed that the *Ricaras* have moved to the Mandans for fear of being Cut off by the Sieoux of the North; I think it probable that the report is Correct, and a measure which I advised them to as I decended last fall, from a knowledge of their dependance on the Sieoux.

. . . .

It is probably necessary for me to go to Washington to settle my public accounts for moneys expended at this place, of which you have been advised in my last letter of the 18th ulto. On this subject I must request that you will inform me.[3] With every sentiment of respect & esteem I have the honor to be Your Most Obedent Hb. Servt.

                                           WM. CLARK

ALS, RC (DNA, RG 107, C-282). Addressed; endorsed; received 7 July 1807.

1. Pierre Dorion, Jr. Serving as a guide to the Astorians in 1813, he was killed by Indians.

2. Lt. Joseph Kimball (d. 1810), of New Hampshire, was appointed second lieutenant in the Corps of Artillerists in June 1804, and promoted to first lieutenant in 1806. Clark's letter of 15 May 1807 to Col. Thomas Hunt, requesting Kimball's services, is DNA, RG 107, H-242.

3. Dearborn replied on 8 July that it would not be necessary for Clark to come to Washington (DNA, RG 75, Letters Sent, Bk. B).

271. Jefferson to Lewis

Dear Sir   Washington June 4. 07.

The seeds & other light articles which you entrusted to me for your friends in Albermarle were safely delivered. Your mother returned from Georgia in good health a little before I left Monticello. The horns, which I could not take on with me, were packed in one of 25. boxes, barrels, &c. which I sent round by water. The vessel was stranded, and every thing lost which water could injure. The others I am told are saved, & consequently the horns.[1] They have not yet however got to Richmond. I brought with me from Monticello Mr. Randolph's & my daughter's watches, which I have forwarded on to Mr. Voight, being too valuable to be trusted to a common hand. It is important I should recieve these & my own before I leave this in July for Monticello. Mr. Gallatin will be in Philadelphia on his return to this place 3. weeks hence. Mr. Briggs will be returning from there in about the same time. Each of them have promised to bring one watch if ready, and by yourself I shall hope for the 3d, and trust that Mr. Voight will be so obliging as to have them ready, it being difficult to get good opportunities of conveying a watch safely from Philadelphia to this place. Mr. Randolph has perfectly recovered his health, & all your friends in Albemarle were well. According to Mr. Cole's[2] account we have the hope of seeing you here to the 4th of July. Accept my friendly salutations & assurances of constant affection & respect.

TH: JEFFERSON

ALS, SC (DLC). Endorsed. Reply is No. 275.

1. Perhaps these are the two pairs of horns, one of a moose and one of a wapiti, which now hang in Jefferson's home with labels identifying them as specimens from the Lewis and Clark Expedition.

2. Isaac A. Coles (d. 1841), Jefferson's last private secretary, who stayed on in the same capacity with James Madison until replaced by his brother Edward. The brothers had been raised on the Coles plantation, Enniscorthy, in Albermarle County near Jefferson's home.

272. John T. Jones to Lewis and Clark

Gentlemen   [13 June 1807]

Having been informed that it is your intentions to Publish a Map of your late important Discoveries permit me to congratulate you on such an event—that I presume will not be only highly gratifying to the Publick in general, but also of considerable importance to

You. The Maps of the United States certainly are entitled to some considerable degree of Merit, and a great Number have been Sold but many Gentlemen in this City are waiting for Yours, and I doubt not, but from the very favorable impressions your new Work has made on the Citizens of this wealthy City and I may say in all the principal Cities of the United States, that its success is certain.

The motives I have in addressing you on this subject affords me an oppertunity of recommending to your attention, an improvement I have made in the Art of Varnishing of Maps Drawings and of Paintings—that for brilliancy and duration is allowed to exceed any other attempt of the Kind, I have sold many Maps of the United States of my own Colering and Varnishing which has given great satisfaction. I should be glad to contract with you for that part of the business as also for the Rollers and laying them down, that is to say the finishing part, for it is presumed, that every Purchaser woud wish to have a Map of such value, highly finished. Should you be inclined to attend to what I have here mentioned, it may prove of mutual advantage. If they are already in that state of forwardness that you could send me one, I will return it finished for your approbation and inform you the lowest Terms I can do them for. I could also render you considerable service in procuring you Sales for them, Please to favor me with your Ideas on this subject soon as convenient, and you will oblige Gentlemen Your Obt. hble. servt.

New York June 13th 1807   JOHN T. JONES
No. 95 Broad Street

ALS, RC (MoSHi). Addressed. "Messrs. Lewis & Clarke, Washington." Forwarded to Philadelphia 2 July 1807. A man named John T. Jones was associated with the City Library (New York Society Library) in 1820. The register of artists, engravers, printers, and booksellers of New York, by MC KAY, contains no more pertinent information.

273. William Simmons to Lewis

Sir,   June 17th 1807

Your letter of the 15th Ulto. came duly to hand, and Mr. Jones of the Treasury also suggested your wish to receive the Balance when your account should be adjusted. The engagements of the Secy of War have interfered with my having a particular conversation with him on several points which I deem necessary before I could undertake to pass the account, you must be sensible of the necessity for his Sanction in the passing of Items not particularly provided for; and as you are soon expected at this place, I have thought it advisable to suspend acting on the account until your arrival. You will therefore do well to bring with you any papers or documents which may relate to your expenditures on the Expedition, so as to explain such of the charges as may require it. The charges for Subsistence to the Men are of this description, there being no Receipts or Statement of the amount actually paid by you, as in the case of the Clothing Account. I mention this Item as the most prominent one, which requires the authority of the Secy. of War, others may also require such authority, which will be pointed out when you are present. I am &c.

W. S.

Lbk (DNA, RG 217, Accountant's letterbooks, M:42–43).

274. J. B. Varnum, Jr., to Lewis

Sir,   Washington City June 18. 1807.

Having recently received an appointment from the Secretary of War which will render my absence from this place necessary, previous to your arrival here, and presuming you may be desirous of having a list of the Post Offices to which I have transmitted your prospectus, I have consequently taken the liberty to annex herewith, a copy of the letters written by me, and a list of the several Offices to which they have been addressed with the prospectus enclosed. I have the honor to be Sir, with respect and esteem Your Obedt. Servt.

J. B. Varnum Jr.

Sir,   "Washington City April 9th 1807"

I am authorized by Govr. Lewis to transmit you the enclosed prospectus, with a request that you will do him the favor of offering it for subscription at your Office, and retain the same in your possession, until, by public advertisement or otherwise, you are solicited to return it to this place. I am &c.

(Signed) Joseph B. Varnum Jr.

[A list of 148 post offices follows]

ALS, RC (MoSHi). Addressed, "His Excellency Meriwether Lewis Philadelphia." Though clearly dated 18 June, the letter is postmarked 17 June. Varnum was the son of Joseph Bradley Varnum, a representative and senator from Massachusetts who became speaker of the House in 1810. Young Varnum was about to be given the factorship at Chicago, and this may be the appointment he refers to here.

275. Lewis to Jefferson

Dear Sir.   Philadelphia June the 27th 1807.

I transmit you by Genl. Dearborn your ring and Majr. Randolph's watch. The ring has been reset with the addition of four new brilliants. Knowing it to be a family piece, I directed the workman to reset it in the same stile it formerly was, but regardless of the charge he took the liberty of consulting his own taste on the subject and has made it such as I fear will not prove pleasing to you.

The watch of Mrs. Randolph is in readiness and shall be forwarded by Mr. Gallatin whom I hourly expect from New York on his way to the city of Washington.

Your watch is not yet repared altho' she was put in the possession of Mr. Voight immediately on my arrival at this place; my visits to him on that subject have not been unfrequent since, and he has after many apologies for having retained her so long promised me that she shall be ready in the course of a few days; should I not meet with an earlier opportunity I shall bring her with me on my return to Washington about the 15th of the next month.

Mr. Briggs has not called nor can I learn that he has yet been in Philadelphia.

I sincerely regret the loss you sustained in the articles you shiped for Richmond; it seems peculiarly unfortunate that those at least, which had passed the continent of America and after their exposure to so many casualties and wrisks should have met such destiny in their passage through a small portion only of the Chesapeak.

Mr. Peal is preparing for you the head and horns of the *American Argali*[1] or big horn, which as soon as complete shall be forwarded to Mr. George Jefferson[2] at Richmond. With the most sincere and unalterable frindship Your Obt. Servt.

MERIWETHER LEWIS.

ALS, RC (DLC). Endorsed; received 1 July 1807.

1. Peale wrote Jefferson 30 Aug. that he was sending the mounted head. "The skin on said head cannot be eatten by Insects, & the Eyes are made agreeable to the description of Govr. Lewis." Jefferson acknowledged the letter 24 Sept., saying the head had not yet arrived but that he expected it soon (DLC).

2. Thomas Jefferson's second cousin, member of the Richmond firm of Gibson and Jefferson which handled the President's financial affairs. He went to Lisbon as U.S. consul in 1811 and lost his life on the return voyage.

276. William Simmons to Lewis

Sir,   July 31st 1807

In your Accounts now under examination you are credited with the whole amount of Subsistence of yourself as a Captain, and for that of Capt. Clarke and his black waiter from the commencement to the close of the Expedition to the Pacific Ocean under your direction—and as it appears by the Accounts that large quantities of Provisions were furnished on account of the Expedition by the Public, and more doubtless obtained by trafficking public property with the Indians and other persons, I conceive it would be proper, before I finally close the account to be laid before the Secy. of War for the approbation of the President of the United States, that you should say in writing to be filed with the Statement whether you consider yourself or Capt. Clarke chargeable with any part of the provisions supplied as above, & if so, to what amount.

As a Schedule of the articles purchased for the Expedition has already been handed you, I will thank you to note such of them as have been expended on that account; and to furnish a list of such as you still have in your possession that you consider yourself accountable for. I am &c.

                                                               W. S.

Lbk (DNA, RG 217, Accountant's letterbooks, M:95–96).

277. Financial Records of the Expedition

                                                        [5 August 1807]

Lewis's Account Through 1805[1]

Dr. Meriwether Lewis Capt.

To the United States

1803	To Warrants on the Treasurer	
June 27	for Warrant No. 8957 on account of expences incident to extending the external commerce of the United States	1500
29	for Warrant No. 6966 for 6 Mo. Pay of 1 Lieut. 1 Sergt. 1 Corporal & 10 Privates	450
	do. 6967 for Cloathing of 12 Men 1 Year	312
	do. 6968 for the Pay of an Indian Interpreter 1 Year	150
1804		
Jany. 16	do 7329 to Jos. Stritch[2] for a bill of Exche. dated January 1. 1804 drawn on account	136

[419]

May 15	do. 7584 for a bill of Exche. dated March 29. 1804 drawn in favor of John Hay on account of the Indian Department	159.81
22	do. 7617 for a bill of Exche. dated March 25. 1804 drawn in favor of C. Gregoire[3] on account of Indian Department	1500
June 4	do. 7640 for a bill of Exche. dated February 25. 1804 drawn in favor of Geo. Wallace Jun. on account of Indian Department	33
27	do. 7680 for 3 bills of Exche. dated 14 May 1804 drawn in favor of P. Falconer on account of the Indian Department	274.87
July 5	do. 7690 for 7 bills of Exchange dated 3 May 1804 drawn in favor of P. Chouteau on account of the Osage deputation of Indians to the Seat of Government	1000
13	do. 7704 for 4 bills of Exche. dated May 3. 1804 drawn in favor of P. Chouteau on account of said deputation	200
14	do. 7706 for 3 bills of Exche. dated 3 May 1804 drawn in favor of P. Chouteau on account of said deputation	150
July 16	for Warrt. No. 7707 for a bill of Exchange dated 18 May 1804 drawn in favor of Alexander McNair on account	100
17	do. 7711 for a bill of Exche. dated May 3. 1804 drawn in favor of P. Chouteau on account of the Osage deputation	100
19	do. 7720 for 3 bills of Exche. dated May 10. 1804 drawn in favor of P. Chouteau on account of the public Service	1706.85
	do. 7721 for a bill of Exche. dated May 15. 1805 drawn in favor of P. Chouteau on account of public service	1151.74
	do. 7722 for a bill of Exc. dated May 15. 1805 drawn in favor of Chouteau on account of Osage Deputation	2249.72
	do. 7723 for 4 bills of Exchange dated May 1804 drawn in favor of Aug. Chouteau & Peter Chouteau on account of Pay of the army &c.	233.98
Aug. 2	do. 7756 to James Davidson for 5 bills of Exchange dated St. Louis drawn on account of the Indian Department his Pay &c.	2020.57
4	do. 7757 to John Horsburgh for 2 bills of Exchange dated 3 May 1804 drawn in favor of Peter Chouteau on account of the Osage Deputation	100
20	do. 7788 to John Peter for a bill of Exc. dated May 3 1804 drawn in favor of P. Chouteau on account of Osage Deputation	50

11	do. 7770 to William Whann for a bill of Exchange dated 18 May 1804 drawn in favor of Charles McNair[4] on account of certain advances to his party	100
August 11	for Warrant No. 7771 to William Whann for 2 bills of Exchange dated 19 June 1804 drawn by his Agent Capt. B. Stoddard on account	110
Sept. 17	for Warrant 7822 to John McGowan for a bill of Exche. dated May 3 1804 drawn in favor of P. Chouteau on account of the Osage deputation	100
Octobr. 13	for Warrant 7874 to Thomas Tudor Tucker for a bill of Exche. dated May 3. 1804 drawn in favor of P. Chouteau on account of the Osage deputation	50
Nov. 12	for Warrant No. 7946 to Thomas English for a bill of Exchange dated May 3. 1804 drawn in favor of P. Chouteau on account of the Osage deputation	50
27	for Warrant No. 7965 to William Whann for a bill of Exche. dated 3 May 1804 drawn in favor of P. Chouteau on account of the Osage deputation	250
Decem. 11	for Warrant No. 7992 to Jeremiah Williams & Co. for a bill of Exchange dated May 3. 1804 drawn in favor of P. Chouteau on account of the Osage deputation	100
1805 August 2	for Warrant No. 437 for Wm. Stewart for a bill of Exche. dated May 20. 1805 drawn in favor of Saml. Gwathney[5] on account of Pay of the Army	227.30
24	for Warrant No. 8498 to John Davidson for a bill of Exchange dated May 23. 1805 drawn by his agent Charles Gratiot in favor of Corporal Warfington on account of his Pay[6]	106
Sept. 16	for Warrant No. 8526 to Edgar Patterson for a bill of Exche. dated May 28. 1805 drawn by his agent Charles Gratiot in favor of A. Chouteau on account of the Indian Department	20
18	for Warrant No. 8526 to Edgar Patterson for a bill of Exche. dated April 6. 1805 drawn in favor of R. Jessome on account of his compensation as Interpreter.	220
19	for Warrant No. 8535 to James Davidson for a bill of Exche. dated May 28 1805 drawn by his Agent Charles Gratiot in favor of A. Chouteau on account of the Indian Department	50

[421]

Octo. 4	for Warrant No. 8565 to Walter Smith for a bill of Exche. dated July 28. 1805 drawn by his Agent Amos Stoddard in favor of Aug. Chouteau on account of Wages due B. Lajeunesse & E. Malboeuf[7] while employed by said Lewis	230.83	
7	for Warrant No. 8569 to Walter Smith for a bill of Exch. dated May 28. 1805 drawn by his Agent Charles Gratiot in favor of Aug. Chouteau for arrears due B. Deschamp & Charles Pineau[8]	264.66	
12	for Warrant No. 8587 to Nathan Luftborough for a bill of Exche. dated 28 July. 1805 drawn by his Agent Amos Stoddard in favor of Edward Hampstead for Wages due Francis Rivet[9]	87.50	
18	for Warrant No. 8602 to Nicholas Whelan for a bill of Exchange dated 20 August 1805 drawn by his Agent Amos Stoddard in favor of John Newman on account of Wages due him	41.40	
Nov. 8	for Warrant No. 8644 to Wm. Stewart for a bill of Exche. dated May 20. 1804 drawn in favor of M. Smith[10] on account of Pay of the Army	67	15703.23
1803 May 17	To Caleb Swan Paymasr. Army For Warrant No. 604 drawn by the Secretary of War for his Pay & Subs. from the 1 April to the 30 Sept. 1803	316.86	
Aug. 9	for Warrant No. 645 drawn by ditto for his Pay & Subs. for Oct. Novem. & December 1803	158.64	
11	for Warrant No. 646 drawn by do. for pay of a detacht. under his Commd.	554	
Nov. 15	for Warrant No. 647 drawn by the Secretary of War on account of the Recruiting Service	48	1077.50
July 31	To Israel Whelen Purveyor for this amount paid him pr. receipt dated June 20. 1803 for the purpose of providing Stores for the expedition under his Command		1000
1804 May 21	To Elijah G. Galusha Contractor for sundry articles of provisions furnished the detachment under his Command & for transporting the Same[11]	1703.53	
Sept. 7	for sundry articles of provision furnished on his order & for transporting the Same	847.23	2550.76
1804 March 28	[To William Linnard, Military Agent] To W. Linnard for amount disbursed by		

Thomas B. Steele[12] asst. My. Ag. in Decem.
1803 for Bar Iron   18
for amount disbursed by Lt. Moses Hooke
between July & Novem. 1803 for ferriage
& for a boat, outfits &c.   938.12
for amount disbursed by Lt. W. Swann[13]
in Nov. 1803 for Piloting a Boat, express
hire &c.   168.50
for amount disbursed by Wm. Linnard for
transportation of Goods from Phila. to
Pittsg.   226.98   1351.60

1805
Feby. 20   To William Linnard Military Agent for
           payment made by Lieut. Hooke at Pitts-
           burg for piloting his company to the rapids
           of Ohio   70

1805   To Peter Chouteau Indian Agent
March 31   for amount of Warrant No. 7753 charged
           to him instead of said Lewis, being for a
           bill of Exche. drawn on account of the
           Osage Deputation   300

July 29   for the amount paid Charles Gratiot for
           the balance of his account for sundry pay-
           ments made by him on account of supplies
           & expences incident to exploring Louisiana 13.50
           for payment made on the order of Capt.
           Lewis to Mr. Garrot[14] for pine boards for
           a public Boat   14   327.50
                                                           22080.59

Cr.

1804
July 19   By Peter Chouteau. Indian Agent for
           amount of Capt. Lewis' drafts drawn on the
           Secretary of War in favor of said Chouteau
           on account of the Osage deputation
           amounting to[15]   3000
           Deduct 3 bills returned by Mr. Chouteau
           unpaid   150
                                                   2850

Sept. 7   By Elijah G. Galusha for this amount over
           credited him on settlement of 21 May
           1804 arising on his being allowed 4½ in-
           stead of 4 Cents pr. Ration on 538 Rations
           Whiskey furnished the detachment under
           his Command between December 1803 &
           March 1804   2.69   2852.69
                                                           19227.90

To which add the following drafts advised
of by Captn. Lewis not yet paid

[423]

No. 61—in favor of Chas. McKenzie[16]	133		
No. 62 in favor of Bapteist Lapage[17]	66	199	
		19426.90	

from which deduct the payments marked
thus x which have been made on a/c of
the Pay Subsistence &c. of Capt. Lewis &
the Soldiers

		2648.36
	Ds.	16778.54
appropriation already made		2500
Balance unappropriated	Ds.	14278.54

add the following Bills drawn by Charles
Gratiot not yet presented

one in favor of the Estate of Regis Loisel [18]	81.16	
do. Joseph Graveline[19]	33	
		114.16

Amot. to be appropriated	Ds.	14,392.70

Final Summation of Lewis's Account[20]

Accountants Office August 5 1807

1988
1989 Meriwether Lewis Captn. 1 Regt. Infty. Dr.
To Expedition to the Pacific Ocean. For
so much received by him, being the net
proceeds of the sale of Sundry Rifles, Muskets, powder horns, Shot pouches, Powder,
Lead, Kettles, Axes, & other public property remaining on hand at the termination
of the Expedition to the Pacific Ocean,
which were disposed of at Public Auction
at St. Louis pr. a/c   408.62

For 300 lbs. Voyagers grease[21] purchased
for him by his agent Capt. Stoddard with
which he charges himself, he having deducted the amount from the subsistence of
the men See Voucher No. 85 of Genl. Abst.   50.00   458.62

1988 Sundries Dr. to Meriwether Lewis Capt.
For amount of his account settled this day.

1875 Indian Department, 1804. For disbursements made by him on account of a deputation of Osage Indians who visited the
Seat of Government in 1804 Vizt. For
amount paid Charles Gratiot for 10 Horses,
for 5 10/12 Yards blue cloth & 1 Ell Linnen
for Said Indians.   950.23

For amount paid P. Chouteau for Gunpowder, Strouds, Blankets, bullets, knives,
paint, Guns &c. &c. for Said Indians pre-
vious to their departure from St. Louis.   2249.72

[424]

	For amount paid Peter Chouteau for clothing, Gun Powder, Lead, Deer Skins, Vermillion &c. for the Osage Indians previous to their departure from St. Louis for the Seat of Govt.	339.09	3539.04
1661	Bounties to Soldiers, 1803. For bounty in full paid by him to Charles Floyd, Nathl. Pryer, Wm. Bratton, John Colter, Reuben Fields, Joseph Fields, George Gibson, Geo. Shannon & Jno. Shields men whom he inlisted in 1803 for 5 Years or during the expedition up the Missouri— 9 men @12 drs. each.[22]	108.00	
1754	Expences of Recruiting, 1803. For premium for inlisting the above men.	18.00	
1738	Bounties to Soldiers, 1804. For bounty in full paid Pierre Cruzett, Francis Labuich & John B. Lepage enlisted in 1804 for 5 Years or during the Expedition. See Pay Roll to 10 Oct. 1806.	36.00	
1784	Bounties to Soldiers, 1805. For amount of bounty in full paid the following men transferred from other Companies to his— & whose period of Inlistment expired in 1805, during his absence & whom he reinlisted for 5 Years or during the Expedition Vt. John Ordway, Patrick Gass, John Collins, Hugh McNeal, John Potts, John B. Thompson, Richd. Windser, Peter Wiser & Alexdr. Willard to 10 Oct. 1806—9 men @ 12 drs. each	108.00	
1785	Bounties to Soldiers, 1806. For bounty paid Robert Frazer, Silas Goodrich & Thos. P. Howard, men transferred from other companies to his, & whose period of Inlistment expired in 1806 during his absence & whom he reinlisted for 5 Years or during the expedition—See pay roll to 10 Oct. 1806.	36.00	
1648	Pay of the Army, 1803. For his own pay as Captain from 1 April to 31 December 1803 @ 40 drs. pr. mo. 360.00 For pay of William Clarke as Lieut. on the Expedition from 1 Augt. to 31 Decr. 03. 150.00 For amount paid John Newman a Private of Danl. Bissells Co. from 1 Augt. to 31 Decr. 1803 and sundry men enlisted by himself from dates of Enlistment to 31 decr. 1803. 186.91	696.91	
1727	Pay of the Army, 1804. For his own pay for the Year 1804. 480.00		

[425]

For pay of Wm. Clarke for same time.
360.00
For do. of the non commissioned Officers
& Privates of his detachment from 1 January to 30 Novr. 1804. 1350.82
For pay of do. & do. for December 1804.
264.14   2454.96

1869 Pay of the Army, 1805. For his own pay
for the Year 1805. 480.00
For pay of Lt. Wm. Clarke for same time.
360.00
For pay of Moses B. Reed, private of his
detachment from 1 January to 13 Feb. 1805.
7.00
For pay of the non commissioned Officers
& Privates of his Detachmt. for 1805.
1678.10   2525.10

1800 Pay of the Army, 1806. For his own pay
for the Year 1806. 480.00
For pay of Lt. Wm. Clarke for do. 360.00
For the pay of the non commissioned
Officers & Privates of his detachment from
1 Jany. to 10 Oct. 1806 the day they were
discharged at St. Louis together with an allowance of pay for returning home. 1466.96   2306.96

1887 Pay of the Army, 1807. For his own pay
from 1 January to 2 March 1807 the date of
his resignation. 82.58
For pay of Lt. Wm. Clarke from 1 Jany.
to 28 Feby. 1807 the date of his resignation. 60.00   142.58

1654 Subsistence of the Army, 1803. For his own
Subsistence from 1 Apl. to 31 decr. 115.50
For Subsistence of Lt. Clarke including
his Black Waiter from 1 Augt. to 31 decr.
1803. 49.36   164.86

1788 Subsistence of the Army, 1804. For his
Subsistence for the Year 1804. 228.51
For Subsistence of Lt. Wm. Clarke & his
black Waiter for same time. 228.51   457.02

1804 Subsistence of the Army, 1805. For his Sub-
sistence for the Year 1805. 273.75
For Subsistence of Lt. Clarke & his black
Waiter for same time. 273.75   547.50

1809 Subsistence of the Army, 1806. For his Sub-
sistence for the Year 1806. 244.77
For Subsistence of Lt. Wm. Clarke & his
black Waiter for same time. 244.68
For payments made the non commissioned
Officers & Privates of his Detachment for

balance of Subsistence from 14 May 1804 the time they entered the Missouri to the 1 October 1806 the day they were discharged, together with an allowance for travelling home—a proportion of the Subsistence furnished by the public having been deducted from them on Settlemt. 5458.63

Deduct amount paid Geo. Drewyer an Interpreter for Subsistence, which payment is carried to the expences of the Expedition. 197.71   5260.92

1809 Subsistence of the Army, 1806 continued. For this amount being that part of the Rations &c. furnished by the Public & charged to Capt. Lewis in this account which he considered as intended for the Soldiers of the party, & which he deducted from them on Settlement—the residue being for the support of Boatmen Interpreters &c. & carried to the expences of the expedition. 459.69   6210.06

1857 Subsistence of the Army, 1807. For his Subsistence from 1 January to 2nd March 1807 the date of his resignation. 31.11

For Subsistence of Lt. Clarke & his black Waiter from 1 January to 28 Feby. 1807 the day he resigned. 27.44   58.55

1780 Cloathing Department, 1806. For amount paid the non commissioned Officers & Privates of his detachment for arrearages of Cloathing due them at the time of their discharge pr. Roll. 2107.20

Deduct amount of cloathing charged to them by Capt. Lewis. 52.59   2054.61

1989 Expedition to the Pacific Ocean. For amount of sundry articles purchased by him on account of the expedition together with purchases made by others on his account with the payment of which he is charged in this account.[23] 6088.79

For payments made by him to Boatmen Interpreters &c. for services on the Expedition including a payment to William Clark for difference of Pay & Subsistence between a Lieut. & Captn. during the Expedition by order of the President of the U. States. 4931.50

For Sundry disbursements made by him of a Contingent nature, being for his travelling expences &c. making arrangements for

the Expedition, transportation, pilotage, repairs of the rifles of his party &c. &c. 1047.16
For this amount being that portion of the Rations &c. furnished by the Public & charged to Capt. Lewis in this account including 500 lbs. grease also charged to him which he applied to the Support of the boatmen, Interpreters &c. & therefore chargable to this Head—the kegs, transportation &c. being credited him on General Abstract. 1201.43
For payment made Geo. Drewyer for his subsistence as an Interpreter to the Expedition 197.71
For one Uniform Laced Coat, one silver Epaulet, one Dirk, & belt, one hanger & belt, one pistol & one fowling piece, all private property, given in exchange for Canoe, Horses &c. for public service during the expedition & admitted to his credit by order of the Secretary of War.[24] 135.00   13601.59

1796 Indian Department, 1806. For disbursements made for the purchase of Horses & other articles incident to the outfit & for the expences of conducting a party of Mandan Indians from St. Louis to Washington City between 23 Sept. & 31 Decr. 1806. 3009.31
For this amount with which he is charged to H. Rogers for an Indian Horse purchased of him, which Horse died while considered in the public service, & now admitted to his credit by order of the Secretary of War. 44.00   3053.31

1788 Subsistence of the Army, 1804. For Sundry Rations, parts of Rations, & extra do. furnished his Detachment by Galusha, Contractor—for their Subsistence from 16 Decr. 1803 to 12 May 1804 the same having been brought to the debit of Capt. Lewis in this a/c. 605.89
Deduct this sum being part of the foregoing already passed to his credit. 2.69
603.20   38722.25[25]

1. The first of the two documents which summarize the financial aspects of the expedition is this preliminary accounting (DNA, RG 107, L-Misc., 1805), covering expenditures made chiefly before the start of the exploration. It probably was drawn up in early 1806, by War Department accountants, for budgeting purposes. Mrs. Grace Lewis's article (LEWIS (2)) on the financing of the expedition draws primarily on this document. Her analysis of the

records should be used with mine, though I question her inference that much of the money Lewis paid to Chouteau and other St. Louis officials was a kind of diplomatic bribery.

2. Since the bills of exchange were negotiable, and the persons to whom warrants for payment were finally drawn had no connection with the expedition, I make no attempt to identify them.

3. Charles Gregoire (d. 1832), of Philadelphia, had moved to Ste. Genevieve. Another bill of exchange for $1,500 drawn by Lewis in his favor, 28 March 1804, was "for pay of the Army" (DNA, RG 217, Register of Warrants, No. 5).

4. An error for Alexander McNair, who is correctly named in Lewis's notification to Dearborn (DNA, RG 107, Register of Letters Sent, L-159, 18 May 1804).

5. Samuel Gwathney (d. 1850), William Clark's nephew, of Louisville, Ky., and Jeffersonville, Indiana Territory.

6. This draft covered Warfington's pay from the day his enlistment expired, 4 Aug. 1804, until his return from Fort Mandan. His pay for the last seven months of his service in Capt. John Campbell's company, amounting to $49.67, was not issued until 4 Aug. 1806 (DNA, RG 217, Records of the Army Accounting Office, Journal M, p. 6507). When Gratiot notified Dearborn of the draft issued to Warfington, he also listed one for $20.00 to Paul Prèmot [Primaut] (DNA, RG 107, Register of Letters Received, G-161, 23 May 1805).

7. Jean Baptiste Lajeunesse and Etienne Malboeuf, two of Lewis's *engagés*.

8. Two more *engagés*. Deschamps was *patron* of the French boatmen.

9. The occurrence of this man's name in the financial records supports Eva Emery DYE's assertion that he was François Rivet, an early Oregon settler. Clark calls him Reevey. He is the Frenchman who danced on his hands (LEWIS & ORDWAY, 167, 175); was one of the two men met by Lewis and Clark near the mouth of the Cannonball 18 Oct. 1804 (LEWIS & ORDWAY, 155, 167n, 181); was the man who wintered, along with Greinyea [Grenier] at Fort Mandan (JOURNALS, 5:350) and who accompanied Warfington's boat to St. Louis in April-May 1805. Lewis and Clark met him and Grenier again in Aug. 1806 (JOURNALS, 5:349–50). Edward Hempstead is identified as his attorney in DNA, RG 217, Records of the Army Accounting Office, Journal L, p. 5921.

10. An entry in Journal L, p. 6002, lists this man as Meriwether Smith and identifies the payment as "on account of his pay."

11. As itemized in Journal K, p. 5332:

1351 Comp[lete] Rat[ion]s from 16 Decr. 1803 to 31 Jany. 1804, @ 14 5/10 Cents	195.89
36 Rats. Whiskey @ 4 5/10	1.62
88 8/9 Flour @ 4 5/10	4.00
1800 Com. Rats. in Feby. & March 1804 @ 14 5/10 . .	261.00
283 Rats. Whiskey @ 4 5/10	12.74
286 3/4 lbs. Flour—254 8/9 Rats. @ 4 5/10	11.47
6 quarts Salt @ 11 5/10	.69
155 lbs.—137 7/8 Rats. Flour @ 4 5/10	6.20
120 lbs.—96 Rats. Beef @ 4 5/10	4.32
219 Rats. Whiskey @ 4 5/10	9.85

For sundry articles provision delivd. to him at the
Camp opposite the Mouth of Missouri River on 31st
March 1804 including Kegs & bags to contain them . . 1170.25
Paid for transporting Do. from Kaskaskias to Missouri . 5.00
Paid for transporting provision for his detachmt. to
the Camp at the River Dubois 22.50 1703.53

12. Lt. Steele, First Infantry, was assistant military agent at Kaskaskia, and in 1805 was commanding officer of the post.

13. Lt. William Swan (d. 1872) was a first lieutenant, First Infantry, in 1801 and as of 1802 was assistant military agent at Fort Massac. He paid the pilot of Lewis's boat from the Falls of the Ohio to Massac the sum of $35, and he advanced $130 to an express hired by Lewis. To make this disbursement he drew upon military agent William Linnard in favor of Alexander McNair (Swan to Linnard, DNA, RG 92, Box 617). The remainder of the sum was for "Screws Augers &c." (Journal K, p. 5242).

14. Nicholas Jarrot, of Cahokia.

15. Here the War Department transfers from Lewis's account the money he issued to Pierre Chouteau for the expenses of the Osage delegation en route to Washington. In the final accounting, he will still be charged with expenses incurred before the delegation left St. Louis. The sum deducted here was issued to Chouteau in the form of drafts in amounts of $50 and $100 each, to be spent along the way. Lewis advised Dearborn by letter of 18 May 1804 that he had drawn drafts totaling $3,000 in favor of Chouteau, numbered from 7 to 40 and all dated 3 May 1804 (DNA, RG 107, Register of Letters Received, L-152).

16. Journal L, p. 6034, lists this bill of exchange dated Fort Mandan, 4 April 1805, in favor of Charles McKenzie on account of a horse borrowed "for public purposes" which was stolen by a party of Sioux. McKenzie (1774–1855) was a clerk of the North West Company who visited the expedition several times at Fort Mandan.

17. Journal L, p. 6034, lists this bill of exchange dated Fort Mandan, 4 April 1805, in favor of Jean Baptiste Lepage "on account of pay and bounty."

18. This bill was drawn by Charles Gratiot, 28 May 1805 (Journal M, p. 6092), but the purpose of the payment is not stated. The expedition met Loisel (1773–1804), a St. Louis fur trader, on 25 May 1804 as he was coming down from his post on Cedar Island. Perhaps Lewis bought some goods from him. Another payment to Loisel, issued soon after the meeting, was made by Amos Stoddard on Lewis's behalf, 19 June 1804, in the amount of $50 (DNA, RG 217, Register of Warrants, No. 5, Warrant No. 7771). As soon as Loisel reached St. Louis after his meeting with Lewis and Clark, he wrote to Carlos Dehault Delassus, viewing with alarm the inroads of the Americans (28 May 1804, NASATIR (2), 2:735–40). He advanced an idea that he may have got from Lewis, claiming the Americans "believe that their boundaries ought to be considered as the sources of the various rivers which empty by different branches into the Mississippi, although many of those rivers take their rise in the midst of Spanish settlements." He offered himself as an agent to counterpropagandize the Indians against American influence. But he died before the Spanish could act upon his proposal.

19. The payment to Gravelines, made 30 May 1805 by Gratiot (Journal M, p. 6224), was probably his wages for piloting the boat from Fort Mandan.

20. The financial statement that follows is in Journal N, pp. 6964–72, 1807–08. Supporting entries are to be found in many early volumes of the records of the Army Accounting Office, now housed at the General Accounting Office but eventually to be transferred to the Fiscal Branch of the National Archives. Specifically, Lewis and Clark entries may be found in Ledgers B, C, and D (Set No. 1); Journals K, L, M, N, P, and Q; Report Books D, E, and G; and Register of Warrants, No. 5. In 1955 these records were examined by Philip H. Ward and Donald M. Zahn, and the Lewis and Clark entries noted.

21. Lard, deer tallow, or bear fat used as a staple in the diet of French watermen.

22. Here is the source of my belief that the men named are the "nine young men from Kentucky" (BIDDLE, 1:2) who were enlisted especially for the expedition. Elsewhere (No. 89) I suggest that Shannon and Colter were picked up by Lewis as he descended the Ohio, and the others were recruited by Clark in the vicinity of Louisville, Ky., and Clarksville, Indiana Territory.

23. This entry covers the vast amount of supplies and equipment which Lewis purchased in the spring of 1803, set forth in Nos. 53–57.

24. Lewis's uniform coat was traded by Drouillard to the Cathlamet Indians for a canoe in March 1806. Lewis wrote: "I think the U'States are indebted to me another Uniform coat for that of which I have disposed on this occasion was but little woarn" (JOURNALS, 4:176–77).

25. And so we have the "total cost" of the expedition. The figure can be augmented or diminished, depending on how we set the limits of the undertaking. To be inclusive, the cost should include the money spent in getting the Mandan chief back to his people—a sum approaching $10,000— plus the appropriation of $11,000 made by Congress for extra compensation to members of the expedition, and the value of their land warrants. But by defining more strictly what constituted the expenses directly attributable to the expedition, we can reduce the figure considerably. We can subtract, for example, the pay, subsistence, and clothing of the men who already were in service when transferred to Lewis's command; those costs would have accrued without the expedition.

278. Luther Robbins to Lewis and Clark

Messrs. Clark & Lewis   Greene D. Maine October 11th 1807

Haveing received information that you are about Publishing in three Volumes your tower to the Pacific Ocean and that your terms are these to subscribers "21 Dollars for said Volums, this is to inform you that I am Directed to wright you that, Benjamin Alden, William Gilbert, John Cole, and my self wish to subscribe for the three Volums, and your money will be ready when you send said

Books, we wish to have them sent to Portland in the District of Maine, as that is a Commercial Town, if you could make it convenient, if not to Boston and wright me a line on the Subject, at what time the Volums will be ready and to whom I can Apply for them and pay the money to, as I presume you will authorise some person in each State for that purpose. I am Dear sir Your Obedient Servt.

LUTHER ROBBINS

P.S. As I keep the Postoffice you can wright me free. L. R.

ALS, RC (MoSHi). Addressed to Lewis and Clark in Philadelphia.

279. Nathaniel Pryor to Clark

Sir,   St. Louis Oct. 16. 1807.

The Escort under my command for the reconveyance of the Mandane Chief to his nation has been compelled to return to St. Louis without accomplishing that object. You will expect to be informed of the untoward circumstances which have contributed to this failure.

We arrived at the lower villages of the Ricaras at 9 OClock, on the morning of the 9th September. These people, as soon as we came opposite their village, fired several guns, the shot of which came very near us.[1] The sub agent Dorion, enquired in the Sieux Language 'What they meant.' They replied 'Put to shore, we will supply you with corn and oil'—From their hospitalities to our party on a former occasion, I thought it prudent to shew a confidence in those friendly professions, and ordered the Boats to land at the village.

Several of the Sieux, the upper bands of which associated with the Ricaras in this affair, immediately came to the Beach. From them we learned, that the Ricaras and the Mandanes still carried on war with each other, and that two of the former had been lately killed at the river Bullett.[2]

In a very short time the bank was crowded with about six hundred and fifty Indians, all of whom were armed with guns, and many of them with additional warlike weapons. A Mandane woman, who had been a captive for several years came on board from whom I obtained informations, which could probably have been derived from no other quarter.

She informed me that Manuel Lisa a St. Louis Trader had passed up some time before: That he had given the Ricaras, through *compulsion* I conjecture, a number of guns and a considerable quantity

[432]

of powder and ball. This man you recollect obtained a licence from Mr. Bates before your arrival and before the plan which the Government had adopted with respect to the Mandane was known at St. Louis. He was however still at St. Charles and it is not forgotten that Mr. Bates having occasion to visit that village informed him of the change of arrangement in the upper country, and desired him to remain until my Boats should be equipped that he might accompany the expedition.

This, we understood he had consented to do—and his failure in those engagements, has probably obliged him to divert the storm which threatened *his own boat,* by directing the attentions of the Ricaras to *ours.*

He told them, as we learn from this woman, that two boats might be very soon expected; that we had the Mandane Chief on board; and that we were to remain, for the purposes of trade at their villages. On this, they pillaged him of about the half of his goods, and suffered him to pass on, determining in their councils at the same time, to kill him on his return, and to lose no time in preparing to murder the Mandane and his Escort as soon as we should arrive. Being thus completely apprized of their sanguinary purposes, as respected the Mandane in particular, I directed him to secure himself in the cabbin, by building in front a breast work of trunks and boxes. My men were prepared for action, and the Indians about the picketed villages and breast works, appeared to be putting themselves in readiness to commence it. They were observed checking their bullets and driving away their women and children.

The chief to whom you desired me to present a Medal, at length approached my boat. I had no doubt of his wish to serve us; and as he was known to possess influence with his nation, I felt desirous of conciliating him. He presented me a letter from Courtney,[3] who had previously to the arrival of Lisa, been cruelly treated by these barbarians, and informed us that he alone had been friendly to that unfortunate Trader, who owed his safety and ultimate release to his friendly offices.

This chief discovered much uneasiness while conversing with us, and after professing his regard for the Mandane and myself, rejoined his blood thirsty companions by whom his advices were in the sequel overruled. My interpreter was in the mean time, employed in persuading the chiefs to meet in council, and at length succeeded in collecting all of them, except the chief of the upper village.

I should have made a farther effort to procure the attendance of this refracting man; but found that if we consumed the day in

[433]

friendly confidences, we would, as soon as it was dark, fall a more easy sacrifice. I therefore determined to meet them and proceed to the upper villages as expeditiously as possible. My Interpreter here was an old Spaniard [4] whom you probably may not have forgotten. To employ a mediator in whom we have no confidence in such circumstances as this, was infinitely embarrassing; but I was obliged to make use of him on this occasion from the absolute impossibility of obtaining another.

I addressed them somewhat in this manner. 'Your Great American Father has sent me with a few of his soldiers to conduct the Mandane chief to his nation. In our long and laborious journey, we have met with many nations of red People, by all of whom we have been treated with hospitality and kindness. I have repeated to them the talk of their Great Father, whose counsels they will in future pursue. We are not strangers to you: On a former occasion you extended to Louis & Clark the hand of friendship. We feasted in your villages and exchanged mutual benefit. As a proof of the confidence of your Great Father in a continuance of your pacific dispositions, and as an evidence of his personal friendship for your chief, he sends him a large Medal the devices of which may continually remind you of the amicable intercourse which ought always subsist between his People and yours.' I then suspended the Medal to the neck of Grey Eyes[5] as is usual on such occasions.

To this address they made no reply—and in fact from a variety of suspicious circumstances I scarcely calculated on a friendly answer.

We separated, it being understood that we would stop at the *upper* Village to pay our respects to the Chiefs, who perhaps from motives of Etiquette, had refused to attend the council below.

Our Boats proceeded on. Dorion and the Interpreter Jesseaume went by land. The Indians followed in a body, using threats and menaces.

On our arrival about 4 OClock in the afternoon all the Indians were collected on the Beach. They appeared in violent rage. It was necessary as I conceived, to see the chief. It was besides my duty to take on board Dorion & Jesseaume. My men were kept prepared for an attack, and it was doubtless, as prudent to meet it on the beach as to be followed into a river filled with irregular Sand Bars. We put to shore and were directed by the Indians to proceed up a narrow channel near the Beach. Their views in *this,* could not be mistaken and we declined a compliance.

We were then told that we should proceed no farther: we should stay and trade with them. Lisa had told them, it was our *intention* to remain &c. &c. together with various other things expressive of their determination to detain us.

They first seized the Cabel of Chouteau's Barge—as *his* contained merchandize and had no *Soldiers* to defend it, with whom they were, no doubt unwilling to provoke a contest, until they should have the *other* completely in their power. Waving their hands then, the moment they attacked the Barge, they made signals that I might go on. Chouteau 'begged he was not to be abandoned in so dangerous a situation.' I replied 'Make them an offer.' He and a number of his men had previously gone on the Beach, in order to shew an advance of confidence, but these unconscionable Rascals appeared to rise in their demands in proportion as they found their victims within their reach. He at length *did* make them an offer, which, had they not been determined on plunder and blood, ought to have satisfied them. He proposed to leave the half of his goods with a man to trade them.

The chief of the upper village who had refused to attend the Council below, now came on board, and desired by gestures which were readily understood that the Mandane might go on shore with him. On my peremptory refusal to suffer this, he retired as hastily as he had entered.

Mr. Chouteau and several of his men were still on the Beach. Dorion continued in conference—a demand was instantly made of *all* the arms and ammunition;—the chief to whom I had given the Medal, threw it on the ground, and one of the men was struck down with the butt end of a gun. The Indians now raised a general Whoop, and as they retired to the willows, fired on the men, on the Beach, as well as on both Boats in the same instant. I had reserved my fire, and was so fortunate as to reach them, with a well directed volley of Swivels, Blunderbusses and small arms, before they sheltered themselves behind a young growth of Willows at the distance of about sixty yards.

Here, they were rather concealed than defended; and as it would have been madness to leave the Boats of which the Savages would have taken the immediate possession, we continued the fight for about a quarter of an hour when, finding that they were too greatly superior in numbers, I ordered a retreat. My Boat was put off with greater care than Chouteau's. He stuck on a Sand Bar; thro' which his men were obliged to drag the Barge while exposed to the continual fire of the enemy.

To my inexpressible satisfaction, he at length surmounted difficulties which had nearly proven fatal to the whole party.

[435]

We again floated in a narrow rapid current, and continued a retreating combat from both sides of the river for about one hour. It was sunset, and the pursuit was at length checked by the death of one [of] their Sieux leaders.

He had been in my Boat, and was afterwards known by a white bandage which he wore about his head. With about 40 men he was endeavouring to meet us at a point projecting into the stream when he received a Ball which was aimed particularly at him, and appeared to expire in a moment on the Beach. His Partizans gathered about him and we saw no more of them.

During the rapid succession of these events I had no leisure to enquire into the situation of my men. As soon as we imagined our-selves free from pursuit, we lashed our Boats together, and examined their wounds.

Of my own men none were killed. My Hunter's leg was broken. One of the soldiers had a ball through the fleshy part of his leg—and a second was wounded in the hip and arm.[6]

Mr. Chouteau was far less fortunate: He had one man killed on the Beach; one in a Perogue which accompanied his Barge; one on board the Barge and another mortally wounded who died nine days after-wards. Six others of his men were badly wounded but have since re-covered.

This miscarriage is a most unhappy affair. The Mandane is now at the camp, and will be supplied with whatever he may reasonably want until the orders of the Government shall be known with respect to him.[7]

Altho Jesseaume the Mandane Interpreter was of my party, he had quarrelled with his chief and was on board Chouteau's Boat. I am sorry to say that he has been badly wounded in the thigh and shouder.[8] Mr. Bates has ordered him medical attendance in St. Louis, as the Surgeon of the Garrison has been of late too ill to attend to his duties.

After our retreat I felt so sensibly the necessity of obeying the orders of the government with respect to this expedition, that I proposed to the Mandane that he should accompany me through by land. The distance was only about three days march, and by leaving the River, and pursuing an unfrequented route, through the Praires, I hoped to reach the Mandane-Lodges, undiscovered by the Ricaras.

The chief declined this project, alledging the impossibility of accom-plishing it with his wounded Interpreter together with the additional incumbrance of their wives and children.

[436]

If my opinion were asked 'what number of men would be necessary to escort this unhappy chief to his nation,' I should be compelled to say, from my own knowledge of the association of the upper band of the Sieux with the Ricaras that a force of less than 400 men ought not to attempt such an enterprize. And surely it is possible that even one thousand men might fail in the attempt. I have the honor to be very respectfully Your obdt. Servant

NATHL. PRYOR

LS, RC (DNA, RG 107, C-350). Endorsed. Enclosed in Clark to Dearborn, 30 Oct. 1807. The letter is in the hand of Frederick Bates and the phrasing is typically Batesian; apparently he helped Pryor to draft it. Clark received the report while visiting in Louisville, 24 Oct., and immediately sent Dearborn a summary of the affray (DNA, RG 107, C-346). Still in Louisville on 3 Dec., he sent another report by Lt. Joseph Kimball. He also expressed his intention of visiting in Virginia during the winter, and asked Dearborn to write him at Fincastle (C-384).

1. Not only were the Arikaras at war with the Mandans, but they were furious with the Americans over the death of their chief in Washington. Joseph Gravelines was ill-treated when he went to the tribe in the spring of 1807 to tell them of the chief's death (Pierre Chouteau to Dearborn, 7 June 1807, MoSHi).

2. The Cannonball River, entering the Missouri below present Bismarck, N.D., and so called because of stony concretions resembling cannon balls in the vicinity of the river.

3. Charles Courtin, a trader who eludes thorough identification. When Lewis and Clark met traders Dixon and Handcock in Aug. 1806, they said they had spent the last winter with the Teton Sioux "in company with a Mr. Coartong who brought goods to trade" (JOURNALS, 5:329), and that the Sioux had robbed him. As they came on down the river, Lewis and Clark met the boat of a man whom Clark calls Coutau, and who may have been Courtin (JOURNALS, 5:384). In the spring of 1807, Robert McClellan reported that "a Certain Mr. Corton a Kenedian who obtained Licinus to Traide with the Suoix & Poncaws for the year 1806 Proceeds On a voige this spring up the Missouri Expecting to Reach the falls be fore he stops" (to Lewis, 5 April 1807, MoSHi). When the Yankton and Teton Sioux sent a delegation to St. Louis that spring, Clark complained of their treatment of a man named Couteau or Courtean, clearly not Chouteau (to Dearborn, 9 May 1807, DNA, RG 107, C-Misc.). Courtin himself wrote a letter to Frederick Bates 22 June 1807, speaking of the rascality of the Arikaras who had plundered his goods. At the time of his report, the Arikaras would not permit him to leave their village. Bates sent a translation to Dearborn with the comment, "I do myself the honor of enclosing the translation of a letter which I have lately received from a French Trader at the Ricaras' Village. As this letter contains all the evidence which I have of the insecurity of the navigation of the Missouri, I forbear to make comments. Of Courtin I know nothing; it is said that he is respectable." Courtin's letter is enclosed in Bates to Dearborn, 2 Aug. 1807 (DNA, RG 107, B-280).

4. I think he means Joseph Garreau, whose name is variously spelled Garout, Garaut, Garon, etc., and who is identified both as a Frenchman and a Spaniard. He was with the Arikaras in the spring of 1807 when Gravelines delivered Jefferson's message, according to Courtin's letter cited in the previous note. He is the "Mr. Garrow" who showed Lewis and Clark the process by which the Indians made glass beads (JOURNALS, 1:272).

5. Grey Eyes (d. 1823), a principal chief of the Arikaras, described by Clark in 1806 as "a Stout jolley fellow of about 35 years of age" (JOURNALS, 5:351).

6. One of the wounded men was George Shannon; an account of the injury that resulted in amputation of his leg is given in No. 387. It is curious that Pryor does not mention him by name here, and the omission suggests that Pryor wrote Clark a personal account of the attack as well as this official one. After his operation, Shannon was near death for a time (Bates to Clark, [?] Dec. 1807, BATES, 1:248). During his recovery his medical treatment caused Frederick Bates to draw upon the Indian Department for $300.00; at the same time, Bates drew $200.00 in favor of a man named Gibson and $303.00 in favor of Lorimier—a clue to the identity of the other wounded men, since Bates wrote Denis Fitzhugh on 16 Dec. 1807 that he had been obliged to make advances particularly to the wounded men of Pryor's escort. Lewis's account book (MoSHi) contains an entry dated 7 May 1808 showing an expense of $68.27½ for supplies to Shannon during his hospitalization. Lewis first worded the entry as a draft on the War Department for "wages and expenses" of Shannon, then struck out the passage, perhaps indicating that he had decided to pay the bill himself.

7. "The Mandane Chief heretofore happy at the camp, where I have always seen him at the Officers tables, and treated with every kind and hospitable indulgence now insists on being at St. Louis. He is made to believe that he is the 'Brother' and not the 'Son' of the President. . . . How trifling and vexatious!" (Bates to Clark, [?] Dec. 1807, MoSHi).

8. Upon returning to St. Louis, René Jusseaume appealed directly to Jefferson for financial aid. "Je me recommande a vous, Monsieur Le President, et vous suplie de prendre en consideration la position de votre suppliant estropié et hors d'etat de travailler pour avoir obéi a vos desirs en descendant avec le Capn. Lewis et qui est et sera toujours pret a sacrifier le reste de sa vie a votre service" (3 Dec. 1807, MoSHi). He asked to be sent back to the Mandans so that he might return his children to their mother's Mandan parents.

280. Lewis's Receipt to William Woods

Sir,   Ivy Creek, Oct. 28th 1807.

On the receipt of this, you will deliver to William Woods or his order, one complete copy of my work, intitled *Lewis & Clark's Tour*, together with one copy of our large map of a part of North America, being of the best paper and type, as the same or any part thereof shall be published and ready for delivery, hereby acknowledging that I have received thirty one dollars as full compensation for the same.

MERIWETHER LEWIS

To all persons employed in vending and delivering the said works.

ADS, RC (MoSHi). Addressed, "Mr. William Woods Gent."; endorsed, "11th April 1812. Recd. payment in full of Dr. John H. Marks. W. Woods." Another endorsement, "Paid by R. L. for J. M." And another, "Taken in by John Marks to be charged to [. . .] Marks as Representative of M. L." This man may have been the William Woods who was a Baptist minister, or the one who was a surveyor of Albemarle County from 1796 to 1828 (see WOODS, 354, 356).

281. Charles Willson Peale to Jefferson

Dear Sir   Museum [Philadelphia] Jany. 29th 1808.

The Bears[1] I received today, in good health, and tomorrow we shall give them a more spacious Cage. Finding they have a division between them in their present Cage, leads to a suspition that they do not harmonize together, which I should hope is not the case, therefore on changing their habitation, I shall take the precaution of chaining them untill we can know their dispositions. If they can be keept together, it will furnish the opportunity trying whether they will breed in a domesticated State, a desirable object with me. Can we obtain their exact age? The register of the Museum should contain every interristing particular about them, as we hope to see them get their full groath, & also to assertain what they may weigh when they acquire their full size.

A few weeks past I compleated a wax figure of Captn. Lewis & placed it in the Museum, my object in this work is to give a lesson to the Indians who may visit the Museum, and also to shew my sentiments respecting wars.

The Figure being dressed in an Indian Dress presented to Capt. Lewis by *Comeahwait* Chief of Shoshone Nation, who was suspitious that Captn. Lewis ment to lead him into an ambuscade with his Enemies. The figure has its right hand on its breast & the left holds the *Calmut* which was given me by Captn. Lewis. In a Tablet I give the Story in a few words, and then add. "This mantle, composed of 140 Ermine Skins was put on Captn. Lewis by *Comeahwait* their Cheif. Lewis is supposed to say, Brother, I accept your dress— It is the object of my heart to promote amongst you, our Neighbours, Peace and good will—that you may bury the Hatchet deep in the ground never to be taken up again—and that henceforward you

[439]

may smoke the *Calmut* of Peace & live in perpetual harmony, not only with each other, but with the white man, your Brothers, who will teach you many useful Arts. Possessed of every comfort in life, what cause ought to involve us in War? Men are not too numerous for the lands which are to cultivate; and Disease makes havock anough amongst them without deliberatily distroying each other— If any differences arise about Lands or trade, let each party appoint judicious persons to meet together & amicably settle the disputed point." Such I believe to be the sentiments of our friend Lewis, and which he endeavored to instill in the Minds of the various savages he met with in his long & hazardous Tour. I am pleased when ever I can give an object which affords a moral sentiment to the Visitors of the Museum.

I have taken of your precious time by this Scrole, that you may enjoy health & long life is the prayer of your friend,

C. W. Peale

ALS, RC (DLC). Endorsed; received 31 Jan. 1808.

1. Two live grizzly cubs which were sent to Jefferson by Lt. Zebulon Pike. "There was shiped from New Orleans, for your Excelly. in the Brig Neptune Capt. Shepheard Master, bound to Baltamore a pair of Grisly Bears (mail & femail) which I brought from the divideing ridges, of the Pacific, & Atlantic Oceans" (Pike to Jefferson, 29 Oct. 1807, DLC). By the time the letter had reached Jefferson the bears had already arrived. The President told his daughter Anne Randolph of their arrival in a letter of 1 Nov., saying, "These are too dangerous and troublesome for me to keep" (ViWC). He thanked Pike for them 5 Nov. and on the same day offered them to Peale for the Philadelphia Museum (DLC). Peale replied 7 Nov. that he would accept them cheerfully. "It will be very interresting to see the Grisley-Bear brought to his full grown. One of the skins which Govr. Lewis had appeared to me enormously large . . ." (DLC). What eventually happened to them is related by SELLERS, 2:228: "The bears, from playful cubs, grew large and fierce. They would attack anyone, man or beast, who came within their reach. A teasing monkey had arm and shoulder blade torn off by a sweep of the great claws. They met their fate when one of them, one night, broke loose from his cage and stalked into the cellar of Philosophical Hall. The family was in terror, and with reason. Peale closed the cellar door and window, and in the morning entered and shot the creature. The survivor was killed in its cage and mounted with its mate."

282. Frederick Bates to Joseph Charless

Sir, St. Louis 12 Mar. 1808.

I should esteem a particular favor your procuring for me, one, two or three of those western Papers, from different Presses, which contain the Prospectus of Frazier's Journal.

The interest which I take in the compromise of those misunderstandings which have arisen from that Prospectus, urge me to trouble you with the request.

If the Publication of Gov. Lewis on the subject of Gass's & Frazier's Journal can be procured, you would confer an additional favor by transmitting it. For these friendly offices I beg you to command me in return.

SC (MoSHi). Joseph Charless (1772–1834) was the first printer in St. Louis, brought there from Louisville at the instigation of Lewis and others who offered him financial backing. He began publication of the *Missouri Gazette* in 1808, and issued the *Laws of the Territory of Louisiana* in 1809 (KING).

283. Bernard McMahon to Jefferson

Dear Sir,   Philadelphia June 28th 1808

I do myself the pleasure of sending you by this mail a few gooseberries, as a sample of what we may have here, by first obtaining good kinds, and then judicious management. I fear that from the extreme heat of the present weather, they will undergo a fermentation and turn sour before they reach you; at all events, they will perspire and become much less in size than when pulled.

I am happy to inform you that I have fine plants of *all* the varieties of Currants (7)[1] and Gooseberries (2)[2] brought by Govr. Lewis, and of about 20 other *new species* of plants, as well as five or six new *genera;* this will add to natural history and the plants are forthcoming. I will not forget you in due time.

I would be very happy to know when Govr. Lewis may be expected here, and am Sir, Yours with sincere esteem.

                                 BERND. McMAHON

ALS, RC (DLC). Endorsed; received 30 June 1808. Reply is No. 284.
1. I doubt if Lewis and Clark brought back seven species of *Ribes* in addition to the gooseberries. McMahon is probably including their "Arikara currant" or buckbush, *Symphoricarpos orbiculatus* Moench, and the buffalo berry which they said resembled a currant, *Shepherdia argentea* Nuttall.
2. The common variety of gooseberry along the Missouri is *Ribes missouriensis* Nuttall ex Torrey & Gray.

284. Jefferson to Bernard McMahon

Sir   Washington July 6. 08.

I recieved duly your favor of June 28. with the gooseberries in good condition. They were certainly such as I had never seen before in any country, and will excite strenuous efforts in me to endeavor to raise such. For this purpose early in the next year I shall ask of you some cuttings of your bushes, and before that shall send a pretty copious list for a supply of the best kinds of garden seeds, and flowers. I shall be at home early in March for my permanent residence, and shall very much devote myself to my garden. I reserved very few of Govr. Lewis's articles, and have growing only his salsafia,[1] Mandane corn, and a pea remarkeable for it's beautiful blossom & leaf. His forward bean[2] is growing in my neighborhood. I have the tulips you sent me in great perfection, also the hyacinths, tuberoses, amaryllis, and the artichokes. I pray you to accept my thanks for the gooseberries and my respectful salutations.

Th: Jefferson

ALS, SC (DLC). Endorsed.
1. Salsify or oyster plant, *Tragopogon* sp. Jefferson planted "a bed 26 f. long. 2. rows & about 8 f. of a 3d. say 60 f. Missouri great Salsafia. 120 seeds 6. I. apart" (18 April 1807, weather memorandum book, PHi).
2. That is, his *early* bean.

285. Jefferson to Bernard Lacépède

Sir   Washington July 14. 08.

If my recollection does not decieve me, the collection of the remains of the Animal incognitum of the Ohio (sometimes called Mammoth) possessed by the Cabinet of Natural history at Paris, is not very copious. Under this impression, and presuming that this cabinet is allied to the National Institute, to which I am desirous of rendering some service, I have lately availed myself of an opportunity of collecting some of those remains. Genl. Clarke (the companion of Govr. Lewis in his expedition to the Pacific ocean) being, on a late journey, to pass by the big-bone-lick of the Ohio, was kind enough to undertake to employ for me a number of laborers & to direct their operations in digging for these bones at this important deposit of them. The result of these researches will appear in the inclosed catalogue of specimens which I am now able to place at the disposal of the National Institute. An Aviso being to leave this place for some port of France on public service, I deliver the packages to Capt. Haley,[1] to be deposited with the Consul of the United States at whatever port he may land. They are addressed to Mr. Warden[2] of our legation at Paris for the National Institute, and he will have the honor of delivering them. To these I have added the horns of an animal, called by the natives the Mountain ram, resembling the sheep by his head but more nearly the deer in his other parts; as also the skin of another animal resembling the sheep by his fleece, but the goat in his other parts. This is called by the natives the fleecy goat,[3] or, in the style of the Natural historian the Pokotragos. I suspect it to be nearly related to the Pacos and were we to group the fleecy animals together it would stand perhaps with the Vigogna, Pacos and Sheep. The Mountain ram was found in abundance by Messrs. Lewis and Clarke on their Western tour, and was frequently an article of food for their party and esteemed more delicate than the deer. The fleecy goat they did not see but procured two skins from the Indians, of which this is one. Their description will be given in the work of Governor Lewis, the journal & geographical part of which may be soon expected from the press: but the parts relating to the plants & animals observed in his tour will be delayed by the engravings. In the mean time the plants of which he brought seeds have been very successfully raised in the botanical garden of Mr. Hamilton of the Woodlands and by Mr. McMahon a gardener of Philadelphia. And, on the whole, it is with pleasure I can assure you that the addition to our knolege, in every department, resulting from this tour, of Messrs. Lewis and Clarke, has entirely fulfilled my expectations in setting it on foot, and that the world will find that those travellers have well earned it's favor. I will take care that the Institute as well as yourself shall recieve Govr. Lewis's work, as it appears.

It is with pleasure I embrace this occasion of returning you my thanks for the favor of your very valuable works sur les poissons et les cetacees,[4] which you were so kind as to send me through Mr. Livingston[5] & Genl. Turreau,[6] and which I find entirely worthy of your high reputation in the literary world. That I have not sooner made this acknolegement has not proceeded from any want of respect & attachment to yourself, or a just value of your estimable present, but from the strong & incessant calls of duty to other objects. The candour of your character gives me confidence of your indulgence on this head, and I assure you with truth that no circumstances are more welcome to me than those which give me the occasion of recalling myself to your recollection, & of renewing to you the assurances of sincere personal attachment and of great respect & consideration.

TH: JEFFERSON

ALS, SC (DLC). A two-page enclosure lists the contents of the boxes of specimens.

1. A sea captain, not further identified.

2. David Bailie Warden (1772–1845) was appointed secretary to Gen. John Armstrong in Paris, 1804, and became U.S. consul in that city in 1810.

3. More on Jefferson's attempt to classify the mountain goat: "I have lately seen Molina's account of Chili in which, correcting Buffon's classification of the wooly animals, he speaks of one, the Chili hueco, or Chili sheep, which may possibly be the same with the fleecy goat of Govr. Lewis" (Jefferson to Peale, 15 Jan. 1809, DLC). He refers to Juan Ignacio Molina's *Compendio della storia geografica, naturale, e civile del regno del Chile* (Bologna, 1776), translated as *Essai sur l'histoire naturelle du Chili* (Paris, 1789).

4. Two parts of a six-volume work which Lacépède published in Paris, 1798–1803, entitled *Histoire naturelle des poissons*. The parts Jefferson refers to are *Histoire naturelle des poissons* and *Histoire naturelle des cétacées*.

5. Robert R. Livingston (1746–1813), minister to France.

6. The French general Louis Marie Turreau de Linières (1756–1816).

286. Jefferson to Lewis

Dear Sir   Washington July 17. 08

Since I parted with you in Albemarle in Sep. last I have never had a line from you,[1] nor I believe has the Secretary at War with whom you have much connection through the Indian department. The misfortune which attended the effort to send the Mandane chief home became known to us before you had reached St. Louis. We took no step on the occasion, counting on recieving your advice so soon as you should be in place, and knowing that your knowlege of the whole subject & presence on the spot would enable you to judge better than we could what ought to be done. The constant persuasion that something from you must be on it's way to us, has as constantly prevented our writing to you on the subject. The present letter however is written to put an end at length to this mutual silence, and to ask from you a communication of what you think best to be done to get the chief & his family back. We consider the good faith, & the reputation of the nation as pledged to accomplish this. We would wish indeed not to be obliged to undertake any considerable military expedition in the present uncertain state of our foreign concerns, & especially not till the new body of troops shall be raised. But if it can be effected in any other way & at any reasonable expence we are disposed to meet it.

A powerful company is at length forming for taking up the Indian commerce on a large scale. They will employ a capital the first year of 300,000 D. and raise it afterwards to a million. The English Mackinac company will probably withdraw from the competition. It will be under the direction of a most excellent man, a Mr. Astor[2] mercht. of N. York, long engaged in the business & perfectly master of it. He has some hope of seeing you at St. Louis, in which case I recommend him to your particular attention. Nothing but the exclusive possession of the Indian commerce can secure us their peace. Our foreign affairs do not seem to clear up at all. Should they continue as at present the moment will come when it will be a question for the legislature whether war will not be preferable to a longer continuance of the embargo. The Presidential question is clearing up daily, and the opposition subsiding. It is very possible that the suffrage of the nation may be undivided. But with this question it is my duty not to intermeddle. I have not lately heard of your friends in Albemarle. They were well when I left that in June, and not hearing otherwise affords presumption they are well. But I presume you hear that from themselves. We have no tidings yet of the forwardness of your printer. I hope the first part will not be delayed much longer. Wishing you every blessing of life & health I salute you with constant affection & respect.

TH: JEFFERSON

ALS, SC (DLC).

1. Lewis well deserved a scolding for his failure to write. From the time of his parting with Jefferson in the fall of 1807 to his death in the fall of 1809, he wrote him three, possibly four, letters. None of the surviving letters contains more than a perfunctory expression of the warm relationship that had once existed between the two men. Jefferson worried about Lewis's failure to keep him informed. After writing the present letter he followed with further messages on 21 and 24 Aug., from Monticello, commenting on Indian affairs in particular. In the last letter he repeated his concern for the Mandan chief: "I am uneasy, hearing nothing from you about the Mandan chief, nor the measures for restoring him to his country. That is an object which presses on our justice & our honour. And farther than that I suppose a severe punishment of the Ricaras indispensable, taking for it our own time & convenience. My letter from Washington [above] asked your opinions on this subject" (DLC). At about this time, Jefferson saw a newspaper clipping of a letter that Lewis had written to Governor Harrison on Indian affairs (see No. 390, note 2). In discussing it with Dearborn, he said, "But it is astonishing we get not one word from him" (12 Aug. 1808, DLC). Lewis's failure as a correspondent was not an entirely new trait; his friend Tarleton Bates told Frederick Bates, in a letter of 20 July 1801, "Meriwether Lewis is silent though he promised to write weekly . . ." (MoSHi). Another notable lapse appears in Lewis's correspondence with Amos Stoddard. The two men were friends, or at least were well acquainted, when the expedition headed up the river in 1804. And Stoddard had consented to serve as Lewis's agent. But after returning from the Pacific, Lewis did not communicate with Stoddard for three years—and then only when he needed something—although Stoddard had written him "several friendly epistles" (No. 299).

[445]

2. John Jacob Astor (1763–1848), who was then organizing the American Fur Company.

287. Bernard McMahon to Jefferson

Dear Sir,   Philadelphia Jany. 17th 1809

. . .

I am very anxious to learn when Governor Lewis may be expected here, as I have detained a man in my house upwards of twelve months, drawing & discribing his plants, which he left with me for that purpose. This was accomplished in May last as far as it could be done in the absence of Govr. Lewis, and he told me on his leaving this City he expected to be here again in that month. This man, who is completely adequate to the task, is becoming very uneasy, and I wish him not to leave the neighbourhood till the arrival of Mr. Lewis, by whose particular instructions only, he can finish the drawings of some very important, but imperfect specimens.

I am sorry to give you so much trouble; hope you will excuse me, and am Sir, With Respect and Esteem, Your Sincere Wellwisher,

BERND. McMAHON

ALS, RC (DLC). Endorsed; received 19 Jan. 1809. McMahon repeats his anxiety to see Lewis in a letter to Jefferson of 13 Feb. 1809 (DLC).

288. Agreement for Return of the Mandan Chief

[24 February 1809]

Articles of Agreement made and Indented, at the Town of St. Louis in the Territory of Louisiana the Twenty fourth day of February in the Year of our Lord One thousand eight hundred and Nine, by and between His Excellency Meriwether Lewis, Governor of the said Territory of Louisiana, and Superintendent of Indian affairs, within the same for and on behalf of the United States of America, on the one part, and the Undersigned members of and belonging to the Saint Louis Missouri Fur Company of the other part.

Witnesseth that the said Company, for and in consideration of the articles, stipulations, and conditions hereinafter contained on the part of the said Meriwether Lewis, have covenanted and agreed, and do hereby covenant and agree to and with the said Lewis, his successor in office, heirs, Executors, and Assigns, to and for the sole use, behoof and benefit of the said United States, as follows. To wit:

First. To engage and raise One Hundred and Twenty five effective men (of whom Forty shall be Americans and expert Riflemen) who together shall form a Body of Militia of this Territory, and act in a Military Capacity, on an Expedition from the said Town of Saint Louis, to the Mandan Villages, on the River Missouri, for the safe conveyance and delivery of the Mandan Chief, his Wife, and child, to the Mandan Nation—the members of which body thus raised for the purpose [assigned] shall be [approved. . .].[1]

Second. The said Company shall furnish the said detachment for the aforesaid expedition, with good and suitable Fire Arms, of which Fifty at least shall be Rifles, and a sufficient quantity of good Ammunition, the quantity and quality of all of which shall be approved of by the Governor of this Territory.

Third. The command of the said detachment shall be given to Peter Choteau, the United States Agent for the Osage Nation of Indians (who will be specially commissioned and instructed by the Governor for that purpose) until the said expedition shall arrive at the Mandan Nation or villages, and at that place or the last of them, the military functions of the said Choteau, and the officers appointed under him for this Service shall cease and expire.

Fourth. The said Company shall provide comfortable, and suitable accommodations on board of Covered Barges, for the said Mandan Chief, his wife, and child, and for Jesson (the Interpreter) his Wife and child, and shall furnish them and each of them with a sufficiency of Good and wholesome Provisions for their, and each of their Consumption, from the day of their embarkation, until their arrival at the Mandan Nation—the said accomodations in this article mentioned, to be approved of by the Governor of this Territory.

Fifth. The said Company shall also provide and furnish accommodations in some of their Barges or Boats, for Two other Interpreters, and transport them therein as far as the said Peter Choteau agent as aforesaid shall direct and shall also furnish them with a sufficiency of good and wholesome provisions for their consumption, so long as they shall continue with the said Company. The said accommodations to be approved of, and the Interpreters to be such as shall be for that purpose selected by the Governor aforesaid.

Sixth. The said Company shall safely deliver the said Mandan Chief, his Wife and Child, Jesson (the Interpreter) his Wife, and Child, at the said Mandan Village, as soon as practicable after the departure of the said intended Expedition from Saint Louis, and shall defend them from all Warlike and other attacks, by force of arms, and every other means to the extent of their power, and at the

[447]

risque of the lives of the said detachment and shall moreover use and employ their and each of their diligent exertions for the health, preservation and safety of the said Mandan Chief, his Wife, and Child, Jesson (the Interpreter) his Wife and child, and for preventing of any accidents to them, each and all of them. And if Unfortunately, the said Mandan Chief, his Wife and child, Jesson (the Interpeter) his Wife and Child, or all or either of them, should by any unavoidable accident, or the death of all or either of them, <*be prevented from being*> fail to be transported to the said Mandan Village, not by reason or through the fault, neglect, omission, want of care, or want of diligence, on the part of the said Company and detachment, the same being sufficiently proven to the Government of the United States, or to the particular officer or person charged and authorized to that effect, then the said Sum of Seven thousand dollars herein after mentioned, shall be fully paid as is within [covenanted]. If on the contrary the said Mandan Chief, his Wife, and Child, Jesson, his Wife and child, should not be by the said Company safely delivered at the Mandan Nation or Village, through the fault, omission, neglect or want of defence on the part of the said detachment, then the said Company shall not be entitled to the sum of Seven thousand dollars, herein after covenanted to be paid nor any part thereof; and all Sum or Sums of money by the said Lewis advanced to the said Company by reason of this agreement, shall in the latter case, be by the said Company refunded and paid to the said Lewis, his Successor in office, heirs, Executors, or assigns on request—for the use and benefit of the United States.

Seventh. The said Company shall cause the said expedition, and detachment to embark and Start from Saint Louis aforesaid, on or before the Twentieth day of April next, and to proceed with all convenient and necessary Speed to the place of destination—and in case of any unforeseen accident, preventing the same before or on that day then the said Expedition, shall without any pretence of delay whatsoever embark, start, and proceed as aforesaid, on or before the Tenth day of May then next, under the penalty for default thereof of paying to the said Lewis, his successor in office, Heirs, Executors or assigns, to and for the sole use, behoof and benefit of the said United States, the sum of three thousand dollars, lawful money of the United States.

Eighth. The said Company shall safely convey such Goods, wares, Merchandizes articles, and utensils, as the Governor of the Territory shall deem necessary to send as Presents to the Indians of the Missouri, either by the said Agent Peter Choteau, or by the said Mandan Chief.

Ninth. The said Company shall immediately after the safe arrival at the Mandan Village, of the said Mandan Chief, his Wife, and Child, said Jesson, [his] Wife and child, despatch a Messenger to the G[over]nor of this [Terr]itory, with a Written report giving him inform[ation] thereof.

And the said Meriwether Lewis, for and on behalf of [the] said United States, and for and in consideration of the article[s of con]ditions, stipulations, and covenants herein before contained on the p[art] of the said members of the Saint Louis, Missouri fur Company, doth here[by] promise and covenant to and with the said Company their Heirs, a[nd] assigns as follows. To wit.

First. To pay to the said Company, their assigns, certain attorney or attornies or to their authorized agent the sum of Seven thousand Dollars lawful money of the United States; the one moiety or half Part thereof on the request of the said company, or a majority of the members thereof after the said detachment is fully formed, completed, armed furnished and equipped to the approbation of the Governor of this Territory, and the remaining Moiety or half part, when in[formation] as aforesaid shall have been received from the said Company by the said Governor, that the stipulations and Covenants herein before contained on the part of said Company have been fully, completely and *bona fide* performed and fulfilled.

Second. The said Lewis shall not before the last day fixed herein for the departure of said expedition, Licence or <*permit*> authorize any other person or persons to ascend the Missouri any higher or farther up the said River, than the Mouth of the River La Platte, for the purpose of Trading with the Indians. Nor permit any party accompanying the said detachment or any other party, to ascend the River, go before or in advance of the said detachment commanded by said Choteau from the mouth of the said River La Platte, to the Mandan Village.

And it is further Mutually understood, agreed and Covenanted by and between the parties aforesaid, that in the absence of the Governor of this Territory, the direction and approbation of General William Clarke of Saint Louis, in all matters and things in which the direction and approbation of the said Governor is required in this Agreement, shall be as good, effectual and binding on the parties aforesaid, as if the same were given by the said Governor of this Territory personally.

For the true and faithful performance of each and every of the conditions, covenants and Stipulations herein before contained the

[449]

said parties respectively, do hereby jointly and severally bind themselves, their Heirs, Executors, administrators and assigns each to the
other in the Penal Sum of Ten thousand dollars, lawful money of
the United States.

In Testimony whereof the parties aforesaid have herewith inter-
changeably set their hands and Seals the day, and Year, and place
first before written.

Signed, sealed and delivered	MERIWETHER LEWIS
[in the] presence of—	PRE. CHOUTEAU
the words "be prevented from being"	MANUEL LISA
in the sixth article on the second page	WM. MORRISON
being first erased, and the words	BEN. WILKINSON[2]
"fail to be" interlined at the same	A. P. CHOUTEAU
place, and the word "Permit" in the	
Second article on the third page erased,	
and the word "authorize" interlined	
before signing.	
Wm. Clark	
E. Hempstead [3]	

ADS (MoSHi).

1. Several words missing.

2. Benjamin Wilkinson, a St. Louis merchant, in partnership with Risdon
H. Price after 1808.

3. Edward Hempstead (1780–1817), St. Charles and St. Louis attorney,
deputy attorney general for the districts of St. Charles and St. Louis in
1809–11, and delegate to Congress from Missouri Territory in 1812–14.

289. Lewis to Henry Dearborn

Sir,   St. Louis March 7th 1809

My bill of exchange No. 23 of this date in favor of Benjamin
Wilkinson agent of the St. Louis Missouri fur company for the
sum of *fifteen Hundred dollars* is on account of a contract which I
have made with that company, who are thereby bound for the consideration of seven thousand Dollars to convey in safety the Mandan
chief and Jessomme his interpreter with their families to the Mandan
Villages on the Missouri, for which purpose the said company are
likewise bound to raise or organize arm and equip at their own expense One hundred and forty effective Volunteers to act under my
orders as a body of the Militia of this Territory, and to furnish

what ever may be deem'd necessary for the expedition, or to insure its success. Yr. Obt. Svt.

MERIWETHER LEWIS

ALS, RC (DNA, RG 107, L-273). Endorsed.

290. Lewis to William Eustis

Sir, St. Louis May 13th 1809.

My Bill of exchange No. 26 of this date in favour of Peter Chouteau or order, is on account of, and in part for, certain ammunition Tobacco and Paint, which has been furnished by the Said Chouteau, and which under my orders has been appropriated in the following manner—It is deposited with Major Chouteau who has been appointed to the command of a detachment of the Militia of this Territory who are directed to convey the Mandan Cheif to his Village, to be transported at the expence of the Missouri St. Louis fur Company who constitute that body of Militia, and under the direction of the Major, is to be expended if necessary by being distributed among such friendly Indians as he may think proper to take with him as auxiliaries to Insure the safe conveyance of the Mandan Cheif in passing the Aricare Village, if the ammunition &c. is not thus expended it is to be returned to this place for the use of the United States or to be paid for by said Chouteau out of his annual compensation as Indian Agent.[1] I am with much respect Your Obt. Servt.

MERIWETHER LEWIS

Note after this there was another bill No. 27. 15th May for 440 Dollars for the ballance of this account—amounting to 940 Dollars.

LS, RC (DNA, RG 107, L-Misc.). Eustis was now Secretary of War, having succeeded Dearborn at the end of Jefferson's administration in March 1809.

1. A copy of Chouteau's bond for $940 and a receipt for the powder, lead, vermilion, and tobacco that he bought with the money, are in DNA, RG 107, C-1809, unregistered series. The bond is undated; the receipt is dated 16 May 1809.

291. Lewis to Pierre Chouteau

(Copy)

Sir St. Louis June 8th 1809

The principal object contemplated by the military Expedition which has been prepared and placed under your command, is that of

[451]

conveying the mandane cheif and his family in Safety to their Village; I consider the honour and Good faith of our Government pledged For the success of this enterprize; You will therefore consider its accomplishment as parimount to every other Consideration connected with the expedition, and will consequently take such measures on Your Voyage as may appear best calculated to insure it's success. That the aricare nation should be severely Punished for their unprovoked attack on the party under the Command of Ensign Pryor in September 1807, is also devoutly to be wished, as well for the reputation of our Government, as for the security which it would give to the future navigators of the river Missoury. I deem it improper to trammil your operations by detailed and Positive Commands as to the plan of procedure, but shall content my self with mearly sketching the outline of a Plan which it is my Wish should be pursued, provided it be Found in the Course of it's execution to Comport with the important objects of the expedition. You will Proceed without unnecessary delay from hence to fort Clark,[1] where you will submit the detachment to the inspection and muster of Captn. Climson, the commanding officer of that Post, who has been requested to discharge that duty.

The hostile of the Aricars, render it necessary that you should adopt war measures in the commencement, or at least that you should be prepared to meet them with a force sufficiently strong to insure a successfull issue, should a decision by arms Become necessary to terminate the existing differences between us, or to effect the safe return of the Mandane chief to [h]is Village. For this Purpose you may engage an auxiliary force not exceeding three hundred men from the most friendly and confidential Indian nations whom you may meet on your way, to cooperate with the detachment against the Aricares. You will Promise them, as a reward for their Services, the plunder which they may acquire from the Aricares.

The traders and hunters who have engaged to associate themselves with you at the entrance of the Chyen river for the Purpose of passing the Aricares Village, will together with Your detachment Amount at least to two hundred and fifty men, which, in addition to the Indian auxiliaries, of three hundred will Form a body of five hundred and Fifty; a force sufficient Not Onely to bid defiance to the Aricares, but to exterpate that abandoned Nation if necessary.

The entrance of the Chyen river is to be the Grand rendez-Vous of the expedition; You will therefore on Your arrival at that Place, remain seven days, unless sooner Joined by those traders and hunters who have been licenced to enter the Upper Country, and by whom you may expect to be Joined at that Point, in which case, having settled your final plan of operation You will procede to the Aricare Village.

On your rout from fort Clark to the rendezvous you will Cause the Indians auxiliaries to march Generaly some miles in the rear of the detachment, in order that You may Previously apprize the soos mahas and other friendly Indians whom you may meet of the real design of those auxiliaries, and their Pacific Intentions towards them, before they arrive, and With a View more perfectly to Guard against any infortunate collition Between the Auxiliaries and the nations through whose Country they must necessaryly pass, you will cause one or more confidential whitemen and such interpreters as you may think necessary to march by land with them.

I am not unapprized of the versatility of the Indian Character, and the dificulty which is always experienced in Causing them steadily to persevere in any enterprize for a length of time. I have much Confidence in your skill and Judgement in managing those People, from Your intimate Acquaintance with their dispositions habits and customs, however I must suggest as one means of insuring their fidelity that You do not Give them an abundant supply of ammunition untill they shall arrive in the neighbourhood of the Aricares, But to keep them in a Good humour by small Presents of Tobacco & Vermillion, and as much amunition from time to time as will enable them to Procure their necessary food.

Those supplies are to be made to the auxiliaries from the Deposite of those Articles placed in your charge for that Purpose onely.

It is of much importance that you should be informed on Your arrival at the entrance of Chyen river of the true state of the Aricares nation; their disposition towards the citizens of the United States, their dispositions, strength, means of defence &c. and for this Purpose You will, about three weeks previous to Your Arrival at the entrance of the Chyen river, dispatch two or more confidential Indians, of some band in Amity with the Aricares, with orders to Visit their villages obtain the necessary information in relation to them and meet you at the General Rendezvous of Chyen river.

Should those spies discover a sincere and contrite disposition, on the Part of the Aricares for their former agressions, they might be instructed to say [to] them, that if they, the Aricares, would send a deputation of eight or ten of their Principal men to meet you that it was propable peace might be restored and their nations again received in to our confidence and favour. Should such deputation be sent, you will demand of them the unconditional surrender of those individuals among them, who killed any Person in their attack on the Party under the command of Ensign Prior; if they cannot ascertain

[453]

the particular individuals who killed our citizens on that occasion they will in that case be required to deliver an equivalent number with those murdered, from among such of their nation as were most active in stimulating them to the Commission of those murders; these murderers when Delivered will be shot[2] in presence of the nation, they will also be required to Give a suitable Present in horses to the auxiliares whom you may have with you.

These terms being Complyed with on their Part, peace will again be restored, and the merchants permitted to trade with them as usual, not withstanding the Prohibition on that Subject, which has been expressed in the licences recently Granted them for the Indian trade in that quarter.

If on the Contrary the aricares should make no overtures of Peace or fail to Comply with the Conditions before expressed, You will take such measures as you may think best calculated to surprise and cut them off, Provided you conceive you can Effect it without eminently hazarding the Primary object of the expedition, to wit, the safe Conveyance of the mandane Chief to his Village.

Should your force be reduced by the desertion of the Indian auxiliaries or an unwillingness appear on the Part of hunters and merchants associated with You, to cooperate in the enterprize of attacking the aricares, insomuch that you would be induced to doubt the favourable Issue of a Conflict with that nation, You will in such case act on the defencive, consider them as enimies in actual war, avoid all intercourse with them, and in no event whatever are you to make such terms with them, as will Commit the honour of our Government, or such as will prove a bar to their being hereafter Punished in an Exemplary manner for the atrocities of which they have been Guilty.

Should you Make any Prisoners of the Aricares nation, you will either give them to the mandane and minnitare nations, Provided they will in Corporate them with their nations.

On your Voyage from fort Clark to the mandane Village, You will Permit no Party of hunters or traders not Immediately Connected with your Command, to Precede you Under any Pretence Whatever.

You will Treat all the nations whom you may meet On Your Voyage, except the Aricares, in a friendly manner, assure them of the Paternal disposition of our Government towards them, and our determination to render them every service in our Power, so long as they act in a friendly manner towards us and respect the persons and Property of our Citizens who Visit them.

Having accomplished Your Voyage and delivered the Mandane

cheif and suit at his Village in safety, you will Loose no time in assembling the mandan, minitare and Ahwahaway nations in Concil. You will explain to them the cause of the detention of the mandan Chief, and Cause the Presents sent by the mandan Chief, to be distributed by him among them.

You will present the *One eye*,[3] the Great chief of the minitaries, with a large medal and flag in the name of the President of the United States, together with a Bridle and saddle from my self and a Coat from General Clark.

Should you not make Peace with the aricares as you Ascend, you will inform the minitaries mandans &c. that it is the wish of their Great father, that they should be driven out of the Country or distroyed. When these arrangements shall have been made with the mandans and minitaries, you will Immediately return to this Place, unless the season shall be so far advanced that you Conceive you cannot reach St. Louis Before the river is obstructed with ice, in which case, you are at liberty to remain untill the ensuing spring. On your Return to St. Louis you will report your self to the Honble. the secretary at War, as well as to the Govr. of this Territory.

Peter Dorion sub agent [h]as been ordered to join you at the mahas Village and Place himself under your direction. You will also take with you, should you find them necessary, the interpreters, mongrain[4] Graveline, and Bapt. Dorion,[5] Whom you will dispose of as may appear to you best Calculated to promote the Public service. If you make Peace with the aricares, you will leave Graveline with them.

You will Probably meet with sundry american Citizens in the Country of the minitaries and mandans, whose licenses was expired; You will therefore be pleased to renew the licences for two Years of such of them as have conducted themselves with Good faith towards our Government and Propriety towards the Indians; For this purpose you are Furnished with blank bonds, oaths and licenses, which You will have executed according to Law, and bring with you the oaths and bounds and deposite them in the office of the Secretary of this territory, such Persons as for mall Conduct or other substantial reasons, you may deem it Improper [to] Give licences, you will order to return to this Place, and if there does appear a determination on their Part not to Comply, you will arrest them and bring them down by Force, no British agent, Clark, or engage can under any Pretence whatever be Permitted to trade or hunt within this territory, the limits of which, are to be conceive to extend to all that Country watered by the Missoury. Should you meet with the subjects of any

[455]

foreign power within those limits, who are not regularly authorised to trade or hunt therein, you will Give them proper notice to depart in twenty four hours, and if they shall refuse or do not comply you will arrest them like wise and bring them with you to this Place that they may be dealt with according to Law.

Should your short Residence in that upper Country Prevent your seeing those traders and hunters you will leave the Blancks with Colo. Minard who is in such case hereby Fully authorized to act with respect to them as you are herein before directed.

All the Presents which you make to the Indians on Public Account while on your way to the Mandan Village will be made from the Public stock which has been Placed in Your Charge.

I sincerely wish you a Pleasant voyage and a safe Return to your Family and Friends. Your obedient Servant,

(Signed) MERIWETHER LEWIS

Transcript, RC (DNA, RG 107, C-689). Enclosed in No. 308.

1. The post on the Missouri near present Kansas City, Mo., originally called Fort Osage. At this time its commander was Capt. Eli B. Clemson.

2. There is some irresponsible Indian policy here, including the shooting of hostages, the invitation to the Mandans and Minitaris to attack the Arikaras, etc. The willingness of Lewis to extirpate the Arikaras seems to go much further than Jefferson's recommendation (see note under No. 286) that they be severely punished. Lewis's instructions should be compared to the saner measures taken by Chouteau and reported in No. 308.

3. Le Borgne, or "the one-eyed," a principal chief of the Hidatsa or Minitari tribe, was a man of legendary coarseness and brutality. Lewis and Clark had given him their swivel gun on the way down the Missouri in Aug. 1806, "with a view to ingratiate him more Strongly in our favor" (JOURNALS, 5:342).

4. Noel Mongrain, an interpreter.

5. Jean Baptiste Dorion, one of old Pierre Dorion's three sons.

292. William Eustis to Lewis

Sir   War Department, July 15th 1809.

After the sum of seven thousand dollars had been advanced on the Bills drawn by your Excellency on account of your Contract with the St. Louis Missouri Fur Company for conveying the Mandan Chief to his Village; and after this Department had been advised that "for this purpose the Company was bound to raise, organize, arm & equip at their own expence one hundred and forty Volunteers and to furnish whatever might be deemed necessary for the Expedition, or to insure its success"—it was not expected that any further advances or any further agency would be required on the part of the United States. Seven thousand dollars was considered as competent to effect the object. Your Excellency will not therefore be surprized that your Bill of the 13th of May last drawn in favor of M. P. Chouteau for five hundred dollars for the purchase of Tobacco, Powder, &c. intended as Presents for the Indians, through which this expedition was to pass and to insure its success, has not been honored. It has been usual to advise the Government of the United States when expenditures to a considerable amount are contemplated in the Territorial Governments. In the instance of accepting the volunteer services of 140 men for a military expedition to a point and purpose not designated, which expedition is stated to combine commercial as well as military objects, and when an Agent of the Government appointed for other purposes is selected for the command, it is thought the Government might, without injury to the public interests, have been consulted. As the object & destination of this Force is unknown, and more especially as it combines Commercial purposes, so it cannot be considered as having the sanction of the Government of the United States, or that they are responsible for consequences. On another account it was desirable that this Government should have been consulted. Being responsible for the expenditure of Public money & made judges in such cases whether the Funds appropriated by the Legislature are applicable and adequate to the object, it is desirable in all practicable cases that they should be advised and consulted when expenditure is required. As the Agency of Mr. Chouteau is become vacant by his accepting the command of the Detachment it is in contemplation to appoint a suitable character to supply his place. Another Bill of your Excellency's in favor of Mr. Chouteau drawn for materials for erecting an assaying Furnace has not been protected, there being no appropriation of this Department applicable to such an object.

The President has been consulted and the observations herein contained have his approval,—and your Excellency may be assured that they are dictated by a sense of public duty and are perfectly consistent with the great respect and regard with which I have the honor to remain, &c. &c. &c.

Lbk (DNA, RG 107, Letters Sent, 4:177–78). Reply is No. 294. On the same subject, Rodolphe Tillier, former factor at Belle Fontaine, wrote President Madison 27 April 1809. He viewed with dismay the awarding of the $7,000 contract to the St. Louis Missouri Fur Company for the delivery of the Mandan, and questioned the involvement of Lewis and Clark in the venture. "Is it proper for the public service that the U.S. officers as a

Governor or a Super Intendant of Indian Affairs & U.S. Factor at St. Louis should take any share in Merchantile and private concerns" (DNA, RG 107, T-1809, unregistered series).

293. Jefferson to Lewis

Dear Sir   Monticello Aug. 16. 09.

This will be handed you [by] Mr. Bradbury,[1] an English botanist, who proposes to take St. Louis in his botanising tour. He came recommended to me by Mr. Roscoe[2] of Liverpool, so well known by his histories of Lorenzo of Medici's & Leo X. & who is president of the Botanical society of Liverpool. Mr. Bradbury comes out in their employ, & having kept him here about ten days, I have had an opportunity of knowing that besides being a botanist of the first order, he is a man of entire worth & correct conduct. As such I recommend him to your notice, advice & patronage, while within your government or it's confines. Perhaps you can consult no abler hand on your Western botanical observations. I am very often applied to know when your work will begin to appear; and I have so long promised copies to my literary correspondents in France, that I am almost bankrupt in their eyes. I shall be very happy to recieve from yourself information of your expectations on this subject. Every body is impatient for it.[3]

You have seen by the papers how dirty a trick has been played us by England. I consider all amicable arrangement with that nation as desperate during the life of the present King. There is some ground to expect more justice from Napoleon: & this is perhaps favored by the signal defeat he has suffered in the battle of the Danube, which has obliged him to retreat & remain stationary at Vienna, till his army, literally cut up, can be reinforced. In the mean time, the spell of his invincibility being broken, he is in danger of an universal insurrection against him in Europe. Your friends here are well, & have been long in expectation of seeing you. I shall hope in that case to possess a due portion of you at Monticello, where I am at length enjoying the never before known luxury of employing myself for my own gratification only. Present my friendly salutations to Genl. Clarke, and be assured yourself of my constant & unalterable affections.

TH: JEFFERSON

ALS, SC (DLC).

1. English botanist John Bradbury went to St. Louis to do botanical collecting, arriving in Dec. 1809 and spending the rest of the winter there.

In the spring and summer of 1810 he made trips into the wilderness about St. Louis, and left in March 1811 with the Astorians bound for the Oregon country. See his *Travels in the interior of America, in the years 1809, 1810, and 1811* (London, 1817). He found Clark "more intelligent in Natural History than from his few opportunities of intercourse might be expected" (Bradbury to William Roscoe, 24 July 1810, RICKETT, 66).

2. William Roscoe (1753–1831) was an English historian, banker, and devotee of botany. He wrote *The life of Lorenzo de' Medici, called the Magnificent* (London, 1795), and *The life and pontificate of Leo the Tenth* (London, 1805).

3. Even Lewis's brother Reuben was anxious for the publication, writing from the Three Forks of the Missouri 21 April 1809[?] to ask for "a Coppy of your travels through this Country" (MoSHi).

294. Lewis to William Eustis

Sir   Saint Louis August 18th 1809.

Yours of the 15th July is now before me, the feelings it excites are truly painful. With respect to every public expenditure, I have always accompanied my Draft by Letters of advice, stating explicitly, the object of the expenditure: if the object be not a proper one, of course, I am responsible; but if on investigation, it does appear to have been necessary for the promotion of the public Interests, I shall hope for relief.

I have never received a penny of public Money, but have merely given the Draft to the person who had rendered the public service, or furnished articles for public use, which have been invariably applied to the purposes expressed in my Letters of advice.

I have made advances for the Public from time to time in small sums for recovering of public horses which were lost, for forage for them, expenses attending Sales &c. and have retained from the sales of those horses the sum of eighty five Dollars, for which I have ample vouchers. In these transactions, I have drawn no draft, calculating on going forward long since and settleing my Accounts with the Public. The balance of the Sales in Money and Bonds have been lodged with General Clark by the Vendue-Master:—to the correctness of this statement, I call my God to witness.

I have been informed Representations have been made against me, —all I wish is a full and fair Investigation. I anxiously wish that this may reach you in time to pr[e]vent any decision relative to me.

I shall leave the Territory in the most perfect state of Tranquility which I believe, it has ever experienced. I find it impossible at this

[459]

moment, to explain by letter, and to do away by written explanations, the impressions which I fear, from the tenor of your letter, the Government entertain with respect to me, and shall therefore go on by the way of New Orleans to the City of Washington with all dispatch—Thursday next I have appointed for my departure from Saint Louis. I shall take with me my papers, which I trust when examined, will prove my firm and steady attachment to my Country, as well as the Exertions I have made to support and further it's interests in this Quarter.

I do most solemnly aver, that the expedition sent up the Misoury under the Command of Mr. Pierre Chouteau, as a military Command, has no other object than that of conveying the Mandane Chief and his Family to their Village—and in a commercial point of view, that they intend only, to hunt and trade on the waters of the Misoury and Columbia Rivers within the Rockey-Mountains and the Planes bordering those Mountains on the east side—and that they have no intention with which I am acquainted, to enter the Dominions, or do injury to any foreign Power.

Be assured Sir, that my Country can never make "A Burr" of me— She may reduce me to Poverty; but she can never sever my Attachment from her.

Those protested Bills from the Departments of War and Treasury, have effectually sunk my Credit; brought in all my private debts, amounting to about $4,000, which has compelled me, in order to do justice to my Creditors, to deposit with them, the landed property which I had purchased in this Country, as Security.

The best proof which I can give of my Integrity, as to the use or expenditure of public Monies, the Government will find at a future day, by the poverty to which they have now reduced me—still, I shall do no more than appeal to the Generosity of the Government by exposing my Claims.

I had sooner bear any pecuniary embarassment, than attempt, in any manner, to wound the Feelings, or injury in the public Opinion, the present Executive, or either of the Heads of Departments, by complaining of Injuries done me, other than in friendly Expostulations.

I am convinced that the Motives expressed in the latter part of your Letter, are those which have actuated you; but at the same time, I trust that the Motives that induced me to make the Expenditure, will be found equally pure.

Some weeks after making the Contract with the Misoury-Fur-Company, for taking the Mandane Chief to his Village, I received information, through the Sous and Mahas that the Chyenns had joined the Aricaras and were determined to arrest all Boats which might ascend the River. I conceived it necessary, in order to meet the additional Force, and to insure the success of the Expedition conveying the Mandane Chief, to make the further advance with a view, that should it become necessary to engage an auxiliary Force among the friendly Nations through which they would pass, that Mr. Chouteau, the Commanding Officer, might be enabled to acquire such aid by means of those Supplies.

You will find from the enclosed Document, that if Mr. Chouteau does not expend the articles for the purposes mentioned, that he is still held accountable to the Government for such part thereof as may remain unexpended.

With respect to the assaying Furnace, I did conceive that such an Establishment was necessary; but, as there is no Appropriation for such objects, arrangements have been made by me, to meet the protested Bill—and no claim will hereafter be made for that object.[1] as there remain several important Subjects on which I have not yet received an Answer.

I still hope that Mr. Chouteau will not be removed, he is ordered to return this Fall, or as soon as the military Expedition is at an end, which you will recollect, ceases as soon as he arrives at the Mandane Nation.

Col. Augoust Chouteau of this place, his brother, has agreed with me to act in his place Pro. Tem. The Osage Treaty not having been ratified, would, in my Opinion, recommend this Arrangement. I have the honour to be with much rispect Your Obt. Servt.

MERIWETHER LEWIS.

N.B. The reasons for wishing Mr. Chouteau not to be displaced is that if the event takes place before one or the other of the Osages treaties ar ratifyed there will in my opinion be War with that nation.

LS, RC (DNA, RG 107, L-101). Endorsed; received 8 Sept. 1809. The note after the signature is in Lewis's hand.

1. Chouteau actually used but a small portion of the goods he took, and sold the rest to the St. Louis Missouri Fur Company for $754.50 (Chouteau to Dearborn, 10 Jan. 1810, MoSHi). But the goods had been bought with drafts issued by Lewis, and after Lewis's death one of the drafts, for $440.00, was protested. Having endorsed it, Chouteau was accountable; he paid the full amount plus interest and charges. In his letter to the War Department of 12 April 1810 he said he expected the other draft to fail also, and he asked the Secretary for relief (MoSHi).

295. Lewis and Clark: Settlement of Account

Dr.		Crtr.		
To half of this sum paid John Ordway $150[1]	$75	Novemb.	5th borrowed	$100
To do. of this sum paid printer &c. $20[2]	$10		9th do.	50
			15th do.	40
To do. of this sum paid young Varnum $10[3]	$5		20th do.	15
		Aug.	3rd do.	6[9]
To do. Ordway one half of this sum $150	$75	Oct.	7th do.	50
			28th do.	49.50
To do. of this sum paid Hasler for calculations $100[4]	$50	Decr. 27	do.	20
				$330.50
		Jany. 25		1.00[10]
To do. Pursh do. 30[5]	$15	To paid Philipsons[11] act.		70.00
To do. Mr. Varnum 3	$ 1.50	Aug. 20. 1809		401.50
To do. Pursh—40	$20	Cash paid you[12]		52.93
To Barrallet—40[6]	$20			$453.43
To this sum lent York to surch for a negroe man[7]	$ 1	Cash paid you[13]		100.00
				$553.43
To paid for [r]ent of house[8]	$125			

Over paid your acct. on settlement at Washington — $41.60

448.10

1809. To money recved of you for John B. LePages pay, not paid — $116.33

$554.43

Settled this 21st of August agreeably to the above settlement. $554.43

MERIWETHER LEWIS
WM. CLARK

ADS (MoSHi). The document is in Lewis's hand down to but not including the final entry in the left-hand column, and down through the $330.50 in the right-hand column. The rest is in Clark's hand.

1. It is clear from this settlement that Lewis and Clark are dividing the expense of preparing their journals for publication. The two entries showing payments to Ordway total $300.00, the amount they paid for his journal. One installment of $150.00 was paid 18 April 1807 (Lewis's account book, MoSHi), and on this day Lewis also paid him the $266.58 he had coming as a "gratuity allowed by Congress for his services on the expedn."

2. "$20. To this amount paid for paper to print prospectus of my voyage &c. . . ." (undated entry, Lewis's account book).

3. "$10. Paid Varnum for distributing the prospectus of my work" (13 May 1807, Lewis's account book).

4. Ferdinand Rudolph Hassler (1770–1843) was a Swiss mathematician who would later organize the U.S. Coast and Geodetic Survey. He had been appointed instructor of mathematics at West Point in Feb. 1807, and now had agreed to make the calculations necessary for the determination of longitudes from the observations of Lewis and Clark. Lewis's account book dates this payment 3 May 1807, "Paid Hassler in advance for celestial observations."

5. The two entries for Pursh here are reflected in Lewis's account book: on 10 May 1807 Lewis paid him $30 "for assisting me in preparing drawings and arranging specemines of plants for my work," and on 26 May he paid $40 "in advance" for the preparation of drawings.

6. Thwaites renders the name "Burraht" in the JOURNALS, 7:363n, thus concealing the role of John James Barralet (c.1747–1815), eccentric Irish engraver who came to the U.S. in 1795 and was now established in Philadelphia at the corner of Eleventh and Filbert Streets. A receipt in the Clark Papers (MoSHi) reads: "Rcd. of Governor Lewis the Sum of Forty Dollar for two Drawings water falls in full. John James Barralet. July 14 1807."

7. "Gave York this sum to bear his expences when he went in surch of a negroe man of Genl. Clark's in St. Charles dist. $4" (30 Aug. 1808, Lewis's account book).

8. "Paid this sum for the rent of the house in which Genl. Clark resides. $125" (July [1808], Lewis's account book).

9. Lewis borrowed this amount from Clark and loaned it to his brother Reuben 3 Aug. 1808, according to his account book.

10. "Borrowed of Genl. Clark this sum at a card party in my room. $1" (25 Jan. 1809, Lewis's account book).

11. Probably Joseph Philipson of Philadelphia, who operated a store in St. Louis after 1807. Lewis owed him $890 at the time of his death (Memorandum of Lewis's debts, Lewis-Marks Papers, ViU). The entry here dates from 6 Jan. 1809 when, according to the account book, Clark paid Philipson $70 on Lewis's behalf. JENNINGS, 49, describes a land transaction involving Philipson and the Lewis estate in 1810.

12. "On final settlement made this day between Genl. Clark and myself he paid me this sum. $53" (21 Aug. 1809, Lewis's account book).

13. Lewis owed Clark $100 at the time of his death, according to the memorandum in the Lewis-Marks Papers.

296. Benjamin Smith Barton to Jefferson

Sir,   [14 September 1809]

I have, at this time, in the press a new edition of my work on the dialects of the American Indians. This edition will be, in many respects, much more correct and satisfactory, as well as more ample, than the former, which you have seen. I am extremely anxious to possess specimens—no matter how small,—of the languages which

Mr. Lewis met with beyond the Missisippi. I will think myself much gratified, and honoured, if you will transmit to me, as early as your convenience may suit, such specimens. I do not ask, or wish for, copies of the *entire* vocabularies: but only a good selection of about ten or twelve words, from each of them. I need not tell you what words those should be. I am less anxious about the language of the Osages, as I have a tolerable specimen of this. Of the Mandan, I have only 4 or 5 words. Of the Pawnees, not one upon which I wish to depend. I shall not fail to make a public acknowledgement of the source from which I receive the words.

. . . .

I am, Sir, with very great respect, Your obedient & humble servant, &c.

Philadelphia September 14th, 1809.   B. S. BARTON

ALS, RC (DLC). Endorsed; received 20 Sept. 1809. Reply is No. 300.

297. Lewis to James Madison

Dear Sir,   Chickesaw Bluffs, September 16th 09

I arrived here \<yesterday\> about \<2 Ock\> P.M. \<yesterday\> very much exhausted from the heat of the climate, but having \<taken\> medicine feel much better this morning. My apprehension from the heat of the lower country and my fear of the original papers relative to my voyage to the Pacific ocean falling into the hands of the British has induced me to change my rout and proceed by land through the state of Tennisee to the City of washington. I bring with me duplicates of my vouchers for public expenditures &c. which when fully explained, or reather the general view of the circumstances under which they were made I flatter myself \<that\> they \<will\> receive both \<sanction &\> approbation \<and\> sanction.

Provided my health permits no time shall be lost in reaching Washington. My anxiety to pursue and to fullfill the duties incedent to \<the\> internal arrangements incedent to the government of Louisiana has prevented my writing[1] you \<as\> more frequently. \<Mr. Bates is left in charge.\> Inclosed I herewith transmit you a copy of the laws of the territory of Louisiana. I have the honour to be with the most sincere esteem your Obt. \<and very humble\> Obt. and very humble Servt.

MERIWETHER LEWIS

[464]

ALS, RC (MoSHi). Endorsed. Lewis's lack of fluency in this letter is often cited as evidence that he was not quite himself in the period immediately preceding his death. Words which he inserted between lines are in roman type, in angle brackets, while struck-out words are shown in the usual italics and angle brackets.

1. Lewis altered this word to "wrinting."

298. Jefferson to Benjamin Smith Barton

Dear Sir   Monticello Sep. 21. 09.

I recieved last night your favor of the 14th and would with all possible pleasure have communicated to you any part or the whole of the Indian vocabularies which I had collected, but an irreparable misfortune has deprived me of them. I have now been thirty years availing myself of every possible opportunity of procuring Indian vocabularies to the same set of words: my opportunities were probably better than will ever occur again to any person having the same desire. I had collected about 50. and had digested most of them in collateral columns and meant to have printed them the last year of my stay in Washington. But not having yet digested Capt. Lewis's collection, nor having leisure then to do it, I put it off till I should return home. The whole, as well digest as originals were packed in a trunk of stationary & sent round by water with about 30. other packages of my effects from Washington, and while ascending James river, this package, on account of it's weight & presumed precious contents, was singled out & stolen. The thief being disappointed on opening it, threw into the river all it's contents of which he thought he could make no use. Among these were the whole of the vocabularies. Some leaves floated ashore & were found in the mud; but these were very few, & so defaced by the mud & water that no general use can ever be made of them. On the reciept of your letter I turned to them, & was very happy to find that the only morsel of an original vocabulary among them was Capt. Lewis's of the Pani language of which you say you have not one word. I therefore inclose it to you, as it is, & a little fragment of some other which I see is in his handwriting but no indication remains on it of what language it is. It is a specimen of the condition of the little which was recovered. I am the more concerned at this accident as of the 250 words of my vocabularies and the 130 words of the great Russian vocabularies of the languages of the other quarters of the globe, 73. were common to both, and would have furnished materials for a comparison from which something might have resulted. Altho I believe no general use can ever be made of the wrecks of my loss, yet I will ask the return of the Pani vocabulary when you are done with it. Perhaps I may make another attempt to collect, altho' I am too old to expect to make much progress in it.

I learn with pleasure your acquisition of the pamphlet on the astronomy of the antient Mexicans.[1] If it be antient & genuine, or modern & rational it will be of real value. It is one of the most interesting countries of our hemisphere, and merits every attention.

I am thankful for your kind offer of sending the original Spanish for my perusal. But I think it a pity to trust it to the accidents of the post, & whenever you publish the translation, I shall be satisfied to read that which shall be given by your translator, who is, I am sure, a greater adept in the language than I am. Accept the assurances of my great esteem & respect.

TH: JEFFERSON

ALS, SC (DLC).
1. Barton had offered to send him a pamphlet on the astronomy of the early Indians which he had received from Mexico and was planning to publish in translation.

299. Lewis to Amos Stoddard

Fort Pickering, Chickesaw Bluffs.

Dear Majr.   September 22nd 1809.
I must acknowledge myself remiss is not writing you in answer to several friendly epistles which I have received from you since my return from the Pacific Ocean. Continued occupation in the immediate discharge of the duties of a public station will I trust in some measure plead my apology.

I am now on my way to the City of Washington and had contemplated taking Fort Adams and Orlianes in my rout, but my indisposition has induced me to change my rout and shall now pass through Tennessee and Virginia. The protest of some bills which I have lately drawn on public account form the principal inducement for my going forward at this moment. An explaneation is all that is necessary I am sensible to put all matters right. In the mean time the protest of a draught however just, has drawn down upon me at one moment all my private debts which have excessively embarrassed me. I hope you will therefore pardon me for asking you to remit as soon as is convenient the sum of $200. which you have informed me you hold for me. I calculated on having the pleasure to see you at Fort Adams as I passed, but am informed by Capt. Russel[1] the commanding officer of this place that you are stationed on the West side of the Mississippi.

You will direct to me at the City of Washington untill the last of December after which I expect I shall be on my return to St. Louis. Your sincere friend & Obt. Servt.

MERIWETHER LEWIS

ALS, RC (MoSHi). Addressed, "Majr. Amos Stoddard Fort Adams"; endorsed. Markings indicate that the letter was forwarded 4 Oct. from Fort Adams to Washington.

1. Capt. Gilbert Christian Russell, of the Fifth Infantry, commanding Fort Pickering at Chickasaw Bluffs, the site of present Memphis, Tenn. For his role in the last days of Lewis's life, see No. 346.

300. James Neelly to Jefferson

Sir,   Nashville Tennessee 18th Octr. 1809

It is with extreme pain that I have to inform you of the death of His Excellency Meriwether Lewis, Governor of upper Louisiana who died on the morning of the 11th Instant and I am sorry to say by Suicide.

I arrived at the Chickasaw Bluffs on or about the 18th of September, where I found the Governor (who had reached there two days before me from St. Louis) in very bad health. It appears that his first intention was to go around by water to the City of Washington; but his thinking a war with England probable, & that his valuable papers might be in dainger of falling into the hands of the British, he was thereby induced to Change his route, and to come through the Chickasaw nation by land; I furnished him with a horse to pack his trunks &c. on, and a man to attend to them; having recovered his health in some digree at the Chickasaw Bluffs, we set out together. And on our arrival at the Chickasaw nation I discovered that he appeared at times deranged in mind. We rested there two days & came on. One days Journey after crossing Tennessee River & where we encamped we lost two of our horses. I remained behind to hunt them & the Governor proceeded on, with a promise to wait for me at the first houses he came to that was inhabited by white people; he reached the house of a Mr. Grinder about sun set, the man of the house being from home, and no person there but a woman who discovering the governor to be deranged, gave him up the house & slept herself in one near it. His servant and mine slept in the stable loft some distance from the other houses. The woman reports that about three o'Clock she heard two pistols fire off in the Governors

[467]

Room: the servants being awakined by her, came in but too late to save him. He had shot himself in the head with one pistol & a little below the Breast with the other—when his servant came in he says; I have done the business my good Servant give me some water. He gave him water, he survived but a short time. I came up some time after, & had him as decently Buried as I could in that place—if there is any thing wished by his friends to be done to his grave I will attend to their Instructions.

I have got in my possession his two trunks of papers (amongst which is said to be his travels to the pacific Ocean) and probably some Vouchers for expenditures of Public Money for a Bill which he said had been protested by the Secy. of War; and of which act to his death, he repeatedly complained. I have also in my Care his Rifle, Silver watch, Brace of Pistols, dirk & tomahawk; one of the Governors horses was lost in the wilderness which I will endeavour to regain, the other I have sent on by his servant[1] who expressed a desire to go to the governors Mothers & to Montic[e]llo: I have furnished him with fifteen Dollars to Defray his expences to Charlotts-ville; Some days previous to the Governors death he requested of me in case any accident happened to him, to send his trunks with the papers therein to the President, but I think it very probable he meant to you. I wish to be informed what arrangements may be considered best in sending on his trunks &c. I have the honor to be with Great respect Yr. Ob. Sert.

JAMES NEELLY

U.S. agent to the Chickasaw Nation

The Governor left two of his trunks at the Chickasaw Bluffs in the care of Capt. Gilbert C. Russell, Commanding officer, & was to write to him from Nashville what to do with them.

ALS, RC (DLC). Endorsed; received 21 Nov. 1809. Maj. James Neelly was the Indian agent for the Chickasaws from July 1809 to June 1812. He probably was the man of that name who served as a cavalry officer in the Tennessee Volunteers under Andrew Jackson in the War of 1812.

Lewis's death is pertinent to this work only as it affected the publication of the journals; the documents I use are meant to be representative, not comprehensive. My comments on this topic are in the notes for No. 346.

1. John Pernier, a free mulatto, Lewis's valet and servant.

301. C. and A. Conrad and Co. to Jefferson

Sir   Philada. November 13th 1809

When Captn. Lewis was last in Philadelphia we contracted with

[468]

him to publish his travels & then since incurred considerable expences in preparing for the publication. The accounts received here yesterday by the Nashville newspapers of his decease induce us to use the freedom to advise you of the contract. That such a contract was made should be known to whoever has controul over his M.S. and not knowing who to apply to we have after some hesitation presumed to address ourselves to you, as most likely & most willing to point out to us what we ought to do.

It is with much regret & some apprehension of incurring your Displeasure that we address you on this painfull subject so soon after the unfortunate circumstance that gives occasion for it. But the consideration that it is not alone our individual interests, but those of our country and of science, that are promoted by forwarding the publication, (already much too long delayed) we hope will be deemed some excuse for troubling you, and perhaps may induce you to take the further trouble to inform us where and to whom we are now to look for the copy. Govr. Lewis never furnished us with a line of the M.S. nor indeed could we ever hear any thing from him respecting it tho frequent applications to that effect were made to him. With the highest Respect Yours &c.

C. & A. Conrad & Co.

ALS, RC (DLC). Endorsed; received 22 Nov. 1809. In the hand of John Conrad. Reply is No. 304.

302. Charles Willson Peale to [Rembrandt Peale]

Nov. 17. [1809]

The Vessel being detained longer than I expected has given me the opportunity of telling you some disagreeable intelligence, which I have had some reluctance to credit, but it comes now with so many circumstances as to force a credit to it. Governor Lewis has distroyed himself. It is said that he had been sometime past in bad health & showed evident signs of disarrangement, and that having drawn bills for the payment of public services, which were protested because no specific funds had been provided, this mortification completed his despair. He was on his way to Washington, when at a tavern he shot himself by two shots. This not being effectual he completed the rash work with a Razor. I have received a number of Articles by the way of New Orleans which he had sent to the Naval officer of that Port & by letter directed him to forward them to me. Consisting of Indian dresses, pipes, arrows, an Indian pot entire, Skins of Beavers

[469]

& others &c. with some minerals &c. I expected that he intended to have described them on his arrival here as I did not receive any letter with them.

. . . .

C. W. PEALE

ALS, SC (PPAmP). An addition to a letter of 28 Oct. 1809 in the Charles Willson Peale letterbooks, X, 105. The addressee is not given but obviously is Rembrandt.

303. Memorandum of Lewis's Personal Effects

[23 November 1809]

Memorandum of Articles Contained in two Trunks the property of Governor Lewis of Upper Louisiana Left in care of William C. Anderson[1] Near Nashville Tennessee and taken charge of by Thomas Freeman[2] to be safe Conveyed to Washington City—Nashville 23rd Novr. 1809.

Taken in presence of Captn. Boote[3] U. States Army—Captn. Brahan[4]—Thomas Freeman & Wm. C. Anderson

	*One Old Port folio containing a few papers of no consequence
	*One Tomahawk—handsomely moun[te]d
I.A.C.	One ½ pint silver Tumbbler
	*One pair of red slippers
forwarded to Richmond	One Black broadcloth coat
forwarded do.	Two striped summer coats
forwarded do.	Five vests
	*Two Pair Nankeen Panteloons
forwarded do.	One pr. black silk Breeches
	*Two Cotton shirts—one Flanl. do.
forwarded do.	One pr. old flannel Drawers
	*Six pr. of short stockings
	*Two pr. cotton stockings
	*Three pr. of silk stockings
	*One Cambrick Handkerchiff
forwarded	One cotton do. two Band.—old. Do.
	*One small bundle of Medecin
Depts.	One small bundle of Letters & Vouchers—of consequence

[470]

Dept. War	One Plan & View of Fort Madison[5]
	*Two Books of Laws of Upper Louisa.[6]
W.C.	One Book an Estimate of the western Indians[7]
	*One old Razor case—no Razors
I.A.C.	One Horizontal silver Watch
T. Jefferson	One small Package containing the last will and Testament[8] of Govr. Lewis Deceas'd & one check on the Bank of New orleans for 99 58/100 dollars
forwarded to Richmond	One Round Portmteau Trunk
W.C.	One Handsome dressed Sea Otter skin
I.A.C.	One Ladies Pocket Book
Th. Jefferson	One Memorandum Book
W.C.	Two small bundles containing silk for dresses—for Mr. Clark
Pret. U.S.	A Transcript of Records &c.
W.C.	Nine Memorandum books
W.C.	Sixteen Note books bound in red morocco with clasps[9]
Th. Jefferson	One bundle of Misceleans. paprs.
War Dept.	No. 2 Returns of Militia—papers not acted on
Th. Jefferson	One bundle papers indorsed—"From the Drawer of my Poligt. [polygraph][10]
P.U.S.	One do. papers relative to the Mines
War Dept.	One do. Public Vouchers
Th. Jefferson	One do. "Taken from the drawer of my Poligraft
W.C.	Six note books unbound
Th. J.	One bundle of Indorsed Letters &c.
War Dept.	One do. of McFarlane's acct. for the outfit of Salt Petre expedn.[11]
War Dept.	One journal of do.
W.C.	One bundle of Maps &c.
W.C.	One do. "Ideas on the Western expedition[12]
War Dept.	One bundle of Musterrolls
State Dept.	One do. Vouchers for expendrs. Dept. State
W.C.	One do. Vocabulary
W.C.	One do. Maps & Charts

[471]

War Dept.	One do. Vouchers for expenditures in the War Departmt.
Th. Jefferson	One Bundle of papers marked A
W.C.	One Sketch of the River St. Francis with a small Letter Book
Th. Jefferson	One do. containg. Commissn. and Diploma
P.U.S.	One do. Sketches for the President of the U. States

N. Those articles marked in the Memorandum with a Star are left in a Square black Trunk (the property of Govr. Lewis) in care of Wm. C. Anderson—the trunk not being of convenient shape & size for Packing.

THOS. FREEMAN

Washington Jany. 10. 1810

The bundles of Papers referred to in the above memorandum were so badly assorted, that no idea could be given of them by any terms of general description. Many of the bundles containing at once, Papers of a public nature—Papers intirely private, some important & some otherwise, with accts. Receipts. &c. &c. They were all carefully looked over, & put up in separate bundles. Every thing public has been given to the President or proper dept. Every thing relating to the expedition to Genl. Clarke, & all that remained has been sent to Mr. Jefferson to be delivered to Mr. Meriwether, to the care of Mr. Geo. Jefferson the following articles, viz.[13]

In a Small Trunk contained in the larger one
1. Broadcloth Coat
2. Summer Do.
5. Waiscoats
1. Pair black Silk Breeches
4. Handkerchiefs
3. Old flannel ——.

In the large Trunk a Pistol case—containing a Pocket Pistol—3 Knives &c. &c.
8 Tin Canisters containing a variety of small articles of little value.
A Sword, Tomahawk, Pike blade & part of the Handle—
A very small Trunk.

I. A. COLES

[In margin:] N.B. The trunk will be sent by the first vessel to Richmond, addressed to Wm. Meriwether[14] to the care of Rob. Gordon mercht. of that place.

I. A. C.

AD (ViU—Lewis-Marks Papers). The manuscript is in Clark's hand except for the notes added by others. The marginal notations, excluding asterisks, apparently were added after the articles listed had reached Washington (see No. 311).

1. Not identified. There were many William Andersons in the counties surrounding Nashville, but the records examined for me by Gertrude Morton Parsley, reference librarian of the Tennessee State Library and Archives, show none with a middle initial *C*. A possible candidate is William Clough Anderson, who left Hanover County, Va., in 1785 and migrated to Kentucky. He was related to Richard Clough Anderson, who married Clark's sister Elizabeth.

2. Probably the man who supervised the government exploration of the Red River in 1806. See No. 180.

3. Capt. William R. Boote, of New Hampshire, First Infantry.

4. Capt. John Brahan, of Virginia, Second Infantry.

5. Not found. Only two crude plans of Fort Madison have been located. One was made by Lt. Alpha Kingsley before he began to build the post (Kingsley to Dearborn, 22 Nov. 1808, DNA, RG 107, K-51); the other was done by factor John Johnson in Jan. 1810 (DNA, RG 75, Drawer 43). There is a description of the two-story factory building in a document headed "Valuation of the factory at Fort Madison," 20 Nov. 1810, in papers labeled "Piqua, Illinois Bayou, Fort Madison, 1808–14" (DNA, RG 75).

6. *Laws of the Territory of Louisiana* (St. Louis, 1809).

7. See JEFFERSON.

8. Perhaps not his final will; see No. 311. The will assumed to be his last is in ViU (transcripts in MoSHi and DNA, RG 49, Special Acts, Box 1).

9. These and the morocco-bound notebooks in the next entry comprise the bulk of the expedition journals.

10. Lewis's polygraph went to Gilbert C. Russell. A "Memo of M. L. property about St. Louis as given by Pernia," in John Hastings Marks's hand, reads: "Gave his writing Machine to Capt. Russell" (Lewis-Marks Papers, ViU).

11. The saltpeter caves were located in the region of the Meramec, Gasconade, and Black rivers. For a description of one, see SCHOOLCRAFT, 11–14. Two McFarlanes were involved in the expedition sent in the summer of 1808 to explore these caves. Lewis's account book (MoSHi) contains an entry for 13 Aug. 1808 showing a draft on the Secretary of War in favor of James McFarlane for $271.00, for wages of persons employed in exploring the caves. And in a letter from Lewis to Col. Thomas Hunt, 2 June 1808 (MoSHi), he asks the Colonel—commanding Cantonment Belle Fontaine—to shoe the horses of Lewis McFarlane and a Mr. Shannon who were going on the expedition. How long the exploration lasted I cannot say; but on 31 Oct. 1808 the factor at newly established Fort Madison paid Lewis McFarlane for his services as *patron* of a boat loaded with factory goods shipped to that post (DNA, RG 75, Drawer 43, Johnson's account with Kingsley). James McFarlane was a trader whom Lewis later sent on a mission to regulate trade and intercourse with the Osage Indians of the Arkansas River and to bring the chiefs in for a treaty council. When Lewis died he owed James McFarlane $718.45 (Memorandum of Lewis's debts, Lewis-Marks Papers, ViU).

12. The nearest I can come to this is an essay at the end of the BIDDLE narrative, "Observations and Reflections on Upper Louisiana" by Lewis, written either late in 1806 or in 1807 (internal evidence is conflicting). Part of it first appeared under the nom de plume "Clatsop" in the *Missouri*

Gazette for 2 Aug. 1808, with the heading, "Observations and reflections on the subject of governing and maintaining a state of friendly intercourse with the Indians of the Territory of Louisiana, No. 1." No other installments appeared. I do not know on what evidence Mrs. Grace Lewis bases her speculation that Lewis wrote many other anonymous articles for the *Gazette* and, indeed, may be considered a kind of behind-the-scenes editor of that journal. His role in founding the paper, and in bringing editor Joseph Charless to St. Louis, is set forth in Mrs. Lewis's unpublished master's thesis (LEWIS (1)). She further asserts that Lewis may have contributed articles of political and social comment to the *National Intelligencer,* written under such names as Atticus, Moderation, and Sydney, during his service as Jefferson's secretary.

13. Two items, a miniature of Lewis and his watch chain, were overlooked when this inventory was made. Dr. William Dickson, of Nashville, sent them to Jefferson in a letter of 20 Feb. 1810 (DLC). In acknowledging their receipt on 20 April, Jefferson said he was sending the items to Lewis's mother. "The deplorable accident which has placed her in the deepest affliction, is a great loss to the world also; as no pen can ever give us so faithful & lively an account of the countries & nations which he saw, as his own would have done, under the guidance of impressions made by the objects themselves" (DLC).

14. William Douglas Meriwether brought the two trunks, one inside the other, to Charlottesville from Richmond, reporting 8 May to John Hastings Marks [?] that he had done so (Lewis-Marks Papers, ViU). Meriwether (1761–1845) had served as Lewis's guardian after the death of the stepfather, and was now active in settling his affairs. He was representative from Albemarle County for the 1809–10 session of the General Assembly of Virginia.

304. Jefferson to C. and A. Conrad and Co.

Messrs. Conrad & Co.   Monticello Nov. 23. 09.

On my return after an absence of a fortnight, I yesterday recieved your letter of the 13th. Govr. Lewis had in his lifetime apprized me that he had contracted with you for the publication of his account of his expedition. I had written to him some time ago to know when he would have it ready & was expecting an answer when I recieved the news of his unfortunate end. James Neelly, the U.S. agent to the Chickasaws, writes me that 'he has his two trunks of papers (at Nashville, I suppose, from whence his letter is dated) amongst which is said to be his travels to the Pacific ocean; that some days previous to his death he requested of him (Neely) in case any accident happened to him, to send his trunk, with the papers therein *to the President,* but he thinks it very probable he meant, *to me,* and wishes to be informed what arrangements may be considered best in sending on his trunks &c.' I am waiting the arrival of Genl. Clarke, expected here in a few days, to consult with him on the subject. His aid & his interest in the publication of the work may render him the proper depository to have it prepared & delivered over to you. But my present idea is (if he concurs) to order it on to the President, according to his literal desire, and the rather because it is said that there are in his trunks vouchers for his public accounts. Be assured I shall spare no pains to secure the publication of his work, and when it may be within my sphere to take any definitive step respecting it, you shall be informed of it by, Gentlemen, Your most obedt. servt.

TH: JEFFERSON

ALS, SC (DLC). Endorsed.

305. Jefferson to James Madison

Dear Sir   Monticello Nov. 26. 09.

. . . . .

I inclose you a letter from Majr. Neely, Chickasaw agent, stating that he is in possession of 2. trunks of the unfortunate Governor Lewis, containing public vouchers, the manuscripts of his Western journey, & probably some private papers. As he desired they should be sent *to the president* as the public vouchers render it interesting to the public that they should be safely recieved, and they would probably come most safely if addressed to you, would it not be advisable that Major Neely should recieve an order on your part to forward them to Washington addressed to you, by the stage, & if possible under the care of some person coming on? When at Washington, I presume, the papers may be opened & distributed, that is to say, the Vouchers to the proper offices where they are cognisable; the Manuscript voyage &c. to Genl. Clarke who is interested in it, and is believed to be now on his way to Washington; and his private papers if any to his administrator, who is John Marks, his half brother. It is impossible you should have time to examine & distribute them; but if Mr. Coles could find time to do it, the family would have entire confidence in his distribution. The other two trunks which are in the care of Capt. Russel at the Chickasaw bluffs, & which Pernier (Govr. Lewis's servt.) says contain his private property, I write to Capt. Russell, at the request of Mr. Marks, to forward to Mr. Brown at N. Orleans to be sent on to Richmond under my address. Pernier says that Governor Lewis owes him 240. D. for his wages. He has recived money from Neely to bring him on here, & I furnish him to Washington, where he will arrive pennyless, and will ask for some money to be placed to the Governor's account. He rides a horse of the Governor's, which with the approbation of the Administrator I tell him to dispose of & give credit for the amount in his account against the Governor. He is the bearer of this letter & of my assurances of constant & affectionate esteem.

TH: JEFFERSON

ALS, SC (DLC). To this letter President Madison replied 11 Dec. 1809: "I have written to Major Neely, according to your suggestion, and shall follow it, also, as to the distribution of Govr. Lewis's papers when they arrive" (DLC).

306. Peale's Memorandum of Specimens and Artifacts

[December 1809]

Articles collected by Merriweather Lewis Esqr. and William Clark Esqr. in their voyage and Journey of Discovery, up the Missouri to its source and to the Pacific Ocean.

A hat manufactured by a Catsop woman near the Pacific Ocian; from whence it was brought by Capts. Clarke & Lewis.

Legings of the Pallatepallers, residing on Lewis'es River, west of the Rocky mountain.

Cap, worn by the women of the Plains of Columbia.

The Tail feathers of the Eagle, much prized by the Indians of North America, who convert them into various ornimental and war-like dresses—these being a pattern for a war-cap would be esteemed by them equal in value to two good horses.

An Indian Pot, found in digging a well at the great Saline near St. Gennevieve, about 17 feet under the surface of the Earth, accompanied by various broken Pots &c. It is supposed that at some former period a walled well had been there.

A Large Mantle, made of the Buffalow skin, worn by the Scioux, or Soue, Darcota Nation.

A small Mantle of very fine wool, worn by the Crow's nation Menetarre.

Legings, ornamented with the hair & scalps taken by the Indian who wore it, and marked with stripes shewing the number he had scalped. Of the Soue Nation.

Two very handsomely ornamented Tobacco pouches, ornamented with Porcupine Quills, and Tin, &c. Of the Saux[1] Tribe.

A Tobacco Pouch, from the Ioway's.

Another, from the Raneird's or Foxes.

A handsomely ornamented belt, from the Winnebagou's or Puount's.

[476]

Wampum, of various discriptions, indicating Peace, War, Choice of either, Hostilities commencing, and a disposition for them to ceace &c. From different nations.

Tobacco Pouch not ornimented sent by the Sacks.[2]

Moccosins, worn by the Otoe's.

Do. from the Soue's.

A Piece of White Buffaloes skin, from the Missouri.

A great number of arrows from diferent Tribes of Saux. And a Bow.

A handsome Belt worn by the Saux as a garter.

2 ornaments, worn round the neck, by the nations of the Plains of Columbia.

Amulets—taken from the shields of the Blackfoot Indians who attacked Captn. Lewis and were killed by himself and party on the 27th of July 1806. near the Rocky Mountain.

Feathers which were at various times presented to Captn. Lewis and Clarke by the principal Chiefs of the nations inhabiting the Plains of Columbia, whose custom it is to express the sincerity of their friendship by cutting feathers from the crowns of their War Caps and bestowing them on each as they esteem.

Roots, presented to Captn. Lewis on the 24th of June 1806 by Neeshneparkeooh, the great chief of the Pottotepallers as an emblem of the poverty of his nation which he discribed in a very pathetic manner.

Bread, used and formes the principle article of food among the Pattotepallers and other Indian Nations west of the Rocky mountains and is called by them cows[3]—it is pripared from the bulb of an umbellaferous plant to which they give the same name. these bulbs are pounded between two stones while in a succulent state and then exposed to the sun untill dry when they assume the appearance and consistance of this specimen. This article for many weeks constituted the principal part of the food of Lewis and party, while in that country.

The Roots of Cows. So called by the Pallatepallers with whom it forms a principal article of food.

Bulbus Roots. These bulbs form the food of many Indian Nations residing within and west of the Rocky Mountain. They are called by the Pallotepallers Quaw-mash.[4]

Bread. This is called Passhequo-quaw-mash being only a varied preparation of the quaw-mas bulb.

Bread. This forms a principal article of food among the Enesher, Skillute, Pishquitpahs[5] and others residing near the great falls of the

Columbia River, and is called by them Shappellel—it is prepared from the Bulb of an umbellaferous Plant to which they give the same name—these bulbs are pounded between two stones while in a succulent state and then exposed to the sun untill dry when they assume the appearance and consistance of this specimen. This article for several weeks constituted the principle part of the food of Capt. Lewis and party.

A Bag prepared of grass by the Pishquilpahs on the Columbia River.

A Water-cup of the natives who resides in the Plains of Columbia, made of the same grass.

Spanish Dollar obtained by Captn. M. Lewis, from the Pallotepallers —a nation inhabiting Lewis's River within the Plains of Columbia, who had never previously seen white-men.

A Cap worn by the natives of Columbia River, and the Pacific Ocean.

Stone, Spear points, from the natives inhabiting the Rocky Mountains.

2 Silver Midals, of George the 3d of England, obtained from the Foxes and one from the Socks, or Saukeys.

Four Pipes, or calmets from the nation Saux, of the following tribes, Yankton, on the River La Moine—Teton on the Misuri 1200 miles up—Sharone's 1400 miles up the Misuri—Dacoto's or Sue's.

One of the Puount, called Winebagou. Near Dog Plains, Missippi.

One of the Fox's and one belonging to White Skin, the Chief of the Foxes. Missippi.

3 from the Sauke's on the Missippi.

2 from the Ioway's on the River Lamaine.

One given to the company by White Pigeon.

One made by the Saux, inhabiting the Dog Plains.

A Dress made of Crow or Raven Skins, worn by the Police Officers of the Saux, nation.[6]

The Dress worn by Captn. Lewis &c.[7]

A number of Minerals &c.

Presented at diferent periods, through the President of the United States, Thomas Jefferson by Govener Meriweather Lewis and General William Clarke, in company, who collected them on their journey & —General Clark.

AD (PHi). Entries on pp. 43–45 of Peale's "Memoranda of the Philadelphia Museum," a folio blank book in which Peale recorded accessions.

1. He may mean either the Sauks or the Sioux here; later he uses the word, as well as Soue and Dacoto, for the Sioux.

[478]

2. A pouch such as this from the Peale collection is now in the Peabody Museum, Harvard University (see WILLOUGHBY, 638–39).

3. Cowish, *Cogswellia* sp., an herb of the Columbia River valley.

4. Quamash or camass, *Camassia quamash* (Pursh) Greene.

5. The Wenatchee tribe, also called the Pisquow.

6. See Clark's description in the Biddle notes, No. 326. This specimen is now in the Peabody Museum (WILLOUGHBY, 637–38 and plate 37d).

7. This garment may be the hunting shirt now at the Peabody Museum, identified by its original label as "Indian Hunting Shirt made of Buffalo skin. This was formerly owned and worn by Capt. Clark in his Exploring Expedition. Presented to Peale's Museum by Capt. Lewis and Clark" (WILLOUGHBY, 640–41).

307. Jefferson to C. and A. Conrad and Co.

Messrs. Conrad & co.   Monticello Dec. 11. 09.

I wrote you on the 23d of Nov. in answer to yours of the 13th of that month.[1] I soon after concluded to write to the President suggesting to him the expediency of his ordering Govr. Lewis's two trunks from Nashville by the stage to Washington, there to have the papers assorted & deliver those respecting his expedition to Genl. Clarke soon expected. Genl. Clarke called on me a few days ago. He is named one of his executors by the Governor; & informed me that he had desired the trunks to be sent on to Washington under the care of Mr. Whiteside,[2] the newly elected Senator from Tennessee. He is himself now gone on to Washington, where the papers may be immediately expected, & he will proceed thence to Philadelphia to do whatever is necessary to the publication. I salute you with respect.

TH: JEFFERSON

ALS, SC (DLC). Endorsed.

1. See Nos. 301 and 304.

2. Jenkin Whiteside (1772–1822), Knoxville, Tenn., attorney who served in the Senate from 1809 to 1811.

308. Pierre Chouteau to William Eustis

Sir,   Saint Louis December 14th 1809.

I had the honor of addressing you on the 22nd ultimo announcing the safe arrival of the Mandan Chief, his wife and family at their Nation and my return here.

At the date of that letter I had proposed to Give you a detail of the incidents on that Voyage in person, but am now informed by the Superintendant of Indian affairs that from the absence of some of the Indian Agents from the territory my actual presence cannot without endangering the Public Service be dispensed with— as Soon however as is praticable, I shall unless otherwise directed from Your Department, leave this for Washington City.

In the mean time, in order to Complete the duties required of me by the written instructions of the late superintendant of Indian affairs dated June 8th 1809 (a Copy Whereof I now have the honor to Inclose)[1] as well as to show that those instructions have been my sole and only Guide in conducting this Expedition; those incidents which have Occured in the Prosecution of it are now submitted. Sensible that the detail will be lengthy, and Perhaps uninteresting, I still deems it my duty as a public agent to lay before the Government a minute & faithful account, that it may be seen whether my conduct merits a Continuance of that Confidence the Government have placed in me or 'Whether I have forfeited it.

Conformably to the orders of Governor Lewis before alluded to, I took the Command of the expedition for the Conveyance of the mandan Chief, his wife and family to their nation. One expedition with the same object in view had failed, it was impressed upon me that where the honour and Good faith of the Government was pledged and where I might be of service, that I ought not to hesitate, and the command though full of danger was accepted the more cheerfully, the detachment proceeded to fort osage where it was inspected and mustered by Captn. Clemson. The Panis, otto and Kanzas tribes of indians were there waiting for me with loud Complaints because there were no merchants among them, and praying that some might be sent—they were referred to Governor Lewis—the expedition left fort Osage and proceeded on, and saw no other Indians untill it arrived at the mahas, there at the request of those indians we went with the mandan chief to the mahas Village. About forty leagues from this fell in with a band of three hundred & fifty of the sioux, who, had dailay and continual communication with the Indians further up the missoury. From them I learned that the sioux had formed themselves into twelve or fourteen bands, who alledging that they had been promised a plenty of Goods, and cheap, and deceived for two Years, would be deceived no longer, and conceiving that the Boats of the expedition, were loaded with merchandize, they intended each Band to seize a boat. After this we met large numbers of the Prairie Sioux, one of the most barbarous tribes of Indians, who are said to be from two thousand five

[480]

hundred, to three thousand strong—the Chiefs of this tribe said they remembered me, that I had treated them with Great hospitality at Saint Louis, and on that account the party should not be molested, and I am convinced that to Persuasion and favor, and not to the strength of the detachment, is to be attributed our having peaceably passed that nation. Agreably to my Instructions, I attempted to avail my self of an auxiliary force of three hundred Sioux, to Cooperate with the detachment against the Ricaras and was refused, they said one tribe ought not to countenance any attempt to distroy another, and if I still persisted in that resolution my self and party might be distroyed before we reached the ricaras. For the more perfect safety of the mandan chief and his family, as well as to secure success to the enterprise, I then determined to Engage some of the Chiefs of the Sioux to accompany us to the Ricaras, and succeeded in procuring six of the principal chiefs. The expedition then departed, and arrived and encamped on the Bank of the river near the ricaras. There the detachment made a martial appearance and conducted with perfect Good order—the Ricaras expecting their Village was to be attacked, sent away their Old men, women and children. Eighteen or twenty of the Chiefs and principal men of the mandan nation fearing that another attack might be made on the party who were bringing their Chief, had been waiting the arrival of the detachment several days, and came to our encampment. Those chiefs with the chiefs of the sioux who had accompanied us, then demanded the pardon of the ricaras. Without giving them any assurances, I expressed a desire that some of the chiefs of the ricaras might come to my Camp. Four of their chiefs soon after came, to whom I expressed my astonishment that no more of the chiefs of their nation had come. They replied that the alarm in their nation was Great,—and the others dare not come. The day being far advanced I dismissed them under a promise of returning to the Concil the next morning with more of their chiefs, none of them however appeared. I sent an Interpreter to them to enquire the reason, who was told that their nation were more alarmed and unless *hostages* were Given to them, they would not again appear at the Council. Anxious to hold a Council with their nation; four of the Principal persons of the detachment were Given as hostages. Eight of their principal chiefs immediately came to the Council. I told them that their Great father the president of the United States had sent me to conduct the mandan chief to his village a second time. The first time you Permitted Yourselves to fire upon the colours of your father, and to attack his men. I have orders to destroy your nation, but the

[481]

chiefs of the sioux and mandan nations have United together and interceded for your pardon. At their particular request, I shall Ground my arms, untill new orders can be received from your Great father who alone can pardon or destroy. You may now call Back your old men, your wives and children, who have fled and Secreted themselves. The mandan Chief who had hitherto been kept in the boat was sent for. I Presented him to them and observed to them, this chief and his family are under the safe conduct and protection of the United States, I am obliged to deliver them at their village, and if any of your tribes shall dare to molest them, I shall put fire to your Villages. The chiefs of the ricaras then took the mandan chief by the hand, saying, if they fired upon him the first time, it was because the principal chief of the nation was then absent, that the death of their Chief in the United States had been the Cause of Great dissatisfaction In their nation, but that he might with Great safety now pass in their Villages without fearing any thing. It may be proper to observe here, that five or six hundred of the ricaras believing that they would be attacked had Provided themselves with Guns, Amunition and Horses. The hostages were returned and the detachment then embarked for the Mandan Nation, where it arrived without further obstruction.[2] I then caused the mandan nation to be assembled, as also the minnitari and ahwapaway nations of Indians, in Council, and presented to them the mandan chief, his wife and family, who were received with the Greatest demonstration of Joy, I explained to them the causes of his detention.

I then demanded of him the presents which had been sent by him to be distributed among these nations, he replied that the presents he had brought were not to be distributed, they were all his own, this seemed to occasion Jealousies and difficulties among all the tribes, and the more so as "One Eye" the Great Chief of the minnetaries had in a quarrel a few days before murdered one of the principal men of the mandans. I then Presented to "One Eye" the large medal and flag in the name of his Great Father the president of the United States, and as a token of the amity & Friendship of the United States towards his nation and to Prevent Any further misunderstandings between the Mandan's and Minnetaries and to appease the Jealousies which had been Created by the refusal of the mandan Chief to have the presents distributed, I distributed among them Sixty Pounds of Powder, and one hundred & Twenty Pounds of the Ball which had been furnished for the Contemplated War fare with the Ricaras, and ten pounds of Ver-

[482]

million, and one hundred and fifty Pounds of tobacco, which seemed to restore harmony amongst them.

Two days before my arrival at the mandan Village Information was Given me, that three persons belonging to the British north west company were at the Village. I Immediately sent forward an Express desiring them to await my arrival But they feared being detained and departed: they however Informed a white man who resides at the mandan Village, that the north west Company had erected a fort at the three forks of the Missoury. This information is believed to be true from the Circumstance of about thirty american hunters, who had used to visit the mandan Village, not being seen nor heard of since about Eighteen months. Had my orders not required my immediate return from the mandan's, I should have ascertained the truth or falshood of the report.

On my return I saw at the river Platte Messrs. McClellan, Crooks and Miller[3] who were licensed to trade & Hunt in the Upper Parts of the Missouri. In passing the *Prairie Sioux* they with a party of Forty chosen men had been stopped, and Fortunately saved themselves by stratagem, taking advantage of the Night and returned to pass the winter where I saw them. These Indians it is feared will continue to be troublesome, and Commit depredations upon the traders untill they are regularly supplied with merchandize.

I have thus Given You a faithful and I trust satisfactory detail of a voyage in which I have encountered many difficulties and dangers, and which was by me undertaken with the most pure motives, and in obedience to the express orders which I Conceived my self bound most rigidly to obey.

If the Confidence of the Government in me has been or is about to be diminished, I shall not fail to regret it as one of the Most unfortunate events of my Life.

Honored with the appointment of *Indian Agent* my Constant endeavors have not been spared, to discharge its duties, for the advantage of the Government and with Credit to my self. In this as in other offices, there are cases in which that feelings of the officer are some times Put to the test. And it had been my Unfortunate Case, to Experience much of it. Did not Justice to my own reputation require it, I should now be silent on that Subject. For a considerable time previous to my departure on the expedition with the mandan chief, I could not be considered in any other light, than as a mere nominal agent, without Powers to exercise or duties to perform. Sub agents for the particular tribes for which I was appointed, were made without my Knowledge or Consent: they assumed my Powers without reporting to me or having any Communication with me. Measures were taken without my advice, or if perchance I was Spoken to, it was only to approve of measures already adopted, and the execution of them perhaps begun. I could not be responsible for measures I had never Counselled, and in the Execution of which I had no hand. I suffered rather than Complain, still hoping that a different Course would be Pursued. Under Circumstances like these the Command of the detachment before mentioned was accepted.

Every act of mine as Indian Agent I have attentively reviewed. Particular orders, I have never intentionally departed from, and my sound discretions had been always exercised where no line of Conduct was marked out for me; which my former accounts rendered will prouve when the department of Indians affair was left to my discretion, and I feel a Pride in Knowing that I have Earnestly sought to fulfil the duties of my office with integrity, and to Promote the best Interest of the United States. I have the Honor to be, with Great Respect Sir, Your Most Obedient Servant,

PRE. CHOUTEAU agt.

LS, RC (DNA, RG 107, C-689). Endorsed; received 31 Jan. 1810. No. 291 enclosed.

1. No. 291.

2. The party arrived at the Mandan village on 24 Sept. after a passage of 101 days (*Missouri Gazette*, 16 Nov. 1809).

3. Robert McClellan, Ramsay Crooks, and Joseph Miller, engaged in the fur trade. McClellan and Crooks were partners from 1807 to 1810, then dissolved their partnership to join the Astorian expedition under Wilson P. Hunt (CHITTENDEN, 1:159–62).

309. Bernard McMahon to Jefferson

Dear Sir,   Philadelphia Decr. 24th 1809

With many thanks I acknowledge the receipt of the fine collection of seeds you were pleased to send me some time ago, and would have done this much sooner, were I not in daily expectation of receiving from London a variety of esculent vegetable seeds, that I wished to send you some of, at the same time. Having received them by the Ship Coramandel which arrived here a few days ago, I do myself the pleasure of sending you by the same mail that conveys this letter, some early cabbage & cauliflower seeds &c., and shall send you by subsequent mails several other seeds for your spring sowing.

I am extremely sorry for the death of that worthy and valuable man Govr. Lewis, and the more so, for the manner of it. I have, I believe, all his collection of dried specimens of plants, procured during his journey to the pacific ocean, and several kinds of *new* living plants, which I raised from the seeds of his collecting which you and himself were pleased to give me. In consequence of a hint, to that effect, given me by Govr. Lewis on his leaving this City, I never yet parted with one of the plants raised from his seeds, nor with a single seed the produce of either of them, for fear they should make their way into the hands of any Botanist, either in America, or Europe, who might rob Mr. Lewis of the right he had to first describe and name his own discoveries, in his intended publication; and indeed I had strong reasons to believe that this opportunity was coveted by ————[1] which made me still more careful of the plants.

On Governor Lewis's departure from here, for the seat of his Government, he requested me to employ Mr. Frederick Pursh, on his return from a collecting excurtion he was then about to undertake for Doctor Barton, to describe and make drawings of such of his collection as would appear to be new plants and that himself would return to Philadelphia in the month of May following. About the first of the ensuing Novr. Mr. Pursh returned, took up his abode with me, began the work, progressed as far as he could without further explanation, in some cases, from Mr. Lewis, and was detained by me, in expectation of Mr. Lewis's arriv[al,] at my expence, without the least expectation of any future remuneration, from that time till April last; when n[ot] having received any reply to several letters I had wro[te,] from time to time, to Govr. Lewis on the subject, nor being able to obtain any in[dication] when he probably might be expected here; I thought it a folly to keep Pursh longer idle, and recommended him as Gardener to Doctor Hosack of New York, with whom he has since lived.

The original specimens are all in my hands, but Mr. Pursh, had taken his drawings and descriptions with him, and will, no doubt, on the delivery of them expect a reasonable compensation for his trouble.

As it appears to me probable that you will interrest yourself in having the discoveries of Mr. Lewis published, I think it a duty incumbent on me, to give you the preceding information, and to ask your advice as to the propriety of still keeping the living plants

[485]

I have, from geting into other hands who would gladly describe and publish them, wthout doing due honor to the memory and merit of the worthy discoverer. I am Sir, With the most sincere esteem, Your wellwisher, &c.

BERND. MCMAHON.

ALS, RC (DLC). Endorsed; received 3 Jan. 1810.
1. For the name omitted here, EWAN suggests either Pursh himself or French botanist F. A. Michaux. It is possible that Henry Muhlenberg's anxiety to obtain specimens might also have aroused McMahon's suspicions (see No. 225).

310. Clark's Memorandum on the Journals

[c. January 1810]

Enquire what has been done by G. L. with Calculations—engraving Printing Botany. The papers relitive. Samples.

If a man can be got to go to St. Louis with me to write the journal & price.

The price of engraving animals Inds. & Maps Paper & other expences.

Get some one to write the scientific part & natural history—Botany, Mineralogy & Zoology.

Praries—muddiness of the Missouri. Volcanic apperns.

Natural Phenomena—23 vocabularies & plates & engraving.

AD (MoSHi). In Clark's hand. On the reverse of the folded sheet: "Sewelel —Small Brown animal inform Mr. Jefferson this name"; and a list of names as follows—"Col. Edgar, Mr. Jefferson, Doctr. Farrar, G. Shannon, Mr. Meriwether, Cap. Brashan, Cap. Chambers, Fitzsimons." John Edgar was a Kaskaskia merchant and trader, and judge of the Randolph County court; see No. 387 for Bernard Farrar; Capt. Talbot Chambers of Pennsylvania was in the Fifth Infantry; "Cap. Brashan" is probably John Brahan, already identified. Fitzsimons is unidentified.
The conjectural date fits the time when Clark was traveling to Philadelphia to arrange for publication of the travel narrative. He was still in Washington about 1 Jan. 1810, but told his brother Jonathan that he was setting off next day for Philadelphia (Jonathan to George Rogers Clark, 3 Feb. 1810, WHi).

311. Isaac A. Coles to Jefferson

Dear Sir,   Washington Jany. 5th 1810.

I take the liberty of sending you by this day's mail, all the private Papers of the late Govr. Lewis, & of asking the favor of you to suffer them to remain at Monticello, until called for by Mr. Wm. Meriwether, for whom they are intended.

On the arrival of the Trunks at this place they were opened by Genl. Clarke and my self, when every thing of a public nature was given to the Dept. to which it properly belonged, every thing relating to the expedition to Genl. Clarke, & all that remained is contained in the five little bundles now directed to you. A large Trunk which had been left in one of the rooms up stairs in this House, was also opened, and was found to contain several things of little value, which, with the clothes sent in the two Trunks from Tennessee, & other articles too bulky to be given to the mail, I shall have put up & shipped for Richmond. His watch & one or two other articles of value, I will either carry to Virginia my self, or give them to Genl. Clarke should he get off before me. You will find that one of the little Packet's contains copies of letters from Govr. Lewis—another letters addressed to him, notes &c—a third Recipts, Acct. &c.—a fourth commissions & diploma's & the fifth a little memorandum Book with some money & his Will. The Will Genl. Clarke informs me is not his last, & that there is another in the hands of a Gentleman soon expected to arrive here. I have not been able to learn how it differs from the one inclosed.

The President has sent to my Brother Edward [1] to take my place, & I am waiting here to know the decision of the House, & to discharge the very few duties that I am still permitted to perform until he arrives, which will be in the course of a week, if he comes at all, of which I entertain much doubt. I beg to be presented to Mrs. Randolph & to add my best wishes for your happiness.

I. A. COLES

ALS, RC (MHi). Endorsed; received 8 Jan. 1810. Jefferson acknowledged the letter 8 Jan., saying, "Govn. Lewis' papers shall be disposed of as you desire" (DLC).

1. Edward Coles (1786–1868) served Madison as private secretary from 1809 to 1815. He became governor of Illinois in 1822.

312. William D. Meriwether to John Marks

Dear Sir   Richmond January 5th 1810

I have this moment recieved a letter from Mr. Coles at Washington announcing the arival there of Meriwether Lewis trunks and papers, which Genl. Clark and himself have examined; they have found a will dated the 11th of Septbr. which gives every thing to your mother, but they suppose that not to be his last will. Meriwethers private papers will be sent to Mr. Jefferson, by Mr. Coles to be delivered to me on my return to Albemarle, he says they are of no value except to his mother and friends. His watch and other things of value Genl. Clark or Mr. Coles will take to Albemarle with them. Every thing relating to the expedition is put into the hands of Genl. Clark. I expect Meriwethers trunks will be sent to this place from Washington with such things as are too bulky for the stage and if they are I will send them up to Milton by a careful waterman.

I have got an order on the treasurer for the interest on your warant and will send the money whenever you shall desire it. A bill has been brought in authorising the auditor to divide certificates, (and progressing into a law). I will have your certificate divided into two according to your wish, unless you should direct otherwise. I will bid you adieu for the present requesting that you will remember me afectionately to your mother and family, and remain yours with sincerity,

W. D. MERIWETHER

ALS, RC (MoSHi). Addressed, "John Marks   Albemarle."

313. Joel Barlow to Benjamin Rush

Dear Sir   Kalorama 11 Jany. 1810

I hope to do you a pleasure as well as my self by commending to your kind attention & friendship Genl. Clarke the companion & colleague of the late Govr. Lewis in the voyage of discovery across the continent. He visits your city to bring forward the publication of that interesting work which Lewis undertook & has left in an unfinished state.

General Clarke's personal merit & the importance of his object render him worthy of the aids that your men of Science may be able to give him. Accept, my dear Sir, our best wishes for your self & family.

JOEL BARLOW

ALS, RC (PPAmP). Addressed; endorsed.

314. Jefferson to Bernard McMahon

Sir   Monticello Jan. 13. 10.

. . . .

Before you recieve this you will probably have seen Genl. Clarke the companion of Governor Lewis in his journey, & now the executor of his will. The papers relating to the expedition had safely arrived at Washington, had been delivered to Genl. Clarke, & were to be carried on by him to Philadelphia, and measures to be taken for immediate publication. The prospect of this being now more at hand, I think it justice due to the merits of Govr. Lewis to keep up the publication of his plants till his work is out, that he may reap the well deserved fame of their first discovery. With respect to Mr. Pursh I have no doubt Genl. Clarke will do by him whatever is honorable, & whatever may be useful to the work. Accept the assurances of my esteem & respect.

TH: JEFFERSON

ALS, SC (DLC). Endorsed.

315. William D. Meriwether to Clark

Dear Sir   Richmond January 22nd 1810

I presented your favour of the 11th instant to Mr. Wirt,[1] the person who had informed me, that he would look over the journal of your travels, and correct it if necessary; but that he only means to correct the gramatical errors that it may contain, and to strike out the minutia, that may make it tedious to the reader, (which I was informed (by Mr. Peter Carr)[2] that Mr. Jefferson said, was all that the work wanted to fit it for the press, but if it was necessary to copy the journal, that it would take more time than he could spare from the professional business by which he lives, and it was understood between us, that it should be first acertained, that Mr. Jefferson, would not undertake the work.

I think it very extraordinary that the United States should set up a claim to the work of your own hands, they have a right to a copy of the chart, and such notes as relate to the geographical situation of the country, but can have no right to claim your journal, my friend Meriwether and yourself have been illy rewarded for the service which you have rendered your country and I hope you will not put it in their power to rob you of your just right.

I wish very much to see you, and if it is necessary that I should go to Washington, will do so if the weather will admit and I can get off in time, and if I cannot I will meet you in Albemarle, on your way home. Write to me as soon as you receive this, and let me know how long you will be in Washington or when you will be in Albermarle; I expect the assembly will rise in about a fortnight, however I shall not wate for that event if I go to Washington. On

[489]

your return from Philadelphia if you will advise what you think had best be done with respect to the publication of your journal, I will give you my opinion; in the mean time, any steps that you may take, will be agreeable to me.

I am sorry to find that there is a probability of our friends property not being suffitient to pay his debts, but on account of his reputation and his eridition, Mr. McFarlane seems very anxious to get his money, he has duned me already for M. L. bond of 780$, and an acct[?] of 25" 50 cts, I wrote to him that I had no funds in my hand of our friend nor had I qualified as his Executor. Inform Mr. Coles that I have received the bundle of letters and list of Articles which he forwarded by mail and that I am much obliged to him for the trouble which he has taken in examining the papers &c. of our Det. friend. I will bid you adieu for the present and remain yours with sincerity,

W. D. MERIWETHER

ALS, RC (MoSHi). Addressed, "Gen. William Clark Washington City"; endorsed, "Ansd. To meet at his house 12th Inst. W. Meriwether." Reply is No. 316.

1. William Wirt (1772–1834), Richmond attorney, and Attorney General of the U.S. from 1817 to 1829.

2. Peter Carr (1770–1815) was the son of Dabney Carr and Jefferson's sister Martha.

316. Clark to William D. Meriwether

Dear Sir   Philadelphia Jany. 26th 1810

Since my arrival at this place I have been employed in serching for the Materials left in this City by the late Govr. Lewis, reletive to our discoveries on the Western Tour. Most of the plants have been classed and drawings made of them by a Mr. Purch who has removed to New York and taken those drawings with him. I have sent to that place [to] pay Persh for his work and precure the drawings & Discriptions of him. The original specimens of those plants, some birds, animals and a fiew Minerals I have found. Mr. Peal has drawn three of the berds, the Braroe & Antilope, and an engraveing has been made of the Big Horn and horned Lizard [1]—imperfect drawings have been made of the falls of the Missouri, & Columbia. I have not found some of the memorandoms, nor the Calculations of Longitude &c. I find some dificuelty of getting a proper scientifcul Charrutor to Compile that part of the work relitive to Botany, Mineralogy & Zoology, however I do not dispare. As to the Naritive which is the most important part, I shall depend on the gentleman you mention who resides in Richmond, to write that part, and shall go to that place to see him. I hope it is Mr. Wort, and if it is I shall be under no apprehension, as I believe him one of the first writers in this Country.

I hope to see or here from you on my arrival at Washington on the Subject of my last letter to you. I should also be Much gratified to reciving a letter from you after you recive this.

Washington City 2nd Feby. 1810

Sir   I intended to have sent the foregoing to you from Philadelphia but for the want of time to finish the letter before I left that place, I did not send it, as I intended. I recved your letter of the 22nd Ulto. on my return to this place to day and am sorry to find that Mr. Wort Cant write our naritive.[2] I shall be obliged to get a gentleman in Philadelphia to write it, whom I would have engaged when in that place had I have known that Mr. Wert would or could not write it. I intended to go to Richmond but as Mr. Wert cant write our book must make arrangements at this place and return home by your house. I shall set out from this about the 7 or 8th and shall be at your house about the 12th Instant when I hope to see you and talk over all the affairs of our mutual much lamented friend. Yours with Sincerity,

WM. CLARK

ALS, RC (PHi). Addressed, "William D. Meriwether Esqr.   Member of Assembly   Richmond Va."

1. As I interpret this passage, Peale drew the birds, the badger, and the pronghorn, but not the mountain sheep or the horned toad. Two of the three birds now in PPAmP are reproduced elsewhere in this volume; the other Peale drawings and the mountain sheep are not located; and in another note, Pietro Ancora is associated with the drawing of the horned toad.

2. A probable reason for Wirt's refusal to undertake the editing is found in his letter to Jefferson of 18 Jan. 1810 (DLC). He discusses the book he is busily writing on the life of Patrick Henry, and says he hopes to have it finished by summer unless the ill health of his family should again send him traveling. The work was published as *Sketches of the life and character of Patrick Henry* (Philadelphia, 1817).

317. Clark to Ferdinand Rudolph Hassler

Sir   Philadelphia 26th Jany. 1810

The Calculations which you made of the Celistial Observations taken by the late Govr. Lewis (& myself) on the late expedition to the Pacific, are not found among his papers. And as I can't hear

[491]

of them in this City, I flatter my self with a hope that those Calculations with the M[em]orandoms are in your possession; if they are, I must request you to send them to Mr. John Conrad of this place. If the Originals are not in your possession, and you have a Copy, may I request the favor of you to send the Copy or an extract of the result of such Calculations as you have in your possession, to Mr. Conrad. Accept the assurance of my highest respect and esteem. Your Obt. Servt.

Wm. Clark

ALS, RC (NN). Enclosed in John Vaughan to Hassler, 26 Jan. 1810. Vaughan writes, "Annexed is a letter from Genl. Clark who went with Lewis reply to it early—as he proposes to print." Vaughan's letter is addressed "Mr. F. R. Hasler   Schenectady   State of New York."

318. John Conrad to Clark

Dear Sir   Philadelphia Jany. 29 1809 [1810]

This will be handed to you by my partner & my friend Mr. Fielding Lucas.[1] I introduce him to you because I think him worthy your acquaintance and that he may apologize to you for my failing to meet you in Balto. as appointed. For some time past I have been afflicted with biles &c but I thought I would have been well enough to leave home tomorrow. I find however that I was mistaken and cannot without the hazard of being laid up on the road start before the next day. Should you by any chance be detained one day longer than you intended in Baltimore I will surely have the pleasure to see you.

I can have nothing to communicate respecting your book til my brother returns from New York when I hope to advise you that the <specimens> drawings &c have been received from Pursh. If I do not see you in Baltimore I hope to overtake you in Washington or in Virginia.

I had not time to call on C. W. Peale to day but will to morrow, to ask him for the use of his likenesses of you & Govr. Lewis[2] to engrave from. I dare say he will not hesitate to allow it & it may as well be going on & be ready before the other engravings, of which we have yet to get the drawings, crowd upon us, by & by.*
I am Dr. sir very respectfully yours

John Conrad

[In margin:] *In about three months I will if not dissapointed, send you copies of them.

[492]

ALS, RC (MoSHi). Addressed, "General Wm. Clarke Gadesbys tavern Baltimore." Conrad has inadvertently dated the letter 1809.

1. Fielding Lucas, Jr. (1781–1854), partner in the Baltimore firm of Conrad, Lucas, and Company. The partnership was dissolved in 1810 when Lucas bought the stock and continued in the bookselling trade. For more about his career and his relationship with the Conrads, See FOSTER (1).

2. Reproduced after p. 106.

319. John Conrad to Clark

Dear Sir   [February 1810]

Conformably to your request I have come on to this place for the purpose of consulting with you respecting your book. I have been busy all the morning hunting for you in this wonderfull city & failing to see you have concluded to leave this note at your lod[g]ings to say that I am at Catons tavern on the capital hill where I will be glad to see you this afternoon or evening as I am under the necessity of returning to Baltimore in the morning. There are two or three friends with me, we have ordered dinner at 4 oClock and will be much obliged by your company. Should you be engaged to dinner I hope you will at all events make it convenient to call some time in course of the evening, but I hope we shall have the pleasure of your compy. to dinner. Very respectfully Yours,

JOHN CONRAD

ALS, RC (MoSHi). No date, but apparently written a few days after Conrad's letter to Clark of 29 Jan. 1810 (No. 318). Addressed, "Genl. Wm. Clarke Prest"; endorsed, "Papers relitive to Journal & engravings."

320. Charles Willson Peale to Rembrandt Peale

Dear Rembrandt   Museum Phila. Feb. 3d 1810

.   .   .   .

I have begun this letter without knowing by what conveyance I shall send it, perhaps by a vessel which goes from New York with french papers, said to sail in about 10 days. Genl. Clark has put their Journal in train to be printed, Doctr. Barton is [to] edit the Botanical part, the narative to be wrote of a Person in Richmond, the name I forget. I would rather Clark had undertaken to have wrote the whole himself and then have put it into the hands of some person of talents to brush it up, but I found that the General was too diffident of his abilities. I would rather see a single narrative with

[493]

such observations as I am sure Clark could have made on the different Nations of Savages & things, which the Notes taken by Capt. Lewis probably passed over unnoticed.

. . . .

C. W. PEALE.

ALS, SC (PPAmP).

321. Clark to Nicholas Biddle

Dear Sir   Near Fincastle Virga. 20th Feby. 1810

I expected to have had the pleasure of hereing from you previous to my setting out from Philadelphia but as I did not recive a note from you at that time calculated on receiving a letter at this place from you on the subject of writing my Western Tour &c. As I have been disappointed in hereing from you on this subject feel my self much at a loss to adress you. I shall not employ the gentleman in Richmond to write the Book whom I mentioned haveing in view, from his offer made previous to my seeing you. I have calculated on your writing for me, and if you will undertake this work, Cant you Come to this place where I have my Books & memorandoms and stay with me a week or two; read over & make yourself thirily acquainted with every thing which may not be explained in the Journals? If you will come it may enable me to give you a more full view of those parts which may not be thirily explained and enable you to proceed without dificuelty. Such parts as may not be full, I can explain and add such additional matter as I may recollect. I brought the books with me to Copy such parts as are intended for the Botanical work which I shall send to Doctr. Bartin, and will deliver the Books to you if you will engage to write the Naritive &c. I mentioned to Mr. John Conrad of Philadelphia to request you to come on here if possible and spend a short time, I am at present with Col. Hancock my father in Law who is on a retired and plesently situated [place] in View of the Town of Fincastle. Should you Come on to this place, I would advise the rout by Hagerstown Winchester & Staunton in the *Stage* which passes this place once a week.

Please to write me on the receipt of this letter your intentions and accept my Highest respect & esteem. Your Obt. Sevt.

WM. CLARK

ALS, RC (DLC—Biddle). Addressed; endorsed. Reply is No. 322. Nicholas Biddle (1786–1844), Philadelphia attorney, publisher, diplomat, and financier, had served in the American legations of England and France before 1807. After 1812 he edited the magazine *Port-Folio* for a time, and in 1822 became president of the Bank of the U.S. An excellent recent biography is by GOVAN.

322. Nicholas Biddle to Clark

Sir,   Philada. March 3. 1810

I have to acknowledge the receipt of your letter of the 20th Feby. which reached me yesterday. Before you receive this my brother's note will have apprized you that it will be out of my power to undertake what you had the politeness to offer, and the only object of the present is to renew my regret at being obliged to decline complying with your wishes. My occupations necessarily confine me to Phila., and I have neither health nor leisure to do sufficient justice to the fruits of your enterprize and ingenuity. You cannot be long however without making a more fortunate selection, but if I can be of any assistance to you here in the proposed publication it shall be very cheerfully given. Being with high respect Yr. Obt. St.

N. BIDDLE

ALS, SC (DLC—Biddle).

323. Jefferson to William D. Meriwether

Dear Sir   Monticello Mar. 14. 10.

The bearer now comes for the trees you have taken care of for me, that is to say, my half of them. Where there is only a single one of a kind, do not risk the taking it up. A graft from it another year will do as well for me. Be so good as to have the roots of those sent well wrapt in straw to keep the cold air from them.

I have some claim on Governor Lewis's estate for monies furnished him some time before he set out on his Western expedition.[1] I do not recollect it's amount, having never looked into it since that time but I have a loose idea of somewhere about 100. D. I have no doubt you will find it stated among his papers. I mention it at present merely for your information, and leave it to the convenience of the estate. I am Dr. Sir Your's affectionately,

TH: JEFFERSON

ALS, SC (DLC). Endorsed.

1. For Lewis's promissory note to Jefferson, and Jefferson's memorandum of the amount owing to him, see No. 49.

324. Nicholas Biddle to Clark

Sir,   Philadelphia Saturday March 17. 1810.

I had the pleasure of writing to you on the 3d inst. upon the subject of your intended publication. Being unwilling to disappoint you I was afraid of undertaking a work which I feared I might not be able to execute to my own or your satisfaction. Having since then seen Mr. Conrad & Dr. Barton, what I learnt from them, joined with a prospect of better health & more time than I had originally expected induced me to consent provided you had not in the mean time, as I thought probable, made a better choice. Mr. Conrad mentioned to me to day that your last letter of the 9th inst. represents you as under no engagement of that sort. I will therefore very readily agree to do all that is in my power for the advancement of the work; and I think I can promise with some confidence that it shall be ready as soon as the publisher is prepared to print it. Having made up my mind to day, I am desirous that no delay should occur on my part. As therefore you express a wish that I should see you, I am arranging my business so as to leave this on Wednesday next, & take the route by Hagerstown Winchester &c. In this way I hope to make you a short visit very soon after the receipt of my letter. In the mean time I remain with high respect Yrs. &c.

N. BIDDLE

ALS, SC (DLC—Biddle). Reply is No. 325.

325. Clark to Nicholas Biddle

Dear Sir   Fincastle Vga. March 25th 1810

I was extreamly sorry to find by your letter of the 3rd inst. that your health was bad, and that your Occupation would Confine you to Philadelphia, and would not afford your leasure to Comply with my wishes of writing my Journals &c. The proffered assistance in the later part of your letter, creates much solicitude and my most sincere acknowledgement for the friendly Sentiments it contained.

I am much gratified by Mr. Conrads letter of the 13th inst. to learn, the state of your health; and that you are willing to undertake the writing of my Journal and to have it ready for publication in 12 months &c.

Mr. Conrad also informs me that you will Comply with my wish to see me at this place before I set out to the Westward; the roads are now fine and I hope your health may have permitted you to have set out before this time. I must request you to Come on, as soon as possible, as my business call me to Louisiana; and nothing detains me, but the business I wish with you.

With the highest respect & esteem I am Yr. Ob. Sevt.

WM. CLARK

ALS, RC (DLC—Biddle). Addressed; endorsed.

326. The Nicholas Biddle Notes

[c. April 1810]

The following notes, written by Biddle during his visit with Clark in Virginia, are found in two volumes of the Lewis and Clark journals at the American Philosophical Society Library. The notes begin in a small blank book, partially filled, and are continued in the pocket journal which Lewis used while descending the Ohio in the summer of 1803. Inside the front cover of the first book is a penciled notation: "The notes contained in this book are in the hand-writing of Nicholas Biddle. [*signed*] Edward Biddle. May 17th 1917." The first leaf is blank except for a doodle or drawing on the verso. The next recto page contains the words "A Ricara a chief of Mandan 22 Feby. 1805" in Nicholas Biddle's hand. The text starts on the verso of the second leaf, or p. [4].

All the text that follows is in Biddle's hand except as noted. It is variously written in red ink, black ink, and pencil, and many passages have been crossed out as if Biddle had marked them off during the writing of his narrative.

The value of these notes lies partly in the new material they contain and partly in what they reveal about Biddle's method of collating the journal entries with Clark's supplementary remarks. I have not attempted a detailed comparison of this information with that in the journals, but have thought it useful to indicate a number of instances where the notes differ from, or add to, the Biddle narrative and the journals of the expedition.

Qu: as to Minetarees.[1] Who are.
Inf: as to Bees as high as the Kanzas.

1. I have conventionalized some of Biddle's usages and have used a period after every sentence or phrase where one would normally appear. As usual, I have identified only those rivers, locations, and Indian tribes which today bear different names—and which have not been identified earlier in the volume.

Qu: as to complexions of Indians.
Beavers huts.
Indian emigrations.
Games & amusements.
Fish.
Islands.
Soil.
Rocks.
Birds.
Quadrupeds.
Prairie wolf.
Barking squirrels.
How many chiefs.
War & village.
Indian hair.
Ricaras who &c. reflecting laws.
Manner of hunting buffaloe.
Mode of curing cous.
Buffaloe Dance & the other dances.
Productions, manufactures.
Tobacco of Mandans.
Indian maps.
Jugglers? Aug. 23. 1805.
Sweating houses Octr. 11. 1805.
Burial ground. Do.
Drums Qu: Oct. 16.
Oct. 13. Kimooenim.
Oct. 10. Palapallasin[?].
End of 7. Pierced nose Nation.
Qu: as to mad woman Oct. 10.
Qu: as to Sokulk nation's habits &c. Octr. 17. 1805.
Qu: as to art of speaking by signs.
Mandan criers at funerals. Presents to them.

None of the Indians of the Columbia had seen white people—there were some at the falls or below 6 miles[?] who had seen white people on the Sea coast.

Qu: mode of drying & pounding fish. Mode of wolf catching Octr. 25.

Qu: Music flute &c. of Indians.

Qu: as to clucking Oct. 27.

Letters & communications from Capts. Clark & Lewis dated about

7. March 1805 published in the papers of that time & also Capt. Clarks letter to his brother published about Octr. 1806.

A book of information published by govt. in which acct. of the voyage. Quere.

Quere as to setting on heels on the Columbia.

Qu: Vancouver & Cook wrong as to inlaying canoes with men's teeth. No they are with shells.

Qus: Ven. Complaint.

Qus: if women Venl[?] or men.

Qus: mode of trade, choosing friend & making presents.

Feby. 14. 1806. Passage across from At. to Pac.

Qu: as to tame rattle snakes in Rocky mountains.

March 27. 1806. Qu: Hulloo-et-tell Indians—who &c.

Qu: Skil-*loot* & Echeeloot changed.

Qu: Skin canoes of the Missouri.

Compare McKenzie's vocabularies of Indians at head of Col[umbi]a. with ours at the junction of it with Lewis's & see if same nation.

Qu: as to Chaboneau's wife meeting Snake Indian prisoner & not being able to speak with her &c. &c.

Shotoes not Choteaus.

March 30. 1806. See as to bathing.

Qu: Columbia Valley or Wappetoe Valley.

Qu: if map is large enough.

Qu: Clackstars & Killamucks trading together up Creek.

Qu: Man with Snakes.

Qu: No oysters.

Qu: Man never saw a gun.

Qu: Man with Uncle.

Qu: Indian orthography.

Qu: Clatsop language more resembling ours in pronunciation & more easy to learn than that of any other language. They not accentuate the last syllable as most Indians, but rather the first.

Qu: People above the falls come to river in fish season & thence go back into the plains. As soon as snow is over they go into the plains to get roots. Occupied in the drying & preparing &c. till the Salmon comes up about May at the falls—then they crowd to the river commonly only the North Side for fear of Snake Indians, there they continue till fish become unfit for use about 1st Sept. This over they *cache* or hide their fish return to the plains which they do till snow fall. Then they go to the foots of the mountains or creeks that have timber & build their lodges taking with them their

[499]

fish for which they have returned. (Quamash they gather in the fall.) During winter they do catch deer, elk, &c. Their trade is chiefly before or after the fish season except that those on Cataract river come down during the Fish Season. All these Indians reside in Columbian plains. Their homes are mere temporary mat lodges by the river. Below the falls they are fixed permanently in houses. Below the great rapids they hunt some roots in their own villages & shoot deer (these the Eleeshoot & Kelluclectiquam). Below the rapids also stationery go down for the Wappatoe roots.

Qu: Twisted hair & broken arm? May 8. 1806.

Indian Speeches.

Osage story of Beaver.

Qu: Mode of flattening heads & [. . .] Flatheads stupid.

Qu: as to depth of water & tide for ships may come up the Columbia.

Qu: as to good situations on it for Settlements.

Qu: as to York &c.

Qu: as to Ind. mode of catching horses June 2. 1806.

The Summer dress of the People from the mouth of Lewis's river to the Echeeloots is—for the men nothing but a robe thrown over shoulder—for the women, no robe, a mat over the shoulders, & some the skin of a goat (those who are rich enough) and a truss drawn very tight. In winter on the sea coast no mocassins, or other cloathing in addition to their summer dress (in winter women wear a sort of vest of sea otter in addition men nothing.

Qu: Sister as fee.

Qu: Some Chopuniesh are flatheads women chiefly the men lower down. Fright at Mussel Shell rapids.

Qu: as to giving an account of what was previously known of each river.

Swallowing arrow.

Great medicine backward.

Carvers robe story true.

Pretend to die & be cured by conjrs.

Qu: Fur trade.

Qu: [. . .].

Qu: No. of men Sgt. Ordway had in the Canoe 10 July 1806.

26 July 1806. Qu: as to hands. Blood on.

Qu: [. . .] Island at Mandans.

Qu: number of women &c. to one warrior.

Qu: York has wife.

Qu: who are Paunch Indians.

[500]

Qu: Dr. Wistar's story.
Qu: McFarlane saw Indians burn warriors.
Qu: Ootlashoots are called Flatheads.
Adoption in wars.
Where both work [. . .] sexes.
Qu: Cause of Missouri muddiness.
Qu: Kickapoos.
Qu: [. . .].
Private vengeance &c.
Qu: Medicine bag.
[*Two entries heavily ruled out. Also on this page, drawing of a human head.*]
If women or men amorous.
Qu: Charbono.
Description of common dance.[2]
Chopunniesh[3] make hole in ground (& other mountn. Inds.) large enough to hold corpse which is wrapped up in skins & placed longitudinally so as not to be altogether below the earth. On each side of the body, stones are placed to the height of the body on which stones sticks &c. earth is thrown to support other stones which are placed then over the grave. [*Drawing of burial site.*]
Oct. 16. 1805. *Drums* [. . .]: a skin or parchment of deerskins or goat sk. stretched over sticks &c.—a sort of tambourin or something like a racket held in one hand & stick in another.
The Mandans have a procession at funerals of relationship &c. but besides his relatives there are people who go habitually to funerals for the sake of getting something, for before the procession starts the wives give clothes of deceased &c. to those who make the greatest show of grief.
None of the Indians on Columbia above falls had seen white people. The Shoshonees & Chopunnish a few had seen white people but that was when taken prisoners—below falls some had seen whites having gone down to Ocean.
The music consists of tambourin or drum—singing & a flute or rather a sort of whistle, at their dance they play on tambourin & sing only.
The *clucking* extends all below the falls—a sound difficult to

2. To this point, Biddle has mainly been listing questions he means to ask Clark, or subjects he wishes to pursue later. Now he begins to set down the answers to most, but not all, of these queries.
3. The Nez Percé Indians of central Idaho, southeastern Washington, and northeastern Oregon.

describe—but more like a hen or duck guttural & disagreeable—intermixed with their talk & incorporated into their language.

All the nations at falls & below both women & men sit upon the calves of their legs & heels—like a frog exactly except that these people open their legs wide when they sit.

In the trade of the Mandans & Ricaras with the Northern Indians—these last come within 20 miles & camp—or into town at once—every man of the North makes a *comrade* of the Mandan or Ricara with whom he has to deal, & makes him a present of someone of his articles of traffic. He returns one of equal or greater value—the gift is made because each knows what the other generally wants—if a man gives his comrade something & that comrade has not got it he will procure it from a friend & give it to him. In this the trade consists each knows the other's wants, & the tarif of exchange is known, there is not much room for imposition.

The Chopunnish man whose horses we used &c. at falls was a professed gambler who went about the country subsisting on games. He was generous to us. When he got to Wallawallahs lost all his horses.

The Indian Snake woman whom Chaboneau's wife met was from up the Multnomah. Chab's wife understood some words [that] were like hers, but did not understand her enough to hold conversation—*At the Falls.*

Saw no oysters on the Pacific Ocean.

[. . .] at head of Jefferson Capt. Clark (about 24 Aug. 1805) met a chief of the Shalatoohs[4] who had come over to see the Shoshonees. He was astonished & pleased to see White People. The Indians who had seen us had described to him ourselves & the effects of our gun —which he was anxious to see. He sent a young man for a beaver (there was one brought up) & asked if I would show them upon beaver. I made Collins take beaver about 40 or 50 [feet?] hold him up by tail, & I shot him in head. Chief ran up to Beaver & astonished to see hole. He wished to know if it was the noise that had killed beaver—looked at the gun, looked at me, at the party & then brought up his mule & wanted me to accept of it which I declined, but rode him to the village at the chief's particular request. He came cautiously & slowly at first towards us.

Ships of burden can come up the Columbia to near the great rapids

4. Also Shallattos, Shallattas, Shall-lat-tos. A small band, "probable number of souls" totaling 100, on the Klickitat River, which empties into the Columbia in Klickitat County, Wash. MOONEY regards them as a band of the Wenatchee tribe.

(the foot) at the upper end of the Wappatoe valley[5]—*certainly* as high as *Multnomah*.

<Osage story of Beaver.>

Indians catch horses by forming a noose & holding the coil in other hand, throw it round horses neck while he is running—this done on foot or horseback—either when horses are wild or when sent out to pasture &c.

York made Inds. believe that he had been wild like bear & tamed. Ricara man shut him up with his wife—those who had seen whites & not blacks thought him something strange & from his very large size more vicious than whites. Those who had seen neither made no difference between white & black.

Examine number of men who accompanied Sgt. Ordway down Missouri.

In taking vocabularies great object was to make every letter sound.

A Clatsop whom I had cured of some disorder brought me out of gratitude his sister—who was anxious to join in her brothers good intentions. She staid two or three days in next room with Chabono's wife. She was quite moritified at being refused by C. She declined the solicitations of the men.

(Tie tight their ankles to make legs swell. Chinooks & Clatsop women.)

Put down Castahanas[6] as an Independent nation. See McKenzie's map.

Calculate for one warrior in the rovers of the plains four women & children. On both sides of Rock Mountains & in the mountains— below Columbia falls not so numerous say 3-½.

Ricara invitait York chez lui, et lui presentait sa femme. York y consentit & il se retira [. . .] de la maison pour empecher que l'affaire ne fut interrompue. Pendant qu'on y etoit un de ses comrades [. . .] le chercher, et le maitre de la maison ne voulait pas le laisser entrer avant que l'affaire fut terminée.

The Indians on heads of St. Francis & Apple Cr. Shawnees Dels. had meeting of chiefs last summer (1809) for the govt. of their tribes. Numbers of crim[ina]ls brought before them were sentenced for various offences. 17 of them were burned on the St. Francis & Apple

5. The valley of the Columbia, so named by Lewis and Clark because of the quantities of wapatoo, *Sagittaria latifolia* Willd., the rootstocks of which were an important part of Indian diet.

6. A name that Lewis and Clark seem to apply to the Arapahoes, along with the names Gens de vache, Kunnanarwesh, Canenaviech, etc. HYDE, 185, suggests that this tribe may have been part of the Comanche group known to the Cheyennes and Arapahoes as Kwaharis.

Cr. A variety of crimes. A woman formerly burned not far from Ohio (White river) for witchcraft. *Prophet*[s] have been burned on our frontiers—but neither prophets nor burnings beyond our frontier Indians.[7]

Prisoners among Mandans are adopted as their children & bring them up (& other Missouri nations) make slaves of the women. One particular man takes boy prisoner into his family.

The same practice in the mountains. The boy whose toes we cut off[8] was an adopted boy & yet father anxious for him. On the Sea Coast they make slaves of women & boys.

Where the mode of living is such as enables the women to share in the labors which procure it they are better treated. The hunters (or village hunters) as the Mandans Minit[aree]s &c. treat their women as subservient. For these the hunting is the chief employment (the women taking care of corn which they consider as inferior). Among the wandering warlike Hunters [*above the line:* Assiniboins] women treated still worse—to the west where they fish the women partake in labors & are more esteemed. & even take care of horses, which the women do on this side.

Among those who live on roots & on the Sea Coast still more so—sometimes in trade ask wife's opinion which Mandans &c. never do.

The Kickapoos are perhaps bands of Taways [Ottawas], live on the heads of the Kaskaskia & heads of Illinois about 2 or 300 men.[9]

The muddiness of Missouri, owing to its running thru a rich level country of thick dark loam mixed with a small proportion of very fine sand. Being very crooked & the descent great & regular its waters wash away the banks which mingle with the stream. The channel of the Missouri is narrow too—not much wider at St. Charles as at the Mandans where it is 500 yds.

Saw nothing like Indian writings or characters.

If man kills another his relations avenge it—it is an affair of private vengeance—the band or the chief does nothing (where there is no whiskey &c. they do not kill each other—that is the bane for they

7. Not in the narrative, not in the journals; the incident postdates the expedition. The St. Francis River and Apple Creek are both affluents of the Mississippi, the St. Francis emptying in Phillips County, Ark., and Apple Creek emptying between Perry and Cape Girardeau counties, Mo.

8. A frostbite case (JOURNALS, 1:246, 251).

9. In his narrative, p. 5, Biddle identified the Kickapoo tribe on the basis of this and a later entry in his notes. He also made a notation in the journal manuscript (see JOURNALS, 1:26) to the same effect. The journal manuscripts contain a number of emendations and additions in Biddle's hand, probably made during his visit with Clark.

kill when drunk revenge when drunk) rarely tho' sometimes a family is appeased by presents and the mediation of friends.

When a person of one band kills one of another it is always war. A man is killed. His relations go & kill as many or more of the offending band. Horse stealing, woman stealing are less cause of offense & may be made up.

Woman stealing not uncommon. One of the Borgne's[10] wives was not stolen but ran off with a man—her lover before marriage. After some time the man remained away she came home & returned to her father's house. The Borgne hearing of it went there, & after smoking for some time with the father, the old men of the village alarmed for the consequence of his going followed him & strove to appease him. He smoked quietly with them. At length rising to go he took his wife by the hair & when he got her as far as the Door tomahawked her before all, & said that if any of her relations dared to avenge her he would be found at his lodge ready to meet her [him]. He was not always so cruel—some years after a similar event occurred one of his wives went off & staid some time with a man who could not support her as she wished & they returned to the village & she came penitent to the Borgne. The Borgne sent for the lover who expected death. He asked them if they still loved each other & on their answering yes dismissed them with a present of three horses (a handsome present) & gave the wife to the man.

The *medicine bag* of about 2 feet long is a large bag containing roots pounded dirt[?] &c. which they alone know how to appreciate, valuable presents or whatever is most esteemed. This is suspended in the middle of the lodge. No man dare to touch it but the owner. It is an object of religious fear, sacred—& its sanctity makes it the safest place to put medals or their most valuable things. Besides this the Indians have small bags which they keep in the medicine bags & take out & wear round their waists & necks as amulets charms against particular evils.

The Sioux respect old age less than other nations (the Mandans respect old people). An old man asked me as I was talking to the chiefs if I could cure the pains in his back &c. A young man in whose charge he was [said] that he should not wish to be restored you are old & have lived long enough & it is time for you to die. The old man said he was right—that he should die soon & begged that he might be buried with his face down towards his old village that the little wolves might eat him, and as soon as possible he might return

10. Le Borgne, a principal chief of the Minitari (Hidatsa), already mentioned in No. 291.

to his relations. The old man died soon after & was buried as he wished. This story proves [. . .]. They, when their old people cannot follow the bands, leave them water & some provisions & leave them to die. Westward more respectful.

The Mandans had venereal. Ricaras too. Minitarees—Shoshonees—Chopunnish—mouth of Kooskooskee—all the way down quite to the Sea Coast. They can cure not gon[orrhe]a, not lues[11] which is excessively bad on Sea Coast.

Prairies caused by fire originating as we have mentioned.[12]

Prairie countries generally level thinly watered, very rich.

Charboneau.

The Indians generally are not fond of women as we are. The women those with whom we had anything to do were not deficient in ardour.

The Villagers have the most numerous families—the Hunters next —the fishermen &c have smaller families than the Hunters (they live miserably on the Columbia—middle plains—and children die under the operation of head flattening—& there is a great want of means of subsistence.

At the common Dances [of the] Sioux & Westrn. Indians women & men dance separately—women shuffle—men jump—men dance *first* then women. Some men have drums & sing. Any man comes out & recites any thing, they then take it up & sing it & dance to it. In the war dance the man will recite some war exploit after he has done they sing & dance to it—then another will come out in the same way.

Strawberry Island is said to have some appearance of cultivation—it was afterds. found that those appearances were occasioned by the digging for roots.

In Osage River mammoth bones found.[13]

Men & women for cholic balancing themselves on sharp stick—Mandans.

Indians (all) have no fixed hours for eating. A man when hungry direct their squaws to get some food.

As to beaver see Aug. 2. 1805.

[*The remainder of the book is blank except for the last two leaves, which contain a list of dates showing entries copied out for Dr. Barton; a crude drawing of a flathead Indian and a sketch showing the manner*

11. That is, syphilis.

12. Lewis and Clark believed that deforestation by fire was the cause of prairies. A later note brings the subject up again.

13. In the vicinity of the Pomme de Terre, an affluent of the Osage. Clark notes "mammoth bones" here on the manuscript map which he prepared for Biddle.

of flattening heads, in Clark's hand; and the following in Biddle's hand:

> Gen. Clark enquire at St. Louis about *Crow* or *Paunch* Indians.
> Indian Speeches.
> Osage story of Beaver.

The notes then continue in the Lewis journal, occupying pages not filled by Lewis. The volume begins with Lewis's entry of 30 Aug. 1803, and the first section of notes ends with his entry of 18 Sept. 1803. The Biddle notes then resume after this notation: "The following pages in handwriting of Nicholas Biddle. E. Biddle. May 17/17."]

The Prairie are not as one would suppose from the name, meadows or bottoms but a sort of high plain or rolling colline—without timber —some high forests retain timber—but generally along margins of creeks & rivers most timber—caused by waters stopping fire & by the vegetation there not becoming dry as soon as the other to catch the trees—& also because for that reason Indians do not burn the grass being greener. Sometimes a little elevation will stop fire & leave trees on it—you see them decaying more or less, a sound copse will the first year or two lose its cotton wood (which is like our lombardy poplar) then more stubborn trees, at last all. Indians set fire for fresh pasture for deer. This Prairie ground extends from the Wabash to the Mountains tho' less near Wabash than more westward. Between St. Louis & river Platte more timber, less prairie because better watered, but beyond Platte to mountains where hunting nations & less water, the prairies more extensive. Over the mountains the same appearance.

May 16 1804 Wednesday. St. Charles <*people not generally industrious*> country around rich but generally speaking not well cultivated as the inhabitants subsist chiefly by Indian trade & by hunting, so that their industry is chiefly confined to their gardens which are in good order. This village like all those of the Illinois country has a common field in the neighborhood which is enclosed by one fence & subdivided into lots of which each inhabitant has the usufruct merely—the limits of each inhabitant's possession is clearly defined— granted originally by the commandant, but by custom & prescription it has descended from father & son & the usufructuary right may be assigned or sold. Country lot attached to town lot.[14]

From St. Charles to the mouth of the river a rich bottom—timber mostly confined to the mouth of the river—on the south side generally high, tolerably well timbered & rich.

14. The last two sentences are not in the narrative or journals.

May 22. 1804. On the Bonhomme creek there is a settlement of Americans who cultivate the rich lands on the sides of the creek.

May 23. 1804. From St. Charles to Osage Woman river[15] a ridge of high lands extends at a greater or less distance from the banks of the river. Between it & the river are fine rich bottoms—on the opposite side of the hills high dry & fertile but thinly timbered—on the Sth. of the Missouri high & woody—the ridge of hills runs on both sides. From Osage Wm. to Osage same appearance but the lands better from the heads of the creeks to the river lands are interspersed with groves of timber.

May 25. 1804. As to Sioux Indians the name is given by the French qu: as to the mode of spelling by them—the Amns. [Americans?] call them *Soos*—the Indians call themselves Dacota.

May 15. The party & provisions started from Wood river in boats but accompanied by two horses to bring back the fruits of the hunting &c.

May 27. 1804. The large island called Otter Island fine fertile soil about 10 miles long—narrow—high situation—one of the richest of the Missouri—lies close to the right shore of the river where Otter river empties into the Missouri. The creek & island called Loutre island.

May 30. The river Gasconnade 100 miles from mouth of Miss[our]i, runs about 150 miles about a north East course thro' a hilly country —on its banks are a number of saltpetre caves, and it is supposed there are lead mines near it.

June 2d. At 40 poles from the junction of the rivers is a high & com[mandin]g position on the Missouri from which delightful prospect &c. (Substitute this.)

June 3. The Osage—a rich country is fed by it—its general course is about W.S.W. it runs thro' a plain country.

8th of June. Mine river[16] forks about 5 or 6 leagues up: at the forks are some very rich salt springs: & in the Summer the west fork of Mine river is so much impregnated with salt that for nearly thirty miles the water is not palatable. Several branches of the Manitou & Good womans river,[17] & the river Saline[18] itself are equally tainted. This all in Summer when water is low. Captn. Clark went out this

15. Now Femme Osage Creek, emptying into the Missouri in St. Charles County, Mo.

16. The Lamine River, emptying in Cooper County, Mo.

17. Moniteau Creek and Bonne Femme Creek, emptying in Howard County, Mo.

18. Petite Saline Creek, emptying in Moniteau County, Mo.

morning on the South side, and after travelling parallel to the river came down Mine river & joined the party. The country thro' which he passed rich & fine.

9 of June. About 4 miles from the Cliff of Arrows[19] to the S.E. is a large lick & salt spring—220 gallons make a bushel of salt—which proves it's strength.

10 June 1804. Large island called Chicot or Stump island Qu:

13 June 1804. The Missouris are the nation who gave the name to the river.

23 June 1804. This little island is separated from the northern bank of the Missi. by a narrow channel which cannot be passed in boats being choked by trees &c. which have been deposited by the stream. Directly opposite to it on the southern shore of the river is a high commanding position 95 feet high, 72 above high water mark which overlooks the river which is here very narrow. The situation is highly favorable for a military position—and a post for trading with the Indians.

Add in a note that in the year 1808 Sept. the U.S. built a fort & a factory at this place[20]—most convenient place for trading with the Osage, Kanzas & Ayauways.[21] The first of these tribes reside near the river of the same name about 80 or 90 miles nearly South of this since called *Fort Clarke* or Fort Osage and at considerable distance from the mouth of the river. They consisted of the Great Osage the Little Osage tribe—& the Arkansa band of Osage. The first consists of about 600 men & lived in a village on the East side Osage river. The little Osage of about half that number reside at a village 6 miles distant from them off the river. The Arkansa band, a detachment or colony of the Osage who left them many years ago under the command of a chief called Big foot is settled on the Vermillion branch of the Arkansa river. (Add in a note that since this time the Great & little Osage have taken up their residence near Fort Clarke or Ft. Osage. Osage next Minitarees stoutest men we have seen.

The Ayauways reside on the Moine river[22] consist of about 350 men —distant about 80 or 90 miles from the same place (Ft. Clarke).

June 26. A few miles up the Blue river are quarries of Plaster of Paris since worked & brought down to St. Louis. *Parroquets* a small kind of parrots.

19. Arrow Rock, in Saline County, Mo.
20. By saying "add in a note," Biddle reminds himself to use this material as a footnote only, since it does not concern the expedition.
21. The Ioway Indians.
22. The Des Moines River, entering the Mississippi below Keokuk, Iowa.

June 28th. The Kanzas takes its rise in the <*plains from which the Platte*> black hills or Côte Noir between the rivers Arkansa & Platte.

29 June. The appearance of the country from the Osage to the Kanzas is beautiful, a level land enriched with many streams of fine running water, and covered with timber—on the south side very fine land great proportions of plains—on the north a beautiful rich country well timbered to[o].

13 June 1804. There are no remains of the Missouri village. On the island opposite to where it formerly stood, was once a French fort (see DuPratz His. of Natchez)[23] of which there are now no appearance —the island having been since inundated & was washed away most probably.

29 June. From St. Charles to the two Charletons,[24] a ridge of high lands borders the river at a small distance from the banks leaving between the river & the hills fine rich bottoms. <*Beyond the hills are high dry & fertile land but thinly timbered.*> From the mouth of the Charletons the hills recede from the river giving greater extent to the bottoms—but again strike the Missi. for a short distance near Grand River and again at Snake creek.[25] From that point they again leave the river and do not approach it till above the Saukee prairie[26] where they are comparatively low & small. Thence they diverge & reappear at the Chariton Carta[27] from which they are scarcely if at

23. Antoine Le Page du Pratz, *Histoire de la Louisiane, contenant la découverte de ce vaste pays; sa description géographique . . . les moeurs, coûtumes & religion des naturels . . .* (Paris, 1758). The English translation, a copy of which Lewis and Clark carried with them, was *The history of Louisiana, or the western parts of Virginia and Carolina; containing a description of the countries that lie on both sides of the River Missisipi . . .* (London, 1763). Le Page du Pratz was a French engineer who came to Louisiana in 1718 and who once supervised a French post among the Natchez Indians. His commentary on the Natchez is the source of the misnomer that Biddle uses here.

24. The Chariton and Little Chariton, both emptying in Chariton County, Mo.

25. Wekenda Creek, emptying in Carroll County, Mo.

26. Biddle terms this "a large and beautiful prairie, called Sauk prairie, the land being fine and well timbered on both sides of the river" (BIDDLE, 1:16). The expedition was in present Ray County, Mo., near the mouth of Crooked River.

27. After returning home and looking over his notes, Biddle was puzzled by this name. He wrote Clark 7 July 1810 (No. 330), "What is the real name & spelling of the stream called *Sharriton Carta,* and also the *Two Charletons.* Get some of the Frenchmen at St. Louis to put them down exactly as they should be printed." Clark replied 8 Dec. (No. 336), "See the enclosed for Chieroton Scarty wrote by a French man. . . ." But the Frenchman's version

[510]

all discernible till they strike the Missouri nearly opposite the Kanzas. Beyond this ridge the land is high & fertile—below the Osage the land is but thinly timbered but above that river, the country is finer & covered with wood to near the heads of the creeks beyond which are rich & extensive plains. On the south side of the Missouri the same ridge of hills extends in almost an unbroken chain from the mouth of the river to the Kanzas tho' decreasing in height beyond the Osage. This ridge continues nearer the river than that on the north side. The land resembles that on the north except in being less woody the lands being rich & immediately beyond the hills extending into plains. The streams too are better than on the north side, so that the land on the south side may be considerable preferable to those of the north. The land becomes better timbered & watered as you approach the Kanzas.

See Ordway July 13 & Journal same day.

From the Kanzas to the Nadaway the hills go up on each side of the river at a distance between 4 to 8 miles from each other. The hills are about nearly equally distant from the river except that on the north of the Missouri the hills from the little Platte to opposite the old Kanzas village are farther from the river than the southern hills, & gave greater extent to the bottoms on that side. From the Nadaway to beyond the river Platte the bottoms grow wider to the north as the hills leave the river. See after July 20, 1804.

July 2d 1804. As to the old village of the Kanzas see *DuPratt's Hist. of Natchez.* No remains of the village nor of the fort. The fort about a mile back of the town which it commands. The spring fine. Recognize the traces of the fort which was small. Some remains of chimnies. This party at the fort probably cut off as there seem no remains of them or history of their success. DuPrat speaks of an expedition under <Montcalm> Bourgemont.[28]

July 12. This river Nemahaw takes its rise in the same place nearly with the Blue river & Saline river between which it flows.

is not present with the letter. Coues supplies the answer: "For 'Charaton Scarty' read *Charretins ecartes,* i.e. two creeks, each named Charretin, which are separated or divergent in their courses, though emptying together into the Missouri" (BIDDLE-COUES, 1:31n). He adds: "There are a pair of creeks in Clay Co., Mo., which exactly answer this description, and are in just the right place," but he does not name them and I have not identified them.

28. Etienne Véniard de Bourgmont, a French army officer who served along the Mississippi and who prepared in 1714 an "Exacte Description de la Louisiana" (GIRAUD). Chapter X of DU PRATZ concerns Bourgmont's mission, as commandant of Fort Orleans on the Missouri, to the Padoucas and other tribes along the river, and no doubt this is why Clark is aware of him.

[511]

July 12. The two kinds of cherries are 1st the wild cherry peculiar to that country—2d the choke cherry which we saw now for the first time.[29]

July 20 (See 17th). The tumors of the people were biles that broke out under the arms on the legs & generally in the parts most exposed to action. They discharged after remaining some days. This without any medicine except a poultice of elm bark or Indian meal. This not attended with any other sickness—painful or troublesome so as to prevent their working—ascribed to the muddy water of Missouri. See July 15.[30]

See 29 June 1804[31]—river Missouri & are not seen again from the river except occasionally & then at a distance till they return to the river 27 miles above the river of Platte at the ancient village of the Ayauways. On the South side the hills continue near to the river from the village of the Kanzas up to the river Platte. The soil &c. on both sides nearly the same, timbered thinly—& better calculated for settlements than the land above the Platte.

From the Ayaway village the northern hills leave the river & do not approach again till Floyd's river 320 miles from the Ayaways. The southern hills continue near the river from the Platte to Council Bluffs[32] 50 miles beyond the Platte. From that place they leave the river & retire to a considerable distance until it again returns to the water near the Mahar village about 200 miles from Council bluffs. Beyond the Council bluffs the river passes thro' a plain rich country—open high grass, very little timber. The great difference between the land above & below the Platte is that the lower is more open & less timbered. The southern hills after continuing near the river by the Mahar villages again disappears and does not return till the cobalt bluffs about 44 miles (by water) from the Mahar villages. From thence to the Yellow Stone river about 1000 miles from cobalt bluffs

29. Their wild cherry is probably the black cherry, *Prunus serotina* Ehrh., and their choke cherry the common chokecherry, *P. virginiana* L. The latter is widely distributed, and it is surprising that they do not encounter the species before 12 July. Perhaps they are seeing for the first time the western form, *P. virginiana demissa* (Nuttall).

30. A slightly more extended statement on boils than those in the narrative and journals.

31. This entry is continued from above, and is one of several instances in which Biddle inserts material out of context—pointing to the likelihood that an earlier draft of these notes may have existed.

32. Like every other editor of Missouri River journals, I feel obliged to note that the Council Bluffs of Clark's day is not the present site of Council Bluffs, Iowa, but is a location on the west side of the river above Omaha, Neb.

the hills follow the course of the Missouri near its banks without receding scarcely at all. The Northern after running a few miles near the Missouri at Floyd's river recede from it at the Sioux river whose course they follow, and tho' again partially visit the Missouri at White Stone R.[33] where they are low yet they do not return to it till beyond James river. After this the hills continue.

These hills from Wood river to the cave are the same height about 150 feet beyond which they become higher to the Osage. Beyond they are not so high. Generally tho' their height varies until the anct. fortns. [ancient fortifications] thence to the Mandans higher after the Mandans to the Muscle Shell river lower from the M. Shell river to Maria's river, the hills much higher, from 300 to 500 feet, & the bottoms very narrow so that it appears like passing thro' a range of high country. From Maria's river to the falls the hills are lower about 2 to 300 feet beyond that place to the mountain the hills are partially scattered & low in height.

On the north side the height of the hills were uniform about 150 feet occasionally to 200 or 300 feet thence from Wood river as high as Muscle Shell river thence to the mountains the country on each side of the Missouri is nearly the same. These hills continue near the river which is now compressed within a narrow space by the approaching hills up as high as the mountains, coming near each other from about one to three miles wide from James river to the Muscle Shell river after which they approach nearer to the river leaving little bottom till you come to Maria's river thence at nearly the same distance as far as the commencement of the falls where the hills approach the water's edge. Above the falls the hills are scattered & low. The hills generally speaking below the Platte composed of a good soil generally timbered—above that river the soil of the hills better but with very little timber—black rich soil.

Don't forget that the plains above Muscle Shell not so good as those below. See Lewis's July 5, 1805 & my June 22, 1805.

July 27. These mounds indicate the position of the ancient village of the Ottoes. This tribe which was formerly numerous, but being reduced by wars moved to the river Platte from this place to be near the Pawnees under whose protection they placed themselves.

July 28. The Ayauways who lived here were a branch of the Ottoes; from which place they emigrated to the Le Moine river.

August 3. Fairfong brought 6 chiefs (Introd[uce]d by Fairfong acc[ordin]g to rank the day before and a number of attendant warriors from the Ottoes & Missouris—chiefs—we told them of the change of

33. The Vermillion River, entering the Missouri in Clay County, S.D.

govt., promises of protection advice &c. Each of the chiefs answered in his turn accg. to rank. They expressed their joy at the change of govt., their hopes that we would recommend them to their great father to obtain trade, necessaries &c. We recognized the chiefs by presenting them medals &c. After the speaking we asked who were the head men. They pointed and the principal chiefs—asked for arms for defence as well as for hunting—& begged us to mediate a peace between them & the Mahars with whom they were at war. We said if they would accompany us to the Mahars we would do so. They declined for fear of being killed by the Mahars. We then promised our assistance to procure a peace.

Missouris & Ottoes speak nearly the same language.

The Indian names.

We ăh rūsh năh.[34]

Acknowledging a chief is a ceremony which confirms his power, & is generally done by the U.S. by putting a medal round his neck &c.

The man Liberté[35] whom we sent for the Ottoes never returned. He went to the Ottoes & told them where we were but never came back himself.

17 August. Setting a prairie on fire is the common signal made by traders to apprize the Indians of their arrival at any place. This also made by different nations of Indians & being seen at a distance serves as an indication of any particular subject that they have previously agreed on.

9 Sept. These creeks have a right of asylum but not so sacred as Pipe Stone creek (see ante) nations at war cease hostilities & intermingle—afterwards renewed as soon as they leave the vicinity. See 21 Aug. 1804.

22 Sep. The hills near the river are washed[?] in gullies in passing over which the mockasons are rotted by some mineral substances.

The small islands of recent formation are generally covered with the common willow, wide leaved & narrow leaved—as they grow

34. The Petit Voleur or Little Thief, principal chief of the Oto tribe, called *We ar ruge nor* by Clark in the journals and *Wear ruge nor* by Lewis in his speech to the Otoes (No. 129).

35. This man, who deserted the party 29 July 1804, has not been satisfactorily identified. Ordway calls him Jo Barter, and I am inclined to think that both these names are phonetic distortions of La Barthe or Labbadie. There is an approximation of these latter names in Clark's field notes (CtY) for 4 July 1804, when he lists one of the *engagés* as J. Le bartee. A man named Joseph Labadee was a petition signer during this period (TERR. PAPERS, 13:328) and one named Labbadie is called an amanuensis for Chief White Hair of the Osages (TERR. PAPERS, 14:467).

larger & stouter the cotton comes up & both trees are very thickly planted on the islands.

21 Augt. Between Cobalt bluffs[36] to Anct. Fortifn. Above the river Scioux Capns. L. & Ck. and the greater part of the men were affected from time to time with a little griping & disagreeable sensations in the stomach (the biles which had afflicted them before had gone off) this was ascribed to a scum which was discovered on the surface of the water near the southern shore about the Cobalt Bluffs. They were ordered to agitate the water & disperse the scum and draw the water from some depth instead of taking it from the surface—on which the sickness ceased, the men recovered.

24 Sept. Evans was a man sent by a company in Wales to explore the Missouri in order to discover if as reported there were any Welsh Indians. He went as high as the Mandans in 1796-7 and died after his return to the Illinois. Evans went under the protection of Mackey Agent for the Company formed for exploring the Missouri which afterds. fell thro'. Mackey went as high as the Mahars. Now lives near St. Louis. Evans was two years in the Indian country—made a map—he returned with a convn. that there were no Welsh Indians. He met with no one single word of Indian words that agreed with his own language—that there were one or two words that sounded like Welsh words but their meaning was entirely different—he believed that there was no foundation for it. That the Indians were Aborigines not Welshmen. The origin of this idea was that there [were] Welshman imigrants before Columbus who had peopled America & the remains of them were on the Missouri. Fillson in His Histy, of Kenty.[37] printed about 1784 says that soon after the Illinois regt. took possession of that country about 1779 a party of Indians came down Missouri to the Illinois & that a Welshman of Capt. Chaplin's[38] comy. conversed with them in Welsh. Col. Clark (brother of Capt. Clarke who then commd. the regt. never heard of this event. Capt. Chaplin (tells Capt. Clark) he had not a Welshman in his

36. Bluffs on the western shore above present Sioux City, Iowa. The explorers thought they contained "Alum, Copperas, Cobalt, Pyrites; a Alum Rock Soft & Sand Stone." Clark wrote: "Capt. Lewis in proveing the quality of those minerals was Near poisoning himself by the fumes & tast of the *Cobalt* which had the appearance of Soft Isonglass. Copperas & alum is verry pisen" (JOURNALS, 1:116).

37. John Filson, *The discovery, settlement and present state of Kentucke* (Wilmington, Del., 1784). The discussion of the Welsh Indians is on pp. 95–97.

38. Capt. Abram Chapline, of Lincoln County, Ky. He served under George Rogers Clark in the Illinois Regiment (BODLEY, 282).

comy. nor did he ever hear of such an occurrence. The real truth was that no one was able to speak with them in their own language (they were thought to be Mahars) but Col. Clark being desirous of speaking with them a man named Murdock who was familiar with Indian manners & habits made himself understood by them & interpreted for them. But he was not a Welshman nor did he belong to the army. This book reached England & Mr. Eraschett[39] when in Engd. was applied to by some Welshmen who had formed a compy. for the purpose of verifying the account. Evans was the agent of that company.

Mackey explored the country watered by the *Qui courre*,[40] & the Loup fork of the river Platte.[41]

26 Sept. These Indians shave their heads all except a tuft on the top which they suffer to grow long—& plaited it hangs down their shoulders—when mourning for the loss of relations they cut off their

39. "Eraschett" is all I get from Biddle's note, but the man might be Richard Crawshay, an ironmaster who hoped to settle Welsh ironworkers in Pennsylvania. It also could be William Pritchard, a Philadelphia printer and bookseller who was in London in 1791 and was visited by men concerned with discovering the Welsh Indians. The best recent discussion of the subject is by WILLIAMS, who deals with the Welsh background of John Evans, his interest in the Indians, his St. Louis connections, and his voyage up the Missouri.

40. La Rivière qui Court, now the Niobrara, entering the Missouri in Knox County, Neb.

41. DILLER (4) treats James Mackay's 1796 exploration, the route of which Clark entered on his Fort Mandan map. The best account of Mackay's involvement with the search for the Welsh Indians is told by himself in his manuscript, "Notes on Indian Tribes" (MoSHi): "About the time I had in view to ascend the Missouri a number of well informed persons of both Europe and America believed the probability of a tribe of Welch Descent's being somewhere near the headwaters of the Missouri & some exaggerated accounts given of the Paducas by some persons, who probably never saw them added considerable strength to that belief. The name Paduca was considered as synonymous with *Madoc,* a Welch Prince who, about six or seven hundred years ago sailed from Wales toward the west with a number of vessels & people & never returned. . . . From these & some other circumstances (all of which is said to have been found in the ancient records of Wales) it was supposed that the Paducas were the remains of Prince Madoc's Colony." Mackay says that he heard nothing of a Welsh tribe during a tour of the Northwest and the upper reaches of the Missouri, but he believes it to be a possibility. On his way from New York to Louisiana in 1794 he met a Welsh doctor, John Rees [Rhys], who gave him a small vocabulary of the Welsh language. Rhys told him of John Evans, who already had gone west to start the search. Upon arriving in St. Louis, Mackay hired Evans as an assistant and, he says, they had ample opportunity to discover that neither the Padoucas nor any other tribe in that part of the country could speak Welsh or a similar tongue.

[516]

hair. The men wear leggings of dressed antelope skins—the leggings come up to their hips—antelope skin white—fastened to a girdle round the waist of dressed Elk Skin or if it can be obtained of cloth leggings often ornamented along the seams (which flap over about two inches outside) with the hair of the Scalps they have taken which is scattered in tufts from the hip down to the ancle; tucked under the waist is a small breech cloth about a foot wide which hangs down over the pudenda & passing between the legs is again tucked under the girdle. This breech cloth made of cloth old blanket or skin—the girdle about one inch wide. The mocassins of buffaloe skin dressed, the hairy side inwards, soaled with thick elk skin parchment this in winter —the summer mocassins of deer or elk skin dressed without hair soaled with elk skin & when in great style from the heel of each mocassin is dragged after them the entire skin of a polecat. Above the girdle comes a loose robe or mantle of buffaloe skin dressed with the hair on & next the skin in fair weather, in damp weather the skin outside, this is either thrown over the arm or wrapped round the body. In addition to this in winter they were [wear] a sort of shirt like ours of skin or cloth coming over their body & arms. Squaws the same style of features &c. as the men—mocassins like the men leggings of the same materials but do not come beyond the knee. A loose shift of skins without sleeves fastened over the shoulders by a string falls to nearly the ancles. Some ends of the skin fall from their armpits down the arm a little way—sometimes a girdle over the shift. Over this is thrown a robe like that of the men. The robes dressed white adorned with porcupine quills. Men (& women particularly) fine white teeth. The women's hair suffered to grow, parted from the forehead across the head where it is clubbed & either hangs down or is collected into a bag.

In girdle or carried in their hands the men carry an entire polecat skin for their *bois roulé* or the inner bark of a species of red willow which is dried in sun or by fire, then rubbed between the hands & broken into small pieces when it is either mixed with tobacco or smoked alone—the pipe is of red earth—the stem is of ash highly decorated with feathers hair & porcupine quills, & about 4 or 3 feet long. The Tetons a cunning vicious set.

25 Sept. 1804. The soldiers of *the chief hugged the mast.* In this nation as in many other Indian tribes (most) the chief appoints one or two Indians whose office it is to keep the peace—a sort of police officer—his office is generally for some days at least till the chief appoints another. Their authority is supreme. They suppress all noise or riot—strike a chief of 2d order if necessary—persons sacred while

in office—punish anyone by striking him—no opposn. to his authority. They generally accompany the chief & if ordered by him to do any duty however dangerous it is a point of honor for the soldier to die rather than desist or refuse to obey. They are known generally by having their bodies blacked but their distinguishing mark are several 2 or 3 stuffed raven skins so fixed on the small of the back in such a way that the tails stick horizontally off from the body fixed to the girdle (One in Peales Museum back part)[42] on his forehead a raven skin split in two tied round his head with the beak sticking out from his forehead.

28th Sept. *Chiefs pride.* I threw him tobacco saying to chief you have told us you are a great man—have influence—take this tob[acc]o & shew us your influence by taking the rope from your men & letting go without coming to hostilities.

1st Octr. The Chayenne Indians now reduced to 300 men rove on the heads of this river & sometimes visit the Ricaras on the Missouri above. They came from the heads of the Red river & were once more numerous. The invasions of the Sioux drove them westward. In their progress they halted on the Southern side of the Missouri below the Warriconne[43] where their ancient fortifications are still seen. Driven from that place they now retired to the Chayenne. Their Indian name is Shar-ha.

The Indian summer of our country is caused wholly by the smoke of the forests of the western country. In autumn when leaves &c. dry this fire runs with great rapidity—the plain for miles is on flame the plain has been for this long time encroaching on the wood—a tree if its bark is not tough dies the first year—the grass being so high— if strong the bark is injured or loosened & the second year it may fall —others (the oak & hickory) resist for three or four years & then falls after which it lies on the ground & the next year dies (the aspen, ash cherry &c. burn up at once). Sometimes at St. Louis the grass of these burnings are wafted in the streets when the plains at a distance 15 or 20 miles—some days it is quite dark with smoke—plains so dry that pipe or accident will set them on fire—the neighboring Indians sometimes fire the grass on fire in the fall in order to catch the game which then comes to enjoy the fresh pasture which springs up (vegetation comes up [. . .] after burning) others burn for signals.

Aug. 17. 1805. Capt. Clark with the Indian women & Shabona were

42. And still extant. See No. 306. The reference to Peale is not in the narrative; the rest of the paragraph was used by Biddle for his entry of 26 Sept. 1804 (pp. 89–90).

43. Little Beaver Creek, entering the Missouri in Emmons County, N.D.

on shore when the woman who was 100 yds ahead began to dance & shew every sign of joy turning back to Capt. C. pointing to the Indians whom he saw in front & sucking her fingers to indicate that it was her native tribe. They advanced & joined the Indn. & Capt. Lewis as they came towards the camp, an Indian woman who had been taken came out & recognized Shabona's wife as the companion in her captivity having been taken at the same time & afterwards excaped. When Shabs. wife joined the party she sat down and was about to interpret when in the person of Cameahwait she discovered her brother. She jumped up, ran & embraced him, & threw her blanket over him & cried profusely. He seemed moved tho' not to the same degree that she was. After some talk between them she resumed her seat & attempted to interpret for us, but was frequently interrupted by her tears. After council was over she was informed by the women (all of whom knew her) of the death of all her family except two brothers & a nephew a son of her oldest sister since dead (only one brother present). The nephew a small boy she adopted immed[iatel]y.

Aug. 23. 1805. Qu: as to jugglers.

Sept. 5. 1805. Our convn. with the Tushepaws was held thro' a boy whom we found among them; a boy a Snake (Soshonee) by birth who had been taken prisoner by some northern band retaken by the Tushepaws whose language he had acquired. I spoke in English to Labieche in English—he translated it to Chaboneau in French—he to his wife in Minnetarée—she in Shoshoné to the boy—the boy in Tushepaw to that nation.

See for Mandan customs 9 Jany. 1806.

The throne of the Mandans generally descends from the chief to his son if he is able, or promises to be able to direct the military movements of the warriors. Sometimes an aged chief will relinquish in favor of his son the honors & the hazards of the royal authority. But the power of a chief is rather the influence of character than the force of authority. He shares all the labors of his warriors, is exempted from none of their services, & is only the first among his equals. The 2d & 3d chiefs usually rise by the authority which bravery never fails to give, & sometimes obtain almost equal consideration with the first. There seems to be no particular election no particular external distinction, but as there power is merely the acquiescence of the warriors in the superior merit of a chief, so it is indicated merely by superior valor. Sometimes however a trader for his own purpose gives a medal or flag to any prominent individual. This (& particularly the last) is a symbol of their being recognized abroad & gives new consequence to the person who is now said to be made chief. These chiefs are either

[519]

war or village chiefs. The village chiefs seem to be the most known & permanent. In war any adventurous young man may propose a campaign—he circulates it among the village that on such a night & such a place he will start in pursuit of the enemy. He arrives in the morning at the spot & waits until evening (for they never go to war in the day time) for those whom his influence may indicate to follow him. His successes may make him a chief (6 or 7 chiefs sometimes in a village—The chief does nothing without consulting the old men—no war—no punishment of indivls. This council formed not by appointment, but the most respectable old men are asked for their advice.

The religion of the Mandans seems to consist in the belief of one great Spirit presiding over their fortunes. This Spirit must be of the nature of a good genius, since it is associated with the healing art, and the great Spirit is synonimous with *great medicine* a name which is also applied to every thing which they cannot comprehend. They also believe in a future state. The tradition connected with it, is that the Mandan nation originally lived in a village underground near a lake. A grapevine which grew above them extended its roots down & opened to the people the view of the land above. They immediately ascended by means of the vine, but after half the nation had come to upper day, a *pregnant [above the line:* big bellied][44] woman heavier than the rest broke the vine as she was climbing up, & the remaining inhabitants are still underground. When the Mandans die, the good will rejoin their ancestors in the subterraneous village, being able to cross the lake—the bad burthened by their sins cannot go across.

Each man selects for himself his particular object of reverence or as they term his medicine. This may be either some invisible being or even some animal. To the first he will frequent sacrifice whatever they possess of most value or most acceptable to the Spirit. A Mandan once said I was the other day owner of 17 horses, but I have made an offering of them to my medicine." He had in fact taken all his wealth his horses gone out into the plain, turned loose the horses whom he thence forward abandoned & committed to the care of his medicine. The horses less religious, took care of themselves. The dead are buried on scaffolds (Qu:) and animals sacrificed to them, or brought up & attached to their tombstones & left to perish. Sometimes they attach other valuable things to the tomb. See April 20 1805.

Polygamy is allowed among the Mandans. When a man becomes enamoured of a damsel which the free intercourse between the sexes permits him to do without

44. In the narrative, Biddle uses the phrase "corpulent woman."

[*Here Biddle encountered the second section of Lewis and Clark journal entries. He turned to the back of the book and began to fill the pages in back-to-front order.*]

difficulty, her dispositions are learnt by means of a friend who will communicate his intentions to the lady. This being known, the lover comes at an appointed time, bringing with him as respectable a retinue of horses as his finances will command. These he ties near the house where the lady resides, and then retires. The friend now arrives at the house and draws the attention of the father to the horses. He goes out & with affected or real ignorance enquires whose they are. The friend takes that opportunity of forwarding the lover's suit. If the father be not satisfied with the lover or his fortune, he says no more. The lover alarmed for his success brings all the horses he can procure. If this be satisfactory, the father takes the horses & puts them among his own. The lover then comes & is presented to his wife. No ceremony occurs, the husband & wife live with & serve the father till the birth of the first child when they go to housekeeping. If the young lady be the eldest daughter, the husband is at the same time virtually married to all the younger daughters whom he has a right to claim at the age of puberty. The grant of an eldest daughter is therefore a greater favor than that of one of the younger females. When the young people go to housekeeping the father returns them as many horses as the son in law had given him at the time of marriage. The wom[e]n afflicted with both sorts of vl. [venereal?] which were given to the men.

At the Mandan fort we had killed a buffaloe & put head on bow of the boat. An Indn. coming by—very cold day, he stopped—took out pipe smoked his pipe, & offered it to Buffl. mouth—this done 15 minutes or 20. He came into the fort. On enquiry this B. head was found to be his Medicine. Know no cure for lu. ven. but the gona. they can cure. (Smoking great ceremony—generally smoke to their medicine—that is give the mouth of the pipe to the object of their veneration.)

July 5. 1806. Shields & others I had sent out to examine the route which the Oolashoots we had met last fall had taken across the mountain when we had seen them 4 & 5 Sept. 1805 said he had found a large trail which turned up the hill from the creek 3 miles higher, an easterly branch of the creek we had come down last fall. Shannon found a trail not so large, nor so good.

Aug. 3. 1806. This river from information has its S.W. branches

connected with those of the R. del Nord & the Arkansaw & Platte—
& in the vicinity of the S.E. sources of the Columbia—the parallel
waters of the Missouri (the Madison & Gallatin rivers).

Aug. 14. The chief of the Mine. [Minitaris] Metaharta told us with
tears that our return reminded him of our good counsels that his
son contrary to our pacific advice had gone to war & been killed &c.

18 Aug. 1806. The Mandans were 7 on one side [*above the line:*
west]—2 on the other side—the 7 reduced 1st to 5 then went up to
Ricaras on W. Side forming themselves into two villages. The two
into one went up & settled east (before the 7 moved) nearly opposite
Ricaras & then joined the two formed out of the 7. Still further
reduced the 3 Mandans moved up to where they now are settling in
3 villages. The two who had gone together settled on the N. West
& one that was alone on S. East. Mackay found them in that way—
Still reduced the seven villages joined into *one* about [*blank*]. When we
returned a quarrel had reduced this N.W. Village for a part went to
S. East ville. & joined them.[45]

On the Arkansaw (south Side) one village & some scattering Choctaws on the White R.—about 200 men—band of our Choctaw nation
in the Mississi. territory. Above the Choctaw village on the same side
of the Arkansaw are the Quapaws (see Pike). On Red River below all
are the Caddos—west—on head of Red River.[46]

Indian Nations

The Chickasaw's, a band of the Chickasaw Nation of Georgia wander occasionally in Louisiana opposite the Chickasaw bluffs on the
river St. Francis West side. They may amount to about 100 men
—they cultivate the earth and have a town on the St. Francis. Next
above them on the St. Francis are two towns of *Cherokees* of about
250 men the bands of the Cherokee nation in Tennassee. Then come
the Delawares who have two towns on St. Francis one town on Apple
Cr. a branch the Mississipi & a few scattered Delawares about St.
Louis & a small town on the Mississippi near Apple Creek in all
about 300. These with an equal number on White R. in Indiana are
all the remains of the great Delaware nation.

Then the Shawnees have one settlement on Apple Creek, & another
high up the Gasconnade, & the remainder on the Glase[47] River a
branch of the Miami of Lake Erie—about 400 men in Louisa. &

45. Biddle wrote a passage similar to this in the JOURNALS, 5:347–48.
46. This paragraph is not in the narrative or journals.
47. Clark seems to mean the Auglaize River in Indiana, not the stream
which shows on his and other maps as the Glase or Glaize River entering
the Mississippi below Apple Creek.

150 on La Glése, remains of the Shawnees who formerly lived (about 1780) on the two Miamis of the Ohio.

Near St. Genevieve roving about are the Piories, a band of about 30 men—the only remnant of a large nation of the same name who formerly lived on the Eastern side of the Mississi.

Opposite Ste. Genevieve in the town of Kaskaskia, live in a part of the town (now Seat of govt.) by themselves the Kaskaskia tribe of about 15 men the remains of a numerous people of Kaskaskias who lived in the same place.

Roving about the settlements sometimes on Missouri sometimes the Gasconnade & the Osage are the tribes of *Potawatamies* & *Taways* the first from the Illinois near Lake Michigan the 2d from the Illinois river—sometimes joined & sometimes separate—in the whole not more than 20 men—hunting &c. The Kickapoos on the heads of Kaskaskia river also hunt about the Illinois settlements—bands of these people hunt on the Missouri the whole about 200 men.

The *Ayauways* live in one village on the river (about 200 men) *Des Moines*. Above them on the Mississipi in several villages live together the Saukes and Renards about 800 men who sometimes pass the Missi. to their original seats on the Rocky river a branch of Mississi.—on both sides of the river 500 men. Above them the Renards who live on the Mississi. up to near Prairie de Chien on the West side of Missi. about 250.

Above these are the difft. bands of *Sioux* (see Elsewhere) as high as Crow Wing River.

The Winnabagos & Milliawaky's[48] wander between Lake Michigan & the Missi. & the Rice Indians[49] a small band on Green bay.

Above the *Sioux* on Leach lake & the heads of the Mississipi are the *Chippeways* about 600 men, besides their bands on the Red river of Lake Winnepec & Assiniboin Riv. where they [are] called "Kinstenaus[50] (See McKenzie) and the Algonquins on Rainy lake the lake of the Woods & about lake Winnepeg near the mouth of Red River.

Following the Missouri up the Osage are the Osage Indians (See Elsewhere note).

48. "A former village with a mixed population of Mascoutens, Foxes, and Potawatomi, situated on Milwaukee r., Wis., at or near the present Milwaukee, in 1699" (HODGE, 1:863).

49. The Menominee Indians, on and near the Menominee River in Wisconsin. The name means "wild rice men."

50. The Cree Indians. A contraction of Kristinaux, which was the French form of the name they called themselves—Kenistenoag (SWANTON, 554). Lewis and Clark used a number of variations: Christanoes, Christinaux, Knistanoux, Knistenaux.

On the Kanzas river are the tribe of Kanzas of about 370 men on the south side of the river near the mouth the Blue Water river—formerly lived on the Missouri above R. Kanza in 2 villages S. Side of Missouri speaking same language.

(Delawares & Shawnees not understand each other—*Dels.* rough—*Shans.* soft gentle.[51]

Ottoes & Missouris on the R. Platte about 200 men come next (see elsewhere notes) lower down the Platte than the Pawnees.

Then come Pawnees (See also note). Then the *Mahars* once very numerous—above Platte—not more than 300 men.

Then The Poncarars[52] band of Mahars above the river Qui court about 50 men—formerly about 400 men now reduced.

Then come the *Sioux* see elsewhere note.

Then the Chayennes on the river Chayenne formerly of the same river a branch of Red river of the Winng.

The Ricaras come next (see elsewhere note).

The Mandans next (see also note).

The Minitarees, are in two villages on Knife river [*blank*] miles from the Mandans on East side. Upper Mandan vill. is about 2 miles above the lower on W. Side. The Maharha village is at the mouth of Knife river on the same side with & 3 miles above the lower Mandan village—about 50 men. This Maharha vill. is the town of the Ahaharways (Qu.) this name—who as the Mandans say formerly lived South on the Missouri, then came for protection to near where the Mandans lived formerly in 9 villages whence they emigrated to where they now live under & near the protection of the Minnetarees whose language they understood in part.

Above the Ahharways on Knife Creek about a mile above Ahharways vill. live Minnitarees Mataharta on South Side of Knife. The acct. given of them by Minnetarees proper is that they came many years ago come from the plains & settled near them about 150 warriors.

About 1½ mile above them on opposite side of Knife R. beautiful low plain is the village of Minnetaree proper (same language with very little if any difference from Min. *Metaharta* Qu. means of the willows—about 450 warriors. They say they grew there & were ordered by their Great Spirit to reside there so that they would not agree to go & live on Rochejaune for Great Spirit had said if they moved they

51. Most of the preceding information under the heading "Indian Nations" is not in the narrative or journals because the tribes were not encountered on the expedition. From this point in the summation Biddle makes use of the information in various ways.

52. The Poncas in northeastern Nebraska.

would all die. The Mandans however say (see Mandan Chiefs talk vol. 14) that the Minnitarees *came & settled by them*—they perhaps mistook the emigration of Ahharways for one of Minnitarees—id. qu. These Minnitarees (who are what McKenzie calls Fall Indians) say that they have relations on the Saskashawan whom they did not know of till they met them in their war parties & in fighting them were astonished at discovering that they spoke their own language. These probably the Minnitarees of Fort de Prairie whom McKenzie calls Fall Indians. The roving Indians on the Saskashawan were first known by English who called them Fall Indians & when they found those of the Missouri speaking same language called them also Fall Indians. Afterwards when it was known that the Missouri Fall Indians were called Minitarees those who spoke the same language on the Saskashawan were called Minitarees on Fort de Prairie residing near the Establishment in the Prairie on that river. The Minitarees are called by the French gros ventres—by the English big bellies—names applied also to all the Fall Indians.

The Ahharways are called Wattasons see note in this book of May 10. 1805.

Next on the Rochejaune are The *Kee heet sa* or *Friends to all* as they call themselves. Crow or Raven Indians as they are called by French & English—two bands (see No. 14) Crows speak Minnetaree language.

The Missouris were formerly numerous & seated on Missouri below mouth of Grand river near mouth then reduced by the Saukees & took refuge among the Little Osage who then lived on the Missouri 20 miles higher up on opposite side. The Little Osage reduced by the Saukees & Inds. East of Mississipi, moved to the Great Osage on Osage river the Missouris went to join the Ottoes on the Platte who had already taken protection under the Pawnees.[53] Besides these two bands is a third who hunt on Clarks fork called Al la ka we ah or Paunch[54] Indians of 300 lodges & 800 men *Qu. as to those Crows & Paunch* at St. Louis.

A vast extent of country on both sides of the mountains is loosely occupied by the Snake Indians[55] (French Les Plaies) a great & nu-

53. Biddle bracketed this paragraph, perhaps to remind himself that it is out of sequence.

54. Apparently a band of Crows.

55. Lewis and Clark usually mean the Shoshonis when they mention the Snake Indians. But they do not have a clear concept of the Shoshonean peoples. For their failure to distinguish between the Northern Paiute and the Shoshoni Indians, and for some of their other difficulties with the ethnology of the Northwest, see RAY & LURIE.

merous people speaking the same language so far as to render themselves intelligible to each other, but connected neither by a common Indian name nor governt. The tribes which rove on the Missouri are 1st. The Shoshonees and Hootsootahah's[56] live in the Rock Mountains on the Heads of the Missouri Wisdom Jefferson & Lewis river—the 1st of 150 men—2d of about 100 men—on the heads of Madison's river are a band of Snakes called *Ne may* of 150 men.

The *Pohah* band live on the East fork of Lewis river above the Shoshonees 200 men.

On the head of the Rochejaune live the Yep pi band of Snakes of 200 men.

All to the South in different bands roaming in the Rock mountains nearly to the Spanish Settle[men]ts on the heads of the Arkansaw are the *Liahtan*[57] tribes.

On the westward of the Rock mouns. (& within them) on the West fork of Lewis as far down as The Portpella R.[58] live the Shoshonees (in description join them with those of East fork of Lewis river) same as those of E. Fork—no particular tribes. The same nation of Snakes is also situated on the heads of the Multnomah where they call the most remote the Shababoah, lower down on another fork the Callapposwah as low as the Falls of the Multnomah; and on the heads of the Tawarnahiooks[59] a band of Tawarnahiooks a branch of Snakes. The whole Snake nation may be 20,000 Souls.

On the heads of Clarks river are placed a wandering band of Oat-lash-oots a part of the great Tushipaw nation situated on the N. side the same river near the Wayton Lake. These Ootlashoots rove on Clarks river in Spring & Summer & in the Winter go up that river —cross over to the heads of Missouri where they are joined by the Shoshonees—& venture as far down as the Rochejaune to meet their friends the Crow Inds. There are 3 other bands of Tushipaws (see large book.

The next nation are the *Chopuniesh* divided into five bands—The Pallotpallah who live on the Koskooskee above its forks the Chopunniesh proper who live on Kooskooskee below its forks & on Colters

56. The Hootsootahahs are not identified.

57. Also Alitan, Aliatan—Clark's word for the Snakes or Shoshonis. Here he probably means the Comanches, which he seems to identify as a branch of the Snake tribe (JOURNALS, 6:107).

58. Possibly the stream identified in BIDDLE-COUES, 3:1255, as Pine Creek in Union County, Ore.

59. Lewis and Clark applied this word to a band of Indians and to a river. The river is the Deschutes (as is also Clark's River, when located in north central Oregon). The Indians are the Northern Paiute (RAY & LURIE, 365).

creek the *Kimooenim* who live on Lewis rivr. above the entrance of Kooskooskee & up Lewis's river to its forks.

Willetpo band residing under the S.W. mountains on a small river running into Lewis's called The Weaucum.

The *Willewah* band on the Willewah river which runs into Lewis on S.W. side below its forks.

& The Chopunnish of Lewis's River who live on that river between the mouth of Kooskooskee and entrance of Lewis's river into the Columbia.

The Sayennom band on N. Side of E. Fork of Lewis's Rr. from its junction to the Rocky Ms. & on Lamaltar Creek.

The Oalashoots are not *The* Flat Heads, the Chopunnish are Pierced nose. The real Flatheads are those in the plains of Columbia below Chopunish to the Falls or rather[?]

These nations from Ocean to falls understand each other. Columbian falls are from near mouth of Kooskooskee to falls.

Esheeloot village is the great mart of trade.

After Chopunniesh come Sokulk &c.

In going up river saw the com[mo]n honey bee as high as beyond the Osage—on our return saw them near the Kanzas in trees like all bees. The comn. bee is not a native rem[embe]r introduction in large quantities into Kentucky none in Illinois when French settled there— now all over that country—they are advancing up Missouri we saw them in large numbers.[60]

Indian comp[lexio]n like that of our frontier Indians, except the Ootlashoots who are lighter than the others than any we have seen— they are also larger than Shoshonees—the Mandan chief here was the whitest man of his nation. On the Westn. Side the complexion nearly similar the Chopunnish to the Clatsops tho' these last have a deeper tinge—in general the Fishing nations are somewhat darker than the hunters—the Chopunnish are no so dark as the Clatsops— for the Chopunnish are only half fisherman & ½ hunters—Shoshonees & Chopunnish wash their faces the fishers dirty & not wash. The two Squaws of Chaboneau were Shoshonees but the one from the adjoining the Tushepaws was lighter than the other who was from the more Southern Indians[61]—the Chopunneish too fish on both sides of river being not afraid of or in alliance with Shoshonees.

60. Clark's reference to the introduction of the honeybee into Kentucky is not in the narrative or journals, though both sources mention the absence of the bee on the upper Missouri.

61. The woman from near the Tushepaws was Sacagawea. The other wife of Charbonneau is not named in the journals.

One of our men Potts originally a dark complexioned man who was like all the party nearly naked during summer on his return was as dark as any of these Indians—having first lost his skin, which pealed off & then became hard & no longer swelled &c.—others of the party not so much affected by it.[62]

The B[eaver]s along the sides of the rivers & in ponds. Sometimes a dam across creek. Sticks 2 feet in length & two or four inches round interwoven so as to stop channel sufficiently (& if necessary mud placed before it)—the rest of dam formed of mud the dam perhaps 2 or 3 feet wide sometimes in middle of pond if shallow, a sort of bed of mud raised to surface of water on which a floor of sticks interwoven, and an arch of sticks forming a sort of upper story or cage the entrance below surface of water & thro' the mud to upper story which is about 18 inches in the interior & 3 feet in height above surface of water.

By side of river hole under water made & worked upwards in the bank five or 6 feet where they make a hold of 4 or 6 feet diameter. If water washes away the bank so as to expose the passage to their hole, they cover it so as to form a sort of covered way with sticks 2 or more feet thick.

No particular facts as to Indian emigration. Our Indian woman said & it is generally known that the Shoshonees Liatans & other Snakes of the Mountains formerly lived in the plains on this side & by war were obliged to take refuge in mounts. The Ootlashoots too say that they once were in the plains & were forced to retire. We have seen how many have been reduced &c. Ottoes Pawnees &c. When <Mackay> [. . .] Tru[t]eau saw the Poncars they were (1796 or 7) nearly 300 men they lived in village tended corn &c. now 50 wanderers. When we saw Mahars in going up they had deserted their village & taken to roving we advised them to return & cultivate corn & gave them some to begin with. On our return they had begun to cultivate and now unite cultivation with roving. [When a nation gets reduced they][63] They were at war with the Sioux, we left Durion with the Yankton Sioux to mediate a peace which he did & the Mahars resumed culture. When a nation gets reduced it is obliged to take to roving to avoid its enemies.

The amusement most common among all is dancing chiefly at entertainments. Our frontier Indians play cards—in the Western moun-

62. This paragraph is not in the narrative or journals.
63. The brackets are Biddle's. This passage is still further indication that Biddle may have been copying from an earlier draft of the notes. The same phrase occurs at the beginning of the next sentence.

tains, they are very fond of horse racing & foot racing for wagers. Single horse racing & a purse also. Some ten or twelve run at a time to a certain point from 3 miles back again. On the Columbia near Ocean the game with hands[?] (described). None of the nations except Sioux fond of drink. The Mandans no—the Ricaras have seen its effects on traders who brought it there without being tempted. The Ricaras said when we offered it that they were surprized that their Father would present them a drink which would make them fools. Their idea as expressed to Tabo a trader is that no man can be their friend who would tempt them to make themselves fools.[64] Even on the Columbia they never asked us for drink nor did any Indians we saw possess any intoxicating liquor—they did however [As we went down the Fishing season just over & the sore eyes then were worse than when we came up][65] Seem (the Indians on Sea Coast) love to take Tobacco smoke so as to produce intoxication.

Smoking is habitual with Ricaras Mandans (that is with the men of consideration not the mass who only smoke in ceremonies. The Ricaras & Mandans cultivate tobacco of two species peculiar to them. All this side (viz. Osages &c.) cultivate our common tobacco. Shoshonees have a particular plant (described) as have also the Chopunnish one similar. But among those only the people of note—Down in the plains we rather introduced the custom in great ceremonies, in the plains it is not at all habitual to smoke—some do not know it.

In the Col. plains below the Chopunniesh smoking is by no means so habitual tho' still used in their councils—but becomes more so near the falls—beyond which to the Ocean it becomes much more usual, & on the Sea coast tobacco is in the highest demand. The blue beads occupy the place which gold has with us. White beads may be considered as our silver—while tobacco hol[d]s a middle rank between them. The tobacco most admired (if not the only one Qu: see book) is our tobacco.

<18th May> 19th Octr. 1805. The alarm was occasioned by their thinking that we were supernatural & came down from the clouds. They had seen us fall from the clouds. In fact while on opposite side of the river unseen by them I had shot this white crane flying & it came down by me I then jumped into a canoe & while going across river I shot a duck flying who also fell. These shots (having never heard a gun) a few light clouds then passing, the fall of the birds & our immediately landing & coming towards them convinced them we were from above—this idea increased by my lighting my pipe with

64. Tabeau makes a similar statement in his journal (TABEAU, 171).
65. The brackets are Biddle's.

[529]

my burning glass in the house which had no roof. This told us after we had left us by the Chopunniesh chief by whose mediation we had pacified them.

Missouri most covered with islands below the Platte—the river changes its beds often—the bed of Missouri chiefly mud, the coarse sand thrown out by the Platte) there are many sandbars which stop the mud of the Missouri which then fills up to the height of the bar along the shores &c. Willows then grow on it first year—which strengthen against freshes—the mud accumulates & the sand too—the cottonwood is now added & the gradual accession makes the island rise up to the highest waters of the river—in the bends of the river water washes across & forms peninsulas & gradually islands. Like Mississipi the Missouri is constantly washing on one side & making on the other near the still waters of the bends. *Islands* again fill up with mud & ponds left.

Generally speaking fine soil up the Missouri to the river Platte fine soil thin timbered well calculated for settle[men]t. Above Platte open wanting timber quite up to mountains—not so good for Settlet. on acct. of scarce timber, and bad water up to near mountains—the creeks having not much water & what there is is brackish. In the mounts. fine water & vallies capable of good cultivation—the East Side of the mounts. not so well timbered as the West. From the foot of the Mounts. near Kooskooskee for 40 or 50 miles west a fine rolling lightly timbered country, which then descends into the Columbian plains which reach to the falls on each side of river forming a high broken land capable of culture (good land) (no timber) in the middle of the plains there is a district of flat & sandy country which rises again at the falls to the same style as before. Below the falls the mountains continue to Quicksand river[66] when it opens into the Wappatoe valley which continues to near mouth of Chicarlieskit,[67] when it closes & continues mountainous all within nearly 20 miles of Sea coast when it gradually descends to the mouth of the Columbia —low flat & marshy tho' immediately at Point Disappointment *land* is high.

There is always a Principal chief—then a Second chief & a third & sometimes more—these are the village chiefs—the war chiefs make them selves by their exploits—tho' in fact the 2d & 3d chiefs are war chiefs—the village chief—

Some old man or 1st chief generally begins a council—a chief who is young will sometimes open a council by saying that such a one is

66. Sandy River, entering the Columbia in Multnomah County, Ore.
67. The Hellgate River.

old & wise & that what he shall say is from him—The old man will then speak. Generally speaking all the Indians we saw have hair naturally—that on their head coarser & thicker than ours they have also hair on their chins arms & private parts. There is however very little hair on breasts & general parts of the body. They extract all the hair that appears by means of tweezers supplied by the traders & made by themselves of brass wire. Some times however they suffer it to grow a little on the chin & other parts when it comes to some length, but grows straight both on chin armpits & private parts—but when it is suffered to grow it does not grow as thick as with us— women have it but generally not much on parts. I have seen an instance of a man who had as much as I have. This hair does not come on them as early as on us—men of twenty five having hair something like our boys of 16—tho' the men ripen as soon as ours do. The women are ripe sooner than do ours but still their hair is more backward. The women of the Mandans stretch the clythoris for sake of ornament so that some have it as long as five or 6 inches.

Among Minitarees if a boy shows any symptoms of effeminacy or girlish inclinations he is put among the girls, dressed in their way, brought up with them, & sometimes married to men. They submit as women to all the duties of a wife. I have seen them—the French call them Birdashes.[68]

Buffaloe hunted on horseback by the hunters with arrows—they incircle their head & gradually drive them gently to a plain or fit place for movements of horse. Then they go in near buffaloe cows (which are always preferred) & shoot him with arrows (close up to him) till wound is mortal, then go to another till quiver exhausted. Then collect their prey. The squaws & attendants in the rear come up & skin &c.

A field [of] corn is gathered part just when it is ripening & what we call roasting ears—this they eat as roasting ears, or dry it by taking off the outward husk leaving enough to plat the eyes [plait the ears?] together & then hang them in the sun to dry—the rest of the field is gathered when it is riper & harder—it is dried in the same way— the first shrivels but still keeps soft & is used thro' winter boiled— the other is harder & is generally pounded & made into cakes the first is mixed with meat & soup &c. on the frontiers called Tossemonòny see Ordway Decr. 30. 1804.

There is what is called a medicine danse—when a man wants to

68. *Berdache*, a hermaphrodite or a homosexual. Lewis and Clark first encountered such deviants during the winter among the Mandans, when "a number of Squars & men Dressed in Squars Clothes" came to camp with corn to sell (JOURNALS, 1:239).

do honor to his medicine or make sacrifice to it he announces that on such a day the sacrifice of horses or other property is to be devoted to those virgins or young ladies who will join in the Medicine dance. This is performed in the open field—everybody may go—whoever among the girls of the village chooses to join may do so. In the day it takes place the girls are perfectly naked—the giver of the Dance has his medicine—bafaloes head &c. if a substantial object—or medicine bag if ideal—after dancing sometimes the girl prostrates herself & remains the reward of impudence sè quelqu'un a la hardiesse de lui faire la cour en presence de tout le monde—car, il n'est pas permis de la fairè a l'écart quelquefois un jeune a l'audace[?] d'entreprendre l'aventure[?] pour se distinguer parmi ses compatriotes.

Corn beans pumpkins & tobacco the principal culture of Mandans & Ricaras who exchange them for skins horses &c. with the more northern Indians.

Indian maps made on skins or mats may be given to you, by individuals, but are not kept permanently among them. Sometimes in sand, hills designated by raising sand, rivers by hollow &c.

The Juggler (of the Wallowallah) told his nation when we returned that he had predicted it &c.—that he had got it from the moon. There appears to be among the Shoshonees & Chopunnish a kind of Juggler who is a prophet & enjoys more or less considn. In other bands the Juggler is a sort of Doctor as among Osages who cures disorders & brings people to life. These are called great medicine men—others of a less note swallow arrows which they do by taking out the barb, throwing their heads back & thrust the arrow all the way down their throat &c. &c.[69]

Sweating houses made of various sizes, forms &c. some like oven of mud & sticks—the patient goes in, with a number of heated stones & some water—he pours it on the stones till he has steam sufficient for his purpose—two or sometimes several go in together—it is a great offence for one friend to decline going with another when invited— it is a social amusement. This is the form among the mountains Rock. On the Columbia plains the form is a hollow in a bank (6 or 8 foot square) of a river—side near river closed up with mud &c. —& is all closed except a hole 2 feet square on top—a number of men seated round the room [above the line: (used for almost all diseases inflammation—pains—universal &c.)]—they have water & stone—on our frontiers the sweat house made of wickered work of willows arched about 4 feet high covd. with skins or mats stones & water—

69. STODDARD, 425, said he had seen an Osage juggler swallow an arrow eighteen inches long; it appears to have been a standard part of the repertory.

but only one can go in at time—our neighbors Indians all have this last. All nations have it near running water & plunge into cold (Tho' our frontier Inds. do not always. Better doctors than westward) water & return again sometimes to warm.

[*Here Biddle left off filling the pages back-to-front and returned to normal order. Beginning at the end of the Lewis and Clark journal material, he filled the remaining blanks with the notes that follow. The notes are preceded by this entry: "The following pages conclude the notes in handwriting of Nicholas Biddle with the exception of 1 page in lead-pencil. Edward Biddle. May 17/17."*]

On the acquisition of Louisiana the Cong. U.S. by law (*Qu:*) appropriated the sum of $— for the purpose of exploring the country. This sum was placed at the disposition of the Prest. Capt. Lewis of U.S. army then Secy. of Prest. and Capt. Clark formerly of the army were appointed by the Prest. to command an exploring party the object of which was to discover the nearest water comm[unicatio]n between the Atlantic & Pac[ifi]c Oceans. "Course & source of the Missouri (trading with Indians information &c.) & the most convenient water comn. from thence to the Pacific ocean" [Prest. Jeffn. to Capn. Lewis 4 July 1803]. Capns. Lewis & Clark were equal in rank & authority in the expedn.[70] Capn. Lewis haveing received the necessary instructions from the Prest. at Washington joined Capn. Clark who then resided at Louisville. From that place they proceeded together by water to St. Louis. Thence to the mouth of Wood river. The winter of 1803–& 4 was employed in disciplining the soldiers & making the necessary preparations for setting out in the spring. The party consisted of Capns. Lewis & Clark, 3 sergeants & about 50 men (*Qu:*) The men were of three discriptions—1st robust young American citizens from the neighborhood of Louisville—2d soldiers of the U.S. army—3d French Engagés or watermen. All these men were enlisted for the particular service—the soldiers being previously released from their engagements to the U.S. The provisions consisted of [see list of necessary stores in No. 3]. To these were added a large quantity of articles to be used as presents to the Indians [see list of presents in No. 3]. The original design of Capns. Lewis & Clark was to go up the Missouri in boats from Louisville [St. Louis] after wintering at Charette. The Spanish commander not being apprized of the Cession of Louisa. objected. The officers then encamped at Wood river (mouth) for the winter, intending to ascend the river on the side opposite the Spanish jurisdn. The

70. The brackets here and following are Biddle's.

[533]

party was formed of 9 young men who joined at Clarksville[71] (Falls of Ohio)—14 soldiers who volunteered from the U.S. army—2 engagés or French watermen—(an Interpreter & Hunter) & a negro servt. of Captn. Clarke. To these were added at Wood river a corporal & 6 soldiers—& 9 French watermen who were engaged to accompany the party as far as the Mandan nation for the purpose of carrying. These 9 + 14 men engaged all as privates & 3 sergts. were appointed out of them by Capns. Lewis & Clarke. The men were enlisted to serve during the expedn. & to submit to the rules &c. prescribed by Capns. L & C or either of them. These addns. to the party were for carrying the stores as well as for protection in case of hostilities from the Indians who were most to be dreaded from Wood river to the Mandans.

The distances may all be found in No. 14.

The party on Starting from Wood river had one large Keel boat of about 55 Keel decked 10 feet in stern & ten feet in bow—drew three feet water—with one square sail—rowing 22 oars—cabin & forecastle (& two large periauges). The lockers of the boat capable of being raised as to form a breast work in case of attack & when down to secure the baggage from rain or the inspection of the Indians.

The low bottoms of the Missouri from the mouth to the Rock Mountains are covered generally with the cotton tree, which grows to the size of 3 feet diameter & rise to the height of 80 or 100 feet. Some ash see 21 June 1804.

Tho' frequently said that the boat was with difficulty got over bars &c., it is to be understood that in the channel of the river there was also water enough for much deeper vessels, but the rapidity of the current obliged us to go near the shore & creep up along the sides. At no place can the Missi. be forded from the mouth to the falls.

When speaking of the Inhabs. of the Platte mention the Pawnees. About 10 leagues [*above the line:* not 15 leagues 21 July 1804] from the mouth live the Ottoes—beyond the Ottoes about 5 leagues up the river are the Pawnees who are about 700 men. The Pawnees are divided into 4 bands. The Principal band is the one above consisting of 500. 2d the Republican Pawnees who formerly lived [*above the line:* 250 men] on the Republican fork of the river Platte, & now reside with the principal band. 3d The Pawnees Loups or Wolf Pawnees live on the first large fork of the river Platte about 90 miles S.W. of the Main Pawnees [*above the line:* 280 men]. The 4th

71. The place of enlistment of the "nine young men from Kentucky" is not mentioned in the narrative or journals.

band now lives on the Red river & consists of about 400 men high up the river. Called Pawnées Piqués (tattooed). These Indians the Pawnées Piqués formerly lived on the Kanzas & Arkansaws, & have been driven by the Osages who were always at war with them to the Red.

All these Indians live in villages & raise corn. During the intervals of culture rove after buffaloe.

The Pawnees once very numerous divided since 1797 into many tribes, cut off &c. &c.

Beyond them on the Platte between the black mountains & the Rock mountains are the Kă ñi nā viĕsch [72] supposed to be originally a band of Pawnees whom they left to colonize. They do not live in villages but rove thro' the plains. Their number is estimated at 400 men. Still further to the Westward are the We tă pă hā tŏ & Kiăwàs on heads of the Platte who amount to 200 men living together for mutual protection. They are conjectured to have been a tribe formerly of the Padukas—as are also the Castahana of about 300 men—the Sta-i-tan or Kites[73] of 100 men—the Ca-ta-ha of 75 men— the Do-ta-mi of about 30 men—all these rove about the heads of the river Platte & the Rocky mountains. These are the colonies of the Padukas,[74] a large nation once settled between the upper parts of the river Platte and the river Kanzas. Bourgemont visited the Perdukas who then lived up the Kanzas river in the country now occupied by the Kanzas tribe (no remains of the Perduka nation except those branches mentioned—

26 Aug. The village of Petit Arc has no remain except the mound of earth about 4 feet high which surrounded the scite of the old village.[75]

72. The Arapaho Indians.

73. Interlined, and obviously referring to the Kites, is this passage: "(most fierce of all) Don't give way nearly [. . .] because fly i.e.: go on horseback."

74. "The Paducas Tribe (who live South of Chy-enn River & on the headwaters of Rivers del-nort & Missouri, does not seem to be of the same race with those nations arround them from whom they differ in almost everything. They are more honest, peacable & sincere in all their transactions— friendly to each other & Courteous to Strangers. Their manners more approaching civilization, their skin more fair, their Countenance more open and agreeable & their features in a Great Degree, resembling White People" (James Mackay, in "Notes on Indian Tribes," MoSHi). HYDE believes these people were the Plains Apaches.

75. Here the Biddle text is interrupted by slightly more than a page of penciled notes in Lewis's hand. They are faint and appear to have been hurriedly scrawled, perhaps when Lewis visited the Big Bone Lick in the fall of 1803. Lewis lists the dimensions of some fossil remains, "Tusk. Length 10.7. Thickness at root, 1.7," etc.

30 of Aug. This Society held in more respect than the Chiefs [*above the line:* seats in council superior]—they are formed principally of young men of 30 or 35 years.

31st Aug. The Sioux or Dacorta originally settled on the Mississipi & called by *Carver*[76] Nadowessiay. Now subdivided into tribes viz:

1. Yankton or bois brulé about 200 men inhabit the Scioux Demoine & Jacques rivers.

2d. The Tetons of the burnt woods about 300 men rove on both sides of the Missouri about White river & Teton river.

3. Tetons Okandandas of about 150 men on Missouri (both sides) below the Chayenne river.

4. Tetons Min-na-kenozo 250 men on both sides of the Missi. above the Chayenne.

5. Tetons Sa-one on both sides of the Missi. below the Warricone river about 300 men.

6. Yanktons of the plains or Big devils who rove on the heads of the Scioux, Jacques & Red river about 500 men.

7. *Wah pa tone* on the St. Peters above its mouth 200 men.

8. Min da war car ton or proper Darcota or Sioux nation—these possess the original seats of the Scioux, and are what are commonly called Scioux—on both sides of the Mississipi about the falls of St. Anthony. 300 men.

9. Wah pa too ta (or Leaf beds live up on each side of the St. Peters below Yellow Wood river 150 men.

10. Sisatoone 200 men on the heads of the St. Peters. [*Above the line:* see Feby. 28. 1805.][77]

The original seats of the Scious were on the Mississipi above & below St. Peters & on St. Peters. A numerous tribe—being the first to learn the use of fire arms they conquered or drove westward their weaker neighbors & are now scattered over their conquered territories. The language is similar thro' the tribes who are acquainted with each other. They meet annually on the river Jacques—those on the Mississipi trading with those on the Missouri. (Hennepin[78] & Carver mention these Scioux.)

76. Jonathan Carver (1710–80), explorer, author of *Travels through the interior parts of North America* (London, 1778).

77. This enumeration, virtually identical to the one in BIDDLE, 1:61, 62, is quite different from the one Clark used in his journal entry of 31 Aug. 1804 (JOURNALS, 1:132–33). The Biddle listing represents Clark's understanding of the Sioux as of 1810.

78. Louis Hennepin (1640–1701?), Franciscan Recollect friar who explored in North America and whose publications are subject to much correction. He wrote *Description de la Louisiane* (Paris, 1682), *Nouveau voyage* (Utrecht, 1696), and *Nouvelle découverte* (Utrecht, 1697).

[*Above the line:* to come in at 13 Novr. 1804.] Farther on to the north between the Assiniboin river & the Missouri are the two tribes or bands of *Assiniboin Menatopa* of 200 men on the rivérre à Souris or Mouse river—and Assiniboin called Gens de Fee on both sides of White Earth river of 250 men.

Still beyond these wandering on the heads of the Milk, Porcupine & Marthy's river are the Assiniboin called Big Devils of 450 men.

Farther North West on the north side of the Askaw[79] is another band of Assiniboins of 500 men and on the north fork of Saskashawan river another band of Assiniboin (Stone Scioux) of 200 men. [*Above* "(*Stone Sioux*)": West.] These two bands may be considered as roving on the Saskashawan.

A common language designates these as the descendants of or detachments from the Scioux—they say that the Scioux are their relations, the Scioux altho' often at war with them still acknowledge them as connected by blood with their nation.

(See McKenzie's Account of the Stone Indians.)

Aug. 31. 1804 Supt. [Supposition?] The name half man probably arose from the modesty of the warrior who when complimented on his exploits would say I am no warrior I am only a half man &c.[80]

12 Octr. 1804. The Ricaras. They are colonies of Pawnees who emigrated from that nation. They formerly lived on the Missouri below the Chayenne thence a part of them emigrated to the neighborhood of the Mandans with whom they were in alliance,* a war breaking out between them & the Mandans they came down the river about 1798 & fixed at their present position. They were seen 20 odd years ago by Mr. Shoter [*corrected to:* Chouteau] of Louisville when they lived below the Chayenne in a number of villages. In this new settlement the inhabitants of the villages who had first emigrated kept together in two villages forming what may be considered the Ricaras proper. The third village was composed of those remnants of the different villages who had escaped the war. As their village was composed of nine different tribes of Ricaras, a difference of pronunciation & some difference of language may be discovered between them & the Ricaras proper. The two lower villages about 150 men each—the upper 300 men.

15 Octr. Ricara women better looking than the Scioux—both are lech[er]ous and the men by means of interpreters found no difficulty in getting women. This without the husbands knowledge—the women

79. "Askaw or Bad river a fork of the Saskashawan" (JOURNALS, 6:106).
80. In the narrative, p. 59, Biddle alters this passage from a mere speculation of Clark's to an actual occurrence at the council: ". . . it was explained to have its origin, probably, in the modesty of the chief," etc.

desire it to be kept secret—the husbds. &c. give wives & sisters to strangers. Anecdote of York man afraid of him.

14 Novr. 1804. For the Knistenaux see McKenzie.

Note the *Fall Indians* of McKenzie are a branch of the Minitarees: speaking the same language.

The Knistenaux & Algonquins are bands of Chippeways.

The *Stone* Indians of McKenzie are Assiniboins.

5th Jany. 1805. Buff[alo]e Dance—a dance for the benefit of the old men. They, about the time Buffe. is scarce, appoint a man to harangue village saying buffe. is far off & they must have a feast to bring them back—name a certain night & place for it. The young married men prepare provisions (a platter) pipe & tobacco which they take to the feast—their wives accompy. them with nothing on except a robe or mantle round them—feast in a house—the old men assemble first seat thems[elves] in a ring on skins cross legged around a fire in the middle of the house. They have before them a sort of small doll dressed like a woman—when the young men & their [wives] arrive the young man chooses the old one whom he means to favor—& to whom he gives the provisions—the old men eat—after which the young man gives the old man a lighted pipe & smokes with him—the [young man] then asks the old man in a whining tone to do him honor by indulging himself with his wife which he brings up to him—the old man follows the woman out of the door. After smoking a particular o.m. appointed for the purpose takes the image in his arms carries her out of doors lies down on it with the appearance of copulation. This is the signal for the young men who are in the rear of the circle with their wives behind them to lead them up to o.m. naked except the robe. The woman arrived out of doors unfolds her robe lies down & invites & receives his embraces. Sometimes the o.m. can scarcely walk. If the old man wants to get a present from husband goes only to the door—the wife informs the husband who sends for a robe & some articles of dress & throws at the feet of the old man & begs that he will not despise or disgrace him, but return to his wife. If present insufficient still lingers till increased by husband. If he receives it he is bound to go. The o.m. if he cannot do the substantial service must go thro' the forms which saves the honor of the parties. This ceremony over—the o.m. smoke together & the y.m. dance together. Indian women do not dance together ever. White men are always considered as o.m. & are generally preferred by the Squaws because they will give probably some present and for other obvious reasons.[81]

81. In the narrative, pp. 150–51, Biddle describes this erotic dance in Latin.

13 Jany. When the Mandans go out in a body to hunt, the game is divided. When a single one kills any thing—those of his neighbors send a Squaw for some. She comes sits down—without saying any thing—the hint is understood & part given to her without pay.

17 Feby. The Sioux & roving tribes (except the Sioux of the St. Peters) raise no corn—only the Mandans Ricaras & Minnetarees Osage Kanzas Ottoes Pawnees Mahars raise corn. The rovers not but live chiefly on buffaloe.

22d Feby. 1805. The nations sometimes choose one of a different tribe a 2d or 3d chief (adopting them) but never a 1st chief.

10 May 1805. The Ahnahawa's as they call themselves are called Wattasoons by the Mandans—by the Fr: Soulier Noir or Shoe Indians—their village is Mahaha.

9 March 1805. In this interview with Capt. Lewis the Borgne said that some foolish young men of his nation had informed him that there was a black man in the party & wished to know if it was true. The negro was brought up. The Borgne was astonished—examined him closely—spit on his hand & rubbed to in order to rub off the paint. The negro pulled off the hand[kerchie]f from his head & shewed his hair—on which The Borgne was convinced that he was of a different species from the whites.

April 9th. The lava is the boiled earth hardened by exposure &c. Exbt. of pumice Stone.

April 14th. Pumice Stones coming down the Little Missouri. Lepage the Frenchm. who joined us at the Mandans & who had come down the L. Missouri says hills all up there are burnt as on Missi. No other volcanic appearance there.

Assiniboins sell their daughters and wives to traders & instances are known of their taking their own daughters for their own wives.

April 15. The waters & drains Capt. Clark saw are the first sources of the Mouse river which take the rise from the high lands on the banks of the Missouri—& thence go to the Winipeg—hills nigh the Missouri narrow bottom between, on the other side not one mile from river these streams begin.

April 29. Antelopes destroyed by their curiosity—when they first see the hunter they run for ½ mile ahead in a straight line—if he lies on his belly & lifts up his hat, arm, & foot, the animal curious to see the object, returns on a trot, & sometimes goes & comes 2 or 3 times, till within reach of the rifle. They leave their party to go & look at a wolf, who then seizes them.

May 29. "More timber" &c. Here we seem to have passed the

[539]

ridge of hills of the Côte Noir[82] & arrive in a plain open country &c. A great deal of beaver on the Judith which rises in the Rock Mountains *with* the Shell & *near* the Rochejaune rivers.

"Indian woman." She had been taken by Minitarees from the Snake Indians on the Rock Mountns.—who sold her as a slave to Chaboneau who married her & by whom he had a son. She was taken into the party with her husband at the Mandans as an interpr. She understood Snake & translated into Minitaree which she had learnt as well as her husband who translated to us.

May 29. At Thompson creek & Bull Creek below Judith's River seem to terminate the last ridges of the Black Mountain—the hills where are the large walls are comparatively small.

Sunday. The difference between the Missouri & Maria's the first of which is tolerably clear & the latter turbid very muddy is occasioned by the formers running thru a hilly ridge & the bed is a coarse gravel up to the mountains while Maria's river goes thro' a level open rich soil and subdivided into many small streams rising within the mountains. The Missouri being less divided into Branches.

Oct. 31. 1805. From falls nearly to Great Shoot[83] there is not much descent. A little above the shoot river widens is gentle & becomes like a pond with trees or stumps on each side where there appear to have been flats on the north Side near the Islands the mountain seems to have been undermined & fallen in upon the islands, thro' large rocks into the current. On the South Side the mountain comes to the waters edge but has not the same appearance of having fallen in. These rocks continue in the water for 7 miles from Strawberry to Brant island.

Novr. 12. 1805. Dexterity of Indians in canoe. The canoe contains 4 oarsmen & a Steersman—generally woman. The oarsmen sit two and two upon their knees or sitting on their heels. When the waves are high, and the boat is going on one side, the man sitting to windward with his paddle, steadies the boat by throwing his body towards the upper side & catches the water by sinking his long paddle very deep with the same stroke sendg. on the canoe.[84]

Novr. 15. Vancouver wrong in placing an island off Cape Adams— there is a shoal—Qu. if Vanr. mentions a shoal or an Island. Haleys bay badly put in in Vancouver. The course pretty much as he says

82. The Black Hills, of which Lewis and Clark had only a vague notion.
83. For "Shoot" read "Chute."
84. Not in the narrative or journals; more applicable to Clark's entry of 11 Nov. (JOURNALS, 3:215) than of 12 Nov.

of the river. No islands off the mouth. Capt. Clark on hill at least 1500, saw 50 or 60 miles in clear weather yet saw no island. Great many *rocks* 15 or 18 miles Southerly of Point Adams but no island.[85]

Novr. 15. No Chinnooks suffered to come into camp. This spread about, & whenever a man wanted to come into camp—he would call out "No *Chinnook*.[86]

O   hole

.   .   pins   the two pins

O   checker

placed about 1 foot apart, they roll about 10 feet—if go into hold thro' the pins—win—if thro' pins not in hole—not lose—if outside of pins—lose. Checker about 1 inch diamr.

14 Jany. 1806. This trade is carried on chiefly by N. Engl[ande]rs. They trade to the *E. Indies,* carry from the U.S. trinkets old arms &c. with which they trade for what they can get of sea otter & elks skins particularly—these they take (the elk Skin) further north & exchange for Sea Otter which they take to the East Indies. (Qu. if China.)

Feby. 1. Vancouver & Cook both wrong about images inlaid with men's teeth (Cook) or Otter teeth (Vanr.). It is with Shells. The shells white of a small muscle so that when driven in the outside resembles teeth. [*Small sketch of shell here.*]

Feby. 15. The Indians in the Rocky Mountns. near on the other side geld their horses & take particular pains—the horses below the mouth of Lewis's river not, at least not so common.

Feby. 15. The best route would be up Missouri to the falls—thence by land across the Rocky mountains to Kobolieskit Creek down which to Clarks river where Trav. Rest Creek falls in—up that creek to its forks then by land across the hills to Kooskooske—down that to Columbia.

Until we came to the falls we saw no one who had seen the ocean —above the falls it is considered as a rem: circ. to have visited them.

Those who had seen the ocean described it by its roaring sound, and a gesture representing its waves.

4 Sept. 1806. Floyds grave. A chief of one of the Sioux bands encamped near it, lost one of his sons. He had Floyds grave opened & his son put in with Floyd for the purpose of accompanying him to

85. There is no criticism of Vancouver's cartography at this place in the narrative, but Clark complains of it in the JOURNALS, 3:226.

86. The use of "No Chinook" as a password is not in the narrative or journals.

[541]

the other world believing the white man's future state was happier than that of the Savages.[87]

April 3. 1806. The Clackstar also carry on trade with the Killamucks.

April 11. 1806. Omit the acct. of tomahawk, biscuit[?] Swippeton &c. Questionable.[88]

April 6. 1806. The Multnomah nation is placed on the Wappatoe Island opposite the mouth of Multh. river and the inlet which forms the island. The 1. Cathlacomahtups—the 2. Cathlanaquiahs, 3. the Clahinnatas. the 4. Cathlacumups—the 5. Clanaminumums—the 1st & 3 of which are on the inlet, the 2d 4 & 5th on the island, are so many tribes of the Mult[nomah]. None of them have a distinguished chief except the Multnomahs. Above on the creek falling into the inlet is the *Clackstar*[89] nation (1200 souls) forms a separate people. On the Northern side of the river the Chotos & Quathlapottle as also the Cathlahaws lower down (who have their old village on Deer Island) may be considered as tribes of the Multnomah—as may indeed the Clackstar nation (the houses are all alike—the neighbors speak of the Multnomah nation as great &c.)

From the mouth of the Columbia to the Multnomahs, embracing the Chinnooks—the Clatsops, the Wakiacums & the Cathlamahs speak the same language [*above the line:* understand each other]. The Chiltz[90] & the N.W. Indians speak a different language. The Killamucks[91] speak a different language from them all.

There is a difference between the Clatsops & the Skilloots a little diff. which becomes greater between Skilloots & Wappatoe Islds. inhabs. & still greater between them & those till the rapids. The [. . .] still resemble that of the Chilucketiqua's above the great rapids where the clucking style begins but tho' different, still all intelligible to each other.

From the great rapids to the neighborhood of the great narrows on thro' the Mountains to the beginning of the plain Country the Chilucketiquaws embraces several bands. (Smackshops A small difference or rather a great similarity between the Echeloots & the

87. Not in the narrative or journals. It is not clear whether the grave of Floyd was disturbed before Lewis and Clark came back past the site in Sept. 1806, or later.

88. This incident about a biscuit alleged by an Indian to have come from a white trader named Swippeton is not in the narrative, but is told in the JOURNALS, 4:268.

89. Also called the Clatskanie, and now extinct. At one time they occupied the prairies along the Chehalis River in Washington, but by 1910 had been reduced to three persons (SWANTON, 458).

90. The Chehalis Indians.

91. The Tillamook Indians.

Chilluckitiquaws. But beyond the falls an entire difference, so much so that the Echeeloots language is quite different from that of the Eneeshur their neighbors above the falls, not 8 miles from each other (The Echeeloots are between the great narrows & the Falls.)

The *Shahalas* embrace four tribes two above & two below the great rapids—& the little colony of Neckokee near the Multnomah where they gather Wappatoe.

(The Echeeloots have a near resemblance in language to the Chilluckitequaws. They also have the clucking tho' not so much as the Chilws.

Trade (See small book). The people near the Rocky Mts. [*above the line:* Choponneesh &c.] bring a few skins &c. for robes (which they either kill themselves or procure by trafficking horses for them with the Tushepaws) bear grass (white) on the mountains. Down to the lower Indians about the falls (the great emporium) & exchange with them for Wappatoe, Pounded fish &c. &c. To this market the Indians of the Columbian plains brings mats, silk grass, rushes, root bread called chapelell. The Chilluckitiquaws & Eleeshoots are the carriers between the great falls & the Indians of Wappatoo valley—who bring wappatoo & the fish peculiarly. Lower down berries & trinkets from the whites & sea coast fish are brought to the market.

The Chopoonish do not bring so many skins as they [do] horses & grass & peculiar roots as Quamash. Those at the falls have a peculiar animal the skin of which is prized below.

Those in the Columbian plains which extend from the falls to the Rock Ms. are the most wretched of all the Inds.

April 28, 1806. The Shoshonee prisoner had been taken from that part of the Shoshonee nation residing to the South on the Multnomah & sometimes visiting the heads of the Wallawallah creek. Our Shoshonee belonged to the mountains on the other side near the head of the Missouri. Their being able to understand each other by means of a common language convinced that the Shoshonee of Both sides of the Rock Mountns. are the same.[92]

May 10. 1806. Generally the Indians between the Rock Mountains & the Falls—that is those who had had no intercourse with the whites were more [. . .] & hospitable than those below, i.e.: those who had known & been corrupted by European connexion [*above the line:* Chopunnish]. The chiefs above the falls more respected &

92. Sacagawea's ability to converse with the Shoshoni prisoners is in the narrative and journals, but the explorers' resulting speculation about the relationship of the two Shoshonean bands is not.

had greater influence than those below. The Wallawalla chief the greatest we met with.

June 17. 1806. "Travelers Rest cr. & as our horses who might have perhaps reached that place could not have sustained the journey should we lost the route"—The reason of our having no guide was that the Indians had declared that the hills were impassable. One of them had attempted & returned we met him. We therefore were safe in leaving our baggage &c. in the mountains—because the Indians would not attempt it again—if they did their only route was by where we were—& as to the Instruments they were safe from touch because they were conceived to be great medicine & therefore sacred. Some of our papers only left.

July 22. 1806. The reason why it was wished that Maria's river should extend to 50° north was that as our boundary is to be formed by a line due west from lake of the Woods to the Mississi., & the Mississi. river not answering that purpose it was hoped that a river parallel to it would go far enough north to satisfy the treaty boundary the lake of Wds. being 49° 37″ at its northern extremity.

13 Sept. 1806. We had among us several men who had been accustomed to drink a great deal—others who had not—this last observed that the liquor seemed as it always did—the others after a long privation were perfectly weaned from it, & did not care any thing about it. *But they* after relapsed into their old habits.

Among Snake Indians in one of the towns a Snake Indian supposed to have been killed having been wounded & scalped by the Minnetarees of F. de Prairie arrived having recovered on field of battle & escaped to woods. He brought with him two large rattle snakes whose teeth he had extracted. They were tamed by him wrapped themselves round his body—bosom &c.—knew him—boys amused thems[elve]s with playing with them & fretting them with sticks—the name of the Snake Indians got by their being remarkable for taming snakes of which they have many in their country.

For bite they use a poltice of the plant (see Mandan—Haney's account) applied externally & accompanied by heat to excite perspiration.

23 Aug. 1805. Here at Berry my guide shewed me a road which went up Berry Cr. & passed over to a large river which ran to the North on which Indians lived of another nation. Not perfectly understand & went on till night. He now informed. We went on & came to another road which cut off as he had told us a great bend of the river on this we saw another road coming in from the

N. down a small creek which we were following. The road here forked one from the N. & the other down to Lewis R[ive]r then in sight. Here he told me Indians came down this Cr. from N. (he mentioned their name Tushepaws) & that they came to fish on Lewis R[ive]r having no Salmon on their river [*above the line: down to the fish wiers*]. I now got him to make a map in the sand. He made the two roads we had passed lead N. to two forks of the same large river Clark's riv. He had been to these Tushepaws, & had seen Indians who had come across the mountains. The next day he said we could go no further this way we were on without passing often the river, but might take one of the two roads we had seen. I came back to the forks of the road where he made me a new map more particular which convinced me that he knew there was a way from where Lewis's party was (Shoshonees) to the great river he mentioned without coming the route I had taken which was impracticable for horses—that he had gone from Clarks river with the Tushepaws over to another river (which must be Koskooskee) to fish where he had met Indians from other side of m. He promised to go & shew it to me. I returned to where I had left my men & sent on my guide to Capt. Lewis & he confirmed to our Ind. woman what he had told me by signs. The Shoshonees all opposed it, they said there was a river but that the road led over to the fish wier, but not across the mountains. The guide persisted & we determined to try.[93]

Compare McKenzie's vocabularies of Indians on the heads of the Columbia with ours at junction of it with Lewis's & see if same nation.

Almost all the people whom we saw west of the Ry. Mounts. flatten their heads more or less. The Chopunniesh nation & Shoshonees confine the practice to the women, but it extends to many of the men even as we approach the falls & below that universal. It is done in infancy the child is laid on board & corded down its head flat on the board over this a piece of board is fixed by strings so as to form a lid which is put up or down at pleasure.

The Flatheads were a much inferior race to those where the practice did not prevail—understanding, all the qualities [*end of manuscript*]

93. Biddle works most of this paragraph into his narrative, but it is much less fully dealt with in the journals. An addition in Clark's hand to the journal entry of 23 Aug. may have been made while Clark and Biddle were reviewing the material, and at the time Biddle made these notes.

327. Clark to Henry Dearborn

Sir   Fincastle 15th April 1810

I must request the favor of you to inform me, if the *estimate* of expenditures for the Indian department in Louisiana for the year 1810 meets your approbation; or such parts as you may think proper to autherise.

Since my return from Washington, I have been closely employed makeing such arrangements of my journal, and Memorandoms, as are necessary for the edition. Mr. Nicholis Biddle (the gentleman who writes the Naritive) left us yesterday. He has been with me nearly three weeks takeing such Notes as will enable him with the explanations made on such parts of the journals as required it, to proceed without dificulty. Such parts as relate to science only, have been selected and sent on by Mr. Biddle to Doctr. Barton, and shall place in his hands the specimens of plants &c.

In a fiew days I shall set out with my family to St. Louis and shall proceed on without makeing any unnecessary delay. I have the honor to be with every sentiment of the highest respect and esteem Your Obt. H. Sert.

WM. CLARK

ALS, RC (DNA, RG 107, C-105).

327a. The Nicholas Biddle Prospectus

[c. May 1810]

PROPOSALS

By C. & A. CONRAD & Co.

FOR PUBLISHING

THE HISTORY

OF THE

Expedition of Captains Lewis and Clarke,

THROUGH

The Continent of North America.

Performed during the years 1804, 1805 and 1806, by order of the Government of the United States

———————

The appearance of the Work, which was announced for publication nearly three years ago, has been retarded by a variety of causes, among which the melancholy fate of Captain Lewis is already known and lamented by the nation. This delay, although it has disappointed the public expectation, and given rise to several imperfect accounts of the journey, may be the less regretted, as the residence of both Captains Lewis and Clarke in Louisiana, has enabled them greatly to extend and mature their knowledge of the country which they describe. All their original papers and journals, together with the curious and scientific objects procured by them, are now carefully collected; and from these materials, improved by personal communication with Capt. Clarke and others who accompanied him, the detailed and authentic history of the expedition will be offered to the public.

Of this enterprize, planned by our own government, and achieved through great dangers by our own countrymen, little need be said to attract the attention of the American people. The sources of the Columbia and Missouri rivers, which had eluded all former research, have been fully explored, and a line of intercourse—the future path of civilization—connects the Atlantic and Pacific oceans. Vast regions are now opened, to reward the spirit of commercial adventure, and to receive, hereafter, the overflowing tide of our own population. Entire nations, varying at once from ourselves and from each other, have been revealed to the curiosity of the civilized world, while science is enriched by new and valuable acquisitions.

It cannot yet be ascertained into what compass these abundant materials may be compressed. The work will however consist of two parts:

First, the narrative of the Journey, comprizing minute descriptions of every interesting object relative to the country through which the travellers passed, or the different nations whom they visited. This will be accompanied by a large and elegant map of the whole route and the countries adjacent, from the most accurate information. Engravings, by the first artists, of the cataracts of the Missouri, as well as of the falls, narrows, and rapids of the Columbia; and a number of plates illustrative of the persons, dresses, habitations, weapons, utensils, &c. &c. of the most remarkable tribes of Indians, will be interspersed through the work. An itinerary of the route, and an inquiry into the means of rendering the fur trade of North America more beneficial to the United States will also be added. This part of the work will be prepared for the press by a gentleman of this city.

The second part will be devoted to the discoveries, and the information acquired by Captains Lewis and Clarke in the several

[547]

departments of botany, mineralogy and zoology. To which will be annexed, meteorological tables kept with great accuracy during the route, and a new and copious collection of Indian vocabularies. This branch of the work is committed to Dr. BENJAMIN S. BARTON, and will be embellished with engravings of the objects of natural history most worthy of attention. The present arrangement will enable all persons to subscribe for the entire work or either division of it.

The price of the first part, which will consist of two octavo volumes, will be ten dollars, including the map. The second part will be sold at eleven dollars.

Subscriptions received by the Publishers, No. 30, Chesnut street, Philadelphia, and by the principal Booksellers in the United States.

Printed copy (ICHi). No other copies located. The brochure consists of four pages, and in present condition measures 5⅝ by 9⅛ inches. I date it soon after Biddle's return from his visit to Clark in Virginia (see his reference to it in No. 330).

A blank form at the end of the prospectus provides space for subscribers' names.

328. Clark to Benjamin Smith Barton

Louisville Kenty 22th May 1810

Dear Sir: You will have seen Mr. N. Biddle who was with me some time at Fincastle and recved from him a Copy of such part of my journal as I had Copied from the Original, which I hope with the assistance of the specimins and what information the young gentleman who will hand you this letter (Mr. George Shannon) Can give you at sundry times, may enable you to proceed in the Scientific part of my work, which I am extreemly happy to find you are willing to engage in. I have wrote to Mr. Peale requesting him to permit you to discribe all & every of the animals &c. which he has received from the late Lewis and myself. The dreid specimins of plants, I requested Mr. McMahon (when in Phila.) to delivir to Mr. Conrad, who will place them in your hands. I have also requested Mr. McMahon to supply you with living specimins when he may have Two or more— and to give you every opportunity of inspecting them in his Garden &c. On this subject I have instructed Mr. Shannon. I have given Mr. M. a hint about the necessity of making the specimins sacredly private between yourself himself & myself and Mr. Shannon &c. As to my self I can't have the smallest objection to your adding parts of the materials or matter of your own, in the Scientific work,

[548]

by way of notes: or as you mention in your letter to me. The friends or relations of my late Companion make some objection to any thing more than what relates to the discovery &c.

Inclosed is as much as I could Collect of the Origin and present state of Fincastle. As to population, it varies. I waited from the time I recved your letter untill I set out on my journey for a Clear View of the Peaks of *Otter* to make a Drawing for you, the weather being Cloudy & Smokey privented my having a few of any <*thing*> portion of the Mountain and have it in my Powor only to shew You by a line the irregular appearence of the top of those Mountains about that place as they appear from Fincastle.

Mr. George Shannon was with me on the NW. Tour and Can give you information on points which I hope may be useful to you and Mr. Biddle & in the work. This young man is in pursuit of an education and profession by which he may be enabled to make his liveing. His Charretor is without blemish, poss[ess]ing a heart undesguised. He is highly rispected at the University at Lexington where he has been for the two last years. The Friendly advice and attention which you may please to bestow on this young man will be greatfully receved by him, and Confur a great Obligation, on Your Most Obt Hble Svt.

WM. CLARK

ALS, RC (MB). Addressed; endorsed; received 14 Aug. 1810.

329. Clark to Nicholas Biddle

Dear Sir   Louisville May 22nd 1810
This will be handed to you by Mr. George Shannon the young man I spoke to you about, who was with me on the N.W. expedition; he has agreed to go to Philadelphia and give such information relitive to that Tour as may be in his power. This Young Gentleman possesses a sincere and undisguised heart, he is highly spoken of by all his acquaintance and much respected at the Lexington University where he has been for the last two years. Any advice and friendly attentions which you may show to this Young Man will be greatfully acknowledged by him, and Confur an additional obligation on me.

Mr. S. Connections are respectable. Since the misfortune of loseing his leg, he has been studiously employed in persute of an education to enable him to acquire a profession by which he can make an honorable & respectable liveing—he wishes to study Law and practice in the Western Country.

[549]

May I request of you to give him such advice or assistance as may be agreeable & Convenient to you to enable him to prosue those studies while in Phila. Accept my highest respect & Friendship.

WM. CLARK

ALS, RC (DLC—Biddle). Addressed; endorsed.

330. Nicholas Biddle to Clark

Dear Sir,   Philadelphia July 7. 1810

I have delayed writing to you for some time not, as I am sure you will be persuaded from any inattention, but from finding in the progress of my labors I had a number of enquiries to make from you & thinking it would be better to collect them at once than to trouble you with a variety of small matters in detail. I am besides the worst correspondent in the world & the consequence is that although ever since my return to Philadelphia I have been engaged seven or eight and even more hours a day on our work, I could scarcely bring himself [myself] to devote half an hour to any of my friends.

I need not tell you that I arrived safe at this place; that the map[1] was immediately forwarded to Mr. Hassler, and that Dr. Barton received all his papers. On consulting with Mr. Conrad he agreed with me in opinion that it was much better to have a large connected map of the whole route & the adjacent country; than to form an atlas of detached parts. The map can embrace as many degrees of latitude as you think your Indian information will authorize, and on a scale perhaps somewhat larger than that which you have already made, though if you think it would be too laborious or would [invite] the risk of any inaccuracies the present size may be made to answer. It can then be either divided into two parts so as to fold in the work; or given separately if too inconvenient to go into the book. The portages of the Columbia & Missouri[2] we have already & they will form very interesting charts which may be put into the work opposite to the pages which contain a description of them. The only other part which I think it would be well to have on a larger scale than it is contained in the general map is the passage of the Rock mountains. That is, the country comprized between the head of Jefferson's river northward to the point where you struck the Kooskooskee and extending eastward to the falls. As that square is so important a part of your route it would be desirable that it should be shewn very distinctly. In all other respects your present map, on a scale rather larger & diminished or increased as to degrees of latitude as you may judge best, will be quite sufficient.

On my arrival I found that proposals were circulating here for a second edition of Gass's journal,[3] which I thought it best to stop by announcing immediately our work & therefore published the Prospectus.[4] I see also by the English journals that some man in England has printed a sort of account of the expedition compiled from Gass chiefly & from the documents which you & Captain Lewis sent to Congress.[5] The work seems to have met with a favorable reception in England which is a good sign for our own.

I have been very industriously with it, and although I find it occupies much more of my time than I expected & is more laborious, I am by no means discouraged.[6] I rise habitually at 5 O'Clock every morning & by constant exertion feel myself advancing in it. To day I have sent you & ten men up into a bottom to look for wood to make canoes after the unhappy failure of your iron boat; so that you see how far I am. There are in the library here a great number of volumes which I must read in order to be perfectly at home among all the Indians who have ever been in Louisiana, and have sent to France for one or two which could not be procured here. Observing in Dupratz, a work of much interest which he quotes Dumont's Historical memoir of Louisiana, I have sent to France for it & hope it may give much light on the situation of the country as far as it was known before you explored it.

I find that Gass's journal in the original manuscript[7] is also deposited in our library, & at my service. Ordway's which is much better than Gass's is really very useful: & as these two as well as your's & Captain Lewis, and my own notes are all to be examined, in order to leave nothing omitted, the labor is by no means light. But I have my health much better than I expected & therefore hope to get along smoothly at last.

Your map will I suppose be delayed considerably till you hear from Mr. Hassler. We have been looking for Shannon who has not yet arrived, but who is not we trust detained by any misfortune.

I must now begin my catechism of enquiries with which you remember I importuned you not a little when I had the pleasure of seeing you but being desirous of as much accuracy as possible I must get you to give me some information on all these points.[8]

1st. What is the real name & spelling of the Stream called *Sharriton Carta,* and also the *Two Charletons.* Get some of the Frenchmen at St. Louis to put them down exactly as they should be printed. How also do they write the name of the animal which is called a *Braro.*

2. I should like to know, as it is disagreeable to mispell names, what is the name of the trader who built a factory on Cedar island, a Mr. *Lucelle* we have him now.

3. Are the band of the Tetons which you met called by the French *bois roulé* which may allude to their smoking rolled wood, or *bois brulé* burnt woods. It is of some consequence to be accurate & I presume there will be no difficulty in ascertaining it exactly.

4. Are you perfectly sure as to the name of the Chayenne nation. The French have been in the habit of calling the Indian tribes after some animals, and the resemblance of sounds would incline us to believe that the true name might be Chien or Dog Indians. Mr. Mackay you observed thought that the name was Chayenne. It would be well not to err & if you can get any information in addition to what you have it might render us more safe.

5. The Baker's Ovens Islands are written down four le tourtre. See if this be not incorrect. I am not certain whether you have any where mentioned the Indian name of the Columbia. If you recollect it let me have it; though possibly as I have not yet got so far on our route it may be in the journals & escaped my memory.

6. Have the Mandans or any other nation you met any particular mode of reckoning time such as week month year, beyond the mere differences of cold & heat. This might be curious as well as their mode of counting distances, measures &c.

7. Are there two Turtle mountains one on the north the other to the South of the Mandans; they are so marked on the map, but do you know any thing of them particularly, for they are but slightly mentioned in the journal.

8. You took a memorandum as to the speeches of the Indians. I have seen in the papers two songs taken from the Osage Chiefs by Dr. Mitchell, and if you have or can get any well authenticated translations of those kind of things they would make the work more interesting. A very literal & close translation would of course be preferable.

9. In addition to this if you have any information as to any system of signs by which you were able to communicate with the Indians, or which enables different tribes to converse together I should like to have it. To you who understand all these things so well, they do not perhaps appear curious because they are familiar. But in our towns, and in Europe too where we know nothing of Indians every little matter is a subject that excites curiosity. Thus for instance with what particular gestures &c. you would make an Indian whom

you were to meet understand all your common inquiries of routes &c. &c.

10. With the Mandans you are in constant habits of Trading, and therefore know them well. This will at once enable us to be accurate, & will give a reason why we should be so since a mistake would be more readily perceived. I wish therefore you would give me any particulars which you happen to remember as to their government, manners &c. &c. Have they for instance in their cultivation a common field, or does each man's squaw tend a spot for the use of each particular family. The number of squaws, &c. &c. Am I perfectly right when I say that the three nations, who reside together are the two villages of Mandans one village (called Mahahas) of Ahnahaways, and two of Minnetarees. I observe in the papers that Mr. Chouteau has returned to St. Louis. He perhaps can say something.

11. Describe if you can a game among the Mandans which is mentioned only in Ordway's journal, but which a gentleman told me Capt. Lewis described to him as resembling billiards very much.

12. The name by which the Minnetarees call the Muscle Shell river is left in blank. Do you remember it?

13. Do you know what is the Indian name of Medicine river.

14. What is in fact the Indian name for medicine or Great medicine. I should like to know that as well as

15th. Everything you know as to the nature of the Great medicine, & all other superstitions—such as the Osage story about a beaver, witches, jugglers & any matter of that sort.

16. The name by which every tribe of Indians call the Missouri if they call it differently, or if there is but one name what is it.

17. In the English review to which I allude, complaint is made that Gass mentions buffaloe paths but does not say what they are. Tell me every thing about them. Are they paths by which the buffaloe go to water, large or small—very numerous, very long—in the plains—by the rivers? &c. &c.

18. Have you heard any thing else of the old fortifications near the Osage, or elsewhere on this side of that of which you made a draft.

19. Give me all the information which you can as to the trade of the Western Country & all that you would wish to be made public as to the nature extent & estimated advantages & profits of your Fur Company.

20. At 5 July 1804 we speak of the remains of the 2d Kanzas village. If you recollect describe what remains these are.

When you have leisure & inclination I wish you would let me hear

[553]

from you on all these matters[9] & add anything else which you may learn for I suppose you increase every day your knowledge of Indian affairs. There are you know a great many things of very little consequence, but still it is of some importance not to be wrong when we speak of them.

If ever you reach this far through my letter, you will perceive that when I do begin it is difficult to stop me. I hope however you will not imitate me in deferring your answer, & that you will follow my example in the length of it. In the mean time I remain with my best respects to Mrs. Clarke, & my warmest wishes for your fine little son Yr's very sincerely

NICHOLAS BIDDLE

ALS, SC (DLC—Biddle). Reply is No. 336.

1. Apparently this map has not survived; it is not the one used in the Biddle edition.

2. An undated note in the Clark Papers (MoSHi) reads: "The two Drawings of the Falls of the Columbia and Missouri are in the possession of Mr. Murray and Mr. Lawson Engravers. Mr. Lawson lives in Pine Street between 8th and 9th Streets. Mr. Lawson will direct Mr. Clark to Mr. Murray." The men named are George Murray (d. 1822) and Alexander Lawson (1773–1846).

3. An edition was issued from Philadelphia by Mathew Carey in 1810. In the same year, a French version appeared, entitled: *Voyage des capitaines Lewis et Clarke, depuis l'embouchure du Missouri, jusqu'à l'entrée de la Colombia dans l'Océan Pacifique; fait dans les années 1804, 1805, et 1806, par ordre du gouvernement des Etats-Unis . . . par Patrice Gass . . .* (Paris, 1810).

4. See No. 327a.

5. The so-called apocryphal Lewis and Clark, entitled: *The travels of Capts. Lewis & Clarke, from St. Louis, by way of the Missouri and Columbia rivers, to the Pacific Ocean; performed in the years 1804, 1805, & 1806, by order of the government of the United States. Containing delineations of the manners, customs, religion, &c. of the Indians, compiled from various authentic sources, and original documents, and a summary of the statistical view of the Indian nations, from the official communication of Meriwether Lewis . . .* (London, 1809). A Philadelphia edition was published by Hubbard Lester in the same year. The book was a composite, based partly on Gass but also containing two of Clark's letters; an account of certain Indian tribes by Mackenzie; an abridged version of Lewis's "Statistical view"; some extracts from Jefferson's *Message from the President;* an essay of Jonathan Carver's published without credit to the author; and some miscellany. As the years wore on, and no "official" Lewis and Clark narrative appeared, public demand brought forth still another edition of the spurious work, this one "by William Fisher, Esq.," entitled: *An interesting account of the voyages and travels of Captains Lewis and Clark, in the years 1804, 1805, and 1806; giving a faithful description of the River Missouri and its source—of the various tribes of Indians through which they passed—manners and customs— soil—climate—commerce—gold and silver mines—animal and vegetable pro-*

ductions interspersed with very entertaining anecdotes . . . (Baltimore, 1812). There were two Baltimore editions in 1812 and another in 1813; also a Philadelphia edition in 1812, and others issued from Dayton, Ohio, as late as 1840 and 1851.

6. But he sounded pretty discouraged three months later in a letter to Edward Watts: "Dr. Barton & myself have undertaken to publish the papers of Capts. Lewis & Clarke, but as the chief labor falls upon myself, I find it excessively troublesome, & for some months past have been obliged to devote to it a most persevering & undivided attention" (5 Oct. 1810, DLC—Biddle).

7. A curious statement, for the manuscript journal kept by Gass has not been found. By "our library" he probably means the library of the American Philosophical Society, but he might also mean that of the Library Company of Philadelphia.

8. Clark answers some of the following inquiries in No. 336.

9. As a reminder to Clark, Biddle had jotted down in one of the journals (No. 4, MoSHi) a short list of desiderata—probably when he had visited Clark in the spring:

"Mem. Enquire at St. Louis into the Situation & number of the Crow Indians &c. which, if either, of their bands is called the Paunch Indians.

"Also for some Indian speeches.

"Story of the Osage on the subject of the Beaver.

"Send to Mr. Biddle every thing authentic & not yet published on the subject of the Fur Trade."

Clark had added to this:

> Get an Indian Song
> About the Fur Trade
> Fur Compy.

331. Nicholas Biddle to David Bailie Warden

Dear Warden,   Philadelphia July 7th 1810

. . . .

I am about to give you some trouble for which I know not how to apologize. You will before this have heard of the death of Captain Lewis who went to the Pacific & who was on his way to the seat of government, intending to devote himself to composition of his travels. On his decease application was made to me to become the editor which with my usual indolence I declined, but after much more persuasion than the subject was worth I have consented to compose the work in conjunction with Dr. Barton who takes charge of the Specimens of natural history which they collected. I find it exceedingly troublesome, for not a word was prepared for the press by Captain Lewis & the papers are very voluminous. In the course of the undertaking I am desirous of consulting a work which is not to be procured

[555]

here but which is no doubt common at Paris. It is called, as I find its name in a translation of Dupratz "An historical memoir of Louisiana by Mr. Dumont." [1] You will oblige me much if in the course of your enquiries you could procure me that book, or indeed any other relative to the early history of that country, particularly of upper Louisiana which the French once possessed & therefore no doubt described & will point out how I may reimburse you whatever they may cost.

. . . . .

God bless you in haste Yrs. ever,

N. BIDDLE

ALS, SC (DLC—Biddle Family Papers).
1. *Memoires sur la Louisiane, composés sur les memoires de M. Dumont* (Paris, 1753). The translator of the English version of Du Pratz cited Dumont in footnotes, and also added a brief section quoting him on tobacco, indigo, and mining in Louisiana. (DAVIS (1) discusses both works and the relationship of the two authors.) Biddle repeated his request for the book in a letter of 9 Aug. 1810, saying that he was eager to obtain anything on the subject of French settlements in Upper Louisiana (DLC—Biddle). Warden was vitally interested in the progress of the work, and inquired about it frequently.

332. Ferdinand Rudolph Hassler to [Robert Patterson]

Dear Sir.   Schenectady 12th August 1810

Some few days ago I received a letter from Mr. Vaughan by which I am very sorry to be informed that he is considerably unwell, I hope it will not be of serious consequences and only transitory, I shall be happy to hear soon of his entire recovery.

This circumstance obliges me to disturb You with these lines, relating to the calculations of Capt. Lewis Voyage of which Mr. Vaughan sent me lately the chart, which I compared now with the results before obtained and was now some time ingaged in scrutinising the whole as far as my means reached. I could not go at it before because of the severe sickness of my younger girl who is now recovered from death and in full restablishment, after more than 2 month's severe sickness.

I had many preparatory Calculations to make to ascertain different points relating to the Elements of the calculation, in calculating backwards from the circumstances & times given what ought to have been observed, so the Err:s Ind:as were otherwise indicated than usually in Math: Obs: the needle was red once at the north, once at south

[556]

point &c. &c. After this having made what I could without a chart, which had been promised in the begining, together with the other journals (having only one, in a fair copy, which I see has many faults in writing) I am now in the following difficulties relating the positions of some interesting points.

1. The point of Departure, Mouth of River Dubois opposite Missouri Ct. Lewis determines Lat: 38° 55′ 20″ Longit: 89° 57′ 45″ and so I admitted it till I had the chart. But this gives long: about 93° 11′ to this place and sets it opposite Illinois west of the Mississipi. A large map of Hutchins 1778 [1] an other large map copy of Arrowsmith &c. what I could consult gives this place about 2° more west Long: than the confluent of Ohio in Missisipi, this point is determined by Mr. Ferrere[2] 89° 06′ which will not agree well together. I therefore tryed to conclude backwards from further points which gives me as follows

From No. 14 two means of results from (Distances give   97° 11′ 15″

  98   14   15

The chronometrical determination would give   95   53   55
Calculating as the observations were intended for
and taking the point of departure as he sets it down.
The differences   1   17   20

  2   20   20

from the results of the (Dist: would give   91   15   05
by the addition to the Departure, Longitude of this
Dep: 92   18   05

which would place this point nearer the determination of other maps and the chart itself. So does also the comparison taken from No. 3 by a similar operation; the Departure is = 91 07 05. These results fall all between Chart & numerical Datas given and pretty near the commun maps. But C. L. sais that his Long. is result of 7 Sets of (Dist: "and may be depended on with safety to 2 or 3 minutes of a *degree*." He gives the chronometrical determination 90° 00′ 20″ wherefore the chronometers rate of going was determined at the mouth of the Ohio, with which I just compared it. Which result would you advise me to adopt? The latitude is in the Chart some minutes more south but upon that I think is not to see (it agrees *there* about with Hutchins, & Arrowsmith copy).

2. My journal in hands goes till Fort Mandan No. 51. The latit: of it Capt. L. gives by mean 47° 21′ 04″ but the Chart 46° 15′ about where lais here the error, I must think in the Chart because C. L. has different results which I calculated over and found only such dif-

ferences as show me that he was not full equal to me in his prop. parts &c. The longitude he determines by the ☽ Eclipse 14th Jany. 1805. The two ends only =

$$6^h \; 37^m \; 31^s = 99° \; 22' \; 45''$$
$$6 \quad 37 \quad 47 = 99 \quad 26 \quad 45$$

But taking the time he indicates for the observation and supposing it corrected (therefore reduced, as he has made the calcul.) I find there a mistake of just 1^h which gives reduced for these two results when compared with the nautical Almanac

Long $\begin{smallmatrix} 114 \; 22 \; 30 \\ 114 \; 27 \; 30 \end{smallmatrix}$ as You will find from $\begin{smallmatrix} 13^h \; 41^m \; 30^s \\ 14 \quad 39 \quad 10 \end{smallmatrix}$ which he gives for

the times of observation, without saying if true, mean, or watch, time. The Chart places this point nearly 103°. The Lunar Distances give somewhat diverging results above 114°—but I will calculate them once more, having discovered the above error, with the new suppositions for the full accuracy of the prop: parts. What Do You advise me to relay upon here? For the intermediate parts I have no mean of comparison till I have further Elements; when I come to the south Sea I have some again, by Cooks and Portlof & Dixons Voyages,[3] for his Chart leads him just about 1° & 2° south of Nutka sound and between two determined points of C. Cook.

I have constructed a Chart Projection upon the principles which I mentioned You on occasion of that of Mr. Garnett, for the Lat. 38°—48° upon the Elements from the last measurements compared

&c. &c. in the scale $\dfrac{1}{2,000,000}$ where I could therefore make all con

structions with accuracy & ease. In less than a fourthnight I shall have pillaged fully the journal I have in hand and to do more I want the subsequent journ: and if a chart is wished containing all determinations and a sketch which Gen. Clarke can then fill with more particulars if wished, I want also the journal of Courses and bearings over the whole, this might give me besides this the, allmost absolutely necessary, advantage of determining those intermediate points of this journal, for which I have not Elements enough; which are numerous, and correct others, or decide on the choice of the observations.

But I should wish to have the originals if possible, be they how they will, they will direct far better than fair copies, which are never faultless. The work is tedious in itself and much more when the very elements must on all possible supposition be tried. I have made more than double the calculations for this purpose than for what will appear in the results.

We have now about 4 weeks more vacancies which would be the

[558]

most convenient time for me to give to this work. I should therefore wish to have it as soon as possible, with directions upon the way in which one wishes the result, if map & Astron: Result, or only the last. If I had had all means, above, I should have done with it about 3. years ago. I shall make as much haste as possible to compleat the whole, when I have the other Elements.

Pray to give our best compliments to Mrs. Patterson and family, and accept my best wishes for Your constant welfare. I remain allways with perfect esteem and sincere attachment Dear Sir Your devoted St.

F. R. HASSLER

ALS, RC (DLC—Biddle). Endorsed. The letter is endorsed by Biddle, but apparently was sent to Robert Patterson.

1. Thomas Hutchins (1730–89), surveyor and geographer, had published a map entitled *A new map of the western parts of Virginia, Pennsylvania, Maryland and North Carolina; comprehending the River Ohio, and all the rivers, which fall into it; part of the River Mississippi, the whole of the Illinois River, Lake Erie, part of the Lakes Huron, Michigan, &c., and all the country bordering on these lakes and rivers* (London, 1778).

2. Not identified.

3. Nathaniel Portlock (1748?–1817) and George Dixon (d. 1800?), British naval men who explored the Northwest coast of North America in 1785–89. Portlock published *A voyage round the world* (London, 1789).

333. Jefferson to Benjamin Smith Barton

Dear Sir   Monticello Oct. 6. 10.

. . . .

When we had the pleasure of possessing you here, you expressed a wish to have some of the Ricara snap beans, and of the Columbian Salsafia brought from the Western side of the Continent by Govr. Lewis. I now inclose you some seeds of each. The Ricara bean is one of the most excellent we have had. I have cultivated them plentifully for the table two years. I have found one kind only superior to them. But being very sensibly so, I shall abandon the Ricaras. I have not yet raised enough of the Salsafia to judge of it. Govr. Lewis did not think it as delicate as the kind we possess. His family cherish his memory with all the fondness his singularly valuable qualities merited. To them he was ever most affectionate and devoted. They are very anxious, when his work shall have been published, & the MSS. of course no longer necessary for that, to recieve them back to be preserved in the family as a kind of relick. It is one of the most worthy families in our state, and one which it is a singular pleasure to me to gratify & serve, especially in whatever relates to my late friend the governor. If you can be instrumental towards having the Manuscripts preserved & returned to the family, I shall feel it as a very particular obligation. Accept the assurances of my constant esteem & respect.

TH: JEFFERSON

ALS, SC (DLC). Endorsed. Reply is No. 335.

334. Nicholas Biddle to [John Vaughan]

[c. 13 October 1810]

1st. The river Dubois according to the manuscript of Captn. Clarke which forms the text of the narrative 38° 55′ 17″ the longitude 87° 57. 45. In my map which is larger and done with more care than that of Mr. Hassler the situation corresponds with those calculations & is I know, almost directly opposite to the mouth of the Missouri. In the same map the 87° degree of longitude crosses the mouth of the Ohio. I incline to think that the slight sketch sent to Mr. Hassler is not to be trusted as to longitude for I understood that its only object was to designate in a general way the places at which the observations were made and of which Mr. Hassler was to fix the longitude by calculation.

2nd. Fort Mandan is mentioned in the manuscript to be in longitude 99. 24. 45—the map has it in 101. There is error somewhere yet it seems difficult to correct it for all that relates to the eclipse in my papers is as follows:

"15 Jany. 1805. This morning between 12 and 3 OClock we had a total eclipse of the moon. A part of the observations necessary for our purpose in this eclipse we got—which is

at 12ʰ 57. 54 total darkness of the moon
at 1. 44. end of total darkness
at 2. 39. 10 end of the eclipse"

I presume that the time here noted cannot be apparent time or time ascertained by an altitude; nor can it be mean time if by that phrase be meant as I understand time obtained from an altitude corrected by adding or subtracting the equation from the nautical Almanac, since in neither of these cases is it probable that a mistake so great as that of an hour could have occured. But it appears as if the time must be that given by the chronometer at the moment. For in the first place that was the most simple & the probability is that simplest plan was adopted. In the second place from the manner in which

[560]

the note is made, the silence of the two other persons who kept Journals, and from the circumstance that the young man of the party who is now here knowing nothing of it, it seems probable that the eclipse came on them rather unawares and that having made no preparation, they took the only way in their power of recording the precise time. If therefore they took the time by the chronometer which Mr. Hassler thinks might have been fixed for the Ohio or the mouth of the Missouri, the difference of the hour may perhaps assist the calculation of the longitude—for they had travelled 1600 estimated miles on a course somewhere about northwest.

4th. Judging from what I have heared Captn. Clarke mention I had supposed that he expected from Mr. Hassler the astronomical results only, on obtaining which he proposed making the map himself. But on this subject, as well as that last mentioned Mr. H. might perhaps receive every information by writing to him.

5th. I think it is of importance that Mr. Hassler should possess at least all the courses bearings, & distances during the whole route and I should wish him to see the map I have. But unfortunately the map itself as well as the original journals are so indispensably necessary for my own share of the work that I cannot part with them.

N. BIDDLE

(copy)

Transcript, RC (NN). Enclosed in John Vaughan to Hassler, 13 Oct. 1810. "The annexed from Mr. Biddle shd. have gone sooner, but was accidentally mislaid."

335. Benjamin Smith Barton to Jefferson

Dear Sir;   [16 October 1810]

I have received your kind letter, with the seeds & Mr. Vater's book. I beg you to accept of my thanks for your attention. Mr. Vater, I find, has made very free use of my publication on the American languages, but not, indeed, without acknowledgments, in several instances. I have not time at present, to study his book. I think, Sir, we should not be too liberal in sending our collections of vocabularies abroad: I mean, before we shall have published them in America.

In regard to Mr. Lewis's papers, I assure you, and I beg you, Sir, to assure his friends, that they will be taken good care of; that it is my sincere wish to turn them, as much as I can, to his honour & reputation; and that they shall ultimately be deposited, in good order, in the hands of General Clark, or those of Mr. Conrad, the publisher.

During the Governor's last visit to Philadelphia, there was some difference between him and me; originating *wholly* in the illiberal and [. . .] conduct of some of my enemies here, who laboured, not without some effect, to excite uneasiness in his mind, as to my friendship for him. I cherish with respect, the memory of your friend; and believe me, Sir, the manner in which you speak of him, in your letter, will act not feebly in making me careful of his fame. His fate was, indeed, melancholy and unhappy: but similar has sometimes been the fate of the best and wisest of men.

.   .   .   .

Permit me to request you to present my respects to Mr. & Mrs. Randolph & family, and be assured of the sincere & high regard with which I am, dear Sir, Your obed. friend, &c.,

B. S. BARTON
Oct. 16. 1810.

ALS, RC (DLC). Endorsed; received 21 Oct. 1810.
Acknowledged by Jefferson 22 Oct. 1810: "With respect to his [Lewis's] just reputation, I know it will be safe in your hands, and the successful achievement of his great and bold enterprize, is gratefully felt by the world, and with dispositions to embalm his memory." Jefferson sent another reminder to Barton 11 Sept. 1811 that the publication of the Lewis and Clark material should be expedited, pointing out that the findings of John Bradbury in the West had given that botanist "a great mass of information, which will immediately pass the Atlantic, to appear first there. . . . With respect therefore to your work, as well as Govr. Lewis's, I am anxious that whatever you do, should be done quickly." And again, 3 April 1813, Jefferson wrote: "When shall we have your book on American botany, and when the 1st volume of Lewis & Clark's travels? Both of these works are of general expectation, and great interest, and to no one of more than to myself" (DLC).

336. Clark to Nicholas Biddle

My Dear Sir   St. Louis Decr. 7th 1810
I had the pleasure of receiving a letter from you dated 7th July which was truly gratifying to me, with much satisfaction I learned the progress which you had made in the Naritive. I have not herd what progress doctr. Barton is makeing, I hope verry good. I have nearly finished a large Connected Map[1] which I shall send on by the next mail. I wish the whole or such part of it anexed as you may think proper and in such a way as you may think best, the map is made on a scale which I think will please you.

[562]

I am much indebted to you for the information Contained in your letter, and am sorry it is not in my power at present to give you half the information on the several points requisit for our work I could wish. Inclosed I send you the Osage Tredition som names of places &c.

The Map will not be Corrected by Celestial observations, but I think verry correct.

The points of Information which you mention I will give as far as I have Collected Viz.

1st. See the inclosed for Chieroton Scarty wrote by a French man— also Blaireau.

2nd. In sted of Lucelle—it is Loisel—See the inclosed for the name of the Indian tribe *Bois Brulé*.

4th. See inclosed for the name of the nation called Chayenne.

5th. See inclosed for Bakers Oven &c.

6th. The Indians you mention recon time by pointing to the Suns position, by no. of nights, no. of Moons No. of Summers & Numbers of Winters. Mainey reckon from Winter to Summer one year and from Summer to Winter another, but the most of the Tribes reckon by winters, the[y] have a name for every Moon, denoting the progress or Decline of Vegitation Animals Feish &c. Enquire of Mr. Shannon for particulars if you please—they do not recon by weeks. The[y] Count distan[c]es by nights or the place of the Sun from Sunrise.

7th. There are two Turtle Mountains on[e] at the head of Knife River & the other on Mouse river, one of which on Knife river I shall Call Turtle hills as they are low mountains, those on Mouse river are not high nor ruged in a open leavel plain elevated Covered with timber on the top of which there are lakes.

8th. I have not been able to get an Indian Song as yet. I will try and get one.

9. Please to enquire of Mr. Shannon for the language of signs used by Indians &c.

10. The Chiefs Generally point out the Spot for each to cultivate, when they do not each family takes as much Groun as he wishes so that he does not interfer with any other who has been in previous possession. You are right when you say that the 3 nations reside together. 2 v. of Mandans one village of (Mahaha or of *Ar wah cah ways* & 2 Minnitarees. Mr. Peter Chouteau is not a man to secure information from, he Knows but little about the Indians of the upper Missouri. Mr. Shannon is much better acquainted with them.

11. I cant describe the Game among the Mandans mentioned in O[rd]ways journal if Shannon cant no one in this country can the

Interpeter who is now with me cant describe it, it resembles Billiards very much.

12. The Minnetaries call the Muscle Shell river *Maŕ âh tucke* (arjá or River).

13. Medicine River is called *Mâh-hó-pâh. âjá.*

14. Medicine is called *Mahopah,* Great Medicine is called *Mah hossah leash kit.*

15. Different nations call the Missouri different names. Most called it Troubled water—[. . .].

17. Please to ask Mr. Shannon to describe the Buffalow Pathes to you.

18. I have not learnt any thing new of any fortifications except one on Lamoin[?] on which river there are also rich Lead mines. Silver is found on Chayenne R. as I am told by Indians.

19. I have not Collected much about the fur trade as yet to send you.

20. The remains of the Two Kanzas Vilages spoken of. Some appearance of earthen houses [. . .].[2] Part of stone chimneys where an old fort at a short distance from the upper village which was occupied by the French. The Ottoes believe that they came from the Earth and will return to the earth, and again return on earth. The ponch Indians inhabit the Country near the waters of California, and of the Crow nation as I have lately been told, now bear another name I wish to leave them out altogether as they are not quit[e] certain as to their Origin. Please to accept my best wishes. Yours Very Sincerely,

WM. CLARK

Prey write to me as often as you can Conveniently—The post is waiting and I have not time to read what I have wrote—

ALS, RC (DLC—Biddle).

1. This map is in the Western Americana Collection of Yale University Library. The descriptive title in the cartouche reads: "A Map of part of the Continent of North America From Longitude [*blank*] W. of Washington City to the Pacific O[cean] and between Lattitude 35 and 52 North. . . . Shewing Lewis & Clarks rout over the Rocky Mountains in 1805 on their rout to the Pacific from the United States. By William Clark. Laid down by a Scale of 50 Miles to the Inch." With a few exceptions the map is identical to that done by Philadelphia engraver Samuel Harrison (1789–1818) for Biddle. The most notable exceptions are these: (a) The manuscript map covers much more territory because, as Biddle explains in No. 343, practical limitations made it necessary to truncate the original for publication. The published version excludes everything below the Kansas River and above the bend of Clark's River. (b) A notation on the manuscript map, in Clark's hand, reads: "Mr. W. P. Hunts rout in 1811." This does not appear—and could not have appeared—on the published version,

since the Hunt expedition postdates Clark's submission of the map to Biddle. (c) On the original, Clark changed the name of the Tongue River to Powder River and assigned the name Tongue to the next river west. These labels occur uncorrected on the published version.

Almost certainly, the Yale map was used as the basis for the engraved version in BIDDLE. "The map from which the plate was made, is in my possession at this place," Clark wrote Jefferson in 1816 (No. 390). It passed to Yale from Clark descendants, and a facsimile was published in four sheets by the Yale University Library in 1950.

2. Several words illegible.

337. Clark to Nicholas Biddle

Dear Sir   St. Louis Decr. 20th 1810

I herewith Inclose to you a Map which I have drawn for my Book, it is much more Correct than any which has been before published, it is made on the same scale of the one you have, containing more Country, I wish you to anex as much of it to the book as you think best, you will observe that I have not inclosed it in lines. The Ohio is not Correct, mearly shows the rivers as they mouth. I am sorry that I could not get the Calculations from Mr. Hosler to Correct the Map, but, I hope it will doe without. This package is inclosed to the Secty. of War to be forwarded.[1]

I have not Collected any information since my last letter to you.

I think I mentioned having heard a rumbling noise at the falls of Missouri, which was not accounted for, and you accounted for them by similating them to Avelanches of the Alps.

Please to give my Compliments to Geo. Shannon and accept my sincere friendship. I shall write you again soon.

WM. CLARK

ALS, RC (DLC—Biddle). Addressed; endorsed.

1. Clark to the Secretary of War, 20 Dec. 1810, enclosed for Biddle a package containing "a Map which I have made since my return to this place of the Country West of the Mississippi, & intended to accompany my Journal, one Vol. of which I expect will be out this winter" (DNA, RG 107, C-314).

338. Clark to Nicholas Biddle

Dear Sir   St. Louis Jany. 24th 1811

I hope you have received my several letters my new map, and sundry other papers relative to such information as I could collect. Inclosed I sent you some rough notes which I made at the Mandans the 1st year of my tour, perhaps you may Collect from this something which you may wish to Know. A Copy of these notes were sent to Mr. Jefferson from the Mandans &c. I send this as I have sent several other papers thro' the Secty. of War. I should be hapy to here from you on the subject of my book. Accept the assurance of my highest respect & esteem, Your Friend,

WM. CLARK

ALS, RC (DLC—Biddle). Addressed; endorsed.

339. Clark to George Shannon

Dear George   St. Louis 20th Apl. 1811

I have not recived a letter from you since the 15. of Decr. and feel extreemly anxious to hear from you, I have wrote to you several letters which I fear you have not received, if you had receved them you certainly would have written to me in answer to some of them. I hope you are in good health and that your mind is easy—let nothing weigh heavy on your mind, write to me freely. I wrote to you on the subject of your Claim on the Government which I hope has been satisfactory for the present.

I should be verry glad to know how my business goes on, I am at present quit[e] uninformed. I wrote to you about som Goods, and waited an answer untill Feby when I found it necessary to send to Baltimore for them <which placed me to some Disadvantage.> What is Dr. Barton about, pray write me all about my Book and such prospects as I have before written to you. Pray speak to Doctr. Barton for me and ask him to inform me the state of progress he [is] makeing.

I am glad to hear that our Frend Conrad has not lost by the condt. of the young man who drew money on his Credit. Give my best repects to him and Mr. Biddle. Tell them I have not heard from them for a length of time. I hope you are in the most perfect health. Please to give Mrs. Clarks and my afft. respects to John Croghan and accept yourself of our sincere wishes. Yrs. &c.

W. C.

This place is pretty much as it was when you was here, I have purchd. a store of goods—$8700 and sent on for more. Manuel is gone to the Mandans to Desolve & settle the Missouri Compy. Imogration is rapid. Several young Lawyers [. . .][1] come forward. My nephey is very sick.

AL, SC (MoSHi). Endorsed, "a Copy to Geo. Shannon 20 Apl. 1811."
1. Manuscript torn; one or more words possibly missing.

340. John Colter's Receipt to Edward Hempstead

John Colter

    vs.

Edward Hempstead, admr.

of Meriwether Lewis dec.   **[28 May 1811]**

Judgment of the Court of Common Pleas, St. Louis district—March
June 1811.

Received of Edward Hempstead the sum of three Hundred & Seventy
five Dollars and Sixty Cents in full of the Judgment in the above case:
—Witness my hand & Seal May 28. 1811.

Witness—   JOHN COLTER{Seal}

John Kerr

DS (MoSHi). Endorsed, "John Colter vs. Lewis, admr. Rect. for $377.60.
No. 10." Lewis seems to have pocketed the grant Colter received from the
government for his role in the expedition, expecting to repay it later.
Colter had a great deal of trouble recovering the money. He claimed
after Lewis's death that Lewis owed him $559, being $380 in pay and
allowances plus $179 in extra pay granted by Congress. He sued the estate
through his attorney, J. A. Graham, and finally received the judgment
shown here.

341. Nicholas Biddle to James Monroe

My dear Sir,   Philada. June 6, 1811

. . . . .

There is a matter which I intended to mention to your predecessor
but which it gives me far more pleasure to communicate to yourself.
You know I believe that I am preparing for publication Lewis &
Clarke's travels. Among other subjects of enquiry, they were desirous
of finding some branch of the Missouri which, by reaching as far
north as the Lake of the Woods, might enable us to rectify the error
in the Treaty of 1794, relative to our northern boundary. Captain
Lewis ascended one of the branches (Maria's river) but before he
reached what he thought the parallel of the Lake of the Woods, the
river turned westward & he was obliged to return, though he expresses a
belief that one or more of the other branches would answer the purpose. If I recollect aright, your treaty in 1806 made provision for
future amicable adjustment, but in the present state of things it
would be desirable not to say any thing which might revive any
injurious pretensions on the part of England, and to mention our

own claims in the most favorable manner. I have understood, tho'
I scarcely know whence, that the English commentary on the treaty
would make the boundary line decline from its western course, so as
to strike the small lakes at the head of the Mississippi. All this however you know much better than I do, and if you think the subject
might be introduced in such a way as to be useful in future, or that
the mention of it, either geographically or politically, can be any wise
important, it would gratify me to hear from you in relation to it.

. . . . .

NICHOLAS BIDDLE

ALS, RC (DLC—Monroe Papers).

342. Nicholas Biddle to Clark

Dear Sir,   Philada. June 28. 1811
    I have duly received your letter inclosing the notes of information
in answer to my enquiries and also that accompanying. Since I wrote
to you I spent the greater part of last winter in the legislature at
Lancaster, but by diligence have at length been able to get completely thro' the manuscripts and am now ready to put the work to
the press as soon as Mr. Conrad wishes it. The map is now in train
for engraving & the plates the subject of which Mr. Shannon & myself
selected are in the hands of the artists. In this as in many other
matters I have derived much assistance from that gentleman who is
very intelligent and sensible & whom it was worth your while to send
here. There remains but one more matter about which I am desirous
of enquiring—that is with regard to the rank between Captn. Lewis
& yourself. You mentioned I recollect that you went on terms of perfect
equality in the command. The act of Congress granting you compensation seems to make some difference with regard to your rank, and I
am very desirous of having that matter settled, so as to prevent the
possibility of any unpleasant reflections in future on the part of the
friends of either of you. Will you be good enough to state precisely
how that stood between you, so that I may be enabled to do justice
to you both. I should desire to have an answer on this subject as
soon as you can conveniently, and then I believe I shall be possessed
of almost all the auxiliary information I desire.
    My winter's essay at legislation was more agreeable than I had
anticipated—it has however brought me into some trouble, for I
am obliged now to make an oration before the whole city on the
fourth of July,[1] which in our heats is more fatiguing than a elk

[568]

hunt among the Shoshonees. As Mr. Shannon tells me that some of his letters have failed, I send a copy of this to the Secretary at war. With my best respects to Mrs. Clarke I remain Yrs. Sincerely,

N. B.

AL, SC (DLC—Biddle). Endorsed, "To Genl. W. Clarke June 28. 1811, I believe not sent but the one of July 8. 1811 preferred."

1. Published as *Oration delivered before the Pennsylvania State Society of the Cincinnati on the Fourth of July MDCCCXI* (Philadelphia, 1811).

343. Nicholas Biddle to Clark

Dr. Sir,   Phila. July 8. 1811

I have had the pleasure of receiving your several letters inclosing the papers of information which I had requested, and also the map. The information was very valuable, & combined with what I have learnt from Mr. Shannon who I find very intelligent & sensible leaves me nothing to wish on the points I mentioned. I am now happy to inform you that altho' I was interrupted by a campaign in the legislature during the last winter, yet by diligence I have got through the work and am ready to put it to press as soon as Mr. Conrad pleases. The map we thought would be too expensive and rather too large as you sent it. We therefore concluded that it was best to take off some degrees from the top & bottom so as to make it illustrate the route principally & not go higher north than the bend of Clarke's river. This will be quite enough for the work & Mr. Conrad thinks that the whole map might then be engraved & sold separately to advantage. The engravings were marked off by Mr. Shannon & myself & are now in the hands of the artist. But engraving is always a tedious work particularly engraving maps so that I do not know when ours will be completed. All that has depended on myself has been forwarded with as much expedition as I could possibly give to it. There is one and only one more thing about which I wish you would give me information. It is the exact relative situation in point of rank & command between Captain Lewis & yourself. I think you mentioned to me that your commission was that of Lieutenant of Engineers which placed you completely on an equality with Captain Lewis who was a captain of Infantry or Artillery. I am desirous of being correct and I will get you to state to me whether I have understood you precisely so as to avoid all error on that subject. With my compts. to Mrs. Clarke I remain Yrs. sincerely,

N. B.

AL, SC (DLC—Biddle). Reply is No. 345.

344. Clark to George Shannon

Dear George   St. Louis August 8th 1811

I have been sick since I recved your last letters, and at this time only in health sufficient to write a part of a letter at a time. Your last letters have given me much satisfaction i.e. those of the 15. & 18. June &c. I had been led to believe that your situation was excessively disagreeable in Phila. and was uneasy about you, and proposed in my last to you to join me in trade at this place. Knowing as I do that you could turn your mind to any prosute. But when I recved your last letters I felt sorry that I had said any thing about Trade to you. I found your situation at Noristown was more agreeable your mind more Composed and prospect more flattering.

On the Subject of Trade, do just as your feel an inclination join or let it alone. On that of Law do prosisely as your inclination leads you, you shall get every aid in my power in either deturmonation, or both if you should be enclined to embarke in both. Inclosed I send you Wilson P. Hunts Draft on his brother Ajaniah of Lamberton of N. Jersey for $240. I cant sell your land warrant for a price which pleases me and shall not dispose of it for less than it is worth.

I send you herewith inclosed Invoices of such goods as are wanting at this place which are not filled with names of any merchant except Messrs. C. Conrad and Co. I wish you to put the name of the Merchant after you find we can trade with him, such as you may find proper. If you do not join I impower you to sign my name to the order—if you do join, the firm must be in the name of G. Shannon & Co.

I shall send Ben[1] to Louisville and from there send this letter by some merchant to Phila. and request them to see you. If you find that I can get goods on good terms, I wish you to get some of the Kenty. merchants to Chuse them—and must request you to attend to the purchase of them make the bargain, head the orders, or give receipts in my name for such goods and the amount which may be recived, or sign in my name when the amt. of the order can be filled. You will find several orders for nearly the same articles, they were intended for different houses.

If you should think proper to join in Trade the firm must be in the name of G. Shannon & Co. and all signatures must be made in the name of the Company; and arrangements made with different houses to furnish supplies on as long a credit as possible.

I can send a Bill which will Bring money to Pittsburgh or Philadelphia as you may find it necessary to Defray the expense of

Transportation in the event of your either sendg. or bringing on goods.

I must request you to write to me imediately after you recive this, inform me your intentions, if you will purchase goods, if I must send on money, the amount, to what place I must send it—or if you think it an unfavourable time to purchase goods, or that they can't be had,—I shall rely on you, and not say you have done wrong, let your deturmonation and acts on this subject be what they may.

I wish also you to say something about my Books & Map and the prospects of their being published. Accept my Consider[ations &c.]

W. C.

If the goods were sent by some merchant to Louisville I would send to meet them, or even at Pittsburgh. Perhaps some merchant may be in Phila. would undertake to bring them on in the event of your not comeing &c. W. C.

AL, SC (MoSHi). Endorsed, "a Copy to G. Shannon 8 Augt. 1811."

1. Benjamin O'Fallon (c.1792–1843), Clark's nephew, later an Indian agent in Missouri Territory.

345. Clark to Nicholas Biddle

Dear Sir   St. Louis 15th August 1811

By the last mail I had the honor of receiving your letter of the 8th of July, which I do assure you gave me much pleasure; as well to hear from you as to learn that you had got thro' the work and had it ready for the press as soon as Mr. Conrad pleased.

I hope Mr. C. is getting it in a state of forwardness,—I feel convinced that your arrangement of the Map is a good one, I wish it was engraved and out.

You express a desire to know the exact relation which I stood in Point of Rank, and Command with Captain Lewis—*equal in every point of view*—(I did not think myself very well treated as I did not get the appointment which was promised me. As I was not disposed to make any noise about the business have never mentioned the particulars to any one, and must request you not to mention my disapointment & the Cause to any one.

In March 1791 I was appointed a Lieut. in Waynes army and was kept on Command about 18 months before I joined the Main Army. When I joined, I was anexed to a Chosen Rifle Company of which I had the Command, and received a Staff appointment, both of which I retained untill after the Treaty at Greenville and at the time of takeing possession of the Western posts, I *resigned* and returned to a Farm in Kentucky on which I lived several years in bad health (Capt. Lewis was appointed an Ensign and arranged to the Company which I commanded a fiew months before I resigned). During the time I [was] liveing on my Farm in Kenty. I had frequent Reasons to Visit the Eastern States & Washington where I became Acquainted with the Presidt. Mr. Jefferson. In 1803 I was applied to by Captain Lewis by Letter, who was then Private Secty. to the President, to accompany him on an Expedition to the Pacific, stating the genl. plan and objects, and offered by the apprbn. of the President to place me in a situation in every respect equal to himself, in rank pretentions &c. &c. On those Conditions I agreed to undertake the expedition made my arrangements and set out, and proceeded on with Capt. Lewis to the Mouth of the Missouri where we remained the winter 1803 made every necessary arrangement to set out early in spring 1804. Every thing arranged I waited with some anxiety for the Commission which I had reasons to expect (Capt. of Indioneers) a fiew days before I set out, I receeved a Commission of 2nd Lieutenant of Artillerist. My feelings on this Occasion was as might be expected. I wished the expidetion suckcess, and from the assurence of Capt. Lewis, that in every respect my situation Command &c. &c. should be equal to his viewing the Commission as mearly Calculated to autherise punishment to the soldiers if necessary, I proceeded. No difficuelty took place on our rout relative to this point. On my return to this Town I inclosed the Commission to the Secty. of War and wrote to him that the Commission had answered the purpose for which it was intended &c.

I do not wish that any thing relative to this Comsn. or appointment should be inserted in my Book, or made known, for very perticular reasons, and I do assure you that I have never related as much on this subject to any person before. Be so good as to place me on equal footing with Cap. Lewis in every point of view without exposeing any thing which might have taken place or even mentioning the Commission at all.

I hope you will do me the honor to write to me often and without reserve. Accept the acknowledgements of Mrs. Clark and my self for the friendly sentiments expressed in the latter part of your letter and accept of our warmest wishes for your health and hapiness. I remain Your Sincere Friend,

WM. CLARK

ALS, RC (DLC—Biddle). Addressed; endorsed.

346. Statement of Gilbert C. Russell

[26 November 1811]

Governor Lewis left St. Louis late in August, or early in September 1809, intending to go by the route of the Mississippi and the Ocean, to the City of Washington, taking with him all the papers relative to his expedition to the Pacific Ocean, for the purpose of preparing and puting them to the press, and to have some drafts paid which had been drawn by him on the Government and protested. On the morning of the 15th of September, the Boat in which he was a passenger landed him at Fort Pickering in a state of mental derangement, which appeared to have been produced as much by indisposition as other causes. The Subscriber being then the Commanding Officer of the Fort on discovering his situation, and learning from the Crew that he had made two attempts to kill himself, in one of which he had nearly succeded, resolved at once to take possession of him and his papers, and detain them there untill he recovered, or some friend might arrive in whose hands he could depart in safety.

In this condition he continued without any material change for about five days, during which time the most proper and efficatious means that could be devised to restore him was administered, and on the sixth or seventh day all symptoms of derangement disappeared and he was completely in his senses and thus continued for ten or twelve days. On the 29th of the same month he left Bluffs, with the Chickasaw agent the interpreter and some of the Chiefs, intending then to proceed the usual route thro' the Indian Country, Tennessee and Virginia to his place of distination, with his papers well secured and packed on horses. By much severe depletion during his illness he had been considerably reduced and debilitated, from which he had not entirely recovered when he set off, and the weather in that country being yet excessively hot and the exercise of traveling too severe for him; in three or four days he was again affected with the same mental disease. He had no person with him who could manage or controul him in his propensities and he daily grew worse untill he arrived at the house of a Mr. Grinder within the Jurisdiction of Tennessee and only Seventy miles from Nashville, where in the apprehension of being destroyed by enemies which had no existance but in his wild immagination, he destroyed himself, in the most cool desperate and Barbarian-like manner, having been left in the house intirely to himself. The night preceeding this one of his Horses and one of the Chicksaw agents with whom he was traveling strayed off from the camp and in the Morning could not be found. The agent with some Indians stayed to search for the horses, and Governor Lewis with their two servants and the baggage horses proceeded to Mr. Grinders where he was to halt untill the agent got up.

After he arrived there and refreshed himself with a little Meal & drink he went to bed in a cabin by himself and ordered the servants to go to the stables and take care of the Horses, least they might loose some that night; Some time in the night he got his pistols which he loaded, after every body had retired in a seperate Building and discharged one against his forehead without much effect—the ball not penetrating the skull but only making a furrow over it. He then discharged the other against his breast where the ball entered and passing downward thro' his body came out low down near his back bone. After some time he got up and went to the house where Mrs. Grinder and her children were lying and asked for water, but her husband being absent and having heard the report of the pistols she was greatly allarmed and made him no answer. He then in returning got his razors from a port folio which happened to contain them and siting up in his bed was found about day light, by one of the servants, busily engaged in cuting himself from head to foot. He again beged for water, which was given him and so soon as he drank, he lay down and died with the declaration to the Boy that he had killed himself to deprive his enemies of the pleasure and honor of doing it. His death was greatly lamented. And that a fame so dearly earned as his should finally be clouded by such an act of desperation was to his friends still greater cause of regret.

(signed) Gilbert Russell

The above was received by me from Major Gilbert Russell of the [*blank*] Regiment of Infantry U.S. on Tuesday the 26th of November 1811 at Fredericktown in Maryland.

J. Williams

D (InU—Williams Papers).

At the time of Lewis's death, Russell was commanding the fort at Chickasaw Bluffs (Memphis), Tenn. His earlier statements on the tragedy consist of two letters he wrote to Jefferson in Jan. 1810, both now in DLC. In the first (4 Jan.) he mentions Lewis's illness upon arrival at the fort, and says: "His situation I tho't rendered it necessary that he should be stoped until he would recover, which I done, & in a short time by proper attention a change was perceptible and in about six days he was perfectly restored in every respect & able to travel." Russell enclosed an undated memorandum from Lewis regarding shipment of some baggage he was leaving behind, and added that Lewis had put his land warrant up for sale. Lewis's own note in his account book, 17 Sept. 1809 (MoSHi), says he has sent his land warrant to New Orleans, to be sold for $2 an acre or more, the money to be deposited in the branch bank there or in Washington, subject to his order or that of William D. Meriwether for the benefit of his creditors. The warrant was not sold; it became a part of the property Lewis left to his mother.

Russell's second letter to Jefferson (31 Jan.) discusses Lewis's alleged intemperance and the possibility that the free use of alcohol contributed to his suicide. Jefferson acknowledged both letters 18 April 1810, saying, "He [Lewis] was much afflicted & habitually so with hypocondria. This was probably increased by the habit into which he had fallen & the painfull reflections that would necessarily produce in a mind like his" (DLC).

Thoughtful men still hold opposing views on whether Lewis killed himself or was slain. Conflicting testimony and the absence of solid documentation has made the case a difficult one, and a strong oral tradition claiming murder has been hard for observers to ignore.

I am inclined to believe that Lewis died by his own hand. The present statement by Russell, not previously published, does much to strengthen that belief. The problems that beset Lewis when he became governor of Louisiana Territory were vastly different from those he had faced on the expedition. A courageous and resourceful man, even if admirably fitted to lead an exploring party, is not necessarily the best man to govern a frontier territory. Lewis made some doubtful decisions, encountered opposition, and found a bitter and influential enemy in Frederick Bates. He ran afoul of some petty hairsplitting in Washington regarding his drafts, and believed himself at the point of financial ruin. He was under strong pressure to publish an account of his expedition, and had announced to the world that he was preparing it; but at the time of his death he had not, according to his publisher, produced a single line of manuscript. He had unaccountably drifted away from his close relationship with Jefferson. And apparently he had lapsed into intemperance.

That Clark clearly believed him capable of suicide is shown by his anguished statement upon learning of Lewis's death: "I fear O! I fear the weight of his mind has overcome him . . ." (Clark to Jonathan Clark, 28 Oct. 1809, typed copy in KyLoF from an unlocated original).

The most recently published study of Lewis's death is by PHELPS. His conclusion: "In the absence of direct and pertinent contemporary evidence to the contrary, of which not a scintilla exists, the verdict of suicide must stand."

347. George Shannon to Nicholas Biddle

Dear Sir,   Norristown Jany. 23d. 1812.

I am anxious to obtain the place of *judge advocate,* in this new Army which is to be raised. If you can aid me in procuring the appointment you will do me a great favour. I have just now written to Genl. Clark on the same subject. Perhaps you can give me some necessary advice. I remain Dear Sir, Your Obt. Srt.

GEORGE SHANNON

ALS, RC (DLC—Biddle). Addressed.

348. George Shannon to Nicholas Biddle

Dear Sir,   Norristown Feby. 5th 1812

I have this moment had the pleasure to receive both your favours of the *first Instant,* which corroborate my own opinion, formed upon mature reflection. I wrote to you precipitately, and have since regreted it; not however, from any diffidence in my abilities to perform the duties of the office, with a proper dignity and correctness, but from a consciousness of my want of the necessary degree of celebrity and standing in society, to justify an expectation of the success of my application. However, as I have already requested Genl. Clark to recommend me, I believe that I will not now countermand my request. I believe too, as you have suggested it, that I will write to Mr. Clay[1] on the subject; and then let things take their natural course: for I have by no means set my heart upon the acquisition of this office. The ardour of my desire to obtain it is very much abated. I beg you to accept my sincere thanks for the trouble which I have given you. Your polite and friendly offer of assistance, will, when an occasion occurs, be accepted with gratitude. With the highest respect & esteem I remain yr. obt. Svt.

GEORGE SHANNON

ALS, RC (DLC—Biddle). Addressed; endorsed.

1. Henry Clay (1777–1852), Kentucky statesman, helpful to Shannon on many occasions.

349. Termination of Lewis's Account

Accountant's Office
March 4th 1812

I certify that there is due to the Estate of the late Meriwether Lewis, deceased—the Sum of Six hundred & thirty six Dollars 25/100 being the balance of his Account for disbursements made for the conveyance of the Mandan Chief, and his family to his Village on the Missouri River—including the Damages, Interest and Cost of Protest of three Bills of Exchange drawn by him on this Department, in May 1809, for said purposes, which were protested for non-payment—now admitted in conformity to the decision of the Secy. of War; which Sum is to be transmitted by the Treasurer of the United States to Edward Hempstead, Administrator of the Estate of said Lewis, deceased, at St. Louis.

W[ILLIAM] S[IMMONS]

Lbk (DNA, RG 217, Report Book G, 173).

350. George Shannon to Nicholas Biddle

Dear Sir, Norristown April 24. 1812.

Under the impression that I should remain pretty much in the city, when I last wrote to Genl. Clark, I requested him to direct his letters to me, to your care. I expect he is now on the Ohio, on his way to this country, and that he will write to me from Louisville. If you receive any letters for me, before I go to the city, will you be so good Sir, as to send them to me at this place? Yours Sincerely,

GEORGE SHANNON.

ALS, RC (DLC—Biddle). Addressed; endorsed.

351. Nicholas Biddle to Clark

Dear Sir, Phila. July 4. 1812

I have been for some time anxiously expecting you in Phila., but observing by the papers that you were at Louisville about the middle of June I write this in expectation that it will find you in Pittsburgh.

It is now almost a whole year since on the 8th of July 1811 I wrote to you that I had completed the work agreeably to our engagement, & was ready to put it to the press whenever Mr. Conrad chose. Since that time I have been constantly endeavoring to commence the publication not only from a regard to the interests of both of us, but because while this work remained on my hands it interfered very much with all my other occupations, besides that the work would lose some of its interest by so much delay. Last winter I was prevented from going to the legislature chiefly by a desire to stay & superintend the printing. Yet notwithstanding all my exertions the publication has been prevented from time to time till at last Mr. Conrad's difficulties have obliged him to surrender everything to his creditors & give up business.[1] This misfortune is very much to be regretted on his account, & I am sorry that we did not know sooner that he would not be able to publish. But since things have taken this turn, it is perhaps better that the printing was not begun than that we should be entangled with his assignees, since now we can place it in other hands. I have already spoken to Mr. Bradford[2] one of the best booksellers here & if we come to an arrangement we can soon print the work. I am in hopes that he will take it on the same terms as Mr. Conrad did, but Mr. Conrad has been so embarrassed & occupied that they have not yet been able to understand each other. In a few days however I expect that some agreement can be made & then we can proceed vigorously & soon get the volumes out.

I am about leaving town for a short time in order to take my mother in law[3] to the sea shore for the benefit of her health—but I hope to be back by the time you are in Phila. & we can then talk over all that concerns the work. In the mean time it will give me great pleasure to hear from you. With my Compts. to Mrs. Clark who I understand accompanies you, I am truly Yrs.

N. B.

To the second copy added: The above letter was sent to Pittsburgh, but lest you should not take that route I inclose this to the Secy. at War in Washington.

July 5. 1812.

AL, SC (DLC—Biddle). Reply is No. 352.

1. On Conrad's business affairs, see a note under No. 262.
2. Samuel F. Bradford (1776–1837), a partner with John Inskeep in the firm of Bradford & Inskeep, 4 South Third Street, Philadelphia, which took over publication of the Biddle narrative when Conrad failed.
3. Mrs. Margaret Craig, mother of Biddle's wife Jane, and widow of Philadelphia merchant John Craig.

352. Clark to Nicholas Biddle

Dear Sir   Washington City Aug. 6th 1812

On my arrival at this place I recved your letter of the 4th of July, in which you inform me the falue [failure] of Mr. Conrad, and the state of our Work. Mr. Conrad has disapointed us both I find; he has disapointed me in a way I had not the smallest suspicion of. I think we might have expected from him some intimition of his situation which would have prevented a delay of the work. I hope you have suckceeded in engageing Mr. Bradford to print the work, and in makeing such other arrangements as you may have thought best. I expect to go on to Philadelphia in a week or ten days, when I hope to have the pleasure to meet you; as I shall take Indian Chiefs with me, it will not be in my power to stay in your City as long as I could wish. I must therefore intrude on your goodness and assistance.

Mrs. Clark and my two Sons came on with me as far as Hagers Town from thence they proceded to Col. Hancocks to remain untill our deficultes are adjusted to the N.W. Accept of my warmest Solicitations. Yours Truly,

WM. CLARK

ALS, RC (DLC—Biddle). Addressed; endorsed.

353. Clark to Nicholas Biddle

Dear Sir   Philadelphia September 5th 1812

I had the pleasure of receiving your letter of the 24th ulto.[1] two days ago at this place, and am extreemly sorry that you were not in the City dureing the time of my remaining in the place, which has been four days, my only Individl. business here was to see you, and make some arrangements respecting the publication of the work (Lewis & Clarks Journal). From the situation of my publick duties I am Compelled to return tomorrow without effecting the Objects of my wishes.[2] I have expected you for two days, and have delayed one longer than the Contract made with the man to carry the Indian Chiefs to Pittsburgh autherised. I am a publick officer and must move with a parcel of people (Indians) who are placed under my charge.

Can't I purswade you to become *Interested* in Lewis & Clarks work, I hope you will Concent, and under that hope I take the liberty of offering you the half of every profit arrising from it if you will attend to it, have it Completed as far as it is possible and necessary, prented published &c. including the advances which have and may be necessary &c.

If you will agree to this proposition (which I hope you will) please to write to me at Pittsburgh or Louisville, inclose agreements which I can execute there; and I will send you orders for such specimins &c. as are in the hands of Mr. Conrad and other gentlemen in this City.

Should you not incline to become interested in this way, be so good as to write to me at Pittsburgh, and give me your oppinion on this subject.

I have not seen Mr. Bradford, thinking it probable you would become interested and Could make a much better bargain with him than I could.

Doctr. Bartain says he can do his part in a very short time. Should you become interested you will in Course employ some other person if the Doctr. should not please you.

Please to write to me as soon as possible, and accept the assurance of my highest respect and Esteem. Yr. Most Ob. Hl. Sevt.

WM. CLARK

I leave you the reduced map & one impression. Mr. Conrad has others & a plate.

ALS, RC (DLC—Biddle). Addressed; endorsed.
1. Not found.

2. On the day that Clark wrote this letter, Fort Madison went under a three-day siege that ended with the burning of the factory building. On Lake Michigan, Fort Dearborn had fallen a few days before. Whether Clark's presence on the frontier could have reduced this violence is debatable—but his influence with the Indians was great. His absences from his St. Louis post are worth noting. On 1 June 1807 (No. 270) he asked Dearborn if he might come to Washington to settle his accounts, and Dearborn replied that this was not necessary. But he left St. Louis that fall and was in Louisville by late Oct. 1807. He did not return from that trip until July 1808. He remained in St. Louis until Sept. 1809, then left for Virginia (and during this trip received word of Lewis's death). He visited Fincastle, Philadelphia, and Washington, was in Louisville in May, and returned to St. Louis 1 July 1810. His next departure occurred in 1812; in August of that year he was in Washington, having brought his family east for the duration of the war. He was back as far as Louisville in Oct. 1812 but was asking Secretary of War Eustis to recall him to Washington so that he could work on his book. Apparently this request was granted; he was in Washington in Feb. 1813 and in Philadelphia in March. In Sept. 1814 he wrote Biddle that Mrs. Clark probably would require another visit to the physicians of Philadelphia. In the six-year period of June 1807 to June 1813, Clark was absent from his post at least thirty months. He was a devoted public servant, and his long absences were rather typical of frontier officeholders; much of this time away from office was spent in arduous travel; but, nevertheless, some of his absences do not appear excusable.

354. Clark to William Eustis

Sir   Louisville Kty. Octr. 24th 1812

· · ·

My Dear Sir I hope you have Considered favorably on the subject I last spoke to you. My Familey are in Virginia without the necessary arrangements made for their continuing there, and the frequent alarms must prevent my takeing them to the frontiers for some time—I shall be obliged to go to Virginia this Winter to make some necessary arrangements there—and I could wish if it is Consistent, to proceed on as far as Philadelphia, to push the publication of Lewis & Clarks Tour, which has been neglected two years— Caused principally by my absence so far on Publick business, and the falue [failure] of a *Buck seller* whome I had employed to Carry it on after Govr. Lewis Death. When I was last in Philadelphia my delay was so short that I could not make the arrangements necessary to Carry on that work. I am well aware of the necessity of men employed by the government being at their posts, but as in the Winter Season not much is done; I hope my absence on the present ocasion may

[580]

not be disapproved of; and that you will find it Convenient to Call me on by Washington. I hope you will do me the honor to write to me on this subject as soon as possible, to enable me to mak some necessary arrangements in time.

Do me the honor to make my Compliments acceptable to Mrs. Eustis; and accept the assurance of my highest respect & veneration. Your Most Obt. Hl. Sert.

WM. CLARK

ALS, RC (DNA, RG 107, C-496). Addressed; endorsed; received 3 Nov. 1812.

355. John Conrad to Nicholas Biddle

Dear Sir   [12 November 1812]

Johnson & Warner[1] have, at last, positively declined making any sort of offer for Genl. Clarkes book, & from their conversation seem to have so incorrect an idea of the value of the work and probable profits arising from the publication of it, that it would in my opinion be useless to make them an offer. There is not the smallest probability of their acceding to a fair & reasonable one. Mr. Dobson[2] also appears to have little inclination to embark in the work and declines making proposals for it. I can now I believe do nothing more in the business for you or Genl. Clarke, unless you will permit me to substitute *advise* for services. If I may do this, I will say decidedly, agree to Mr. Bradford's offer. It is I am confident the best bargain you can make for Genl. Clarke. The copyright I presume will be in him (Genl. C.) & I suppose he will derive the entire benefit of the sale of the M.S. in England. Yours sincerely,

JOHN CONRAD
Philada. Nov. 12. 1812

ALS, RC (DLC—Biddle).

1. Jacob Johnson and Benjamin Warner, stationers and booksellers, 147 Market Street, Philadelphia.

2. Thomas Dobson and Son, booksellers, 41 South Second Street, Philadelphia.

356. Clark to Nicholas Biddle

Dear Sir   At Col. Hancocks in Virginia January 24th 1812 [1813]

I have not had the pleasure of receiving a letter from you since your favor of the 15th of September, and am entirely uninformed as to

[581]

the Journal, in a fiew days I shall set out and hope to have the pleasure of seeing you in Philadelphia towards the latter part of next month, Mrs. Clark wishes to accompany me & spend a fiew days in your City, and flatters herself with the hopes of becoming acquainted with your Family.

The young man who will hand you this Benja: oFallon is my nephew who goes on to Phila. for the purpose of purchasing a small assortment of Merchandize to take on to St. Louis. Any advice or attentions you may find it Convenient to give this young, and unexperienced lad in his way, will be greatfully acknowledged by him and add additional obligations on Your Sincere Obdt. Hl. Sevt.

WM. CLARK

ALS, RC (DLC—Biddle). Addressed; endorsed. Reply is No. 357. Inadvertently dated 1812 by Clark.

357. Nicholas Biddle to Clark

Dear Sir   Phila. Feby. 23. 1813

I received with great pleasure your letter by Mr. Fallon to whom I shall be very glad to render any assistance in my power & hope soon to have the satisfaction of taking you by the hand.

The times have thrown some obstacles in the way of our work which have prevented its making as much progress as I could have wished. Soon after you left us I consulted Mr. Bradford, but finding his terms not such as I thought advantageous I made proposals to all the booksellers in town. The stagnation in that branch of business however was so great that no one was willing to embark in it, and after a great deal of fruitless negociation I was obliged to return & on the advice of Mr. Conrad accept Mr. Bradford's proposals. This I was desirous of deferring in hopes of obtaining better terms, but none could be had owing to the nature of the times. I now wait only for the engravers who will soon I hope finish their work and then we can strike off the printing immediately & in a little time the work will be published. The agreement with Mr. Bradford you will see when you arrive, but as I am not sure whether you are not already on this side of Washington I will add no more than that I am very sincerely Yrs.

N. B.

AL, SC (DLC—Biddle).

358. Clark Assigns Power of Attorney

[29 March 1813]

I William Clark of the Missouri territory do hereby constitute Nicholas Biddle of Philada. my lawful attorney in all things relative to my transactions with Bradford & Inskeep or any other persons concerned in the publication of Lewis & Clark's Travels, and do hereby empower him for me to demand, recover & receive all my claims & rights thereto, or to the profits thereof—make such arrangements and commence such legal processes, consent to such compromises as he may judge proper & generally to do every thing relative to the said work as fully as I could were I personally present—with power also to make such substitutes as he may think advisable, Hereby ratifying whatever he or his substitutes may lawfully do in the premises. In witness whereof I have set my hand & seal hereto this 29th day of March 1813 at Philadelphia.

Witness at signing   WM. CLARK {seal}

The words "demand recover & receive
all my claims & rights thereto or to
the profits thereof" being previously
interlined

Benj. O'Fallon

DS (NjP). The document is in Biddle's hand. Endorsed, "Wm. Clarke to N. Biddle Power of Atty." Notations in the hand of Elliott Coues, "Text is Mr. Biddle's handwriting," and "autograph signature of Clark."

359. Jefferson to Bernard McMahon

Dear Sir   Monticello May 30. 13.

I just now recieve information from my old friend Thouïn of the national garden of Paris that he has sent me a box of seeds of 270. kinds of trees of every sort for either use or ornament. This box, Mr. Warden informs me, he sends by Mr. Breuil of the schooner Bellona, bound to Philadelphia. If you will be so good as to watch the arrival of this vessel, perhaps already arrived, this letter may suffice to authorise the delivery of it by Mr. Beuil to you, to whom I should send it were it to come here, as being the best mode of fulfilling the intentions of the benevolent giver. If you could make up a collection of the seeds of the plants brought to us by Governor

Lewis[1] from beyond the Missisipi, it would be a just and grateful return which Mr. Thouïn merits at our hands. He expresses to me a great desire for the plants of the region beyond the Missisipi. If within the reasonable compass of the mail, it will come safest to me thro' that. If larger, the stage is a good conveyance if a passenger can be found who will take charge of it. Such opportunities to Richmond must be almost daily with you, and if addressed to Messrs. Gibson & Jefferson there it will come safely to me. Accept the assurances of my great esteem and respect.

TH: JEFFERSON

ALS, SC (DLC). Endorsed.

1. McMahon had been working with the Lewis and Clark plants faithfully since he first received the seeds and cuttings. He wrote Jefferson 28 Feb. 1812 that he was sending him a number of cuttings:

"No. 1. Ribes odoratissimum (mihi). This is one of Capt. Lewis's, and an important shrub, the fruit very large, of a dark purple colour, the flowers yellow, showey, & *extremely fragrant.*

"No. 2. Symphoricarpos leucocarpa (mihi) [*S. albus* (L.)]. This is a beautiful shrub brought by C. Lewis from the River Columbia, the flower is small but neat, the berries hang in large clusters are of a snow white colour and continue on the shrubs, retaining their beauty, all the winter; especially if kept in a Green House. The shrub is perfectly hardy; I have given it the trivial English name of Snowberry bush.

"No. 3. The Yellow Currant of the river Jefferson; this is specifically different from the other, but I have not yet given it a specific botanical name" (DLC).

Jefferson acknowledged receipt of the cuttings 11 Oct. 1812, saying that only one of the snowberry cuttings had failed and that the rest now "shew some of the most beautiful berries I have ever seen" (DLC). The currants and gooseberries also were flourishing. He sent cuttings to his friend Madame Noailles de Tessé, in Paris, 8 Dec. 1813, calling the plant "a very handsome little shrub, of the size of a currant bush. . . . We call it the Snow-berry bush, no botanical name being yet given to it, but I do not know why we might not call it Chionicoccos, or Kallicoccos" (DLC).

360. Jefferson to Paul Allen

Sir   Monticello Aug. 5. 13.

Not being able to go myself in quest of the information respecting Govr. Lewis which was desired in your letter of May 25.[1] I have been obliged to wait the leisure of those who could do it for me. I could forward you within a few days a statement of what I have collected, but more time would improve it, if the impression of the work will not be delayed. I will ask the favor of you therefore to name the latest time which the progress of the other part will admit, by which time you shall not fail to recieve it. My matter may fill perhaps 20 8vo. pages, and as these may be paged independantly of the body of the work, I suppose it may be the last sheet printed.

Of General Clarke I shall be able to give you nothing. He was indeed born within 2. miles of Charlottesvill, & 4. of the place of my birth in the county of Albermarle, but he was so much my junior, that before I could know him, his father removed to another part of the country. Accept the assurance of my great respect.

TH: JEFFERSON

ALS, SC (DLC). Endorsed. Reply is No. 361. Paul Allen (1775–1826), of Providence, R.I., was an editorial assistant on the *Port-Folio* under Joseph Dennie and Nicholas Biddle, and by 1816 was established in Baltimore as editor of the *Morning Chronicle*. Biddle's ostensible reasons for turning the Lewis and Clark project over to him are given in No. 366. It is difficult to say how much Allen contributed to the final manuscript, but the fact that he was promised $500 for the task of putting it into shape indicates that Biddle left a considerable amount of work to be done.

1. Not found.

361. Paul Allen to Jefferson

Dear Sir   Philadelphia Aug. 18 1813.

I have in consequence of the reception of your letter & the prospect which it gives Me of rendering the work more compleat by the addition of Gov. Lewis biography prevailed upon the Booksellers to delay the publication of the first volume as it was not originally contemplated to have done. Their plan was to publish the first volume as soon as it was struck off & to have the second published with all possible expectation afterwards. But Sir I apprehend your delay has done Me a benefit as a publication in the manner contemplated would unquestionably have done an essential injury to the work. I am now authorized by the Booksellers to say that they will wait four weeks for the communication which You have obligingly condescended to promise. [The] works will now all be published at once, & your communication will be placed in the front of the Narrative. If Sir it would not suit amidst the multiplicity of your other engagements to finish the biography at the time which the Booksellers have stipulated I think that I might venture to add a procrastination of three or four weeks on my own responsibility. You would confer an essential obligation by informing Me at an early period whether either & which of these portions of time would best enable You to fulfill your benevolent engagement. I am not

[585]

apprehensive that the fulness of Your Biography will be an obstacle to its publication now that I have prevailed upon the Booksellers to procrastinate the volume. I wish very much to enliven the dulness of the Narrative by something more popular splendid & attractive. The publick taste has from a variety of adventious causes been gorged to repletion on fanciful viands & the most nutritive & invigorating aliments will not be relished unless seasoned with Something of that character. Biography partakes to a certain extent of this quality, & is essentially connected with subjects dear to every heart. I am Sir with sentiments of esteem Yours &c.

P. ALLEN

ALS, RC (DLC). Endorsed; received 14 Sept. 1813.

362. Jefferson to Paul Allen

Sir   Monticello Aug. 18. 1813.

In compliance with the request conveyed in your letter of May 25. I have endeavored to obtain, from the relations & friends of the late Governor Lewis, information of such incidents of his life as might be not unacceptable to those who may read the Narrative of his Western discoveries. The ordinary occurrences of a private life, & those also while acting in a subordinate sphere in the army, in a time of peace, are not deemed sufficiently interesting to occupy the public attention; but a general account of his parentage, with such smaller incidents as marked early character, are briefly noted, and to these are added, as being peculiarly within my own knolege, whatever related to the public mission, of which an account is now to be published. The result of my enquiries & recollections, shall now therefore be offered, to be enlarged or abridged <according to your better judgement> as you may think best, or otherwise to be used with the materials you may have collected from other sources.[1]

Meriwether Lewis late Govr. of Louisiana was born on the 18th of Aug. 1774. near the town of Charlottesville in the county of Albemarle in Virginia, of one of the distinguished families of that state. John Lewis one of his father's uncles was a member of the King's council, before the revolution, another of them, Fielding Lewis, married a sister of Genl. Washington. His father Wm. Lewis was the youngest of 5. sons of Colo. Robert Lewis of Albemarle, the 4th of whom Charles was one of the early patriots who stepped forward in the commencement of the revolution, and commanded one of the regiments first raised in Virginia and placed on Continental establishment. Happily situated at home with a wife and young family, & a fortune placing him at ease, he left all to aid in the liberation of his country from foreign usurpations then first unmasking their ultimate end & aim. His good sense, integrity, bravery, enterprize & remarkable bodily powers marked him an officer of great promise; but he unfortunately died early in the revolution. Nicholas Lewis the 2d of his father's brothers commanded a regiment of militia in the successful expedition of 1776 against the Cherokee Indians, who, seduced by the agents of the British government to take up the hatchet against us, had committed great havoc on our Southern frontier, by murdering and scalping helpless women & children according to their cruel and cowardly principles of warfare. The chastisement they then recieved closed the history of their wars, prepared them for recieving the elements of civilisation which zealously inculcated by the present government of the U.S. have rendered them an industrious, peaceable and happy people. This member of the family of Lewises, whose bravery was so usefully improved on this occasion, was endeared to all who knew him by his inflexible probity, courteous disposition, benevolent heart, & engaging modesty & manners. He was the umpire of all the private differences of his county, selected always by both parties. He was also the guardian of Meriwether Lewis, of whom we are now to speak and who had lost his father at an early age. He continued some years under the fostering care of a tender Mother, of the respectable family of Meriwethers of the same county, and was remarkable even in infancy for enterprize, boldness & discretion. When only 8. years of age, he habitually went out in the dead of night alone with his dogs, into the forest to hunt the raccoon & opossum, which, seeking their food in the night, can then only be taken. In this exercise no season or circumstance could obstruct his purpose, plunging thro' the winter's snows and frozen streams in pursuit of his object. At 13. he was put to the Latin school and continued at that untill 15. when he returned to his mother, and entered on the cares of his farm, having, as well as a younger brother, been left by his father with a competency for all the correct and comfortable purposes of temperate life. His talent for observation which had led him to an accurate knolege of the plants & animals of his own country, would have distinguished him as a farmer; but at the age of 20. yeilding to the ardor of youth and a passion for more dazzling pursuits, he engaged as a volunteer in the body of militia which were called out by Genl. Washington, on occasion of the discontents produced by the Excise taxes in the Western parts of the U.S. and from that situation he was removed to the regular service as a lieutenant in the line. At 23. he was promoted to a Captaincy & always attracting the first attention where punctuality & fidelity were requisite, he was appointed paymaster to his regiment. About this time a circumstance occurred which leading to the transaction which is the subject of this book, will justify a recurrence to it's original idea. While I resided in Paris John Ledyard [2] of Connecticut arrived there, well known in the U.S. for energy of body & mind. He had accompanied Capt. Cook in his voyage to the Pacific ocean, and distinguished himself on that voyage by his intrepidity. Being of a roaming disposition, he was now panting for some new enterprize. His immediate object at Paris was to engage a mercantile company in the fur-trade of the Western coast of America, in which however he failed. I then proposed to him to go by land to Kamschatka, cross in some of the Russian vessels to Nootka sound, fall down into the latitude of the Missouri, and penetrate to and thro' that to the U.S. He eagerly siesed the idea, and only asked to be assured of the permission of the Russian government. I interested in obtaining that M. de Simoulin M.P. [minister plenipotentiary] of the Empress at Paris, but more especially the Baron de Grimm M.P. of Saxe-Gotha her more special agent & correspondent there in matters not immediately diplomatic. Her permission was obtained & an assurance of protection while the course of the voyage should be thro' her territories. Ledyard set out from Paris & arrived at St. Petersbg. after the empress had left that place to pass the winter (I think) at Moscow. His finances not permitting him to make unnecessary stay at St. Petersburg he left it, with a passport from one of the ministers, & at 200. miles from Kamschatka was obliged to take up his winter quarters. He was preparing in the spring to resume his journey, when he was arrested by an officer of the Empress, who by this time <*from the caprice or* [. . .]> had changed her mind,[3] and forbidden his proceeding. He was put into a close carriage & conveyed day & night, without ever stopping, till they reached Poland where he was set down & left to himself. The fatigue of this journey broke down his constitution, and when he returned to Paris his bodily strength was much impaired. His mind however remained firm and he after this undertook the journey to Egypt. I recieved a letter from him, full of sanguine hopes, dated at Cairo, the 15th of Nov. 1788. the day before he was to set out for the head of the Nile on which day

[588]

however he ended his career and life. And thus failed the first attempt to explore the Western part of our Northern continent.

In 1792. I proposed to the A.P.S. that we should set on foot a subscription to engage some competent person to explore that region in the opposite direction that is, by ascending the Missouri, crossing the Stony mountains, and descending the nearest river to the Pacific. Capt. Lewis being then stationed at Charlottesville on the recruiting service, warmly sollicited me to obtain for him the execution of that object. I told him it was proposed that the person engaged should be attended by a single companion only, to avoid exciting alarm among the Indians. This did not deter him. But Mr. André Michaux a professed botanist, author of the Flora Boreali-Americana, and of the histoire des chenes d'Amerique, offering his services, they were accepted. He recieved his instructions, and when he had reached Kentucky in the prosecution of his journey, he was overtaken by an order from the minister of France then at Philadelphia to relinquish the expedition, & to pursue elsewhere the Botanical enquiries on which he was employed by that government; and thus failed the 2d attempt for exploring that region.[4] <*When in 1803. Louisiana was ceded to the U.S. a knolege of the Missouri was no longer an object of mere geographical curiosity, but was become highly interesting to the nation, all the country covered by the waters running into the Misipi constituting the extent of their new acquisition in the upper country. Capt. Lewis was now become my private Secretary, and on the first mention of the subject he renewed his sollicitations to be the person employed. My knolege of him, now become more intimate, left no hesitation on my part. I had now had opportunity of knowing his character intimately*>

In 1803 the act for establishing trading houses with the Indian tribes being about to expire some modifications of it were recommended to Congress by a confidential message of Jan. 18. and an extension of it's views to the Indians on the Missouri. In order to prepare the way the message proposed the sending an exploring party to trace the Missouri to it's source, to cross the highlands and follow the best water communication which offered itself from thence to the Pacific ocean. Congress approved the proposition and voted a sum of money for carrying it into execution. Captain Lewis who had then been near two years with me as private secretary, immediately renewed his sollictations to have the direction of the party. I had now had opportunities of knowing him intimately. Of courage undaunted, possessing a firmness & perseverance of purpose which nothing but impossibilities could divert from it's direction, careful as a father of those committed to his charge, yet steady in the maintenance of order & discipline, intimate with the Indian character, customs & principles, habituated to the hunting life, guarded by exact observation of the vegetables & animals of his own country, against losing time in the description of objects already possessed, honest, disinterested, liberal, of sound understanding and a fidelity to truth so scrupulous that whatever he should report would be as certain as if seen by ourselves, with all these qualifications as if selected and implanted by nature in one body, for this express purpose, I could have no hesitation in confiding the enterprize to him. To fill up the measure desired, he wanted nothing but a greater familiarity with the technical language of the natural sciences, and readiness in the astronomical observations necessary for the geography of his route. To acquire these he repaired immediately to Philadelphia, and placed himself under the tutorage of the distinguished professors of that place, who with a zeal & emulation, enkindled by an ardent devotion to science, communicated to him freely the information requisite for the purposes of the journey. While attending too, at Lancaster, the fabrication of the arms with which he chose that his men should be provided, he had the benefit of daily communication with Mr. Andrew Ellicot, whose experience in Astronomical observation, and practice of it in the woods, enabled him to apprise Capt. Lewis of the wants & difficulties he would encounter, and of the substitutes & resources offered by a woodland and uninhabited country. *<It was deemed necessary, also to provide an Associate properly qualified to succeed to the direction of the enterprize, in the event of accident to Capt. Lewis. He proposed Capt. William Clarke of Ohio, brother to Gl. Geo. Rogers Clarke, who was approved without hesitation.>*[5]

Deeming it necessary he should have some person with him of known competence to the direction of the enterprise, & to whom he might confide it, in the event of accident to himself he proposed William Clarke, brother of Genl. Geo. Rogers Clarke, who was approved, and with that view recieved a commission of captain.

In April 1803. a draught of his instructions was sent to Capt. Lewis & on the 20th of June they were signed in the following form. [Here insert the instructions verbatim.]⁶

While these things were going on here, the country of Louisiana, lately ceded by Spain to France, had been the subject of negociation at Paris between us & this last power; and had actually been transferred to us by treaties executed at Paris on the 30th of April. This information recieved about the 1st day of July, increased infinitely the interest we felt in the expedition, & lessened the apprehensions of interruption from other powers. Every thing in this quarter being now prepared, Capt. Lewis left Washington on the 5th of July 1803 and proceeded to Pittsburg where other articles had been ordered to be provided for him. The men too were to be selected from the military stations on the Ohio. Delays of preparation, difficulties of navigation down the Ohio, & other untoward obstruction retarded his arrival at Cahokia until the season was so far advanced as to render it prudent to suspend his entering the Missouri before the ice should break up in the succeeding spring. From this time his journal, now published, will give the history of his journey to and from the Pacific ocean, until his return to St. Louis on the 23d of Sep. 1806. <*He reached Washington accompanied by Capt. Clarke, about the middle of Feb. 1807. Congress being then in session.*> Never did a similar event excite more joy thro' the United States. The humblest of it's citizens had taken a lively interest in the issue of this journey, and looked forward with impatience for the information it would furnish. Their anxieties too for the safety of the corps had been kept in a state of excitement by lugubrious rumors, circulated from time to time on uncertain authorities, and uncontradicted by letters or other direct information from the time they had left the Mandan towns on their ascent up the river in April of the preceding year 1805, until their actual return to St. Louis.

It was the middle of Feb. 1807. before Capt. Lewis with his companion Clarke reached the city of Washington where Congress was then in session.[7] That body granted to the two chiefs and their followers, the donation of lands which they had been <*promised*> encouraged to expect in reward of their toils & dangers. Capt. Lewis was soon after appointed Governor of Louisiana, and Capt. Clarke a General of it's militia and agent of the U.S. for Indian affairs in that department.

A considerable time intervened before the Governor's arrival at St. Louis. He found the territory distracted by feuds & contentions among the officers of the government, & the people themselves divided by these into factions & parties. He determined at once, to take no side with either; but to use every endeavor to conciliate & harmonize them. The even-handed justice he administered to all soon established a respect for his person & authority, and perseverance & time wore down animosities and reunited the citizens again into one family.

Governor Lewis had from early life been subject to hypocondriac affections. It was a constitutional disposition in all the nearer branches of the family of his name, & was more immediately inherited by him from his father. They had not however been so strong as to give uneasiness to his family. While he lived with me in Washington, I observed at times sensible depressions of mind, but knowing their constitutional source, I estimated their course by what I had seen in the family. During his Western expedition the constant exertion which that required of all the faculties of body & mind, suspended these distressing affections; but after his establishment at St. Louis in sedentary occupations they returned upon him with redoubled vigor, and began seriously to alarm his friends. He was in a paroxysm of one of these when his affairs rendered it necessary for him to go to Washington. He proceeded to the Chickasaw bluffs where he arrived on the 16th of Sep. 1809. with a view of continuing his journey thence by water. Mr. Neely, agent of the U.S. with the Chickasaw Indians arriving there two days after, found him extremely indisposed, and betraying at times some symptoms of a derangement of mind. The rumors of a war with England, & apprehensions that he might lose the papers he was bringing on, among which were the vouchers of his public accounts, and the journals & papers of his Western expedition, induced him here to change his mind and to take his course by land thro' the Chickasaw country. Altho' he appeared somewhat relieved, Mr. Neely kindly determined to accompany & watch over him. Unfortunately, at their encampment after having passed the Tennissee one day's journey, they lost two horses, which obliging Mr. Neely to halt for their recovery, the Governor proceeded under a promise to wait for him at the house of the first white inhabitant on his road. He stopped at the house of a Mr. Grinder, who not being at home, his wife alarmed at the symptoms of derangement she discovered, gave him up the house, and retired to rest herself in an outhouse; the Governor's & Neely's servants lodging in another. About 3. oclock in the night he did the deed which plunged his friends into affliction and deprived his country of one of her most valued citizens whose valour & intelligence would have been now imployed in avenging the wrongs of his country and in emulating by land the splendid deeds which have honored her arms on the ocean. It lost too to the nation the benefit of recieving from his own hand the Narrative now offered them of his sufferings & successes in endeavoring to extend for them the boundaries of science, and to present to their knolege that vast & fertile country which their sons are destined to fill with arts, with science, with freedom & happiness.

To this melancholy close of the life of one whom posterity will declare not to have lived in vain I have only to add that all facts I have stated are either known to myself, or communicated by his family or others for whose truth I have no hesitation to make [myself] responsible: and I conclude with tendering you the assurances of my respect & consideration.

Th: Jefferson

ALS, SC (DLC); RC (DLC) in photostat only.

1. The first paragraph is written in narrow measure in the margin of the manuscript.

2. On Ledyard, see several letters in Appendix 1. Here Jefferson claims to have originated the idea that Ledyard should attempt to walk across the continent from the Northwest coast. Acually it was Ledyard's own plan, probably conceived more than two years before he met Jefferson (AUGUR, 125).

3. Jefferson now believes the Empress Catherine granted Ledyard passage, then retracted the permission. No such permission was given, as Jefferson later discovered.

4. An indulgent treatment of Michaux's activities in the U.S. on behalf of his own government. See Jefferson's instructions to Michaux and other material on this topic in Appendix 1.

5. First version of this deleted sentence: "Capt. William Clarke of Ohio, brother of Gl. Geo. Rogers Clarke, was the choice of Capt. Lewis & was approved without hesitation."

6. The bracketed words are Jefferson's, referring to that version of his instructions to Lewis which appear in this volume as No. 47.

7. Jefferson is writing from memory and is not too exact about details. Lewis reached Washington in late Dec. 1806, and Clark followed some weeks later.

363. Biographical Sketch of Lewis

[c. 18 August 1813]

M. Lewis, born August 18, 1774 in Albemarle. At first went to common day schools, learning to read, to write & Arithmetic with ordinary facility, he was early remarkable for intrepidity, liberality & hardihood, at eight years of age going alone with his dogs at midnight in the depth of winter, hunting wading creeks when the banks were covered with ice & snow. He might be tracked through the snow to his traps by the blood which trickled from his bare feet. At eleven years old he was taken from his mother and remained untill thirteen with his guardian, when he was past to Latin schools kept by Pr. Everett Parson Maury & Parson Wardell. From eighteen to twenty he remained on his farm an affectionate son and an assiduous and attentive farmer, observing with minute attention all plants and insects which he met with. In his twentieth year he joined a volunteer corps as a private under T. Walker against the insurgents. During the same year he was appointed lieutenant in the U.S. army. In his twenty third year he was promoted to a Captaincy and returned to Albemarle to recruit. He again joined the army and acted as paymaster untill he was made private secretary to the President.

(DLC). The handwriting is not identified. Endorsed by Jefferson, "Lewis Meriwether." Although the undated document is filed after No. 149 in the Jefferson Papers, it probably is information gathered by Jefferson while compiling data for his memoir of Lewis (No. 362). Note that it covers the early period of Lewis's life only; for the period after Lewis became his secretary, Jefferson seems to have relied on his own files and his memory.

364. Jefferson to Nicholas Biddle

Sir   Monticello Aug. 20. 13.
    In a letter from Mr. Paul Allen of Philadelphia, I was informed that other business had obliged you to turn over to him the publication of Govr. Lewis's journal of his Western expedition; and he requested me to furnish him with any materials I could for writing a sketch of his life. I now inclose him such as I have been able to procure, to be used with any other information he may have recieved, or alone, if he has no other or in any way you & he shall think proper. The part you have been so good as to take in digesting the work entitles you to decide on whatever may be proposed to go out under it's auspice's; and on this ground I take the liberty of putting under cover to you, and for your perusal, my letter to Mr. Allen, which I will request you to seal & hand on to him. I am happy in this occasion of expressing my portion of the thanks all will owe you for the trouble you have taken with the interesting narrative, and the assurance of my sentiments of high esteem and respect.

                                                            TH: JEFFERSON

    ALS, SC (DLC). Reply is No. 366.

365. Jefferson to Paul Allen

Sir   Monticello Aug. 20. 13.
    In my letter of the 5th inst. I requested what time you could give me for further enquiry on the subject of the life of Govr. Lewis. I

have since satisfied myself that there is no more matter within my reach. And being about to set out on a journey, on which I shall be absent three weeks, I have concluded it best to forward you without delay the sketch I have been able to prepare. Accept with it the assurance of my great respect.

TH: JEFFERSON

P.S. Not knowing who is to print the work, I will ask the favor of you to desire the printer, when the work is compleat, to send me thirteen copies, 3 of them neatly bound, the rest in boards (for transmission to Europe). The best conveyance is by the stage, addressed to Gibson & Jefferson, merchants of that place, who will pay the transportation and forward them to me. They would be still safer, if any passenger to Richmond would take them under his care. The amount shall be remitted on reciept of the printer's bill.

ALS, SC (DLC). Reply is No. 368.

366. Nicholas Biddle to Jefferson

Sir,   Andalusia on the Delaware Sept. 28. 1813

My residence in the country during the Summer has prevented me from answering sooner your very polite note of the 20th of August covering a communication to Mr. Allen which was immediately transmitted to him. It is now a long time since I was tempted by the request of Genl. Clark & other friends as well as by the natural interest of the subject to undertake the composition of the narrative part of the travels of Messrs. Lewis & Clark whilst Dr. Barton took charge of the objects of natural history connected with the work. I had written off roughly nearly the whole when other occupations interposed, & on Genl. Clark's visit here last spring I gave up the manuscripts to Mr. Allen who was to take the rude outline as I had left it, add from the original journals whatever had been omitted in the first rapid sketch—mould the whole as he thought best and superintend the publication. He informs me that about one half of the second & last volume of the narrative is printed & that the whole will appear shortly. The introductory notice of Govr. Lewis is very interesting & the account of the previous projects for exploring the country west of the Mississipi contains new & curious information. You mention the assistance of the Baron de Grimm. You may not perhaps have seen the correspondence of that gentleman which was published last year at Paris. I have received it & if I thought the perusal of it would gratify you would forward it to you at Monticello, the more willingly as I know that you regard with interest the literary occurrences of France. This correspondence however, tho' in five large Octavo volumes does not reach lower than the year 1782, a circumstance which diminishes in some degree its value to us.

My estimable friend Mr. Correa spent a short time with me on his way northward to embark for Europe. I am delighted at his visit to Monticello, since the sentiments with which he returns from it, have raised our country in his estimation & will do us much honor abroad. They have also added greatly to the respectful consideration with which I am sincerely Yrs.

N. BIDDLE

ALS, SC (DLC—Biddle); RC (DLC). Endorsed; received 10 Oct. 1813.

367. Jefferson to F. H. Alexander von Humboldt

My dear friend and Baron   Dec. 6. 13.

· · · · ·

You will find it inconcievable that Lewis's journey to the Pacific should not yet have appeared; nor is it in my power to tell you the reason. The measures taken by his surviving companion Clarke, for the publication, have not answered our wishes in point of dispatch. I think however, from what I have heard, that the mere journal will be out within a few weeks in 2. vols. 8vo. These I will take care to send you with the tobacco seed you desired, if it be possible for them to escape the thousand ships of our enemies spread over the ocean. The botanical & zoological discoveries of Lewis will probably experience greater delay, and become known to the world thro' other channels before that volume will be ready. The Atlas, I believe, waits on the leisure of the engraver.

Altho' I do not know whether you are now at Paris, or ranging the regions of Asia to acquire more knolege for the use of man, I cannot deny myself the gratification of an endeavor to recall myself to your recollection, of assuring you of my constant attachment, and of renewing to you the just tribute of my affectionate esteem & high respect and consideration.

TH: JEFFERSON

ALS, SC (DLC). Baron Friedrich Heinrich Alexander von Humboldt (1769–1859), German naturalist and statesman, had traveled in North America and made important geographical observations.

368. Paul Allen to Jefferson

Philadelphia Dec. 18. 1813.

I trust that Your Excellency will do Me the justice to believe that Your request with regard to the volumes of Lewis & Clarke would have been complied with long since & the books transmitted if the works had not been unexpectedly detained in the hands of the Printer.[1] They have now arrived at the conclusion of the work excepting the diary of the weather &c. which comes in at the appendix. The delay has been occasioned by the press of other avocations which the Printers have been obliged to turn their more immediate attention to, particularly periodical works. My reason for troubling Your Excellency is an apprehension that You would deem me neglectful of Your request of which believe Me Sir I am utterly incapable. With regard to the biographical [sketch] which you so condescendingly furnished Me with, I have to offer my sincerest thanks accompanied I must confess with some little chagrin that it was out of my power to requite the obligation. My mind was for sometime wavering on the propriety of annexing to Your biographick sketch a particular account of the melancholy death of Capt. Lewis. That account has already been published by the late Alexander Wilson Esqr. the celebrated Ornitholgist. But as this might notwithstanding in all human probability wound the sensibility of surviving relatives & friends, I deemed it the most expedient to err on the side of humanity & rather to veil the severity of bibliographick fact than to have my motives misunderstood by the recital. I should have been much gratified by annexing a sketch of the life of Gov. Clarke but that has been long since abandoned as unattainable. The misfortune in such cases is that with regard to many of the Men who have adorned the character of their Country it *is by one single act that they have rendered themselves illustrious.* When that act is told the whole of the life of the Individual so far as the Publick is interested becomes already known & precludes interesting biography. Thus this hazardous expedition is the only part of Capt. Lewis's [. . .] life which were he now alive he would be willing probably to submit to public Notice. It was on one occasion only that his great talents were put to the proof & then they were found adequate to the emergency.

It is commonly believed by Mankind that when one of [. . .] Beings displays talents commensurate with the [. . .][2] them forth, that the whole of his previous life must exhibit some traces of that character. This is a great mistake which may be illustrated by an anecdote of my Countryman the late Gen. Greene. When he was a Militia General in Rhode Island he addressed a petition to the Legislature of that State mentioning that a bill of six shillings of Continental currency was accidentally washed to pieces in his jacket pocket & praying compensation. Yet this was the same Nathaniel Greene who afterwards delivered the southern States from the tyranny of England! Your Excellencys humble Servt.

P. ALLEN

ALS, RC (DLC). Endorsed; received 31 Dec. 1813.

1. Bradford and Inskeep did not notify Jefferson until 12 April 1814 (MHi) that they had shipped him thirteen copies, including one complimentary copy. The bill dated 7 April amounted to $68.75. Jefferson wrote them 17 Aug. that while he had received their bill on 22 April he had not received the books until 15 Aug. He enclosed payment and thanked them for the free copy (MHi).

2. Two or more words concealed by a mend in the manuscript.

369. Nicholas Biddle to Clark

My Dear Sir,   Phila. March 23. 1814

I have at last the pleasure of informing you that the Travels are published—that they have sold very well I understand, and have been well thought of by the readers. Henceforward you may sleep upon your fame which must last as long as books can endure. Mr. Bradford has I presume sent you a copy of the work. The gentleman who revised & prepared it for the press, Mr. Allen is a very capable person, & as I did not put the finishing hand to the volumes I did not think it right to take from him the credit of his own exertions & care by announcing personally the part which I had in the compilation. I am content that my trouble in the business should be recompensed only by the pleasure which attended it,[1] and also by the satisfaction of making your acquaintance which I shall always value. I could have wished that your time had permitted you to revise the whole of the work as no doubt some errors & inadvertencies have from the nature of the volumes & the circumstances attending the publication crept into them. I hope however that you will not find them very numerous or important.

All my family as well as my self have lately been in the greatest affliction from having lost in the course of 2 month's time my mother in law Mrs. Craig & my own son. In order to recruit Mrs. Biddle's health & spirits we mean to undertake a journey as soon as the weather permits, to the upper part of Virginia where we shall probably pass the whole of the summer. In the course of our ride I may perhaps see your good friends at Fincastle.

There is nothing of much political importance stirring here. We are all expecting peace shortly, & then I hope your fur trade & your fine western country will flourish more than ever.

I forward a letter lately sent to me for you.

Let me hear from you often. Neither you nor I are great letter writers but I will always be happy to learn that you are well & your affairs prosperous. With my Compts. to Mrs. Clarke I am yrs. truly,

N. BIDDLE

ALS, SC (DLC—Biddle). Reply is No. 370.

1. I have found no evidence that Biddle received the slightest remuneration for his months of toil on the Lewis and Clark publication. When I asked Biddle's biographer, Thomas P. Govan, about this curious fact, he reminded me that Biddle was married to one of the richest women in America and could hardly have been interested in payment. By assigning the Lewis and Clark project to Allen, Biddle preserved the anonymity which he also observed on the *Port-Folio*. His friends knew what he had done; public acclaim did not matter. As Govan points out, Biddle always seemed to do the "right thing," and his associates expected it of him. Clark's expressions of gratitude seem almost perfunctory, as if the labor that Biddle had put into the book was quite a natural thing.

370. Clark to Nicholas Biddle

Dear Sir   St. Louis Septr. 16th 1814

I do assure you that I was extreemly concerned for the loss you have met with in your familey, my own feelings enables me to know what those of a fond parent must be towards his child. I hope Mrs. Biddle has born her loss in such a way as [not] to have injured her health, and that you both are at this time in perfect health. I have not heard of your being in the upper part of Virginia, and fear the dificulties on your Coast will prevent your intended visit to Virginia. We have alarming accounts of the depredations of the Enemy in Meryland & Virginia. The accounts are more favourable from Niagara. I assure you that I have had my hands full in the Territory an emence number of Indians & som of British to oppose & but fiew men to stand to their post, our small force has had a great deel of fighting on very unequal terms. In the spring I assended the Mississippi and built a Fort at Prarie de Chien,[1] which has been taken since by the British & Indians from Mackanack, after some hard fighting, Genl. Howard[2] who has the Command at this time of the Troops at this point finds a good deel of dificulty to keep the frontier from Breaking with all the aid I can give him of Militia & friendly Indians. However I expect we shall keep the enemy off this season.

I have borrowed a Copy of my Book which has reached this place but have not had time to read it as yet.

I think it not improbable that Mrs. Clark will have to take another Trip to Phila. Her Breast continues to be sore & enlargens. She has been at the Sulpher Springs for six weeks without any proceivable change for the better. I am apprehensive it will termonate in a Cancer. Doctr. Phisicks[3] advice on the subject would be a Cordual to her feelings.

Let me hear from you often. We shall ever be glad to hear from you and your familey and that you may all enjoy health & hapiness is the sincere wish of your sincer friend,

WM. CLARK

17th. Mrs. Clark has written to me to day to request you to give her love to Mrs. Biddle & accept her best wishes for yourself. I have enclosed to you a letter to Col. Williams Covering $25 for the Military Philosophical Society, which leter I must beg you to send to the Col.

ALS, RC (DLC—Biddle). Addressed; endorsed.

1. Clark, now governor of Missouri Territory as well as superintendent of Indian affairs, had led an expedition of five armed gunboats up the Mississippi in May. His force had occupied Prairie du Chien, constructed a fort which was christened Fort Shelby, and the expedition had at first seemed a glowing success. But in July the post came under heavy attack by British and Indian forces, and was lost (GREGG, 328–34).

2. Brig. Gen. Benjamin Howard, commanding the forces in the western portion of military district No. 8, including militia, mounted rangers, and the First Infantry Regiment (Secretary of War to Howard, 10 April 1813, DNA, RG 107, Letters Sent, 6:359).

3. Dr. Philip Syng Physick (1768–1837), a Philadelphia physician.

371. In Account with Bradford & Inskeep

[1815]

Lewis & Clarks Travels in a/c Currt. with the Estate
of Bradford & Inskeep

Dr.

1813
March 29 To Cash paid S. Lewis[1] for making Sundry
              Alterations in plates   20 50

August 18	" ditto paid Wm. Kneast[2] for Engraving	75	
Septem 29	" ditto " Mrs. Garrett for folding	48	50
1814			
January 28	" ditto " Henry Charles[3] for Copper-plate Printing	77	50
March 5	" ditto " Saml. Harrison for Engraving Large Plate	325	64
April 27	" ditto " for folding	55	40
29	" 1 Copy overcharged to West & Blake	4	80
May 29	" additional discount allowed Cramer & Co.[4] Pittsburg	23	33
June 8	" O. C. Greenleaf for 7 Copies del. to Bradford & Read, Boston	28	
11	" Printing 2000 Copies Circulars &c.	1145	30
	301 Reams Printing Paper @ 500	1505	
	3 " Copperplate do. 1600	48	
	4 " Large India do. 2500	100	
	Cash Paid for Boxes of Advertising &c.	40	
		3496	97

To Amount of Bills not paid yet viz.

Gaskill[5] for binding 387.95 ⎱
Desilver[6] "   do.   220.82 ⎰ 686 27
Charles "   Cop
    printing   77.50 ⎰

Bad Debts & Copies not paid for

26 Copies to St. Pleasants[7]
    decd.   105 ⎱
125   "   Sundry Booksellers   677.55
    failed   572.55 ⎰

Not paid for

18 to J. Kennedy Alex.   72 ⎱
50 " Fitzwhylsome &
    Co.   201.25
3 " Wm. Graydon   13.50 ⎰ 520.58
36 " E. J. Coale[8]   145
10 " Wm. T. Gray   40.82
12 " Essex & Co.   48.01 ⎰

	1884	40
Balance	154	10
	5535	47

[601]

1814

February 20 By 55 Copies Sold to J. Hoff ⁹ 221.50
           1 " " J. Vaughan 6 — 227 50
March 1 " 36 " " E. J. Coale Balt. — 145
           50 " " Fitzwhylsome & Co. Rich. — 201 25
           18 " " J. Kennedy Alex. — 72
    3 " 50 " " Ronalds, Swords, Eastburn
           & Co.¹⁰ New York — 206
    4 " 27 to Johnson & Warner 109
         8 " Sundry Persons 32 — 141
       26 " S. Pleasants Richmond — 105
       10 " Wm. T. Gray Fredericksburg — 40 82
    5 " 59 " Sundry Persons in N. York — 246
    7 " 30 " Eastburn & Co. " " — 126
      175 " Sundry Booksellers in N.Y. Boston &c. — 782 55
    9 " 3 " Wm. Graydon Harrisburg — 13 50
   10 " 90 " Sundry persons in Philada. — 376 "
   12 " 90 " " Booksellers in Philada. &
           New York — 357 65
   14 " 40 " " ditto ditto — 185 33
   17 " 9 " " ditto ditto — 36 34
   21 " 62 " " ditto ditto — 246 25
   22 " 33 " " New York & Pittsburg — 159
   23 " 72 " " ditto — 281 45
   24 " 9 " " A. A. Inskeep — 34 80
   25 " 65 " " Charleston & Phila. — 293 75
   30 " 3 " " Philadelphia — 13 30
April 7 " 18 " " ditto &c. — 87 09
    9 " 20 " " ditto — 79 36
   18 " 13 " " ditto — 52 20
   19 " 7 " " Collins & Co. N. York — 28
May 9 " 1 " " George Zollock — 7
   12 " 40 " " in Baltimore — 170 01
   17 " 26 " " Phil. — 118 66
   30 " 1 " " Kimber & Co. — 6 67
June 9 " 16 " Copies in New York & Boston — 60
   24 " 1 " T. Leiper — 6
July 8 " 8 " Johnson & Warner — 32 66
   10 " 2 " A. Small — 10
   30 " 1 " J. Brown — 5 84
      14 " J. D. Clifford — 60 80

[602]

				1 " R. Fielding	6 00
Sep 30	"	1	"	Johnson & Warner	5 84
Oct 31	"	12	"	Essex & Co.	48 01
Nov 7	"	1	"	R. O. Weightman	4
Dec 8	"	1	"	John Vaughan	6
15	"	1	"	Johnson & Warner	5 84

```
               92 " Sold to Sundry Booksellers
                    for Cash                       552 00
                         disct. 50 pr. ct.   276 00
                                                    276
           60 "         do @ 140 pr. vol.           168
                                                   5535 47
                              By balance            154 10
```

        Remaining on hand 392 Vol. 1st
                           390 "   2 wanting plates
                            35 Copies wanting index &c.
                            38 "   bds complete
                            23 "   sheep do.
        156 Copies deficient, supposed to be destroyed in binder
        or printer hands or never received from Printer—

(NjP). In the manuscript, credit and debit columns are arranged side by side; they have been divided here to simplify typography.

1. Samuel Lewis (1754?–1822), Philadelphia draftsman and engraver. A man identifying himself as Samuel Lewis, Sr., wrote Jefferson a long appeal on 14 Jan. 1801 (DLC) from the "debtor's apartment" of the prison in Philadelphia, asking for help. He said he had been an aide in the War Department against whom a shortage had developed, and now had a volume of maps in preparation. Undoubtedly the maps were those later published in *A new and elegant general atlas, comprising all the new discoveries to the present time; containing sixty-three maps, drawn by* [Aaron] *Arrowsmith and* [Samuel] *Lewis* (Philadelphia, 1804). The publisher was John Conrad.

2. William Kneass, engraver, Filbert and Twelfth Streets, Philadelphia.

3. Henry Charles, copperplate printer and map publisher, 117 North Fifth Street, Philadelphia.

4. Zadok Cramer's publishing house, the firm of Cramer, Spear and Eichbaum.

5. Benjamin Gaskill, bookbinder, 18 Bank Street, Philadelphia.

6. Thomas or Robert De Silver. As listed in BROWN, both men were Philadelphia bookbinders, operating separately at times and in 1812 as a partnership. In 1814 they seem to have had separate shops, Thomas at 220 High and 14 South Seventh, and Robert at 110 Walnut Street.

7. Jefferson referred to "the late Mr. Pleasants" on 12 Oct. 1816, in

transferring his book buying to Fitzwhylson and Potter, in Richmond. He had previously done his Richmond book buying from Pleasants (DLC).

8. Edward J. Coale, bookseller. Lakin's *Baltimore directory and register* for 1814 and 1815 lists him as operating at 176 Baltimore Street.

9. John Hoff, printer at 48 Cherry Street, Philadelphia, in the period 1803–09 (BROWN).

10. No such firm is listed by MC KAY, but he lists Eastburn, Kirk & Co., Wall and Nassau Streets, 1814–16; Thomas A. Ronalds, 188 Pearl Street, 1809–20; and Thomas and James Swords, 160 Pearl Street, 1803–20.

372. Nicholas Biddle to [Samuel F. Bradford or John Inskeep]

Sir,   Harris[burg]h Jany. 22. 1815

You will readily believe that it has given me much pain to hear of your misfortunes. With your industry & talents however no misfortunes can be irreparable & I hope that you will soon be able to get through your difficulties & again be prosperous.

The chief purpose of my writing at present is to ask your attention to the affairs of my friend General Clarke. <*When Mr. Conrad was unfortunate the books belonging to the late General Pike continued to be his property & were preserved for him.*> I hope that you will be able to make some arrangement to preserve for him the books which may be unsold & secure his share of those already disposed of. After all the toils & hazards which he has undergone, the only remuneration he expected was from the profits of his book, and I should be sorry that he should not derive all the emolument from that source to which he is entitled. The management of that concern he always confided to your liberality & justice—& I therefore rely on your exertions to do the best for him under present circumstances. I should be glad to hear from you on this subject as soon as you have leisure & remain Yrs. respy.

N. BIDDLE

ALS, SC (DLC—Biddle).

373. Nicholas Biddle to Clark

My dear Sir,   Harr[isburg]h March 12. 1815

I am very sorry to inform you that among the effects of the war among trading people in Phila. has been the insolvency of Messrs. Bradford & Inskeep. I have been confined to this place during the winter as a member of the Senate, but as soon as I heard of their misfortune I wrote a letter to Mr. Bradford of which the following is a copy.

[Dated Harrh. March 12. 1815].[1] To this letter I received an answer which I have not at present by me, but in which he tells me that he had apprized the assignees of your claims & would do what he could in the business. I since made a short visit to Phila. & endeavored to procure the accounts but in the confusion & bustle of a recent failure they were not able to make them out. Being obliged to return to the legislature I left the papers in the hands of a friend—a gentleman of the law, whom I directed to consult with the assignees & do what was necessary. The legislature will adjourn tomorrow & I will then go to Phila. & look into the business. If the peace had come a few weeks sooner the misfortune of these persons would have been prevented but as it is the failure is for a very large amount.

I have been passing a very disagreeable winter here at a distance from my family. You too have been very busy with public affairs, but I hope the peace will bring you leisure & prosperity. Will it not also induce you to pay us a visit. I should be very glad to see you again. I hope Mrs. Clarke's health is better. Remember me to her with great respect & believe me to be with great Esteem & regard Yrs. sincerely,

N. BIDDLE

ALS, SC (DLC—Biddle). Clark replied 18 June 1815, lamenting the failure of his publisher. "The steps you have & may think proper to prosue for the purpose of obtaining my proportion of Books, Papers, amount of sales &c. will not only meet my approbation, but my sincerest thanks for the interest you take as my friend" (DLC—Biddle).

1. The bracketed phrase is Biddle's. He must mean Jan. 12, referring to our No. 372.

374. Charles Chauncey to Thomas Astley

Sir,   [10 May 1815]

I have examined the statement, concerning Lewis & Clarke's Travels, which you were so obliging as to furnish me, and will take the liberty of stating the principles, upon which, I conceive, the account should be settled.

The agreement between Genl. Clark and Messrs. Bradford & Inskeep was, That the latter should cause the work to be printed, to the number of two thousand copies, and do. pay all the expenses. That out of the first monies received from the sale, in the first place 500 Drs. shd. be pd. to Genl. Clark's attorney in fact (for Mr. Allen), in the next place, Messrs. Bradford & Inskeep shd. be reimbursed the expenses of publication, and then the net profits shd. be equally divided between the parties to the agreement.

The account should be stated & settled, I think, under this agreement, as upon a joint undertaking & interest. As against the joint property, which I consider the Edition to be, should be charged all the expenses of publication including the 500 Drs. for Mr. Allen; and the balance of the joint property, which is the net profits is then to be equally divided. If Messrs. B. & I. previously to their failure received any part of their share of the profits, it of course reduces their interest in the residue; & that residue is to be disposed of—so as to place Genl. Clark upon an equal footing with them. The assignment by B. & I. placed the ass[ign]ees, exactly in the situation of B. & I. themselves, and the settlement shd. now take place precisely as it would between Genl. Clark & B. & I. if no assignment had taken place. It would not, I apprehend, be just or legal, to consider the assignees as entitled to a moiety of the Books on hand, and Genl. Clark as a creditor of B. & I's for a moiety of the monies received then by B. & I. over the amt. of their disbursements; which I presume from the statement furnished me, has been contemplated by the assignees as the correct mode of adjustment.

After the assignees shall have considered of these suggestions, I should be happy to hear from them on the subject. I am, Sir, very respectfully, Yours,

CH. CHAUNCEY

May 10, 1815

P.S. I am under an impression, that Mr. Biddle has informed me, that Mr. Allen has recd. $200 on acct.

ALS, RC (DLC—Biddle). Charles Chauncey, counselor at law, 85 Walnut, Philadelphia, was assigned by Biddle to handle Clark's interest. Thomas Astley is listed as a merchant, 6 Yorks Building, in the 1816 *Directory*, and is probably a member of the firm of Astley & Brooks, "assignees of Bradford & Inskeep," 63 South Fifth Street. The Brooks of this firm might be Samuel Brooks, merchant, 161 Walnut.

375. Moses Thomas to Nicholas Biddle

D Sir
[17 July 1815]

I offer to take the whole of "Lewis & Clarke's Expedition" at a discount of fifty per cent from the retail price & 6 months credit (security for the payment shall be given if required) on condition of having the refusal of the copyright & plates when this edition is disposed of—it is to be understood that no other edition of the work is to be printed until the present shall be sold. With respect Yr Obt. Svt.

July 17th 1815.   M. THOMAS

ALS, RC (NjP). Addressed.

376. Thomas Astley to Charles Chauncey

Dear Sir   [30 November 1815]

I have been attending to the business of Lewis & Clarke's Journal, but I find that in order to give you a proper view of it, it will be necessary to draw out a statement of the account, from the commencement of the business to the present time. I have set a person to work to do this, but it is long, & it will take some days to complete it. In the mean while I have had an account taken of the stock on hand, which appears to be as follows—

392 copies	1st Vol	nearly all wanting Plates, & in the
390 "	2d Vol	hands of the binder for security of his charges against the work
31 copies	1st Vol	in boards, not complete
39 "	2d Vol	Do Do wanting Plates & table of contents—in the hands of the binder
23 sets	complete	bd sheep
39 "	"	in boards

I think either you or Mr. Biddle mentioned to me that Mr. B had had an offer for the Stock & the Copy-right. Will you be good enough to inform me the terms of the offer, & the person who made it.

May I also trouble you for a copy of the agreement between Genl. Clarke & Bradford & Inskeep relating to the work. I have not been able to lay my hands on Mr. Bradford's copy of this instrument. I am very truly Your Obed. Srvt.

30th Nov. 1815.   THO. ASTLEY

ALS, RC (NjP). Addressed.

377. Jefferson to José Corrèa da Serra

Monticello Jan. 1. 16.

. . . .

The death of Dr. Barton revives my anxiety to recover the MS. journals of Capt. Lewis, for the satisfaction of his family; and may at

[607]

the same time facilitate it. He had promised me sacredly that he would see to it's restoration, and as you were so kind as to say you would attend to it on your return to Philadelphia, I now earnestly entreat your aid for this object. Knowing nothing of what is doing, or intended to be done as to the publication of the papers respecting the natural history & geography of the country, you will oblige me by any information you can obtain on this subject. The right to these papers is in the government, as may be seen by the instructions to Capt. Lewis. They were left in his hands that he might derive to himself the pecuniary benefits of their publication, on the presumption they would certainly be published. If that presumption is to fail, the government must reclaim them; and it is to put this object into an effective course that I wish for information what is doing, or likely to be done. I know I should have the concurrence of Genl. Clarke in this, were he within the timely reach of consultation, and I shall not fail to advise with him as soon as I can do it understandingly.

· · · ·

TH: JEFFERSON

ALS, SC (DLC). Endorsed. José Francisco Corrèa da Serra (1750–1823), Portuguese diplomat, botanist, and priest, spent nearly nine years in America from 1812 to 1820. He was a friend and correspondent of Jefferson and other learned Americans of the period. For a collection of his letters, see CORREA. In reply to this letter, he said, "Several times have I called on Mrs. Barton and twice on Mr. Pennington her brother, who has great influence on her, and assists her in the arrangement of her affairs, but I am not more advanced than in the beginning. The Dr. has left such an immense heap of papers, and in such disorder; the reclamations for papers and books are so many, that I conceive how the poor Lady is embarrassed how to do. . . . But I hope there will be an end in this suspense; you will know the result" (16 Feb. 1816, DLC). Dr. Barton had married Mary Pennington in 1797; her brother was Edward Pennington, of Philadelphia.

Jefferson's interest in preserving and publishing the findings of the expedition has been evident in earlier correspondence, but he may have been particularly stimulated at this time by Peter S. Du Ponceau (1760–1844), lawyer and ethnologist. As corresponding secretary of the newly formed Historical and Literary Committee of the American Philosophical Society, Du Ponceau had written Jefferson 14 Nov. 1815 (DLC), soliciting his help in locating historical manuscripts for deposit with the Society. Jefferson had replied 22 Jan. 1816 (DLC) that he would do what he could to aid in the search for such materials.

378. José Corrèa da Serra to Jefferson

Dear Sir   Philadelphia 29 March 1816
    At last Mrs. Barton has sent me a little morocco bound volume,

[608]

part of Capt. Lewis journal containing his observations from April 9 of 1805 to February 17 1806, and the meterological observ. for July August September 1805, together with the drawing of a quadruped which he calls the Fisher.[1] As the chaos of his library begins to clear, by the separation of printed books which are sold to the hospital I doubt not the remaining papers of Capt. Lewis may be found, but you could help me much by sending me a description of their external appearance, and their probable volume, because Mrs. Barton who acts in all this very honestly (but does not permit any body, to search the papers of her husband, but by what I understand only herself and her brother who is also a very honest person) will be much helped in finding them. In the mean time I expect your directions about what I am to do with the volume I have got, and the others that may appear.

I hope you have enjoyed perfect health, and your winter probably has not been so capricious as in Pennsylvania, where after very pleasant weather, we have felt two rather severe snow storms since the middle of the month.

Marshall Grouchy has been here a few days in the same hotel with Mr. Short whose acquaintance he is. I have spoken with him, and he did not seem to me very sanguine in his expectations about what is going in Europe. From his account Bonaparte's talents did not shine in the last years of his political existence. I remain with the highest respect and esteem Most sincerely Yours,

J. Corrèa de Serra

ALS, RC (DLC). Endorsed; received 19 April 1816.
1. The volume of Lewis's observations is Codex P, and the drawing of the fisher—*Martes pennanti* (Erxleben)—is in vol. 7 of the Lewis and Clark journals and miscellaneous papers (PPAmP). Corrèa sent this little volume by way of Jefferson's granddaughter, Ellen Wayles Randolph (1796–1876), who was then visiting in Philadelphia (Corrèa to Jefferson, 12 May 1816, and Jefferson to Elizabeth Trist, 25 April 1816, both in MHi).

379. Clark to Nicholas Biddle

Dear Sir   St. Louis March 31st 1816
It has been a long time since I have had the pleasure of a letter from you. Your last was on the Subject of Mr. Bradfords falue [failure], and your intention of precureing the Books for me of the assignees &c. I must request the favor of you to inform me what has been done with the Books specimens &c.

I am unacquainted with the progress which Mr. Bradford had made, and as yet have not been able to precure any of those which have been printed.

I have never heard from Doctr. Barton nor do I know what he has done in his part—as he is dead, and most probably has not complyed with his contract, would it not be best to secure the specimens and papers placed under his control? If you think the measure correct, and it would not give you too much trouble, I would be oblige to you to apply for and receive them of his Extrs. &c.

As Doctr. Marks (the half Brother of Govr. Lewis has expressed to me in a letter some Concern about his brothers interest in the Books,[1] and asked of me for a power of atty. to receive of the publisher the Books, I must request you to deliver to the order of his Mother Mrs. Marks, such Books Papers &c. as you may think Govr. Lewis's Heirs should receive at least fully the one half of my part.

As to news we [hear] nothing interesting, the hostile Indians are about to make peace, which will produce Tranquility once more in this quarter which we have not enjoyed for several years.

The Country is already beginning to populate and the tide of imigration is bending it's course up the Missouri. The only obsticle is the want of Lands to purchase.

I sincerely wish it was in my power to visit you this spring or summer, but the duties assigned to me in this Country will employ me [the] greater part of the year. I hope you will favor me with a letter when convenient which I hope will be frequently.

Mrs. Clark has been unwell for several months and at this time confined to her bed. She joins me in Compliments most respectfully to yourself and Lady; and with the highest respect & sincerely Your mo. obt. hl. Sevt.

WM. CLARK

ALS, RC (DLC—Biddle). Addressed; endorsed. Reply is No. 382.

1. In the Eva Emery Dye papers at the Oregon Historical Society are notes purporting to paraphrase a letter from Clark to John Hastings Marks, 29 March 1816, original not located. Clark refers to Marks's inquiry of 18 Jan. 1810 [1816], then summarizes the unfortunate history of the publication. He agrees that some of the books and papers should go to Mrs. Marks—Lewis's mother—and concludes, "Any measures which the mother & relatives of my dear friend wishes should be adopted relative to his Travels & will meet my hearty co-opperation."

380. [Canceled.]

381. Jefferson to José Corrèa da Serra

Dear Sir   Poplar Forest April 26. 16.

Your favor of Mar. 29. was recieved just as I was setting out for this place. I brought it with me to be answered hence. Since you are so kind as to interest yourself for Capt. Lewis's papers, I will give you a full statement of them.[1]

1. Ten or twelve such pocket volumes, Morocco bound, as that you describe, in which, in his own hand writing, he had journalised all occurences, day by day, as he travelled. They were small 8vos and opened at the end for more convenient writing. Every one had been put into a separate tin case, cemented to prevent injury from wet. But on his return the cases, I presume, had been taken from them, as he delivered me the books uncased. There were in them the figures of some animals drawn with the pen while on his journey. The gentlemen who published his travels must have had these Ms. volumes, and perhaps now have them, or can give some account of them.

2. Descriptions of animals and plants. I do not recollect whether there was such a book or collection of papers, distinct from his journal; altho' I am inclined to think there was one: because his travels as published, do not contain all the new animals of which he had either descriptions or specimens. Mr. Peale, I think, must know something of this, as he drew figures of some of the animals for engraving, and some were actually engraved. Perhaps Conrad, his bookseller, who was to have published the work, can give an account of these.

3. Vocabularies. I had myself made a collection of about 40. vocabularies of the Indians on this side of the Missisipi, and Capt. Lewis was instructed to take those of every tribe beyond, which he possibly could: the intention was to publish the whole, and leave the world to search for affinities between these and the languages of Europe and Asia. He was furnished with a number of printed vocabularies of the same words and form I had used, with blank spaces for the Indian words. He was very attentive to this instruction, never missing an opportunity of taking a vocabulary. After his return, he asked me if I should have any objection to the printing his separately, as mine were not yet arranged as I intended. I assured him I had not the least; and I am certain he contemplated their publication. But whether he had put the papers out of his own hand or not, I do not know. I imagine he had not: and it is probable that Doctr. Barton, who was particularly curious on this subject, and published on it occasionally, would willingly recieve and take care of these papers

after Capt. Lewis's death, and that they are now among his papers.

4. His observations of longitude and latitude. He was instructed to send these to the war-office, that measures might be taken to have the calculations made. Whether he delivered them to the war-office, or to Dr. Patterson, I do not know; but I think he communicated with Dr. Patterson concerning them. These are all-important: because altho', having with him the Nautical almanacs, he could & did calculate some of his latitudes, yet the longitudes were taken merely from estimates by the log-line, time and course. So that it is only as to latitudes that his map may be considered as tolerably correct; not as to its longitudes.

5. His Map. This was drawn on sheets of paper, not put together, but so marked that they could be joined together with the utmost accuracy; not as one great square map, but ramifying with the courses of the rivers. The scale was very large, and the sheets numerous, but in perfect preservation. This was to await publication, until corrected by the calculations of longitude and latitude. I examined these sheets myself minutely, as spread on the floor, and the originals must be in existence, as the Map published with his travels must have been taken from them.[2]

These constitute the whole. They are the property of the government, the fruits of the expedition undertaken at such expense of money and risk of valuable lives. They contain exactly the whole of the information which it was our object to obtain for the benefit of our own country and of the world. But we were willing to give to Lewis and Clarke whatever pecuniary benefits might be derived from the publication, and therefore left the papers in their hands, taking for granted that their interests would produce a speedy publication, which would be better if done under their direction. But the death of Capt. Lewis, the distance and occupations of General Clarke, and the bankruptcy of their bookseller, have retarded the publication, and rendered necessary that the government should attend to the reclamation & security of their papers. Their recovery is now become an imperious duty. Their safest deposit as fast as they can be collected, will be the Philosophical Society, who no doubt will be so kind as to receive and preserve them, subject to the orders of government; and their publication, once effected in any way, the originals will probably be left in the same deposit. As soon as I can learn their present situation, I will lay the matter before the government to take such order as they think proper. As to any claims of individuals to these papers, it is to be observed that, as being the property of the public, we are certain neither Lewis nor Clarke would undertake to convey away the right to them, and that they could not convey them, had they been capable of intending it. Yet no interest of that kind is meant to be disturbed, if the individual can give satisfactory assurance that he will promptly & properly publish them. Otherwise they must be restored to the government, & the claimant left to settle with those on whom he has any claim. My interference will, I trust, be excused, not only from the portion which every citizen has in whatever is public, but from the peculiar part I have had in the design and execution of this expedition.

To you, my friend, apology is due for involving you in the trouble of this inquiry. It must be found in the interest you take in whatever belongs to science, and in your own kind offers to me of aid in this research. Be assured always of my affectionate friendship and respect.

Th: Jefferson

ALS, SC (DLC). Jefferson wrote to Corrèa 5 June 1816, acknowledging receipt of the single journal volume that Corrèa had mentioned 29 March. Jefferson also congratulated him on his appointment as Spanish minister to the U.S. (DLC).

1. For a more recent statement, see Elliott Coues's description in *Proceedings* of the American Philosophical Society, 31 (1893), 17–33, reprinted by Thwaites in the JOURNALS, 6:411–23, in condensed form. It was Coues who first termed the manuscript notebooks "codices" and assigned them alphabetical designators; Thwaites followed Coues, and it now seems likely that we shall continue to refer to the individual journals as Codex A, Codex B, etc., except for those which have come to light since Coues's time.

2. He is mistaken in supposing that the map sent to Hassler was later published in BIDDLE. It is suggested by WHEAT, 2:46n, that these sheets may have been given subsequently to Maximilian, Prince of Wied.

382. Nicholas Biddle to Clark

Dear Sir   Phila. May 29. 1816

I received some time since your letter of the 31st March which I would have answered sooner but from the want of something decisive to communicate. I still labor under the same inconvenience but will not longer delay informing you of the state of your concerns here. On receiving the news of Mr. Bradford's failure I immediately interfered in your behalf. But the concerns of his estate were very complicated, his assignees had other business of their own to attend to, so that altho I was constantly urging a settlement in person & during my absence at Harrisburg employed a friend of mine a gentleman of the bar to follow up the business it was not until the latter end of April last that we received from the assignees their account. The true principle on which alone an account could be settled seems to be this. The work should be charged with all the expenses of publishing and the $500 to Mr. Allen. All the profits above that amount to be equally divided between you and Mr. Bradford's assignees. This is according to the agreement and decidedly the most favorable to yourself, since if you were to be made a creditor of Mr. B & the work thrown into the mass of his effects the chances would be much more against you.

The expences of printing & of the maps &c. have been so great that added to bad debts & commissions to other booksellers will absorb almost all the proceeds of the sales. The number remaining unsold are in boards and in the hands of the binders, who are not yet paid for binding those already sold, and when the expence of completing them is paid they will not I fear do much more than cover their own expences. This will depend on the terms on which they can be disposed of & I have been endeavoring to negociate with some book seller to take the remaining copies pay the debts & give some surplus. But no book seller has offered more than 45 or 50 per cent on the retail price. This is a great sacrifice, but if the books remain in their present state they will be wholly unproductive & it would take years to wait till they would sell by retail.

The only chance by which we can hope to gain much is: To procure from the assignees a relinquishment of their claim to any future edition. If they can be induced to do this the work will then remain in your hands unrestricted, and you will be in possession of the copper plates. With these you may be able to contract for another edition by which I trust you may yet make something. But of any immediate profit from the present there are not grounds for much expectation. I will send shortly the account of the assignees & will then let you know if I can succeed in obtaining a good price for the remaining copies and from the assignees a renunciation of their claims on a future one.

Dr. Barton died without having I believe done any thing towards his share. I have applied to the proper authority & am promised whatever can be found in relation to the work.

I cannot express to you how much I am disappointed at the unfortunate result of this business. I was in hopes that after having sacrificed a great deal of time & some money (in travelling to Virginia) —after renouncing all claim for the trouble of almost two years I should at least have had the pleasure of seeing you enjoy something to reward for your long laborious & honorable services. I have been much disappointed. It is not indeed much of a consolation that the trade of bookselling has been of late years a very ruinous one, that few books now do more than pay their own expences and that you suffer like many others from the effects of bankruptcy. But you may find more comfort in reflecting that nothing can deprive you of the glory acquired by that expedition & I hope you will be able to indemnify yourself for the disappointment by judicious management in your young & thriving country. I am now at my country house, but shall go in a day or two to Phila. to hear from the Booksellers & the assignees.

Mrs. B joins me in compts. to Mrs. Clarke whom we should be very glad to see again & I am always yrs sincerely,

N. B.

AL, SC (NjP). Endorsed. A draft containing many revisions and deleted passages, including some figures on the state of the enterprise which Biddle evidently decided not to include.

383. José Corrèa da Serra to Jefferson

Dear Sir   Philadelphia 16. June. 1816

. . .

Three other pocket books of Capt. Lewis have been found among the papers of Dr. Barton, and that was all that existed in the Drs. hands, but all the remaining papers concerning that expedition I have found deposited with Mr. Nicholas Biddle, who tells me he is ready to give them, on receiving an intimation to do so, from Genl. Clarke from whom he had them. You see that I have done every thing in my power to satisfy your wishes, and you may be sure that will be the case in every occasion to serve you.

. . .

I remain with the highest esteem and respect Most sincerely yours,

J. Corrèa de Serra

ALS, RC (DLC). Endorsed; received 10 July 1816. Reply is No. 385.

384. Nicholas Biddle to Charles Chauncey

Dear Sir,   Andalusia June 25. 1816
On looking over the account furnished by the Assignees
of Messrs. Bradford & Inskeep it appears that the whole

proceeds of sales are	5535.47
From which are to be deducted for	

Bad debts 677.55
Copies not paid for 520.58 ⎫ 1198.13

leaving as the sum actually earned by B. & Inskeep from the work	4337.34
It appears further that the whole payments were	3496.97
From which must be deducted DeSilver's acct. which though included among the payments is found on the opposite side of the acct. marked still unpaid, say	77.50
	3419.47

[To this] may be added the advance of part of the $500 payable to Mr. Allen out of the first proceeds. This sum is not charged by the assignees but having been paid by me & allowed by Messrs. B. & I. should be credited to them. This sum was not as I supposed $200 but only

123.00

The whole payments then were	3542.47
The whole Receipts	4334.34
Leaving a nett Balance of	791.87

to be shared between General Clark & the Assignees. That is the work owes thus far of undivided profits to Genl. Clark $395.93.

The debts due *by* the work are:

To Gaskell DeSilver & Charles   686.27
To Allen the remainder of the $500   377.00
1163.27

The debts due *to* the work are

Bad debts 677.55
Unpaid copies 520.58 ⎫ 498.13

These debts to the work however wear so unpromising an appearance that I am afraid they will contribute but little—if at all—to liberate the work from the $1163.27 still claimed from the proceeds. On consulting with the Booksellers, it seems that nothing more can be accomplished by the sale than barely to defray the expences of putting them into a saleable condition & then paying the debts. Under these circumstances it has occurred to me that the only way of obtaining any thing for Genl. Clark would be to procure a clear & unrestricted right to the use of the copper plates &c. of any future edition & then let him make [what] he can of them. How far the assignees have any right whatever to share in a future edition, or whether the right stipulated for in the agreement can be fairly construed to extend beyond the booksellers whose insolvency has rendered them unable to provide for such an edition you can judge better than myself. The assignees are however in possession of the copper plates which would spare much of the expence of any future edition & are of course desirable. I submit therefore for your consideration whether it would be well to make this offer to the Assignees. You owe to Genl. Clark $395.93. Indeed it might be said that out of the $791.87 nett profits Mr. Allen's $377 should be first taken & the balance divided, which would make the Assignees $584.43 in debt. Now if you will deliver up all the copies of the work with the copper plates debts & every thing connected with the work & will release all claim on any future edition, we will release to you the $385.93[1] or the $584.43 & ingage to pay the debts of the work.

The advantages of such an arrangement to the Assignees would be apparent. They would be released from the claim of the $385.93 & from the claims on the work. They would give up the books which can never do more than pay those claims & as to the future copy right it would not be an object of sale to any booksellers even if the Assignees had the right to part with it, since a bookseller would not desire to connect himself with a stranger whose interference would give him much trouble. The advantages to Genl. Clark would be, the prospect of covering the debts by the sale of the books & the hopes of profit by a future edition.

Will you be so good as to turn this in your mind & if you think the offer a safe one on the part of Genl. Clark communicate with Mr. Astley on the subject & I will see you in a few days to know whether any thing can be done. Mr. A. I believe leaves town in the hot weather and it might therefore be well to see him if convenient before he goes. In hopes of seeing you shortly I remain Yrs. truly & respy.

NICHOLAS BIDDLE

ALS, SC (NjP). Addressed. An earlier draft is present, plus a sheet of Biddle's calculations upon which he based the letter.

1. The correct figure, according to Biddle's calculations, is $395.93. He wrote $383.93 throughout his first draft, then corrected the figure in the present draft. He failed to correct at every occurrence in this copy, but probably did so in his fair copy to Chauncey.

385. Jefferson to José Corrèa da Serra

Dear Sir   Monticello July 20. 16.

I returned from Poplar Forest about a week ago, and found here your favor of June 16. I learn with sincere regret your rheumatic indisposition; and the more as it strikes so directly at your summum bonum of botanical rambles. Would it not be well to direct these toward Augusta Springs, which we consider as specific for that complaint? They are but about 80. or 90. miles from Monticello. But of this we will say more when we have the pleasure of seeing you here; which from the 'few weeks' of your letter of June 16 we daily hope. Mr. Gilmer is also daily expected by his friends. I am very glad to learn that 3. more of Capt. Lewis's volumes are found, and hope the rest will reappear in time, as no one could think of destroying them. As to the astronomical observations & the Vocabularies, I will write to Genl. Clarke to obtain his order for their delivery to the war-office, to which they belong. Besides the notoriety of the fact that the expedition was under public authority, at public expence, & for public objects and consequently that all it's results are public property, in the XIVth page of the life of Capt. Lewis prefixed to the History of his expedition, it will be seen that the Astronomical observations were expressly directed to be rendered to the War office, for the purpose of having the calculations made by proper persons within the U.S. If on these considerations Mr. Biddle would think himself authorised to deliver these papers to the order of the Secy. at war I will sollicit such an order to be given in favor of such person as the Secretary may engage to make the calculations. But if Mr. Biddle has any scruples of delicacy with respect to Genl. Clarke I shall not press it, but wait an answer from him, which will only add 3. or 4. months to the delay already incurred. I hope my anxieties and interference in this matter will be excused, when my agency in the enterprise is considered, and that the most important justification of it, still due to the public depends on these astronomical observations, as from them alone can be obtained the correct geography of the country, which was the main object of the expedition.

I thank you for the new recipe for the cement. I think it more easily practised than the former one, which, by the bye I have recovered. I had stuck the paper into a little Cornelius Nepos which I had in my pocket at the Natural bridge, and had replaced the volume on it's shelf at Poplar Forest without observing the paper. I am in the daily hope of seeing you, and the more anxiously lest the recurrence of my calls to Bedford should repeat the last year's misfortune. But as the next visit to that place has nothing to fix it to a day, it can be accomodated to your movements if known without the least inconvenience. Ever & affectionately yours,

TH: JEFFERSON

ALS, SC (DLC). Endorsed.

386. Jefferson to Clark

Dear Sir   Monticello Sep. 8. 16

The travelling journal of Govr. Lewis and yourself having been published some time ago, I had hoped to hear that something was doing with the astronomical observations, the Geographical chart, the Indian vocabularies, and other papers not comprehended in the journal published. With a view to have these given to the public according to the original intention, I got a friend to apply for them to Mr. Biddle, in whose hands I understood them to be, referring him for authority to the instructions inserted in the life of Govr. Lewis prefixed to the journal. He said he could not deliver them even to the War-office, without an order from you. It is to sollicit this order that I now trouble you, and it may be given in favor either of the war office or of myself. If the latter, I should deliver the Astronomical observations to the Secretary at War, who would employ some one to make the calculations, to correct the longitudes of the map, and to have it published thus corrected; and I should deliver the papers of Natural history & the Vocabularies to the Philos. society, at Philadelphia, who would have them properly edited, and I should deposit with them also for safe keeping the travelling pocket journals as originals to be recurred to on all interesting questions arising out of the published journal. I should receive them only in trust for the War office to which they belong, and take their orders relating to them. I have received from Dr. Barton's ex[ecuto]rs 4. vols. of the travelling pocket journals, but I think there were 11. or 12. The rest I suppose Mr. Biddle has. I hope the part I have had in this important voyage, will excuse the interest I take in securing to the world all the beneficial results we were entitled to expect from it, and which would so fully justify the expences of the expedition incurred by the United states in that expedition. I salute you with constant friendship and respect.

Th: Jefferson

ALS, RC (MoSHi); SC (DLC). Addressed, "General William Clarke Governor of Missouri St. Louis"; endorsed, "Mr. Jefferson ansd. 10th Oct. 1816." Reply is No. 390.

387. Clark to Henry Clay

Dear Sir   St. Louis Missouri Territory September 11th 1816

Mr. George Shannon a very worthy and valuable man residing in Lexington, (with whome I presume you are acquainted) accompanied me to the Pacific Ocean, and on that expedition was one of the most active and useful men we had. In the early part of the year 1807. Mr. Shannon was employed by me (as Agent for the government) to accompany and assist the Mandan Chief on his return to his Nation, Sixteen hundred miles up the Missouri—for which he was to receive Twenty five Dollars per Month. The Ricaras Tribe opposed the return of the Mandan Chief and in an attack which they made on Mr. Shannon and this party, wounded him severely with a Ball through the Leg which resulted in the amputation of his leg a short time afterwards.

The Certificate of Doctr. Barnard G. Farrar[1] herewith inclosed will shew the nature of the wound and the extent of injury sustained by Mr. Shannon.

In bestowing pensions upon individuals the object of the government should be, and doubtless is, [to] alleviate the misfortunes of all, and above all, of the meritorious men who suffer in the service of the Country. And from a througher knowledge of the worth of Mr. Shannon, and an acquaintance with his services, I feel no hesitation in pronounceing him worthy of their benevolent notice. As to the amount of Pension, it is altogether a matter of opinion; but for myself, I conceive Mr. Shannon justly entitled to, at least one half of the Salary he was receiving from the government, at the time this misfortune befell him, which has occasioned his disability.[2] I have the honer to be with high respect Your Mo. Obt. & Respectful H. Sert.

WM. CLARK

[Enclosure]
I certify that I was called to visit George Shannon esqr. on the 31th of October 1807 and that I found one of his legs in a state of gangrene caused by a ball having passed through it, and that to save his life I was under the necessity of amputating the limb above the knee, the loss of which constitutes in my opinion the first grade of disability. Given under my hand at St. Louis this 11th of Sept. 1816.

B. G. FARRAR

ALS, RC (DNA, RG 15A, OWIF 24807).
1. Bernard G. Farrar, a Virginian who first practiced medicine in Frankfort, Ky., and who located in St. Louis in 1807. He was elected to the territorial assembly in 1812.
2. Clark is not trying to get Shannon a pension, but an *increase* in pension. It had taken Shannon a long time to get on the pension rolls, and not without Clark's help. The Secretary of War wrote Clark 8 Aug. 1809, "It is not proper that the pension of George Shannon should be paid out of the Funds for the Indian Department: every soldier who is disabled in the service of the United States is entitled to a pension; but he must take

[620]

the course prescribed by Law, to enable him to receive it" (DNA, RG 75, Letters Sent, Bk. C). A monthly pension of $8 was awarded Shannon by a special act of Congress, 2 Aug. 1813, to begin 1 Jan. 1814. Apparently Clark wrote the above letter when Shannon was gathering support for a new petition to Congress, asking for an increase. Clay's intervention may also be assumed; a note on one of the pension documents for this period says, "Speak to Mr. Clay." And a note from Clay's office 18 May 1816 reads, "The Speaker of the House of Reps. [Clay] respectfully requests that Mr. Shannon's Case may receive the particular attention of the War Dept." Shannon filed his petition for an increase 1 Oct. 1816, saying he felt he had been pensioned "at a rate which he humbly conceived below the just standard." By act of Congress of 3 March 1817, the pension was increased to $12. (The foregoing information is from Shannon's pension envelope, DNA, RG 15A, OWIF 24807.) Clay seems to have acted as Shannon's agent for the collection of the pension. A receipt of Shannon to Clay, 18 Oct. 1816, for $18, states, "which with what he has heretofore paid me amounts to two hundred & eighty eight dollars, being three years of my pension recd. by him" (Thomas J. Clay Coll., DLC).

Something must have happened to the first land warrant issued to Shannon for his service with the expedition. He petitioned for renewal, and the petition was approved 16 April 1814. On 2 Nov. 1815 he assigned Clay his warrant for 320 acres "in virtue of a special Act of Congress passed for my benefit, founded upon services rendered by me on the Expedition of Capn. Lewis & Clarke to the Columbia River. . . ." He also assigned Clay the power of attorney to draw his pension. The document is endorsed in Clay's hand: "I do Certify that the power of Attorney of which the within is a copy was signed by George Shannon and attested by the subscribing witnesses thereto in my presence. 23d. Dec. 1815. [signed] H. Clay" (OWIF 24807).

A bill to grant Shannon 640 acres of land as compensation for his injury failed to pass Congress in March 1822 (Annals of the Congress of the United States, 38:314, 315).

Shannon studied law at Transylvania University, Lexington, Ky., and was practicing in Lexington by 1818; he was a member of the Kentucky House of Representatives in 1820 and 1822 (COLLINS, 2:170). Later he was a state senator and U.S. attorney in Missouri. Among the raw materials for a biographical study of Shannon are two compositions (MoSHi) that he may have prepared as classwork at Transylvania. One is a seven-page AD dated 20 Dec. 1809 on the subject of "disinterested benevolence." The other is a nine-page AD on dreaming, dated 30 Dec. 1809. "As to the question 'whether there be any thing prophetic, in dreams, or not' I must if I give my opinion, answer in the affirmitive. It is however no more than an opinion, for I believe I cannot support it by any arguments."

388. Thomas Astley to Charles Chauncey

Dear Sir   Philadelphia 18 Sept. *1816*.

I have gone into another examination of the amounts relating to Lewis & Clarke with the view of replying to Mr. Biddle's letter of

the 25th June last. For the sake of perspicuity, I will re-state the
account in the manner Mr. Biddle has done it, with such corrections
as appear to be necessary, & you will be good enough to compare the
two statements together.

The whole proceeds of the sales		5535.47
Deduct for bad debts	677.55	
Copies not paid for	520.58	1198.13
Leaving the sum actually received by Bradford & Inskeep from the work		4337.34
pr. Contra		
The whole of payments as pr. acct.		3496.97
To which add for the sum engaged to be* paid to Mr. Allen—who is Dr. on the Books of Bradford & Inskeep, for goods sold to him & on the same books for cash paid him by Mr. Biddle	864.66 123.00 —— 987.66	
From which take for Lewis & Clarke	500.00	500.00
And Mr. Allen is a debtor to B & I beyond the full sum engaged to be paid him on acct. of Lewis & Clarke	487.66	
Making the sum actually paid by Bradford & Inskeep, on acct of the work		$3996.97
From the whole of the Receipts		4337.34
Deduct the whole of the Payments		3996.97
and there remains the balance of		340.37
Half of which belongs to Genl. Clarke		$ 170.18½

The books on hand will do nothing more than barely pay the debts
due upon them (& for which they are pledged) & defray the expenses of putting them into a saleable condition, as Mr. Biddle has
ascertained; and to release them it will be necessary to advance
$686.27. From the Copies unpaid for, we may probably collect 200
to 250 Dollars.

Believing this statement to be as nearly correct as it can be ascertained at present, as to the manner in which the concern will wind
up—I propose to you, in order to close accounts betwixt Genl. Clarke &
us—That we give up to you the Copy Right of the work, & the Copper
Plates belonging to it, with all privileges of new editions—and that
you relinquish to us, all that remains of the books on hand, & the

debts due upon the work, we engaging to pay all the claims due to the printers binders &c. The Copy-right with the Plates may, I think, very fairly be estimated at 600 to 700 Dollars—and we only derive benefit from the balance of $170.18½ & from the outstanding debts valued at $250—together about $420. It will be proper for us however to stipulate that no proceedings towards the publishing of a new edition of the work shall take place within six months, that we may have time to complete the books on hand, & that we shall first use the Plates for such maps &c. as may be wanting in them. I am very truly Dear Sir Your most obed. svt.

THO. ASTLEY

I return you inclosed, Mr. Biddle's letter.

[*In margin:*] *Mr. Biddle is wrong in deducting 77.50 for Desilver —one acct. amounting to this sum has been paid to Charles (not Desilver) & another similar acct. is still owing to him.

ALS, RC (NjP). Addressed.

389. Clark to Nicholas Biddle

Dear Sir [10 October 1816]

I must request the favor of you to deliver to Mr. Jefferson, or to his order all the papers you may have received in my behalf relating to the Astronomical Observations, the Geographical Charts, the Indian Vocabularies, and other papers not comprehended in the journal of Lewis & Clarks Travils which have been latterly published, and the Specimins which were in the possession of Doctor Barton— also the traveling pocket journal. And obg. Yr. Friend & Ob. St.

Missouri Territory WM. CLARK
St. Louis October 10th 1816

ALS, RC (NjP). Endorsed.

390. Clark to Jefferson

Dear Sir Saint Louis October 10th 1816

I had the honor of Receiving your letter of the 8th of Septr., by the mail, and with much pleasure comply with the contents.

It has ever been my wish, that the Travelling journal of Govr. Lewis & myself, the astronomical observations, the Geographical Chart, the Indian Vocabularies and all subjects of Natural history should be

[623]

given to the public in the best possible manner, and agreeably to the original intention. And for that purpose I have been twice to Phila. and have used all the means which have been in my power without the success contemplated.

The Naritive has been published, but I have not been so fortunate as to precure a single volume as yet. After the death of my friend Govr. Lewis, finding the arrangements he had made relative to the publication had failed, and the greater part of the astronomical observations with the plates and drawings which he had directed to be made were not to [be] found. A new contract was made with Messrs. Bradford & Inskep, to print & publish that part, and the cientific part also, which was to have been (by contract) prepared in Six Months from the time by Doctr. Barton. In these arrangements I have been also disappointed.

Since the falue [failure] of Bradford & Inskep, and the death of Doctr. Barton my agent Mr. Nicholas Biddle has been requested to collect all the Books, papers, Specimens, &c.

Previously to my making the last arrangement, I had conversation with the then Secretary of War on the subject of publishing Lewis & Clarks Journal map &c., he thought it important, but could promis no assistance at that time.

It is with pleasure that I inclose you an Order on my friend Mr. Biddle for the papers in his possession relating to the Astronomical Observations, the Geographical Charts, the Indian Vocabularies, and other Papers not comprehended in the journal of Lewis & Clarks Travels laterly published, and the specimins which were left in the possession of Doctr. Barton. Also the Traveling pocket Journals.

From the mortification of not having succeeded in giving to the world all the Results of that expedition, I feel relief & gratitude for the interest which you are willing to take, in effecting what has not been in my power to accomplish.

Some time ago, I requested Mr. Biddle to deliver to Mrs. Markes's order, the half of all the Books he may have received in my behalf. The map from which the plate was made, is in my possession at this place; it is rough and has not been corrected and comprehends the Connection of Country from Lat. 34° to 50° N. If you think it adviseable, I will make a new map of the same size of the one I have, corrected by such matireals as I have precured since the last was made. Otherwise I shall take the liberty of sending the one I have to you.[1]

The Missouri River on which there is such emence tracts of fine

[624]

Country calculated for rich & populous settlements, and watering an emence space in which there is much welth in furs, Peltr[i]es, minerals, dies &c. is tolerably well understood but not in sufficient use. The Lands on the lower portion of that river is settling fast, the middle portion (or as high up as the Big Bend or White river) is Crowded with Traders, but the upper and richer portion has had no American Citizen since the falue of the Missouri Co. in 1811 and I am under great apprehentions that the British will take possession of that rich Tract by the way of Assinniboin & Saskassion rivers as they have done at the mouth of the Columbia, and on Lewis & Clarks rivers: If a larger and over bearing company Cannot be formed of American Citizens with sufficient Capital to keep them out. I think such a Co. could be formed with some Countrimen and a little aid from the government.

The present population of this Territory would most probably amount to about 35 or 40.000 Soles. Since peace was made with the Indians on the Mississippi the emogration has been emence bending their Course to the Missouri principally. Landed property has risen which has inrichened the old inhabitants and reconsiled them to our government much more than formerly.

In the exurcise of Govr. of this Territory I have suceed in the worst of times with more approbation than I had expected. Laterly a Small and disappointed party has sprung up deturmined to vex & Teaze the executive.

I am happy to have it in my power to say to you that I suceed in Keeping the Indians of the Territory (except those high up the Mississippi) in peace. The Torments of this frontier was pirduced by the Tribes East of the Missippi & high up that River. The dificueltes & responsibilities however were great, and in some instancs I was compeled to vary from princpal,[2] and Let the Missouri Tribes at war against those of the Mississippi to prevent the British influence amogst the Missouri tribes as also to prevent a Coeletion which would have destroyed our settlements at a blow.

Please to accept the assurance of my highest respect and veneration and best wishes for your health and hapiness. Yours Most Sincerly,

WM. CLARK

ALS, RC (PPAmP). Endorsed; received 2 Nov. 1816. This letter was originally enclosed in Jefferson's to Du Ponceau, 7 Nov. 1817 (No. 399).

1. There is no record that Jefferson responded to this suggestion or that Clark sent him a map.

2. A view of principle not shared by all frontier administrators, and

particularly not by Lewis. As governor of Louisiana Territory, Lewis had written Harrison: "I have in several late conferences with the Shawnese, Delawares, Kickapoos, Soos, Saues [Sauks], Jaways [Ioways], &c. declared the Osage nation no longer under the protection of the United States, and set them at liberty to adjust their several differences with that abandoned nation in their own way, but have prohibited their attacking them except with a sufficient force to destroy or drive them from our neighborhood" (26 July 1808, clipping from a Philadelphia newspaper, DNA, RG 107, P-1808, unregistered series).

391. Clark to Nicholas Biddle

Dear Sir   St. Louis October 17th 1816

I have not had the pleasure of a line from you since the latter part of June, should be extreemly gratified in hearing from you on the subject of my Book &c. I fear the half Brother of my old friend Lewis is displeased with me, probably without knowing the state of that work.

A short time past I received a letter from Mr. Jefferson on the subject of the part of Lewis & Clarks Travels relating to natural history asking of me an order on you for the astronomical observations, the geographical charts, the Indian vocabularies and other papers not comprehended in the journal published, and the Traveling pocket journal, 4 vols. of which he says he has received from the Ext. of Doctr. Barton. His object is to deliver the astronomical & geographical to the War Dept. to be calculated and the map Corrected, the other parts to the Philos. Society of Phila. I have complied with the requisition from reasons he assigned &c. You will be the best judge of the papers to be delivered. And excuse I hope the trouble I have and must continue to give you on a subject on which I am greatly interested.

I have had troublesome time during the war, & since making peace with the Indians which is nierly accomplished—have to contend now with a little news paper abuse for my political course.

This Territory is populating uncommonly rapid, the imigration from all quarters is imence principally bending the Course to the Missouri.

Mrs. Clark joins me in affectionate remembrance to you and Mrs. Biddle and would be hapy in seeing you once more. I solicit you with const. friendship and respect. Yrs Sincerely,

WM. CLARK

ALS, RC (DLC—Biddle). Addressed; endorsed.

[626]

392. Nicholas Biddle to Clark

Dear Sir,   Andala. (near Phila.) Octr. 21. 1816

My last was of May 29. informing you of the state of your business. After examining the account presented by the assignees, I sent the following letter to Mr. Chauncey, the gentleman who has taken charge of the affair during my absence.

[here insertd my letter to Mr. Chauncey dated Anda. June 25. 1816]

To this communication no reply was received until the following from Mr. Astley to Mr. Chauncey. [here inserted that letter dated Phila. Septr. 18. 1816][1]

I have copied these letters that you might see exactly how things stand & make up your mind as to the offer of the assignees to give up their claim to the copy right and the copper plates if we give up our claim on the books. Of the propriety of agreeing to the proposal you can judge as well as my self. If I have any advice to give it would be, on a view of the whole circumstances to accept the proposal. If you retain a share in the unfinished books you will have to make such a sacrifice in order to get rid of them at once, as will almost absorb if it does not exceed the profits, or else after making the advance of $686 to the binders wait some years for the gradual sale of the books. With a clear copy right and the copper plates you might perhaps sell the whole to a bookseller & thus make something out of the concern at last. Mr. Chauncey is of the same mind. If you would consent to the proposal I will endeavor to procure for you in addition some copies of the work, but I do not wish to give Mr. Astley any decisive answer until I hear from you. I have delayed writing to you until I heard from Mr. Allen at Baltimore about his account as represented by Mr. Astley. From him I did not receive a letter till this day. The sooner you can communicate your decision to me, the better, as I shall spend the winter at Harrisburg, and if you wish me to do any thing about the copy right you may freely command me. Very truly yrs,

                                    N. B.

AL, SC (DLC—Biddle).
1. The brackets are Biddle's.

393. Mathew Carey to Nicholas Biddle

Dear Sir   [6 December 1816]

Agreeably to your wishes, I have reflected on the subject on which we conversed yesterday, & submit the result.

As neither Capt. Lewis nor Capt. Clark ever recd. a single cent for the copy right of the work from which they ought to have recd. from 1500 to 2000 Dollars, it appears to me extremely hard indeed, that the survivor is now called upon to relinquish his claim on the copies that remain on hands, as a bonus for a relinquishment of the copyright on the part of the assignees of Bradford & Inskeep.

In pro conscientia[?] the assignees have no claim on the copy right. Neither they nor their principals ever gave an equivalent for it. It therefore appears to me to require but a moderate degree of re-flexion on their part & a slight attention to the holy rule, "Do as you wd. be done by"—to induce them to transfer the title to the rightful claimant.

I am no lawyer. And I have lived long enough to know that there is too often a deadly warfare between law & equity. But I profess to know somewhat of common sense & equity. And I am clear that whatever support law may afford the claims of the assignees, equity sets her face against them.

Two modes of settling the controversy present themselves to my mind.

The first—to submit the facts to the decision of three or four intelligent Booksellers.

The other—to divide what remains of the Books* between the assignees & Captain Clark & the heirs of Capt. Lewis—the copy right being relinquished by the former to the latter. Your obt. hble. Servt.

Mathew Carey

Decr. 6 1816

*each party paying a share of the demands on the work.

ALS, owned by Donald F. Hyde, New York, N.Y. Mathew Carey (1760–1839) was a prominent Philadelphia publisher and bookseller.

394. Nicholas Biddle to Charles Chauncey

Dr. Sir   Phila. Decr. 7. 1816

I was very desirous of having your further advice in relation to the remaining copies of Lewis & Clarkes work, & of conversing with Mr. Astley on the subject. But being obliged to leave town tomorrow, I am under the necessity of asking the favor of you to look over the inclosed papers & confer with Mr. Astley as to the best way of disposing of the property to the mutual advantage of both parties. I mentioned to you that Mr. Astley had some time since proposed an arrangement in which I did not feel at liberty to acquiesce. Perhaps in considering the subject together, you can suggest some more eligible mode of adjusting the matter & prevent a delay which cannot but injure the sale of the work. I will thank you, in case any thing should occur, to drop me a line to Harrisburg. Very respy. yrs.

N. B.

AL, SC (DLC—Biddle).

395. Mathew Carey to [Nicholas Biddle]

Dear Sir,   26 December [1816]

I have attended to the business you confided to me—& am sorry to say there does not appear to me much if any chance, of any thing for Gen. Clarke.

Mr. Astley enquired what I wd. give for the copyright—& when I offered some observations on the justice of the claims of your friend, cut me short at once, with a declaration that that affair was not submitted to the consideration of Your obt. hbl. Servt.

Decr. 26   MATHEW CAREY

ALS, RC (DLC—Biddle).

396. Clark to Nicholas Biddle

Dear Sir   St. Louis Decr. 28th 1817 [1816]

Your letter of the 21st of October informing me of the state of my business with the ass[ignee]s of Messrs. Bradford & Inskeip in relation to the publication of Lewis & Clarks Journal was only received a few days ago. The proposition made by Mr. Astley as recommended by you meets my decided approbation. I have written to the mother of the late Govr. Lewis (Mrs. Marks) & sent her a statement of the accounts,[1] and asked her to assent to the arrangement. This measure is important to me as it enables me to satisfy the old lady who I have reasons to believe has been persuaded that profit arrising from that work has been received.

I wish something done with the Copy Right but what should be done I cant say, must leave it to your own judgement and better experience. I am realy sorry that you have been at so much trouble in acting for me. I console myself that I may yet have it in my power to do you a service; Mrs. Clark joins me in Compliments, respectfully

[629]

to Mrs. Biddle & hope you will accept my best wishes. Your Obt.
Hble. Servant,

WM. CLARK

LS, RC (DLC—Biddle). One of the few Clark letters in this collection
not in his own hand. It is addressed by Clark; endorsed by Biddle.
Anticipating the turn of the year, Clark mistakenly dated the letter 1817.

1. A copy of Biddle's letter of 21 Oct. 1816 (No. 392) in an unidentified
hand is in the Lewis-Marks Papers (ViU). It probably is the "statement of
accounts" mentioned by Clark.

397. [Clark to Jefferson]

Dear Sir   St. Louis Feby. 1st 1817.

I have taken the liberty of inclosing under cover to you a letter
to Mrs. Marks, and a Copy of a letter and statement of the publication
of Lewis & Clarks Journal &c. from Mr. N. Biddle, which I latterly
received.

The population of this Territory is rapidly increasing and very
widely extending itself, the Lands on the Missouri having greatly
the advantage as respects fertility of soil & health, draws the greatest
emigration in that direction.

For the last three or four years, party spirit appeared to have almost
subsided, but laterly it has been revived, and increases by the aid of the
old partizans. Accept of my best wishes for your health & happiness.
With the highest respect I have the honor to be Your Ob. Hbl. Servt.

Photostat (MoSHi). An unsigned clerk's copy with no indication of sender
or receiver, but almost certainly addressed to Jefferson. Original not found.

398. Jefferson to John Vaughan

Dear Sir   Monticello June 28. 17.

Your two letters of the 2d and 18th have been recieved in due
time. Mine of the 7th had partly anticipated your requests of the 2d.

I thank you for the advance to Mr. Girard, and now inclose 70. D.
to cover it in bills of the Virginia bank which I understand pass
with you. The duplicates you advise for Cathalan & Debures, I
had sent thro' the Secretary of State's office. I shall be glad to subscribe for the volume of transactions now in the press, and ask the
favor of you to have my name placed on the subscription paper.
But I have nothing to offer for insertion in it. In earlier life when
I should from inclination have devoted myself to pursuits analogous

to those of our society, my time was all engrossed by public duties, and now without either books or memory I could offer nothing which would do credit either to the society or myself. You enquire for the Indian vocabularies of Messrs. Lewis and Clarke. All their papers are at present under a kind of embargo. They consist of 1. Lewis's MS. pocket journals of the journey. 2. His Indian Vocabularies. 3. His astronomical observations, particularly for the longitudes. 4. His map, and drawings. A part of these papers were deposited with Dr. Barton; some with Mr. Biddle, others I know not where. Of the pocket journals Mr. Correa got 4. out of 11. or 12. from Mrs. Barton & sent them to me. He informed me that Mr. Biddle would not think himself authorised to deliver the portion of the papers he recieved from Genl. Clarke without his order; whereon I wrote to Genl. Clarke, & recieved his order for the whole some time ago. But I have held it up until a Secretary at War is appointed, that office having some rights to these papers. As soon as that appointment is made, I shall endeavor to collect the whole, to deposite the MS. journals & Vocabularies with the Philosophical society, adding a collection of some vocabularies made by myself, and to get the Secy. at War to employ some person to whom I may deliver the astronomical papers for calculation, and the geographical ones for the correct execution of a map; for in that published with his journal, altho' the latitudes may be correct, the longitudes cannot be. I wait therefore only for this appointment to begin my endeavors for a compleat collection and distribution of these papers. The historical committee were so kind as to send me Colo. Byrd's MS. journal of the survey of the boundary between N. Carolina & Virginia. I am in negociation with the family to obtain his private journal of the same expedition containing much matter not in the public one, equally curious, and equally worthy of being printed. As soon as I obtain a definitive answer I shall return them theirs, and the other also if I can obtain leave. Accept my friendly and respectful salutations.

TH: JEFFERSON

ALS, RC (PPAmP). Addressed; endorsed; received 4 July 1817.

399. Jefferson to Peter S. Du Ponceau

Dear Sir   Monticello Nov. 7. 17.

A part of the information of which the expedition of Lewis and Clarke was the object has been communicated to the world by the publication of their journal; but much & valuable matter remains yet uncommunicated. The correction of the longitudes of their map is essential to it's value; to which purpose their observations of the lunar distances are to be calculated & applied. The new subjects they discovered in the vegetable, animal & mineral departments are to be digested and made known. The numerous vocabularies they obtained of the Indian languages are to be collated and published. Altho' the whole expence of the expedition was furnished by the public, and the information to be derived from it was theirs also, yet on the return of Messrs. Lewis & Clarke the government thought it just to leave to them any pecuniary benefit which might result from a publication of the papers, and supposed indeed that this would secure the best form of publication. But the property in those papers still remained in the government for the benefit of their constituents. With the measures taken by Govr. Lewis for their publication, I was never acquainted. After his death Govr. Clarke put them, in the first instance, into the hands of the late Dr. Barton, from whom some of them passed to Mr. Biddle, and some again, I believe, from him to Mr. Allen. While the MS. books of journals were in the hands of Dr. Barton, I wrote to him on behalf of Govr. Lewis's family requesting earnestly, that, as soon as these should be published, the originals might be returned, as the family wished to have them preserved. He promised in his answer that it should be faithfully done. After his death, I obtained, thro' the kind agency of Mr. Correa, from Mrs. Barton, three of those books, of which I know there had been 10. or 12. having myself read them. These were all she could find. The rest therefore, I presume are in the hands of the other gentlemen. After the agency I had had, in effecting this expedition, I thought myself authorised, and indeed that it would be expected of me that I should follow up the subject, and endeavor to obtain it's fruits for the public. I wrote to Genl. Clarke therefore for authority to recieve the original papers. He gave it in the letters to Mr. Biddle and to myself, which I now inclose, as the custody of these papers belonged properly to the War-office, and that was vacant at the time. I have waited several months for it's being filled, but the office still remaining vacant, and my distance rendering any effectual measures, by myself, impracticable, I ask the agency of your committee, within whose province I propose to place the matter, by making it the depository of the papers generally. I therefore now forward to them the 3. volumes of MS. journals in my possession, and authorise them, under Genl. Clarke's letters, to enquire for and to recieve the rest. So also the astronomical and geographical papers, those relating to zoological, botanical, and mineral subjects, with the Indian vocabularies, and statistical tables relative to the Indians. Of the astronomical and geographical papers, if the Committee will be so good as to give me a statement, I will, as soon as a Secretary at war is appointed, propose to him to have made, at the public expence, the requisite calculations, to have the map corrected in it's longitudes and latitudes, engraved and published on a proper scale: and I will ask from Genl. Clarke the one he offers, with his corrections. With respect to the zoological, vegetable & mineralogical papers & subjects, it would perhaps be agreeable to the Philosophical society to have a digest of them made, and published in their transactions or otherwise. And if it should be within the views of the historical committee to have the Indian vocabularies digested and published, I would add to them the remains of my collection. I had thro' the course of my life availed myself of every opportunity of procuring vocabularies of the languages of every tribe which either myself or my friends could have access to. They amounted to about 40 more or less perfect. But in their passage from Washington to this place, the trunk in which they were was stolen and plundered, and some fragments only of the vocabularies were recovered. Still however they were such as would be worth incorporation with a larger work, and shall be at the service of the historical committee, if they can make any use of them. Permit me to request the return of Genl. Clarke's letter and to add assurances of my high respect & esteem.

TH: JEFFERSON

P.S. With the volumes of MS. journal, Mrs. Barton delivered one by mistake I suppose, which seems to have been the journal of some botanist. I presume it was the property of Dr. Barton, & therefore forward it to you to be returned to Mrs. Barton.

ALS, RC (PPAmP). Endorsed. Reply is No. 400.

400. Peter S. Du Ponceau to Jefferson

Dear Sir   Philadelphia 5th Dec. 1817

The two letters which you have done me the honor to write to me, dated the 6th & 7th ultimo, have been laid by me before the Historical Committee of the Philosophical Society, together with the valuable manuscripts which accompanied them. They have directed me to return you their warm thanks for these fresh instances of your enlightened & unwearied Zeal in the Cause of Science & literature, &

for the promotion of the best interests of your Country. I shall not particularly designate the MSS. which we have received, it is Sufficient to Say that all those mentioned in your letters as forwarded by you have come to hand, & will be disposed of according to your wishes.

Mr. Biddle, who is a Member of our Historical Committee has promised to assist us in obtaining the remainder of Messrs. Lewis & Clark's Manuscripts. He is at present, I presume, actively employed with Mr. Vaughan in effecting this desirable object. The Committee will consider themselves as the Depositories of these papers for all useful purposes, & subject to the orders of the Government. They & the Society in their respective Departments will in the mean while exert themselves to make them Subservient to the great objects of their institution.

The Committee are highly pleased with your kind offer to Present them with your remaining Indian Vocabularies, which will be to them a highly valuable gift. They are now in possession of a considerable & interesting collection of materials relating to the manners, customs & languages of the Indians, enough, indeed, to make a handsome Octavo Volume. These Vocabularies will add much to this collection, & will be received with gratitude.

. . . .

I have the honor to be with the greatest respect Sir, Your most obed. hum. Servt.

PETER S. DU PONCEAU

ALS, RC (DLC). Endorsed; received 23 Dec. 1817.

401. Clark to Nicholas Biddle

Sir,   Washington 27th Jany. 1818

In consequence of our conversation this morning I have thought it best to leave you this Memorandum of what I will thank you to do for me with regard to the manuscripts of our expedition.

The papers which were to be delivered to Mr. Jefferson were, if I recollect right chieftly, if not entirely confined to the Scientific part of the journey. Of this, however, I am not certain, and you will therefore please to examine the order which I gave to Mr. Jefferson and conform to it strictly. The journal of Serjeant Ordway I must request you to send me by the first convenient opportunity.[1]

In giving up the papers to the Society agreeably to my order in favor of Mr. Jefferson, you will also stipulate with the officers of the Society that I or any agent of mine shall at all times, have the

[634]

full use of the papers to be employed for any future edition of the work. With the highest respect I have the honr. to subscribe my self Your Friend

WM. CLARK

ALS, RC (NjP). Addressed, "Nicholas Biddle Esquire of Philadelphia at Mr. Tennisons"; endorsed.

1. Not sent. The Ordway journal was still among the Biddle family papers when they were turned over to the Library of Congress in 1913.

402. Nicholas Biddle to William Tilghman

Dear Sir, Philada. April 6. 1818

I have the pleasure of depositing with the Historical Committee the papers & books which accompany this letter, in compliance with the request of Governor Clark in his letter to me of the 10th of October 1816 transmitted by Mr. Jefferson.

It may perhaps be useful to add such notices of other objects connected with them, as may enable the Committee to extend its researches.

It was in the Spring of 1810 that I received from Governor Clark in Virginia, & brought to Philadelphia the papers & documents deemed necessary for the publication of the Travels. They consisted of,

1. A large map of the country between the Mississipi & the Pacific illustrating the course of the journey.

2. A map for Mr. Hassler who was in the State of New York and engaged in some astronomical calculations for the work.

3. Some documents for Dr. Barton.

4. The manuscript journal of Serjeant Ordway, one of the party.

5. The pocket Journals of the expedition.

Of these,

1. The map after the draft was made from it for the engraver was delivered by the draftsman, Mr. Lewis, to Governor Clark when last in Phila. about the year 1813.

2. The other map was forwarded by Mr. Vaughan to Mr. Hassler, who in his letter dated Augt. 12. 1810 at Schenectady mentions the receipt of it.

3. The documents for Dr. Barton, were delivered to him immediately after my arrival in Phila. Not having received any list of them from Govr. Clark I of course took none from Dr. Barton, and as I was merely the bearer of them, my recollection is not as accurate as it

[635]

would have been had they fallen more immediately under my examination. My impression however is that the packet for Dr. Barton consisted of small manuscript books & some papers. The books were chiefly extracts relative to objects of natural history taken from the original Journal now deposited with the Committee. The papers were Indian vocabularies, collected during the journey. They formed, I think a bundle of loose sheets each sheet containing a printed vocabulary in English with the corresponding Indian name in manuscript. There was also another collection of Indian vocabularies, which, if I am not mistaken, was in the handwriting of Mr. Jefferson.

I have turned to my letter to Governor Clark dated July 7. 1810, the first to him after my arrival at Phila., in hopes of finding some further particulars, but the letter merely states in general terms "I need not say that I arrived safe at this place—that the map was immediately forwarded to Mr. Hassler, and that Dr. Barton received all his papers." In the preface to the printed travels which, being published in Phila. whilst Dr. Barton was there, must be presumed to have been correct it is stated that "those parts of the work which relate to the various objects of natural history observed or collected during the journey, as well as the alphabets of the Indian languages are in the hands of Professor Barton, and will it is understood, shortly appear." This was in 1814.

I have mentioned these particulars so minutely because the description may perhaps enable some of the Committee to recognize the vocabularies, which I incline to think were the only things delivered by me to Dr. Barton not included in the volumes now deposited.

4. The journal of Serjeant Ordway was I believe a private purchase from that person. Governor Clark in his letter to me of the 24 Jany. 1818 desires me to send it to him.

5. The Journals of Messrs. Lewis & Clark from the beginning to the end of the journey are contained in the 14 volumes, all of which are now deposited. There is besides one volume of astronomical observations & other matter by Captain Lewis, a small copy book containing some notes by Captain Lewis—the rough draft of his letter to the President from St. Louis announcing his return— and two Statistical tables of the various tribes of Indians west of the Mississipi made by Governor Clark.

These are all the observations which occur to me as promising to be useful to the Committee. Very respectfully yrs.,

NICHOLAS BIDDLE

ALS, RC (PPAmP); SC (DLC—Biddle). Endorsed, "received & read to the Historical Committee April 8, 1818. See Minutes." A transcript (DLC) carries a signed notation in the hand of John Vaughan: "N.B. J. V. as Secy. gave receipt (for the Documents) in which was included an engagement to give free access to Capt. Clarke, should he want to issue another edition of the Travels & Expeditions." An added note, not in Vaughan's hand, reads: "It would be very desirable to procure the Journal of Sergeant Or[dway] from Capt. Clark to be Deposited in like manner, subject to his inspection or even future order—Mr. Biddle has it yet in his possession."

William Tilghman (1756–1827), chief justice of Pennsylvania, was elected president of the American Philosophical Society in 1824.

403. John Vaughan to Nicholas Biddle

Received April 8. 1818 of Nicholas Biddle

Fourteen volumes of the Pocket Journal of Messrs. Lewis & Clark.

A volume of astronomical observations & other matter by Captain Lewis.

A small copy book containing some notes by Captain Lewis.

A rough draft of his letter to the President from St. Louis announcing his return.

Two Statistical tables of the Indian tribes west of the Mississipi river made by Governor Clark.

All which are deposited with the Historical Committee in compliance with the request of Governor Clark in his letter to Nicholas Biddle dated Octr. 10. 1816 & forwarded to the Historical Committee by Mr. Jefferson.

It is understood & agreed on the part of the Historical Committee in receiving these books & papers, that Governor William Clark his heirs or assigns shall at all times have the full use of them for any future edition of his Travels. By order of the Historical Committee.

> JN. VAUGHAN Recording Secy.
> of the Hist. & Lit. Class
> of the Am. Phil. Socy.

DS, RC (DLC–Biddle). The document is in Biddle's hand.

For a summary of the negotiations through which the journals were acquired, see the minutes of the Historical and Literary Committee of the American Philosophical Society, especially the entries for 19 Nov. 1817 and 8 April 1818 (JOURNALS, 7:405–07). Vaughan and his colleagues apparently failed to learn anything of the materials which had been sent to Ferdinand Hassler. An entry in the minutes for 19 Nov. 1817 reads: "J. Vaughan reported that the astronomical papers had been in the hands of Mr. Hassler who had given up the calculations in despair." The entry for 8 April 1818 lists the map which Biddle had sent to Hassler to aid in his work, and adds: "this may be in his hands."

404. Clark to Nicholas Biddle

Majr. Croghans Near Louisville, Kty.
My Dear Sir   October 28th 1821

Majr. Biddle affords me an oppertunity of writing to you a fiew lines. I have not had the pleasure of receiving a letter from you since I saw you last in Washington; will you be so obliging as to write me in what state my concern is in with the Trustees of Mr. Bradfords estate and if I have any prospects of gaining any thing from the publication of L & Clarks Book &c. If any Books are recovered for me please send a Copy to me, as but few are to be met with in this Country & none to purchase & I have never found any. Parden the trouble I give you and accept of the best wishes of your sincer friend,

WM. CLARK

ALS, RC (NjP). Addressed; endorsed.

404a. Clark's List of Expedition Members

[c. 1825–28]

Men on Lewis & Clarks Trip

Capt. Lewis Dead
Odoway Dead
N. Pryor at Fort Smith
Rd. Windser on Sangamah Ills.
G. Shannon Lexington Ky.
R. Fields near Louisville
Wm. Bratten near Greenville Ohio
F. Labieche St. Louis
R. Frazier on Gasconade
Ch. Floyd Dead   Alr. Willard Mo.
P. Gass Dead   Geo. Drulard Killed
J. Collins do.   Tous. Charbono Mand[ans]
J. Colter do.   ⌈Se car ja we au Dead [1]
P. Cruzate Killed   ⟨Tousant Charbon[o] in
J. Fields do.   ⌊ Wertenburgh, Gy.[2]
S. Goodrich dead
G. Gibson dead
T. P. Howard
H. Hall

[638]

H. McNeal   dead
J. Shields   do.
J. Potts   Killed
J. B. Le Page   dead
J. Thomson   Killed
Wm. Warner   Vir.
P. Wiser   Killed
[J.] Whitehouse
[R.] Warpenton
[J.] Newman

AD, owned by Everett D. Graff, Winnetka, Ill. This document appears on the front cover of Clark's cash book and journal for 1825–28 and seems, according to internal evidence, to have been written during those years. Surely Clark was the only person who could have drawn up such a roster at this time and included the present status of the expedition members; yet the roster is only as reliable as Clark's information could make it. He is incorrect, for example, in listing Gass as dead (see Nos. 408, 410, 411). We may expect him to have the most reliable information about those members of the party who were still in the West.

1. The notation that Sacagawea was dead by 1825–28 is the most interesting piece of intelligence that Clark presents here, because it tends to contradict a popular belief. Sacagawea was never acclaimed as a real heroine by the American public until she was, in a sense, rediscovered by Eva Emery DYE in 1902. Then the task of elevating her to an even loftier position in history was assumed by Grace Raymond HEBARD, who wrote *Sacajawea, a guide and interpreter of the Lewis and Clark Expedition, with an account of the travels of Toussaint Charbonneau, and of Jean Baptiste, the expedition papoose* (Glendale, Calif., 1933). Mrs. Hebard believed that Sacagawea had survived the rigors of her youth and was the very old Shoshoni woman of the same name who lived, until late in the nineteenth century, in the Wind River country of Wyoming. Other historians have been inclined to suspect that Sacagawea may have died on the upper Missouri in 1812, in view of trader John Luttig's journal entry of 20 Dec.: "this Evening the Wife of Charbonneau a Snake Squaw, died of a putrid fever she was a good and the best Women in the fort, aged abt 25 years she left a fine infant girl" (LUTTIG, 106). But, since Charbonneau had at least two wives, both Shoshoni, the matter has remained in doubt. In 1941 the Wyoming Historical Landmark Commission erected a monument to Sacagawea on U.S. highway 287, two miles east of her supposed grave in a Shoshoni burial ground.

Although Clark's notation here is not conclusive, it cannot be dismissed lightly. We are hardly justified in saying, "If Clark is wrong about Gass, then perhaps he is also wrong about Sacagawea," for the cases are different. Gass had gone back to Virginia and severed his contacts with the West, but Sacagawea, her husband Charbonneau, and her children were Clark's concern for many years after the expedition. He cared about them and felt a kind of responsibility for them. It is difficult to believe that he could have been wrong about Sacagawea's death.

[639]

2. For "Tousant" read "Jean Baptiste." It has always been supposed that Charbonneau had three children, Jean Baptiste, Toussaint, and Lizette. I am indebted to Dale L. Morgan for the suggestion that there may only have been two, and that a misunderstanding has arisen because his contemporaries commonly called Jean Baptiste by his father's name, as Clark does here. At this time Jean Baptiste was in Württemberg, Germany, as the ward of Prince Paul, who met the young man while on a trip up the Missouri and took him abroad in 1824. The two returned to St. Louis in 1829.

405. Franklin Wharton to James Barbour

Sir   Crawford Court House, A. Terr. Feby. 28th, 1826

Capt. N. Pryor of this Territory has requested me to use means towards obtaining a liquidation of a just claim,[1] which he supposes he has against the U.S. Will you allow me to present its nature and solicit your answer to certain inquiries.

Capt. Pryor was the first person who volunteered his services in Lewis and Clark's expedition. He accompanied them through all their excursions and was finally sent in command of the party, to take back the Mandan chief and family to their homes. Of the event of this, you are aware. From that time to the period, when he derives his claim, he was engaged in extensive and dangerous business among the Indian Tribes.

About eighteen months before the late war, he was licensed by the Gov. of Missouri, as a trader among the Weenibagoes or Puans, on the Eastern Mississipi, Ter. of Missouri, at a place called De-Buque's Mines. At that place he was transacting a profitable business, had buildings erected as well as a smelting furnace, and was rapidly distributing through the Tribes the comforts and conveniences of civilization. About six months before the War, he received a letter from Gov. Clarke, requesting him to endeavour to find out Tecumseh or the Prophet. The execution of this duty, a duty performed at the wish of the Government—a duty delicate and hazardous in the extreme, rendered Capt. P. an object of hostility and enmity with the natives. From receiving the letter of the Gov. the Captain had heard nothing of a war likely to ensue. He was actively and industriously engaged in his occupation. On Christmas day and even after of the year '12 the Winbagoes were trading peaceably with him. On the 1st of Jany. 13 about 12 O'clock in the day, eight of the tribe came to his house, with their war accoutrements, and offered violence. They would not let him leave his dwelling. About sun-down of the same day, sixty arrived, shooting down the oxen in the yard and killing two of his men. They rushed on him, and was in the act of putting him to death, when by the politic dissimulation of a female in the house, they were averted for the moment from their intention. They then placed him in the house with a sentinel over him, intending to burn him in it. While they were plundering his stores and ravaging his premises, with the greatest difficulty, he made his escape. After crossing the Mississippi on the cakes of ice, he was still the object of pursuit to the hostile Indians. They were not so soon to forget his endeavorous for Tecumseh. They robbed him of all they [he] had in the world: they entirely destroyed every article of his property. Capt. P. only claims the original amount of his goods, amounting to 5,216$ 25 cents. He asks not the freight on them: he asks not what they were actually worth to him—he asks nothing for his buildings, his furnaces, his cattle, save two, which were shot down before his face. He, in fact, asks for less than what he conceives to be his just claim. And his reason is; for that which he seeks a remuneration he can positively swear to the amount. He will not add more, as he cannot remember certainly the value.

Capt. Pryor is a man of real, solid, innate worth. His genuine modesty conceals the peculiar traits of his character. He was a brave and persevering officer in the attack on New Orleans. He has the most thorough knowledge of the Western country; has been on considerable service to the U.S., and the benefit he has conferred on the Indian Tribes is gratefully acknowledged by them. He has been frequently urged by Gov. Clarke the Supt. of Ind. Aff. and by Gen. Miller,[2] the late Gov. of this Territory to forward this claim. But he has refused. His own exertions have hitherto been his support. Again robbed and plundered by the savages, viz. Cherokees he is left in a situation, where the money would be of service to him. His want drives him to that, which hitherto his conscious pride prevented. You will observe, that it was six months after the declaration of war, this transaction occurred. Yet had the traders no knowledge of it. The British Indian allies, received it first through their emissaries. It was not known at St. Louis 'til months after it took place. And does not Capt. P's claim derive additional support, from the fact that Gov. Clark was bound to give notice of the war, and at the time, such notice had not been given. The Capt. was trading under the license and protection of the U.S.; by an act of the U.S. of which he was ignorant, he was deprived of his property and his home. You will also please to remember that, the tribe was allied with the English troops. I am not aware, Sir, that this claim falls under your cognizance, of this much, I am certain, that, if you cannot *officially* interest yourself in it, its details will ensure your warm and generous support. The eloquent advocate of the abstract rights of man, will not lend a cold and feeble support, to what has connection, with the more kind and gentle feelings of humanity. If not inconsistent with your duty, would you be pleased to answer these enquiries.

Does this demand come within the scope of those, which have hitherto been termed just and equitable by the U.S.? If it bear no analogy to the former claims allowed, is it your opinon, that it is a fair one against the U.S.? What measures are necessary to place it before the proper authority, and what is that authority?

During the spring Gen. Clark has promised to have the necessary depositions taken. . . .

A letter will reach me, directed to "Dardanelle," Crawford Co. A.T. I have the honour to be Yr. Obt. Servt.

FRANKLIN WHARTON

Printed, PRYOR. The original is in DNA, RG 75. Wharton had military connections which probably made his name familiar to the Secretary of War. His father was Lt. Col. Franklin Wharton of the Marine Corps, and his older brother was Col. Clifton Wharton, of the Army. James Barbour (1775–1842) was Secretary of War from 1825 to 1828.

1. Upon Pryor's return from the unsuccessful attempt to return the Mandan chief in 1807, he was sent to Cantonment Belle Fontaine, where on 3 May 1808 he became a second lieutenant (Belle Fontaine order book, MoSHi). When in August of that year a company from the First Infantry was sent up the Mississippi to establish Fort Madison, under Lt. Alpha Kingsley, Pryor was second in command. In the spring of 1809, when an Indian attack on the fort was threatening, Pryor was sent to St. Louis with a request for support—and on the basis of his information Lewis called out a detachment of militia for a fruitless march to Fort Madison (*Missouri Gazette,* 5 April 1809 and subsequent issues).

His resignation from the army, sent from Fort Madison, was accepted as of 1 April 1810. He then moved 200 miles up the river to the mining region a few miles above the mouth of the Galena, in what was by then Illinois Territory, to trade with the Indians and operate a lead-smelting furnace. Although not in partnership with Pryor, the ex-sutler from Fort Madison, George Hunt, was trading in furs and lead at the same location. It was here that both men were to suffer from the Indian unrest created by the Battle of Tippecanoe.

Gen. Harrison had fought the Indians on Nov. 7, along the Wabash, and a party of Winnebagoes from a village on the Rock River, near the Mississippi, had been embroiled in the clash rather by accident. They were not a part of Tecumseh's forces, but had been returning from a visit to the British in Canada and had stopped to spend the night with Tecumseh's band at Tippecanoe. In the battle, the visiting Winnebagoes had lost twenty-five men. Returning to their village on the Rock River, they had brooded a while, then set out for the Galena River mines to seek vengeance. A party

[642]

of about 100 warriors arrived early 1 Jan. 1812 and attacked the trading establishments of Pryor and Hunt. Neither man had heard of the Tippecanoe encounter; they were completely unprepared for a hostile visit. Alexander Willard was on his way upriver from St. Louis to warn them, but he failed to arrive in time.

Two of their laborers were killed, but Hunt and Pryor escaped. They were saved, as William Clark wrote to the Secretary of War, "by some Sock & Fox Squaws who lived with the young men declaring they were English men" (13 Feb. 1812, TERR. PAPERS, 14:518–19).

At first Pryor was reported dead, but eventually he made his way down the river. The representations made by Wharton on his behalf are grossly inaccurate. Pryor's claim for remuneration is based on two assertions: that he was singled out for attack because of his mission regarding Tecumseh (about which I know nothing), and that the country was at war and he should therefore have been warned. There is no evidence that the attacking Indians knew of his mission, whatever it had been; and clearly the country was not at war, for the incident occurred six months before the declaration of War with Great Britain. He *should* have been warned, and Clark was trying to do so by sending Willard, but the government was under no obligation to warn or protect him. He was a civilian, operating independently and at his own risk.

Pryor was again commissioned by the army in 1813, serving as first lieutenant and captain in the Forty-fourth Infantry until disbanded in 1815. There are biographical notes in the article from which this letter is reprinted, in JAMES (4), 6–7, 117–19, and in FLOYD, 16. For the attack at the mines, see the anonymous narrative (by George Hunt) in *Michigan Historical Collections*, 8:662–69, 12:438–50, reprinted and somewhat re-arranged in VAN DER ZEE.

2. James Miller (1776–1851), governor of Arkansas Territory from 1819 to 1825.

406. Clark to Albert Gallatin

Sir,   Washington City March 31st 1826

On my return from New York I had the honour of receiving your letter of the 16th Instant & do assure you it is with much regret, that I cannot answer your letter as I could wish, for the want of references which I have not with me at this place, however I will endeavour to answer such parts of it as I can from memory.

Govr. Lewis undertook to publish our Voyage to the Pacific, he visited Philadelphia in 1807 & 1808 for that purpose, employed Mr. Conrad booksellers of that place to conduct & publish the work, and placed in his hands some engravings &c; a Mr. Perche was employed by him, to make drawings from Specimens & descriptions; some specimens were lodged with Mr. Peale; others in relation to Botany placed in the hands of Mr. McMahan, and part cultivated in his garden near Germantown.

After Govr. Lewis's death the papers, memorandums &c, were delivered to me by Mr. Madison among which were a part of the vocabularies and only a part of the celestial observations which had been taken by us. Soon after the death of my friend Lewis Mr. Conrad failed and some of the papers and plates were never recovered. I employed Messrs. Bradford and Inskeep of Philadelphia to conduct the publication of which I was advised to divide, that part relating particularly to Natural History Doctr. Barton was employed to arrange & write in a specified time by Contract which he failed to perform, all memorandums, descriptions, Specimens &c. was either placed in his possession or subjected to his examination. The other materials were left with Mr. Biddle, from which to write the work published, and which came out as soon after as could be expected. The vocabularies were as I believe placed in the hands of Dr. Barton and if they have not been placed by order of Mr. Jefferson in possession of the Historical Committee of Philadelphia must yet remain in the possession of the executors of Dr. Barton. I authorized Mr. Jefferson to receive the papers, books specimens &c. which I have reason to believe he deposited with the Historical Committee, as I recollect having Mr. John Vaughns receipt for 14 volumes of the pocket journal, astronomical observations &c. delivered by Mr. Biddle in 1818. I recollect of no receipts of deliveries by Dr. Bartons Excrs. neither do I recollect of any copies retained by me at Saint Louis, except the Original Map. If the books, papers & specimens which were in the hands of Dr. Barton, have not been disposed of by Mr. Jefferson, they must yet be in the possession of the Excrs. of Dr. Barton. I will write to Mr. Jefferson and learn the disposition which he has made of those papers &c. and advise you of the steps which may eventually be necessary for their recovery. I discovered no affinity between the Language of the Mandans and that of either, the Sioux, Osage, Minatarees or any other Tribe known to me; The language of the Shoshone or Snake Indians, is spoken by the Tribes along the Eastern borders, & within the Stoney Mountains, from the Missouri as far S.E. as the Spanish Settlements & West of the mountains for some distance down the Molknoma River.

I am inclined to believe that all the Tribes through which I passed residing West of those mountains as low as the falls of Columbia originally spoke the same language. From the falls of Columbia to the Sea Coast the language is very different from those nearer the Rocky Mountains and from the affinity, a peculiar pronunciation of their language, and the custom of Flattening their

[644]

foreheads it is probable they were all originally the same Nation. It may not be amiss to observe that there is a great affinity of Language between the Blackfoot, Minataree & Crow Indians—between the Pawnee & Aurickara—between the Osages, Kansas, Mahas, Poncas, Quapaws & Caddors—& between the Ottoes, Missouri Ioways & Winebagoes.

The best means and most proper persons to procure more extensive vocabularies than we now possess of the Western Tribes, is by making it the duty of the Several Indian Agents by an order from the Secry. of War.

Most of those bands alluded to in the relation of my Voyage or the Map annexed are the remnants of the once powerful nation of Padoucas, now become so reduced that only few bands are at this time known.

It will afford me great pleasure at all times to give you any information which may be in my Power. Please to accept an assurance of the very high respect with which I have the honor to remain Sir, Yr. Mo. Obt. Servt.

WM. CLARK

LS, RC (NHi). Addressed, "Albert Gallatin Esqr.   Baltimore   Maryland"; endorsed.

407. Clark to James Barbour

Superintendency of Ind'n Affairs.
Sir   St. Louis, Aug. 4th, 1827

Since the death of the Sub Agent of the Arkansas Band of Osages, no appointment has been made to fill the vacancy. As the situation of that Band requires a Sub Agent of respectablity and influence, I have employed Capt'n Nathaniel Pryor, at the rate of $500 per ann. and given him a temporary appointment of Sub Agent. His influence among the Indians generally, in that quarter, his capacity to act and be serviceable, added to his knowledge of the Osage language, would it is believed justify his receiving the appointment and pay of Sub Agent and Interpreter, which would enable him to perform those duties which Col. Arbuckle,[1] and the Choctaw and Osage Agents have suggested in their letters which I have the honor to enclose. Capt. Pryor served with me, on an expedition to the Pacific ocean in 1803, 4, 5, and 6 in the capacity of 1st Sergeant; after which he served as an officer in the Army, and was disbanded after the last war. When out of Service, he has pursued the Indian trade, in which he has been unfortunate, first by the Winnebagoes, who took every article he had and for which he has a claim before Congress, and since by casual occurrences in his commercial pursuit on the Arkansas.

Capt. Pryor's long and faithful services and his being disabled by a dislocation of his shoulder[2] when in the execution of his duty under my command, produces an interest in his favor and much solicitude for bettering his situation by an office which he is every way capable of filling with credit to himself and usefulness to his government. I have the honor to be With high respect Your most obt. servt.

WM. CLARK

Printed, PRYOR. The original is in DNA, RG 75.

1. Col. Mathew Arbuckle, Seventh Infantry, with headquarters at Cantonment Gibson, later Fort Gibson, in present Oklahoma.

2. "Sergeant Pryor in takeing down the mast put his Sholder out of Place, we made four trials before we replaced it" (Clark in the JOURNALS, 1:229).

408. Patrick Gass to John H. Eaton

Sir   Wellsburgh, Brooke County, Va., March 12th 1829

I am reluctantly compelled to trouble you with the present application relative to the conduct of the agent for paying pensions in Richmond. On the 11th June 1815 I was placed on the pension list,[1] Roll of the Virginia Agency, for total inability, having lost the sight of my left eye whilst in the service of the United States during the late war—received a pension certificate for $8. per month, dated Octr. 21st 1816, and continued until lately to receive my pension. Some years ago, the Agent at Richmond demanded that I should be examined bienually, and which I have hitherto complied with, but he lately objected to the *form* of the Surgeons certificate, and now absolutely refuses to pay my pension, unless such form as he says the law demands be complied with, and which the Surgeons here refuses to grant—because, they say, they do not know that I was put on the Roll for *total* inability, and I having nothing to shew but my pension certificate, which does not discribe the *degree* of disability. By the inclosed application for my pension in the Spring of 1828, and which was returned because of the informality of the Surgeons certificate, it will be seen that, if I am subject to be at all examined, the Surgeons have given such certificate, as my situation warranted. The words interlined and underscored, "is total being" were inserted

[646]

by the agent at Richmond, and the word "is" erased; and returned to the gentleman that applied for my pension, as the proper form, and without complying with which, as will be seen by the agents letter of the 1st Decr. last, also inclosed, my pension will not be paid; and then again another examination must take place in September following.

When I first complied with the demand that I should be examined by two Physicians, or Surgeons, I furnished the agent that was to receive my pension with a note, protesting that I was exempted from such examination by the law of the 3d. March 1819 and the regulation of the Secretary of War of the 23rd. These expressly excepts from examination those invalid pensioners to whom "pension shall have been origonally granted for a total disability, in consequence of the loss of a limb, or other cause which cannot either in whole or in part be removed." I am unacquainted with any other law or regulation on the subject than those referred to; and as I am now nearly sixty years of age, having no real or personal property, except wearing appearl, and not able to procure, entirely, my subsistance by manual labor, being severly afflicted by rheumatic pains, the effect of severe and continued exertions in the service of my country, since I was capable of carrying arms until the close of the late war. And permit me to add here that in the years 1804, 5 & 6 I accompanied Captains Lewis and Clarke to the Pacific Ocean, and on our return had published my dailey Journal, which book I am informed is honored with a place in the library of Congress; that at the commencement of the late war I inlisted with Captain Kingsley at Nashville in the Year 1812 in the 1st regmt. Infantry— in March 1813 moved to Fort Massack—thence to Belle-fontaine on the Missouri—then assisted in building a small fort on the Mississipi, called "Independance." In 1814 decended the Mississippi and acended the Ohio river to Pittsburgh, under the command of Col. Nichols[2]—thence marched to Presque-isle—Fort Erie—Chipewa —and was in the battle at Lundays lane, under Captn. Symmes[3]— after that battle returned to Fort Erie—where we were canonaded by the British for about seven weeks, and was finally marched to Sackets harbor, and discharged[4] in June 1815, having obtained from the Surgen general a certificate of *total* disability on account of the loss of the sight of my left eye, whilst in service.

My humble request is that the agent for paying pensions at Richmond may be ordered to pay my pension; and that, if I am subject to be examined, that he will admit such certificate as the Surgeons are willing to grant—namely—that my disability does still

[647]

continue, as when first placed on the pension Roll. May I without being considered as too troublesome, solicit an answer. I have the Honor to be, Your most Obdt. Servt.

PATR. GASS.

LS, SC (DNA, RG 15A, OWIF 25097). John H. Eaton was Secretary of War, 1829–31.

1. Gass was the last survivor of the expedition, dying in 1870. The letter presented here and the two affidavits (Nos. 410, 411) contain some fresh biographical details. A summary of his pension status filed in OWIF 25097 verifies his own statement about the date and amount of his pension. This pension, it should be noted, was awarded for an injury he suffered in the War of 1812, not for his service with the expedition.

2. Probably Col. A. Y. Nicoll, who was adjutant and inspector, 1807–12, and a colonel from March 1813 until his resignation in June 1814.

3. John Cleves Symmes (d. 1829) was commissioned ensign in 1802 and was a captain when discharged in 1815. He earned a moment of fame with his "holes in the poles" theory, based on a belief that the earth is hollow and habitable within. For this aspect of his career, see MITTERLING, 67–82.

4. His discharge is filed in the pension envelope, listing him as about five feet seven inches tall, dark complexion, gray eyes, dark hair; occupation, carpenter; enlisted 25 Aug. 1812, discharged 19 June 1815.

409. Joshua Pilcher to the Commissioner of Indian Affairs

Superintendy. of Indian Affs.

Sir: St. Louis, Augt. 26, 1839

On the 21st inst. Toussaint Charbonneau, the late Mandan Interpreter, arrived here from the Mandan villages, a distance of 1600 miles, and came into the office, tottering under the infirmities of 80 winters, without a dollar to support him, to ask what appeared to me to be nothing more than just, and I accordingly have paid his salary as Interpreter for the Mandan sub-agency, for the 1st & 2d quarters of this year, with the understanding that his services are no longer required. This man has been a faithful servant of the Government—though in a humble capacity. He figured conspicuously in the expedition of Lewis and Clark to the Pacific, and rendered much service. For the last fifteen years, he has been employed as the Government interpreter at the Mandans, and never received notice of the intention of the Department to dispense with his services, until some time in July, in consequence of the remote situation of the post. Under these circumstances I thought, and still think it but right that he should be paid, and believe it will meet your sanction, to be charged, (as there has been no allottment for that sub-agency), to the contingent account of the District. I am, Sir, Your mo. ob. st.

JOSHUA PILCHER, Supr. In. Affs.

ALS, RC (DNA, RG 75). Apparently the payment to Charbonneau was allowed. The letter is endorsed, "File." Joshua Pilcher (1790–1843) succeeded Clark in 1838 as superintendent of Indian affairs at St. Louis.

410. Pension Petition of Patrick Gass

[23 December 1851]

To the Senate and House of Representatives in Congress Assembled. The Petition of the Undersigned, *Patrick Gass,* respectfully showeth:

That in the year 1799, he being 28 yea[r]s of age, he enlisted [1] in the Regular Army at Carlisle Pa. and joined the 10th Penna. Regiment, under Col. Thos. L. Moore.—at the expiration of his term of enlistment was honorably discharged—that he subsequently re-enlisted under Maj. Cass—was stationed for a short time at Harper's Ferry—thence removed to Pittsburg, where Maj. Cass resigned.—thence he was removed to Kaskaskia, Illinois Territory, under Gen'l. Wilkinson.—That, while here, he volunteered in the Expedition to the Rocky Mountains, in 1803, under *Lewis & Clark,* was appointed by them a Sergeant, and, pursuant to their order, kept a regular and full Journal, during the 3 years of great toil and privation that Command underwent. The incidents of that Expedition to the Mouth of the Columbia River are a part of history, and need no recital here. In 1812 he again enlisted in the regular Army, under Genl. Bissell and served faithfully, as a Private, through nearly all of the sanguinary engagements of that period—receiving many *flesh* wounds—but was never a week on the sick list, save once, when *he suffered the loss of one eye* at the Battle of Lundy's Lane.[2] In 1815, when Peace was declared by the respective Governments of the U.S. & Great Britain, he was honorably discharged—and returned to his home in Western Virginia, and applied himself to acquiring a respectable maintenance. But a constitution, impaired & broken by long service in the Army, precluded him, for many years, from gaining more than a mere livelihood, even assisted by the welcome yet small pension allowed him by the Government. In 1831 he married—and in 1847 his wife died, devolving on him the sole care and education of a large and infant family. Age, with its concomitant decrepitude and helplessness, has

[649]

now overtaken him, and driven him to the verge of indigence, and rendered physical labor impossible. He finds that were it not for the benificent, yet very small amount received annual from the Government—too meagre, indeed to provide even the necessaries of life for his motherless children—he must inevitably be cast on the cold charity of the world, from which his feelings revolt with indescribable dread. Virginia is not blest with any system of general education, and, hence, he has no opportunity to school his children.

In view, therefore, of the years and strength your Petitioner has expended in the service of the U.S.—in view of the 3 years of suffering endured in the Expedition to the Rocky Mts., from which such incalculable good enured to this Country—in view of his numerous, small and helpless family—in view of his extreme age, (81), and incapability to maintain and educate this family, knit to him by the dearest & strongest ties of earth, and whom he has the honest pride to make respectable and intelligent citizens—he most earnestly prays your honorable body, to grant him an appropriation sufficient to make his few remaining years comfortable, & his death solaced by the pleasing reflection, that the country which he so long and faithfully served, has enabled him to bequeath to his offspring the priceless heritage of a free and happy people—a wholesome and substantial Education.

And your Petitioner will ever pray &c.

PATK. GASS

Virginia—Brooke Co. to wit:—Personally appeared before me the undersigned, a justice of the Peace, in & for the said County, that[?] Gass, and made oath that he is the identical Patrick Gass mentioned in the above memorial, as having rendered services to the U.S. in the "Lewis & Clark Expedition," & elsewhere. Given under my hand & seal this 23rd day of Decr. A.D. 1851.

SAMUEL L. MARKS[?] J.P.

DS, RC (DNA, RG 15A, OWIF 25097).
1. Another Gass affidavit, drawn 9 March 1855, adds the following: "He served as a private, then sergeant, in the company of Capt. Graham of the 10th Pennsylvania Regulars, having enlisted at Huntington County, Pa., in May 1799 for the term of the then existing differences between France and the United States." He served thirteen months and was discharged at Little York, Pa., in June 1800.
2. His assertion that he lost an eye at Lundy's Lane is false, and this seems to be the first time he has made the claim. His medical certificate of 5 June 1815 states that he lost his left eye in Sept. 1813 due to an injury sustained "at Fort Independence on the Mississippi, Missouri Territory." The present document has misled Earle R. Forrest, who prepared the

introduction for a recent edition of Gass's journal (Minneapolis, 1958). Forrest presents a facsimile of this affidavit, offering it as proof that Gass had not "lost the sight of an eye while 'chopping wood' "; but he overlooks the medical certificate.

411. Affidavit of Patrick Gass

[17 February 1854]

Virginia, Brooke County, to wit: This day before me Joseph Applegate a Justice of the Peace in and for the County and state foresaid, personally came *Patrick Gass,* a resident of the County & state aforesaid, who being first duly sworn, according to law, doth, on his oath say, that he is eighty three (83) years of age, that he was born in Chambersburg, Cumberland (now Franklin) County, State of Penna., on the 12th day of June, one thousand seven hundred & seventy one (1771)—that in the year one thousand eight hundred & three (1803) in the month of November of said year last aforesaid, at Caskaskia, in the (then) Territory of Illinois, he volunteered under Capts. Lewis & Clarke, appointed by Prest. Jefferson, on an Expedition of Discovery to the Mouth of the Columbia River, on the Pacific coast—that the Expedition consisted (of permanent volunteers, on the banks of the Debois or Wood River, about 18 miles above St. Louis) of thirty one (31) persons, exclusive of the two Capts. afore-named. That in the latter part of April, or first of May of the year one thousand eight hundred & four, affiant, at the direction of said Captains, commenced the keeping of a daily journal of incidents of the progress of the Expedition—that in August of the last aforenamed year, the duty Sergeant of the Expedition, [*blank*] Floyd, died a short distance from Council Bluffs, & Capts. Lewis & Clarke ordered an election to fill the vacancy, occasioned by the death of said Sergeant, & that affiant was elected duty sergeant, which post he, affiant, held till the Company was disbanded. After incredible hardships, intense suffering from inclement weather, hunger, thirst, through an hitherto unexplored & savage wilderness, affiant says, the Company reached the mouth of the Columbia River, in November A.D. one thousand eight hundred & five (1805)— where they remained, on the sea coast till March A.D. one thousand eight hundred & six, at which time they evacuated their little fort (erected during their stay at the mouth of said River, & so called, after the tribe of Indians (Clatsup) inhabiting that region. That the said Company incurred the same imminent perils on their return home which began as before stated in March 1806, & closed by reaching

St. Louis on the 23rd day of Sept. one thousand eight hundred & six (1806) where the Company was disbanded—he affiant, receiving from the said Capts., a Certificate of Honorable Discharge & testimony of valuable Services rendered said Company, during said Expedition. That in the year one thousand eight hundred & seven (1807) said affiant had published & circulated his Journal, in advance, he believes, of that of Lewis & Clarke—a copy of this Journal of his keeping, affiant states, has been recently sent to Z. Kidwell, M.C. from this District, & to which he refers for more detailed particulars of said Expedition. Affiant further states that he enlisted in the war of 1812, under General Bissell, Capt. Sims; & the recruiting officer (Kingsley) demanded of said Affiant his original Certificate from Capts. Lewis & Clarke, alledging that it was unsafe for any soldier, no matter how loyal, to have such a paper in his possession, while in service. That, after said war, affiant has often sought to regain said Certificate, but has always failed in obtaining the address of Kingsley. Hence, affiant, further takes it the Certificate is hopelessly lost. Affiant further says that he was first married in the year one thousand eight hundred & thirty one (1831)—that his wife died in the year one thousand eight hundred & forty six (1846)—that he is left with a family of six children, & has no pecuniary means whatever to procure for them what he most desires, a liberal, or at least, a substantial English Education. That two of his children died prior to the death of his wife, & the six still surviving are of tender years (the youngest not yet 8 years (eight) old,—Affiant further states that George Shannon, brother to Hon. Wilson Shannon, M.C. from Ohio, was a member of the aforesaid Expedition under Capts. Lewis & Clarke. Affiant further says that he has from time to time learned of the deaths respectively of all, he believes, of the members of said Company, and does not know of a single surviving member, save himself. He does not know of any one who could now identify him as the Patrick Gass of that Expedition—but desires to add, that he never yet heard it questioned, by any one—that his own vivid recollection of the scenes of that Expedition, & his own physical marks of its hair-breadth escapes, leave no room for doubt in his mind at least. And further deponent saith not.

PATR. GASS

Sworn to & subscribed before me, Joseph Applegate a Justice of the Peace in & for the County of Brooke & state of Virginia, & I hereby certify that I believe the Affiant Gass to be of the Age stated; that I have been personally acquainted with him for thirty five years; that he has during that time been a resident of this County, that he is a man of respectability, & worthy of full credence, & that I verily believe all & singular his statements to be true. Given under my hand & seal this 17th day of February A.D. 1854.

JOSEPH APPLEGATE {seal}

DS (DNA, RG 15A, OWIF 25097).

The purpose of this affidavit is not clear; it may have been an attempt to establish Gass's identity as an authentic survivor of the expedition. In this connection it is worth noting that Clark, in his list of expedition members described under No. 404a, believed Gass to be dead in the late 1820's. I have made no attempt to verify the identity of the man who here calls himself the Patrick Gass of the expedition, but his signature closely matches Gass's signature of 1807.

The Committee on Private Land Claims issued the following statement in Report No. 215, H.R., 33d Cong., 1st sess., 23 June 1854: "The government is now giving to the actual settlers in Oregon three hundred and twenty acres of land. The donation of this quantity of land to actual settlers is a ready means to induce population, and convert the wilderness into blooming and cultivated States; and while the committee, under the circumstances and position of the Oregon Territory, readily recognise the propriety and justness of such an application of the lands in that distant and unprotected quarter, they also think that something may be due for the remnant of that small band who accompanied Lewis and Clark in their long, perilous and laborious expedition. . . . The petitioner not only fought in defence of his country, but his labors contributed to the extension of its borders and the possession of the magnificent and important valleys on the Pacific slope. . . . Mr. Gass, it is believed, is the only survivor of that expedition . . . he is too old and helpless, and with a numerous family of small children, to go to Oregon for the land that his boldness discovered, and his valor defended; and he thinks, and the committee concur with him, that the government should compensate him out of its public lands. . . . The committee report the accompanying bill for his relief."

To summarize the land grants received by Gass: he received Warrant No. 6 for 320 acres in 1807, when all members of the expedition were rewarded. He received Warrant No. 7460 for 160 acres for his services in the War of 1812. He received Warrant No. 27894½ for 320 acres by special act of Congress, 4 Aug. 1854. There are also indications in his pension file that he applied for bounty land on the basis of his 1799–1800 service, and that his application was rejected.

Appendix I

These letters, very lightly annotated and intended to be representative, not exhaustive, deal with four American plans to send exploring parties to the Pacific between 1783 and 1793. Three of the proposed explorations, those of George Rogers Clark, John Ledyard, and André Michaux, were either originated or abetted by Jefferson. As for the fourth—an abortive attempt by the War Department to send Lt. John Armstrong across the continent—there is no indication that Jefferson ever knew of it.

The approach to George Rogers Clark was hardly a plan; it was merely a suggestion. The others reflect a common defect in the thinking of the planners—skimpy preparation. Ledyard's project typifies this point of view: he thought he could walk from the Pacific to the civilized places of the U.S., protected only by a couple of dogs and a winning way with Indians. His biographer, Helen Augur, defends this "lone traveler" theory of exploration and disparages the well-equipped Lewis and Clark Expedition. "More than once Lewis and Clark almost failed because of the extreme difficulty of transporting their gear. . . . Lewis and Clark present a picture of a group of Americans encysted in their equipment . . ." (AUGUR, 187–88). But if it was equipment that often deterred Lewis and Clark, it was also equipment that made their success possible; and Ledyard, even if he had managed to cross the West with two dogs and an Indian pipe as he hoped, could have brought back little useful information.

412. Jefferson to George Rogers Clark

Dear Sir   Annapolis Dec. 4. 1783.

I received here about a week ago your obliging letter of Oct. 12. 1783. with the shells and seeds for which I return you many thanks. You are also so kind as to keep alive the hope of getting for me as many of the different species of bones, teeth and tusks of the *Mammoth* as can now be found. This will be most acceptable. Pittsburg and Philadelphia or Winchester will be the surest channel of conveyance. I find they have subscribed a very large sum of money in England for exploring the country from the Missisipi to California. They pretend it is only to promote knolege. I am afraid they have thoughts of colonising into that quarter. Some of us have been talking here in a feeble way of making the attempt to search that country. But I doubt whether we have enough of that kind of spirit to raise the money. How would you like to lead such a party? Tho I am afraid our prospect is not worth asking the question. The definitive treaty of peace is at length arrived. It is not altered from the preliminaries. The cession of the territory West of Ohio to the United states has been at length accepted by Congress with some small alterations of the conditions. We are in daily expectation of receiving it with the final approbation of Virginia. Congress have been lately agitated by questions where they should fix their residence. They first resolved on Trentown. The Southern states however contrived to get a vote that they would give half their time to Georgetown at the Falls of Patowmac. Still we consider the matter as undecided between the Delaware and Patowmac. We urge the latter as the only point of union which can cement us to our Western friends when they shall be formed into separate states. I shall always be happy to hear from you and am with very particular esteem Dr. Sir Your friend & humble servt.,

TH: JEFFERSON

ALS, RC (WHi). Addressed; endorsed in several hands. In Jefferson's index of letters it is recorded under Dec. 5, and the subject is given as "bones—expdn. tow[a]rds Calfa."

413. George Rogers Clark to Jefferson

Sr   Richmond Feby 8th 1784

Your favour of the 4th Decr. last came safe to hand. I should have given you an answer sooner but some part of the subject required serious attention in a person in my ciutation. It gives me pleasure to suppose you my friend originating from the Idea I have of your sentiments. The Bones you wish for will undoubtedly be sent to you without some misfortune should happen me as I am now divesting myself of a trust that I have long suffered in & hope in future to have pleasure in private connections. Your proposition respecting a tour to the west and North west of the Continent would be Extreamly agreable to me could I afford it but I have late discovered that I knew nothing of the lucrative policy of the world supposing my duty required every attention and sacrifice to the Publick Interest but must now look forward for future Support. Should Congress risolve to have the western Country Explored I should take pleasure in lending all the aid in my power as an Individual. It is what I think we ought to do. But pardon me when I inform you that I

[655]

think our Ideas of this Business is genly. wrong. Large parties will never answer the purpose. They will allarm the Indian Nations they pass through. Three or four young Men well qualified for the Task might perhaps compleat your wishes at a very Trifling Expence. A tolerable subsistance on their return might procure them. They must learn the Language of the distant Nations they pass through the geography of their Country antient Speach or Tradition, passing as men tracing the Steps of our four Fathers wishing to know from whence we came. This would require four or five years, an Expence worthey the attention of Congress, from the Nature of things I should suppose that you would require a genl. Superintendant of Indian affairs to the westward as the greatest body of those people live in that quarter. I should have no objections in serving them. I shall set out for the Falls of Ohio in a few Days whare I expect to reside perhaps for Life. Lets. that you might think of Honouring me with might be sent by the way of Pittsburg. Such favours will be always gratefully receiv'd. I am Sr with Respect your obedt. Servt.

G R CLARK

ALS, RC (ViHi). Addressed; endorsed.

414. John Ledyard to Jefferson

London Novr. 25th 1786

My friend, my brother, my Father,—I know not by what title to address you—you are very very dear to me. Embrace the dear Marquis la Fayette for me: he has all the virtues of his country without any of its little foibles. I am indeed a very plain Man, but do not think that mountains or oceans shall oppose my passage to glory while I have such friends in remembrance—I have pledged myself—difficulties have intervened—my heart is on fire—ye stimulate, & I shall gain the victory. Thus I think of you—thus I have thought of you daily—& thus I shall think of you <*untill it ceases to be a virtue to think— with regard to myself this cannot be the case while either of you exist*>. After all the fair prospects that attended me when I last wrote—I still am persecuted—still the slave of <*fortune*> accident & the son of care. The Ship I embarked in was seized by the Custom house & is this day exchequered. If a small subscription now begun in London <*in my favour*> by Sr. Joseph Banks & Doctr. Hunter will enable me to proceed you will probably hear from me at Hamburgh: if I arive at Petersbourg you most certainly will <*hear from me*>. You see the course I was purs[u]ing to fame reverted &

I am now going across Siberia as I had once before intended from Paris this time twelve month—what a twelve months! I do defy fortune to be more malicious during another. I fear my subscription will be small: it adds to my anxiety to reach those dominions where I shall not want money—I do not mean the dominions that may be beyond death: I shall never wish to die while you the Marquis & Mr. Barclay are alive:—pray Sr. if that dear and genuine friend of mine is any where near you do me the honour to present me sur mes genoux devant lui—Ja'adore son coeur genereux. May I beg to be presented to Mr. Short to Commodore Jones & to Colo. Franks if with you: <a present je pense comme lui de la gouvernement de cet pays ici—tout est un cabal meme dans leur [. . .]us—heureusment pour moi j'entend bien a don[ner] des coups du poins, & have litteraly been obliged to thrash 5 or 6 of these haughty turbulent & very insolent people: one of them at the theatre where I assure you one is still more liable to insult than in the streets even>. I have just parted with Colonel Smith: he is well & is trying also to do something for me. I hear yo[u] have not been very well lately, tho now better—take care of your health for the sake of our Country & for his sake who begs the honor to subscribe himself with all possible respect & esteem Sr. your very humble & most obedt. servant

JNO LEDYARD

ALS, RC (NHi). Endorsed; listed in Jefferson's index of letters as received 20 Dec. 1786.

415. John Ledyard to Jefferson

Sir   St. Petersbourg March 19th 1787
It will be one of the remaining pleasures of my life to thank you for the many instances of your friendship to me & wherever I am to pursue you incessantly with the tale of my gratitude.

If Mr. Barclay should be at Paris let him rank with you as my next friend: I hardly know how to estimate the goodness of the Marquis la Fayette to me—but I think a french nobleman of the first character in his country never did more to serve an obscure citizen of another than the Marquis has done for me: & I am as sure that it is impossible (without some kind of soul made expressly for the purpose) that an obscure citizen in such a situation can be more gratefull than I am: may he be told so & with my Compliments to his Lady: my Compliments wait on Mr. Short, Commodore

[657]

Jones & Colo. Franks if at Paris—with thanks for their favours also. If I was sure Mr. Barclay was at Paris I would write him, for no man less acquainted with him esteems him more than I do, believing verily that of such as him consisteth the Kingdom of heaven. I cannot tell you by what means I came to Petersbourg, & hardly know by what means I shall quit it in the further prossecution of my tour round the world by Land: if I have any merit in the affair it is perseverence, for most severely have I been buffeted—& yet still am I even more obstinate than before—& fate as obstinate continues her assaults. How the matter will terminate I know not: the most probable Conjecture is that I shall succeed, & be kicked round the world as I have hitherto been from England thro Denmark, thro Sweeden, thro Sweedish lapland, Sweedish finland & the most unfrequented parts of Russian finland to this Aurora Borealis of a City. I cannot give you a history of myself since I saw you, or since I wrote you last: however abridged, it would be too long: upon the whole, mankind have used me well, & tho I have as yet reached only the first stage of my journey I feel myself much indebted to that urbanity which I always thought more general than many think it to be, & was it not for the villianous laws & bad examples of some Governments I have passed thro I am persuaded that I should have been able to have given you still better accounts of our fellow creatures.

But I am hastning to those countries where goodness if natural to the human heart will appear independant of example & furnish an annecdote of the character of man not unworthy the attention of him who wrote the declaration of American Independence.

I did not hear of the death of Monsieur de Vergenes untill I arived here. Permit me to express my regret at the loss of so great a man & of so good a man. Permit me also to congratulate you as the minister of my Country on account of the additional commercial privileges granted by france to america & to send you my ardent wishes that the friendly spirit which dictated them may last forever: I was extremely pleased at reading this account, & to heighten the satisfaction I felt I found the name of la Fayette there. There was a report a few days ago of which I have heard nothing since, that the french ships under the Command Capt. Lapereux had arrived at Kamchatka. There is an equipment now on foot here for that ocean & it is first to visit the NW Coast of America: it is to consist of four ships. This & the equipment that went from here 12 months since by land to Kamchatka are to cooperate in a design of some sort in the northern pacific Ocean—the lord knows what—nor does it matter what with me

—nor need it with you, or any other Minister or any Potentate southward of 50° of Latitude. I can only say that you are in no danger of having the luxurious repose of your charming climates disturbed by a second incursion of either Goth Vandal Hun or Scythian. I dined to day with Doctr. Pallas Professor of Natural history &c &c— an Accomplished Sweed: my friend: has been all thro European & asiatic Russia. I find the little french I have of infinite service to me: I could not do without it <*the little I have*>: it is a most extraordinary language: I believe that wolves, rocks, woods & snow understand it, for I have addressed them in it & they have all been very complaisant to me: but I dined in a shirt that I had worn *four* days. I have but *two:* & I suppose when I write you next I shall have none.

We had a Scythian at table that belongs to the royal society of Physicians here: the moment the savage knew me, & my designs he became my friend & it will be by his generous assistance joined with that of Doctr. Pallas that I shall be able to procure a *royal passport* without which I can not stir: but this must be done thro the application of the french Minister (there being no American one here) & to whose secretary I shall apply with Dr. Pallas to morrow: & beg liberty to Make use of your name & the Marquis la fayettes as to my character. As all my Letters of recommendation have been English & as I have been hitherto used by them with the greatest kindness & respect I first applied to the English Embassy: but with[out] success: the ostensible apology was that the present political moment between England & Russia would make it disagreeable for the English minister to ask any favour: but I saw the reason—the true reason in the specula of the secretarys eye—& so damn his eyes— which in this case particularly I concieve to be polite language: I hate ill nature & pity a fool.

Sir, I have waited on the Secretary of the french embassy who will dispatch my Letter with one of his accompanying it to the Count Segur to morrow morning. I will endeavour to write you again before I leave Petersbourg & give you some further accounts of myself. In the meantime I wish you health. I have wrote a very short Letter to the Marquis. Adieu!

I have the honor to be with respect & friendship Sr. your much obliged & most obt. & most hbl. Servt.

LEDYARD

ALS, RC (NHi). Addressed; endorsed; recorded in the index of letters as received 25 May 1787 at Bordeaux.

416. John Ledyard to Jefferson

Sir   Town of Barnowl in Siberia July 29th 1787

You will find this town by the Russian charts situated in about the Latd. 52°: & Longd. 100: it is near the town of Kolyvan & in the province of Kolyvan: the residence of the Governor of the province. It is near the silver mines & has a foundery in it wch produces anualy 650 poods of silver bullion besides some gold. A pood is 36 pounds english: it is also situated near the salt lakes wch produces more to the revenue than the mines. I am 4539 versts from petersburg & have 4950 versts to go before I arive at Okotsk, & if I go to Peter & Paul in Kamchatka I have 1065 versts more to go before I see that ocean which I hope will bear me on its boosom to the coast of America. How I have come thus far & how I am still to go farther is an enigma that I must disclose to you on some happier occasion. I shall never be able without seeing you in person & perhaps not even then to inform you how universaly & circumstantialy the Tartars resemble the aborigines of America: they are the same people—the most antient, & most numerous of any other, & had not a small sea divided them, they would all have still been known by the *same name*. The cloak of civilization sits as ill upon them as our American tartars— they have been a long time Tartars & it will be a long time before they are any other kind of people. I shall send this Letter to Petersburg to the care of Doctor Pallas Professor, of the royal Academy president, & historyographer to the Admiralty. I hope he will transmit it to you together with one to the Marquis in the mail of the count de Segur. I hope you & your friends & mine enjoy as much good health as I do which is of the purest kind—but notwithstanding all the vigour of my body—my mind keeps the start of me & anticipates my future fate with the most sublimated ardour. Pity it is that in such a career one should be subjected like a horse to the beggarly impediments of sleep & hunger.[1]

The Banks of the large Rivers in this country every where abound with something curious in the fossil world. I have found the leg-bone of a very large animal on the banks of the Oby & have sent it to Dr. Pallas & told him to render me an acct. of it hereafter. It is either the Elephant or Rinoceros bone, for the latter Animal has also been in this country: there is a compleat head of one in a high state of preservation at Petersburg. I am a curiosity myself in this country: those who have heard of America flock round me to see me: unfortunately the marks on my hands procures me & my Countrymen the appelation of wild-men. Among the better sort we are somewhat more known: the Governor & his family get a peep at the history of our existance thro the medium of a Septennial pamphlet of some kind. We have however two Stars that shine even in the Galaxy of Barnowl, & the healths of Dr. Franklin & of Genl. Washington have been drank in compliment to me at the Governors table: I am treated with great hospitality here—hitherto I have fared comfortably when I could make a port any where—but when totaly in the Country I have been a little incommoded: hospitality however I have found as universal as the face of man.

When you read this—perhaps 2 months before you do If I do well I shall be at Okotsk where I will do myself the honour to trouble you again & if possible will write more at large.

If Mr. Barclay should be with you I pray you present me to him—my compliments wait on all my Parisian friends—remember that I am & always shall be with the highest esteem & gratitude Sr. yr. much obliged most obt. hbl servt.

LEDYARD

ALS, RC (NHi). Endorsed.
1. Before revision, this passage read: "It is certainly a pity that in such a career I should be. . . ." Then he wrote, "I feel the indignity," and struck it out.

417. Henry Knox to Josiah Harmar

(Secret)
Dear Sir   War Office 20 December 1789

The subject I am about stating to you must be retained by you as a profound secret, and I depend on your honor not to communicate thereon now or hereafter excepting with the Governor of the Western Territory who I shall refer to you.

It is important that the official information of all the western regions should be as precise and as extensive as the nature of things will admit. You will therefore exercise your mind in obtaining such information. Devise some practicable plan for exploring the branch of the Mississippi called the Missouri, up to its source and all its southern branches, and tracing particularly the distances between the said branches and any of the navigable streams that run into the Great North River which empties itself into the gulf of Mexico. In order that you may better comprehend my Idea I send you a map of the said river, and its conjectural relation to the Missouri.

You will easily see that this object cannot be undertaken with the sanction of public authority. An enterprizing Officer with a non commissioned Officer well acquainted with living in the woods, and perfectly capable of describing rivers and countries, accompanied by four or five hardy indians perfectly attached to the United States would in my opinion be the best mode of obtaining the information requested. Could you engage two such parties, and send them off at different periods of one of two months distance from each other, it is highly probable that one if not both would succeed and return. I am not authorized to make any stipulations on this subject, but I pledge myself unequivocably that if the parties should succed that I will exert myself to the utmost that they shall not only be satisfactorily but liberally rewarded on their return. Endevor therefore by all means to find suitable characters for this hardy enterprize, and having found them dispatch them as soon as possible. I say nothing about their equipments or the manner of their being furnished leaving that to your and the Governors judgement, and those to whom you may confide the direction of the enterprize. Pocket compasses would be necessary to their success, and Pencils and papers to assist their remarks.

Were it practicable to make the operation with Canoes it would be most satisfactory. I am Dear Sir with great esteem Your most humble Servant,

H. KNOX

LS, RC (MiU-C—Harmar Papers, vol. 12). Maj. Gen. Henry Knox (1750–1806) was Secretary of War from 1785 to 1794. Brig. Gen. Josiah Harmar (1753–1813) was commander of the forces on the Ohio River.

To this letter Harmar replied 20 Feb.: "I shall shortly do myself the honor of writing to you again, as I am making preparations to endeavor to carry into effect what was communicated to me in your Secret letter of the 20th December. It will be a very difficult dangerous undertaking. I wish to have the Governor's opinion upon it, as he must now be at Kaskaskias; however if there is a practicability, it shall be attempted" (Harmar Lbk. G).

Extracts from these letters on the Armstrong expedition appear in STORM.

418. Henry Knox to Josiah Harmar

(Private)

Sir,   War Office 16 January 1790.

In addition to my letter to you on the subject of exploring the country and Waters, on which you were to consult the Governor of the Western Territory, that the party employed on that business should be habited like indians in all rispects and on *no pretence whatever,* discover any connection with the troops—of course they will not take any written orders with them. I am Sir with great Esteem Your Most Obedient Servant,

H. KNOX

LS, RC (MiU-C—Harmar Papers, vol. 12). Addressed; endorsed; received 5 March 1790.

419. Josiah Harmar to Arthur St. Clair

Dear Sir   Head Quarters, Fort Washington February 20th 1790

I have had the honor of receiving your letter[1] from Fort Steuben dated the 26th Ult. and observe that your detention so long there, was occasioned for want of provisions. We have been upon the point of Starvation here, ever since my arrival. I have no great opinion of Major Doughty's Mission & another is on foot, which I think to be really difficult & hazardous. The Copy of the Secret Letter sent me from the War Office I do not think proper to commit to paper, for fear of accident, but Lieut. Armstrong (whom I have ordered to undertake the Tour if practicable) can fully inform you the Nature of the business, as the contents of the Letter have been communicated to him, & he has taken notes in such a manner as to be able to give you an exact Copy of it. I have written to the War-office that I wished very much to have your Excellency's opinion upon this Subject, before I ordered the Officer to proceed; I must therefore beg, that you will be pleased to give it. It seems very much upon the too adventrous establishment. If your Excellency should be of opinion, that it is adviseable for him to undertake it, be so Kind as to afford him your advice, & assistance upon the Occasion, as it is impossible for me at this distance to make the necessary Arrangements for that purpose. This is the Subject which the Secretary at War has written to you that we were to consult about; Mrs. Harmar desires to be most Affectionately remembered to you, & Major Sargent. Believe me ever Dear Sir Yours Sincerely,

JOS. HARMAR

[In margin:] Favored Pr. Lieut. Armstrong

Lbk (MiU-C—Harmar Lbk. G). Arthur St. Clair (1734–1818) was governor of the Northwest Territory.

1. St. Clair had written Harmar 26 Jan. 1790: "The Secretary at War has mentioned something that you and I should consult about, but did not tell me what—it was right not to commit it to paper, for it might have miscarried. I can do nothing but guess . . ." (Harmar Papers, MiU-C).

420. Josiah Harmar to John Armstrong

Sir   Head Quarters, Fort Washington February 20th 1790.

I have already made you acquainted with the business which you have to undertake, provided the Governor of the Western Territory should Judge it adviseable. If not, You are to Return from the Illinois Country to Post Vincennes, & explore the Wabash River, & give me a particular report of its communication with Lake Erie, the depth of the Water, the distances &c. & if it can be done with safety, proceed to the Miami Village, in which case it will be necessary to have an Escort of Friendly Indians to accompany you. You will endeavor to Return to Head Quarters by Land, after this business is effected. I wish you a Safe Tour, & am with great Esteem & Regard Your hum. Servt.

Jos. Harmar
Lt. Col. Com. 1st U.S. Regt.

Lbk (MiU-C—Harmar Lbk. G). John Armstrong (1755–1816), of Pennsylvania, became a lieutenant in 1789 and captain in 1790, and served for a time, after his military career, as treasurer of the Northwest Territory.

421. Josiah Harmar to John Armstrong

Sir   Head Quarters, Fort Washington. March 8th 1790.

Since the communication I made to you, another Letter has been Received from the War Office dated the 16th January last, & Received the 5th Inst. which mentions, "That the party employed on that business should be habited like Indians in all respects, and on *no pretence whatever,* discover any Connection with the Troops, of Course they will not take any written orders with them." Acknowledge the Receipt of this Letter, and govern yourself accordingly; you may then burn it. Persevere in the undertaking, if the Governor should judge it adviseable, as you find by this last Letter, that it is expected the business must commence, & be pursued. I am Sir with esteem Your hum. Serv't.

Jos. Harmar
Lt. Col. Com. 1st. U.S. Re[gt.]

Lbk (MiU-C—Harmar Lbk. G). Armstrong reached Kaskaskia and the counsels of Governor St. Clair late in March, and accompanied the Governor to Cahokia. On 1 May 1790, St. Clair wrote to Knox: "Mr.

Armstrong has been here for sometime, in consequence of your communications to General Harmar, who made me acquainted with them by him. It is, sir, I believe, at present, altogether impracticable. It is a point on which some people are feelingly alive all over, and their jealousy awake. Indians to be confided in, there are none; and if there were, those who would be most proper, and others, are now at war . . ." (ST. CLAIR, 2:138). He wrote to Harmar from Cahokia in May, giving him the same information (ST. CLAIR, 2:144).

422. [John Armstrong to Josiah Harmar]

Sir   Fort Washington 2d June 1790

Agreeable to your Orders of the 20th February I proceeded to Kaskaskias by way of the Rapids of Ohio Post vincennes & the Missisippi and reached Kaskaskias on the 28th of March. Having communicated to the Governer of the Western Territory the business on which I was detached after exercising his mind on the occasion he observed it was not only a dificult task, but one that in his opinion could be executed in the character of a trader only, and even in that there is a dificulty, as there are by Government fixed Posts for Traders to assemble at and a certain quaintity of goods permited to go to each Post. The Spanish commendent knows the quaintity of Firs that country produces yearly, and the quaintity of Goods necessary for the Natives. As to Indians well attached to the United States I know not where they are to be found, but by making generous presents to some of those nations on the Missouri I have no doubt but in a Tour of eighteen Months or two years the necessary infermation might be obtained, promised rewards will not secure an indian to your interest. I presume the Governer has wrote you fully on this subject. It is a business much easier planed then executed, and should I again be called on to go on this Service I should chuse to be equiped for the Tour. The adventurer ought to be furnished with a convenience made of Oil cloth for the purpose of securing his papers when traveling by Land, a half faced Camp or Tent of the same would also be necessary and is very portable. If it is a matter of consequence to the United States I am of opinion there would be less dificulty in the execution at present than at an afterday. I have procured an invoice of the goods necessary for the Trade of that country, and conceive a connexion with some of the Traders might take place, and this business executed with very little expence to the Public. After visiting St. Genavive & St. Louis

[665]

on the 2d May I took my departure for post vincennes from whence
I set out on the Morning of the 13th May in company with two
Indians and after proceeding* two days on the course for this place
one of my companions falling sick & the other being Lame they
would proceed no ferther on that route, I then with much dificulty
prevailed on them to take a course for the Rapids of Ohio, assuring
them I knew the way & that in four Suns we would reach that place
where I arrived on the 25th. I found my companions attentive trusty
fellows.

While at S. Louis I obtained some infermation respecting the
country I was to have explored which is contained in the inclosed
Notes. I also inclose you a Map of the Missouri which I copied at
St. Louis as also one of the Illanois River & its connexion with Lake
Michagon explained by remarks made by the drawer of the Original
I am Sir with respect your obt. Servt.

* I found from the hostile disposition of the Indians on the
Wabash that it was unsafe to attempt exploring that & the Moami
Rivers &c.

D (MiU-C—Harmar Papers). Also present with this report are (a) an
undated, unsigned manuscript of four pages, endorsed, "Discription of the
Illanois river," which begins, "The better to discribe the Illanois River
I shall give an account of it as I found it last September in decending
it"; (b) a manuscript map of the Illinois; (c) a manuscript map identified
by Colton STORM as a tracing of Jacques Nicholas Bellin's "Carte de la
Louisiane et des Pays Voisins . . ." of 1750, apparently the one that
Armstrong describes above; (d) Armstrong's expense account, 2 June 1790,
"for himself & Servant, totaling one hundred and ten dollars and thirty
nine ninetieths of a Dollar."

423. Josiah Harmar to Henry Knox

Sir   Head Quarters, Fort Washington June 9th 1790

. . . .

Lieutenant Armstrong, whom I detached sometime since, to endeavor
to carry into effect your Secret orders, returned to this post on the
2nd Inst. After proceeding with the Governor from Kaskaskias to
Cahokia, and informing him the business he was sent upon, the
Governor was of opinion that it was neither prudent nor practicable
to undertake it. He has made several observations to me upon the
Country, which he obtained from persons who had explored it for

[666]

some distance, those notes & maps when arranged, I shall do myself the honor to transmit to you, together with an account of his expences.

. . . .

I have the honor to be Sir with perfect esteem & Respect Your most hum. & obedt. Servt.

Jos. HARMAR
Lt. Col. Com. 1st U.S. Regt.

Lbk (MiU-C—Harmar Lbk. A). Endorsed, "Original forwarded pr. Lieutenant Ford—duplicate pr. Govr. St. Clair." Armstrong's report and maps were sent to Knox 3 Aug. 1790 and were acknowledged 14 Sept. by Knox: "Lieut. Armstrong's . . . reports shall be submitted to the President of the United States" (Harmar Papers, vol. 12).

424. Jefferson to George Washington

[22 January 1793]
Th: Jefferson has the honor to inclose to the President the subscription paper he has proposed for enabling the Philosophical society to send Mr. Michaux on the mission through the country between the Missisipi & South sea, and he will have that of waiting on him tomorrow morning on the subject.
Jan. 22. 1793.

AL, SC (DLC).

425. George Washington to Jefferson

Dear Sir,   Philadelphia 22d. Jan. 1793
Nothing occurs to me as necessary to be added to the enclosed project.
If the Subscription is not confined to the members of the Philosophical Society I would readily add my mite to the means for encouraging Mr. Michaud's undertaking—and do authorise you to place me among & upon a footing with the respectable sums which may be Subscribed. I am always Yours.

G. WASHINGTON

ALS, RC (DLC). Endorsed; received 22 Jan. 1793.

426. Agreement of Subscribers to André Michaux's Expedition

[Philadelphia, 22 January 1793]

Whereas Andrew Michaux, a native of France, and inhabitant of the U.S. hath undertaken to explore the interior country of North America, from the Missisipi along the Missouri and Westwardly to the Pacific ocean, or in such other direction as shall be advised by the American Philosophical society, and on his return to communicate to the said society the information he shall have acquired of the geography of the said country, it's inhabitants, soil, climate, animals, vegetables & minerals, & other circumstances of note:

We the subscribers, desirous of obtaining for ourselves relative to the land we live on, and of communicating to the world, information so interesting to curiosity, to science, & to the future prospects of mankind, promise for ourselves, our heirs, exrs. & admrs. that we will pay, to the sd. Andrew Michaux, or his assigns the sums herein affixed to our names respectively, one fourth part thereof on demand, the remaining three fourths whenever, after his return, the sd. Philosophical society shall declare themselves satisfied that he has performed the sd. journey, & that he has communicated to them freely all the information which he shall have acquired & they demanded of him. Or if the sd. Andrew Michaud shall not proceed to the Pacific ocean & shall reach the sources of the waters running into it, then we will pay him such part only of the remaining three fourths as the said Philosophical society shall deem duly proportioned to the extent of unknown country explored by him in the direction prescribed, when compared with that omitted to be so explored.

And we consent that the bills of exchange of the sd. Andrew Michaux for monies said to be due to him in France shall be received to the amount of 200 Louis & shall be negociated by the sd. Philosophical society and the proceeds thereof retained in their hands to be delivered to the sd. Andrew Michaux on his return after having performed the journey to their satisfaction, or if not to their satisfaction, then to be applied towards reimbursing the subscribers the fourth of their subscription advanced to the sd. Andrew Michaux.

We consent also that the sd. Andrew Michaux shall take to himself all benefit arising from the publication of the discoveries he shall make in the three departments of nat. history, animal, vegetable & mineral, he concerting with the sd. Philosophical society such measures for securing to himself the sd. benefit, as shall be consistent with the due publication of the said discoveries.

[668]

In witness whereof we have hereto subscribed our names and affixed the sums we engage respectively to contribute.

AD, SC (DLC). André Michaux (1746–1802), French botanist, had traveled widely in the eastern U.S., and his abilities had led Jefferson and other members of the American Philosophical Society to suppose that he was their best hope for a transcontinental expedition. Jefferson's account book contains an entry for 1793: "Apr. 28. pd. ¼ of my subscription for Michaud's journey to Pacific sea 12.5" (BETTS, 207). For further information on the amounts of money subscribed by members, and its disposition, see JOURNALS, 7:204–05. Michaux had gone as far as Kentucky when it became clear that his chief aim, supported by officials of the French Republic, was to raise a western force to attack Spanish possessions beyond the Mississippi. When the scheme was disclosed, Michaux was recalled by his government.

427. Jefferson to David Rittenhouse

Dear Sir   Philadelphia Apr. 11. 1793.
I received yesterday your note on the subject of Michaud's instructions, and think it would be better to have a meeting of the society that they may accept the charge proposed to them by the subscribers, and may appoint a committee to draw instructions, and a person to collect the fourth of the subscriptions & pay it to Mr. Michaud. My attendance on the society will be precarious, as it must depend on the weather: but I hope you will attend & have the thing done right. I am Dear Sir yours affectionately,

TH: JEFFERSON

ALS, RC (PPAmP). David Rittenhouse (1732–96), astronomer and instrument maker, was president of the American Philosophical Society, 1791–96.

428. Jefferson to André Michaux

To Mr. Andrew Michaud.   [30 April 1793]
Sundry persons having subscribed certain sums of money for your encouragement to explore the country along the Missouri, & thence Westwardly to the Pacific ocean, having submitted the plan of the enterprize to the direction of the American Philosophical society, & the Society having accepted of the trust, they proceed to give you the following instructions.
They observe to you that the chief objects of your journey are to find the shortest & most convenient route of communication between the U.S. & the Pacific ocean, within the temperate latitudes,

& to learn such particulars as can be obtained of the country through which it passes, it's productions, inhabitants & other interesting circumstances.

As a channel of communication between these states & the Pacific ocean, the Missouri, so far as it extends, presents itself under circumstances of unquestioned preference. It has therefore been declared as a fundamental object of the subscription, (not to be dispensed with) that this river shall be considered & explored as a part of the communication sought for. To the neighborhood of this river therefore, that is to say to the town of Kaskaskia, the society will procure you a conveyance in company with the Indians of that town now in Philadelphia.

From thence you will cross the Missisipi and pass by land to the nearest part of the Missouri above the Spanish settlements, that you may avoid the risk of being stopped.

You will then pursue such of the largest streams of that river, as shall lead by the shortest way, & the lowest latitudes to the Pacific ocean.

When pursuing these streams, you shall find yourself at the point from whence you may get by the shortest & most convenient route to some principal river of the Pacific ocean, you are to proceed to such river, & pursue it's course to the ocean. It would seem by the latest maps as if a river called Oregan interlocked with the Missouri for a considerable distance, & entered the Pacific ocean, not far Southward of Nootka sound. But the Society are aware that these maps are not to be trusted so far as to be the ground of any positive instruction to you. They therefore only mention the fact, leaving to yourself to verify it, or to follow such other as you shall find to be the real truth.

You will, in the course of your journey, take notice of the country you pass through, it's general face, soil, rivers, mountains, it's productions animal, vegetable, & mineral so far as they may be new to us & may also be useful or very curious; the latitude of places or materials for calculating it by such simple methods as your situation may admit you to practice, the names, numbers, & dwellings of the inhabitants, and such particularities as you can learn of their history, connection with each other, languages, manners, state of society & of the arts & commerce among them.

Under the head of Animal history, that of the Mammoth is particularly recommended to your enquiries, as it is also to learn whether the Lama, or Paca of Peru is found in those parts of this continent, or how far North they come.[1]

The method of preserving your observations is left to yourself, according to the means which shall be in your power. It is only suggested that the noting them on the skin might be best for such as are most important, and that further details may be committed to the bark of the paper birch, a substance which may not excite suspicions among the Indians, & little liable to injury from wet or other common accidents. By the means of the same substance you may perhaps find opportunities, from time to time, of communicating to the society information of your progress, & of the particulars you shall have noted.

When you shall have reached the Pacific ocean, if you find yourself within convenient distance of any settlement of Europeans, go to them, commit to writing a narrative of your journey & observations & take the best measures you can for conveying it by duplicates or triplicates thence to the society by sea.

Return by the same, or such other route, as you shall think likely to fulfill with most satisfaction & certainty the objects of your mission, furnishing yourself with the best proofs the nature of the case will admit of the reality & extent of your progress. Whether this shall be by certificates from Europeans settled on the Western coast of America, or by what other means, must depend on circumstances.

Ignorance of the country thro' which you are to pass and confidence in your judgment, zeal, & discretion, prevent the society from attempting more minute instructions, and even from exacting rigorous observance of those already given, except indeed what is the first of all objects, that you seek for & pursue that route which shall form the shortest & most convenient communication between the higher parts of the Missouri & the Pacific ocean.

It is strongly recommended to you to expose yourself in no case to unnecessary dangers, whether such as might affect your health or your personal safety: and to consider this not merely as your personal concern, but as the injunction of Science in general which expects it's enlargement from your enquiries, & of the inhabitants of the U.S. in particular, to whom your Report will open new feilds & subjects of Commerce, Intercourse, & Observation.

If you reach the Pacific ocean & return, the Society assign to you all the benefits of the subscription beforementioned. If you reach the waters only which run into that ocean, the society reserve to themselves the apportionment of the reward according to the conditions expressed in the subscription. <If you do not reach even those waters, they [refuse all reward, and reclaim the money you may have received h]ere under the subscription.>[2]

[671]

They will expect you to return to the city of Philadelphii to give in to them a full narrative of your journey & observations, and to answer the enquiries they shall make of you, still reserving to yourself the benefits arising from the publication <*of such parts*> of them. <*as are in the said subscription reserved to you.*>

AD (PPAmP); SC (DLC). Jefferson's file copy is identical except for the stricken passages.

1. In the margin beside the preceding two paragraphs, Jefferson wrote: "Here it is proposed to insert the contents of the annexed paper." The paper is not present.

2. That portion of the deleted matter in square brackets is missing (trimmed) from the PPAmP copy, and has been supplied from the DLC copy.

Appendix II

ELLIOTT COUES AND HIS EDITION OF THE BIDDLE NARRATIVE

When bookseller and publisher Francis P. Harper suggested to Elliott Coues in 1891 that he prepare a new edition of the Biddle narrative, Harper was approaching a capable man for the task. As an army surgeon, Coues had been stationed at various western posts and knew the region well. As an ornithologist and zoologist he was familiar with the natural history of the area. As naturalist for the Northern Boundary Survey Commission, in 1873–74, he had traveled more than a thousand miles of the Lewis and Clark route. He was a fluent writer with a liking for history.

Coues was not anxious to undertake the work, however, for he had just finished seven years of arduous labor on the *Century dictionary*—as author of thousands of zoological definitions—and he was about to leave his home in Washington, D.C., for a few months' rest in California. But he was interested enough to write Harper, on 16 August 1891: "This reprint I think you will agree with me should be verbatim et literatim et punctuatim after the original. Even to copying of typographical errors. . . ."[1] Having laid down a rule that he, of all men, could never follow, he went off to California and was still there in midyear of 1892 when Harper offered him $500–$750 to prepare the new edition.

By 17 July of that year he had looked over a copy of the Biddle version and decided to take on the assignment. His first report to Harper revealed the failing that was ever to mar his reputation as an editor—an inability to refrain from tampering with the prose he was editing.

You should understand that the original 'Lewis and Clarke' was very badly edited from the rough field-notes of the explorers, after these notes, in a chaotic state, had had a precarious existence for seven to ten years & went through various hands after Capt. Lewis blew his brains out in 1808 or thereabouts. The printer, Inskeep probably did the best he could with the copy furnished him, but it is wretchedly set up, the pointing in particular being terrific, the spelling often very funny, and the 'parts of speech' dislocated in a thousand places. . . . While I think you will agree with me

1. Letters between Coues and Harper quoted here and below are in the Western Americana Collection, Yale University Library.

that it would *not* be desirable, even if it were possible, to 'recast' or 'rewrite' the work—for you must be able to assure your public that you are giving them the original genuine 'Lewis & Clarke,' without abridgement or alteration—yet I can in going over the book put in the necessary touches, to make 'the nouns & verbs agree,' &c., and thus insure some degree of literary excellence, without presuming to so much as recast a single sentence.

Working from his summer home in North Carolina, Coues began to prepare his notes with the aid of reference books sent him by Harper. He thought the work would fit into one large-octavo volume, or two at the most, but when he began to send in his annotations he received a quick notice from the alarmed Harper that he was far too verbose. His notes threatened to exceed the original text.

Coues did not discover until he had begun to receive galleys that the correct spelling of "Clarke" was Clark, and he had to check back through his work and change the spelling of the name (he overlooked a few instances). But a much more startling discovery soon held up production even longer. By August 1892, Harper had learned of the existence of the original manuscript journals. Coues told him in a letter of 21 August that the location of such journals would prove a bonanza, and by 29 September Coues had found out the location of the journals through Judge Craig Biddle, the son of Nicholas. He told Harper they were held by the American Philosophical Society.

"Let the Philadelphia original manuscript go for the present," Harper told Coues on 14 November. "You have been so fortunate in finding so much important additional material that I think we have enough for our purpose. . . ."

Inexcusable, declared Coues, not to examine the journals. Besides, he wrote on 20 November, it would be "an advertising point that I should think you would be quick to recognize the advantage of."

Carrying a requisition from William Clark's son, Jefferson Kearny Clark, Coues persuaded the officers of the Society to let him take the journals to his home on 17 December 1892 for close study. He at once recognized their value, both as historical documents and as potentially advantageous publishing property.

"Of course we shall not be idiotic enough to ever let the mss. go out of our hands without our keeping a copy. I have an expert copyist already at work making an *exact* copy, word for word, letter for letter, point for point. . . . I think most probably, *after* our present edition . . . you will want to bring out another vol. reproducing the orig. mss. *verbatim*."

The treatment that Coues gave the journals has always been one of the minor scandals of the historical profession. Using the journal

[674]

notebooks almost as printer's copy, he freely interlined the text with his own changes of wording, in keeping with his disregard for the sanctity of documentary material. No one at the Society noticed the damage he had done until the summer of 1903, when Reuben Gold Thwaites was preparing to edit the journals for publication.

Coues had high hopes of making a sensational publication of the journals later. "Meanwhile, however, let us simply possess ourselves of the copy," he wrote Harper on 6 January 1893, "and we can talk about printing it later. . . . Better keep very dark about this!"

By 14 June the book was in type and Coues was toying with the wording of his excessively long title page. It pleased him to point out that it formed a perfectly grammatical sentence, and he told Harper that its very length gave it "an antique look, suitable to our book." The complete title reads as follows: *History of the expedition under the command of Lewis and Clark, to the sources of the Missouri River, thence across the Rocky Mountains and down the Columbia River to the Pacific Ocean, performed during the years 1804–5–6, by order of the government of the United States. A new edition, faithfully reprinted from the only authorized edition of 1814, with copious critical commentary, prepared upon examination of unpublished official archives and many other sources of information, including a diligent study of the original manuscript journals and field notebooks of the explorers, together with a new biographical and bibliographical introduction, new maps and other illustrations, and a complete index.*

The edition was off the press by late August, but Coues kept the journals until December because his copyist had not yet finished reproducing them. In the meantime he and Harper ran afoul of the Clark family in St. Louis over the question of who was to receive the earliest copies of the limited, numbered edition. Coues wrote Harper, 24 July 1892:

Item, about Mr. W. H. [William Hancock] Clark, who has evidently got a fishbone crosswise in his throat. Of course we do not want to hurt his feelings, and could not afford to offend him. *He must be pacified*—if not for his own sake, then for the memory of his illustrious grandpa. It would never do to get the numerous and influential Clark family down on the book! They have no doubt got enough of old William's stuffing in them to raise hell, if they took a notion. . . . Now you do this: write W. H. C. the politest and most deferential letter you can concoct. Illuminate his grandfather, & let the reflected glory alight on his own head. Say how infinitely you value his genealogical charts, which you could hardly have got along without, and that you know your editor prizes them not less highly. Say how very sorry you are you did not ascertain his wishes sooner regarding Nos. 1, and 2 of the large paper copies; but that No. 1 had been sold *long* before; but that, the moment Dr. Coues heard of his wishes regarding early copies, he (Dr. Coues) "generously relinquished" Nos. 2 and 3 for himself and Jeff. C. which therefore you have the pleasure of placing at his disposal, &c. &c. . . .

The quotations from the journals, used by Coues in his footnotes, whetted the appetites of his readers for more of the same. Coues and Harper never published an edition of the entire journals as they planned (Coues died in 1899), but in 1904 and 1905 the Thwaites edition of the journals appeared and eclipsed the Biddle-Coues version of the narrative. While the historical value of the original journals is self-evident, and while they rightly deserve to be considered our prime source of knowledge about the expedition, the Coues edition still can be studied with much profit.

It is difficult to forgive Coues for his desecration of original texts. He began his editing of the Biddle book by changing a key word in the first sentence (making "early" read "earnestly"), and proceeded in the same vein throughout the work. He was conscious of the need to preserve the original spelling of proper names; all else he altered to suit his own taste. He did not hesitate to edit Jefferson's letter of 18 August 1813, transmitting a memoir of Meriwether Lewis. The excerpts from the Lewis and Clark journals that he used in footnotes were similarly "improved" in keeping with Coues's schoolmarm approach to the language. Even the appendix, with its meteorological data and observations on natural history, did not escape Coues's editorial eye. He edited this material unevenly, correcting spelling silently at times ("pellicans" to "pelicans") but with brackets occasionally ("mail [male] cottonwood").

What, then, makes Coues a good editor? The amazing breadth of his information. His leisurely, almost gossipy, annotation is complete and generally accurate. His close attention to the rivers, creeks, and landmarks is partly the result of his personal knowledge of the area, partly the product of careful collating of maps. His attention to natural history arises from his lifelong dedication to the subject and from a boyish delight in flora and fauna that is evident in his notations. He is less at home with botany and ethnology than with zoology, but draws upon authoritative sources when his own knowledge wanes.

When Harper grew impatient with delays during the production of the book, Coues reminded him: "Once well done, it is done forever." Never quite true in the writing of history, but still a goal worth trying for.

Appendix III

ACKNOWLEDGMENTS

My first duty is to acknowledge the assistance of the Research Board of the University of Illinois, which made this work possible through a grant-in-aid, and the generosity of the archivists who readily gave permission for the use of their manuscript holdings. It is gratifying to recall that only one document was withheld—by a private owner. Below I list the names of all those librarians, archivists, historians, and others whose interest and helpfulness I am happy to make known.

ALDERMAN LIBRARY
Francis L. Berkeley, Jr., curator of manuscripts
Anne Freudenberg, associate
AMERICAN PHILOSOPHICAL SOCIETY LIBRARY
Gertrude D. Hess, assistant librarian
Richard H. Shryock, librarian
Murphy Smith, manuscripts librarian
BOSTON PUBLIC LIBRARY
Zoltán Haraszti, keeper of rare books
PUBLIC ARCHIVES OF CANADA, OTTAWA
Wm. Kaye Lamb, dominion archivist
CARNEGIE FREE LIBRARY, PITTSBURGH
H. Dorothy English, librarian, Pennsylvania Division
CHICAGO HISTORICAL SOCIETY LIBRARY
Elizabeth Baughman, reference librarian
Mrs. Robert G. Johnson, manuscripts librarian
WILLIAM L. CLEMENTS LIBRARY
William S. Ewing, curator
COLONIAL WILLIAMSBURG LIBRARY
Lynette Adcock, manuscripts assistant
FILSON CLUB
Dorothy Thomas Cullen, curator and librarian
Mabel Weaks, archivist
HENRY E. HUNTINGTON LIBRARY
Robert O. Dougan, librarian
Herbert C. Schulz, curator of manuscripts

UNIVERSITY OF ILLINOIS
  The many members of the library staff, and Elizabeth G. Dulany,
    Donald F. Hoffmeister, Marguerite J. Pease, George White
INDIANA HISTORICAL SOCIETY LIBRARY, INDIANAPOLIS
  Caroline Dunn, librarian
INDIANA UNIVERSITY LIBRARY
  Doris M. Reed, curator of manuscripts
ARCHIVO GENERAL DE INDIAS, SEVILLE
  Rosario Parra, secretary
  José de la Peña, director
LIBRARY OF CONGRESS
  David C. Mearns, chief, Manuscripts Division
MASSACHUSETTS HISTORICAL SOCIETY
  Malcolm Freiberg, editor of publications
  Stephen Riley, librarian
  Warren G. Wheeler, assistant librarian
MISSOURI HISTORICAL SOCIETY
  Dorothy A. Brockhoff, reference librarian
  Mrs. Benjamin D. Harris, assistant manuscripts librarian
  Mrs. Dana O. Jensen, editor of the *Bulletin*
  Mrs. Ernst A. Stadler, manuscripts librarian
  Elizabeth Tindall, reference librarian
  Charles van Ravenswaay, director
MONTANA HISTORICAL SOCIETY LIBRARY
  Virginia Walton, librarian
NATIONAL ARCHIVES
  Robert Bahmer, deputy archivist of the United States
  Mabel E. Deutrich, archivist in charge, Early Wars Branch
  Herman R. Friis, chief archivist, Technical Records Division
  Victor Gondos, Jr., archivist in charge, Civil War Branch
  Oliver W. Holmes, chief archivist, Social and Economic Records
    Division
  Lyle J. Holverstott, archivist in charge, Fiscal Branch
  Jane F. Smith, archivist in charge, Interior Branch
  Philip Ward, assistant archivist, Fiscal Branch
NEW-YORK HISTORICAL SOCIETY
  James J. Heslin, associate director
NEW YORK PUBLIC LIBRARY
  Robert W. Hill, keeper of manuscripts
OREGON HISTORICAL SOCIETY LIBRARY
  Jean Brownell, library assistant
  Kenneth W. Duckett, librarian

[678]

Priscilla Knuth, acting librarian

PAPERS OF HENRY CLAY (UNIVERSITY OF KENTUCKY)
Mary W. M. Hargreaves, editor
James F. Hopkins, editor

PAPERS OF THOMAS JEFFERSON (PRINCETON UNIVERSITY)
Julian P. Boyd, editor

PAPERS OF JAMES MADISON (UNIVERSITY OF CHICAGO)
Donald O. Dewey, assistant editor

HISTORICAL SOCIETY OF PENNSYLVANIA
J. Harcourt Givens, manager, Manuscripts Division
Catherine Miller, Manuscripts Division
R. N. Williams II, director

PRINCETON UNIVERSITY LIBRARY
Alexander P. Clark, curator of manuscripts

VANCOUVER PUBLIC LIBRARY
Peter Grossman, director

VIRGINIA HISTORICAL SOCIETY LIBRARY
Virginius C. Hall, Jr., curator of rare books

STATE HISTORICAL SOCIETY OF WISCONSIN LIBRARY
Josephine L. Harper, manuscripts librarian

YALE UNIVERSITY LIBRARY
Archibald Hanna, librarian, Western Americana Collection

And the following persons whose contributions of time, care, and experience have been invariably helpful:

John Bakeless	John Francis McDermott
Col. Nicholas Biddle, Jr.	Franklin J. McLean
Vardis Fisher	J. T. Maltsberger
Mrs. George Gordon	Dale Morgan
Thomas P. Govan	A. P. Nasatir
Rachel Graham	Ernest S. Osgood
W. Eugene Hollon	Carl P. Russell
Donald F. Hyde	Colton Storm
Catherine Jackson	John Tevebaugh
Richard C. Knopf	Prudence B. Trimble
John L. Loos	Carl I. Wheat

Bibliography

ABEL   Abel, Annie Heloise, "A new Lewis and Clark map,"
                Geographical Review, 1 (May 1916), 329–45.

ALDEN & IFFT   Alden, Roland H., and John D. Ifft, "Early naturalists
                in the far West," *Occasional Papers,* California
                Academy of Science, 20 (1943).

ANDERSON   Anderson, Sarah Travers Lewis, *Lewises, Meriwethers
                and their kin*. Richmond, Va., 1938.

A.O.U.   American Ornithologists' Union, *Check-list of North
                American birds*. 5th ed. [Baltimore], 1957.

A.P.S.   American Philosophical Society, *Early proceedings of
                the American Philosophical Society* [1744–1838]. Phila-
                delphia, 1884.

ATKINSON &   Atkinson, Alfred, and M. L. Wilson, "Corn in Mon-
WILSON   tana," *Bulletin* of the Montana Agricultural College
                Experiment Station, No. 107 (Oct. 1915).

AUGUR   Augur, Helen, *Passage to glory; John Ledyard's
                America*. New York, 1946.

BAKELESS   Bakeless, John, *Lewis and Clark; partners in dis-
                covery*. New York, 1957.

BALDWIN   Darlington, William, ed., *Reliquiae Baldwinianae;
                selections from the correspondence of the late William
                Baldwin, M.D*. Philadelphia, 1843.

BATES   Marshall, Thomas M., ed., *The life and papers of
                Frederick Bates*. 2 vols. St. Louis, 1926.

BEARD   Beard, J. Howard, "Medical observations and practices
                of Lewis and Clark," *Scientific Monthly,* 20 (May
                1925), 506–26.

BETTS   Betts, Edwin Morris, ed., *Thomas Jefferson's garden
                book. Memoirs* of the American Philosophical Society,
                22 (1944).

[681]

BIDDLE   *History of the expedition under the command of Captains Lewis and Clark, to the sources of the Missouri, thence across the Rocky Mountains and down the River Columbia to the Pacific Ocean. Performed during the years 1804–5–6. By order of the government of the United States. Prepared for the press by Paul Allen, esquire.* 2 vols. Philadelphia, 1814.

BIDDLE-COUES   Coues, Elliott, ed., *History of the expedition under the command of Lewis and Clark, to the sources of the Missouri River, thence across the Rocky Mountains and down the Columbia River to the Pacific Ocean, performed during the years 1804–5–6, by order of the government of the United States. A new edition. . . .* 4 vols. New York, 1893.

BILLON (1)   Billon, Frederic L., *Annals of St. Louis in its early days under the French and Spanish dominations, 1764–1804.* St. Louis, 1886.

BILLON (2)   ———, *Annals of St. Louis in its territorial days from 1804 to 1821.* St. Louis, 1888.

BIOG. DIR.   *Biographical directory of the American Congress, 1774–1949.* Washington, 1950.

BODLEY   Bodley, Temple, *George Rogers Clark.* Boston, 1926.

BOYD   Boyd, Julian, ed., *The papers of Thomas Jefferson.* Princeton, N.J., 1950———.

BROWN   Brown, Glenn, and Maude O. Brown, "A directory of the book-arts and book trade in Philadelphia to 1820," *Bulletin* of the New York Public Library, 53 (1949), 54 (1950).

BURTT-DAVY   Burtt-Davy, Joseph, *Maize, its history. . . .* London, 1914.

CARTER   Carter, Clarence E., "The Burr-Wilkinson intrigue in St. Louis," *Bulletin* of the Missouri Historical Society, 10 (July 1954), 447–64.

CHARDON   Abel, Annie Heloise, ed., *Chardon's journal at Fort Clark, 1834–1839.* Pierre, S.D., 1932.

CHINARD   Chinard, Gilbert, *Volney et l'Amérique d'aprés des documents inédits et sa correspondance avec Jefferson.* Baltimore, 1923.

CHITTENDEN   Chittenden, Hiram M., *The American fur trade of the far West.* Reprinted. 2 vols. Stanford, Calif., 1954.

CLAIBORNE   Claiborne, W. C. C., *Official letter books . . . 1801–1816.* 3 vols. Jackson, Miss., 1917.

CLARKE   Clarke, Charles G., "The roster of the Lewis and Clark Expedition," *Oregon Historical Quarterly,* 45 (Dec. 1944), 289–305.

COLLINS   Collins, Richard H., *History of Kentucky.* 2 vols. Covington, Ky., 1874.

CORREA   Davis, Richard Beale, ed., "The Abbé Correa in America, 1812–1820," *Transactions* of the American Philosophical Society, n.s., 45 (1955).

COUES (1)   Coues, Elliott, "An account of the various publications relating to the travels of Lewis and Clarke, with a commentary on the zoological results of their expedition," *Bulletin* of the Geological and Geographical Survey of the Territories, No. 6, ser. 2 (1876), [417]–44.

COUES (2)   ———, ed., *New light on the early history of the greater Northwest; the manuscript journals of Alexander Henry . . . and of David Thompson. . . .* 3 vols. New York, 1897.

COUES (3)   ———, "Notes on Mr. Thomas Meehan's paper on the plants of Lewis and Clark's expedition across the continent, 1804–06," *Proceedings* of the Academy of Natural Sciences of Philadelphia (1898), 291–315.

COX   Cox, Isaac Joslin, *The early exploration of Louisiana.* University Studies. Cincinnati, 1906.

CRAWFORD   Crawford, Helen, "Sakakawea," *North Dakota Historical Quarterly,* 1 (April 1927), 5–15.

CRISWELL   Criswell, Elijah Harry, *Lewis and Clark: linguistic pioneers.* University of Missouri Studies, vol. 15, no. 2. Columbia, 1940.

DAVIS (1)   Davis, Andrew M., "The journey of Moncacht-Apé," *Proceedings* of the American Antiquarian Society, 2 (April 1883), 321–48.

DAVIS (2)   Davis, Richard Beale, *Francis Walker Gilmer; life and learning in Jefferson's Virginia.* Richmond, Va., 1939.

DE VOTO   DeVoto, Bernard, *The course of empire.* Boston, 1952.

DILLER (1)   Diller, Aubrey, "Maps of the Missouri River before Lewis and Clark," *Studies and essays . . . in homage to George Sarton,* New York [1946], 505–19.

DILLER (2)   ———, "An early account of the Missouri River," *Missouri Historical Review,* 45 (Jan. 1951), 150–57.

DILLER (3)   ———, "A new map of the Missouri River drawn in 1795," *Imago Mundi,* 12 (1955), 175–80.

[683]

DILLER (4)   ———, "James Mackay's journey in Nebraska in 1796," *Nebraska History*, 36 (Jan. 1955), 123–28.

DOUGHTY   Doughty, J. and T., *The cabinet of natural history and American rural sports*. 2 vols. Philadelphia, 1830–32.

DOUGHTY & MARTIN   Doughty, A. G., and Chester Martin, eds., *The Kelsey papers*. Ottawa, 1929.

DOUGLAS   Douglas, Jesse S., "Lewis map of 1806," *Military Affairs*, 5 (Spring 1941), 68–72.

DUNLAP   Dunlap, William, *Diary*. Collections of the New-York Historical Society. 2 vols. New York, 1930.

DU PRATZ   Du Pratz, Antoine Le Page, *Histoire de la Louisiane, contenant la découverte de ce vaste pays; sa description géographique . . . les moeurs, coûtumes & religion des naturels. . . .* Paris, 1758. English translation: *The history of Louisiana, or the western parts of Virginia and Carolina; containing a description of the countries that lie on both sides of the River Missisipi. . . .* London, 1763.

DYE   Dye, Eva Emery, *The conquest; the true story of Lewis and Clark*. Chicago, 1902.

ELLICOTT   Ellicott, Andrew, *The journal of Andrew Ellicott . . . for determining the boundary between the United States and the possessions of his Catholic Majesty in America. . . .* Philadelphia, 1803.

EWAN   Ewan, Joseph, "Frederick Pursh, 1774-1820, and his botanical associates," *Proceedings* of the American Philosophical Society, 96 (1952), 599–628.

EWERS (1)   Ewers, John C., "Hair pipes in plains Indian adornment," *Bulletin* of the Bureau of American Ethnology, 164 (1957), 37–85.

EWERS (2)   ———, *The Blackfeet; raiders on the Northwestern plains*. Norman, Okla., 1958.

FLOYD   Floyd, N. J., *Biographical genealogies of Virginia-Kentucky Floyd families*. Baltimore, 1912.

FORREST   Forrest, Earle E., "Patrick Gass, carpenter of the Lewis and Clark Expedition," *Bulletin* of the Missouri Historical Society, 4 (July 1948), 217–22.

FOSTER (1)   Foster, James W., "Fielding Lucas, Jr., early nineteenth century publisher of fine books and maps," *Proceedings* of the American Antiquarian Society, 65 (1955), 161–212.

[684]

FOSTER (2)   Foster, Augustus John, *Jeffersonian America; notes on the United States of America collected in the years 1805-6-7 and 11-12.* . . . Edited by Richard Beale Davis. San Marino, Calif., 1954.

FREEMAN &   [Freeman, Thomas, and Peter Custis], *An account of the Red River in Louisiana drawn up from the returns of Messrs. Freeman and Custis to the War Office of the United States.* . . . Washington, 1807.
CUSTIS

FRIIS   Friis, Herman R., "Cartographic and geographic activities of the Lewis and Clark Expedition," *Journal of the Washington Academy of Sciences,* 44 (Nov. 1954), 338-51.

GASS   Gass, Patrick, *A journal of the voyages and travels of a corps of discovery, under the command of Capt. Lewis and Capt. Clarke of the Army of the United States, from the mouth of the River Missouri through the interior parts of North America to the Pacific Ocean, during the years 1804, 1805 & 1806. Containing an authentic relation of the most interesting transactions during the expedition,—a description of the country,—an account of its inhabitants, soil, climate, curiosities and vegetable and animal productions.* Pittsburgh, 1807.

GIRAUD   Giraud, Marcel, "Etienne Véniard de Bourgmont's 'Exact Description of Louisiana,'" *Bulletin* of the Missouri Historical Society, 15 (Oct. 1958), 3-19.

GOVAN   Govan, Thomas Payne, *Nicholas Biddle, nationalist and public banker, 1786-1844.* Chicago, 1959.

GREGG   Gregg, Kate L., "The War of 1812 on the Missouri frontier," *Missouri Historical Review,* 33 (1938), 3-22, 184-202, 326-48.

GUTHRIE   Guthrie, William, *A new geographical, historical, and commercial grammar; and present state of the kingdoms of the world.* 2 vols. Philadelphia, 1815.

HAGAN   Hagan, William, *The Sac and Fox Indians.* Norman, Okla., 1958.

HAGUE   Hague, Arnold, "An early map of the far West," *Science,* 10 (4 Nov. 1887), 217-18.

HALL &   Hall, E. Raymond, and Keith R. Kelson, *The mammals of North America.* 2 vols. New York, 1959.
KELSON

HARLAN   Harlan, Richard, *Fauna Americana: being a descrip-*

[685]

tion of the mammiferous animals inhabiting North America. Philadelphia, 1825.

HARRIS Harris, Burton, *John Colter, his years in the Rockies.* New York, 1952.

HARRISON Esarey, Logan, ed., *Governors' messages and letters; messages and letters of William Henry Harrison.* 2 vols. Indianapolis, 1922.

HEBARD Hebard, Grace Raymond, *Sacajawea, a guide and interpreter of the Lewis and Clark Expedition, with an account of the travels of Toussaint Charbonneau, and of Jean Baptiste, the expedition papoose.* Glendale, Calif., 1933.

HEITMAN Heitman, Francis B., comp., *Historical register and dictionary of the United States Army.* 2 vols. Washington, 1903.

HERNANDEZ Hernandez, Francisco, *Nova plantarum, animalum et mineralum Mexicanorum historia.* . . . Rome, 1651.

HODGE Hodge, Frederick W., *Handbook of American Indians north of Mexico. Bulletin* of the Bureau of American Ethnology, 30 (1907). 2 vols.

HOLMAN & Holman, Albert M., and Constant R. Marks, *Pioneer-*
MARKS *ing in the Northwest.* Sioux City, Iowa, 1924.

HOWE Howe, Mark Anthony De Wolfe, "The capture of some fugitive verses," *Proceedings* of the Massachusetts Historical Society, 43 (1910), 237–41.

HYDE Hyde, George E., *Indians of the high plains; from the prehistoric period to the coming of Europeans.* Norman, Okla., 1959.

INGERSOLL Ingersoll, Ernest, "An adventure in etymology," *Scientific Monthly,* 44 (1937), 157–65.

JACKSON (1) Jackson, Donald, ed., *Black Hawk: an autobiography.* Urbana, Ill., 1955.

JACKSON (2) ———, "William Ewing, agricultural agent to the Indians," *Agricultural History,* 31 (April 1957), 3–7.

JACKSON (3) ———, "Old Fort Madison, 1808–1813," *Palimpsest,* 39 (Jan. 1958), 1–64.

JACKSON (4) ———, "Some books carried by Lewis and Clark," *Bulletin* of the Missouri Historical Society, 16 (Oct. 1959), 3–13.

JACKSON (5) ———, "Lewis and Clark among the Oto," *Nebraska History,* 41 (Sept. 1960), 237–48.

[686]

JACKSON (6)　　　———, "A new Lewis and Clark map," *Bulletin* of the Missouri Historical Society, 17 (Jan. 1961), 117–32, with separate map.

JACKSON (7)　　　———, "The race to publish Lewis and Clark," *Pennsylvania Magazine of History and Biography*, 85 (April 1961), 163–77.

JACOB　　　Jacob, John G., *The life and times of Patrick Gass, now sole survivor of the overland expedition to the Pacific, under Lewis and Clark, in 1804–5–6.* Wellsburg, Va., 1859.

JAMES (1)　　　James, Edwin, *An account of an expedition from Pittsburgh to the Rocky Mountains, performed in the years 1819 and 1820.* . . . 2 vols. Philadelphia, 1823.

JAMES (2)　　　———, "On the identity of the supposed pumice of the Missouri . . . ," *Annals* of the Lyceum of Natural History of New York, 1 (1823), 21–23.

JAMES (3)　　　James, James A., *The life of George Rogers Clark.* Chicago, 1928.

JAMES (4)　　　James, Gen. Thomas, *Three years among the Indians and Mexicans.* Edited by Walter B. Douglas. St. Louis, 1916.

JANSON　　　Janson, Charles William, *The stranger in America.* London, 1807.

JEFFERSON　　　*Message from the President of the United States communicating discoveries made in exploring the Missouri, Red River and Washita, by Captains Lewis and Clark, Doctor Sibley, and Mr. Dunbar; with a statistical account of the countries adjacent.* . . . Washington, 1806.

JENNINGS　　　Jennings, Sister Marietta, *A pioneer merchant of St. Louis, 1810–1820; the business career of Christian Wilt.* New York, 1939.

JEWITT　　　Jewitt, John Rodgers, *A narrative of the adventures and sufferings of John R. Jewitt, only survivor of the crew of the ship Boston.* . . . Middletown [Conn.], 1815.

JOURNALS　　　Thwaites, Reuben Gold, ed., *Original journals of the Lewis and Clark Expedition, 1804–1806, printed from the original manuscripts in the library of the American Philosophical Society and by direction of its committee on historical documents, together with*

[687]

	manuscript material of Lewis and Clark from other sources . . . now for the first time published in full and exactly as written. 8 vols. New York, 1904–05.
KAPPLER	Kappler, Charles J., ed., *Indian affairs; laws and treaties.* 2 vols. Washington, 1904. Also published as U.S. Serials 4623–24.
KEATING	Keating, William H., *Narrative of an expedition to the source of St. Peter's River.* 2 vols. Philadelphia, 1824.
KING	King, Roy T., "The territorial press in Missouri," *Bulletin* of the Missouri Historical Society, 11 (Oct. 1954), 73–81.
KINGSTON	Kingston, C. S., "Sacajawea as a guide—the evaluation of a legend," *Pacific Northwest Quarterly,* 35 (Jan. 1944), 2–18.
LARSELL	Larsell, O., "Medical aspects of the Lewis and Clark Expedition," *Surgery, Gynecology, and Obstetrics,* 85 (Nov. 1947), 663–69.
LEWIS (1)	Lewis, Grace, "'His Excellency Meriwether Lewis and the first publications west of the Mississippi River,'" master's thesis, University of Texas, Austin, 1948. Unpublished.
LEWIS (2)	———, "Financial records: expedition to the Pacific," *Bulletin* of the Missouri Historical Society, 10 (July 1954), 465–89.
LEWIS (3)	———, "The first home of Governor Lewis in Louisiana," *Bulletin* of the Missouri Historical Society, 14 (July 1958), 357–68.
LEWIS & ORDWAY	Quaife, Milo M., ed., *The journals of Captain Meriwether Lewis and Sergeant John Ordway kept on the expedition of western exploration, 1803–1806.* Madison, Wis., 1916.
LONG	Long, John, *Voyages* [of 1768–88], in *Early western travels,* edited by Reuben Gold Thwaites. 32 vols. Cleveland, 1904–07.
LOOS (1)	Loos, John Louis, "A biography of William Clark, 1770–1813," doctoral dissertation, Washington University, St. Louis, 1953. Unpublished.
LOOS (2)	———, "William Clark's part in the preparation of the Lewis and Clark Expedition," *Bulletin* of the Missouri Historical Society, 10 (July 1954), 490–511.
LUTTIG	Drumm, Stella M., ed., [John C. Luttig's] *Journal of*

a *fur-trading expedition on the upper Missouri, 1812–1813.* St. Louis, 1920.

MC BRIDE   McBride, John R., "Pioneer days in the mountains," *Tullidge's Quarterly Magazine of Utah,* 3 (July 1884).

MC GILLIVRAY   McGillivray, Duncan, "Account of the wild North-American sheep," *Medical Repository,* 6 (1803), 237–40.

MC GIRR   McGirr, Newman F., "Patrick Gass and his journal of the Lewis and Clark Expedition," *West Virginia History,* 3 (1942), 205–12.

MC KAY   McKay, George L., comp., *A register of artists, engravers, booksellers, bookbinders, printers and publishers in New York City, 1633–1820.* New York, 1942.

MACKAY   Quaife, Milo M., "Extracts from Capt. Mackay's journal—and others . . . ," *Proceedings* of the State Historical Society of Wisconsin [for 1915], (1916), 186 ff.

MC KELVEY   McKelvey, Susan Delano, *Botanical exploration of the trans-Mississippi West, 1790–1850.* Jamaica Plain, N.Y., 1955.

MACKENZIE   Mackenzie, Alexander, *Voyages from Montreal, on the River St. Lawrence, through the continent of North America, to the frozen and Pacific Ocean; in the years 1789 and 1793. . . .* 2 vols. London, 1801.

MASSON   Masson, Louis François Redrigue, *Les bourgeois de la compagnie du Nord-Ouest; recits de voyages, lettres et rapports inedits relatifs au Nord-Ouest canadien.* 2 vols. Quebec, 1889–90.

MATHEWS   Mathews, Mitford M., ed., *A dictionary of Americanisms on historical principles.* Chicago, 1951.

MEANY   Meany, Edmond S., "Doctor Saugrain helped Lewis and Clark," *Washington Historical Quarterly,* 22 (1931), 295–311.

MEEHAN   Meehan, Thomas, "The plants of Lewis and Clark's expedition across the continent, 1804–1806," *Proceedings* of the Academy of Natural Sciences of Philadelphia (1898), 12–49.

MILLER &   Miller, Gerrit S., Jr., and Remington Kellogg, "List
KELLOGG   of North American recent mammals," *Bulletin* of the U.S. National Museum, No. 205 (1955).

MITCHILL   [Mitchill, Samuel Latham], "Lewis's map of the part of North America which lie between the 35th and 51st degrees of north latitude from the Mississippi and the upper lakes to the Pacific Ocean," *Medical Repository,* 2nd hexade, 3 (Nov.-Dec. 1805, Jan. 1806), 315–18.

MITTERLING   Mitterling, Philip I., *America in the Antarctic to 1840.* Urbana, Ill., 1959.

MOONEY   Mooney, James, "The aboriginal population of America north of Mexico," *Miscellaneous Collections* of the Smithsonian Institution, 80 (1928), No. 7.

MORTON   Morton, Samuel George, *Synopsis of the organic remains of the Cretaceous group of the United States.* Philadelphia, 1834.

NASATIR (1)   Nasatir, A. P., "John Evans, explorer and surveyor," *Missouri Historical Review,* 25 (Oct. 1930–July 1931), 219–39, 432–60, 585–608.

NASATIR (2)   ———, ed., *Before Lewis and Clark.* 2 vols. St. Louis, 1954.

ORD   Ord, George, "Account of a North American quadruped . . . Rocky-Mountain sheep, Ovis montana," *Journal* of the Academy of Natural Sciences of Philadelphia, 1 (May 1817), 8–12.

PEAKE   Peake, Ora Brooks, *A history of the United States Indian factory system, 1795–1822.* Denver, 1954.

PENNANT   Pennant, Thomas, *Arctic zoology.* 2 vols. London, 1784–87.

PENNELL (1)   Pennell, Francis W., "Travels and scientific collections of Thomas Nuttall," *Bartonia,* No. 18 (1936), 7.

PENNELL (2)   ———, "Historic botanical collections of the American Philosophical Society and the Academy of Natural Sciences of Philadelphia," *Proceedings* of the American Philosophical Society, 94 (1950), 137–51.

PHELPS   Phelps, Dawson A., "The tragic death of Meriwether Lewis," *William and Mary Quarterly,* ser. 3, 13 (July 1956), 305–18.

PICOLO   Picolo, Francis Maria, "An extract of a memoir, concerning the discovery of a passage by land to California," *Philosophical Transactions* (London), No. 317 (1708), 232–40.

PIKE   Coues, Elliott, ed., *The expeditions of Zebulon Montgomery Pike to headwaters of the Mississippi River, through Louisiana Territory, and in New Spain, during the years 1805–6–7.* 3 vols. New York, 1895.

[690]

PRYOR "Documents: Captain Nathaniel Pryor," *American Historical Review,* 24 (Jan. 1919), 253–65.

PURSH Pursh, Frederick, *Flora Americae septentrionalis; or, a systematic arrangement and description of the plants of North America; containing, besides what have been described by preceding authors, many new and rare species, collected during twelve years travels and residence in that country.* 2 vols. London, 1814.

RAY & LURIE Ray, Verne F., and Nancy Oestreich Lurie, "The contributions of Lewis and Clark to ethnography," *Journal* of the Washington Academy of Sciences, 44 (Nov. 1954), 358–70.

REES Rees, John, "The Shoshoni contribution to Lewis and Clark," *Idaho Yesterdays,* 2 (1958), 2–13.

REID & GANNON Reid, Russell, and Clell C. Gannon, "Birds and mammals observed by Lewis and Clark in North Dakota," *North Dakota Historical Quarterly,* 1 (July 1927), 14–36.

RICKETT Rickett, H. W., "John Bradbury's explorations in Missouri Territory," *Proceedings* of the American Philosophical Society, 94 (1950), 59–89.

RITTER Ritter, Abraham, *Philadelphia and her merchants.* Philadelphia, 1860.

ROBINSON (1) Robinson, Doane, "Lewis and Clark in South Dakota," *South Dakota Historical Collections,* 9 (1918), 514–96.

ROBINSON (2) ———, "The medical adventures of Lewis and Clark," *South Dakota Historical Collections,* 12 (1924), 53–66.

ROYCE Royce, Charles C., comp., *Indian land cessions of the United States.* Bureau of American Ethnology, Annual Report, No. 18. Washington, 1896–97.

RUDD Rudd, Velva E., "Botanical contributions of the Lewis and Clark Expedition," *Journal* of the Washington Academy of Sciences, 44 (Nov. 1954), 351–56.

RUSH Corner, George W., ed., *The autobiography of Benjamin Rush.* Princeton, N.J., 1948.

RUSH LETTERS Butterfield, Lyman H., ed., *Letters of Benjamin Rush.* 2 vols. Philadelphia, 1951.

RUSSELL Russell, Carl P., "The guns of the Lewis and Clark Expedition," *North Dakota History,* 27 (Winter 1960), 25–33.

[691]

ST. CLAIR   Smith, William H., ed., *The St. Clair papers.* 2 vols. Cincinnati, 1882.

SARGENT   Sargent, Charles Sprague, "The first account of some western trees," *Garden and Forest,* 10 (Jan. 1897), 28–29, 38–40.

SCANLAN   Scanlan, P. L., "Nicholas Boilvin, Indian agent," *Wisconsin Magazine of History,* 27 (Dec. 1943), 145–69.

SCHOOLCRAFT   Schoolcraft, Henry R., *Journal of a tour into the interior of Missouri and Arkansaw . . . performed in the years 1818 and 1819.* London, 1821.

SEBA   Seba, Albertus, *Locupletissimi rerum naturalium thesauri accurata description . . . per universam physices historiam.* 4 vols. Amsterdam, 1734–65.

SELLERS   Sellers, Charles C., *Charles Willson Peale.* 2 vols. Philadelphia, 1947.

SETZER   Setzer, Henry H., "Zoological contributions of the Lewis and Clark Expedition," *Journal* of the Washington Academy of Sciences, 44 (Nov. 1954), 356–57.

SHIPTON   Shipton, Clifford K., *The American bibliography of Charles Evans.* Vol. 13, 1799–1800. Worcester, Mass., 1955.

SIMPSON   Simpson, George Gaylord, "The beginnings of vertebrate paleontology in North America," *Proceedings of the American Philosophical Society,* 86 (1942), 130–88.

SMITH (1)   Smith, James S., and Kathryn Smith, "Sedulous sergeant, Patrick Gass," *Montana,* 5 (Summer 1955), 20–27.

SMITH (2)   Smith, Margaret Bayard, *Forty years of Washington society.* New York, 1906.

SOWERBY   Sowerby, E. Millicent, comp., *Catalogue of the library of Thomas Jefferson.* 5 vols. Washington, 1952–59.

STANLEY   Stanley, L. L., "Medicine and surgery of the Lewis and Clark Expedition," *Medical Journal and Record,* 127 (1928), 275–78, 306–07, 364–66, 536–40, 598–99, 655–58.

STATUTES   Peters, Richard, ed., *The public statutes at large of the United States of America.* Boston, 1845——.

STETSON   Stetson, Sarah P., "William Hamilton and his 'Woodlands,'" *Pennsylvania Magazine of History and Biography,* 73 (1949), 26 ff.

STODDARD   Stoddard, Amos, *Sketches historical and descriptive of Louisiana*. Philadelphia, 1812.

STORM   Storm, Colton, "Lieutenant Armstrong's expedition to the Missouri River, 1790," *Mid-America*, 25 (July 1943), 180–88.

SWANTON   Swanton, John R., *The Indian tribes of North America. Bulletin* of the Bureau of American Ethnology, 145 (1952).

TABEAU   Abel, Annie Heloise, ed., *Tabeau's narrative of Loisel's expedition*. Norman, Okla., 1939.

TEGGART   Teggart, Frederick J., "Notes supplementary to any edition of Lewis and Clark," *Annual Report,* American Historical Association (1908), 1:185–95.

TERR. PAPERS   Carter, Clarence C., ed., *Territorial papers of the United States*. Vol. 13, Territory of Louisiana-Missouri, 1803–06. Washington, 1948. Vol. 14, Territory of Louisiana-Missouri, 1806–14. Washington, 1949.

THOMPSON   Thompson, Charles N., *Sons of the wilderness: John and William Conner*. Publications of the Indiana Historical Society. Indianapolis, 1937.

TODD   Todd, Charles B., *Life and letters of Joel Barlow, LL.D.* New York, 1886.

TRUE   True, Rodney Howard, "Some neglected botanical results of the Lewis and Clark Expedition," *Proceedings* of the American Philosophical Society, 67 (1928), 1–19.

TRUTEAU   Abel, Annie Heloise, "Trudeau's description of the upper Missouri," *Mississippi Valley Historical Review,* 8 (June-Sept. 1921), 149–79.

TUCKER   Tucker, Sara Jones, comp., *Indian villages of the Illinois country*. Part 1. Illinois State Museum, Scientific Papers. Springfield, Ill., 1942.

VAN DER ZEE   Van der Zee, Jacob, ed., "Old Fort Madison: some source materials," *Iowa Journal of History and Politics,* 11 (Oct. 1913), 517–45.

VENEGAS   Venegas, Miguel, *Noticia de la California*. . . . Madrid [1757]. English translation: *Natural and civil history of California*. 2 vols. London, 1759.

VINTON   Vinton, Stallo, *John Colter*. New York, 1926.

WAGNER   Wagner, Henry R., *Cartography of the Northwest coast of America*. 2 vols. Berkeley, Calif., 1937.

[693]

WAGNER-CAMP Wagner, Henry R., *The plains and the Rockies; a bibliography of original narratives of travel and adventure, 1800–1865.* Revised by Charles L. Camp. Columbus, Ohio, 1953.

WEDEL Wedel, Waldo R., "Observations on some nineteenth century pottery vessels from the upper Missouri," *Bulletin* of the Bureau of American Ethnology, 164 (1957), 91–114.

WHEAT Wheat, Carl I., *Mapping the Transmississippi West.* 3 vols. San Francisco, 1958–60.

WHEELER Wheeler, Olin D., *The trail of Lewis and Clark, 1804–1904.* 2 vols. New York, 1904.

WILL Will, Drake W., "The medical and surgical practice of the Lewis and Clark Expedition," *Journal of the History of Medicine,* 14 (July 1959), 273–97.

WILLIAMS Williams, David, "John Evans' strange journey," *American Historical Review,* 54 (Jan.-April 1949), 277–95, 508–29.

WILLOUGHBY Willoughby, Charles C., "A few ethnological specimens collected by Lewis and Clark," *American Anthropologist,* n.s., 7 (Oct.-Dec. 1905), 633–41.

WILSON Wilson, Alexander, *American ornithology; or, the natural history of the birds of the United States.* 9 vols. Philadelphia, 1808–14.

WOLLON & "Augustus J. Foster and 'The Wild Natives of the
KINARD Woods,' 1805–1807," *William and Mary Quarterly,* ser. 3, 9 (April 1952), 191–214. Introductory note by Dorothy Wollon and a note on illustrations by Margaret Kinard.

WOODS Woods, Edgar, *Albermarle County in Virginia.* Charlottesville, Va., 1901.

Index

The following abbreviations are used: LCE for Lewis and Clark Expedition, ML for Meriwether Lewis, TJ for Thomas Jefferson, and WC for William Clark.

Abel, Annie Heloise, 135–36, 372n
Academy of Natural Sciences of Philadelphia: LCE specimens at, 240n, 355n, 399n
Adams, Calvin, 349n
Adams, John Quincy: parody on Barlow poem, 362n
Aechmorphorus occidentalis. See Grebe, western
Agent, contractor's, 101
Agent, military: Hooke to leave post as, 115
Agriculture, Indian: on WC list, 159
Ahwahaway, Ahwahharway Indians. *See* Hidatsa Indians
Alden, Benjamin, 431
Algonkin Indians: location, 523
Alitan Indians. *See* Comanche Indians
Allen, J. A., 294n
Allen, Paul: letters from, 585–86, 597–98; letters to, 584–85, 586–93, 594–95; re memoir of ML, 584–85, 585–86, 594, 596; re Biddle narrative, 585n, 595, 597–98, 599n, 606, 614, 616, 622, 632
Alston, Willis: letter from, 361; letter to, 363–64; re LCE compensation, 361, 363–64
Alum, 228
American Philosophical Society, 44, 161n, 166, 220, 231, 236n, 239n–40n, 258–59, 263, 264, 276, 301, 308, 355n, 361, 555n, 589, 667–72. *See also* Journals, preservation of

American State Papers, 140n, 300n, 364n
Amoureux, Michel: letter from, 412–13
Ancora, Pietro: draws horned toad, 277n, 411n, 491n
Anderson, Alexander: as publisher, 241n
Anderson, Edmund, 100
Anderson, Elizabeth, 473n
Anderson, Jane, 100
Anderson, Richard Clough, 473n
Anderson, William G.: holds trunks of ML, 470
Animals: new species from LCE, 292–97. *See also* common names of species
Ankedoucharo, 305–06
Antelope, pronghorn. *See* Pronghorn
Antilocapra americana. See Pronghorn
Anville, Jean Baptiste d', 28, 32, 53
Aplodontia rufa. See Beaver, mountain
Apostle's River: in ML report, 320; in WC report, 326
Apple Creek: as boundary, 182; Indians on, 503; mentioned, 522
Arapaho Indians: Truteau lists, 139; WC lists, 229, 503; location, 535
Arbuckle, Mathew, 645
Arctomys citillus, 241n
Argali. *See* Sheep, mountain
Arikara Indians: Truteau describes,

138; parole for chief, 210n; WC discusses, 229, 537; passenger on barge, 237n; delegation of, 242, 257; illness and death of chief, 261–62, 266, 278, 303, 306; chief characterized, 272–73; names of chief, 305–06; condolences from TJ, 306; village as rendezvous, 312; fear of Sioux, 414; and Pryor expedition, 432–38; punishment of, 452, 453–55; and Chouteau expedition, 481; mode of trade, 501; and York, 503; venereal diseases, 506; raising of tobacco, 529; re liquor, 529; WC re language, 645; mentioned, 229, 461

Arkansas River: explorations, 137, 218; jack rabbits on, 171; salines on, 180–83; settlements on, 193; Indians on, 509, 522, 535; mentioned, 141, 201, 522

Arketarnawhar, 306n

Arms and ammunition: estimated cost, 8–9; itemized, 70; authorization for, 75–76; pocket pistols, 91; ML tests, 107; muskets on swivels, 175; denied to Indians, 257; muskets to sons of Arikara chief, 305; muskets to Indian delegation, 307–08; ML's pistol, 472; Shallatto chief's reaction to firearms, 502. See also Gunpowder, Knives, Lead, Rifles, Tomahawks

Armstrong, John: letter from, 665–66; letters to, 664, 664–65; expedition, 661–67

Arrow Rock, 509

Arrowsmith, Aaron: identified, 23n; map of 1795 cited, 48n; TJ orders map, 56; mentioned, 24, 28, 155, 603n

Artifacts: collected by LCE, 476–79

Artillerists, Corps of, 172

Askaw River: Indians on, 537

Assiniboine River: on Hay's route, 155; North West Company on, 214n; Pryor sent to, 314; in ML's report, 321, 322; Indians on, 523, 537; mentioned, 229, 311, 314, 625

Assiniboin Indians: hostility, 322; treatment of women, 504; location, 537

Astley, Thomas: letters from, 607, 621–23; letter to, 605–06; as assignee of Bradford & Inskeep, 606n, 607, 621–23, 627, 629

Astley & Brooks, 606n

Astor, John Jacob: TJ re his company, 444–45, 446n

Astragalus sp.: as remedy for bites, 221n

Asyndesmus lewis. See Woodpecker, Lewis'

Athabaska, 321

Auglaize River: Indians on, 522

Augur, Helen: quoted re Ledyard, 654

Aurora (Philadelphia), 346n, 355n, 386n, 393n, 411

Axes: issued to ML, 101

Ayawa, Ayowa Indians. See Ioway Indians

Ayres, Stephen: re journal, 275n

Aythya collaris. See Duck, ring-necked

Bache, Catharine, 134

Bache, William F., 134, 166

Bachman, John, 294n, 295n

Badger, American: WC lists, 229; specimen sent, 235, 263; as new species, 263; Peale re, 268; TJ lists, 291; re Peale drawing, 490, 491n; mentioned, 551, 563

Baillet, François: supplier, 78, 81

Baker's Ovens Island, 552

Baldwin, William: re LCE plants, 354n

Banger, Timothy, 90n

Barbour, James: letters to, 640–43, 645–46

Barclay, Samuel, 381n

Barge. See Boats

Barlow, Joel: letters from, 361–63, 488; identified, 309; re naming rivers for ML and WC, 361–62; poem honoring ML, 362n

Barnhill, Robert: supplier, 78, 91, 98

Barralet, John James: makes drawing for journals, 462, 463n

Barter, Jo. See Liberté

Barton, Benjamin Smith: letters from, 271, 275–77, 463–64, 561–62; letters to, 16–17, 271–72, 272, 289, 465–66, 548–49, 559–60; re planning LCE,

16–17, 44, 52; *Elements of botany*, 96, 99n; re wc's list of queries, 161n; re pronghorn, 238n; re lce specimens, 240n, 271; re mountain sheep, 240n; re prairie dog, 241n; re wapiti, 242n; re cottonwood, 275–76; re Indian languages, 289n; re jack rabbit, 293n–94n; to describe horned toad, 302; re lce, 354n; as Pursh's employer, 398, 399n, 485; re portrait of, 410; re Indian vocabularies, 463–64; to write scientific report of lce, 493, 494, 496, 546, 548–49, 555, 566, 579, 595, 607–08, 608–09, 609–10, 614, 615, 619, 623, 624, 626, 631, 632, 635–36, 644; re preserving lce papers, 561–62; re death of, 607–08, 610; mentioned, 51, 108, 293n, 397n, 506, 562

Barton, Mrs. Mary, 608n, 609

Bartonia ornata, 399n

Bartram, John, 275, 276n

Bartram, William, 238n

Basq, Mr.: French geographer, 5, 6n

Bass, William A.: letter to, 77

Batavia, Java, 65

Bates, Frederick: letter from, 440–41; letter to, 134; attitude toward ml, 134n, 575n; buys Drouillard's warrants, 345n; drafts petition for lce men, 380n; and Pryor expedition, 433; and Shannon's injury, 438n; re dispute over journal publication, 440–41

Bates, Tarleton: letter from, 134; identified, 1n–2n; re John Conner, 134; re ml as correspondent, 445n

Bates, Thomas F., 134n

Baume, Joseph: interpreter for Indian delegation, 289n

Bayou River: as boundary, 182

Beads: purchased, 72, 86; blue preferred by Indians, 74, 75n, 375; wc re, 529

Beans, Arikara: tj raises, 559

Beans, early: tj raises, 442

Bear: abundance of, 224, 227; mentioned, 229, 322

Bear, grizzly: skins sent, 234; previous knowledge of, 295n–96n; origin of

name, 296n; sent to tj, 296n; Peale re, 296n; Pike's live specimens, 440n

Beaver: in fur trade, 138–39; abundance, 318, 540; shooting of, 502; wc re dams, 528

Beaver, mountain: as new species, 294n; mentioned, 486n

Beck & Harvey: suppliers, 78, 87

Beef: purchased, 430n

Bees. *See* Honeybee

Belle Fontaine. *See* Cantonment Belle Fontaine

Bellet, François. *See* Baillet, François

Belmont County, Ohio, 126n

Benoit, Francis Marie, 180, 197

Berdaches: among Minitari and Mandan Indians, 531

Berry, John G., 381n

Berry Creek, 544

Berton, Mine of (Mine à Berton), 192

Bewick, Thomas: *General history of quadrupeds*, 241n

Biddle, Edward, 497, 503, 533

Biddle, Jane Craig, 578n, 598

Biddle, Nicholas: letters from, 495, 496, 550–55, 555–56, 560–61, 567–68, 568, 569, 577–78, 582, 595–96, 598–99, 604, 604–05, 613–15, 615–17, 627, 628–29, 635–37; letters to, 494–95, 496–97, 549–50, 562–65, 565, 565–66, 571–72, 575, 576, 577, 578, 579–80, 581, 581–82, 594, 599–600, 606–07, 609–10, 623, 626, 627–28, 629, 629–30, 634–35, 637, 638; invited to write lce narrative, 494; declines, then accepts, 495, 496; notes from interview with wc, 497–545; inquiries to wc, 550–55, 568, 569; re Dumont memoir, 555–56; Hassler queries, 560–61; query to Monroe, 567–68; progress reports to wc, 577–78, 582; re wc's power of attorney, 583; withdraws as editor, 595–96, 598, 599n; deposits lce papers in American Philosophical Society Library, 635–36

Big Beaver River: Indians on, 536

Big Belly Indians. *See* Gros Ventre Indians

Big Blue (Bluewater) River: Indians on, 524

Big Bone Lick (Ky.): ML visits, 126–30; location, 131n
Big Hole River: Indians on, 526
Big Horn River, 540
Big Muddy River: ML describes, 318; Indians on, 537
Big Sioux River, 228
Big Track, Osage chief, 201, 509
Big White. *See* Sheheke
Birch, bark of: for use as paper, 62
Birds: drawings by Peale, 490; new species from LCE, 297–98. *See also* common names of species
Bissell, Daniel: letter to, 103; to provide LCE volunteers, 103, 125; men from company of, 370n; mentioned, 102n, 164, 176n, 237n, 649
Bissell, Russell: letters to, 103, 103–04; to provide LCE volunteers, 103, 103–04, 125, 370n, 372n; men from company of, 372n; mentioned, 121, 237n
Black Cat (Mandan chief), 314
Blackfoot Indians: hostility, 341; Potts killed by, 381n; artifacts, 477; WC re language, 645
Black Hills, 228, 229, 510, 535, 540
Black River: saltpeter caves on, 473n
Blacksmith: with LCE, 144
Blainville, Henri Marie: re megalonyx, 16n
Blair, Neb., 293n
Blaireau. See Badger, American
Blankets: purchased, 70, 98; in Indian trade, 139
Blarina brevicauda. See Shrew, short-tailed
Blondeau, Maurice: re Indian population, 198n
Blue River: quarries on, 509
Bluffs, along Missouri River: WC describes, 513
Boar, wild: fossil remains, 132n
Boats: William Dickson to supply, 38; iron-framed, 39–40, 73, 233, 551; ML's Ohio River crew, 67, 126n; keelboat purchased, 73, 99; delays in building keelboat, 112, 115, 121–22, 125; ML buys pirogue, 122, 126n; gunwales for pirogue, 180; barge

returns to St. Louis, 233, 242; pirogues built, 329, 339; boards for boatbuilding, 423; WC describes LCE keelboat, 534; Indians as canoemen, 540; mentioned, 110, 196, 317
Bobcat: as new species, 297n
Bodega y Cuadra, Juan: Pacific explorer, 5
Boilvin, Nicholas: presents ore specimens, 192; identified, 195n; re Indian population, 198n; as Indian agent, 304
Bois Brulé Indians. *See* Sioux Indians
Boley, John: on boat crew, 237n
Bollman, Justus Erich: ML to pay, 43
Bonasa umbellus sabini. See Grouse, Oregon ruffed
Bonhomme Creek, 508
Bonne Femme Creek, 508
Books, consulted and carried: Vancouver's *Survey*, 13n; tables requisite and *Nautical almanac*, 45n, 96, 99; Miller's *Sexual system of Linnaeus*, 70; Kirwan's *Elements of mineralogy*, 96; Barton's *Elements of botany*, 96; Kelly's *Spherics*, 96
Boote, William R., 470
Botany: TJ asks Barton's help re, 16–17; Rafinesque re, 217–18; LCE contributions discussed, 355n–56n. *See also* common names of species
Boundaries. *See* Louisiana, boundaries of
Bounty, enlistment, 102, 177
Bounty lands: of John Marks, 101
Bourgmont, Etienne Véniard de: re western mission, 511; visits Padoucas, 535
Bradbury, John: re Indian corn, 239n; to botanize in West, 458–59; *Travels*, 459n; re WC's knowledge of natural history, 459n; TJ re, 562n
Bradford, Samuel F.: letter to, 604; as assignee for John Conrad, 394n; as partner of John Inskeep, 577, 578n, 579, 581, 598, 605, 614. *See also* Bradford & Inskeep
Bradford & Inskeep: as publishers of Biddle narrative, 578n, 598n, 644; financial failure, 601–04, 604, 604–05, 605–06, 606–07, 607, 609–10,

613–15, 615–17, 621–23, 627–28, 628–29, 629
Bradford & Read, 601
Bradhurst and Field: draft to, 409
Brahan, John, 372n, 470, 486
Brant, white, 229
Brant Island, 540
Braro. *See* Badger, American
Bratton, William: one of "nine young men," 118n; listed, 366, 638; named in compensation act, 378; re warrant, 381n; in financial records, 425
Brent, Robert: at testimonial dinner, 362n
Brent, William: as TJ's secretary, 42n, 166
Briggs, Isaac: confers with ML, 45n; re finding longitude, 244, 246n; mentioned, 370, 415, 418
Brooks, Samuel, 606n
Broome, William: supplier, 78, 90
Broughton, William Robert: ascends Columbia River, 46; Lacépède cites, 109
Brown, Francis: supplier, 78, 92
Brown, J., 602
Brown, Samuel, 355n
Brown, William, 132n
Browne, Joseph, 257n
Bruff, James: letter from, 215–16; sends news of LCE, 215; commands Upper Louisiana, 215n; mentioned, 216n, 243n, 248
Brulé Indians. *See* Sioux Indians
Brush Creek: land warrants, 101
Bryan, Guy, 144n
Bryan and Morrison, 157n, 189
Bubo virginianus occidentalis. See Owl, Montana horned
Buchanan, William: U.S. consul, 65
Buckbush, 441n
Buckongahelas' Town: Delaware Indian village, 40n
Buffalo: abundance, 224; robes sent to TJ, 234; WC re Indian hunting of, 531; paths, 553, 564; mentioned, 128, 295n, 338, 521
Buffalo dance, 538
Buffon, Georges Louis Leclerc, Comte de, 47, 268
Buford County, N.D., 319n

Bull Creek, 540
Burial, Indian: Nez Percé mode, 501
Burr, Aaron, 140n, 387, 460
Burwell, William A.: as TJ's secretary, 4n, 43n
Bustamente y Guerra, José: Pacific explorer, 5
Bustard, John: draft to, 348
Butler, James D., 346n
Butler, John: obtains Frazer prospectus, 346n

Cabra, cabri, cabrie, *cabril. See* Pronghorn
Cache River, 7
Caddo Indians: attacks on, 304; location, 522; WC re language, 645
Cadron, Etienne: notes on salines, 180–82
Cahokia, 41n, 118, 131, 135, 137, 144n, 157n, 167, 177n, 335, 591
Calculations, astronomical: Ellicott discusses, 23–25. *See also* Hassler, Ferdinand Rudolph; Observations, astronomical
Callarado River. *See* Colorado River
Camassia quamash. See Quamash
Cameahwait: Peale re, 439–40; meets sister, Sacagawea, 518–19
Cameron, Murdoch: as trader, 312
Caminabiche, Canenaviech Indians. *See* Arapaho Indians
Camp, equipment for, 70–72, 95
Campbell, John: identity discussed, 124n; Lt. Campbell furnishes LCE volunteers, 370n, 371n; mentioned, 227n
Campbell, Robert, 393n
Canachites canadensis franklinii. See Grouse, spruce
Canada: routes of traders, 63–64; mentioned, *passim*
Canis latrans. See Coyote
Canis lupus. See Wolf, gray
Canisters, lead: for powder, 79, 98
Cannonball River, 437n
Canoe: William Dickson to supply, 38; listed, 73; to return from LCE with journals, 232; Indian handling of, 540
Canton, China: in fur trade, 321

Cantonment Belle Fontaine, 371n, 383n, 457n, 473n, 642n, 647
Cape Adams, 540
Cape Girardeau: district of, 152, 182, 183n
Cape Horn: LCE may return via, 65
Cape of Good Hope: LCE may return via, 65
Carey, Mathew: letters from, 627–28, 629; issues Gass journal, 554; re failure of Bradford & Inskeep, 627–28, 629
Carlisle Barracks (Pa.), 112
Carmichael, George Washington, 164
Carmick, Daniel: as courier, 261, 263, 267n
Carpenter (joiner): with LCE, 144
Carr, Peter, 489
Carr, William C., 344
Carson, Alexander: alleged member of LCE, 373n
Cartouche boxes: purchased, 97
Carver, Jonathan: *Travels*, 536n; mentioned, 500, 554
Casa Calvo, Marqués de: letters from, 173–75, 185–86, 210–12; letters to, 142–43, 186–87; on intercepting LCE, 210–12
Castahana Indians. *See* Arapaho Indians
Cataha Indians: location, 535
Catherine, Empress of Russia: re Ledyard, 588
Cathlamet Indians, 542
Catlett, Hanson: re army contract, 168n
Cayuga Indians: Truteau lists, 139
Cedar, dwarf, 392
Census, Upper Louisiana: ML discusses, 151–54
Centrocercus urophasianus. *See* Grouse, sage
Cervus canadensis. *See* Wapiti
Cevallos, Pedro: letters to, 4–7, 14–15, 173–75, 183–89, 210–12; re proposed LCE, 4–6; receives notice of pending LCE, 14–15
Chaboillez, Charles: letter to, 213–14
Chain, surveyor's: recommended to ML, 48; purchased, 69, 82, 96
Chamberlain, Jason, 214n

Chambers, Talbot, 486n
Chancellor, William, & Co.: supplier, 78, 89
Chandler, John, 397n
Chapline, Abram, 515
Chapman, Matilda: supplier, 78, 88
Charbonneau, Jean Baptiste (Pomp): WC offers to educate, 315; mentioned, 317, 640n
Charbonneau, Lizette, 640n
Charbonneau, Toussaint: letter to, 315–17; WC offers aid, 315–16; ML re his service, 369; in compensation act, 378; re land warrant, 382n; re wives, 527; discharge as interpreter, 648–49; mentioned, 317, 519, 540, 638, 639n
Chardon, F. A.: journal cited, 325n
Chariton River, 510
Charles, Henry: printer for Biddle narrative, 601; engraver of plates, 616, 623
Charless, Joseph: letter to, 440–41; mentioned, 474n
Charlevoix, Pierre François: cited by Barton, 276
Charts. *See* Maps
Chauncey, Charles: letter from, 605–06; letters to, 607, 615–17, 621–23, 628–29; re Biddle narrative, 605–06, 607, 615–17, 621–23, 627, 628–29
Cheetham, James: letter to, 55–56
Chehalis Indians, 542
Chehalis River: Indians on, 542
Cherokee Indians: in Louisiana Territory, 522; hostility, 587
Cherry: WC lists, 357n
Cherry, black: WC mentions, 512
Chevallié, J. A., 156n
Cheveux Blancs. *See* White Hair
Cheyenne Indians: Truteau lists, 139; WC lists, 229; WC discusses, 518; location, 524; Biddle queries name, 552; mentioned, 461, 503
Cheyenne River: trading house site, 310; in ML's report, 321; as rendezvous, 452; Indians on, 524, 536; silver on, 564
Cheyenne River (branch of Red River, north): Indians on, 524

Chicarlieskit River. *See* Hellgate River

Chickasaw Bluffs (Tenn.): and death of ML, 464, 467, 468; mentioned, 522, 592

Chickasaw Indians: oppose sale of land, 12; location, 522

Chicot Island, 509

Chillucketiqua, Chilluckitiquaw Indians, 542, 543

Chiltz Indians. *See* Chehalis Indians

Chinook Indians, 503, 541, 542

Chipmunk, Townsend's: new species, 294n

Chippewa Indians, 40n, 523

Choctaw Indians, 273, 522

Chokecherry: wc mentions, 512

Chouteau, Auguste: letter to, 161–63; queried by ML, 161–63; presents specimens, 193; presents chart of Mississippi, 193; sends news of LCE to TJ, 219n; re arms to Indians, 257n; agent pro tem, 461

Chouteau, Auguste Pierre: with Mandan expedition, 411, 414, 450

Chouteau, Paul: interprets for Indian delegation, 289n; mentioned, 305n

Chouteau, Paul Liguest, 305n

Chouteau, Pierre: letters from, 242–44, 248–49, 479–84; letters to, 247–48, 451–56; leads Osage delegations, 168, 198, 203, 208, 209n, 246, 247–48, 260, 308; re Osage orange, 170; agent for LCE, 191n, 192n; presents ore specimens, 192; sends TJ news of LCE, 219n, 291n; discusses Indian delegations, 242–43; re live specimens, 248–49; in post-expedition party, 325n, 362n; named Osage agent, 382; in financial records, 420; commands Mandan expedition, 447, 451, 451–56, 479–84; financial difficulties, 457, 460, 461; agency jeopardized, 457; mentioned, 175, 189n, 198n, 215n, 217, 262, 277n, 537, 553, 563

Chouteau, Pierre, *fils*: ML recommends for West Point appointment, 172n

Christie, William, 349n

Christy, J. P., 344

Chronometer, Arnold's: recommended, 23, 48; how to protect, 25; Voigt to clean, 49; Ellicott to regulate, 49; TJ discusses, 45, 49; characteristics, 51; purchased, 88, 96; bill for cleaning, 91

Church, Dr. John, 133, 134n

Cincinnati: ML directs mail to, 117; mentioned, *passim*

Cinnebar, 228

Cipher: carried by ML, 9–10

Clackstar Indians, 542

Claiborne, William C. C.: letters from, 250, 253; letters to, 248–49, 252; re live specimens, 248–49, 250, 252, 253; mentioned, 137, 169, 180

Clarckia pulchella, 399n

Clark, George Rogers: letters from, 7–8, 655–56; letters to, 325–30, 330–35, 654–55; re Fort Jefferson, 7; recommends brother wc for post, 7–8; invited by TJ to lead expedition, 8n, 654–55, 655–56; re Welsh Indians, 515; mentioned, 119n, 590

Clark, John, 319n

Clark, Jonathan: receives wc papers, 226, 227n; mentioned, 330n, 486n

Clark, William: letters from, 110–11, 112–13, 113, 117–18, 118–19, 123–24, 164–65, 175–76, 178–79, 195–96, 203–08, 213–14, 226, 226–27, 227–30, 230, 230–31, 309–13, 313–15, 315–17, 325–30, 330–35, 347, 359, 387–88, 411–12, 414, 490–91, 491–92, 494–95, 496–97, 546, 548–49, 549–50, 562–65, 565, 565–66, 566, 570–71, 571–72, 578, 579–80, 580, 581–82, 599–600, 609–10, 619–21, 623, 623–26, 626, 629–30, 630, 634–35, 638, 643–45, 645–46; letters to, 57–60, 115–17, 124–26, 135–36, 144–45, 167–68, 177–78, 179–80, 382–83, 385, 387, 415–16, 431–32, 432–38, 489–90, 492–93, 493, 495, 496, 550–55, 568, 569, 577, 582, 598–99, 604–05, 613–15, 619, 627; brother George R. recommends, 7–8; invited to join ML, 57–60, 572; re commission, 60, 172–73, 179, 347, 568, 569, 571–72; re land patents, 101n; accepts ML's invitation, 110–11, 112–13, 113;

progress reports to ML, 117–18; contacts John Conner, 118–19; at Big Bone Lick, 131n, 442; receives Mackay map, 135; from Kaskaskia by water, 145; re map for TJ, 193; sends journals to TJ, 226, 230–31; report from Fort Mandan, 227–30; builds Fort Osage, 275n; aids Charbonneau, Sacagawea, 315–17; ML commends, 323–24; illness, 329; testimonial dinner for, 362n; promotion proposed, 375; nomination as lieutenant colonel fails, 376, 376n; appointed superintendent of Indian affairs, 376n; re land warrants, 380n, 383; re engagement, 388; McKeehan praises, 402–03; settles account with ML, 462–63; as ML's executor, 479; arranges to publish account of LCE, 486, 490–91, 494, 496–97; interviews with Biddle, 497–545; sends Shannon to Biddle, 549; data and map to Biddle, 562–65; in fur trade, 566, 570–71; offers partnership to Shannon, 570–71; re ML's death, 575n; trips east, 580n; power of attorney to Biddle, 583; re Indian hostilities, 599–600; re preservation of LCE papers, 609–10, 623, 623–24; re Shannon's pension, 619–20; discusses publication of Biddle narrative, 624; re Missouri Territory, 624–25; lists location of LCE members, 638–39; employs Pryor as agent, 645

Clark, Mrs. William, 578, 580n, 582, 600, 610

Clarke, Daniel, 141n

Clark's River. See Deschutes River

Clarksville, Indiana Territory, 8n, 316, 330n, 533

Clatskanie Indians, 542

Clatsop Indians: clothing, 476; language, 499; mentioned, 503, 527, 542

Clavijero, Francisco: cited re horned toad, 276, 277n

Clay, Henry: letter to, 619–21; buys Shannon's warrant, 381n, 621n; re Shannon's pension, 619–21

Clearwater River: in ML's report, 320,

321; in WC's report, 326, 328; Indians on, 526; mentioned, 476, 506, 530, 541, 545, 551

Clemson, Eli B.: escorts Arikara chief, 274; builds Fort Osage, 275n; mentioned, 452, 480

Clifford, J. D., 602

Climate: TJ instructs ML to study, 63

Clothing: furnished to boat crew, 67; for Indian delegation, 260; Pryor to barter for, 314; ML's note re, 393n; ML's uniform coat traded, 431n; in ML's effects, 470, 472. See also Uniforms

Clyma, William P., 198

Coal, 228

Coale, Edward J.: bookseller, 601

Cobalt: bluffs of, 512, 514; illness due to, 515

Code. See Cipher

Coffee: Pryor to barter for, 314

Cole, John, 431

Coles, Edward, 415n, 487

Coles, Isaac A.: letter from, 486–87; mentioned, 415, 475

Colhoon, Mr.: mentioned by ML, 100

Collins, John: sells warrant, 345n; receives pay, 348n; listed, 366, 638; WC's appraisal, 370n; named in compensation act, 378; re land warrant, 381n; in financial records, 425; mentioned, 502

Collins & Co., 602

Collinsville, Ill., 145n

Colorado River: in ML's report, 320; in WC's report, 326

Colter, John: one of "nine young men," 118n; re joining LCE, 125n; listed, 366, 638; brief biographical statement, 371n; named in compensation act, 378; re land warrant, 381n; re compensation, 384; in financial records, 425; claim against ML, 567; mentioned, 180

Colter's Creek, 526–27

Columbia, Valley of the. See Wappato Valley

Columbia River: Pichon mentions, 22; Lacépède discusses, 46–47; TJ re, 65; re south fork of, 225; described, 320; in ML's report, 320, 321, 322,

323; in wc's report, 325, 326, 327, 328; Barlow re name, 361–62; re drawing, 392; snowberry from, 584n; mentioned, *passim*

Comanche Indians: to intercept LCE, 188; location, 526; mentioned, 273

Comegys, John G., 349n, 381n

Commission, blank: War Department to provide, 102; text, 104

Commission, wc's: captaincy denied, 172–73; ML comments, 179; wc returns commission, 347; wc comments, 571–72

Compasses, 48, 69, 82, 96

Compensation: promised to LCE members, 60, 65–66, 177; Congress inquires re, 361; Dearborn recommends, 363–64; men eligible for, 366–69; act provides for, 377; petition of men re, 378–79; McKeehan deplores, 402; Colter sues for, 567n

Conner, John: letter to, 118–19; invited to join LCE, 37–38, 44, 116, 118, 118–19; declines, 123, 125, 130, 134

Conrad, Andrew, 394n

Conrad, C. and A., and Co.: letter from, 468–69; letters to, 474–75, 479; re publication of journals, 394n, 397n, 468–69, 474–75, 570

Conrad, Cornelius, 394n

Conrad, John: letters from, 393–94, 492–93, 493, 581; identified, 393n–94n; re publication of journals, 492, 493, 494, 550, 569, 579, 581, 582, 644; financial failure, 566, 577–78; mentioned, 140n, 397n, 469, 548, 603n, 604

Conrad, Samuel, 394n

Contractor, army: to supply LCE, 145; visits camp, 168; re kegs, 180. *See also* Galusha, Elijah G.; Rumsey, Nathan

Cook, James, 5, 6n, 28, 499, 541, 558, 588

Cook River, 5

Copper ore, 273

Corn: supplies of, 176; as food, 233; Mandan seed sent to TJ, 234; Arikara, 239n; cultivation discussed, 239n, 531, 538; Mandan, 239n, 442;

quarantine, 239n, 355; TJ sends to Monticello, 358n

Corrèa da Serra, José: letter from, 608–09, 615; letters to, 607–08, 611–13, 617–18; re the megalonyx, 16n. *See also* Journals, preservation of

Cost, LCE. *See* Financial records

Cotton: cottonwood as substitute for, 277n

Cottontail, desert: and LCE, 294n

Cottonwood: TJ re, 272; substitute for cotton, 277n; wc mentions, 530, 534

Coues, Elliott: re identification of Heney, 221n; notations on documents, 236n; as zoologist, 293n; re LCE species, 294n, 297n, 298n, 356n, 392n; re LCE manuscripts, 583n, 613n; edits Biddle narrative, 673–76

Cougar, 47

Council Bluffs: LCE at, 512

Courtin, Charles (Coartong, Coutau, Corton, Courtney): identity discussed, 433, 437n

Courtney, Charles. *See* Courtin, Charles

Cousin, Barthelemi, 217

Covington, Ky., 131n

Cowish: use of, as Indian food, 477, 498

Coxe, Tench, 397n

Coyote: collected by LCE, 235, 267, 295n

Craig, Isaac, 114, 115n, 134n

Craig, Mrs. Margaret, 578n, 598

Cramer, Spear and Eichbaum, 601, 603n

Cranberry: collected by LCE, 392n

Crataegus douglasii. *See* Haw, black

Crawford, Lewis: Indian agent for ML, 190, 196, 243; collects vocabularies, 212–13, 221

Crawshay, Richard: re Welsh Indians, 516n

Credit, letter of: issued to ML, 65, 105–06

Cree (Kristinaux) Indians: location, 523

Croghan, John, 566

Croghan, Lucy, 230

Croghan, Nancy, 164

tion, 137; Indians on, 139, 216n, 221–22, 243n, 509, 523, 536; described, 196–97; trading house near, 305n; fortifications on, 564; lead mines on, 564; mentioned, 189, 513
De Tessé, Mme. Noailles: receives LCE plants, 584n
Dickinson College, 391n
Dickson, William: re LCE boat, 38, 41n, 53; re ML's watch, 474n
Dinsmore, James, 351
Districts, Upper Louisiana: organization, 182, 183n; re map, 194
Dixon, George, 558, 559n
Dobson, Thomas, and Son, 581
Dogs, as food, 328, 339
Dog Soldier, 203n
Donaldson, James Lowry: letter from, 360; in charge of LCE shipment, 360
Dorion, Pierre: brings news of LCE, 219n; re his pay, 262, 263n; as Indian agent, 412, 414; and Pryor expedition, 432, 435; and Chouteau expedition, 455; mentioned, 528
Dorion, Pierre, Jr., 414
Dotami Indians, 535
Dougherty, Joseph, 107, 108n, 255
Drouillard, George: arrives with recruits, 144; listed, 317, 638; at Marias River, 342; buys Whitehouse's and Collins' warrants, 345n; sells warrants, 345n; in financial records, 427; trades ML's coat, 431n
Drum, Indian, 501
Duane, William, 140n, 392
Dubois, Camp: WC arrives at, 147; area described, 164; mentioned, 144n, 227n
Dubois River. See Wood River
Dubreuil, Olympia, 372n
Dubuque, Julien, 168
Duck, ring-necked: and LCE, 297n
Ducks: abundance of, 224
Dufief, Nicholas Gouin, 52, 53n
Dunbar, William: letter from, 250–51; letters to, 244–46, 290; on finding longitude, 250–51; mentioned, 18n, 270, 299
Dunlap, William, 210n, 274n–75n
Dumont, M.: Memoires sur la Louisiane, 551

Du Ponceau, Peter S.: letter from, 633–34; letter to, 631–33; re preservation of LCE journals, 608n, 631–33, 633–34; mentioned, 161n
Du Pratz, Le Page: re site of fort, 510; Histoire de la Louisiane, 510, 511, 551; re Dumont memoir, 556n
Dye, Eva Emery, 121, 610n

Eagle: plumes, in Indian dress, 476
Eagle, calumet, 229
Eagle's Feather, 306n
East Indies: in fur trade, 321–22, 541
Easton, Rufus, 257n, 381n
Eaton, John H.: letter to, 646–48
Eaton, William, 377n
Echelute (Echeloot) Indians, 542–43
Eclipse, lunar, 560
Edgar, John, 486
Education, of Indian children: TJ authorizes, 64
Eggplant, 357n
Elk. See Wapiti
Ellicott, Andrew: letters from, 23–25, 36–37, 45, 45–46; letter to, 51; re instruction to ML, 23–25, 40, 41n, 45; Journal, 25n; map, 28; re artificial horizon, 36; re theodolite, 48; re finding longitude, 270; mentioned, 49, 570
Ellicott, Joseph, 41n
Elliott, Stephen, 354n
Ellwood, John, 263, 264
Elmslie, John, Jr.: U.S. consul, 65
Eneeshur Indians, 543
Engagés. See Voyageurs
Engineers, Corps of, 172
England: Gallatin re British trade, 32; informed of LCE, 61; ML's apprehensions re, 464, 467; boundary treaties, 568; influence on Indians, 625; mentioned, passim
English, Thomas, 421
Eppes, John Wayles, 155
Eppes, Maria Jefferson, 157n
Eraschett, ——: re Welsh Indians, 516
Essex & Co., 601
Eustis, William: letter from, 456–58; letters to, 249, 451, 459–61, 479–84, 580–81; draft of ML refused, 456–58, 459–61

Fort Hamilton, 41n, 116
Fortifications, ancient, 513, 553, 564
Fort Independence, 647, 650n
Fort Jefferson, 7
Fort Madison, 305n, 371n, 372n, 471, 473n, 580n, 642n
Fort Mandan: communications from, 220–21, 221–22, 222–25, 226, 227–30, 230, 231–44; LCE winters at, 222; mentioned, 41n, 224, 227n, 237, 290, 293n, 317, 318, 335n, 365, 557, 560
Fort Massac, 38, 101, 102, 103n, 107n, 116, 118, 125, 144, 164, 176, 203, 243, 308, 372n, 430n, 647
Fort Mifflin, 67n
Fort Orleans: WC discusses, 511
Fort Osage, 182n, 275n, 480, 509
Fort Pickering, 467n, 573
Fort Shelby, 600n
Fossils: TJ's interest in, 16n; from LCE, 132n
Foster, Augustus John, 265n, 325n
Fox, kit, 295n
Fox, red, 229, 235, 263
Fox, swift, 295n
Fox Indians: relations with U.S., 197n–98n, 247n; murders by, 215n–16n; land cession by, 216n; delegation, 242, 259, 265, 266, 289; artifacts, 476; location, 523
France: expeditions by, expected, 27; informed of LCE, 61; re Louisiana Purchase, 116–17. See also Louisiana Purchase, Passports
Franklin, Benjamin, 134n
Frazer, Robert: letter from, 409–10; issues prospectus, 345–46; journal discussed, 346n; map discussed, 346n; bond to, 346n; listed, 367, 638; in compensation act, 378; re land warrant, 381n; delivers WC's commission, 387; witness in Burr affair, 387, 409–10; McKeehan re journal, 400–401; in financial records, 425
Freeman, Thomas, 270, 290, 374, 470, 473n
Friis, Herman, 135n
Fritillaria lanceolata, 399n
Furnace, assaying, 461

Furs and skins: from LCE, 250, 252, 253, 253–54, 255, 256; to Peale, 263, 264, 268
Fur trade: TJ re importance, 10–14; ML re, 321, 322; in WC's report, 327; TJ re Astor, 444–45; Biddle memo, 555n; WC in, 567, 570–71; WC fears loss of, to England, 625

Galena River: lead mines on, 642n
Gallatin, Albert: letters from, 27–28, 32–34; letters to, 31–32, 643–45; interest in LCE, 13n; re maps, 27–28; discusses LCE, 32–34; re Pierre Chouteau, 209n; re appointing ML governor, 351n; mentioned, 415, 418
Gallatin River, 327, 337, 522
Galusha, Elijah G., 168n, 422
Game: abundance, 224, 234; scarcity, 329
Game, Indian: WC describes, 541
Garnett, John, 45, 49, 56, 558
Garreau (Garout, Garaut, Garon), Joseph, 438n
Gasconade River: as boundary, 182; saltpeter caves on, 473n; WC describes, 508; Indians on, 522
Gaskill, Benjamin, 601, 603n, 616
Gass, Patrick: letter from, 646–48; leads detachment, 342; promotion of, 366; named in compensation act, 378; re land warrant, 381n; petitions Congress, 378–79; in financial records, 425; Biddle re journal, 551; re journal, 553, 647; reported dead, 639n; re pension claims, 646–48, 649–51; career summarized, 646–48, 649–51, 651–53; described, 648n; re land warrants, 653n; mentioned, 346n
Gazette (Pittsburgh, Pa.), 330n, 391, 407n
Geese: abundance, 224
Gens des Vaches Indians. See Arapaho Indians
Gerardia sp.: as remedy for bites, 221n
Gibson, George: one of "nine young men," 118n; in trading party, 313; listed, 367, 638; in compensation

[707]

act, 378; re land warrant, 381n; petitions Congress, 378–79
Gibson, John, 349n
Gifts, Indian. *See* Goods, Indian
Gilbert, William, 431
Gillaspy and Strong: suppliers, 78
Gilmer, Francis Walker, 101n
Glaize River, 522
Gmelin, Samuel, 276, 277n
Goat, mountain: and LCE, 297n; TJ re, 443, 444n
Goforth, Dr. William, 126, 132n–33n
Gonorrhea. *See* Venereal diseases
Goodrich, Silas: listed, 367, 638; in compensation act, 378; petitions Congress, 378–79; re land warrant, 381n; in financial records, 425
Goods, Indian: listed, 72–73; purchased, 83–99, *passim;* prices listed, 93–99; John Hay to help pack, 157n; TJ discusses, 374–75
Gooseberries, 389n
Gopher, northern pocket, 295n
Goshen (Indiana Terr.), 145n
Govan, Thomas P., 599n
Graham, J. A., 567n
Grand River, 279, 510
Grapes: WC sends seed, 230
Gratiot, Charles: letters from, 189, 217; identified, 168; re plant specimens, 170; re bills of exchange, 189; agent for ML, 191, 236–37, 430n; re horned toad, 192; answers queries of ML, 217; sells horses to ML, 350; in financial records, 421; mentioned, 177, 227n
Gratiot, Charles, *fils,* 168, 172n, 189
Gravelines, Joseph: on boat crew, 237n; re death of Arikara chief, 303, 304; interpreter, 304, 307; LCE meets, 305n; in financial records, 424; among Arikaras, 437n; re Chouteau expedition, 455
Gray, Robert: re discovery of Columbia River, 46, 47n, 362n
Graydon, William, 601
Grease, voyagers', 180
Great Chute, 540
Great Falls (of Columbia River), 320, 326, 490, 550
Great Falls (of Missouri River), 233,

311, 323, 326, 327, 353n, 490, 541, 550, 565
Grebe, western, 297n
Greene, Nathaniel, 598
Greenleaf, O. C., 601
Greenville, Treaty of, 572
Gregoire, Charles, 420
Grenier (Greinyea), ——, 305n, 429n
Grey Eyes: medal for, 434, 438n
Grinder, Mr. and Mrs.: and death of ML, 467–68, 573, 574, 592
Grossman, Peter, 343n
Gros Ventre Indians, 273, 408n
Ground squirrel, Columbian, 294n
Ground squirrel, thirteen-lined, 294n
Grouse, blue, 297n
Grouse, Oregon ruffed, 297n
Grouse, sage, 297n
Grouse, sharp-tailed: living specimen to TJ, 236, 248–49, 263, 297n
Grouse, spruce, 297n
Gualtheria shallon. See Salalberry
Gunpowder, 70, 73, 87, 97, 99n, 142, 303, 308
Guthrie, William, 292
Gwathney, Samuel, 421
Gymnorhinus cyanocephala. See Jay, piñon

Hagner, P., 77n
Haile, Robert, 381n
Hair ball, buffalo, 192
Haley, —— (trader), 340
Haley's Bay, 540
Hall, Hugh: listed, 367, 638; described, 371n; in compensation act, 378; petitions Congress, 378–79; re land warrant, 381n
Hamilton, James, 41n
Hamilton, John, 41n
Hamilton, William: letters to, 269–70, 389; LCE plants to, 170, 240n, 269–70, 356, 389; employs Pursh, 398n
Hammond, Samuel, 257n
Hamtramck, Francis, 4n
Hancock, George, 388, 494, 578
Hancock, Julia, 388
Hankinson, John, 349n
Harbeson, Benjamin, & Sons: supplier, 78, 85

Hare, American varying, 294n
Harlan, Richard, 294n
Harmar, Josiah: letters from, 663, 664, 664–65, 666-67; letters to, 661–62, 662–63, 665–66
Harper, Francis P., 673–76
Harper's Ferry, Va.: equipment obtained at arsenal, 38–39; ML detained at, 43, 106; mentioned, *passim*
Harrison, William Henry: letters from, 135–36, 140–41, 246–47, 247–48; letters to, 227–30, 242–44; sends map to WC, 135; sends Evans map to TJ, 140–41; re districting of Upper Louisiana, 183n; re Sauk and Fox treaty, 198n; re Indian delegations, 243n, 246, 247–48; re Sioux attitude, 246–47; re Sauk prisoner, 247; sends bear to TJ, 296n; mentioned, 41n, 266, 445n
Harrison, Samuel, 564n, 601
Harvey & Worth: suppliers, 78, 83, 89
Harvie, Lewis: letter to, 41–43; TJ's secretary, 41–43, 42n; mission to France, 43n, 166; mentioned, 107, 155, 157n
Hassler, Ferdinand Rudolph: letter from, 556–59; letter to, 491–92; works on LCE astronomical calculations, 462, 491–92, 550, 551, 556–59, 560–61, 565, 613n, 635
Haw, black, 170–71
Hawkesbury, Lord. *See* Jenkinson, Robert Banks
Hawkins, John I.: letter to, 410–11
Hay, John: letter from, 219–20; re Mackay map, 135; ML meets, 145; re journal, 155; translates for ML, 155; annotates Mackay journal, 156n; assists LCE, 156n–57n; ML recommends for subagency, 172n; sends news of LCE, 219; in financial records, 420; mentioned, 20n, 157n, 175n, 343n
Health, Rush's rule for, 54–55
Hebard, Grace Raymond, 639n
Heiskel & Sowers, 353
Hellgate River, 530
Hempstead, Edward, 429n, 450, 467
Henebury, Patrick, 144

Heney, Hugh: letter to, 309–13; contact with LCE, 214n; presents bite remedy, 220, 221n, 544; asked to work for LCE, 309–13, 314
Hennepin, Louis, 536
Hernandez, Francisco: re pronghorn, 238n; re horned toad, 276
Hessler, John, 91n
Hewes, Thomas: U.S. consul, 65
Hidatsa Indians: in fur trade, 322; hostility of, 342; treatment of women, 504; venereal diseases, 506; WC re villages, 524; *berdaches*, 531; WC re language, 644; mentioned, 222, 236, 315, 317, 455, 482, 497, 525, 539, 544, 554, 563
Hoff, John, 602, 604n
Holmes, Abel, 90n
Honeybee: WC re range of, 497, 527
Honeysuckle, 357n
Honoré, Louis Tesson, 198n
Hooke, Moses: letter from, 119–20; letters to, 101–02, 115, 203; furnishes supplies and assistance, 101–02; re joining LCE, 113–14, 115, 117, 134; reports departure of ML, 119; in financial records, 423; mentioned, 110, 112
Hootsootahah Indians, 526
Hopkins, Samuel, 409
Hoppas-straps, 74
Horizon, artificial: carried by LCE, 24, 25, 36, 45, 48, 69
Horn, powder, 70, 90, 97
Horsburgh, John, 420
Horses: pack horses for ML, 4n; in transporting supplies, 53–54; pulling boats, 122, 124; corn for, 144; of Indian delegations, 203, 259, 260; Warfington to use, 226; of Shoshoni Indians, 233; cottonwood as food for, 272; Pryor transports, 312, 313–14, 341; cheapness, among Indians, 320; purchased, 328, 338, 339; as food, 328, 339; on Marias River expedition, 341; theft, by Indians, 342, 408n, 430n; Gratiot sells, 350; Werner uses, 385; ML re sale, 460; ML loses, 467; Indian method of catching, 503; in Mandan religion, 520; in Mandan mar-

riage, 521; racing, among Indians, 529; gelding, 541; in Indian trade, 543; mentioned, 243, 291n, 508

Hosack, Dr. David, 399n, 485

Howard, Benjamin, 599–600

Howard, Thomas Procter: re pay, 348; listed, 367, 638; described, 371n; in compensation act, 378; re land warrant, 381n; in financial records, 425

Hudson's Bay, 12, 33, 48n, 229, 295n

Humboldt, Friedrich Heinrich Alexander von, Baron: letter to, 596; re finding longitude, 245

Hummingbird, broad-tailed, 298n

Hunkpapa (Sioux). *See* Sioux Indians

Hunt, Ajaniah, 570

Hunt, George, 642n

Hunt, Thomas: letter to, 384; re return of Sheheke, 383n, 384; mentioned, 414, 473n

Hunt, Wilson P., 349n, 373n, 564n, 570

Hunt and Hankinson, 409

Hunter, Dr. George, 218

Hurst, Henry, 8n

Hutchins, Thomas: re map of, 557, 559n

Hydrometer, 69

Ibex. *See* Sheep, mountain

Illinois River, 12, 504

Illinois Trading Company, 138

Indians: estimated cost of goods for, 8–9; act to establish trade, 10–12; instructions to LCE re, 62–63; described by Truteau, 138–39; re removal to west side of Mississippi, 148; Welsh, search for, 156n, 167n, 515–16; WC's list of queries re, 157–61; WC discusses, 227–30, 497–545, *passim*, 530–31; assist LCE, 325–30, 330–35, *passim*; attack LCE, 342, 408n; goods preferred, 374–75; manners and customs, 497–545, *passim*; manner of dress, 516–17; artifacts, 518; recreation, 528–29; re liquor, 529; tobacco used by, 529; buffalo hunting, 531; corn among, 531; medicine dance, 531–32; sweating houses, 532; language, 542–43;

trade, 543 and *passim;* sign language, 552; jugglers, 553; game played, 558, 563; reckoning of time, 563. *See also* Delegations, Indian; names of individual tribes

Indian Trade, Superintendent of, 172n

Ingels, George W., 90n, 91n

Inskeep, A. A., 602

Inskeep, John: letter to, 604; partner of Samuel F. Bradford, 578n. *See also* Bradford & Inskeep

Instructions, to LCE: cabinet members comment upon, 32–34, 34–36; TJ sends to ML: text, 61–66; partial copy, 66n

Instruments: astronomical, 8–9, 48–49, 49, 69, 82, 93, 99; plotting, 48, 69, 82, 96; surveying, 48, 82; surgical, 80

Interpreters: Conner offered post as, 37, 116, 118, 118–19; Dearborn authorizes, 102–03; Fairfong, 219n; Dorion, 219, 220n; Jusseaume, 313, 314n, 315; Charbonneau, 315, 648; Drouillard, 368; Tushepaw prisoner, 519; mentioned, 134, 144n, 232, 248, 289, 304, 447

Ioway Indians, 190, 196, 212–13, 259, 265n, 265, 284, 289, 476, 509, 512, 513, 523, 645

Irvine, William: letter to, 76; re supplies for LCE, 38, 76, 81n

Jack rabbit, white-tailed, 171, 172n, 229, 235, 263, 293n

Jackson, Andrew, 468n

Jackson, David: supplier, 78, 88

James River (Va.), 12

James (Jacques) River, 228, 513, 536

Janey. *See* Sacagawea

Jarrot, Nicholas, 145, 423

Jay, gray, 298n

Jay, piñon, 298n

Jefferson, George, 418n, 472

Jefferson, Thomas: letters from, 1–2, 2–3, 16–17, 17–18, 18–19, 21, 31–32, 41–43, 43, 44, 44–45, 49–50, 55–56, 61–66, 68, 104–05, 105–06, 107–08, 109–10, 136–40, 163, 165–66, 199–200, 200–203, 216–17, 218–19, 244–

[711]

uscript, 468–69; TJ reports status of ML papers, 474–75, 479; WC memo re, 486; William Wirt asked to edit, 489; WC searches for material, 490–91; Peale comments, 493–94; Biddle declines, then accepts, invitation to prepare narrative, 494, 495, 496; second Conrad prospectus, 546–48; Biddle's queries to WC, 550–55, 562–65, 568, 569; spurious edition issued, 551, 554n; Hassler queries, 560–61; Biddle re boundaries, 567–68; financial failure of Conrad, 577–78, 579; search for new publisher, 581; power of attorney to Biddle, 583; TJ writes memoir of ML, 584–85, 585–86, 586–93, 594, 595; Biddle explains his withdrawal, 595–96; publication completed, 598; financial failure of Bradford & Inskeep, 604, 604–05, 605–06, 606–07, 609–10, 613–15, 615–17, 621–23, 627–28, 628–29, 629; WC discusses publication, 643–44

Journals, preservation of: 468, 471, 472, 473n, 474–75, 475–76, 479, 486–87, 489, 559–60, 607–08, 609, 609–10, 611–13, 615, 617–18, 619, 623, 623–24, 626, 630–31, 631–33, 634, 634–35, 635–36, 637

Juan de Fuca, Strait of, 5

Judith River. See Big Horn River

Jugglers, Indian, 498, 532

Juniperus horizontalis. See Cedar, dwarf

Jusseaume, René: pay to, 236n; interpreter, 313, 314n, 315, 325n, 434, 436, 447, 448, 449, 450; petitions TJ, 438n

Kamschatka, 588

Kansas Indians: Truteau lists, 139; delegation of, 265, 284, 289; hostility, 272; old village of, 511, 553, 564; location, 523; WC re language, 645; mentioned, 480, 509, 535

Kansas River: ML may ascend, 131; re exploration of, 201; source, 510; Indians on, 523, 535; mentioned, 33, 224, 227, 260, 511, 564n

Kaskaskia, 38, 50, 102, 103n, 113, 116, 121, 125, 133, 137, 144n, 145, 163, 164, 177, 203, 430n, 504, 523

Kaskaskia Indians: remnants of, 523

Keelboat. *See* Boats

Kelly, P., 77

Kelly, Patrick: *Spherics* purchased, 96, 99n

Kelsey, Henry, 295n

Kennedy, J. Alexander, 601

Kickapoo Indians: chief visits camp, 167; delegation of, 265; location, 523; mentioned, 501, 504

Killamuck Indians. *See* Tillamook Indians

Kimball, Joseph, 414, 437n

Kimooenim Indians, 527

King, Nicholas: to make blank map, 27–28; his mapmaking, discussed, 28n, 252

Kingsley, Alpha, 371n, 473n, 642n, 647

Kiowa Indians, 535

Kirwan, Richard: *Mineralogy* purchased, 96

Kite Indians. *See* Crow Indians

Klickitat River, 502

Kneass, William, 601, 603n

Knife River, 524, 563

Knistenaux (Kristinaux) Indians. *See* Cree Indians

Knives: made at Harper's Ferry, 40; purchased, 72, 74, 97; dirk of ML, 107; ML re, 111; Pryor to barter for, 314

Knowlton, Frank Hall, 392n

Knox, Henry: letters from, 661–62, 662–63; letters to, 666–67

Koboliéskit Creek, 541

Kooskooske River. *See* Clearwater River

Kunnanarwesh Indians. *See* Arapaho Indians

Kutenai Indians, 330n

Labadee, Joseph, 514n

La Barthe. *See* Liberté

Labbadie. *See* Liberté

Labiche, Francis: in post-expedition party, 325n; ML re service of, 367; in compensation act, 378; re land

River, 119, 121, 122n, 126–32; visits Delassus, 145–47; reports to TJ, 148–55, 231–42, 317–19; queries Louisiana officials, 161–63; sends maps and specimens to TJ, 192–95; speech to Oto Indians, 203–08; attitude toward British, 214n; edits WC's letter to TJ, 226; *Statistical view,* 299, 554, 636, 637; Indian policy of, 310–13, 625n–26n; author of Clark letters, 313n, 330–35; letter to unknown person, 335–43; illness, 339, 515; accidentally shot, 342; re appointment as governor, 351n, 376, 591; testimonial dinner for, 362n; resigns commission, 376; re land warrant, 380; warns of unauthorized journals, 385–86; portrait painted by Peale, 409–10; Peale re, 439–40; re failure to write letters, 444–45; re return of Sheheke, 446–50; financial difficulties, 456–58, 459–61, 464, 466; settles account with WC, 462–63; alleged derangement of, 467, 469, 473, 574n; re death of, 467–68, 573–75, 592; personal effects, 470–74, 486–87; will and testament, 471, 473n, 487; "Observations and reflections on Upper Louisiana," 473n; re promissory note, 495; Colter's claim against, 567; service with Wayne, 572; alleged intemperance of, 575n; account terminated, 576; TJ's memoir of, 584–85, 586–93, 594, 595; education, 587; military service, 587–88
Lewis, Nicholas, 587
Lewis, Reuben: letters to, 216–17, 218–19, 251–52, 290–91, 350; receives part of ML's land, 381n; borrows from ML, 463n
Lewis, Robert, 586
Lewis, Samuel, Jr.: re engraving of plates, 601; re atlas, 603n
Lewis, William, 586
Lewis and Clark River, 329
Lewisia rediviva, 399n
Lewis's River. *See* Snake River
Liahtan Indians. *See* Comanche Indians
Liberté: identity discussed, 514

Lignite, 275n
Limestone (Maysville), Ky., 114, 125n
Lincoln, Levi: letter from, 34–36; re political enemies, 14n; re instructions to LCE, 34–36
Linnaeus, Carl, 263, 276, 277n, 298n, 302
Linnard, William: letters to, 53–54, 119–20; to provide team and wagon, 53–54; mentioned, 106, 430n
Liquor: Rush's advice re, 55; rectified spirits, listed, 72; spirits of wine, purchased, 88; Indian use, 158, 199n, 504–05, 529; given to Oto Indian, 219n; wine for sick chief, 308; Pryor to barter for, 314; whisky purchased, 429n; use, on LCE, 544; ML's alleged intemperance, 575n
Lisa, Manuel: to provide boatmen, 168; obstructs preparations, 180; raises mountain sheep, 241n; and Pryor expedition, 432–33; and Chouteau expedition, 450; mentioned, 182n, 197, 566
Lisa, Mme. Manuel, 168
Little Beaver Creek, 518n
Little Chariton River, 510
Little Missouri River, 229, 318, 539
Little Muddy River, 318, 537
Little Sioux River, 228
Little Thief, 203, 208n, 514
Livingston, Robert R., 444n
Lloyd, Nicodemus: supplier, 78, 79n
Lockhart, Pat, 359
Logan, Priscilla: supplier, 78, 82
Log, patent, 69, 96
Loise, Paul, 305n
Loisel, Regis, 424, 552, 563
Long, John, 295n
Long, Stephen: expedition of, 161n, 221n, 293n, 295n, 303n
Longitude, finding of, 28–31, 45, 46, 244–45, 250–51, 290
Loomis, Noel M., 6n
Lorimier, Louis, 152, 155n
Lorimier, V. B., 172n
Louisiana, boundaries of, 137–38, 342, 544, 567–68
Louisiana, Upper, 137, 148–55, 183n, 193
Louisiana Purchase: TJ to Harvie re,

42; Lewis informs wc re, 59, 116–17; TJ to Peyroux re, 105; Wistar mentions, 108; wc has heard of, 113, 118; ML requests copy of treaty, 130; ratification, 135; TJ sends ML treaty, 136; re delivery of territory, 163; wc re taking possession of St. Louis, 164; TJ re, 590–91

Louisville, Ky., 111, 114; mentioned, *passim*

Loup-cervier (lousivire). *See* Lynx

Loup Indians. *See* Pawnee Indians

Loup River, 516

Loutre Island, 508

Lucas, Fielding, Jr., 492, 493n

Lucas, John B. C., 257n

Ludlam, George: supplier, 78, 80

Ludlow, Israel, 41n

Luftborough, Nathan, 422

Lundy's Lane, Battle of, 647

Luttig, John, 639n

Lye, as preservative for meat, 55n

Lynx: specimen sent, 235; mentioned, 263

Lynx canadensis. See Lynx

Lynx rufus fasciatus. See Bobcat

Lyon, Matthew: re army contract, 168n

McBride, John R., 346n

McClallen, John, 41n, 355n

McClellan, Robert, 38, 203, 335n, 437n, 483

McCracken, Hugh, 213

McDermott, John Francis, 6n, 151n, 245n

McFarlane, James: re saltpeter expedition, 471

McFarlane, Lewis: re saltpeter expedition, 471; ML's debt to, 490; mentioned, 501

McGillivray, Alexander, 51n

McGillivray, Duncan, 109n, 241n

McGowan, John, 421

Mackay, James: re journal, 155; visits LCE camp, 157n; wc mentions, 515, 522, 528; re Welsh Indians, 516n; re Padouca Indians, 535; in Biddle query, 552

McKeehan, David: letter from, 399–

408; re Gass journal, 386n, 390–91, 399–408

Mackenzie, Alexander, 5, 22, 26, 28, 33, 56, 108, 156n, 295n, 362, 401–02, 411, 499, 503, 523, 525, 537, 545, 554

McKenzie, Charles, 214n, 424

Mackinac. *See* Michilimackinac

Maclura pomifera. See Osage orange

McMahon, Bernard: letters from, 354–56, 391–92, 398–99, 441, 446, 484–86; letters to, 356–58, 388, 390, 441–42, 488–89, 583–84; re plants and seeds of LCE, 354–56, 356, 357n, 388–89, 389, 391, 441, 484–86, 548, 583–84, 643; re Pursh, 398, 445, 485; mentioned, 354n, 397n, 443

McNair, Alexander, 345n, 420, 430

McNeal, Hugh: listed, 367, 639; at Fort Madison, 321n; in compensation act, 378; re land warrant, 381n; in financial records, 425

McRae, William: letter to, 102; to recruit men for LCE, 38, 41n, 53, 102, 125

Madison, James: letters to, 464–65, 475–76; re instructions to LCE, 34; mentioned, 25n

Madison River, 327, 337, 522

Magpie, black-billed: wc lists, 229; live specimens sent to TJ, 235, 236, 241n, 248–49, 250, 253, 254, 255, 256, 261, 264; as new species, 263, 298n; Peale re, 267, 267–68; Barton re, 271; TJ re, 271–72, 291

Maharha (Minitari village): location of, 524

Mail, 107, 135, 190

Maize. *See* Corn

Malboeuf, Etienne, 237n, 422

Maldonaldo, Lorenzo Ferrer, 5

Malespina, Alejandro: Pacific explorer, 5

Mammoth: remains of, 126–30, 442, 506

Mandan Indians: Truteau re, 139; Mackay and, 156n; LCE winters near, 218, 219n, 222; bow and arrows to TJ, 234; message to, from TJ, 307; Pryor's party to, 313; in fur trade, 322; re return of Sheheke, 382–83, 387, 411–12, 414, 432–38,

diseases among Indians, 373, 506; amputation, 504; colic among Mandans, 506; boils and tumors, 512; illness attributed to cobalt fumes, 515

Medicine bag: described, 505

Medicine River, 341, 553, 564

Meehan, Thomas: re LCE plants, 356n

Megalonyx, remains of, 16

Menard, Pierre, 169

Menominee Indians, 523n

Menominee River, 523n

Meramec River, 153, 182, 192, 473n

Meriwether, William D.: letters from, 487–88, 489–90; letters to, 490–91, 495–96; re ML's affairs, 472, 474n, 486n, 487–88, 490, 575n; re journals, 489–90

Metaharta (Minitari village), 522, 524

Miami Indians, 265

Miami River, 522, 523

Michaux, André: letter to, 669–72; re expedition, 589, 667–72

Michaux, F. A.: and LCE plants, 486n

Michilimackinac: Truteau re, 139; mentioned, 155, 599

Microscope, 69, 82, 96

Mifflin, Benjamin: letter from, 77

Mifflin, John F., 397n

Military agent: duties of, 54n; Hooke serves as, 101n

Military Philosophical Society, 361n

Milk River, 319, 537

Mill, corn: TJ recommends, 44; purchased, 71, 84, 95

Miller, James, 641, 643n

Miller, John: *Sexual system of Linnaeus*, 70, 75n

Miller, Joseph, 483

Milwaukee (Indian village), 523

Minerals: LCE instructed re, 63; specimens, 192, 221n, 228, 234, 240n, 258, 263, 273; lead and silver deposits, 564

Mines, lead, 192

Ming, George, 349n

Miniconjou (Sioux). *See* Sioux Indians

Minitari Indians. *See* Hidatsa Indians

Mint, U.S., 21n

Mississippi River: as boundary, 12,

137, 182, 544, 568; given as LCE route, 38, 44, 58, 119; re source, 63; LCE to camp near, 143; on Hay's route, 155; Indians on, 523, 536

Missouri Company: in fur trade, 156n

Missouri Fur Company. *See* St. Louis Missouri Fur Company

Missouri Gazette (St. Louis), 441n, 473n–74n

Missouri Indians, 202–08, 208n, 227, 242, 259, 265, 284, 289, 509, 510, 524, 645

Missouri River: proposed exploration, 4–6; TJ re importance, 12; Gallatin re importance, 32–33; schedule for reaching, 40; Lacépède on exploration of, 46; TJ instructs LCE re, 61–66; Wistar on true direction of, 108; as boundary, 137, 182, 567–68; described, 138, 164, 227, 510–11, 530; navigation, 222–23, 320, 534; closing, 256–58; ML on condition, 317–18; in LCE reports, 320, 321, 322, 326, 327; Gass re, 407; muddiness, 504; WC re settlements on, 624–25; mentioned, *passim*

Mitchell, John, 32

Mitchill, Samuel L.: letter to, 258–59; publishes Mackay journal, 156n; translates Soulard letter, 156n; declines to publish ML map, 238n; visits Arikara chief, 274n; re pumice, 275n; re Osage songs, 552

Mole, 277n

Mole, Townsend's: and LCE, 293n

Molina, Juan Ignacio, 444n

Monax, 294n

Mongrain, Noel, 455, 456n

Moniteau Creek, 508n

Monroe, James: letter to, 567–68; Biddle query to, 567–68

Montgomery, Samuel, 126n

Montreal, Canada: in fur trade, 321

Montrose, Iowa, 372n

Montucla, Jean-Etienne, 246n

Moose, 242n, 415

Moore, Joshua: re finding longitude, 246n, 270, 290

Moore, T.: pilot's boat for ML, 126n

Moore, Thomas L., 649

Moore, William, 380n

Morgan, John, 394n
Morin, Jean Baptiste, 246n
Morning Chronicle (Baltimore), 585n
Morrison, William: letter to, 189; and
    LCE, 144, 177, 189, 450
Mosquito netting, 71
Mountain goat. *See* Goat, mountain
Mountain sheep. *See* Sheep, mountain
Mount Hood, 47, 109
Mourelle, Antonio Francisco: Pacific
    explorer, 5
Mouse River, 156n, 322, 537, 563
Muhlenberg, Henry: and LCE plants,
    353–54, 486n
Muhlenberg, Capt. Henry: recruits
    obtained from, 67n
Mulford, Clarence, 191
Mullin, Henry K., 248–49
Multnomah Indians, 542
Multnomah River. *See* Willamette
    River
Murray, George, 554
Murray, William Augustus: letter to,
    48; mentioned, 43n, 67, 197n, 126n
Musselshell Rapids, 500
Musselshell River, 513, 540, 553, 564
Mustela frenata longicauda. See Wea-
    sel, long-tailed
Muster rolls, 232

Nadaway River. *See* Nodaway River
Narrative, LCE. *See* Journals, publica-
    tion of
Nasatir, A. P., 6n
Natchez Indians, 510n
National Intelligencer (Washington,
    D.C.), 138, 330n, 362n, 397n, 399,
    474n
*Nautical almanac and astronomical
    ephemeris*, 45n, 99n
Navajo Indians, 188
Navigation, river: 122, 123n, 124, 138,
    181, 196, 222–23, 317–18, 329, 534
Neelly, James: letter from, 467–68;
    re death of ML, 467–68, 474, 475,
    592
Nemaha River, 511
Neotoma floridana. See Wood rat,
    eastern
Netul River. *See* Lewis and Clark
    River

Newman, John: expelled from LCE
    party, 237n, 365–66; injury of, 365–
    66; biographical data, 372n; in com-
    pensation act, 378; re land warrant,
    382n; in financial records, 422, 425;
    listed, 639
Newman, Walter, 372n
Nez Percé Indians: mode of burial,
    501; venereal diseases, 506; WC re
    bands of, 526, 527; use of tobacco,
    529; jugglers, 532; trade, 543; flat-
    tening of heads, 545; mentioned,
    330n, 498, 500, 501, 543
Nichols, F., 13n
Nicoll, A. Y., 647, 648n
Nicotiana quadrivolvus. See Tobacco
Niobrara River, 228, 516, 524
Nodaway River, 511
Nolan, Philip, 185, 273, 275n
Nootka Sound, 59, 340, 588
North West Company, 213, 229, 313–
    14, 321, 322, 483
Northwest Passage, 6n
Norton, Peter, 397n
"Notes on Indian Tribes," by James
    Mackay, 156n, 516n
Nucifraga columbiana. See Nutcrack-
    er, Clark's
Nutcracker, Clark's: and LCE, 298n
Nuttall, Thomas, 161n, 180n, 241n

O'Bannon, Presley Neville, 377n
Observations, astronomical: Patter-
    son's formula, 28–31; instruments
    for, 36; publications for, 45n; ML
    re plans for, 48–49; statistical table
    to ML for, 56; TJ instructs ML re,
    61–62; re Hassler's work, 491–92,
    556–59; Biddle re, 560; TJ re, 612
Odocoileus hemionus. See Deer, black-
    tailed
O'Fallon, Benjamin, 570, 582, 583
O'Fallon, Dr. John, 164
O'Hara, James, 133
Ohio River: defense of, 7; as bound-
    ary, 12; as trade route, 12; lowness
    of, 110, 112, 117, 119, 131; men-
    tioned, *passim*
Oliver, Thomas, 409
Omadi, Neb., 156n

Patterson, William Ewing, 123n, 133

Paunch (Crow) Indians, 525, 564

Pawnee Indians: Truteau describes, 139; delegation of, 208n, 260, 265, 284, 289; parley with LCE, 216; vocabulary, 464, 465, 466; WC describes, 534; re language, 645; mentioned, 227, 303, 513, 524, 528

Pawnee River, 137, 201

Pay, of LCE members: WC re, 118; offered John Conner, 119; ML re, 125; Drouillard's, discussed, 144; Whitehouse's, 175, 176n; ML discusses, 177–78; Werner's, 385; Colter's suit for, 567n. *See also* Financial records

Paymaster, U.S. Army: ML replaced as regimental paymaster, 4n; and LCE, 68; Pike as, 176n

Pea, flowering, 392n, 442

Pea, of Columbian Plains: WC lists, 357n

Peabody Museum (Harvard University), 241n

Peace River, 5

Peale, Charles Willson: letters from, 267, 267–79, 301–03, 308–09, 373–74, 410–11, 439–40, 469–70, 493–94; letters to, 260–61, 263, 264, 360–61, 374; collects mammoth remains, 127, 132n; and LCE specimens, 236n, 260–61, 263, 264, 267–68, 476–79; re horned toad, 277n; draws Indian profiles, 289n; re grizzly bears, 295n, 439, 440n; re pronghorn, 308–09; re diseased Indians, 373; paints portraits of ML and WC, 373, 374n, 409–10, 492; re drawings for LCE publication, 411, 490, 611; re mountain sheep, 418; discusses death of ML, 469; re Biddle narrative, 493–94, 548, 644; mentioned, 241n, 269, 271, 397n

Peale, Raphael, 411

Peale, Rembrandt: letters to, 469–70, 493–94

Peale, Titian R., 294n, 411n

Peau Blanche. *See* White Skin

Pedioecetes phasianellus. See Grouse, sharp-tailed

Pelican Lake, 228

Pennant, Thomas, 241n, 268

Pennington, Edward, 608n

Pennsylvania, University of, 17n, 18n, 19n, 21n

Pensions: Shannon's, 619–21; Gass's, 646–48

Peoria Indians, 523

Pepper: Pryor to barter for, 314

Perisoreus canadensis. See Jay, gray

Perkins, Joseph: letter to, 75–76

Pernier (Pernia), John, 467, 468, 473n

Personnel: number established by Dearborn, 102; escort for ML, 107; Ohio River boat crew, 112; WC re volunteers, 113, 117–18; ML re volunteers, 116, 125; "nine young men from Kentucky," 118n; recruits from Tennessee, 144; ML re morale of party, 224–25, 234; number in party, 225, 232, 323; boat crew identified, 237n; Lewis enumerates, 317; health of, 324; roll of LCE men, 364–69; previous service, 370n–71n

Peter, John, 420

Petite Saline Creek, 508n

Petit Voleur. *See* Little Thief

Peyroux, Henri: letter from, 169; letter to, 104–05; Wistar refers ML to, 108, 109n; reported explorations by, 133; mentioned, 142, 146

Phalaenoptilus nuttallii. See Poor-will

Philadelphia Medical and Physical Journal, 238n, 241n, 277n, 294n

Philadelphia Museum, 132n, 241n, 267, 292, 308, 411, 440n, 478n, 518

Philipson, Joseph, 463n

Phosphorus, 71

Phrynosoma douglassi. See Toad, horned

Physick, Dr. Philip Syng, 600

Pica pica hudsonia. See Magpie, black-billed

Pichon, Louis André, Baron: letters from, 21–22, 22–23

Pickering, Timothy, 51n

Picolo, Francis Maria, 241n

Piegan Indians, 408n

Pike, Zebulon, 147n, 175, 176n, 189, 237n, 296n, 313n, 370n, 440n, 604

Pilcher, Joshua: letter from, 648–49

Pills, Rush's: prescribed for LCE, 55

Pilot, boat, 119n, 126n, 430n, 431n

Pine Creek, 526n
Pineau (Pinaut), Charles, 237n, 422
Pinkney, Ninian, 4n, 371n
Pipes, hair, 175, 176n, 177
Pipestone Creek, 514
Piranga ludoviciana. See Tanager, western
Pirogue, 122, 180, 196, 233. See also Boats
Pistols, 91, 97, 98
Pitapahato Indians, 139
Pittsburgh, Pa.: as point of embarkation, 57, 58; ML arrives at, 110; mentioned, passim
Planesphere, 69
Plants, collected by LCE: specimens sent to TJ, 170–71, 220–21, 231, 235; seeds to Hamilton, 269, 356–57, 388–89, 390; Muhlenberg requests seeds, 353–54; McMahon requests seeds, 354–56; plants discussed, 355n–56n; seeds to McMahon, 356–57, 388–89, 390, 391–92; WC's list of seeds, 357n; McMahon's comments, 391–92, 441, 441–42, 484–86; TJ re, 441–42, 488–89, 562n, 583–84. See also Pursh, Frederick
Platte River: ML promises trading house on, 206; LCE at mouth, 215, 216; re military post on, 262, 266, 278–80; terrain near, 512; Indians on, 524, 534; mentioned, 223, 227, 229, 266, 318, 449, 483, 507, 510, 511, 513, 522, 530, 534
Pleasants, S.: bookseller, 601, 603n–04n
Plum, wild, 171, 357n
Plumbago, 274
Poem, commemorating LCE, 362n
Point Adams, 329
Point Disappointment, 530
Pole, Edward, 79n
Pole, setting: use of, by LCE, 73, 317
Polygraph, of ML, 471, 473n
Pomme de Terre River, 506
Ponca Indians: trade, 139; WC lists, 228; delegation of, 242; location, 524; WC re language, 645
Pond, Peter, 108
Poor-will: as new species, 298n
Poplar River, 318–19, 537

Population: Upper Louisiana, 150; Missouri Territory, 625
Populus angustifolia. See Cottonwood
Populus deltoides. See Cottonwood
Porcupine River. See Poplar River
Pork, for LCE, 176, 234
Port-Folio, 214n, 495n, 585n, 599n
Portlock, Nathaniel, 558, 559n
Portpella River, 526
Posecopsahe. See Black Cat
Potash, 274
Potawatomi Indians, 265, 289, 523
Potomac River, 12
Pottery, Mandan: sent to TJ, 235, 240n, 253; in Peale's museum, 476
Potts, John: paid, 348n; listed, 367, 639; described, 371n; in compensation act, 378; re land warrant, 381n; re death, 381n; in financial records, 425; dark skin of, 529
Pouch, powder, 70, 90
Pouch, shot, 98
Powder River, 564n
Prairie: WC discusses, 507
Prairie dog, black-tailed: villages, mentioned by ML, 182; WC re, 229, 498; live specimen to TJ, 235, 236, 248–49, 250, 253, 254, 255, 256, 261, 263; discussed, 241n; Peale re, 267, 302; Barton re, 271; TJ re, 272, 291; as new species, 294n
Prairie du Chien, Wis., 147n, 372n, 523, 599
Prairie hen. See Grouse, sharp-tailed
Prather, Thomas, 351–52
Presque Isle, Mich., 647
Preston, William: letter to, 179
Price, Risdon H., 349n
"Printeau's journal," 140n
Pritchard, William, 516n
Proctor, Thomas, 131n–32n
Pronghorn: abundance of, 224; name discussed, 225n; WC re, 228, 229, 539; specimen to TJ, 234, 263; species discussed, 238n; TJ re, 263, 291; Peale discusses, 268, 308–09; as new species, 297n; re drawings of, 303n, 490, 491n
Prospectus, of publications: text of Frazer's, 345–46; text of Gass's, 390–91; text of Conrad's first, 394–97;

various states of Conrad's first, 397n; ML re, 386; copies mailed, 417; re Frazer's, 440–41; re costs, 463n; Conrad's second, 546–48, 551
Provenchere, Pierre, 325n, 362n
Prunus serotina. See Cherry, black
Prunus sp. *See* Plum, wild
Prunus virginiana. See Chokecherry
Pryor, Nathaniel: letter from, 432–38; letters to, 313–15, 383–84; one of "nine young men," 118n; mission to North West Company, 312, 313n, 313–14, 314n–15n; listed, 317, 638; leads detachment, 341; in compensation act, 378; re land warrant, 381n; re journal, 405, 408n; re return of Sheheke, 382–83, 411–12, 414, 432–38, 452; claim against U.S., 640–43; later career, 642n–43n; as Indian agent, 645–46; injury to shoulder, 646; mentioned, 372n
Puerta, Sebastian Calvo de la. *See* Casa Calvo, Marqués de
Pumice, 274, 275n, 539
Pursh, Frederick: re Indian corn, 239n; work on LCE plants, 355n–56n, 398, 398n–99n, 446, 485, 486n, 492, 643; payments to, 462, 489, 490

Quadrant, Hadley's, 21, 69, 82, 96, 290
Quaife, Milo M., 156n
Quail, mountain: as new species, 397n
Quamash (camass), as Indian food, 477, 543, 500
Quapaw Indians, 522, 645
Quashquame, 305n, 372n
Quicksand River. *See* Sandy River
Quicourre River. *See* Niobrara River
Quills, 96

Rafinesque, Constantine Samuel: letter from, 217–18; re LCE botany, 218, 294n
Rainy Lake: on Hay's route, 155; Indians on, 523
Rainy River: on Hay's route, 155
Randolph, Martha Jefferson, 157n
Randolph, Thomas Mann, 350, 418
Rattlesnake, 220, 499, 544

Read, James, 114, 115n
Receipt books, 96
Recruiting, for LCE: western officers to assist, 38, 103; Tennessee men, 53, 102, 144; needs listed, 57–58, 116; inducements, 58; funds for, 102; WC re, 111, 113
Red River (north), 155, 200n, 214n, 321, 523, 536
Red River (south), 137, 201, 245, 270n, 300, 304, 522
Reed, Moses B., 180, 237n, 426
Rees, Thomas, 166n
Republican Pawnee Indians. *See* Pawnee Indians
Republican River, 534
Rhys, Morgan John, 165, 166n, 516n
Ricara Indians. *See* Arikara Indians
Riddick, Thomas F., 345n, 349n
Rifles, 40, 70
Rio Bravo, 63, 185
Rio Colorado, 63, 65
Rio del Norte, 28, 32, 33, 47, 227, 522
Rittenhouse, David: letter to, 669
Rivers, western, 32–33, 137, 229, 318
Rivet, François, 305n, 422
Robbins, Luther: letter from, 431–32
Robe, buffalo: sent to TJ, 235
Robertson, John, 100, 101n
Robinson, David C.: letter to, 258
Robinson, John, 373n
Robinson, Dr. John H., 258
Robinson, Robert, 258
Roche Jaune River. *See* Yellowstone River
Rock River, 197n, 523
Rocky Mountains: Mackenzie crosses, 5; Fidler reportedly sees, 47, 48n; Lacépède re, 109; ML re, 233, 320, 321, 323; Mitchill re, 275n; mentioned, *passim*
Rodney, Caesar A., 14n
Rodney, Thomas, 123n, 131n, 132n
Rogers, Hezekiah: letter from, 208–09; Indian approval of, 288; mentioned, 383, 426
Ronalds, Swords, Eastburn & Company, 602
Ronalds, Thomas A., 604n
Roscoe, William, 239n, 458
Ross, David, 127, 132n

Rumsey, Nathan, 168n
Rush, Benjamin: letters from, 50–51, 54–55; letters to, 18–19, 68, 488; aids in planning LCE, 18–19, 44, 50; questions on Indian life and customs, 50–51, 161n; rules for preserving health, 54, 55; mentioned, 109n, 348n, 397n
Russell, Gilbert Christian, 466–67, 468, 473n, 475, 573–75
Russell, William, 348n

Sacagawea: WC offers aid to, 315–16; meaning of name, 316n; meets brother, 518–19; as interpreter, 519; complexion of, 527; language of, 543; death discussed, 638, 639n; mentioned or referred to, 317, 499, 502, 503, 540
Sagittaria latifolia. See Wappato
St. Andrew (Upper Louisiana), 153
St. Anthony, Falls of, 196
St. Charles: LCE departs from, 196; WC discusses, 507; mentioned, 319n
St. Clair, Arthur: letter to, 663; mentioned, 41n
St. Clair County, Ill., 145n
Ste. Genevieve, 64, 105n, 133, 153, 169, 182, 183n
St. Ferdinand, 153
St. Francis River, 153, 182, 194, 472, 503, 522
St. Louis: ML reaches, 142; ML visits, 145; attitude of residents, toward Louisiana Purchase, 164; re maps of, 194; mentioned, *passim*
St. Louis Missouri Fur Company, 446-50, 450, 456, 460, 566, 625
St. Louis River, 155
Saint Memin, C. B. J., 411n
St. Peter's River, 137, 138, 228, 312–13, 321, 536
Salalberry: collected by LCE, 392n
Salcedo, Juan Manuel de: letter to, 142–43; re opposition to LCE, 186
Salcedo, Nemesio: letters from, 183–84, 186–87; letter to, 185–86; identified, 175n
Saline River, 508, 511
Salines: Peyroux is proprietor of, 133; Harrison describes, 141; on Arkan-

sas River, 180–83; ML re, 180–83; salt specimens from, 193; at Ste. Genevieve, 476; on Lamine River, 508; near Arrow Rock, 509
Salsify, 442, 559
Salt, making of, 340
Saltpeter caves: expedition to, 473n; on Gasconade River, 508
Salts, Glauber's: Pryor to barter for, 314
Sandy River, 530
Sangamon River, 372n
Santa Fe, 131
Saskatchewan River, 108, 241n, 321, 341, 525, 537, 625
Saugrain, Antoine, 192, 195n
Saukenuk, 198n
Sauk Indians: Stoddard discusses, 197; relations with U.S., 197n–98n; murders by, 215, 215n–16n, 247n; land cession by, 216n; delegation of, 242, 259, 265, 266, 289; treaty, 247n; Willard as blacksmith for, 372n; artifacts, 476; location, 523. *See also* Fox Indians
Sauk Prairie, 510
Say, Thomas, 293n, 295n
Scapanus townsendii. See Mole, Townsend's
Scott, John B., 257n
Seba, Albertus, 238n, 301
Secrecy, re LCE: 13n, 21, 38, 44, 58, 111
Secretary, to TJ: ML as, 1, 2–3, 3–4; duties of, 4n; Harvie, 42n; Burwell, 43n
Selasphorus platycercus. See Hummingbird, broad-tailed
Serviceberry, 357n
Sewellel. *See* Beaver, mountain
Sextant, 36, 48, 82, 96
Sexual customs, Indian, 503, 506, 532, 537–38, 538, 539
Seybert, Adam, 221n, 240n, 275n
Shalala Indians, 543
Shallatto (Shallattas, Shalatoohs) Indians, 502
Shannon, George: letters from, 575, 576, 577; letters to, 566, 570–71; one of "nine young men," 118n; re joining LCE, 125n; in trading party,

313; re pay, 348n; listed, 367, 638; in compensation act, 378; re land warrant, 381n, 570, 621n; in financial records, 425; wounded on Pryor expedition, 438n, 621n; scouts trail, 521; re publication of Biddle narrative, 548, 549–50, 551, 563, 566, 568, 569; WC offers partnership to, 570–71; re pension, 619–21; mentioned, 473n, 486n, 565, 652

Shappellel, 543

Shaw, George, 276

Shawnee Indians, 38, 372n, 503, 522, 524

Sheep, big horn. *See* Sheep, mountain

Sheep, mountain: specimen to TJ, 235; discussed, 240n–41n, 263; Barton re, 271; in ML's report, 323; Peale prepares head, 418; TJ sends specimen to France, 443; re engraving, 490; mentioned, 291, 316

Sheheke: to descend Missouri, 315; visits Washington, 323, 325n; TJ greets, 350–51; at testimonial dinner, 362n; re return to his village, 382–83, 411–12, 414, 432–38, 445, 446, 446–50, 456–58, 460, 460–61, 479–84

Shields, John: one of "nine young men," 118n; listed, 317, 639; paid, 348n; ML re, 367; in compensation act, 378; re land warrant, 381n; in financial records, 425; scouts trail, 521

Shoemaker, Edward, and Company: supplier, 78, 84

Shoshoni Indians: accompany ML, 328, 338; chief gives costume to ML, 439; venereal diseases among, 506; location, 525–26; former homes, 528; and tobacco, 529; jugglers, 532; naming of Snake Indians, 544; flattening of heads, 545; WC re language, 644; mentioned, 316n, 317, 499, 519, 527, 543, 545, 568

Shrew, pygmy: Barton re, 276, 277n

Shrew, short-tailed: as new species, 293n

Sibley, Dr. George, 299

Sign language: Arikara chief uses, 273

Silver mine: on Cheyenne River, 564

Simmons, William: letters from, 408–09, 416–17, 419; terminates ML's account, 576

Sinclair, John, 50

Sioux Indians: Truteau describes, 138–39; TJ re, 166, 200n; deputation of, 190; location, 196; delegation of, 221–22, 259, 266, 284, 289; hostility, 233, 309–10, 322; Heney and, 309–13; presents for, 314; decline invitation to Washington, 412, 414; and Pryor expedition, 432; artifacts, 476; and Chouteau expedition, 480–81; re old age, 505; dancing, 506; re name of, 508; WC lists divisions of, 536; WC re language, 644; mentioned, 228, 461, 552

Sioux River, 512, 536

Sisseton (Sioux). *See* Sioux Indians

Skillute Indians, 542

Slavery, in Upper Louisiana, 153, 154

Sloth, giant ground, 16

Smackshop Indians, 543

Smallpox, vaccine for, 35, 64, 130, 246

Smith, Charles, 177

Smith, Meriwether, 350n, 422, 429n

Smith, Robert, 199n

Smith, Samuel, 349n, 409

Smith, Walter, 422

Smith T, John, 409–10

Snake Creek, 510

Snake Indians. *See* Shoshoni Indians

Snake River, 320, 326, 328, 526, 527, 541, 545

Snowberry: TJ raises, 584n

Sorex exilis. See Shrew, pygmy

Soulard, Antoine, 148–51, 155n, 194

Soup, portable, 72, 81, 97, 233

South West Point (Tenn.), 38, 144n, 370n, 371n

Spain: opposition to LCE, 4–6, 14–15, 61, 142–43, 167n, 173–75, 183–88, 210–12, 430n

Specimens, live. *See* Grouse, sharp-tailed; Magpie, black-billed; Prairie dog, black-tailed; Toad, horned

Spermophilus columbianus. See Ground squirrel, Columbian

Spermophilus tridecemlineatus palli-

[725]

Toad, horned: TJ receives live specimen, 192, 277n; Barton discusses, 276, 277n; re engraving, 490, 491n; mentioned, 291, 411n

Tobacco: purchased, 72, 85; seed sent to TJ, 234; discussed, 238n–39n; kitefoot, 239n; pigtail, 239n; seed sent to Hamilton, 269; Pryor to barter for, 314; WC lists, 356n; Hamilton re Arikara, 389n; McMahon re Arikara, 391–92; to Indians, 518; WC on Indian use, 529

Tomahawks, 40, 70, 97, 375, 470, 472

Tongue River, 564n

Tools, carpenter, 70–71, 83–84, 95, 98

Transylvania University (Lexington, Ky.), 218n, 621n

Traveller's Rest, 335n

Traveller's Rest Creek, 541, 544

Trist, Elizabeth, 609n

Trist, Hore Browse, 127, 132n, 166, 170, 234

Trumpets, tin, 71, 79, 175

Truteau, Jean Baptiste: TJ sends journal to ML, 138–39, 165; mentioned, 136n, 528

Truxillo, Francisco Xavier de, 186, 187

Trade, Indian, 64, 502

Traders, Canadian, 108, 138, 213, 257

Traders, private, 11, 138, 139, 153–54

Trading house, Indian: government operates, 10–12; ML promises, 206; TJ promises, 281; for Sauks and Foxes, 305n; mentioned, 304, 310

Tucker, Sara Jones, 136n

Tucker, Thomas Tudor, 28n, 421

Turkey, wild, 224

Turner, George, 240n

Turreau de Linières, Louis Marie, 444n

Turtle Mountain, 552, 563

Turton, William, 268

Tushepaw Indians, 328, 339, 342, 519, 526, 543, 545

Tuttle, Ebenezer: on boat crew, 237n

Uniforms: LCE needs listed, 70; instructions for packing, 77; shirts purchased, 88; bill for coatees, 92; purchases, 92

Upper Louisiana: ML's questions re, 161–62; re delivery to U.S., 165; re districting, 182, 183n

Ursus horribilis. See Bear, grizzly

Vaccinium macrocarpon. See Cranberry

Vancouver, George, 5, 6n, 13n, 28, 46, 48n, 53, 109, 343n, 499, 540–41

Vancouver Point, 46

Van Langeren, Michael Floris, 246n

Varnum, Joseph Bradley, Jr.: letter from, 417; payment to, 462

Vaughan, John: letter from, 637; letters to, 45, 560–61, 630–31; re instruments, 36; sends certificate to ML, 166n; re horned toad, 277n; mentioned, 25n, 221n, 300n, 340n, 491n, 556, 561, 602, 644

Venegas, Miguel, 241n, 271

Venereal diseases, among Indians, 157, 506, 521

Vermillion River, 509, 513

Vial, Pedro: re Spanish search for LCE, 188

Vicia americana. See Pea, flowering

Vincennes, 8n, 114, 119

Vivian, John, 381n

Vocabularies, Indian: blank forms provided for, 70; of Ioway and Sioux, 212–13; Stoddard sends to TJ, 221; in ML's report, 323; Barton inquires re, 463–64; TJ re his collection, 465–66; in ML's effects, 471; TJ discusses, 611; Biddle re, 636; mentioned, 499, 503, 545

Voigt, Henry, 48, 51, 52, 91, 415, 418

Volcano, 273, 275n, 539

Volney, Constantin François Chasseboeuf, Comte de; letter to, 291–98, TJ reports re LCE, 291; mentioned, 273, 275n

Voorhis, Eleanor Glasgow, 397n

Voorhis, Julia Clark, 397n

Voyageurs: ML re recruiting of, 125; Chouteau provides, 178; re hiring of, 180; Stoddard's instructions re, 190; discussed, 237n

Vulpes fulva regalis. See Fox, red

Vulpes macrotis. See Fox, kit

Vulpes velox. See Fox, swift

[727]

listed, 368, 638; biographical data on, 372n; as blacksmith, 372n; as express, 372n, 643n; in compensation act, 378; re land warrant, 382n; petitions Congress, 378–79; in financial records, 425

Willetpo Island, 527

William and Mary, College of, 100, 225

Williams, Jonathan: letter to, 360–61; re ML's death, 574; mentioned, 600

Williams, Thomas H., 131n

Williamson, Samuel: supplier, 78, 87

Willow trees, 530

Wilson, Alexander: re magpie, 241n; re Clark's nutcracker, 298n; re Lewis' woodpecker, 398n; and death of ML, 597

Wilson, James, 43n

Wilson, John, 43n

Wilson, Nathaniel: alleged member of LCE, 373n

Wilson, Samuel: alleged member of LCE, 373n

Windsor, Richard: in trading party, 313; paid, 348n; listed, 368, 638; residence, 372n; in compensation act, 379; re land warrant, 382n

Wine, spirits of. See Liquor

Wingate, Joshua: letter from, 76; mentioned, 277n

Winn, John T., 381n

Winnebago Indians, 476, 523, 642n, 643n, 645

Winnipeg River: on Hay's route, 155

Wirt, William: re editing LCE journals, 489, 490n, 491

Wisdom River. See Big Hole River

Wiser, Peter: listed, 368, 639; in compensation act, 378; re land warrant, 382n; in financial records, 425

Wistar, Caspar: letters from, 108–09, 133–34; letters to, 17–18, 353; and planning of LCE, 17–18, 44, 108–09, 130, 133, 161n; inquires re Great

Falls, 353n; mentioned, 397n, 501

Wister, John and Charles Jones: suppliers, 78, 86

Wolf, burrowing. See Coyote

Wolf, gray: as new species, 395n

Wolf, prairie: in Biddle notes, 498

Wolford, Adam. See Woolford, Adam

Wood, Eliza, 393n

Wood, Sarah, 393n

Woodchuck, 294n

Woodpecker, Lewis': as new species, 298n

Wood rat, eastern: as new species, 295n

Wood River, 143, 147, 513, 533, 557, 560

Wood River camp. See Dubois, Camp

Woolford, Adam, 176n, 349n

Worrell, Stephen, 191

Wyaconda Prairie, 198n

Wyandot Indians, 40n

XYZ Company: in fur trade, 322

Yanktonai (Sioux). See Sioux Indians

Yazoo River, 12

Yellowstone River: WC's party on, 309, 311, 312; Pryor descends, 315n; ML describes, 318, 341; Indians on, 525, 526; mentioned, 227, 234, 357n, 512, 540

Yellow Wood River, 536

York (servant of WC), 317, 319n, 462, 463n, 500, 503, 538, 539

Yrujo, Carlos Martínez, Marqués de Casa: letters from, 4–7, 14–15; reports proposed LCE, 4–6, 14–15; mentioned, 143

Yturrigaray, Joseph de, 175n

Zea mays. See Corn

Zimmerman, Catherine, 372n

Zimmerman, Johann Georg von, 277n

Zollock, George, 602

Zoological specimens. See common names of species

COLOPHON

This book has been set in a faithful contemporary re-cutting of Baskerville, one of the great letters from eighteenth-century England. The paper is Warren's Olde Style, laid finish, and the cloth is Bancroft's buckram. The book has been designed by Carroll Coleman.

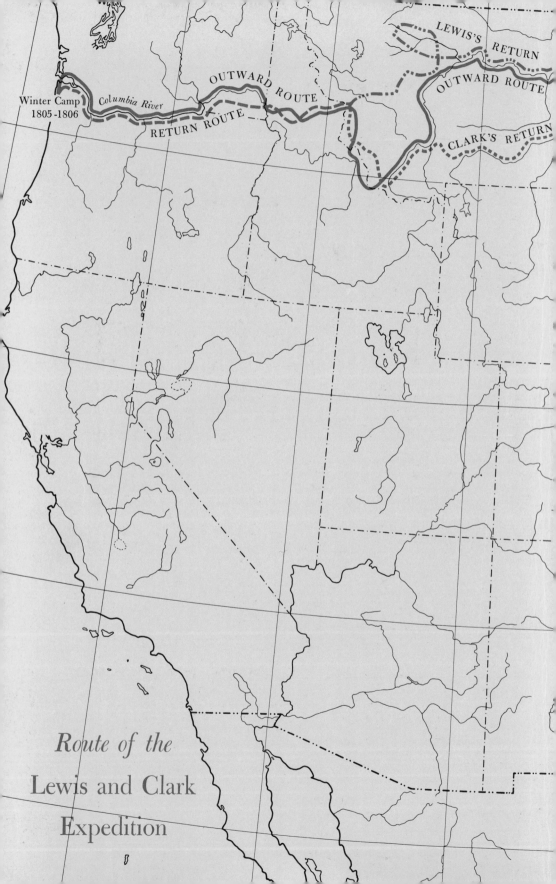

Winter Camp
1805 -1806

Columbia River

OUTWARD ROUTE

RETURN ROUTE

LEWIS'S RETURN

OUTWARD ROUTE

CLARK'S RETURN

*Route of the
Lewis and Clark
Expedition*